HE LIBRARY

at M

INTERNATIONAL COURTS AND
TRIBUNALS SERIES

General Editors: RUTH MACKENZIE, CESARE P.R. ROMANO,
AND PHILIPPE SANDS

Complementarity in the Rome Statute and National Criminal Jurisdictions

INTERNATIONAL COURTS AND TRIBUNALS SERIES

A distinctive feature of modern international society is the increase in the number of international judicial bodies and dispute settlement and implementation control bodies; in their case loads; and in the range and importance of the issues that they are called upon to address. These factors reflect a new state in the delivery of international justice. The International Courts and Tribunals series has been established to encourage the publication of independent and scholarly works which address, in critical and analytical fashion, the legal and policy aspects of the functioning of international courts and tribunals, including the institutional, substantive and procedural aspects.

Complementarity in the Rome Statute and National Criminal Jurisdictions

JANN K. KLEFFNER

OXFORD
UNIVERSITY PRESS

OXFORD
UNIVERSITY PRESS

Great Clarendon Street, Oxford OX2 6DP

Oxford University Press is a department of the University of Oxford.
It furthers the University's objective of excellence in research, scholarship,
and education by publishing worldwide in

Oxford New York

Auckland Cape Town Dar es Salaam Hong Kong Karachi
Kuala Lumpur Madrid Melbourne Mexico City Nairobi
New Delhi Shanghai Taipei Toronto

With offices in

Argentina Austria Brazil Chile Czech Republic France Greece
Guatemala Hungary Italy Japan Poland Portugal Singapore
South Korea Switzerland Thailand Turkey Ukraine Vietnam

Oxford is a registered trade mark of Oxford University Press
in the UK and in certain other countries

Published in the United States
by Oxford University Press Inc., New York

British Library Cataloguing in Publication Data

Data available

Library of Congress Cataloging in Publication Data

Data available

Typeset by Newgen Imaging Systems (P) Ltd., Chennai, India
Printed in Great Britain
on acid-free paper by
CPI Antony Rowe, Chippenham, Wiltshire

ISBN 978–0–19–923845–3

1 3 5 7 9 10 8 6 4 2

General Editors' Preface

The International Criminal Court may exercise jurisdiction only when national courts have declined to investigate, prosecute and try those responsible for genocide, crimes against humanity and war crimes, or when they have shown themselves to be unwilling or unable to do so for proper reasons. This is the 'principle of complementarity', and it has emerged as a cornerstone for the ICC and, perhaps more generally, for the emerging system of international criminal justice.

It is a pragmatic compromise between two opposing, but related, concerns. On the one hand, the principle is meant to protect state sovereignty and reassure governments that the ICC will not have the last word on politically sensitive matters where national legal systems have acted appropriately. On the other hand, it ensures that perpetrators of international crimes within ICC jurisdiction will no longer find any safe haven within complacent or collusive national jurisdictions.

The ICC is the first international judicial body to interface with national courts on the basis of such a principle, at least in a formalized sense. Indeed, the ICTY and ICTR have *primacy* over national courts. Whether complementarity can work in practice remains to be seen. If implemented too strictly, it could paralyze the ICC and consign it to irrelevance. If implemented too loosely, it risks stirring considerable resistance amongst governments, on whose support the ICC depends. Now that the ICC is taking its first tentative steps, an in-depth study of the principle of complementarity, in theory and practice, is needed.

Yet, an analysis of the 'principle of complementarity' has ramifications that go well beyond the ICC. On a higher theoretical level, the principle of complementarity is central to the larger question of whether it is possible to conceptualize, let alone design and implement, a judicial system that functionally integrates the national and the international. As Jann Kleffner acutely remarks, the principle of complementarity raises issues that are at the core of the *International Courts and Tribunals Series*' concerns.

At this time in history, the international criminal law field is a mosaic of jurisdictions. Typically, on any given case, several national courts may potentially exercise jurisdiction (on the basis of territory, active and passive nationality, or universal jurisdiction). At the international level, besides the ICC, currently there are two ad hoc international criminal tribunals (the ICTY and ICTR) and multiple internationalized courts, from Sierra Leone to Cambodia. The trend might be seen to incline towards greater jurisdictional fragmentation. The question of how to regulate the jurisdictional relationships, on both the vertical and the horizontal level, amongst the various jurisdictions is complex. As Dr Kleffner writes: '... [C]omplementarity, which is confined to the relationship between *national criminal jurisdictions* and the *ICC*, supplies only *one* organizational principle and *not all* of those that would be needed before being able to speak of international criminal justice as a *system*. As such, complementarity incites us to think beyond it, and to confront the challenges ahead, in building such a system.' (para 349)

This book is a revised version of Jann Kleffner's PhD dissertation, which he defended in 2007 at the University of Amsterdam. Once again, we are proud to publish this stimulating contribution by an emerging academic who sheds light on the challenges and opportunities created by multiple jurisdictions.

Ruth Mackenzie, University College, London
Cesare P.R. Romano, Loyola Law School, Los Angeles
Philippe Sands, University College, London

June 2008

Contents Summary

Contents

Acknowledgements

This book emanates from my PhD thesis, which I defended in January 2007 at the University of Amsterdam. Throughout the years of research on the topic of complementarity, both prior and subsequent to the finalization of my PhD manuscript, I have benefited from input and support from many colleagues and friends. Writing this book would not have been possible—or the book would at least have taken a radically different form—without them. I am deeply indebted and wish to express my gratitude to them all. Singling out some necessarily entails incompleteness, and vis-à-vis all those not individually mentioned, I can only hope that a collective sincere thank-you will do.

I am particularly grateful to my supervisors, Professor André Nollkaemper and Professor Bert Swart, whose reflections on my research were a continuous source of inspiration and enriched my analysis. I would also like to express my gratitude to Professor M. Cherif Bassiouni, Morten Bergsmo, Professor John Dugard, Professor Willem van Genugten, Professor Göran Sluiter, Professor Harmen van der Wilt, and Professor and Judge Christine van den Wyngaert, for having commented on various aspects of my work. I would further like to thank Morten Bergsmo for having invited me to serve as a member of the Informal Expert Group consulting the Prosecutor of the International Criminal Court on Complementarity in Practice. My thanks also go to the other members of the group—Xabier Agirre, Antonio Cassese, Rolf Einar Fife, Håkan Friman, Christopher Hall, John T. Holmes, Hector Olásolo, Norul H. Rashid, Darryl Robinson, Elizabeth Wilmshurst and Andreas Zimmermann—for the fruitful discussion that we had, much of which has found its way into this book.

At the Amsterdam Center for International Law, I benefited from discussions amongst members of the PIONIER research project on 'Interactions between Public International Law and National Law', funded by the Netherlands Organisation for Scientific Research (NWO). In that context, I am particularly indebted to Professor Erika de Wet for her support. I am especially grateful to Dr Ward Ferdinandusse and Gerben Kor for having been intellectual sparring partners and for their friendship. Thanks also to my research assistants, Helen Dobby and Swen Meereboer, for support in giving the book its current form. I would also like to express my gratitude to the staff of the International Human Rights Law Institute at DePaul University College of Law in Chicago, where I spent some time as a research fellow, with a Scholarship for which I am indebted to the Amsterdam University Fund. Further thanks to the staff of the Geneva Academy of Humanitarian Law and Human Rights, and in particular Professor Paola Gaeta, for having accommodated me and provided a very pleasant and quiet environment for my research sabbatical during which I finalized the manuscript

for this book. Last but by no means least, I thank Cecilia, Mio and Pax for inject-
ing the word 'complementarity' with real-life meaning as the condition of things
(and persons!) that complement one another. I dedicate this book to them.

Jann K. Kleffner

The Hague
March 2008

List of Abbreviations

AfCHPR	African Charter on Human and Peoples' Rights
Afr J Hum Rights	African Journal of Human Rights
AJIL	American Journal of International Law
Am U Intl L Rev	American University International Law Review
AP	Additional Protocol
ASIL	American Society of International Law
BJIL	Berkeley Journal of International Law
BYIL	British Yearbook of International Law
Boston University Intl LJ	Boston University International Law Journal
Bull Crim	Bulletin Criminel
California Western ILJ	California Western International Law Journal
Columbia Human Rights LR	Columbia Human Rights Law Review
Cornell Intl LJ	Cornell International Law Journal
CUP	Cambridge University Press
Duke JCIL	Duke Journal of Comparative and International Law
ECHR	European Convention on Human Rights
ECtHR	European Court of Human Rights
EHRR	European Human Rights Reports
EJIL	European Journal of International Law
Emory ILR	Emory International Law Review
ETS	European Treaty Series
Finnish YbIL	Finnish Yearbook of International Law
GC	Geneva Convention
Houston LR	Houston Law Review
HUP	Harvard University Press
HRC	Human Rights Committee
IACHR	Inter-American Convention on Human Rights
IACtHR	Inter-American Court of Human Rights
IACmHR	Inter-American Commission on Human Rights
ICC	International Criminal Court
ICCPR	International Covenant on Civil and Political Rights
ICJ	International Court of Justice
ICLQ	International and Comparative Law Quarterly
ICRC	International Committee of the Red Cross
ICSID	International Center for the Settlement of Investment Disputes
ICTR	International Criminal Tribunal for Rwanda
ICTY	International Criminal Tribunal for the former Yugoslavia
IHRR	International Human Rights Reports
ILA	International Law Association

ILC	International Law Commission
ILDC	International Law in Domestic Courts
ILM	International Legal Materials
ILR	International Law Reports
ILSA J Intl & Comp L	International Law Students Association Journal of International and Comparative Law
IMT	International Military Tribunal for the Trial of German Major War Criminals
IMTFE	International Military Tribunal for the Far East
IRRC	International Review of the Red Cross
Israel Yb HR	Israel Yearbook of Human Rights
IWPR	International War and Peace Reporting
JICJ	Journal of International Criminal Justice
LJIL	Leiden Journal of International Law
LRA	Lord's Resistance Army
Max Planck UNYB	Max Planck Yearbook of United Nations Law
Michigan JIL	Michigan Journal of International Law
NATO	North Atlantic Treaty Organization
NILR	Netherlands International Law Review
NJIL	Nordic Journal of International Law
NJW	Neue Juristische Wochenschrift
Nebraska LR	Nebraska Law Review
NYIL	Netherlands Yearbook of International Law
NYU J Intl L & Pol	New York University Journal of International Law and Politics
OAS	Organisation of American States
OAU	Organisation of African Unity
OTP	Office of the Prosecutor
OUP	Oxford University Press
PrepCom	Preparatory Committee on the Establishment of an International Criminal Court
RdC	Receuil des Cours
RGDIP	Revue Générale de Droit International Public
RoPE	Rules of Procedure and Evidence
SCSL	Special Court for Sierra Leone
Texas ILJ	Texas International Law Journal
UN	United Nations
UN Doc	United Nations Document
UNGA	United Nations General Assembly
UNSC	United Nations Security Council
UNTS	United Nations Treaty Series
Wisconsin ILJ	Wisconsin International Law Journal
YIHL	Yearbook of International Humanitarian Law
Yale JIL	Yale Journal of International Law
Yale LJ	Yale Law Journal
ZaöRv	Zeitschrift für ausländisches öffentliches Recht und Völkerrecht

Table of Cases

1. INTERNATIONAL

European Court of Human Rights

European Court of Justice

Human Rights Committee

Inter-American Court and Commission of Human Rights

International Criminal Court

International Court of Justice

International Centre for the Settlement of Investment Disputes

International Criminal Tribunal for the former Yugoslavia

2. INTERNATIONALIZED

Special Court for Sierra Leone

3. NATIONAL

Australia

Belgium

Canada

Denmark

Estonia

Sweden

Switzerland

United Kingdom

USA

Table of Treaties

I

Introduction

Traditionally, national criminal jurisdictions have in principle been assigned the exclusive role in investigating and prosecuting the core international crimes of genocide, crimes against humanity and war crimes. Notwithstanding the fact that, on occasion and in response to particular situations, States and the United Nations have established international and, more recently, internationalized criminal tribunals, domestic courts have remained the forum of choice and convenience. States were unwilling to yield their jurisdiction to an international criminal court permanently, since they considered the investigation and prosecution of core crimes as their sovereign prerogative.

International law reflects the traditional presumption in favour of domestic investigation and prosecution of core crimes. Conventional and customary international law details how genocide, crimes against humanity and war crimes are to be suppressed on the national level. It does so by providing definitions of these crimes, which States are entitled or obliged to implement into their national legislation, and by stipulating which jurisdictional bases States are entitled or obliged to establish, and whether and to what extent they are entitled or obliged to exercise jurisdiction. In so doing, international law is far from uniform and does not provide for one coherent and all-encompassing regime for the suppression of all core crimes on the national level. Rather, it establishes different regimes for different core crimes.

Underlying these (disparate) regimes for the national suppression of core crimes is one common presumption: genocide, crimes against humanity and war crimes are the most serious crimes of concern to the international community as a whole. In suppressing them, national courts do not only act in the interest of their immediate constituency, ie their State and the society living in it, but also on behalf of the international community as a whole. In the absence of permanent, genuine enforcement mechanisms on the international level, international law foresees the use of national criminal jurisdictions to fill the void and act in both a domestic and an international capacity.

These expectations have occasionally been met, and States have investigated core crimes, prosecuted those accused of them and convicted those responsible. Overall, however, the record of success of national criminal jurisdictions to fulfil the central task that international law assigns to them has been modest. States have been slow in adopting the necessary legislative frameworks to adequately respond to core crimes. They often lack the jurisdictional provisions, which would enable them to investigate, prosecute and adjudicate cases. Their national laws are flawed as regards the definitions of the crimes or the general principles governing matters such as modes of liability (ie rules governing the perpetration and participation, superior responsibility and defences). More importantly, however, even when States have an adequate legislative framework at their disposal, they often prove unwilling or unable to enforce it. Core crimes are system crimes—crimes that are committed on a systemic level, regularly involving State authorities, *de facto* regimes or organized armed groups in armed conflicts. System crimes habitually have a paralyzing effect on the national judicial system of the State or States, which are primarily envisaged to conduct proceedings: first and foremost, not only the State on whose territory core crimes occurred, but also the State whose nationality the alleged perpetrator and victims possess. Instead of bringing those responsible to justice in independent and impartial proceedings, States remain completely inactive, respond to core crimes by other means, such as truth commissions and amnesties, or conduct criminal proceedings, which do not satisfy internationally recognized standards for the fair and effective administration of criminal justice. What is more, third States have never adequately filled these deficiencies in the national suppression of core crimes by States with a direct nexus to the crime. The adjudication of core crimes on the basis of universal jurisdiction has for a long time proved a dormant concept, and its reinvigoration in recent years has been at least as cumbersome and piecemeal as the prosecution of core crimes by States more directly involved. Exclusive reliance on national suppression of core crimes, in short, has proved deficient in the fight against impunity.

The traditional system of suppressing genocide, crimes against humanity and war crimes has changed with the adoption and entry into force of the Rome Statute of the International Criminal Court (hereafter the Statute).[1] The Statute establishes a permanent International Criminal Court (hereafter ICC or Court) with jurisdiction over genocide, crimes against humanity and war crimes, and eventually, the crime of aggression.[2] The Court has jurisdiction with respect to

---

[1] Rome Statute of the International Criminal Court (adopted 17 July 1998, as corrected by *procès-verbaux* of 10 November 1998, 12 July 1999, 30 November 1999, 8 May 2000, 17 January 2001 and 16 January 2002, entered into force 1 July 2002) A/CONF.183/9 (Rome Statute).

[2] Rome Statute (n 1) Articles 5–8. See also Article 9 on Elements of Crimes, which 'shall assist the Court in the interpretation and application of articles 6, 7 and 8'. The Elements of Crimes were adopted on 9 September 2002 as Doc ICC-ASP/1/3 (part II-B). When reference is made in the following to genocide, crimes against humanity and war crimes within the jurisdiction of the ICC as defined in the relevant provisions of Part 2 of the Statute, the umbrella term 'ICC crimes' will be used. 'ICC crimes' overlap to considerable extent with the concept of 'core crimes' employed in this book to denote the broad categories of genocide, crimes against humanity and war crimes under international customary and conventional law. However, the two terms of 'core crimes' and 'ICC crimes' are not identical. For, the crimes within the jurisdiction of the ICC lag behind, or go beyond, what is criminalized under the broad categories of crimes against humanity and war

crimes committed after the entry into force of the Statute (1 July 2002),[3] and the Security Council, a State Party or the ICC Prosecutor acting *proprio motu* can trigger its jurisdiction.[4] Although aspiring to become a truly universal court, the exercise of the jurisdiction of the ICC is conditioned in the cases of State referrals and *proprio motu* action of the Prosecutor by the requirement that either the State on whose territory crimes of genocide, crimes against humanity or war crimes have occurred is a State Party, or the person accused of such a crimes is a national of a State Party.[5] Notwithstanding this and other limitations, the entry into force of the Statute has been hailed as a 'constitutional moment'.[6] With currently more than half of all States of the world as parties,[7] it is evolving into one of the central elements of an emerging system of international criminal justice for the suppression of crimes of genocide, crimes against humanity and war crimes. It reflects the views of an increasing number of States on how the enforcement of the prohibitions of the most serious crimes of concern to the international community as a whole is to be achieved.

In the quest for agreement on the Statute, the relationship between the ICC and national criminal jurisdictions proved to be a pivotal issue at the heart of States' concerns about their sovereignty. The establishment of a permanent international criminal court, endowed with prospective jurisdiction over crimes committed on States Parties' territory or by their nationals, including officials, inevitably entailed a transfer of one of the core attributes of sovereignty: the exercise of criminal jurisdiction by States. The establishment of the ICC thus necessitated that sovereignty concerns of States be accommodated. At the same time, in answering the question of the relationship between the ICC and national criminal jurisdictions, States sought a formula designed to establish an ICC with the potential of filling the gaps left by the ineffectiveness of national criminal jurisdictions. The debate about the proper relationship between the ICC and national criminal jurisdictions thus evolved with two principal considerations in mind: accommodating State sovereignty and ensuring the criminal accountability of perpetrators of genocide, crimes against humanity and war crimes.

The Rome Statute seeks to strike a balance between these two considerations in providing that the ICC 'shall be complementary to national criminal jurisdiction'.[8] The principle of complementarity is one of the three fundamental

crimes under international customary and conventional law in certain respects. Furthermore, core crimes committed before the entry into force of the Rome Statute and those committed neither on the territory nor by a national of a State Party fall outside the jurisdiction of the Court. This is subject to the exception that the latter 'preconditions to the exercise of jurisdiction', which derive from Article 12 (2) of the Rome Statute, do not apply in case of a Security Council referral.

[3] Rome Statute (n 1) Article 11.   [4] Rome Statute (n 1) Articles 13–16.
[5] Rome Statute (n 1) Article 12.
[6] LN Sadat and SR Carden, 'The New International Criminal Court: An Uneasy Revolution' (2000) 88 Georgetown LJ 381, 395.
[7] Developments after February 2008 are not considered.
[8] Rome Statute (n 1) Preamble, para 10, Article 1, second sentence.

cornerstones of the ICC, alongside its permanent nature and its jurisdiction over the most serious crimes of international concern.[9] The principle translates into the regime governing the admissibility of cases before the Court.[10] It denotes that the Court is only to exercise its jurisdiction if States remain wholly inactive vis-à-vis ICC crimes or, in case States investigate, prosecute and adjudicate cases, if they prove to be unwilling or unable to do so genuinely. According to the principle of complementarity, in other words, national courts retain primary competence to exercise jurisdiction over core crimes. They are envisaged to take pride of place and constitute the first line of defence in the fight against impunity. The ICC, on the other hand, is supposed to function as a 'permanent reserve court',[11] which steps in when effective national suppression of ICC crimes is absent. State Parties and the ICC together thus constitute an enforcement community, which consists of the two layers of national criminal jurisdictions and the Court. Underlying the complementary nature of the ICC is the acknowledgement that 'the international cannot and should not do without the national'. Conversely, however, the principle of complementarity also reflects the intention that the international is designed to supply the deficiencies of the national. The ICC is envisaged as the mechanism through which any gaps left by the deficiencies of domestic suppression are filled, or at least significantly narrowed. What, then, is the potential of complementarity to attain this envisaged aim, and what is its impact on national criminal jurisdictions likely to be? These are the central questions that this book will address.

In examining these questions, the overall objective is to clarify the content of the principle of complementarity. In a narrow reading of the Statute, complementarity fulfils a procedural role: it provides criteria for the admissibility of cases before the ICC and a procedural setting for their application in the course of ICC proceedings. However, my hypothesis is that the content of the principle does not exhaust itself in such procedural matters. Rather, complementarity has wider implications: it stands central in conceptualizing the role of national criminal jurisdictions in the system of international criminal justice, which the Rome Statute seeks to establish, and impacts on the national suppression of ICC crimes. This book aims to identify this wider content of complementarity. In so doing, it proceeds in the following steps.

---

[9] Cf Rome Statute (n 1) Article 1.

[10] The core of that regime is constituted by the Rome Statute (n 1) Articles 17–20 and 53 (1)(b) and Rules 48, 50–62, 133, 181 and 186 of the Rules of Procedure and Evidence (RoPE). The RoPE were finalized on 12 July 2000: see Report of the Preparatory Commission for the International Criminal Court, Addendum Finalized draft text of the Rules of Procedure and Evidence (12 July 2000) UN Doc PCNICC/2000/INF/3/Add.1. In accordance with Article 51 (1) of the Rome Statute, the RoPE were adopted by the Assembly of States Parties and entered into force on 9 September 2002 as Doc ICC-ASP/1/3 (part II-A).

[11] A Bos, 'The Role of an International Criminal Court in the Light of the Principle of Complementarity' in E Denters and N Schrijver (eds), *Reflections on International Law from the Low Countries* (Kluwer, The Hague 1998) 249–259, 253.

Chapter II clarifies the role of national criminal jurisdictions in the suppression of core crimes prior to, and independent of, the Rome Statute of the ICC. An identification of the role of national criminal jurisdictions that can be deduced from international law and of the factual, legal and other factors, which prevent them from fulfilling that role, provides the backdrop for understanding the content of complementarity and its impact on the national suppression of ICC crimes. Chapter III proceeds by describing the context and evolution of complementarity in the Rome Statute. It places complementarity into the broader framework of allocating competences of international criminal tribunals and national criminal jurisdictions and contrasts it with the models of allocation that were adopted in the framework of the Nuremberg, Yugoslavia and Rwanda tribunals. The chapter subsequently traces the evolution of complementarity during the negotiations of the Rome Statute. Chapters IV and V provide an examination of the formal framework of complementarity embodied in the provisions of the Rome Statute. In so doing, a distinction is made between the provisions, which establish complementarity as a legal principle and set forth the criteria for the admissibility of cases before the ICC in Articles 17 and 20 (3) of the Statute (Chapter IV), and the procedural framework for the application, invocation and litigation of complementarity (Chapter V). Chapter VI turns to the question: How much room, if any, does complementarity leave for States not to investigate and prosecute ICC crimes? Or, put differently, to what extent is complementarity based on the idea that States are obliged to investigate and prosecute these crimes? Chapter VII seeks to clarify the potential of complementarity to function as a catalyst for States to fulfil their primary role in suppressing ICC crimes. Finally, Chapter VIII offers some conclusions.

II

National Suppression of Core Crimes

1. Introduction

In order to provide a framework for analyzing the content of the principle of complementarity, including its implications for the role of national criminal jurisdictions in the suppression of core crimes, it is first necessary to analyze that role prior to, and independent of, the Rome Statute. The analysis of this 'decentralized'[1] model of suppression begins with an identification of the role of national criminal jurisdictions that can be deduced from international law and a summary account of the occasions in which States have actually investigated and prosecuted core crimes (2). The chapter then proceeds with an analysis of factual, legal and other factors, which prevent national criminal jurisdictions from suppressing core crimes (3).

2. The Role of National Criminal Jurisdictions

Under international law, national criminal jurisdictions are envisaged to assume, either as a matter of right or of obligation, a central role in the suppression of genocide, crimes against humanity and war crimes. In fact, the suppression of core crimes was principally the *exclusive* domain of national criminal jurisdictions

---

[1] R Wolfrum, 'The Decentralized Prosecution of International Offences Through National Courts' in Y Dinstein and M Tabory (eds), *War Crimes in International Law* (Martinus Nijhoff Publ, The Hague, Boston, London 1996), 233–249. This model of enforcement has also been described as 'indirect': cf M C Bassiouni, 'The Sources and Content of International Criminal Law' in C Bassiouni (ed), *International Criminal Law* (vol I (Crimes) 2nd edn Transnational Publ, Ardsley NY 1999) 3–126, 110, 113 [distinguishing indirect (national) from direct (international) enforcement of international criminal law]. Note, however, that this latter distinction may be misleading in as much as national enforcement of international criminal law may very well be said to be the most direct way of doing so, especially when one considers the domestic—as opposed to the international—role that national criminal jurisdictions play when enforcing core crimes prohibitions. On the simultaneous domestic and international role, see *2.2. National Criminal Jurisdictions as International and Domestic Organs*. From a purely practical point of view, national criminal jurisdictions may also be said to be more direct than international criminal courts and tribunals, as they have a full enforcement system (police, courts, prisons etc) at their disposal. The assertion that national enforcement is 'indirect' thus only holds true to the extent that they fulfil a role as surrogate international organs in the absence of genuine international enforcement bodies.

prior to the entry into force of the ICC Statute. This rule has been subject to some exceptions, consisting of the few occasions on which international criminal courts and tribunals[2] or internationalized criminal courts and tribunals[3] have effectuated the core crimes prohibitions. Due to the exceptional, ad hoc nature of such other criminal justice mechanisms, exclusive national suppression remained the *default mechanism* prior to the entry into force of the Rome Statute. The following sections sketch this role of national criminal jurisdictions vis-à-vis the three core crimes by reference to treaty and customary law (2.1.), before addressing the role of national criminal jurisdictions as agents of the international and domestic legal order (2.2.) and briefly describing empirical developments in national enforcement by providing a concise overview of actual domestic investigations and prosecutions since the Second World War (2.3.).

2.1. Applicable Law Governing the National Suppression of Core Crimes

The law applicable to core crimes is a specific branch of public international law. It contains rules agreed upon by States governing the suppression of conduct of individuals. This body of *international criminal law* thus consists of a blend of *inter-State (horizontal)* norms directed at States[4] and *vertical* norms directed at individuals.[5] By identifying a given conduct as a crime under international law,

---

[2] International criminal tribunals are understood here as judicial bodies established by an international legal instrument, which resort exclusively to international criminal law in deciding the cases before them, and which fulfil a judicial function in as much as the outcome of the process is a legally binding judgment determining the innocence or guilt of individuals. This definition draws in part on the definition of 'international judicial bodies' developed by C P R Romano, 'The Proliferation of International Judicial Bodies: The Pieces of the Puzzle' (1999) 31 NYU J Intl L & Pol 709–751, 713–714. International criminal courts and tribunals thus comprise the International Military Tribunal for the Trial of the German Major War Criminals, established in accordance with its Charter of 8 August 1945, 82 UNTS 280 (Nuremberg Tribunal), the International Tribunal for the Prosecution of Persons Responsible for Serious Violations of International Humanitarian Law Committed in the Territory of the Former Yugoslavia since 1991, established in accordance with UNSC Res 827 (adopted on 25 May 1993) (ICTY), and the International Criminal Tribunal for the Prosecution of Persons Responsible for Genocide and Other Serious Violations of International Humanitarian Law Committed in the Territory of Rwanda and Rwandan Citizens Responsible for Genocide and Other Such Violations Committed in the Territory of Neighbouring States, between 1 January 1994 and 31 December 1994, established in accordance with UNSC Res 955 (adopted on 8 November 1994) (ICTR).

[3] Although the latter are a comparably recent phenomenon, internationalized criminal courts and tribunals had been established prior to the entry into force of the Rome Statute in East Timor, Kosovo and Sierra Leone. See generally C Romano, A Nollkaemper and J K Kleffner (eds), *Internationalized Criminal Courts: Sierra Leone, East Timor, Kosovo, and Cambodia* (OUP, Oxford 2004) 491.

[4] These include rules such as those delineating the jurisdictional bases for prosecutions, the question whether States are under an obligation to exercise that jurisdiction, rules on implementation, etc.

[5] On international criminal law consisting of the mentioned blend of norms, see generally A Cassese, *International Criminal Law* (OUP, Oxford 2003) 19–21 ['hybrid branch of law']. This is not to suggest that the commission of core crimes cannot also entail the responsibility of a State.

the horizontal element of that prohibition recognizes States' right or obligation to exercise one of the core elements of their sovereignty—the enforcement of criminal law—with regard to the prohibited conduct. This would only be different in the theoretical case where the norm in question indicates otherwise, notably by providing for the *exclusive* jurisdiction of an international criminal court. Such exclusivity finds no basis in positive international law.[6] This being the case, the very fact that international law recognizes a given crime indicates that, in the absence of any other forum for suppression, national criminal jurisdictions are at least entitled (and may even be obliged) to assume the role of investigating, prosecuting and punishing core crimes. Otherwise, the prohibition of such crimes would be rendered meaningless as far as the imposition of criminal punishment on the perpetrator is concerned. In the words of the District Court of Jerusalem in the Eichmann judgment: '[...] international law is, in the absence of an International Court, in need of the judicial and legislative organs of every country to give effect to its criminal interdictions and to bring the criminals to trial.'[7]

Several international legal rules confirm and further define the role of national criminal jurisdictions with regard to the suppression of war crimes (2.1.1.), genocide (2.1.2.) and crimes against humanity (2.1.3.). These rules are supplemented by the obligation of States to investigate and prosecute serious human rights violations (2.1.4.).

2.1.1. War Crimes

The regime governing national suppression of war crimes—ie serious violations of international humanitarian law applicable in armed conflict, which entail the criminal responsibility of individuals—finds its basis in a number of treaties and in customary law.

Cf Article 4 of the Draft Code of Crimes against the Peace and Security of Mankind, ILC, 'Report of the International Law Commission on the work of its 48th Session' (6 May-26 July 1996) UN Doc A/51/10 Supplement No 10. See on the relationship between individual criminal responsibility and State responsibility, A Nollkaemper, 'Concurrence between individual responsibility and state responsibility in international law' (2003) 52 ICLQ 615–640; ICJ, *Case Concerning the Application of the Convention on the Prevention and Punishment of the Crime of Genocide (Bosnia and Herzegovina v Serbia and Montenegro)* Judgment of 26 February 2007, General List No 91 [166–179].

  6 The only crime in relation to which the International Law Commission (ILC) has suggested 'exclusive' jurisdiction in its work on the Draft Code is the crime of aggression; cf ibid Draft Article 8, which limits the obligation to take measures necessary to establish jurisdiction to crimes other than aggression as defined in Draft Article 16. For the latter crime, jurisdiction 'shall rest with an international criminal court'. However, the State committing aggression is not precluded from trying its nationals for the crime of aggression. Thus, although the ILC refers to this jurisdictional regime as being governed by the 'principle of exclusive jurisdiction', it does not entirely preclude national suppression of the crime of aggression. For the reasons that led the ILC to suggest such a jurisdictional regime, see Commentaries on Article 8 [14].

  7 *Attorney-General v Eichmann*, District Court of Jerusalem, 36 ILR 5 (12 December 1961) [12].

As far as *treaties on war crimes* are concerned, the four Geneva Conventions of 1949[8] and the First Additional Protocol,[9] the 1954 Hague Cultural Property Convention[10] and its 1999 Second Protocol,[11] the 1994 UN Convention on the Safety of United Nations and Associated Personnel,[12] and a number of treaties relating to the prohibition of the use of certain weapons[13] envisage that the prohibition of these crimes is to be effectuated on the national level. These treaties regularly contain one or more of the following undertakings of States: to make the respective crime punishable and enact the necessary legislation for that purpose, establish certain forms of jurisdiction and exercise that jurisdiction.[14]

Thus the first paragraph of the common provisions in the *Geneva Conventions* on the system of suppression of grave breaches of those conventions[15] imposes a duty on States 'to enact any legislation necessary to provide effective penal sanctions for persons committing, or ordering to be committed, any of the grave breaches'.[16] Paragraph 2 of the respective provisions contains the 'obligation

[8] 1949 Geneva Convention (I) for the Amelioration of the Condition of the Wounded and Sick in Armed Forces in the Field (adopted 12 August 1949, entered into force 21 October 1950) 75 UNTS 31–83; Geneva Convention (II) for the Amelioration of the Condition of Wounded, Sick and Shipwrecked Members of Armed Forces at Sea (adopted 12 August 1949, entered into force 21 October 1950) 75 UNTS 85–133; Geneva Convention (III) relative to the Treatment of Prisoners of War (adopted 12 August 1949, entered into force 21 October 1950) 75 UNTS 135–285; Geneva Convention (IV) relative to the Protection of Civilian Persons in Time of War (adopted 12 August 1949, entered into force 21 October 1950) 75 UNTS 287–417.
[9] 1977 Protocol Additional to the Geneva Conventions of 12 August 1949, and relating to the Protection of Victims of International Armed Conflicts (AP I) (adopted 8 June 1977, entered into force 7 December 1978) 1125 UNTS 3–608.
[10] 1954 Convention for the Protection of Cultural Property in the Event of Armed Conflict. The Hague (adopted 14 May 1954, entered into force 7 August 1956) 249 UNTS 240–288.
[11] 1999 Second Protocol for the Protection of Cultural Property in the Event of Armed Conflict (adopted 26 March 1999) 38 ILM 769–782.
[12] 1994 UN Convention on the Safety of United Nations and Associated Personnel (adopted 15 December 1994, entered into force 15 January 1999) 34 ILM 482–493.
[13] Convention on the prohibition of the development, production, stockpiling and use of chemical weapons and on their destruction (adopted 3 January 1993, entered into force 29 April 1997) 32 ILM 800 (Article VII in conjunction with Article I (1)(b) and (c)); 1997 Ottawa Convention on the Prohibition of the Use, Stockpiling, Production and Transfer of Anti-Personnel Mines and on their Destruction (adopted 18 September 1997, entered into force 1 March 1999) 36 ILM 1507–19 (Article 9).
[14] Cf Geneva Convention I (Arts 49–51) (n 8); Geneva II (Arts 50–52) (n 8); Geneva III (129–131) (n 8); Geneva IV (Arts 146–148) (n 8); Article 28 Cultural Property Convention (n 10); Articles 15–17 of the Second Protocol on Cultural Property (n 11); VII (1)(a) and (c) of the Chemical Weapons Convention (n 13); Article 9 of the Convention on the Prohibition of the Use, Stockpiling, Production and Transfer of Anti-Personnel Mines and on their Destruction (n 13); 1996 Amended Protocol II to the 1980 Certain Conventional Weapons Convention on Prohibitions or Restrictions on the Use of Mines, Booby-Traps and Other Devices (adopted 1996, entered into force 3 December 1998) 35 ILM 1206–17. Several treaties contain further rules on mutual legal assistance between States, extradition, etc; see eg AP I (n 9) Art 88; Second Protocol to the Cultural Property Convention (n 11) Art 19; Convention on the Safety of United Nations and Associated Personnel (n 12) Arts 15–16.
[15] Geneva Convention I (Arts 49–51); Geneva II (Arts 50–52); Geneva III Arts (129–131); Geneva IV (Arts 146–148) (n 8).
[16] Cf Geneva Convention I: Art 49 (1); Geneva Convention II (1): Art 50 (1); Geneva Convention III: Art 129 (1); Geneva Convention IV: Art 146 (1) (n 8).

to search for persons alleged to have committed, or to have ordered to be committed, ... grave breaches, and [each High Contracting Party] shall bring such persons, regardless of their nationality, before its own courts'.[17] While this provision does not specify the jurisdictional bases available to States, the words 'regardless of their nationality' are unanimously interpreted to mean that grave breaches of the Geneva Conventions can be prosecuted on any jurisdictional basis recognized by international law, including universal jurisdiction.[18] Alternatively, the High Contracting Party 'may also, if it prefers, and in accordance with the provisions of its own legislation, hand such persons over for trial to another High Contracting Party concerned, provided such High Contracting Party has made out a *prima facie* case'.[19] The Geneva Conventions thus subject grave breaches to the principle of *aut dedere aut judicare* (either extradite or prosecute).

The provisions of the Geneva Conventions relating to the suppression of grave breaches have been confirmed and supplemented by Part V, Section II (Articles 85–91) of *Additional Protocol I* (1977). While adding substantive provisions with respect to acts described as grave breaches,[20] failure to act,[21] and the duty of commanders,[22] the Protocol affirms that '[t]he provisions of the Conventions relating to the suppression of [...] grave breaches [...] shall apply to the suppression [...] grave breaches of this Protocol'.[23]

A further class of conventional war crimes relates to violations of the *1954 Hague Cultural Property Convention*. Its Article 28 provides that States Parties 'undertake, within the framework of their ordinary criminal jurisdiction, all necessary steps to prosecute and impose penal or disciplinary sanctions upon those persons, of whatever nationality, who commit or order to be committed a breach of the [...] Convention'. While this provision is rather general, and grants States considerable leeway as to the exact framework for suppressing violations of the 1954 Convention, the *1999 Second Hague Protocol for the Protection of Cultural Property in the Event of Armed Conflict* devotes an entire chapter to the refinement

---

[17] Cf Geneva Convention I: Art 49 (2); Geneva Convention II: Art 50 (2); Geneva Convention III: Art 129 (2); Geneva Convention IV: Art 146 (2) (n 8).

[18] See amongst many others M Henzelin, *Le Principe de l'Universalité en Droit Pénal International, Droit et Obligation pour les États de poursuivre et juger selon le principe de l'universalité* (Helbin & Lichtenhahn, Munich, Geneva, Brussels 2000) 351–356.

[19] Cf Geneva Convention I: Art 49 (2) second sentence; Geneva Convention II: Art 50 (2) second sentence; Geneva Convention III: Art 129 (2) second sentence; Geneva Convention IV: Art 146 (2) second sentence (n 8).

[20] AP I (n 9) Article 85 (3), (4).   [21] AP I (n 9) Article 86.   [22] AP I (n 9) Article 87.

[23] AP I (n 9) Article 85 (1). The Protocol also introduces new enforcement elements, such as mutual assistance in criminal matters in connection with criminal proceedings brought in respect of grave breaches and extradition (Article 88), cooperation in situations of serious violations of the Conventions and the Protocol (Article 89), liability of States to pay compensation for the violation of the Conventions' or Protocol's provisions committed by its armed forces (Article 91) and the International Fact-Finding Commission with a facultative competence to 'enquire into any facts alleged to be a grave breach as defined in the Conventions and this Protocol or other serious violation of the Conventions or of this Protocol' (Article 90, 90 (2)(c)(i)).

of that framework.[24] The chapter contains the obligation to 'adopt such measures as may be necessary to establish as criminal offences under its domestic law the offences set forth in [Article 15 (1)] and to make such offences punishable by appropriate penalties'[25] and further establishes a rather detailed jurisdictional regime.[26] According to that regime, States Parties shall establish territorial[27] and active nationality[28] jurisdiction with regard to all such offences, and must establish jurisdiction on the basis of *aut dedere aut judicare* regarding some.[29]

Furthermore, violations of the *1994 Convention on the Safety of United Nations and Associated Personnel* may be committed in the course of an armed conflict and then be regarded to fall into the broad category of 'war crimes'. This can readily be deduced from the scope of the Convention, since it extends to crimes committed against '[p]ersons engaged or deployed by the Secretary-General of the United Nations as members of the military, police or civilian components of a United Nations operation',[30] and such operations include operations for the purpose of maintaining or restoring international peace and security.[31] The Convention provides *inter alia* that States Parties shall make the crimes set out in Article 9 (1) of that Convention 'punishable by appropriate penalties which shall take into account their grave nature'.[32] As in the case of the Second Protocol to the Cultural Property Convention, States Parties are under the obligation

---

[24] Second Hague Protocol (n 11) Chapter 4 (Articles 15–21). For an overview, see T Desch, 'The Second Protocol to the 1954 Hague Convention for the Protection of Cultural Property in the Event of Armed Conflict' (1999) 2 YIHL 63–90, 63–64, 79.

[25] Second Hague Protocol (n 11) Article 15 (2). The provision further reads: 'When doing so, Parties shall comply with general principles of law and international law, including the rules extending individual criminal responsibility to persons other than those who directly commit the act.'

[26] Second Hague Protocol (n 11) Article 16.

[27] Second Hague Protocol (n 11) Article 16 (1)(a).

[28] Second Hague Protocol (n 11) Article 16 (1)(b).

[29] Second Hague Protocol (n 11) Article 16 (1)(c) in conjunction with Article 17 (1). Article 16 (2)(a) further clarifies, however, that the Protocol 'does not preclude the incurring of individual criminal responsibility or the exercise of jurisdiction under national and international law that may be applicable, or affect the exercise of jurisdiction under customary international law'.

[30] Convention on the Safety of United Nations and Associated Personnel (n 12) Article 1 (a)(i).

[31] Ibid Article 1 (c)(i). Some of the crimes penalized in the Convention (cf Article 9) have been declared to amount to 'war crimes' in Article 8 (2)(b)(iii) and (e)(iii) of the Rome Statute of the International Criminal Court (adopted 17 July 1998, as corrected by *procès-verbaux* of 10 November 1998, 12 July 1999, 30 November 1999, 8 May 2000, 17 January 2001 and 16 January 2002, entered into force 1 July 2002) A/CONF.183/9 (Rome Statute), if committed in the course of an armed conflict; see further 246. See also UNSC Res 1502 on the Protection of Humanitarian and UN Personnel (26 August 2003) UN Doc S/RES/1502, preambular para 5 ['*Emphasizing* that there are existing prohibitions under international law against attacks knowingly and intentionally directed against personnel involved in a humanitarian assistance or peacekeeping mission undertaken in accordance with the Charter of the United Nations which in situations of armed conflicts constitute war crimes, and recalling the need for States to end impunity for such criminal acts'.].

[32] Convention on the Safety of United Nations and Associated Personnel (n 12) Article 9 (2).

to establish territorial[33] and active nationality jurisdiction[34] as well as jurisdiction on the basis of *aut dedere aut judicare*.[35] Establishing jurisdiction over such crimes when they are committed 'by a stateless person whose habitual residence is in [a] State [Party]',[36] 'with respect to a national of that State'[37] or 'in an attempt to compel that State to do or to abstain from doing any act'[38] is optional, however. Article 13 of the UN Safety Convention further provides that '[w]here the circumstances so warrant, the State Party in whose territory the alleged offender is present shall take the appropriate measures under its national law to ensure that person's presence for the purpose of prosecution or extradition'.[39] A State Party 'in whose territory the alleged offender is present shall, if it does not extradite that person, submit, without exception whatsoever and without undue delay, the case to its competent authorities for the purpose of prosecution, through proceedings in accordance with the law of that State. Those authorities shall take their decision in the same manner as in the case of an ordinary offence of a grave nature under the law of that State.'[40]

A final set of treaty provisions on the national suppression of war crimes relates to the prohibition of the use of certain *weapons*. Parties to the 1993 Convention on the prohibition of the development, production, stockpiling and use of chemical weapons and on their destruction, for instance, are required to adopt the necessary measures to implement their obligations under this Convention, *inter alia*, by '[p]rohibit[ing] natural and legal persons anywhere on its territory or in any other place under its jurisdiction as recognized by international law from undertaking any activity prohibited to a State Party under this Convention[41], including enacting penal legislation with respect to such activity',[42] and by extending that penal legislation 'to any activity prohibited to a State Party under this Convention undertaken anywhere by natural persons, possessing its nationality, in conformity with international law'.[43]

---

[33] Convention on the Safety of United Nations and Associated Personnel (n 12) Article 10 (1)(a), that jurisdiction extends to crimes committed 'on board a ship or aircraft registered in that State'.
[34] Convention on the Safety of United Nations and Associated Personnel (n 12) Article 10 (1)(b).
[35] Convention on the Safety of United Nations and Associated Personnel (n 12) Article 10 (4).
[36] Convention on the Safety of United Nations and Associated Personnel (n 12) Article 10 (2)(a).
[37] Convention on the Safety of United Nations and Associated Personnel (n 12) Article 10 (2)(b).
[38] Convention on the Safety of United Nations and Associated Personnel (n 12) Article 10 (2)(c).
[39] Convention on the Safety of United Nations and Associated Personnel (n 12) Article 13 (1). Paragraph 2 of the same provision states that [m]easures taken in accordance with paragraph 1 shall be notified, in conformity with national law and without delay, to the Secretary-General of the United Nations and, either directly or through the Secretary-General, to the State where the crime was committed; the State or States of which the alleged offender is a national or, if such person is a stateless person, in whose territory that person has his or her habitual residence; the State or States of which the victim is a national; and other interested States.
[40] Convention on the Safety of United Nations and Associated Personnel (n 12) Article 14.
[41] According to Chemical Weapons Convention (n 13) Article I (1)(b), these prohibited activities include the use of chemical weapons.
[42] Chemical Weapons Convention (n 13) Article VII (1)(a).
[43] Chemical Weapons Convention (n 13) Article VII (1)(b).

Article 9 of the Convention on the Prohibition of the Use, Stockpiling, Production and Transfer of Anti-Personnel Mines and on their Destruction similarly provides that '[e]ach State Party shall take all appropriate legal, administrative and other measures, including the imposition of penal sanctions, to prevent and suppress any activity prohibited to a State Party under this Convention undertaken by persons or on territory under its jurisdiction or control'. Likewise, the 1996 Amended Protocol II to the 1980 Certain Conventional Weapons Convention on Prohibitions or Restrictions on the Use of Mines, Booby-Traps and Other Devices obliges States Parties to 'take all appropriate steps, including legislative and other measures, to prevent and suppress violations of this Protocol by persons or on territory under its jurisdiction or control'.[44] It further clarifies that these measures 'include appropriate measures to ensure the imposition of penal sanctions against persons who, in relation to an armed conflict and contrary to the provisions of this Protocol, wilfully kill or cause serious injury to civilians and to bring such persons to justice . . .'.[45]

Alongside the aforementioned conventional regimes, a number of war crimes lacked codification in instruments with (potentially) universal reach prior to the adoption of the Rome Statute.[46] Accordingly, the suppression of the majority of war crimes committed in non-international armed conflicts,[47] and of a number of war crimes committed in international armed conflicts, was subject to *customary international law*.[48]

---

[44] AP II Conventional Weapons Convention (n 13) Article 14 (1).

[45] AP II Conventional Weapons Convention (n 13) Article 14 (2).

[46] Codifications in the statutes of the international ad hoc tribunals of Nuremberg, Tokyo and ICTY and ICTR, as well as other written sources, such as Control Council Law No 10, were only applicable to very specific circumstances/armed conflicts. While they have proved central elements of a piecemeal customary process, they do not in themselves constitute codifications of a global reach. Similarly, the Draft Code (n 5), while intended to codify core crimes and the legal regime applicable to them, has never been adopted. It is therefore regarded as evidence of customary international law: see *Prosecutor v Anto Furundzija* (Judgment) IT-95-17/1-T, T Ch II (10 December 1998) 227, confirmed by the Appeals Chamber in the *Prosecutor v Tadic* (Appeals Judgment) IT-941-A, A Ch (15 July 1999) 223.

[47] Exceptions relate to cultural property and anti-personnel mines. Cf Article 19 in conjunction with Article 28 of the 1954 Cultural Property Convention and Article 22 (1) (n 10) in conjunction with Articles 15–21 of the Second Protocol to the Convention (n 11). The fact that Article 1 of the Convention on the Prohibition of the Use, Stockpiling, Production and Transfer of Anti-Personnel Mines and on their Destruction, 18 September 1997 (n 13), contains the obligation not to use anti-personnel mines 'under any circumstances', in conjunction with Article 9 is also understood to extend the criminalization of the use of anti-personnel mines to internal armed conflicts. The 1996 Amended Protocol II to the 1980 Certain Conventional Weapons Convention on Prohibitions or Restrictions on the Use of Mines, Booby-Traps and Other Devices (n 14) provides in Article 1 (2) that the Amended Protocol also applies 'to situations referred to in Article 3 common to the Geneva Conventions of 12 August 1949'.

[48] The content of some of the aforementioned Conventions is also generally accepted as amounting to customary international law. The customary status of the prohibition of grave breaches of the Geneva Conventions, for instance, was beyond question even prior to the adoption of the Rome Statute, as evidenced by the universal ratification of the Geneva Conventions, decisions of international courts and tribunals (ICJ, ICTY), and other recent developments, such as the Draft Code (n 5) Article 20 (a)–(c), and the Report of the United Nations Secretary-General, 'The

There is no doubt that customary law envisages that national criminal jurisdictions shall assume an *equally central role* in the suppression of core crimes as treaty law.[49] This role of national criminal jurisdictions is also confirmed by the process of forming customary criminalizations of serious violations of international humanitarian law. One of the sources used to establish such customary rules are national laws relating to, and prosecutions of, the conduct in question.[50] Customary rules thus formed thereby encapsulate that national criminal jurisdictions are competent to prosecute the crime in question.

However, it lies in the nature of customary law that such regimes governing the prosecution of war crimes are less detailed and specific than those established by written instruments.[51] Consequently, a number of questions relating to the exact role of national criminal jurisdictions in their suppression were raised. It was unclear whether these crimes were subject to passive personal jurisdiction[52]

establishment of the International Criminal Tribunal for the former Yugoslavia (1993) (Report pursuant to paragraph 2 UNSC Res 808)' (3 May 1993) UN Doc S/25704 [35, 41–44]. The same applies to those grave breaches in Protocol I that have equally been included in these instruments; see also S R Ratner and J S Abrams, *Accountability for Human Rights Atrocities in International Law—Beyond the Nuremberg Legacy* (2nd edn OUP, Oxford 2001) 86–87. The following analysis will be confined, however, to those war crimes that are subject *exclusively* to a customary regime.

[49] Cf *8–9*.

[50] For the customary criminalization of war crimes in internal armed conflicts, see the reference to such sources in *Prosecutor v Tadic* (Appeals Decision on the Defence Motion for Interlocutory Appeal on Jurisdiction) IT-94-1 App Ch (2 October 1995) 106, 125, 131–132. Implementing legislation adopted after this landmark decision of the ICTY include the Penal Codes of Spain, Finland, Sweden, The Netherlands, Nicaragua, Ethiopia, Slovenia, the Swiss Military Penal Code, the Norwegian Military Penal Code, and the United States War Crimes Act as amended in 1996. For a discussion of these and other laws, see T Graditzky, 'Individual criminal responsibility for violations of international humanitarian law committed in non-international armed conflicts' (1998) International Review of the Red Cross 29–56, 38–44. More recent legislation prior to the adoption of the Rome Statute comprised: Article 320 of the 1997 Penal Code of Paraguay (reproduced in YIHL vol I (1998), 623); Article 1 (a) of the Rwandan Organic Law 8/96 of August 30, 1996 on the organization of prosecutions for offences constituting the crime of genocide or crimes against humanity since 1 October 1990 (ibid, 626); section 2 of the 1997 USA Expanded War Crimes Act (ibid, 644); and the 1998 Irish Geneva Conventions (Amendment) Act amending, *inter alia*, section 4 of the Geneva Conventions Act of 1962 (reproduced in YIHL vol II (1999) 546–547). Post-*Tadic* national case law comprised the Dutch case: *re Knezevic*, Arnhem District Court, Military Division (Chambers), Decision of 21 February 1996, NJ 1998/463, 30 NYIL (1999), 315; Supreme Court, Decision of 22 October 1996, NJ 1998/462; Supreme Court, Decision of 11 November 1997, NJ 1998/463.

[51] On that chronic deficiency of custom, see generally I Lukashuk, 'Customary Norms in Contemporary International Law' in J Makarczyk (ed), *Theory of International Law at the Threshold of the 21st Century—Essays in Honour of Krzysztof Skubiszewski* (Martin Nijhoff, The Hague 1996) 487–508, 488, 496–497.

[52] Cf A Yokaris, 'Les Critères de Compétence des Juridictions Nationales' in H Ascensio, E Decaux and A Pellet (eds), *Droit International Pénal* (Éditions Pedone, Paris 2000) 897–904, 902 [who notes that this jurisdictional basis is 'très discuté']; B Swart, 'La place des critères traditionnels de compétence dans la pursuite des crimes internationaux' in A Cassese and M Delmas-Marty (eds), *Juridictions nationales et crimes internationaux* (Presses Universitaires de France, Paris 2002) 567–589, who concludes from a number of national and regional reports that passive personality jurisdiction 'n'a été adopté que par une minorité d'États représentées' (576). On the other hand, A Cassese seems to suggest that practice supports passive personality jurisdiction

and whether a customary rule of permissive universal jurisdiction had crystallized.[53] Similarly, it was controversial whether States—and which States—were under an obligation to investigate and prosecute customary war crimes.[54]

2.1.2. *Genocide*

As far as the crime of genocide is concerned, the 1948 *Genocide Convention*[55] obliges States Parties 'to prevent and punish' this crime[56] and 'to enact, in accordance with their respective Constitutions, the necessary legislation to give effect to the provisions of the [Genocide] Convention and, in particular, to provide

exercised over war crimes (n 5) 283 ['frequent resort to this ground of jurisdiction to prosecute war crimes'].

[53] In favour of universal jurisdiction: Article 8 in conjunction with Article 20 (f) of the Draft Code (n 5); for further references in support of such an answer in the affirmative, see Amnesty International, 'Universal Jurisdiction—The Duty to Enact and Implement Legislation', AI Index IOR 53/002–018/2001, September 2001, Chapter Three, 7–12, 21–23; J M Henckaerts and L Doswald-Beck (eds), *Customary International Humanitarian Law* (Volume I: Rules, CUP, Cambridge 2005) Rule 157. Against universal jurisdiction over war crimes in internal armed conflicts: M S M Mahmoud, 'Les leçons de l'affaire Pinochet' (1999) 4 Journal du Droit International, 1021–1041, 1025 ['Un tel système [de compétence universelle] ne peut (...) s'appuyer sur les règles du droit coutumier, sauf pour le crime de piraterie']. In a similar vein C Tomuschat, 'The duty to prosecute international crimes committed by individuals' in H J Cremer and H Steinberger (eds), *Tradition und Weltoffenheit des Rechts: Festschrift für Helmut Steinberger* (Springer, Berlin 2002) 315–349, noting that universal jurisdiction 'requires special authorization by the international legal order' (at 327) and that 'it is not easy to prove that serious violations of the rules contained [in Additional Protocol II] may [...] be prosecuted within the judicial system of every State irrespective of existing links with the conflict concerned' (at 334). See also J B Bellinger III and W J Haynes II, 'A US government response to the International Committee of the Red Cross study Customary International Humanitarian Law' (2007) 89 IRRC 443–471, 465–471.

[54] Amongst the abundant pronouncements on the matter, see eg in favour of such an obligation: J M Henckaerts and L Doswald-Beck (eds), ibid Rule 158, 607 ['States must investigate war crimes allegedly committed by their nationals or armed forces, or on their territory, and, if appropriate, prosecute the suspects. They must also investigate other war crimes over which they have jurisdiction and, if appropriate, prosecute the suspects.']; Principle 19 of the Updated Set of principles for the protection and promotion of human rights, Report by Diane Orentlicher updating the Joinet Principles, UN Commission on Human Rights E/CN.4/2005/102/Add.1 Sixty-first session, 8 February 2005 ['States shall undertake prompt, thorough, independent and impartial investigations of violations of human rights and international humanitarian law and take appropriate measures in respect of the perpetrators, particularly in the area of criminal justice, by ensuring that those responsible for serious crimes under international law are prosecuted, tried and duly punished.']. Against: C Tomuschat, ibid 334 ['not easy to prove that serious violations contained [in Additional Protocol II] may nonetheless be prosecuted within the judicial system of every State irrespective of existing links with the conflict concerned. Notwithstanding the question of links, there can be no question of a duty to institute prosecutorial proceedings [...].'].

[55] Convention on the Prevention and Punishment of the Crime of Genocide (adopted 9 December 1948, entered into force 12 January 1951) 78 UNTS 277.

[56] Article I Genocide Convention (n 55). On the meaning and content of these two distinct obligations, see ICJ, *Case Concerning the Application of the Convention on the Prevention and Punishment of the Crime of Genocide (Bosnia and Herzegovina v Serbia and Montenegro)* (n 5) [428–438] (prevention) and [439–450] (punish).

effective penalties for persons guilty of [acts criminalized by the Convention]'.[57] Article VI further provides that '[p]ersons charged with [such acts] shall be tried by a competent tribunal of the State in the territory of which the act was committed, or by such international penal tribunal as may have jurisdiction with respect to those Contracting Parties which shall have accepted its jurisdiction'. Since such consensually established 'international penal tribunal[s]' remained dormant before the coming into existence of the International Criminal Court,[58] the suppressive regime established under the Genocide Convention was thus confined to national criminal jurisdictions exercising territorial jurisdiction.

The prohibition of genocide also had evolved into a norm of *customary international law*[59] and is recognized to have *jus cogens* status.[60] The customary regime applicable to national suppression of that crime is, however, not fully identical with the Convention. Thus it was widely accepted prior to the adoption of the Rome Statute that customary international law had widened the jurisdictional scope over the crime of genocide to allow for the exercise of jurisdiction based on criteria other than territoriality, including active nationality and universal

---

[57] Article V Genocide Convention (n 55).

[58] The only two other international tribunals, which possess jurisdiction over the crime of genocide, the ICTY and ICTR, have been established by Security Council Resolutions under Chapter VII of the UN Charter and thus have jurisdiction regardless of the *specific* consent of States concerned. It has been argued that they therefore fall outside the ambit of Genocide Convention (n 55) Article VI, which requires that Contracting Parties 'have accepted [the] jurisdiction' of the international penal tribunal: see P Akhavan, 'Enforcement of the Genocide Convention: A Challenge to Civilization' (1995) 8 Harvard Human Rights Journal 229–258, 239 ['irrespective of Article VI of the Genocide Convention [. . .] the Security Council has opted to enforce the substantive provisions of the Convention by means of extra-treaty mechanisms']. This is notwithstanding the *general* consent given by UN members to the Chapter VII powers of the Security Council by virtue of which the ICTY and ICTR were established. In its judgment in the *Case Concerning the Application of the Convention on the Prevention and Punishment of the Crime of Genocide* (*Bosnia and Herzegovina v Serbia and Montenegro*), the ICJ came to a different conclusion and held that the ICTY is an 'international penal tribunal' within the meaning of Article VI, with which Serbia and Montenegro was under an obligation to cooperate (n 5) [444–447].

[59] Cf *Reservations to the Convention on the Prevention and Punishment of Genocide* (Advisory Opinion) [1951] ICJ Rep 15, 23. The customary status of the prohibition of the crime of genocide was also confirmed by the Report of the United Nations Secretary-General, 'The establishment of the International Criminal Tribunal for the former Yugoslavia (Report pursuant to paragraph 2 UNSC Res 808)' (3 May 1993) UN Doc S/25704 [45], by judgments of international tribunals (see eg the Judgments of the ICTR in *Prosecutor v Akayesu* ICTR-96-4-T (2 September 1998) [495].; *Prosecutor v Kayishema and Ruzindana* ICTR-95-1-T (21 May 1999) [88]; *Case Concerning Application of the Convention on the Prevention and Punishment of the Crime of Genocide (Bosnia-Herzegovina v Yugoslavia)* (Preliminary Objections) [1996] ICJ Rep 595 [31]; and national courts see eg Federal Court of Australia in *Nulyarimma v Thompson* [1999] Federal Court of Australia 1192 (1 September 1999), <http://www.austlii.edu.au/Federal Court of Australia>.

[60] *Armed Activities on the Territory of the Congo (New Application 2002) (Democratic Republic of the Congo v Rwanda)* Jurisdiction of the Court and Admissibility of the Application, Judgment of 3 February 2006, General List No 121 [64].

jurisdiction.[61] Whether the exercise of that jurisdiction is obligatory, however, was subject to controversy.[62]

2.1.3. Crimes Against Humanity

Prior to, and outside of, the Rome Statute, the regime of national suppression applicable to crimes against humanity—ie acts such as murder, extermination, torture and imprisonment committed as part of a widespread or systematic attack against the civilian population—was governed exclusively by *customary international law*.[63] Similar to the customary regimes of war crimes and genocide, uncertainties surrounded the exact extent of the rights and obligations of States to suppress that crime. These ambiguities relate, *inter alia,* to the question of universal jurisdiction over crimes against humanity,[64] passive personality

[61] See Amnesty International (n 53) Ch VII, 4–13 (with further references and convincing arguments refuting arguments against permissive universal jurisdiction made by a small number of authorities); A Peyró Llopis, *La compétence universelle en matière de crimes contre l'humanité* (Bruylant, Brussels 2003) 128–129. The view is also shared by authors who take a comparatively cautious approach, see eg C Tomuschat (n 53) 331. More cautiously, W A Schabas, *Genocide in International Law—The Crime of Crimes* (CUP, Cambridge 2000) 361–368 [increasing willingness to accept universal jurisdiction but 'existence of more isolated contrary signals may give some pause to suggestions that an international consensus has developed on the subject. The law will only develop in the right direction if States attempt to exercise universal jurisdiction over genocide, and here they show little inclination', at 367–368]. A scope wider than territorial jurisdiction has also been confirmed after the entry into force of the Rome Statute: ICJ, *Case Concerning the Application of the Convention on the Prevention and Punishment of the Crime of Genocide (Bosnia and Herzegovina v Serbia and Montenegro)* (n 5) [442].

[62] Pro: L A Steven, 'Genocide and the Duty to Extradite or Prosecute: Why the United States is in Breach of Its International Obligations' (1999) 39 Virginia Journal of International Law 425–466; M Scharf, 'The Letter of the Law: The Scope of the International Legal Obligation to Prosecute Human Rights Crimes' (1996) 59 Law and Contemporary Problems 41–61, 44; S Landsman, 'Alternative Responses To Serious Human Rights Abuses: Of Prosecution and Truth Commissions' (1996) 59 Law and Contemporary Problems 81–92, 90–91; Amnesty International (n 53) Ch VII, 13–17 (with further references). Contra: C Tomuschat (n 53) 332; A Peyró Llopis (n 61); D F Orentlicher, 'Settling Accounts: The Duty to Prosecute Human Rights Violations of a Prior Regime' (1991) Yale LJ, vol 100, 2537–2615, 2565; A R Carnegie, 'Jurisdiction over Violations of the Laws and Customs of War' (1963) 39 BYIL 402–424, 408–409; K C Randall, 'Universal Jurisdiction under International Law' (1988) 66 Texas Law Review 785–842, 837; ICRC Advisory Service, *Punishing Violations of International Humanitarian Law at the National Level—A Guide for Common Law States* (ICRC, Geneva 2001) 44.

[63] Codifications were limited to the statutes of the Nuremberg and Tokyo tribunals and Control Council Law No 10, in addition to the ICTY and ICTR Statutes (n 2). These instruments, although undoubtedly highly significant in the customary process of defining crimes against humanity, did not contain any rules on national suppression of this crime with universal reach. Cf (n 46).

[64] Pro: Amnesty International (n 53) Chapter V (with further references). Contra: A Peyró Llopis (n 61) 131; J Verhoeven, 'M. Pinochet, la coutume internationale et la compétence universelle, note sous Civ. Bruxelles, 6 novembre 1998' (1999) Journal des Tribunaux 308–315, 313.

jurisdiction[65] and whether crimes against humanity entailed an obligation to investigate or prosecute.[66]

In addition to customary law applicable to national suppression of crimes against humanity as such, the sub-species of the crime of *apartheid* and a number of underlying crimes—ie crimes that amount to crimes against humanity if committed as part of a widespread or systematic attack against the civilian population—were regulated in *treaties*.

The 1973 *Apartheid* Convention[67] contains the undertaking of States Parties to 'adopt any legislative or other measures necessary to suppress [. . .] any encouragement of the crime of apartheid [. . .] and to punish persons guilty of that crime' and to 'adopt legislative, judicial and administrative measures to prosecute, bring to trial and punish in accordance with their jurisdiction persons responsible for, or accused of [the crime of apartheid], whether or not such persons reside in the territory of the State in which the acts are committed or are nationals of that State or of some other State or are stateless persons.'[68] Persons charged with the crime of apartheid 'may be tried by a competent tribunal of any State Party to the Convention which may acquire jurisdiction over the person of the accused or by an international penal tribunal having jurisdiction with respect to those States Parties which shall have accepted its jurisdiction.'[69] As in the case of the Genocide Convention,[70] such an 'international penal tribunal' was never established and the suppression of the crime of apartheid remained (at least in theory)[71] the exclusive domain of national criminal jurisdictions.

Besides the crime of apartheid, other international agreements circumscribe the role of national criminal jurisdictions in the suppression of a number of

---

[65] Pro: A Peyró Llopis (n 61) 129–130; A Cassese (n 5) 283. Contra: see A Yokaris (n 52).

[66] Pro: M C Bassiouni, *Crimes Against Humanity in International Criminal Law* (2nd edn Martinus Nijhoff, Dordrecht 1999) 224; D F Orentlicher (n 62) 2593–2594; Inter-American Court of Human Rights, *Almonacid-Arellano et al v Chile*, Judgment of 26 September 2006, IACtHR Series C No 154 (2006) [114] ['duty to investigate, identify, and punish those persons responsible for crimes against humanity']; Inter-American Court of Human Rights, *Miguel Castro-Castro Prison v Peru,* Judgment of 25 November 2006, IACtHR Series C No 160 (2006) [404] [prohibition to commit crimes against humanity is norm of *ius cogens,* and therefore, the State has the obligation not to leave these crimes unpunished and must ensure effective prosecution and punishment of perpetrators]; Inter-American Court of Human Rights, *La Cantuta v Peru* (Merits), Judgment of 29 November 2006, Reparations and Costs, IACtHR Series C No 162 (2006) [110] [duty to investigate is particularly intense and significant in cases of crimes against humanity]; see also [225]. Contra: M Scharf (n 62) 56–59.

[67] International Convention on the Suppression and Punishment of the Crime of Apartheid (adopted November 30 1973) 1015 UNTS 243.

[68] Apartheid Convention (n 67) Article IV.

[69] Apartheid Convention (n 67) Article V.   [70] Cf (n 58) and text.

[71] No domestic prosecutions for the crime of apartheid have been conducted.

underlying crimes. In particular, *slavery*,[72] *torture*[73] and *forced disappearance of persons*[74] are regulated by treaties. The suppression of these crimes, as envisaged by the respective treaty, applies regardless of whether or not they are committed as part of a widespread or systematic attack against a civilian population.

However, the mechanical transposition of these regimes to the suppression of crimes against humanity if the commission of these underlying crimes reach that threshold (*argumentum a minori ad maius*) has to be approached with caution. For, the difference between crimes against humanity and singular and isolated acts of torture or forced disappearance may very well be reflected in different regimes regulating their suppression.[75] Furthermore, the mechanical transposition of the treaty regimes of underlying crimes to crimes against humanity would result in the latter crimes being governed by a fragmented regime, thereby running counter to its character as a single and identifiable category of core crimes.

However, although the treaty regimes governing underlying crimes do not determine conclusively the national suppression of crimes against humanity as a whole, it is nevertheless useful to describe briefly the treaty regimes applicable to slavery and similar practices, torture and forced disappearance.

National suppression of the crime of *slavery and similar practices* has been regulated in a number of treaties.[76] The earliest such treaty, the 1926 Slavery Convention, provided in general terms that '[t]he High Contracting Parties undertake, each in respect of the territories placed under its sovereignty, jurisdiction,

---

[72] Slavery Convention (adopted 25 September 1926, entered into force 9 March 1927) 60 LNTS 253; 1956 Supplementary Convention on the Abolition of Slavery, the Slave Trade, and Institutions and Practices Similar to Slavery (adopted 7 September 1956, entered into force 30 April 1957) 266 UNTS 3; 1930 Convention Concerning Forced or Compulsory Labour (ILO Convention No 29) (adopted 28 June 1930, entered into force 1 May 1932) 39 UNTS 55; 1957 Convention Concerning the Abolition of Forced Labour (ILO Convention No 105) (adopted 25 June 1957, entered into force 17 January 1959) 320 UNTS 291. The term 'slavery' has been replaced by 'enslavement' in the provisions defining crimes against humanity of the 'Nuremberg Charter', Charter of the International Military Tribunal (8 August 1945) 82 UNTS 280 (Article 6 (c)); 'Tokyo Charter', Charter of the International Military Tribunal for the Far East (19 January 1946) TIAS No 1589 (Article 5 (c)); ICTY Statute (n 2) (Article 5 (c)), ICTR Statute (n 2) (Article 3 (c)) and the Draft Code (n 5) Article 18 (d)). For the similarities between 'slavery' and 'enslavement' as a crime against humanity, see *inter alia Prosecutor v Kunarac, Kovac and Vukovic* ('*Foca*') (Judgment) IT-96-23 (22 February 2001) 518–543 and (Appeals Chamber judgment) IT-96-23/1, Ap Ch (12 June 2002) 106–124. See generally, M C Bassiouni, 'Enslavement as an international crime' (1991) 23 NYU J Intl L & Pol 445–517.

[73] UN Convention against Torture and Other Cruel, Inhuman or Degrading Treatment or Punishment (adopted 10 December 1984, entered into force 26 June 1987) 1465 UNTS 85.

[74] International Convention for the Protection of All Persons from Enforced Disappearance 2006, GA Res 61/177, 20 December 2006, A/RES/61/177; 14 IHRR 582 (2007); Inter-American Convention on Forced Disappearance of Persons (entered into force 28 March 1996) 33 ILM 1429.

[75] Cf International Convention for the Protection of All Persons from Enforced Disappearance, ibid Article 5 ['The widespread or systematic practice of enforced disappearance constitutes a crime against humanity as defined in applicable international law and shall attract the consequences provided for under such applicable international law.'].

[76] (n 72).

protection, suzerainty or tutelage, [...t]o [...] suppress the slave trade'.[77] States Parties 'whose laws do not at present make adequate provision for the punishment of infractions of laws and regulations enacted with a view to giving effect to the purposes of the [...] Convention' are also under an obligation 'to adopt the necessary measures in order that severe penalties may be imposed in respect of such infractions'.[78] The 1956 Supplementary Convention on the Abolition of Slavery, the Slave Trade, and Institutions and Practices Similar to Slavery subsequently expanded the list of prohibited acts, which States Parties were equally obliged to criminalize.[79]

Three years after the entry into force of the 1926 Slavery Convention, the General Conference of the International Labour Organisation adopted the 1930 Convention Concerning Forced or Compulsory Labour (ILO Convention No 29). The latter provided in Article 25 that '[t]he illegal exaction of forced or compulsory labour shall be punishable as a penal offence, and it shall be an obligation on any Member ratifying this Convention to ensure that the penalties imposed by law are really adequate and are strictly enforced'. The 1957 ILO Convention No 105 Concerning the Abolition of Forced Labour later expanded the list of prohibited acts, which '[e]ach Member of the International Labour Organisation which ratifies this Convention undertakes to suppress', thus leaving open whether such suppression must take the form of penal sanctions.

While the aforementioned treaties on slavery and similar practices would seem to grant States considerable leeway as regards the exact regime governing national suppression, the conventional regime relating to the crime of *torture* is far more detailed. Article 4 of the 1984 Convention against Torture obliges States Parties to ensure that all acts of, attempts to commit and complicity or participation in torture are offences under their criminal law and to make these offences punishable by appropriate penalties which take into account their grave nature. The Convention further contains the duty to establish territorial and active nationality jurisdiction in addition to jurisdiction on the basis of *aut dedere aut judicare,* as well as passive nationality jurisdiction 'if [the State Party concerned] considers it appropriate'.[80] Criminal jurisdiction exercised in accordance with internal law is not excluded.[81] Article 6 provides for rather detailed obligations of States

---

[77] Slavery Convention (n 72) Article 2 (a).   [78] Slavery Convention (n 72) Article 6.

[79] Slavery Convention (n 72) Articles 3 (1) [as regards the 'act of conveying or attempting to convey slaves from one country to another by whatever means of transport, or of being accessory thereto'], 5 [as regards the 'act of mutilating, branding or otherwise marking a slave or a person of servile status in order to indicate his status, or as a punishment, or for any other reason, or of being accessory thereto'] and 6 [as regards the 'act of enslaving another person or of inducing another person to give himself or a person dependent upon him into slavery, or of attempting these acts, or being accessory thereto' and 'the act of inducing another person to place himself or a person dependent upon him into the servile status resulting from any of the institutions or practices mentioned in article 1, to any attempt to perform such acts, to being accessory thereto, and to being a party to a conspiracy to accomplish any such acts'].

[80] Torture Convention (n 73) Article 5 (1)–(2).

[81] Torture Convention (n 73) Article 5 (3).

Parties, in whose territory a person alleged to have committed acts of torture is present, either to extradite or to prosecute that person.[82]

Finally, two treaty regimes govern the suppression of the underlying crime of *forced disappearance*. These are the Inter-American Convention on Forced Disappearance of Persons and the International Convention for the Protection of All Persons from Enforced Disappearance. Both conventions contain an obligation to criminalize forced disappearance of persons as an offence under domestic law,[83] to establish jurisdiction on the basis of principles closely resembling those of the Torture Convention[84] and to extradite persons alleged to have committed forced disappearance of persons or, alternatively, to investigate and, if appropriate, prosecute these persons.[85]

One can safely deduce from the foregoing description that, prior to the Rome Statute, international law envisaged national criminal jurisdictions as the central forum for the investigation and prosecution of war crimes, genocide and crimes against humanity. All regimes applicable to core crimes, whether conventional or customary, clearly envisage the respective prohibitions to be effectuated on the national level. However, beyond this generality, no single and unified regime for the national suppression of core crimes existed. Different crimes were governed by different formal sources, and the substance of the respective rules varied. While bearing occasional resemblance, these regimes were heterogeneous and could best be described as a patchwork of norms, notwithstanding attempts to develop a uniform body of law, most notably in the context of the ILC's work on the Draft Code of Crimes against the Peace and Security of Mankind.[86]

2.1.4. *The Obligation to Prosecute Human Rights Violations*
In addition to the aforementioned regimes specifically regulating the national suppression of individual core crimes, human rights obligations further define the role of national criminal jurisdictions. More specifically, universal and regional

---

[82] Torture Convention (n 73) Articles 6–7.

[83] International Convention for the Protection of All Persons from Enforced Disappearance (n 74) Article 4; Inter-American Forced Disappearances (n 74) Article III.

[84] International Convention for the Protection of All Persons from Enforced Disappearance (n 74) Article 9; Inter-American Forced Disappearances (n 74) Article IV. Notable differences from the jurisdictional regime established by the Torture Convention are that the Inter-American Convention does not contain any provision on jurisdiction exercised in accordance with internal law, and that it contains an express prohibition of States Parties 'to undertake, in the territory of another State Party, the exercise of jurisdiction or the performance of functions that are placed within the exclusive purview of the authorities of that other Party by its domestic law'. Such an express prohibition is absent in the Torture Convention.

[85] International Convention for the Protection of All Persons from Enforced Disappearance (n 74) Article 11; Inter-American Forced Disappearances (n 74) Article VI.

[86] (n 5).

human rights treaties have been interpreted by the respective organs responsible for their supervision to impose on States Parties the *obligation* that serious violations of human rights be investigated and those responsible for them prosecuted and punished. Such an interpretation is based on the general provision in these human rights treaties that States Parties shall ensure respect of, or secure the rights embodied in, the respective instrument[87] to all individuals within their jurisdiction, in conjunction with the right to an effective remedy and access to court.[88]

According to the Inter-American Court of Human Rights in the case of *Velásquez-Rodríguez*,[89] this obligation to ensure respect entails that '... States must [...] *investigate, and punish* any violation of the rights recognized by the Convention [...]'.[90] Such obligation does not only arise vis-à-vis violations directly imputable to the State, for instance in cases in which State organs have committed the violation, but may also be violated if the State fails to exercise due diligence to respond to violations or abuses which are not so attributable to it.[91] In other words, the obligation to investigate and punish extends to acts of State organs and non-State actors, subject to the difference that the obligations of States vis-à-vis conduct that cannot be considered their own[92] is governed by the standard of due diligence rather than amounting to a strict obligation of result.

The initial jurisprudence of the Inter-American Court on such an obligation to investigate and punish, confirmed by subsequent decisions of the Inter-American

[87] Cf Article 2 (1) of the International Covenant on Civil and Political Rights (adopted 16 December 1966, entered into force 23 March 1976) 999 UNTS 171 (ICCPR), ['to respect and to ensure...the rights...']; Article 1 of the European Convention for the Protection of Human Rights and Fundamental Freedoms (entered into force 3 September 1953, as amended by Protocols Nos 3, 5, 8, and 11 which entered into force on 21 September 1970, 20 December 1971, 1 January 1990, and 1 November 1998 respectively) 213 UNTS 222 (ECHR) ['shall secure']; Article 1 (1) of the Inter-American Convention on Human Rights (entered into force 18 July 1978) OAS Treaty Series No 36, 1144 UNTS 123 (IACHR) ['to respect...and to ensure...']; Article 1 of the African Charter on Human and Peoples' Rights (adopted on 27 June 1981, entered into force 21 October 1986) OAU Doc CAB/LEG/67/3 rev. 5, 21 ILM 58 (AfCHPR) ['shall recognize...and shall undertake to adopt...measures to give effect...'].

[88] Articles 2 (3) ICCPR; 13 ECHR; 8 and 25 IACHR; 7 (1)(a) AfCHPR (n 87).

[89] *Velásquez Rodríguez* Judgment of 29 July 1988, Inter-American Court of Human Rights (Series C) (No 4 (1998).

[90] (n 89), 166, emphasis added.   [91] (n 89), 172.

[92] On what acts can be considered 'conduct of the State' and the extent to which acts of non-State actors can be directly attributed to a State, see Chapter II of the Articles on Responsibility of States for Internationally Wrongful Acts (2001), reproduced in J Crawford, *The International Law Commission's Articles on State Responsibility—Introduction, Text and Commentaries* (CUP, Cambridge 2002) 91–123.

Court and Commission[93] and other human rights bodies,[94] were considered by some to leave room for argument as to whether the investigation and punishment has to be of a criminal nature.[95] However, several decisions clearly indicate that the obligation 'to investigate and punish' amounts to an obligation to conduct *criminal* proceedings vis-à-vis serious human rights violations.[96]

[93] For decisions of the IACtHR, see for example *Godínez Cruz*, Judgment of 20 January 1989 Series C No 5 [184] *et seq*; *Aloeboetoe et al*, Judgment of 4 December 1991, IACtHR Series C No 11 (1994) 76 *et seq*; *Gangaram Panday*, Judgment of 21 January 1994, IACtHR Series C No 16 (1994); *El Amparo*, Judgment of 18 January 1995, IACtHR Annual Report 1995, 23 *et seq*; *Neira Alegría et al*, Judgment of 19 January 1995, IACtHR Series C No 21 (1995), 41 *et seq*; *Bámaca Velásquez Case*, Judgment of 25 November 2000, IACtHR Series C No 70 (2000) [211–212]; *Barrios Altos Case*, Judgment of 14 May 2001, IACtHR Series C No 75 (2001) [41–44], available at <http://www1.umn.edu/humanrts/iachr/C/75-ing.html>; for decisions of the IACmHR, see for example: Cases No 10.235, 10.454, 10.581, Annual Report IACmHR 1992, 27 *et seq*; 1993, 52, 61; Cases No 10.433, 10.443, 10.528, 10.531, Annual Report IACmHR 1992–93, 110, 118, 128, 136; Report No 1/99 of 27.1.1999, Case 10.480: *Lucio Parada Cea et al*, at [130]; *Carlos Manuel Prada Gonzalez and Evelio Antonio Bolano Castro v Colombia*, Case No 11.710, Report No 84/98, IACmHR, OEA/Ser.L/V/II.95 Doc 7 rev at 72 (1998) [41] *et seq*, available at <http://www1.umn.edu/humanrts/cases/1998/colombia84-98.html>; *Castillo Páez Case*, Judgment of 3 November 1997, Series C No 34 [90]; *Caballero Delgado and Santana Case*, Judgment of 8 December 1995, Series C No 22 [56–58]; *Río Frío Massacre*, Case 11.654, Report No 62/01, IACmHR, OEA/Ser.L/V/II.111 Doc 20 rev at 758 (2000) [73, 75], available at <http://www.cidh.oas.org/annualrep/2000eng/ChapterIII/Merits/Colombia11.654.htm>.

[94] See for instance Human Rights Committee, *Guillermo Ignacio Dermit Barbato et al v Uruguay*, Communication No 84/1981 UN Doc CCPR/C/OP/2 at 112 (1990) [11]; *Tshitenge Muteba v Zaire*, Communication No 124/1982 (25 March 1983) UN Doc Supp No 40 (A/39/40) at 182 (1984) [13]; *Hugo Rodriguez v Uruguay*, Communication No 322/1988, UN Doc CCPR/C/51/D/322/1988, 2 IHRR (1995) 112 [12.3–12.4]. See also Human Rights Committee, General Comment no 20, Article 7, adopted during the Committee's 44th session in 1992, Compilation of General Comments and General Recommendations adopted by Human Rights Treaty Bodies, UN Doc HR1/GEN/1/Rev. 6 at 151 (2003), with respect to the prohibition of torture (Article 7 ICCPR). For jurisprudence of the European Court of Human Rights, see among others *Aksoy v Turkey* (App no 21987/93) [1996] ECHR 68 (18 December 1996) 2287 [98]; *Assenov and Others v Bulgaria* (App no 24760/94) [1998] ECHR 98 (28 October 1998) 3290 [102]; and, *mutatis mutandis*, *Soering v the United Kingdom* (App no 14038/88) [1989] ECHR 14 (7 July 1989) 34–35 [88]; *Selmouni v France* (App no 25803/94) [1999] ECHR 66 (28 July 1999) 79; *Al-Adsani v United Kingdom* (App no 35763/97) [2001] ECHR 761 (21 November 2001) at 38–40; *Kaya v Turkey* (App no 22535/93) [2000] ECHR (28 March 2000) [102–108].

[95] For such doubts, see M Scharf (n 62) 50–51; N Roht-Arriaza, 'Sources in International Treaties of an Obligation to Investigate, Prosecute, and Provide Redress' in N Roht-Arriaza (ed), *Impunity and Human Rights in International Law and Practice* (OUP, Oxford 1995) 24–38, 31. The authors argued that the *Velásquez-Rodríguez* Case was inconclusive on the question, because the Court, in ordering remedies, did not direct the Honduran government to institute *criminal* proceedings against those responsible for the disappearance, despite the fact that the lawyers for the victims' families, the Inter-American Commission and a group of international experts acting as *amici curiae* had specifically made a request to that effect. In light of the absence of any express reference to criminal prosecution as opposed to other forms of disciplinary action or punishment, the obligation to investigate violations, to identify those responsible, to impose the appropriate punishment and to ensure the victim receives adequate compensation does not appear to exclude non-criminal responses per se in their view.

[96] See for instance Human Rights Committee, *Bautista de Arellana v Colombia*, Communication No 563/1993, UN Doc CCPR/C/55/D/563/1993 (1995) [8.6], in which the Committee, while reaffirming that 'the Covenant does not provide a right for individuals to require that the State criminally prosecute another person', held that States Parties to the ICCPR are 'under a duty to

However, the scope of that obligation is territorially limited. States are only obliged to investigate and prosecute those serious human rights violations that have taken place on their territory and/or against individuals '*subject to their jurisdiction*'.[97] These latter terms have been interpreted to mean that the human rights obligations of States Parties to the ICCPR, ECHR or IACHR are primarily territorial. Only in exceptional circumstances do acts performed outside their territory or which produce effects there trigger these States' obligations. This is the case *inter alia* when they exercise control over an area outside their territory or where the human rights violation is committed under the State Party's authority and control through its agents operating in another State.[98] As far as the obligation to investigate and prosecute serious human rights violations is concerned, such an obligation is, as a rule, thus limited to prosecutions on the basis of the principle of territorial jurisdiction. That rule is subject to the exception that the obligation to investigate and prosecute also applies vis-à-vis extraterritorial

investigate thoroughly alleged violations of human rights, and in particular forced disappearances of persons and violations of the right to life, and *to prosecute criminally, try and punish those held responsible for such violations*'; IACmHR, Colombia, *Río Frío Massacre* case (n 93); see also Report No 28/00 of 7 March 2000 adopted by the IACmHR in the *Barrios Altos* Case (referred to in *Barrios Altos Case*, Judgment of 14 March 2001 (n 93) [17]), recommending that the State of Peru 'conduct a serious, impartial and effective investigation into the facts, in order to identify those responsible for the assassinations and injuries in this case, and continue with the *judicial prosecution* of Julio Salazar Monroe, Santiago Martín Rivas, Nelson Carbajal García, Juan Sosa Saavedra and Hugo Coral Goycochea, and *punish* those responsible for these grave crimes, *through the corresponding criminal procedure*, in accordance with the law'. For jurisprudence of the ECtHR, see eg *Kilic v Turkey* (App no 22492/93) [2000] ECHR 128 (28 March 2000) [93] ['[N]o effective *criminal* investigation can be considered to have been conducted in accordance with Article 13 [of the European Convention, providing for the right to an effective remedy] [...] The Court finds therefore that the applicant has been denied an effective remedy in respect of the death of his brother'.] [All emphases added] See also Updated Set of principles for the protection and promotion of human rights, Principle 19 (n 54).

[97] ICCPR (n 87) Article 2 (1) ['within its territory and subject to its jurisdiction']; other human rights treaties include very similar formulations, cf IACHR (n 87) Article 1 (1); ECHR (n 87) Article 1 ['within their jurisdiction']. However, Article 1 of the AfCHPR (n 87) does not include such a specification.

[98] Human Rights Committee, *Delia Saldias de Lopez v Uruguay*, Communication No 52/1979 (29 July 1981), UN Doc CCPR/C/OP/1 at 88 (1984) [12.2–12.3]; *Celiberti de Casariego v Uruguay*, Communication No 56/1979 (29 July 1981) UN Doc CCPR/C/OP/1 at 92 (1984) [10.3]; General Comment No 31 [80], *Nature of the General Legal Obligation on States Parties to the Covenant*, 26 May 2004, UN Doc CCPR/C/21/Rev.1/Add.13 [10]. ECtHR, *Loizidou v Turkey* (*Merits*) (App no 15318/89) [1996] ECHR 70 (18 December 1996) 2234–2235 [52]; *Banković and Others v Belgium and 16 other Contracting States* (App no 52207/99) [2001] ECHR (12 December 2001) [67–73]; *Ilaşcu and Others v Moldova and Russia* (App no 48787/99) [2004] ECHR 318 (8 July 2004) [314–316]; *Issa and Others v Turkey* (App no 31821/96) [2004] ECHR 629 (16 November 2004) [67–71]. Inter-American Commission, *Coard et al v United States*, Case No 10.951, Report No 109/99, IACmHR, OEA/Ser.L/V/II.106 Doc 3 rev at 1283 (1999) [37]. See also *Legal Consequences of the Construction of a Wall in the Occupied Palestinian Territory* (Advisory Opinion) ICJ Reports, 9 July 2004 [107–113]. Note that the aforementioned cases are inconsistent as regards the required *degree* of control, however: see G L Neumann, 'Comment, Counter-terrorist Operations and the Rule of Law' [2004] 15 EJIL, 1019–1029, 1021, 1028 [contrasting decisions and comments of the Human Rights Committee with ECtHR jurisprudence].

human rights violations provided that the victim of the underlying human rights violation is subject to the 'jurisdiction' of a State Party to a human rights treaty.

As far as the legal framework governing national suppression of core crimes is concerned, the obligation to investigate, prosecute and punish serious human rights violations entails that national criminal jurisdictions are assigned a *mandatory* role in investigating, prosecuting and punishing genocide, crimes against humanity and war crimes, which have been committed 'within their jurisdiction'. For, such offences, apart from amounting to international crimes, also regularly amount to serious violations of human rights, such as the right to life, freedom from torture and slavery, and the right to liberty and security of person. To the extent that the specific regimes applicable to the individual core crimes leave the question unanswered as to whether and to what extent the exercise of States' criminal jurisdiction is mandatory,[99] an independent obligation to do so flows from human rights treaties (and customary international law, provided that the abovementioned treaty provisions, from which an obligation to investigate and prosecute is derived, are reflective of custom), subject to the aforementioned limitations with regard to extraterritorial human rights violations.

2.2. National Criminal Jurisdictions as International and Domestic Organs

Although the foregoing analysis has demonstrated that the rules governing the national suppression of core crimes are far from uniform, the role of national criminal jurisdictions is based on the cohesive premise that they are envisaged to operate in both the international and domestic legal orders. In so doing, they fulfil an international as well as a domestic role.

First, national criminal jurisdictions act as *organs of the international community*. The prohibition of genocide, crimes against humanity and war crimes is at the centre of the criminal law of the international community[100] and embodies the most basic common interests of humanity.[101] In the words of the Supreme Court of Israel in the Eichmann case, core crimes

constitute acts which damage vital international interests; they impair the foundations and security of the international community; they violate the universal moral values and humanitarian principles that lie hidden in the criminal law systems adopted by civilised nations. [...] Those crimes entail individual criminal responsibility because they

---

[99] Cf (nn 54, 62 and 66), and text.
[100] J Barboza, 'International Criminal Law' (1999) 278 RdC, 9–200, 24.
[101] A Cassese, 'On the Current Trends towards Criminal Prosecution and Punishment of Breaches of International Humanitarian Law' [1998] 9 EJIL 2–17; T Meron, 'Is International Law Moving towards Criminalization?' [1998] 9 EJIL 18–31. See also the Preamble of the Rome Statute (n 31), which identifies core crimes as 'the most serious crimes of concern to the international community as a whole' (para 4), which 'deeply shock the conscience of humanity' (para 2) and 'threaten the peace, security and well-being of the world' (para 3).

challenge the foundations of international society and affront the conscience of civilised nations. [...] [T]hey involve the perpetration of an international crime which all the nations of the world are interested in preventing.[102]

Core crimes thus 'transcend the individual because when the individual is assaulted, humanity comes under attack and is negated'.[103] On a theoretical level, national courts therefore act on behalf of the whole of humanity within the international legal order whenever they enforce the prohibition of these crimes and have the international community as their constituency.[104] In the absence of genuine international enforcement mechanisms in the form of international criminal tribunals, or to the extent that crimes are beyond the reach of such other mechanisms due to their limited mandate[105] or capacity,[106] national suppression of the core crimes is the only way to effectuate their prohibitions. Only States have the necessary judicial infrastructure, namely a police force, prosecution services, courts and a penitentiary system, at their disposal.[107] Put another way, investigations and prosecutions by national judicial authorities are necessary to instil meaning into the prohibition of core crimes, because no judicial organ could impose punishment in their absence.[108] Much as in other areas of international law, domestic courts and other judicial authorities act as surrogate enforcement

---

[102] *Attorney-General of Israel v Eichmann*, Judgment of the Supreme Court of 29 May 1962, 36 ILR 277 291, 293. In a similar vein, see Spain Constitutional Tribunal, *Guatemalan Genocide Case*, Second Chamber, Judgment of 26 September 2005, No STC/237/2005, summary and discussion by N Roht-Arriaza in (2006) 100 AJIL 207–213, 211 [crimes under the universal jurisdiction principle 'transcend the harm to the specific victims and affect the international community as a whole. Therefore, prosecution and punishment are not only a shared commitment, but a shared interest of all states ... '].

[103] *Prosecutor v Erdemovic* (Judgment) IT-96-22-T (29 November 1996) T Ch I, 28.

[104] H Arendt, *Eichmann in Jerusalem—Ein Bericht von der Banalität des Bösen* (7th edn Piper, Munich/Zurich 1964) 339 ['Nichts ist verderblicher [...] als die weitverbreitete Meinung, dass Mord und Völkermord im Grunde die gleichen Verbrechen seien und dass darum der staatlich organisierte Völkermord "kein neues Verbrechen" darstelle. Das Merkmal des letzteren ist, *dass eine gänzlich andere Ordnung zerstört und eine gänzlich andere Gemeinschaft verletzt wird*.']. Emphasis added.

[105] The limited jurisdiction *ratione temporis* and *loci* of the two ad hoc tribunals for the former Yugoslavia and Rwanda are salient examples, cf Articles 1 and 8 of the ICTY Statute and Articles 1 and 7 of the ICTR Statute (n 2).

[106] For instance, by February 2008, the two ad hoc tribunals (ICTY and ICTR) had indicted a total of 161 persons (ICTY) and 74 persons (ICTR), while estimates of persons who have committed crimes which fall into the jurisdiction of these tribunals are many times higher.

[107] Cf the above-quoted statement of the District Court of Jerusalem in the *Eichmann* case (n 7) and text.

[108] In furtherance of this hypothesis, one leading authority on the enforcement of international law in domestic legal orders goes as far as ascertaining that the application of international law by domestic legal operators, and most prominently amongst them domestic courts, is the *only* way to understand the truly legal function of international law and its binding force, cf B Conforti, 'Cours général de droit international public' (1988) RdC V, tome 212, 9–210, 25–27; the slightly amended translation of his *cours*: B Conforti, *International Law and the Role of Domestic Legal Systems* (Martinus Nijhoff Publ, Dordrecht/Boston/London 1993) 8; and most recently his 'Notes on the Relationship between International Law and National Law' (2001) 3 International Law FORUM du Droit International 18–24, 18.

bodies, which fill the gaps left by the absence of effective centralized judicial enforcement at the international level.[109] Although such a role of domestic courts is at times regarded as merely transitory on the way to a supranational legal order, with centralized enforcement and adjudicating mechanisms of its own,[110] it has not lost its relevance. Quite to the contrary. With international law expanding into areas that were traditionally considered to pertain to States' *domaine réservé* and exclusively subject to domestic law, national judiciaries are called upon to adjudicate cases that involve questions of international law with increasing frequency. What is more, the incorporation into the international legal fabric of meta-national values that are considered fundamental to the international community as a whole entails that domestic jurisdictions enforce these norms.[111] In certain cases, this may even lead to a situation where the nexus between the adjudicating national jurisdiction and the event that gave rise to the proceedings exhausts itself in the fact that the adjudicating State is a member of the international community. In the context of core crimes proceedings, this is most clearly illustrated in the case of the exercise of universal jurisdiction, where none of the traditional grounds for the exercise of jurisdiction (territoriality, active and passive nationality) is present, yet where international law allows or even obliges States to bring perpetrators to justice.[112]

Second, national criminal jurisdictions assume vital functions in the *domestic legal order* in which they operate.

From a *legal* point of view, national criminal jurisdictions operate in the domestic legal order because the legal framework governing national suppression of

---

[109] G Scelle, 'Le phénomène juridique du dédoublement fonctionnel,' in W Schätzel and H J Schlochauer (eds), *Rechtsfragen der Internationalen Organisation—Festschrift für H. Wehberg* (Vittorio Klostermann, Frankfurt am Main 1956) 324–342, 331. As an illustration of domestic courts' conceiving of themselves as such surrogate international bodies, consider the following words of Justice Powell in his Concurring Opinion in US Supreme Court, First National City Bank v Banco Nacional de Cuba, 406 US 759 (1972): 'Until international tribunals command a wider constituency, the courts of various countries afford the best means for the development of a respected body of international law'.

[110] See eg G Scelle, *Manuel de droit international public* (Domat-Montchrestien, Paris 1948) 22; ibid 'Quelques réflexions sur l'abolition de la compétence de guerre' (1954) RGDIP 7–13, 9.

[111] On the development of international law from a 'relational' law of co-existence to an 'institutional' law of cooperation and the gradual development towards a 'universal' law of the world community, see generally C Tomuschat, 'International Law: Ensuring the Survival of Mankind on the Eve of a New Century' (1999) 281 RdC 9–438, 56–90; R Neuwirth, 'International Law and the Public/Private Law Distinction, Zeitschrift für öffentliches Recht' (2000) 55 Austrian Journal of Public and International Law 393–410, 396; A Cassese, *International Law* (OUP, Oxford 2001) 166. For an assessment in the context of law-making, see J I Charney, 'Universal International Law' (1993) 87 AJIL 529–551; D Thürer, 'Modernes Völkerrecht: Ein System im Wandel und Wachstum—Gerechtigkeitsgedanke als Kraft der Veränderung' (2000) 60 ZaöRV 557–603, 558–559; B Conforti (n 108) 22–23.

[112] M Cottier, 'Die Anwendbarkeit von völkerrechtlichen Normen im innerstaatlichen Bereich als Ausprägung der Konstitutionalisierung des Völkerrechts' (1999) 9 Schweizerische Zeitschrift für internationales und europäisches Recht 403–440, 422; C Kress, 'Universal Jurisdiction over International Crimes and the Institut de Droit International' (2006) 4 JICJ 561–585, 567 [in pursuing international crimes on the basis of universal jurisdiction, a State acts 'as...a trustee of the fundamental values of the international community'].

conduct, which amounts to core crimes, includes domestic legal norms to varying degrees. Thus national implementation of core crimes regularly relies on national criminal law and thereby 'domesticates' international law to some extent.[113] At times, such implementation results in the original international norm (virtually) disappearing, as is the case when international crimes are prosecuted as ordinary domestic offences.[114] Even when core crimes can be prosecuted under the rubric of genocide, crimes against humanity or war crimes, some underlying acts, such as 'killing',[115] 'murder'[116] or 'wilful killing'[117] are frequently applied in accordance with domestic law in adjudicating core crimes.[118] The same holds generally true for the principles which together form what is increasingly referred to as 'the general part' of international criminal law governing modes of liability.[119]

[113] M C Bassiouni describes the mutual relationship of national and international law in international criminal law as 'complementary': M C Bassiouni (n 1) 13.

[114] This was the case for example in Germany prior to the adoption of the Code Of Crimes Against International Law (2002) with regard to war crimes and crimes against humanity: R Roth and Y Jeanneret, 'Droit Allemand' in A Cassese and M Delmas-Marty (n 52) 7–29, 12–13. This approach had a long history in Germany, as evidenced by the *Llandovery Castle* judgment of the German Reichsgericht of 16 July 1921, where conviction for a 'violation of the law of nations in warfare', more specifically the act of killing shipwrecked people by firing on lifeboats wherein they had taken refuge, constituted homicide according to Article 222 of the German Penal Code; English excerpts of the decision reproduced in L Erades, 'Interactions between International and Municipal Law—a comparative case law study' in M Fitzmaurice and C Flinterman (eds), *Interactions between International Law and Municipal Law* (TMC Asser Institute, The Hague 1993) 467.

[115] Cf Genocide Convention (n 55) Article II (a).

[116] 'Murder' is one of the acts that amounts to crimes against humanity if committed as part of a widespread or systematic attack directed against any civilian population: cf Article 6 (c) of the Nuremberg Charter (n 72); Article 5 (c) of the Tokyo Charter (n 72); Article II (c) of Control Council Law No 10; 5 (a) ICTY Statute (n 2); 3 (a) ICTR Statute (n 2); 7 (1)(a) Rome Statute (n 31).

[117] 'Wilful killing' is a grave breach of the Geneva Convention if committed as part of an international armed conflict against a person protected by one of the Four Geneva Conventions (n 8): cf Articles 50, 51, 130 and 147 of the Four Geneva Conventions respectively.

[118] See for instance the German *Bundesgerichtshof* in its judgment of 21 February 2001 *Sokolovic Federal Supreme Court (Bundesgerichtshof)*, 3 St R 372/00, BGHSt 46, 292–307, 54 NJW 2728–2732 (21 February 2001) BGH 3 StR 372/00. When interpreting the provision incorporating the crime of genocide into the German Penal Code (§ 220 a), the court confirmed the decision of the lower instance (*Oberlandesgericht Düsseldorf*) and its own earlier jurisprudence that the first alternative of the national provision (section 1 Nr 1, 'killing members of the group') required a finding 'at least of manslaughter' (§ 212) ['§ 220 a Abs. 1 Nr. 1 StGB ist eine Begehungsalternative des Völkermordes, die als Tatbestandsmerkmal die vorsätzliche Tötung eines Menschen voraussetzt, so daß der Sachverhalt, der wegen Völkermordes nach § 220 a Abs. 1 Nr. 1 StGB festgestellt werden muß, jeweils auch einen Verurteilung zumindest wegen Totschlags trägt (BGHSt 45, 64, 70).']. See also Supreme Court of Canada, *R v Finta* (24 March 1994) at 256 ['It is evident that compendious expressions like "murder, extermination, enslavement, deportation, persecution, or any other inhumane act or omission" include acts and omissions that comprise such specific underlying crimes as confinement, kidnapping, robbery and manslaughter under our domestic system of law.'] For a rare contrary example, in which a domestic court gave precedence to the international notion of 'murder' as a war crime under Article 6 (b) of the Charter of the International Military Tribunal (n 72) after the Second World War over the divergent domestic notion of 'murder', see *In re* Ahlbrecht (No 2), Holland, Special Court of Cassation, Judgment of 11 April 1949, in Annual Digest and Reports of Public International Law Cases (1949) case No 141, 396–398, 396–397.

[119] See generally K Ambos, *Der Allgemeine Teil des Völkerstrafrechts: Ansätze einer Dogmatisierung* (Duncker & Humblot, Berlin 2003) 1058; E van Sliedregt, *The Criminal Responsibility of Individuals*

Irrespective of whether the various means of implementation withstand the test of criminalizing conduct which is co-extensive to the prohibited conduct according to international law,[120] national courts act within the domestic legal orders when applying such domestic rules and principles.

A further legal dimension of the role of national criminal jurisdictions as organs of the domestic legal order stems from the fact that practically all core crimes amount *simultaneously* to domestic offences. Accordingly, a conviction for 'killing' as an act of genocide,[121] for instance, can also attract a separate, cumulative conviction for the domestic offence of murder.[122] When applying such domestic offences, national courts are squarely placed within the domestic legal order.

In addition to these legal aspects of national suppression, the domestic role of national criminal jurisdictions stems from the fact that they serve *domestic agendas and constituencies*. These agendas and constituencies may differ, depending *inter alia* on whether national criminal jurisdictions are called upon to operate within or outside periods of transition. They have in common, however, the fact that domestic courts and other legal operators act with an inward-looking perspective.

As far as the State within which core crimes occurred is concerned, its national criminal jurisdiction is expected to function as an instrument of *transitional justice* in the society directly affected by these crimes.[123] In bringing perpetrators to justice, national criminal jurisdictions are presumed to assist in a catharsis, which is part and parcel of (re-)building a peaceful and democratic society based on the rule of law.

Genocide, crimes against humanity and war crimes are regularly both the cause and the consequence of a breakdown of law and order. Armed conflict, widespread or systematic attacks against the civilian population and genocidal policies, commonly implemented with substantial involvement of governmental

---

for Violations of International Humanitarian Law (TMC Asser Press, The Hague 2003) 437. For examples, see the following national reports in International Society for Military Law and the Law of War, 'Compatibility of National Legal Systems with the Statute of the Permanent International Criminal Court' (2003) Recueil XVI, vol 1: Iran (284–285), Israel (293), Netherlands (for modes of perpetration and participation: 325–337).

[120] For further discussion, see *3.1. Obstacles relating to Implementing Legislation*, and Chapter VII.

[121] Cf n 115.

[122] See eg Judgment *Bayerisches Oberstes Landesgericht* of 15 December 1999, 6 St 1/99 - 2 BJs 25/95 - 5 - 2 StE 5/99 (Kuslijc), confirmed by judgment of the *Bundesgerichtshof* of 21 February 2001, Az: 3 StR 244/00, at 3. In a similar vein, see *Polyukhovich v The Commonwealth of Australia and Another* (1991) High Court of Australia, 172 Commonwealth Law Reports 501 FC 91/026 (14 August 1991) ['The Act is not retrospective in operation because it only criminalizes acts which were war crimes under international law *as well as* "ordinary" crimes under Australian law at the time they were committed'. Emphasis added].

[123] See amongst many others R Teitel, *Transitional Justice* (OUP, Oxford 2002); N J Kritz, *Transitional justice: How emerging democracies reckon with former regimes* (United States Institute of Peace Press, Washington DC 1995).

authorities or organs exercising de facto authority, leave the affected society in shatters. When such periods of large-scale victimization come to an end, criminal prosecutions conducted within such societies are presumed to contribute to societal reconstruction and the transition to peace.

The role of national criminal jurisdictions as instruments of transitional justice is primarily a *domestic* one. Their principal envisaged role is to function as organs within the affected society. In comparison with trials in international criminal courts or third states, criminal prosecutions conducted within the affected society bear the potential of more directly influencing—and ultimately reconciling—perpetrators, victims and the affected society at large. They are also presumed to contribute to restoring and consolidating trust into the national judiciary and the rule of law as a peaceful mechanism for transition, and to serve to document past and deter future violations.[124] Domestic prosecutions are seen to diminish the risk of vigilante justice and general scepticism towards the political system, and provide a remedy for the victims and their relatives.[125] While some of these objectives might also be furthered by ordinary domestic criminal law, reliance in varying degrees on international norms governing core crimes fulfils a number of roles. It recognizes that the crimes committed go beyond ordinary domestic crimes and reflects the scale, gravity and systematicity of the committed atrocities. It has also been pointed out that reliance on international norms can help to legitimize the prosecution, because it averts an application of domestic law, which may have become politicized under the past regime.[126] Furthermore, national enforcement of these norms is expected to contribute to internalizing into domestic societies those values that are reflected in the prohibitions of core crimes, whereby they may make the commission of core crimes less likely in the future.[127]

To say that national criminal jurisdictions fulfil a primarily domestic role in transitional societies does not mean, however, that such a role is absent when core crimes are investigated and prosecuted by national criminal jurisdictions *outside transitional contexts*. Judicial authorities of the State may very well decide

---

[124] See generally L E Fletcher and H M Weinstein, 'Violence and Social Repair: Rethinking the Contribution of Justice to Reconciliation' (2002) 24 Human Rights Quarterly, 573–639 [recognizing, however, that criminal trials have limitations with respect to addressing the social and collective forces that led to the violence and suggesting that 'alternative interventions must be considered in synergy with war crimes trials' (367)].

[125] For an overview of criminal justice theories and punishment rationales in the present context, see N Roht-Arriaza, 'Punishment, Redress, and Pardon: Theoretical and Psychological Approaches' in N Roht-Arriaza (ed) (n 95) 13–23; see also M Scharf, 'Swapping Amnesty for Peace: Was There a Duty to Prosecute International Crimes in Haiti?' (1996) 31 Texas International Law Journal 1–41, 12–15. For a socio-legal analysis, see M J Osiel, 'Why Prosecute? Critics of Punishment for Mass Atrocities' (2000) 22 Human Rights Quarterly 118–147.

[126] R Teitel (n 123) 20–21.

[127] J I Charney, 'International criminal law and the role of domestic courts' (2001) 95 AJIL 121–124, 124.

to investigate and prosecute core crimes in response to a domestic constituency of (relatives of) victims, who are nationals of that State, while the crimes were committed in a foreign jurisdiction.[128] In other cases, the State concerned may consider domestic prosecutions necessary in order to preserve the integrity of its domestic legal system[129] and to prevent victims, who have fled to the same State as the perpetrator, to take the law into their own hands.

The foregoing discussion demonstrates that national suppression of the core crimes has both an internal and an external dimension. In applying an amalgamation of both international and domestic norms and serving both international and domestic agendas and constituencies, national criminal jurisdictions fulfil a *concurrent role* in the suppression of core crimes, one *international* and the other *domestic*. In so doing, they cannot be assigned exclusively to the international or the national legal order. Rather, national criminal jurisdictions act as organs of the international and domestic realms in a construct of *role splitting* (*dédoublement fonctionnel/funktionelle Verdoppelung*), chiefly developed in the writings of Georges Scelle:[130] they act as national organs any time they perform a role within the national legal system, while they act as international agents any time they operate within the international legal system.[131] However, when enforcing the prohibition of core crimes, they assume both roles *simultaneously* ('role concurrence'), as they are tasked to protect important legal values of the international community as a whole and at the same time to protect legal values which belong to the national legal order.[132] This is an important departure from Scelle's construct, which assumed that domestic courts act *either* as national organs *or* as agents of the international community.[133] Indeed, this concurrence of roles is borne out by

---

[128] Examples are cases in Italy, France and Spain, in which nationals of these States were victimized in Argentina, Chile and Guatemala during the 1970s. See eg Italy as regards Argentina: 3 YIHL 2000 (Conviction of seven former members of the Argentine military for the murder of Italian citizens during the 'dirty war') 538; Cour d'Assises de Paris: Judgment *in absentia* in the case of *Alfredo Astiz* (16 March 1990), information available at <http://www.trial-ch.org/trialwatch/ profiles/en/facts/p311.html>; Tribunal Supremo (Supreme Court) of Spain: *Judgment in the Case of General Hernán Julio Brady Roche*, Judgment No 319/2004 (8 March 2004), *Recurso de Casación NO:* 1812/2002, *Fallo:* 03/03/2004 (re Chile).

[129] See for example *Rechtbank Rotterdam* re Nzepali ['roi des bêtes'], AO7178 Zaaknr: 10/000050–03, Judgment of 7 April 2004 [torture committed in Congo against Congolese national by Congolese national resident in The Netherlands: 'De ten laste van de verdachte bewezen gedragingen raken evenzeer de Nederlandse rechtsorde, nu hij zich hier te lande heeft gevestigd, en dit te meer nu hij door middel van een asielaanvraag te kennen heeft gegeven van de Nederlandse samenleving deel te willen (blijven) uitmaken.'].

[130] In addition to his writings already referred to (nn 109–110), see eg G Scelle, 'Règles générales du droit de la paix' (1933) 46 Recueil des cours de l'Académie de La Haye 327–703, 358–359.

[131] G Scelle, ibid.

[132] On that 'role concurrence' of national criminal jurisdictions when enforcing the prohibition of core crimes, see O Triffterer, 'Preliminary Remarks: The Permanent International Criminal Court—Ideal and Reality' in O Triffterer (ed), *Commentary on the Rome Statute of the International Criminal Court—Observers' Notes, Article by Article* (Nomos, Baden-Baden 1999) 26–28 [23].

[133] See eg A Cassese, 'Remarks on Scelle's Theory of "Role Splitting" (*dédoublement fonctionnel*) in International Law' [1990] 1 EJIL 1/2, 210–232, 213.

some of the rare instances in which national courts have pronounced on the matter. Thus the Bavarian *Oberlandesgericht* in the Djajic case included among the rationales for its decision to prosecute a Serb defendant for international crimes committed in the former Yugoslavia, the need to safeguard and foster the trust of German citizens in the *national and international* legal order, as well as to show the world that Germany was not sheltering international criminals.[134] Similarly, the French *Cour de Cassation* in the Barbie case stated that crimes against humanity, of which the defendant was accused, *'ne relèvent pas seulement du droit pénal interne français, mais encore d'un ordre répressif international [...]'*.[135] And when Trial Chamber I of the Iraqi High Criminal Court delivered its Final Opinion in the al-Dujail trial, which led to the conviction of Saddam Hussein and a number of other accused, it held:

[T]he actions attributed to the accused in the Al Dujail case, if verified are considered international and internal crimes simultaneously, and the committing of such crimes is considered a violation of the international criminal law and international human law, at the same time considered a violation of the Iraqi law [...].[136]

The question as to whether, and to what extent, domestic courts act as domestic or as international organs, in turn, is a matter of degree, which is influenced by a complex web of factors. These factors include the link to the crime and the primary constituency of domestic proceedings, the way in which international criminal law has been implemented and the self-perception of the judicial organs concerned.

2.3. Empirical Matters: Actual National Suppression of Core Crimes

Although national suppression has a troubled history,[137] national criminal jurisdictions have investigated and prosecuted core crimes on numerous occasions. Indeed, domestic core crimes prosecutions have a long history, starting with the

---

[134] *Djajic* Bavarian High Court (*Oberlandesgericht*) Munich, 2 St 20/96, 51 NJW (1998) 392 (23 May 1997).

[135] Judgment of 6 October 1983, 88 Revue Générale de Droit Internationale Public (1984) 507–511, 508, 87 ILR 125–131, 126.

[136] Case No 1/9 First/2005 *Al Dujail* Lawsuit (Case), Iraqi High Criminal Court (Trial Chamber 1), Case No 1/9 First/2005 Part I, 9 (2006), Final Decisions and Judgment available at <http://www.law.case.edu/saddamtrial/documents/dujail_opinion_pt1.pdf>. See also Iraqi High Criminal Court (Cassation Panel), Case No 1/9 First/2005, available at <http://www.iraq-iht.org/ar/doc/ihtco.pdf>. For the unofficial English translation, see <http://www.law.case.edu/saddamtrial/documents/20070103_dujail_appellate_chamber_opinion.pdf>, p 18 ['the crimes of which the defendants are accused of in the Dujail case form both international and domestic crimes and committing them constitutes a violation of the International Penal Code and the Law of Human Rights while at the same time violating Iraqi laws'].

[137] For further discussion, see *3. Obstacles to National Suppression.*

punishment of war crimes, which can be traced back for centuries.[138] Rather than providing an all-embracing historical overview of such domestic core crimes prosecutions, the following account summarizes developments since the Second World War, which serve as evidence that national prosecutions have not remained a mere theoretical possibility.[139]

After the Second World War, numerous cases were tried in West Germany, both on the basis of Control Council Law No 10[140] and later based on the ordinary German Criminal Code.[141] East Germany also tried a considerable number of cases.[142] Other proceedings were conducted in military commissions, tribunals and courts of the Allied Nations of the Second World War, of States occupied during the war or of those States with their nationals amongst the victims.[143] In parallel to those proceedings, numerous domestic trials for crimes under international law committed by Japanese individuals took place before military tribunals of the Allied Nations and of Asian States on whose territory core crimes

[138] See eg the Henfield's case, 11 F. Cas. 1099 (C. C. D. Pa. 1793) (No 6360), reproduced in J Paust, M C Bassiouni, M Scharf *et al* (eds), *International Criminal Law, Cases and Materials* (2nd edn Carolina Academic Press, Durham 2000) 232–238; R J Pritchard, 'International Humanitarian Intervention and Establishment of an International Jurisdiction over Crimes Against Humanity: The National and International Military Trials on Crete in 1898' in J Carey, W V Dunlap and R J Pritchard (eds), *International Humanitarian Law* (vol 1 (Origins) Transnational Publ, Ardsley NY 2003) 1–87; G Mettraux, 'US Courts-Martial and the Armed Conflict in the Philippines (1899–1902): Their Contribution to National Case Law on War Crimes' (2003) 1 JICJ 135–150.

[139] For more comprehensive overviews, see the surveys available at the following websites: International Committee of the Red Cross, <http://www.icrc.org/ihl-nat.nsf/WebCASE? OpenView>; Prevent Genocide International, <http://preventgenocide.org/punish/domestic/index. htm>; Domestic Jurisprudence on International Criminal Law, <http://www.haguejusticeportal. net/eCache/DEF/6/579.html>.

[140] Control Council Law No 10 of 20 December 1945 [Punishment of Persons Guilty of War Crimes, Crimes Against Peace and Against Humanity], available at <http://www.yale.edu/lawweb/ avalon/imt/imt10.htm>.

[141] For trials under Control Council Law No 10, see Trials of war criminals before the Nuremberg military tribunals under Control Council Law No 10, Vol 1 (1949)–15 (1953), Washington, DC: US Government Printing Office; David Maxwell Fyfe (ed), War Crimes Trials (William Hodge, London 1948–1952). From 1951 onwards, Western German Prosecutions were based on ordinary criminal law: see A Rückerl, *Die Strafverfolgung von NS-Verbrechen 1945–1978* (C F Müller Publ, Heidelberg, Karlsruhe 1979) 41. For a systematic overview of trials involving offences of unlawful killing in West Germany, see D W De Mildt, *Die westdeutschen Strafverfahren wegen nationalsozialistischer Tötungsverbrechen. Eine systematische Verfahrensbeschreibung mit Karten und Registern* (Maarssen Holland) University Press, Munich K.G. Saur Verlag 1998).

[142] A Rückerl ibid 73–74; C F Rüter mentions a total of approximately 17 000 prosecutions for alleged crimes committed during the Second World War, with 1800 for capital offences: 'Door Nederland gezochte oorlogsmisdadigers allang berecht door de DDR—Prof. Rüter krijgt toegang tot Stasi-archieven' (1996) 49 Folia 1–2, 8–11.

[143] For an overview of the laws and regulations providing the legal setting for prosecutions of war crimes in these states, see M W Mouton, *Oorlogsmisdrijven en het Internationale Recht* (A.A.M. Stols Publ, The Hague 1947) 519, 177–202. See also J L Garwood-Cutler, 'The British War Crimes Trials of Suspected Italian War Criminals, 1945–1947' in J Carey, W V Dunlap and R J Pritchard (eds) (n 138) 89–103.

were committed.[144] Prosecutions related to crimes committed during the Second World War continue to date, albeit on a more limited scale.[145]

During the Cold War, the aforementioned prosecutions relating to crimes committed during the Second World War constituted the exception to the rule that national suppression of core crimes was a largely dormant concept.[146] Only since the end of the Cold War can one observe an increase in criminal proceedings vis-à-vis core crimes committed outside the context of the Second World War.[147]

Prosecutions relating to crimes committed in the former Yugoslavia conducted in Bosnia-Herzegovina,[148] Croatia[149] and, more recently, the former FR Yugoslavia (now Serbia)[150] are accompanied by criminal proceedings in

---

[144] P R Piccigallo recounts 920 death sentences and approximately 3000 prison sentences for Japanese defendants between 1945 and 1951, by the US, China, Britain and Australia; and in many different locations, including Japan, Singapore, the Philippines and China: P R Piccigallo, *The Japanese on Trial: Allied War Crimes Operations in the East, 1945–1951* (Univ of Texas Press, Austin 1980) 292. P Osten mentions 2244 trials against a total of approximately 5700 members of the Japanese military between October 1945 and April 1951: P Osten, 'Der Tokioter Kriegsverbrecherprozeß und seine Rezeption in Japan—Japan und das Völkerstrafrecht' Vortrag, gehalten auf den 3. Keio-Tagen, Universität des Saarlands 2.–5. Dezember 2003, available at <http://www.jura.uni-sb.de/projekte/Bibliothek/texte/Osten.html#II>.

[145] See for example France: *Cour de Cassation,* 3 June 1988 (Barbie), 100 ILR 330; *Cour de Cassation,* 6 October 1983 (Barbie), 78 ILR 125; *Cour de Cassation,* 1 June 1995 (Touvier), Bull Crim 1995 547–558; *Cour de Cassation,* 21 October 1993 (Touvier), Bull Crim 1993 770–774; *Cour de Cassation,* 27 November 1992 (Touvier), 100 ILR 358; *Cour d'appel de Paris,* 13 April 1992 (Touvier), 100 ILR 358–364; *Cour de Cassation,* 23 January 1997 (Papon), Bull Crim no 32; *Cour d'appel de Bordeaux,* 18 September 1996 (Papon), cited in A Cassese (n 5) xxxvii; Germany: Götzfried, Regional Court of Stuttgart, Judgment of 20 May 1999, summary in 2 YIHL (1999) 369–370; Italy: Rome Military Tribunal, 22 July 1997 (Hass and Priebke); Military Court of Appeal (Hass and Priebke) 7 March 1998; UK: *R v Sawoniuk,* Court of Appeal (Criminal Division), 10 February 2000; Latvia: Riga District Court, Judgment of 21 January 2000, reported in 3 YIHL (2000) 546–547.

[146] G Werle, *Völkerstrafrecht* (Mohr Siebeck Publ, Tübingen 2003) 17 ['Anwendung völkerstrafrechtlicher Normen durch staatliche Gerichte blieb die seltene Ausnahme'.].

[147] Human Security Centre, *Human Security Report 2005, War and Peace in the 21st Century* (OUP, Oxford 2005) 154–155.

[148] The earliest reported case is that of Savo Ivanovic, who was indicted for war crimes against the civilian population according to Article 142 (1) of the Socialist Republic of Yugoslavia Criminal Code in August 1992, 'Office of the High Representative: Summary of War Crimes and Highly Political Cases in BiH', 1999, 31–33 (on file with author). The mentioned report lists a number of other cases involving charges of violations of international humanitarian law. See also YIHL, Correspondents' Reports, vol 1 (1998) 417; vol 2 (1999) 340–344; vol 3 (2000) 432–436; vol 4 (2001) 460–466.

[149] See for instance Zadar District Court, Judgment of 24 April 1997, case No. K. 74/96; Split District Court, Judgment of 26 May 1997, case No. K. 15/95; Osijek District Court, Judgment of 25 June 1997, case No. K-64/97-53 (all available at ICRC website, n 139). See also YIHL, Correspondents' Reports, vol 1 (1998) 429–430; vol 2 (1999) 352–355; vol 3 (2000) 463–465; vol 4 (2001) 484–487.

[150] See for instance *Prosecutor v Nenad Stamenković, Tomica Jović and Dragisa Petrović*, Military Court of Niš, reported in YIHL, Correspondents' Reports, vol 3 (2000) 494–495 (20 December 2000); *Prosecutor v Nebojša Ranisavljević*, High Court of Bijelo Polje, Montenegro, reported in YIHL, Correspondents' Reports, vol 4 (2002) 487 (9 September 2002); *Prosecutor v Ivan Nikolić*, District Court of Prokuplje, reported in YIHL, Correspondents' Reports, vol 5 (2002) 489 (8 July

third states, such as Denmark,[151] Germany,[152] Sweden,[153] Switzerland[154] and The Netherlands.[155] Likewise, Rwandan national courts are enforcing international criminal law in the aftermath of the 1994 genocide in application of the Organic Law[156] and the law on *gacaca* jurisdictions,[157] with third states having equally conducted criminal trials with respect to this period.[158] Furthermore, proceedings relating to crimes under international law have been initiated in a number of States of the former Warsaw Pact in relation to the occupation or intervention by the USSR[159] and crimes committed by the respective Communist

2002); *Prosecutor v Zlatan Mančić, Rade Radivojević, Danilo Tešić and Mišel Seregij,* Military Court of Niš, reported in YIHL, Correspondents' Reports, vol 4 (2002) 489–490 (11 October 2002).

[151] The *Prosecution v Saric, Eastern Division of High Court* (Third Chamber), 25 November 1994, available at ICRC website (n 139).

[152] *Djajic* Bavarian High Court (*Oberlandesgericht*) Munich, Judgment of 23 May 1997 (n 134); Jorgic High Court (*Oberlandesgericht*) Düsseldorf, 2 StE 8/96 (26 September 1997) Jorgic Federal Supreme Court (*Bundesgerichtshof*) 3 StR 215/98, 19 NStZ (1999), 396–404 BGHSt 45, 64–91(30 March 1999) Jorgic Federal Constitutional Court (Bundesverfassungsgericht), 2 BvR 1290/99, 54 NJW 2001, 1848–1853 (12 December 2000); 21 February 2001, 3 StR 244/00, in 54 NJW (2001), 2732–2734) and *Sokolovic* (OLG Düsseldorf, Sokolovic, 29 November 1999, 2 StE 6/97; BGH, *Sokolovic,* 21 February 2001, 3 StR 372/00; BGHSt 46, 292–307; 54 NJW, 2728–2732).

[153] *Prosecutor v Arklöf,* Judgment of the Stockholm District Court, 18 December 2006, Mål nr B 4084–04.

[154] *In re G,* Military Tribunal, Division 1, available at ICRC website (n 139) (18 April 1997).

[155] Netherlands: *Knezevic* Arnhem District Court, Military Division (Chambers), Decision of 21 February 1996, NJ 1998/463, 30 NYIL (1999); *Knezevic* Military Division Arnhem Court of Appeal, (19 March 1997); *Knezevic* Supreme Court, NJ 1998/463 (11 November 1997).

[156] Organic Law on the Organization of Prosecutions for Offences Constituting the Crime of Genocide or Crimes Against Humanity Committed Since 1 October 1990, Law No 8/96, Rwanda Official Gazette 30 August 1996; O Dubois, 'Rwanda's national criminal courts and the International Tribunal' (1997) 321 IRRC 717–731; M Morris, 'The trials of concurrent jurisdiction: the case of Rwanda' (1997) 7 Duke JCIL 349–374. For a limited selection of cases, see the website of Avocats Sans Frontières: <http://www.asf.be/FR/Frameset.htm>.

[157] Organic Law No 40/2000 of 26/01/2001 setting up «Gacaca Jurisdictions» and Organizing Prosecutions for Offences Constituting the Crime of Genocide or Crimes Against Humanity Committed Between October 1, 1990 and December 31, 1994. For summary overviews of proceedings, see the website of Avocats Sans Frontières, ibid.

[158] See for instance Belgium: *Prosecutor v Alphonse Higaniro, Gertrude Mukangango, Maria Kisito Mukabutera and Vincent Ntezimana,* 'the Butare four' («4 de Butare»), Judgment of the *Cour d'Appel de Bruxelles,* 10 June 2003; Switzerland: *In re N,* Tribunal militaire, Division 2, Lausanne, (30 April 1999); *In re N,* Military Court of Appeal (26 May 2000); *In re N,* Military Court of Cassation (27 April 2001), unpublished, available at ICRC website (n 139).

[159] See eg Estonia: *Prosecutor v V Beskov,* Pärnu County Court No 1–116, (10 March 1999), *Prosecutor v V Loginov,* Järva County Court No 1–95, (17 March 1999), *Prosecutor v J Klaassepp,* Lääne County Court No 1-49/98, (22 January 1999); Tallinn Circuit Court (Court of Appeal) No II-1/183, (6 April 1999), *Prosecutor v M Neverovski,* Pärnu County Court No 1-148 1998, (30 July 1998); Tallinn Circuit Court (Court of Appeal) No 11-1/810, (1 November 1999), *Prosecutor v K-L Paulov,* Põlva County Court (court of first instance) No 1-77/99, (26 October 1999); Tartu Circuit Court (Court of Appeal) No II-1-425/99, (13 December 1999); Supreme Court of Estonia No 3-1-1-31-00; Põlva County Court No 1-055-00 (29 June 2000); Tartu Circuit Court No II-1-333/2000, (5 October 2000), all cases reported in YIHL, Correspondents' Reports, vol 3 (2000) 484–490; Hungary: *Prosecutor v I Váraljai, Gy Pápista, V Józsa,* Supreme Court (25 June 2000), *Prosecutor v S Gulyás Kis and M Pataki,* Supreme Court (11 September 2000), *Prosecutor v B Török and I Korbély,* Supreme Court (20 September 2000) all cases reported in YIHL, Correspondents'

regimes.[160] In addition, proceedings have been conducted in Latin America. These include criminal proceedings relating to the Colombian armed conflict,[161] as well as to crimes committed by members of the Latin American military juntas who were in power in the 1970s and 1980s, with the *Pinochet* case as the most prominent example.[162] Other proceedings were initiated in Belgium under the law on the suppression of serious violations of international humanitarian law[163] against, *inter alia*, high officials of several States, ranging from the former Foreign Minister of the Democratic Republic of Congo[164] to the then acting Prime Minister of Israel,[165] although none of such proceedings had led to actual prosecutions of any of those high-level accused prior to the amendment of the law, which curtailed its jurisdictional reach. In fact, although the large majority

Reports, vol 3 (2000) 518–519; Latvia: *Prosecutor v Yevgeny Savenko*, Kuzeme Regional Court (7 July 2000), reported in YIHL, Correspondents' Reports, vol 3 (2000) 547; Poland: *Prosecutor v Geborski*, reported in YIHL, Correspondents' Reports, vol 3 (2000) 562–563. See also R Satkauskas, 'Soviet Genocide Trials in the Baltic States: the Relevance of International Law' (2004) 7 YIHL 388–409.

[160] See eg Lithuania: *Prosecutor v Pranas Preikšaitis and others*, Vilnius Regional Court, 4 June 2002, *Prosecutor v Bronius Viater and Kazys Kregždė*, Judgment of Vilnius Regional Court, 4 June 2002, *Prosecutor v Vincas Misiunas*, Judgment of Vilnius Regional Court, 30 December 2002, all cases reported in YIHL, Correspondents' Reports, vol 5 (2002) 564–566.

[161] See eg (2000) 3 YIHL 459–462.

[162] For a concise account of proceedings in Argentina and Chile, see P A Barcroft, 'The Slow Demise of Impunity in Argentina and Chile' ASIL Insight, January 2005. For Chilean proceedings against Pinochet, see also (2000) 3 YIHL 447–451. For the decisions of Haitian courts in the so called '*Raboteau*' case, see (2000) 3 YIHL 517. As far as third States are concerned, see on the Pinochet extradition proceedings in English courts, C Warbrick, E M Salgado, N Goodwin, 'The Pinochet Cases in the United Kingdom' (1999) 2 YIHL, 91–117. Besides the proceedings in Spanish courts, which gave rise to the aforementioned extradition proceedings, other proceedings against Pinochet had been instituted in Belgium, see (1999) 2 YIHL 335–340, and in Sweden, see (1999) 2 YIHL 414. Other proceedings in Spain relate to suspects from Guatemala, Argentina and Chile, see eg (2000) 3 YIHL 587–594, the convictions *in absentia* of Gen Manuel Contreras and Brig Raúl Iturriaga (both formerly of the Chilean Directorate of National Intelligence (DINA) <http://www.preventgenocide.org/punish/domestic/> and the case of *Graciela P de L and Others v Scilingo*, Audienca Nacional, Judgment of 19 April 2005, Reference Aranzadi JUR 2005/132318, and Spanish Supreme Court, Judgment of November 2007. On the latter judgment, see R J Wilson, 'Spanish Supreme Court Affirms Conviction of Argentine Former Naval Officer for Crimes Against Humanity' (2008) 12 ASIL Insight Issue 1. Suspects from Argentina and Chile have also been tried in Italy, see eg (2000) 3 YIHL 538. France has also tried an Argentinian suspects, Alfredo Astiz, see (n 128).

[163] *Loi du 16 juin 1993 relative à la répression des violations graves du droit international humanitaire.* These proceedings and the controversies that some of them had sparked resulted in several amendments curtailing the jurisdictional reach of the law, with the last amendment having taken place on 7 August 2003.

[164] This case gave rise to the Judgment of the International Court of Justice of 14 February 2002 in the *Case Concerning the Arrest Warrant of 11 April 2000* (Democratic Republic of the Congo v Belgium) [2002] ICJ Rep 3. For the background to the case, see [13–21] of the judgment.

[165] For detailed documentation, see <http://www.indictsharon.net/>. Other high-profile proceedings included the former President of the Islamic Republic of Iran, Rafsandjani (see (2000) 3 YIHL 431), and US General Tom Franks <see http://informationclearinghouse.info/article3449.htm>.

of prosecutions have been initiated in Europe, proceedings have also been conducted in other continents.[166]

The foregoing cursory overview indicates that the decentralized prosecution of
core crimes has made some advances in recent years.

3. Obstacles to National Suppression

As much as it is clear that national criminal jurisdictions are assigned a central
role in the suppression of core crimes and do at times act accordingly, as endemic
are the factors, that prevent them from fulfilling that role. These factors, which
are together referred to as 'obstacles' in the following discussion, have hampered
domestic enforcement in the past and can reasonably be expected to retain their
relevance in the future. Obstacles to national suppression can take normative and
factual forms, ie they can come about 'by law' or 'by practice'.[167] One can broadly
distinguish between such obstacles relating to the adoption of laws, which allow
for the prosecution of core crimes (3.1.), and those relating to the actual enforcement of such laws (3.2.).

3.1. Obstacles relating to Implementing Legislation

The first set of obstacles relates to the implementation of the international legal
framework for the suppression of core crimes into national law. Absence, delays
of and flaws in implementing legislation may withhold from national criminal
jurisdictions the necessary legal framework to prosecute those accused of core
crimes. Gaps resulting from differences between conduct that can be prosecuted
in accordance with implementing legislation and conduct criminalized under
international criminal law can emerge in relation to the definition of core crimes,
the 'general part' applicable to these crimes[168] and the jurisdiction of national
courts. Examples are numerous, and merely taking a few from different legal systems suffices to illustrate the various manifestations of these obstacles.

---

[166] See for example in Africa: the case against Hissène Habré in Senegal (information available
at <http://www.trial-ch.org/trialwatch/profiles/en/legalprocedures/p86.html> and chronological
account at <http://hrw.org/english/docs/2004/10/29/chad9579.htm>); the Ethiopian 'Red Terror'
Trials, see eg *The Special Prosecutor v Col Mengistu Hailemariam and 173 Others* [unreported]
Federal High Court, Criminal File No 1/87, Decision of Meskerem 29, 1988 E.C. (9 October
1995 G.C.) ILDC 555 (ET 1995), and generally W L Kidane, 'The Ethiopian "Red Terror"
Trials' in M C Bassiouni (ed), *Post-Conflict Justice* (Transnational Publishers, Ardsley NY 2000)
667–694; for Latin America, see (nn 161–162) for pertinent examples; for Asia, see eg Sri Lanka,
Correspondents' Reports (2000) 3 YIHL 594–595.

[167] For this distinction, see K Ambos, 'Impunity and International Criminal Law—A case
study on Colombia, Peru, Bolivia, Chile and Argentina' (1997) 18 Human Rights Law Journal,
1–15, 1.

[168] Cf (n 119) and text.

First, implementation of the *definitions of the core crimes* may be absent or may not correspond to what is criminalized under international criminal law. As regards *absent* implementation, a great number of States have not implemented core crimes into their domestic law, even when the relevant treaties contain an unambiguous obligation to do so.[169] The practice of non-implementation appears to be particularly extensive in the field of customary core crimes, as evidenced by the poor implementation record with regard to crimes against humanity, which many States had not penalized in their national laws preceding the adoption of the Rome Statute.[170] In the absence of such specific provisions, these States can only enforce the prohibition of core crimes by reference to ordinary domestic crimes.[171] However, besides the conceptual difference between domestic and international crimes—the latter being crimes of not only domestic but also international concern—this 'ordinary crimes approach' may entail a number of problems.[172]

On other occasions, domestic core crimes laws may *not correspond* to international criminal law. This may be because States only follow up on their undertakings to criminalize with respect to some crimes but not all; for instance in criminalizing only some of the grave breaches of the Four Geneva Conventions.[173] On other occasions, States adopt domestic rules with a view to implementing core crimes, but the way in which this is done results in the domestic norms diverging

---

[169] For the poor record of States in implementing grave breaches of the Geneva Conventions and Additional Protocol I, see eg K Drzewicki, 'National legislation as a measure for implementation of international humanitarian law' in F Kalshoven and Y Sandoz (eds), *Implementation of International Humanitarian Law* (Martinus Nijhoff Publ, Dordrecht, Boston, London 1989) 109–131, 111–112. See also M Bothe, 'Introduction' in M Bothe (ed), *National Implementation of International Humanitarian Law* (Kluwer Academic Publishers, Dordrecht, Boston, London 1990) xviii. For empirical information, see the implementation database of the ICRC, at <http://www.icrc.org/ihl-nat>. For the margin of appreciation as regards the method of implementation, see W Ferdinandusse, *Direct Application of International Criminal Law in National Courts* (TMC Asser Press, The Hague 2006) 132–136, concluding that the freedom of implementation as regards international law in general also applies in relation to core crimes, notwithstanding some indications to the contrary (at 219–220).

[170] See A Andries, 'Investigations et poursuites des violations du droit des conflits armés: lois et procédures nationals' (1998) 37 Revue de droit militaire et de droit de la guerre 179–223, 189–190; ICRC Advisory Service, (n 62) 45. For the impact of the Rome Statute, see *333–337*.

[171] Cf (n 114) and text.

[172] J K Kleffner, 'The Impact of Complementarity on National Implementation of Substantive International Criminal Law' (2003) 1 JICJ 86–113, 96–99. For further discussion of these problems, see *121–123*.

[173] See eg Article 320 of the Paraguayan Penal Code, Law No 1160/97 Penal Code of the Republic of Paraguay, reproduced in (1998) 1 YIHL 621–623, 623, which expressly incorporates a number of war crimes, but does not cover several war crimes, which are clearly established under international criminal law, including the grave breaches of wilfully depriving a prisoner of war or other protected person of the rights of fair and regular trial and the taking of hostages (Articles 130 of the Third Geneva Convention and 147 of the Fourth Geneva Convention). Paraguay became a party to the Four Geneva Conventions on 23 October 1961 and is therefore under an obligation 'to enact any legislation necessary to provide effective penal sanctions for persons committing, or ordering to be committed, any of the grave breaches': see (n 16).

from the original international rule.[174] Such gaps resulting from domestic legal concepts may even occur when wording is used in the 'domesticated' rule that is identical to the original international rule, but where national courts are, or consider themselves, obliged to give precedence to divergent national concepts.[175]

The implementation of *the general part of international criminal law*[176] have been faced with broadly the same obstacles as have faced the definitions of the core crimes. This is subject to the qualification that some of the rules, which together form the general part of international criminal law, find their origin in general principles of criminal law recognized in (virtually) all domestic legal systems.[177] Since the latter provide for rules on perpetration, participation and defences, it is more often the difference between these principles recognized by *national* law and the *international* principles, rather than the complete absence of rules of domestic law, which results in gaps.[178]

---

[174] The way in which the crime of genocide had been penalized under German law may serve as an example. In contrast to Article 2 (c) of the Genocide Convention (n 55), which refers to the *actus reus* of '[d]eliberately inflicting on the group conditions of life *calculated* to bring about its physical destruction in whole or in part', section 220 a (1) No 3 of the German Criminal Code provides: '[He who] inflicts on the group conditions *apt* to bring about its physical destruction in whole or in part [is liable to punishment].' Emphasis added. Accordingly, German law replaces a subjective element with an objective one. See for a discussion of consequences and relevant jurisprudence, K Ambos and S Wirth, 'Genocide and War Crimes in the Former Yugoslavia Before German Criminal Courts' in H Fischer, C Kress and S R Lüder (eds), *International and national prosecution of crimes under international law: current developments* (Spitz, Berlin 2001) 769–797, 778–789. The provision has been retained in the ICC implementation law: see Section 6 (1) No 3 of the German Code of Crimes against International Law. Similarly, prior to the adoption of the ICC implementing legislation, Dutch law circumscribed the *actus reus* of the crime of 'torture' by reference to the national crime of 'assault': cf Article 1 of the 1984 Torture Act (*Uitvoeringswet Folteringverdrag*). For the situation under the ICC implementing legislation, see Article 1 (1)(d) and (e) of the *Wet houdende regels met betrekking tot ernstige schendingen van het international humanitair recht* (*Wet Internationale Misdrijven*/International Crimes Act), 19 June 2003.

[175] (nn 115–118) and text.   [176] (n 119) and text.

[177] This is not to suggest that these different legal systems recognize uniform 'general parts'. For different models of participation and (often divergent) national underpinnings of other concepts in Anglo-American and Civil law systems, see E van Sliedregt (n 119) 61–64, 69–70, 74–76, 84–86, 103–106, 243–245, 250–252, 264–266, 269–279, 309–313, 329–337. On the process of deducing general principles from national legal systems and transposing them to the legal framework applicable to core crimes, see ICTY, *Prosecutor v Anto Furundzija* IT-95-17/1-T (10 December 1998) 178 ['Whenever international criminal rules do not define a notion of criminal law, reliance upon national legislation is justified, subject to the following conditions: (i) [...] international courts must draw upon the general concepts and legal institutions common to all the major legal systems of the world [...]; (ii) [...] account must be taken of the specificity of international criminal proceedings when utilising national law notions. In this way a mechanical importation or transposition from national law into international criminal proceedings is avoided.']; see also ICTY, *Prosecutor v Erdemovic* (Judgment) IT-96-22-T (29 November 1996) 19–31. See also A Cassese (n 5) 32–35.

[178] See J L F Flores, 'Suppression of breaches of the law of war committed by individuals' (1991) 31 IRRC 247–293, 276–277. Such differences are illustrated by comparing the notions of 'aiding and abetting' in the commission of core crimes on the international level (cf Genocide Convention (n 55) Article III (e)) with the way in which French law criminalizes aiding and abetting by virtue of the concept of 'complicity'. The former does not require the aider and abettor to share the *mens rea* of the principal offender; see for jurisprudence on complicty of the two ad hoc tribunals for the former Yugoslavia and Rwanda, E van Sliedregt (n 119) 88–91. In contrast, French law

Besides these differences between international legal principles and pre-existent domestic legal principles, States have at times also failed to implement those elements of the general part, which evolved specifically with regard to core crimes and which do not correspond to or at least resemble concepts in national criminal law. Chiefly amongst them feature rules governing the responsibility of commanders and other superiors,[179] the exclusion of the defence of superior orders and prescription of law[180] and the irrelevance of official capacity.[181] An example is the Yugoslav criminal code, which penalizes the commission and ordering of war crimes but does not cover command responsibility for failure to act,[182] although Yugoslavia had undertaken to implement Article 86 (2) of the First Additional Protocol[183] by ratifying it in 1977, and had passed a law to implement both Additional Protocols in 1978.[184]

---

requires the accomplice to share that *mens rea* and thus establishes a higher threshold for criminal responsibility: cf C Grynfogel, 'De Touvier à Papon, "la complicité de crime contre l'humanité"' (1998) 78 Revue de droit pénal et de criminologie 758–779.

[179] Cf *US v Tomoyuki Yamashita* 327 US 1, 14–16 (1945). For further post-Second World War jurisprudence and developments in customary and treaty law, including Article 86 of Additional Protocol I (n 9), see K Ambos, 'Superior Responsibility' in A Cassese, P Gaeta and J Jones (eds), *The Rome Statute of the International Criminal Court: A Commentary* (OUP, Oxford 2002) 823–872, concluding that prior to the adoption of the Rome Statute, 'the doctrine of superior responsibility [...was] a well-established principle of customary international law' (at 846–847). See also G Werle (n 146) 462–501, who concurs with K Ambos (n 119) 667, that superior responsibility is an '*originär völkerstrafrechtliche Rechtsschöpfung*' (467 at 464).

[180] See generally for this concept prior to the adoption of the ICC Statute, G Werle (n 146) 137–142; P Gaeta, 'The Defence of Superior Orders: The Statute of the International Criminal Court versus Customary International Law' (1999) 10 EJIL 172–191.

[181] For the position of this rule prior to and independent of the ICC Statute, see P Gaeta, 'Official Capacity and Immunities' in A Cassese, P Gaeta and J Jones (eds) (n 179) 975–989. See also *Case Concerning the Arrest Warrant of 11 April 2000* (n 164) [58]. For a discussion of the judgment, see the symposium in (2002) 13 EJIL 853–899, with contributions from A Cassese, S Wirth and M Spinedi.

[182] Cf Article 144 (war crimes against prisoners of war) of the 1977 Criminal Code, which reads: 'Whoever, in violation of the rules of international law, *orders* murders, tortures or inhuman treatment of prisoners of war, including therein biological experiments, causing of great sufferings or serious injury to the bodily integrity or health, compulsive enlistment into the armed forces of an enemy power, or deprivation of the right to a fair and impartial trial, or who *commits* some of the foregoing acts, shall be punished by imprisonment for not less than five years or by the death penalty'. Emphasis added. On the other hand, Regulation 21 of the 1988 Yugoslavian Military Regulations do provide for superior responsibility for failure to act: reproduced in M C Bassiouni and P Manikas, *The Law of the International Criminal Tribunal for the Former Yugoslavia* (Transnational Publ, Ardsley NY 1996) 660. However, case law indicates that courts have not applied Article XX of the 1988 Yugoslavian Military Regulations to fill the gap contained in Yugoslav criminal law as regards command responsibility for failure to act, as indicated by case law of Bosnian courts, which applied Article 144 until the new Criminal Codes of the Federation of Bosnia and Herzegovina came into force in November 1998: see J K Kleffner, *National Enforcement of International Humanitarian Law: A Case Study of War Crimes Prosecutions in Bosnian Domestic Courts* in H van Harten and Y Donders (eds), *Gepeperde noten* (UvA, Amsterdam 2006) 124–140.

[183] (n 21).

[184] Socialist Federal Republic of Yugoslavia, Law of Ratification of the Geneva Protocols, Medunarodni Ugovori, at 1083 (26 December 1978).

States have also frequently not established *extraterritorial jurisdiction,* especially universal jurisdiction, over (some) core crimes. This is even the case with regard to those crimes for which international law imposes a clear obligation to do so.[185] For instance, prior to the implementation of the Rome Statute into national law, national courts in Italy were unable to exercise universal jurisdiction over grave breaches of the Geneva Conventions.[186]

Even when extraterritorial jurisdiction is established, its applicability has at times been limited to crimes committed in certain periods or places. An example stems from the Australian War Crimes Act 1945 (as amended by the War Crimes Amendment Act 1988), which limits extraterritorial jurisdiction for war crimes to those committed in Europe during the Second World War.[187] Other States have limited extraterritorial jurisdiction by other conditions, such as double criminality.[188] Last but not least, some States have established such jurisdiction for only some core crimes in spite of their international legal obligations.[189] Thus, while Nigeria is a party to the four Geneva Conventions *and* Additional Protocol I, Section 3 (1)–(2) of the Nigeria Geneva Conventions Act 1960 only extends universal jurisdiction to grave breaches of the four Conventions, but was never amended to establish that jurisdiction over the grave breaches contained in Additional Protocol I.

In theory, gaps resulting from absent or defective national implementing laws could be filled without additional legislative action in those States that allow for the direct application of international law by virtue of their constitutions. However, for a number of reasons, including considerations of sovereignty, the separation of powers and legal certainty,[190] this possibility is rarely resorted to in practice.[191]

---

[185] Cf (nn 18–19, 23, 28–29, 34–35, 43, 68, 80, 84).

[186] Cf P Gaeta, 'War Crimes Trials Before Italian Criminal Courts: New Trends' in H Fischer, C Kress and S R Lüder, (n 174) 751–768, 752–753, noting also that courts have not remedied that gap despite the possibility to do so (at 767, n 35) and text. On this latter point, cf also below nn 190–191 and text.

[187] Section 9 (1) 1988 War Crimes Amendment Act (promulgated and entered into force 25 January 1989). In contrast, Article 7 of the Geneva Conventions Act 1957, as amended by the Geneva Conventions Amendment Act 1991, establishes universal jurisdiction over grave breaches of Geneva Conventions and Additional Protocol I without such restrictions.

[188] Cf Article 7 (Part II) (a), section 2 (b) of the Brazilian Criminal Code, which provides that: 'The following shall be subject to Brazilian law, even though committed abroad: . . . II—crimes (a) which through treaty or agreement Brazil is obliged to suppress, . . . Section 2. In the circumstances in subsection II, the application of Brazilian law shall depend on the concurrent existence of the following conditions: (a) the agent is on national territory, (b) the act is also punishable in the country in which it was performed, (c) the crime is included among those for which Brazilian law authorizes extradition, (d) the agent has not been acquitted abroad or has not completed his sentence, (e) the agent has not been pardoned abroad or the penalty has not been extinguished, in accordance with the most favourable law, for any other reason.' English translation from Amnesty International (n 53) Chapter 4a, 33.

[189] See Amnesty International (n 53) Chapter 4b, 44.

[190] For a discussion of these reasons, see W Ferdinandusse (n 169) 99–104, 221–268.

[191] For an overview of relevant case law, see W Ferdinandusse (n 169) 36–84, who concludes at 85 that such general direct application is '[d]ecidedly less common' than other methods of implementation.

In sum, prior to and independent of the Rome Statute, the state of implementing the international legal framework for the national suppression of core crimes was frequently such that national criminal jurisdictions were hampered to assume the central role, which international law envisages them to fulfil.

3.2. Obstacles relating to Enforcement

In addition to those relating to implementation, a myriad of obstacles relate to the actual enforcement of the prohibition of core crimes in domestic proceedings. The primary cause of these obstacles originates in the very nature of core crimes and the context in which they are committed.

These crimes are typically 'system crimes'[192] or 'macro-crimes',[193] ie crimes that are committed with involvement of State or de facto authorities[194] and that rarely occur as isolated or sporadic acts, but rather on a widespread scale.[195] Furthermore, they are typically committed during times of political upheaval, unrest or collective violence between groups, which, as far as war crimes are concerned, amount to armed conflicts.[196] The environment of core crimes is thus one of intense social antagonisms, organized along political, ethnic, religious or other lines, which entail a break-up of social structures into the distinction between 'them' and 'us', 'enemy' and 'ally', and 'good' and 'evil'. Staying neutral is the privilege of a few. Individuals commonly feel compelled to take sides and close the ranks, if only in an attempt to ensure their own survival. Prosecuting members of

---

[192] See eg B V A Röling, 'The Significance of the Laws of War' in A Cassese (ed), *Current Problems of International Law* (Guiffré, Milan 1975) 137–139. See also A Cassese (n 5) 295 ['perpetration... presupposes the complicity, participation, toleration, or acquiescence of State authorities, or which is effected by State agents themselves']; in German literature the corresponding term of '*Systemunrecht*' is sometimes used: cf eg E Lampe, 'Systemunrecht und Unrechtssysteme' (1994) 106 Zeitschrift für die gesamte Strafrechtswissenschaft 683–745.

[193] The terms 'macro-criminality' (*Makrokriminalität*) and 'macro-crimes' (*Makroverbrechen)* are often used in German literature to denote '*systemkonforme und situationsangepasste Verhaltensweisen innerhalb eines Organisationsgefüges, Machtapparates oder sonstigen kollektiven Aktionszusammenhangs*': see eg H Jäger, '*Makrokriminalität. Studien zur Kriminologie kollektiver Gewalt*' (Suhrkamp, Frankfurt/Main 1989) 11; and H Jäger, 'Makroverbrechen als Gegenstand des Völkerstrafrechts' in G Hankel and G Stuby (eds), *Strafgerichte gegen Menschheitsverbrechen: Zum Völkerstrafrecht 50 Jahre nach den Nürnberger Prozessen* (Hamburger Edition, Hamburg 1995) 325–354, 327.

[194] See generally B Swart, *De berechting van internationale misdrijven* (Gouda Quint, Arnhem 1996) 6–7. On the commission of core crimes by members of non-State actors, see eg *Prosecutor v Kupreskic et al* (Judgment) IT-95-16, T Ch (14 January 2000) [551] *et seq* (for crimes against humanity). See also K Ambos (n 119) 51–53.

[195] This is subject to the qualification that war crimes do not necessarily meet the criterion of system-criminality or of widespread commission, as they can be committed as isolated acts by individual soldiers acting on their own initiative: see A Cassese (n 5) 295. Overall, the fact remains, however, that isolated core crimes are an exception.

[196] Although crimes against humanity and genocide do not *require* an armed conflict as a contextual element (cf Article 1 of the 1948 Genocide Convention (n 55); for crimes against humanity, see *Prosecutor v Tadic* (Appeals Judgment) IT-94-I-AR72 (15 July 1999) [249, 251], they often coincide with war crimes.

one's own group is regarded as weakening the efforts to ensure the ultimate aim of the survival of that State or group and to 'overcome the enemy'.

These features reveal the intrinsic dilemma facing national enforcement of the prohibition of core crimes: the mechanism that is envisaged to effectuate these proscriptions is almost inevitably undermined by the very nature of the conduct that is supposed to be suppressed. Core crimes are frequently both cause and consequence of a partial or complete paralyzation of the judiciary of the State on whose territory they occur. The judiciary, as a whole or as individual members, lacks the necessary independence and impartiality;[197] it is incapable of coping with an overwhelming number of perpetrators, because judges and lawyers may have been killed and court buildings destroyed during an armed conflict,[198] or, when such an armed conflict is still ongoing, opposing armed forces exercise control over the territory, which is thereby beyond the reach of the judicial authorities.[199] All these effects on the domestic legal system are regularly felt for a long time after the periods in which core crimes were committed have ended.[200]

Of course, the territorial State is not the only forum in which perpetrators could be brought to justice. However, despite the fact that the obstacles to national enforcement confronting territorial States and third States differ in important respects, the aforementioned characteristics of core crimes do not leave third States unaffected. The political implications of a core crime prosecution may very well be a cause for third States to refrain from conducting or abandoning

[197] For some examples, see the following 'Reports of the Special Rapporteur on the independence of judges and lawyers, Mr Param Cumaraswamy': (1998) UN Doc E/CN.4/1998/39/Add.2 (Colombia), especially [125–153]; (2001) E/CN.4/2002/72/Add.2 (Guatemala), especially [27–42]; (1997) E/CN.4/1997/62/Add.1 (Nigeria), especially [49–59]. Naturally, core crimes are not the doubtful privilege of States with a structurally defunct judiciary, as amply evidenced in the My Lai massacre during the Vietnam War and the abuse of detainees in Abu Ghraib prison in Iraq by US soldiers; UK soldiers violating international humanitarian law (IHL) in Iraq (see 'British soldiers face abuse court martial' *Guardian*, 15 June 2004); Canadian soldiers violating IHL in Somalia (see eg *The Queen v Brocklebank*, Court Martial Appeal Court of Canada, 2 April 1996, and commentary on the decision by K Boustany, 'Brocklebank: A Questionable Decision of the Court Martial Appeal Court of Canada' (1998) 1 YIHL 371–374); Italian soldiers violating IHL in Somalia: see P Gaeta (n 186) 767 (Ercole case). However, if core crimes reach the level of systematicity and pervasiveness as can frequently be witnessed, they are regularly indicative of a systematic lack of independence and impartiality.
[198] See for Rwanda: S Rwagasore, 'The case of Rwanda, in: ICRC Advisory Service' in C Pellandini (ed), *National Measures to Suppress Violations of International Humanitarian Law (civil law systems), Report on the Meeting of Experts* (ICRC, Geneva 2000) 98–106, 98.
[199] In Colombia, for instance, the largest armed opposition group, the Revolutionary Armed Forces of Colombia (FARC), carried out acts in a large demilitarized zone ('*zona de distensión*') between 1998 and 2002, in which arrest warrants were suspended. On crimes committed in this zone and the state of the Colombian judicial system, see generally 'Report of the United Nations High Commissioner for Human Rights on the human rights situation in Colombia' (8 February 2001) UN Doc E/CN.4/2001/15. See also <http://www.cidh.org/countryrep/Colombia04eng/chapter3.htm>, paras 58–59.
[200] For instance, despite efforts of the occupying forces to reinvigorate the German domestic legal system, it took until the mid-1950s for it to develop a proactive stance towards prosecuting Nazi crimes: see Rückerl (n 141) 33–72.

proceedings.[201] These States are also confronted with obstacles of a different kind than territorial States, such as the inaccessibility of evidence and witnesses in foreign jurisdictions.

The most obvious and direct obstacle to national enforcement caused by the aforementioned factors, which also appears to be the most common, is that States remain inactive and do not respond to core crimes by legal means, let alone criminal prosecutions.[202] Even when States do decide to respond to core crimes, however, they frequently substitute criminal prosecutions with amnesties, truth commissions, lustration processes and similar measures (3.2.1.), or obstacles occur in the course of criminal proceedings (3.2.2.).

3.2.1. Substitutes for Criminal Prosecutions

States have frequently replaced criminal prosecutions with alternative responses to core crimes.[203] Each of these substitutes raises a number of questions, including whether they are permissible or, indeed, required under international law, whether they preclude third States from prosecuting or the territorial State to prosecute at a later date, how they relate to each other and whether and under what conditions they may be a wise choice in political terms.[204] However, an analysis of these questions goes beyond the purpose of the present section, which

---

[201] One may only recall high-profile cases such as proceedings against former Israeli Prime Minister Sharon, the former foreign minister of the Democratic Republic of Congo, and US General Franks in Belgium, all of which sparked serious diplomatic rows. In fact, pressure from Israel and the US was finally a factor in amending the jurisdictional clauses of the Belgian law, which provided the basis for these proceedings: see S Smis and K van der Borght, 'Introductory Note to Belgium's Amendment to the Law of June 16, 1993 (As Amended by the Law of February 10, 1999) Concerning the Punishment of Grave Breaches of Humanitarian Law' (2003) 42 ILM 740–748, 745.

[202] See J L Balint, 'Conflict, Conflict Victimization, And Legal Redress, 1945–1996' (1996) 59 Law and Contemporary Problems 4 231–247. The author analyzes 285 conflicts since 1945 and concludes that only 49 of these conflicts were addressed by some form of (legal) redress, ie criminal prosecutions, truth commissions and inquiries, lustration legislation, compensation or amnesty. States remained inactive in the remaining 236 conflicts. Criminal prosecutions were only opted for in 23 of the analyzed conflicts.

[203] That such alternatives *replace* criminal prosecutions goes without saying for some of them, such as blanket amnesties. Others can be adopted in addition to criminal prosecutions, such as truth commissions. See for a discussion of such a concurrent model, W Schabas, 'Internationalized Courts and their Relationship with Alternative Accountability Mechanisms: The Case of Sierra Leone' in C Romano, A Nollkaemper and J K Kleffner (eds) (n 3) 157–180.

[204] On these questions, see amongst many others D F Orentlicher (n 62); Naomi Roht-Arriaza (ed), *Impunity and Human Rights in International Law and Practice* (OUP, New York 1995); L Huyse, 'To Punish or to Pardon: A Devil's Choice' in C C Joyner and M C Bassiouni (eds), *'Reining in Impunity for International Crimes and Serious Violations of Fundamental Human Rights: Proceedings of the Siracusa Conference 17–21 September 1998'* (1998) 14 Nouvelles Etudes Pénales 79–90; M J Osiel (n 125); M Scharf (n 125); J Dugard, 'Is the Truth and Reconciliation process compatible with international law? An unanswered question' (1997) 13 S Afr J Hum Rights 258–268; G Meintjes and J E Méndez, 'Reconciling Amnesties with Universal Jurisdiction' (2000) 2 International Law FORUM du droit international 76–97. On relevant decisions of human rights bodies, see *23–24*.

is confined to a general description of such substitutes in order to provide an understanding of the obstacles that they pose to national prosecutions.

Repeatedly, core crimes have been decriminalized by granting *amnesties* to perpetrators. Such amnesties have a long history and can be traced back at least to the 1648 Westphalian Peace Treaties.[205] In the post-Second World War order, amnesties have been adopted in a considerable number of States in which core crimes occurred.[206] These 'modern' amnesties have regularly a political settlement as their foremost objective and typically reflect a compromise between the agents of the old regime, which may be potentially prosecuted, and the transitional or new government.[207] Their occurrence thus directly relates to the character of core crimes.

States have also substituted criminal prosecutions with *truth commissions,* which are set up at a point of political transition to investigate a past history of core crimes and attempt to paint the overall picture of such crimes.[208] In comparison with amnesties and pardons, truth commissions are a relatively recent phenomenon, and have been multiplying rapidly over the past 30 years.[209] While truth commissions do not necessarily exclude criminal prosecutions of core crimes,[210] they usually do, as they are regularly the result of a political compromise in situations where criminal prosecutions could not be achieved.[211] This is notwithstanding the fact that they may serve some of the same purposes as prosecutions, such as establishing an authoritative record of the crimes committed, providing a forum for the victims and their relatives and sometimes even providing a formal basis for compensation and other forms of reparations.[212] Similarly, States have at times set up *investigatory commissions,* with a narrower mandate for single incidents, as a substitute for criminal prosecutions.[213]

---

[205] Cf Article 2 of the Peace Treaties. Mutual amnesty clauses were regularly included into peace treaties up to the First World War. Thereafter, a new policy of one-sided amnesties emerged, providing for the prosecution of the vanquished and the granting of amnesty to the victors. See F Domb, 'Treatment of War Crimes in Peace Settlements—Prosecution or Amnesty' in Y Dinstein and M Tabory (eds) (n 1) 305–320, 306–310; A M de Zayas, 'Amnesty Clause' in R Bernhardt (ed), *Encyclopedia of Public International Law* (vol 1 North-Holland, Amsterdam 1992) 148–151, 149–150.

[206] For an overview, see A O'Shea, *Amnesty for crime in international law and practice* (Kluwer, The Hague 2002) 21–23, 34–64.

[207] The developments leading to the establishment of the South African Truth and Reconciliation Commission and to the blanket amnesty provided for under the Lomé Peace Accord for Sierra Leone are prominent examples. See J Dugard, 'South Africa's Truth and Reconciliation Process and International Humanitarian Law' (1999) 2 YIHL 254–263, 254–255; A McDonald, 'Sierra Leone's Uneasy Peace: The Amnesties Granted in the Lomé Peace Agreement and the United Nations' Dilemma' (2000) 1 Humanitäres Völkerrecht 11, 11–26, 11–15.

[208] P B Hayner, 'Fifteen Truth Commissions—1974 to 1994: A Comparative Study' (1994) 16 Human Rights Quarterly 597–655, 600, 604.

[209] The first instance was the establishment of the 'Commission of Inquiry into the Disappearances of People in Uganda since the 25th January, 1971' in 1974.

[210] See (n 203).   [211] P B Hayner (n 208) 604–605.

[212] N J Kritz, 'Coming to Terms with Atrocities: A Review of Accountability Mechanisms for Mass Violations of Human Rights' (1996) 59 Law and Contemporary Problems 4, 127–152, 141.

[213] A prominent example is the Israeli Commission of Inquiry into the events at the refugee camps in Beirut, 8 February 1983 (Kahane Commission), set up to investigate a number of Israeli

Reparations, while serving an important function as a remedy for victims of core crimes[214] and offering the possibility of being adopted in combination with criminal proceedings, may also constitute a substitute for criminal prosecutions. In such cases, States adopt measures of restitution, compensation, rehabilitation and satisfaction that aim to relieve the suffering of and afford justice to victims by removing or redressing to the extent possible the consequences of the wrongful acts and by preventing and deterring them,[215] without recourse to the means of criminal law. Thus States implement processes to re-establish the situation for the victim prior to the wrongful acts (restitution);[216] to economically assess damage resulting from the wrongful act and afford an amount of money to the victim or his/her relatives (compensation);[217] to restore the dignity of victims by providing legal, medical, psychological and other care and services (rehabilitation);[218] or to provide satisfaction and guarantees of non-repetition, including measures ranging from an apology to human rights training of the police and armed forces.[219] Reparation measures are primarily substitutes for criminal prosecutions in the territorial State, but third States may also have recourse to them in the form of civil suits for compensation.[220]

governmental officials and military officers who were implicated in the commission of core crimes that occurred in the Palestinian refugee camps of Sabra and Shatila. See Kahane report, available at: <http://www.jewishvirtuallibrary.org/jsource/History/kahan.html>. These investigatory commissions substituting criminal prosecutions have to be distinguished from international and national commissions, whose purpose is to collect evidence of criminality as a first step on the way to criminal proceedings. On the latter, see M Cherif Bassiouni, 'Searching for Peace and Achieving Justice: The Need for Accountability' in C C Joyner and M C Bassiouni (eds) (n 204) 45–70, 60. Examples are the Commission of Experts for the former Yugoslavia established pursuant to Security Council Resolution 780 (1992); the Commission of Experts established pursuant to Security Council Resolution 935 (1994); the International Commission of Inquiry on East Timor established pursuant to Commission on Human Rights resolution S-4/1999/1; and the Indonesian Commission of Inquiry on East Timor, conducted under the auspices of the National Human Rights Commission (Komnas HAM), established by Komnas HAM's plenary session on 23 September 1999, Decree of the Komnas HAM No 770/TUA/IX/99.

[214] See generally A Randelzhofer and C Tomuschat (eds), *State responsibility and the individual: reparation in instances of grave violations of human rights* (Nijhoff, The Hague 1999) 296; R P Mazzeschi, 'Reparation claims by individuals for state breaches of humanitarian law and human rights: an overview' (2003) 1 JICJ 339–347; M Nowak, 'The right to reparation of victims of gross human rights violations' in G Ulrich and L Krabbe Boserup (eds), *Human rights in development Yearbook 2001—Reparations: Redressing Past Wrongs* (Kluwer, The Hague 2003) 275–284; F McKay, 'Civil reparation in national courts for victims of human rights abuse' in M Lattimer and P Sands (eds), *Justice for crimes against humanity* (Hart Publ, Oxford 2003) 283–302.

[215] Cf the Study concerning the right to restitution, compensation and rehabilitation for victims of gross violations of human rights and fundamental freedoms, 'Final Report submitted by Mr. Theo van Boven, Special Rapporteur' (1993) UN Doc E/CN.4/Sub.2/1993/8 [137] Proposed Basic Principle 3.

[216] Ibid, Proposed Basic Principle 8. [217] Ibid, Proposed Basic Principle 9.
[218] Ibid, Proposed Basic Principle 10. [219] Ibid, Proposed Basic Principle 11.

[220] For instance, US courts have broad universal jurisdiction over civil suits for core crimes under the Alien Tort Claims Act and the Torture Victim Protection Act (1991), and a large number of cases have been adjudicated under both these acts. In sharp contrast, criminal prosecutions based on universality have not been conducted except in relation to Second World War offences despite the legal possibility to do so with regard to war crimes: see Amnesty International (n 53) Chapter 4b, 90–105.

Finally, States often respond to core crimes by imposing *administrative* instead of criminal *sanctions*. As in the case of reparations, they may serve important functions in holding individuals accountable for core crimes and do not necessarily exclude criminal proceedings. However, States often replace the latter by such administrative sanctions. They may decide to purge the State apparatus by processes of lustration through which individuals who supported or participated in core crimes are removed or barred from certain positions.[221] In relation to crimes committed by members of armed forces, such sanctions may take the form of disciplinary sanctions in application of the relevant code of military discipline.[222] Or, as far as third States are concerned, suspects may be excluded from refugee status in application of Article 1 F of the 1951 Convention Relating to the Status of Refugees.[223]

In sum, the array of substitutes for criminal prosecutions is wide, and considerable differences exist between them, not least as regards their ability to effectuate some form of accountability, albeit non-criminal. All of them have in common, however, the fact that they are frequently used by States to replace criminal prosecutions.

3.2.2. Obstacles during Criminal Proceedings

Even when States decide to initiate criminal proceedings, a variety of obstacles occur at different stages of such proceedings. As in the case of obstacles to implementation, the following account does not claim to be all-inclusive, but merely illustrates the problems by selecting a few examples from the abundance of material available.

One such obstacle to national suppression is the frequent *inability* of national authorities to carry out criminal proceedings. Such inability may result from the general insecurity in a State embroiled in an armed conflict, which prevents the investigating authorities from collecting evidence and carrying out the search for, and arrest of, suspects.[224] The inability to obtain the suspect or carry out

---

[221] M Cherif Bassiouni (n 213) 62. Lustration can also be seen as a specific form of satisfaction and a guarantee of non-repetition: cf (n 219) and text.

[222] J Verhaegen, 'Legal obstacles to prosecution of breaches of humanitarian law' (1987) 27 IRRC 607–620, 611.

[223] 1951 Convention Relating to the Status of Refugees 189 UNTS 150 Article 1 F excludes persons from the provisions of the Convention 'with respect to whom there are serious reasons for considering that [...h]e has committed a crime against peace, a war crime, or a crime against humanity [...].' See amongst others the symposium in (2000) 12 International Journal of Refugee Law. For empirical evidence of the increasing trend to apply Article 1 F and relevant case law, see Correspondents' Reports (2001) 4 YIHL 416–419 (Australia), 471 (Canada), 608 (US); see also G Gilbert, 'Current Issues in the Application of the Exclusion Clauses, Background Paper for an Expert Roundtable Discussion on exclusion organised as part of the Global Consultations on International Protection in the context of the 50th anniversary of the 1951 Convention Relating to the Status of Refugees' (2001) (on file with author) 42, 5. The increase in applying Article 1 F is not matched by criminal prosecutions.

[224] Cf (n 199) and text.

proceedings may also be caused by the non-cooperation of other States, for example because they refuse to extradite the suspect or to hand over evidence. This may be either a factual matter or one resulting from legal bars to extradition or access to evidence.[225] Other factual obstacles are caused by judicial authorities and witnesses being intimidated[226] or bribed,[227] or evidence suppressed.[228]

Undue delays constitute a further obstacle. If national authorities decide not to commence an inquiry into the facts of a case, or to do so only after a considerable period of time has lapsed, vital evidence may be lost and the memory of witnesses may fade.[229] Suspects may be too old and unfit to stand trial[230] and, if national criminal jurisdictions recognize statutory limitations (at times in spite

---

[225] Recall the refusal of Argentina to extradite Adolf Eichmann to Israel, for example, which ultimately led to his abduction on 11 May 1960 in Buenos Aires. Legal bars to extradition may stem from the absence of an extradition treaty or competing obligations under international law, for instance because the requested State is legally obliged not to extradite a suspect to a State that may impose the death penalty: cf for States Parties to the European Convention on Human Rights, *Soering v the United Kingdom* (n 94). Similarly, the refusal to extradite a suspect may emanate from a State's international obligation not to extradite a suspect to a State where there are grounds to believe that the suspects may be subjected to torture or inhuman and degrading treatment: cf Article 3 of the UN Convention against Torture (n 73). Another example is when the requested State refuses to hand over evidence that it considers to contain state secrets: see J Verhaegen (n 222) 611–613.

[226] For some salient examples, see: for Rwanda, 'Prosecuting Genocide in Rwanda: A Human Rights First report on the ICTR and National Trials' (July 1997), available at <http://www. humanrightsfirst.org/pubs/descriptions/rwanda.htm#rwanda> (at F.2.b.); for the former Yugoslavia, see for instance F M M Florenz, 'The Rule of Law in Kosovo: Problems and Prospects' (2000) 11 Criminal Law Forum 127–142, 133; A Kebo, 'Regional Report: Local Justice, Bosnian-Style' (2001) IWPR's Tribunal Update No 220, May 7–12, 2001.

[227] N Heasley, R Hurley, K Irwin, A Kaufman, N Moustafa and A Personna, 'Impunity in Guatemala: The State's Failure to Provide Justice in the Massacre Cases' (2001) 16 Am U Intl Rev 1115–1194, 1153.

[228] For instance, when a superior knows that a subordinate has committed core crimes but does not submit the matter to the competent authorities for further investigation and prosecution, in violation of clear regulations. For a pertinent case, see ICTY *Prosecutor v Krstic* (Judgment) IT-98-33-T (2 August 2001) 480–482.

[229] There are numerous examples of such delays. For the underlying reasons in Germany in relation to Nazi crimes committed during the Second World War, see A Rückerl, 'NS-Prozesse, "Warum erst heute?—Warum noch heute?—Wie lange noch?"' in A Rückerl (ed), *NS-Prozesse, Nach 25 Jahren Strafverfolgung: Möglichkeiten, Grenzen, Ergebnisse* (CF Müller Verlag, Karslruhe 1972) 13–34. For Italian delays relating to the same period, see P Gaeta (n 186) 751–752.

[230] A prominent example can be seen in the Spanish and Chilean proceedings against Augusto Pinochet, which were hampered by his ailing health, due to which some concluded he was unfit to stand trial. For the decision of the then UK Home Secretary Jack Straw to halt extradition proceedings for reasons of ill-health, see Mr Straw's full Commons speech: Guardian (12 January 2000), available at <http://www.guardian.co.uk/pinochet/Story/0,,194674,00.html>]. Chile's Supreme Court reached a similar conclusion on 1 July 2002: see *The Guardian* 'Pinochet unfit to stand trial, rules court', available at <http://www.guardian.co.uk/world/2002/jul/02/pinochet>. However, this did not put an end to criminal proceedings in Chile against him: for a chronological overview see BBC 'Timeline: The Pinochet legal saga' available at <http://news.bbc.co.uk/2/hi/americas/1209914.stm>.

of international obligations to the contrary[231]), these domestic statutes of limitations may result in investigations not being conducted at a later stage.[232]

Another obstacle hampering domestic criminal proceedings emanates from the exercise of *prosecutorial discretion*. All criminal justice systems establish various degrees of such discretion, which allows national authorities to decline to conduct or to discontinue proceedings on a number of grounds.[233] Prosecutorial discretion can be (ab)used in order to abstain from bringing charges or to enforce the prohibitions of the core crimes selectively.

Such *selectivity* may limit proceedings to those against one side of the conflict[234] or a small fraction of the perpetrators, despite the possibility to charge

---

[231] Some of the Parties to the UN and European Conventions on the Non-Applicability of Statutory Limitations to War Crimes and Crimes Against Humanity still recognize statutory limitations to some extent. See eg for the situation in The Netherlands, which had ratified the European Convention prior to the adoption of the ICC implementing legislation, the Dutch report in International Society for Military Law and the Law of War (n 119) 324–325. The current Dutch ICC implementing legislation retains statutory limitations for a number of war crimes: cf Section 13 of the *Wet Internationale Misdrijven*.

[232] P Gaeta (n 186) 752.

[233] J Verhaegen (n 222) 610–611; R Cryer, *Prosecuting International Crimes—Selectivity and the International Criminal Law Regime* (CUP, Cambridge 2005) 192–194; D D Ntanda Nsereko, 'Prosecutorial Discretion before National Courts and International Tribunals' (2005) 3 JICJ 124–144, 126–130. For a concise overview of prosecutorial discretion, see A Hamzah and R M Surachman, *The Prosecutorial Discretion, A Comparative Study, Barcelona Conference on the law of the world* (World Jurist Association, Washington DC 1991) 40, concluding at 6 that '[e]ven in jurisdictions where the public prosecutor's decision in dropping the case needs the consent of the court, most of the time the court will give a positive response to the demand of the public prosecutor'. Also cf 9–10 [exceptions to the mandatory prosecution principle in Germany and the practice in other States which adopt the mandatory prosecution principle (Italy and Austria)]. For a more detailed discussion of the situation in various States, see 'Survey over the Belgian, Dutch, French, German, UK and US prosecution services' (2000) 8 European Journal of Crime, Criminal Law and Criminal Justice 154–295; L Arbour, A Eser, K Ambos and A Sanders (eds), *The Prosecutor of a Permanent International Criminal Court* (edition iuscrim, vol 81, Freiburg 2000) 197–528; answers to question 13 (duty to investigate) in *Compatibility of National Legal Systems with the Statute of the Permanent International Criminal Court*, XVI Recueils of the International Society for Military Law and the Law of War (2003) vol II, 497–498, 557, 561, 565, 569–572, 603, 611, 615, 619, 621–622, 651, 655, 659, 661, 665, 669, 673, 675, 677, 681, 725, 735, 739, 741, 745, 747, 751, 757–759, 781, 785, 787.

[234] Examples can be found in prosecutions relating to the internal armed conflict that accompanied the 1994 genocide in Rwanda. Notwithstanding indications to the effect that the Tutsi-dominated Rwandan Patriotic Army (RPA) had committed core crimes during the 1994 armed conflict, crimes committed by the (now) Rwandan government's armed forces have so far been neglected by Rwandan national courts. On evidence that crimes have been committed by the RPA, see 'Prosecutor outlines future plans' ICTR Press Release ICTR/INFO-9-2-254.EN (13 December 2000). Similarly, charges brought in national courts in the States of the former Yugoslavia for a long time almost exclusively related to members of the opposing party to the conflict: 'Office of the High Representative: Summary of War Crimes and Highly Political Cases in BiH', 1999 (n 148). See also for Croatia, the various cases referred to at the ICRC website, <http://www.icrc.org/ihl-nat.nsf/WebCASE?OpenView&Start=1&Count=30&Expand=9#9>, all of which relate to Serb accused. Another example relates to crimes committed during the Second World War: cf G Triggs, 'National Prosecutions of War Crimes and the Rule of Law' in H Durham and T L H McCormack (eds), *The Changing Face of Conflict and the Efficacy of International Humanitarian Law* (Martinus Nijhoff, The Hague/London/Boston 1999) 175–191, 179–183.

a larger number of them.[235] Furthermore, the competent national authorities sometimes bring charges only against lower-level suspects, while abstaining from prosecuting suspects on the highest level of military or political authority.[236] Alternatively, they may limit charges to forms of responsibility, which carry a lesser sentence or convey a less direct involvement of the accused; for instance charging him or her for command responsibility because s/he failed to act, rather than for inciting or ordering the commission of core crimes.[237] A different form of selectivity occurs on a purely practical level, when the sheer number of suspects forces the competent authorities to prioritize certain categories of crimes or perpetrators.

One can also observe selectivity in national enforcement of international criminal law by *third States*. For example, proceedings with respect to the conflicts in the former Yugoslavia[238] so far almost exclusively relate to Serb suspects. The broader picture also suggests that charges are often limited to crimes committed in only a limited number of armed conflicts or systematic or widespread attacks against the civilian population, while leaving core crimes committed in other States unaddressed. The latter is most notably the case when national authorities are faced with bringing charges against nationals of 'friendly States', and other cases where bringing charges against suspects is deemed to adversely affect the national interests of the investigating State.

Another obstacle to bringing charges concerns *immunities* enjoyed by suspects under national and international law. Many *national laws* grant immunity to high-ranking public officials, such as the Head of State, members of the cabinet and parliamentary deputies, and thus constitute a bar to prosecutions by the State of active nationality.[239] Immunities under *international law*, on the other hand, protect high governmental officials, diplomats and consular agents from the criminal jurisdiction of foreign States. Here, one has to distinguish between functional immunities, which exclude proceedings against governmental officials engaged in acts of an official nature, and personal immunities, which protect senior governmental officials and diplomats due to their personal status in order to enable them to perform their official functions abroad. The extent

---

[235] While the Indonesian national commission of inquiry (n 213) recommended to the Attorney-General that more than 100 individuals be investigated as suspects of the crimes committed in East Timor in 1999, this recommendation was not followed up. Ultimately, charges were only brought against 18 individuals: see D Cohen, 'Intended to Fail—The Trials before the Ad Hoc Human Rights Court in Jakarta' (2003) 74 International Center for Transitional Justice 5, 8–9.

[236] J Verhaegen (n 222) 619, (n 35); as regards the US proceedings in relation to the My Lai massacre during the Vietnam War, see M Bilton and K Sim, *Four Hours in My Lai* (Penguin Books, London 1992) 322–323; D Cohen (n 235) 5.

[237] See eg the case of Eurico Gutteres, summarized in D Cohen (n 235) 24–28.

[238] See (nn 151–155) for pertinent examples.

[239] See J K Kleffner, 'General Report, The Compatibility of National Legal Systems with the Statute of the Permanent International Criminal Court (ICC), Part II—Procedural Law' (2003) International Society for Military Law and the Law of War, Recueil XVI, vol II, 497–523, 509–510.

of these immunities is subject to considerable debate, at least since the ground-breaking *Pinochet* case.[240] The state of the law, however, appears to be that, while customary international law might arguably have evolved to reject functional immunities with respect to core crimes,[241] personal immunities remain intact. Consequently, proceedings before foreign courts for core crimes are inadmissible with regard to incumbent senior governmental officials, most notably heads of State, heads of government and foreign ministers.[242]

Immunities, whether under national or international law, constitute a particularly relevant obstacle to national enforcement as they relate to governmental officials who are often those involved in core crimes due to the character of such crimes as system-crimes.[243]

A number of obstacles may also result from a *qualification of international crimes as ordinary offences,* despite the presence of a legal framework to do otherwise.[244] Where specific implementing legislation with respect to core crimes provides for broader criminal responsibility than is provided under common criminal law, for instance by excluding the defence of superior order[245] and exclusion from amnesty,[246] qualification as an ordinary offence may preclude the applicability of

---

[240]   *R v Bow Street Stipendiary Magistrate and others, ex parte Pinochet Ugarte* [1997] 2 All ER 97.
[241]   For state practice and arguments in support of such an exception, see P Gaeta (n 181) 979–983; A Cassese (n 5) 267–271; A Cassese, 'When May Senior State Officials Be Tried for International Crimes? Some Comments on the Congo v Belgium Case' (2002) 13 EJIL 853–874, 870–71. See also Article 13 (2) of the Resolution of the Institut de Droit International on 'Immunities from Jurisdiction and Execution of Heads of State and of Government in International Law', adopted at the Session of Vancouver, 2001 (Thirteenth Commission, Rapporteur: Mr Joe Verhoeven). For the contrary position, see G Karl, *Völkerrechtliche Immunität im Bereich der Strafverfolgungen schwerster Menschenrechtsverletzungen* (Nomos, Baden-Baden 2003) 128.
[242]   *Case Concerning the Arrest Warrant of 11 April 2000* (n 164) [58]. Note that the court failed to make a distinction between functional and personal immunities. On that point and further criticisms of the judgment, see A Cassese, 'When May Senior State Officials Be Tried for International Crimes? Some Comments on the Congo v Belgium Case' ibid. See also the other contributions to the symposium on the judgment by S Wirth and M Spinedi (2002) 13 EJIL. See further extensively R van Alebeek, *The Immunities of States and Their Officials in International Criminal Law and International Human Rights Law* (OUP, Oxford 2008).
[243]   Cf 43–45.
[244]   P Gaeta (n 186) 767, (n 45) (referring to the Italian Ercole case); *The Queen v Brocklebank* (n 197).
[245]   Cf (nn 179–181) and text. Thus Article 43 of the Dutch Penal Code provides for superior orders as a justification under certain conditions, while Article 10 of the War Crimes Act and Article 3 of the Genocide Act exclude the applicability of Article 43 in relation to war crimes and genocide. For the situation after the entry into force of the ICC implementing legislation, see Article 11 *Wet Internationale Misdrijven*/International Crimes Act (n 174).
[246]   See for instance Article 3 of the Croatian 'Law on General Amnesty', 20 September 1996, published in *Narodne novine*, No 27/1996, available at <http://www.icrc.org/ihl-nat.nsf/6fa4d3 5e5e3025394125673e00508143/05d747daa8526b23412566020047b072]?OpenDocument> [exempting 'the greatest violations of the humanitarian law which have the character of war crimes' from such amnesty, with Article 3 of the Amnesty Law containing an exhaustive enumeration of these crimes. Consequently, qualification of a core crime as an offence not enumerated in Article 3 of the Amnesty Law could be interpreted to entail that such an offence is covered by the amnesty as long as it falls into the applicability *ratione temporis* in accordance with Article 1 of the Law on General Amnesty].

such a broader framework and replace it by the narrower rules of ordinary criminal law. On a conceptual level, qualification of international crimes as ordinary
offences also conveys an impression of the underlying acts being solely a matter of
domestic law rather than a crime with international dimensions, which not only
concerns the State but also the international community as a whole.[247]

Violations of due process, either to the detriment or the benefit of the accused,
constitutes a further set of obstacles. As to the former, core crimes trials are at
times *unfair*.[248] When suspects are denied the right to select adequate counsel,[249]
the right to be tried without undue delay[250] and the right to be tried by a competent, independent and impartial tribunal,[251] such denials not only constitute violations of the individual's rights, but also undermine the legality and legitimacy
of the trial as a whole in the eyes of the affected society and the international community at large. If one premise underlying national enforcement in the territorial
state is to rebuild (trust in) the judicial system,[252] this aim cannot be achieved by
conducting trials, that disregard fundamental guarantees of due process.

Conversely, a *lack of independence and impartiality* may result in the shielding of perpetrators and unjustified acquittals.[253] The interference of non-judicial

---

[247] Cf *26–28*. See also W Ferdinandusse (n 169) 203–208.

[248] See generally on the right to a fair trial, D Weissbrodt, *The Right to a Fair Trial, Articles 8, 10
and 11 of the Universal Declaration of Human Rights* (Martinus Nijhoff, The Hague 2001).

[249] For example, massive violations of the right to counsel have been observed with respect to
Rwandan genocide trials: M Drumbl, 'Counseling accused in Rwanda's domestic genocide trials'
(1998) 29 Columbia Human Rights LR 545; for Ethiopia, see D Haile, *Accountability for Crimes of
the Past and the Challenges of Criminal Prosecution: The Case of Ethiopia* (Leuven University Press,
Leuven 2000) 71, 39–41. Another illustrative example is the trial *in absentia* of 14 NATO leaders in a Belgrade court. On 21 September 2000, the court sentenced US President Bill Clinton,
UK Prime Minister Tony Blair, French President Jacques Chirac and others to 20 years in prison
each for 'inciting an aggressive war, war crimes against the civilian population, use of prohibited
combat means, attempted murder of the Yugoslav president, as well as with the violation of the
country's territorial integrity' committed during NATO's bombing campaign against Yugoslavia.
Slavisa Mrdaković, who was appointed as defence counsel to French President Jacques Chirac, was
quoted by the news agency Beta as saying, 'If I were the judge, and it's a good thing that I am not,
I would ... take a gun and shoot both Clinton and the other scum for all the evil they have done,'
to applause in the courtroom. In January 2001, the new Serbian justice minister Vladan Batić was
reported as saying that the verdict would be revised, stating that, 'This was not a trial, but a farce, a
comedy ...' (2000) 3 YIHL 494. The judgment was subsequently annulled.

[250] G Triggs (n 234) 187; Drumbl, ibid; on pre-trial detention in Ethiopia, see D Haile, ibid,
38–39; Guantanamo Bay.

[251] See for instance J V Mayfield, 'The Prosecution of War Crimes and Respect for Human
Rights: Ethiopia's Balancing Act' (1995) 9 Emory ILR 553–593, 589–591.

[252] Cf (nn 123–127) and text.

[253] Early examples of such unjustified acquittals, despite clear evidence to the contrary, can
be found in the Leipzig Trials, such as the cases of Lt Karl Neumann (Dover Castle) and General
Steinger: see J Daniel, *Le Problème du Chatiment des Crimes de Guerre d'après les Einseignements
de la Deuxième Guerre Mondiale* (Schindler, Cairo 1946) 33–34. These acquittals prompted the
Belgian and French missions to the Leipzig Trials to leave Leipzig in protest: see ibid, 34. For more
recent examples, see the acquittal of Endar Priyanto before the Indonesian Ad Hoc Human Rights
Court: D Cohen (n 235) 28–31.

authorities in core crimes trials[254] and other irregularities during trial, if not conclusive evidence, are at least indicative of such a lack of independence and impartiality. In addition to these obstacles, which may occur on a case-by-case basis, *structural problems* may equally cause a lack of independence and impartiality. An example of such a problem is 'political corruption', ie the trafficking of influence through the politicized processes for the appointment of judges.[255] If judges and prosecutors obtain their positions through political connections and favours, rather than through merit and ability, they are more likely to consider themselves indebted to the government authorities and individuals who were influential in their appointment. If such authorities and individuals are later implicated in core crimes, which is far from inconceivable due to the nature of such crimes,[256] judges and prosecutors may be less inclined to prosecute and convict them.

Further obstacles to national enforcement of core crimes emanate from *incorrect application* of the law. This may be the consequence of general shortcomings in the education and training of members of the judiciary and therefore not limited to core crimes proceedings. However, a specific problem in relation to international law cases, including core crimes trials, is that misapplication may also in part be attributable to a lack of expertise and familiarity with international (criminal) law among lawyers. These deficiencies in the knowledge of lawyers partly accounts for their falling into more well-known patterns of thought which they find in domestic law.[257] Ultimately, the results are various forms of misapplication, ranging from the wrong classification of a crime[258] to the acceptance of non-existent defences.[259]

Even when all of the aforementioned potential hurdles to national enforcement are overcome, and trials result in a conviction, additional obstacles arise at the *sentencing stage,* in relation to both the imposition and the execution of punishment. The *imposition* of an adequate sentence is to some extent determined by the sentencing tradition of a given criminal justice system, also in relation to the core crimes.[260] Yet, courts at times impose sentences that clearly do not reflect

[254] R Brody and H Duffy, 'Prosecuting Torture Universally, Hissène Habré, Africa's Pinochet?' in H Fischer, C Kress and S R Lüder (eds), (n 174) 817–842, 824–825 [removal of proactive judge].

[255] N Heasley, R Hurley, K Irwin, A Kaufman, N Moustafa and A Personna (n 227) 1149–1150.

[256] Cf 43–45.

[257] W Ferdinandusse (n 169) 105–106. For the comparable problem in general international law, see ILA, 'Third Report of the Committee on International Law in National Courts' (1998) 672–673, 16–17.

[258] See eg Nigerian Supreme Court, *Pius Nwaoga v The State* (1972) [classification, albeit obiter, of murder during the Nigerian civil war as crime against humanity rather than war crime].

[259] See J Verhaegen (n 222) 616–617, (n 30) and text.

[260] See eg Finland: Chapter 11 of the Revised Penal Code, Dealing with War Crimes and Crimes against Humanity, 21 April 1995/578, reproduced in (1998) 1 YIHL 619–621; Article 2 of the Law provides for a maximum sentence of 12 years for an aggravated war crime: ibid 620. On the other hand, see Congo/Brazzaville: Law No 8–98 of 31 October 1998 on the definition and the suppression of genocide, war crimes and crimes against humanity, available at <http://www.

the serious nature of core crimes. These inadequate sentences may be caused by bias on behalf of the court,[261] sometimes even resulting in the imposition of sentences below the legally required minimum.[262] Irrespective of the adequacy of the imposed sentence, obstacles also occur in relation to the *enforcement* of such a sentence. Sometimes, the sentence is simply not executed, is replaced with the imposition of house arrest or is commuted, or the convict is released early or granted clemency, parole or a pardon.[263]

In short, obstacles to effective, independent and impartial domestic criminal proceedings vis-à-vis core crimes occur throughout the entire spectrum of procedural stages.

4. Interim Conclusions

International law envisages that national criminal jurisdictions assume the central role in the suppression of core crimes as organs acting simultaneously in the domestic and international legal orders. States have at times acted in conformity with this premise in the past and one can witness a certain increase in domestic prosecutions of core crimes in recent years.

Notwithstanding these quantitative advances, national suppression frequently faces obstacles on a number of fronts. Chronically, States either do nothing or do something different from that which international law envisages them to do. These obstacles emanate from a complex entanglement of different factors, which are the cause and consequence of core crimes, including those of a political, legal, practical, economic or personal nature. Although obstacles resulting from bad

---

icrc.org/ihl-nat.nsf/WebLAW?OpenView&Start=1&Count=150&Expand=15.4.1#15.4.1>, whose Articles 2, 7, 8–10 provide for the death penalty for genocide, certain crimes against humanity and certain war crimes. See more generally, U Sieber, *The punishment of serious crimes: a comparative analysis of sentencing law and practice* (2 volumes, edn iuscrim, Freiburg, Breisgau 2004).

[261] See for example the findings of an inter-allied commission, composed of representatives of Great Britain, Italy, France and Belgium, on the German Leipzig Trials after the First World War, concluding that the proceedings were biased in favour of the accused and the sentences did not reflect the gravity of the crimes: G Hankel, *Die Leipziger Prozesse—Deutsche Kriegsverbrechen und ihre strafrechtliche Verfolgung nach dem Ersten Weltkrieg* (Hamburger Edition, Hamburg 2003) 103.

[262] Thus, while none of Articles 36–42 of Indonesia's Law 26/2000 Establishing the Ad Hoc Human Rights Court establish minimum sentences below five years in prison, the sentences of several defendants went below this minimum: see D Cohen (n 235) 4 and case overview 56–59.

[263] For an early example, see the execution of sentences following the Leipzig Trials of Dithmar and Boldt in the *Llandovery Castle* case: after having been subjected to favourable treatment, they were given the possibility to escape to Sweden and the Netherlands a few weeks after the judgment, whereupon the German authorities did not take any further action to re-obtain the two convicts: see J Daniel (n 253) 34. The execution of the sentence against Lt. Calley for his role in the My Lai massacre of Vietnamese civilians is a further example: despite sentencing him to hard labour for the length of his natural life on 31 March 1971, his sentence was reduced and he was later paroled, leading to his freedom on 9 November 1974. Cf M Bilton and K Sim (n 236) 339, 353, 354–357.

faith on behalf of various actors (State organs and others in a position to exert influence on the judicial process) may constitute the greater part of the problem, these obstacles do not provide a full picture. For, the criminal process may also be hampered by factual constraints, despite bona fide efforts on behalf of the relevant authorities, and occasionally by requirements emanating from domestic and/or international law, such as the granting of immunity. However, such obstacles have in common the fact that they severely limit the potential of national criminal jurisdictions to conduct proceedings vis-à-vis core crimes, and suggest that, to the extent that States are unable or unwilling to remedy these obstacles themselves, exclusive reliance on States in the suppression of core crimes is illusive.

Underlying national suppression of core crimes is thus the paradox of a clear presumption in its favour, on the one hand, and its chronic deficiencies, on the other. The antipathy of these two facets provokes the question as to how to supply the deficiencies whilst maintaining the room for effective, impartial and independent national suppression. The Statute of the International Criminal Court seeks to answer this question by declaring that the International Criminal Court 'shall be complementary to national criminal jurisdictions'.[264] It is to an analysis of this complementary nature of the ICC that we now turn.

---

[264] Rome Statute (n 31) Preamble, para 10 and Article 1, second sentence.

III

The Context and Emergence of Complementarity

1. Introduction

The obstacles to national suppression of core crimes, and the conceptual premise that core crimes are crimes that are universal in nature and entitle the international community as a whole to act, have led to the (attempted) establishment of international criminal courts and tribunals[1] and—more recently—internationalized criminal courts and tribunals.[2] Such international(ized) courts and tribunals raise the question as to the allocation of their respective competences in relation to national criminal jurisdictions. In practice, this question has been answered on an ad hoc basis in relation to each of the instances in which States have decided to establish international or internationalized criminal courts or tribunals. The model adopted to allocate the respective competences of the International Criminal Court and national criminal jurisdictions is that the ICC shall be 'complementary to national criminal jurisdictions'.[3] In order to provide the general background against which the complementary nature of the ICC

---

[1] For general historical narratives, see amongst many others: M C Bassiouni, 'L'expérience des premières jurisdictions pénales internationals' in H Ascensio, E Decaux and A Pellet (eds), Droit International Pénal (Editions Pedone, Paris 2000) 635–659; H S Levie, 'The History and Status of the International Criminal Court' in M Schmitt (ed), International Law Across the Spectrum of Conflict: Essays in Honour of Professor L.C. Green on the Occasion of His Eightieth Birthday (Naval War College, Newport 2000) 247–261; S Rosenne, 'Antecedents of the Rome Statute of the International Criminal Court Revisited' in M Schmitt (ed), International Law Across the Spectrum of Conflict: Essays in Honour of Professor L.C. Green on the Occasion of His Eightieth Birthday (Naval War College, Newport 2000) 387–420; H Ahlbrecht, 'Geschichte der völkerrechtlichen Strafgerichtsbarkeit im 20. Jahrhundert, unter besonderer Berücksichtigung der völkerrechtlichen Straftatbestände und der Bemühungen um einen Ständigen Internationalen Strafgerichtshof' (Nomos, Baden-Baden 1999).

[2] See generally C Romano, A Nollkaemper and J K Kleffner (eds), International Criminal Courts: Sierra Leone, East Timor, Kosova, and Cambodia (OUP, Oxford 2004).

[3] Rome Statute of the International Criminal Court (adopted 17 July 1998, as corrected by procès-verbaux of 10 November 1998, 12 July 1999, 30 November 1999, 8 May 2000, 17 January 2001 and 16 January 2002, entered into force 1 July 2002) A/CONF.183/9 (Rome Statute) Preamble, para 10 and Article 1, second sentence. The other language versions: 'complémentaire' (French); 'complementaria', (Spanish). Note, however, that the official Arabic version refers to something which can only be translated as 'integrative'.

needs to be understood, this chapter begins with a concise overview of models for allocating the respective competences of international criminal courts and tribunals and domestic courts (2). It then describes how complementarity evolved in the drafting of the Rome Statute (3).

2. Models of Allocation

Whenever a judicial body fulfils functions that can be, or are in fact also, fulfilled by (an)other judicial organ(s), the question as to the mutual relationship and interaction between these organs arises.[4] This holds true for the relationship between domestic courts *inter se*[5] and international(ized) courts and tribunals *inter se*,[6] as much as for the relationship between domestic and international(ized) judicial bodies.[7]

As regards the latter relationship, various generic models of allocating adjudicative functions are conceivable. International and domestic judicial bodies can relate to one another in a system of mutual *exclusivity*.[8] Or they may be envisaged to *share* adjudicative functions and exercise that role concurrently. In the latter case, different principles may govern that concurrent jurisdiction. For instance, the exercise of jurisdiction by domestic courts could be made dependent on an absence of adjudication by an international judicial body; or a reverse model could be adopted, in which adjudication by an international body is conditional on an absence or exhaustion of adjudication by domestic courts.[9] International

---

[4] See generally D W Drezner (ed), *Locating the proper authorities: the interaction of domestic and international institutions* (University of Michigan Press, Michigan 2003) 280.

[5] One can think, for instance, of the relationship between domestic courts, which are called upon to exercise jurisdiction with regard to the same subject matter, and whose competence is defined along the lines of their territorial competence and hierarchy (courts of first instance, second instance, final appeal, etc). Another example is the horizontal relationship between domestic courts of different States.

[6] For international courts and tribunals, see Y Shany, *The competing jurisdictions of international courts and tribunals* (OUP, Oxford 2003) 348.

[7] See generally Y Shany, *Regulating Jurisdictional Relations between National and International Courts* (OUP, Oxford 2007); A-M Slaughter, 'A Typology of Transjudicial Communication' in T M Franck and G H Fox (eds), *International Law Decisions in National Courts* (Transnational Publ, Ardsley NY 1996) 37–69, 39, 42–46.

[8] See eg the *electa una via* principle in the field of investment law, according to which potential claimants have a choice among national and international courts. Selection of one tribunal typically excludes the right of referring the claim to any other competent tribunal: see Y Shany, ibid 36–37.

[9] This is the case in individual complaints procedures for human rights violations: see eg Article 41 (1)(c) of the International Covenant in Civil and Political Rights (adopted 16 December 1996, entered into force 23 March 1976) 999 UNTS 171 (ICCPR), Article 50 of the African Charter on Human and Peoples' Rights (adopted on 27 June 1981, entered into force 21 October 1986) OAU Doc. CAB/LEG/67/3 rev. 5, 21 ILM 58 (AfCHPR), Article 46(1) of the Inter-American Convention on Human Rights (entered into force 18 July 1978) OAS Treaty Series No. 36, 1144 UNTS 123 (IACHR), Article 35(1) of the European Convention for the Protection of Human Rights and Fundamental Freedoms (entered into force 3 September 1953, as amended by protocols Nos 3, 5, 8, and 11 which entered into force on 21 September 1970, 20 December 1971, 1 January 1990, and 1 November 1998 respectively) 213 UNTS 222 (ECHR).

judicial bodies can be competent to review decisions of domestic courts.[10] An international judicial body could also act as a final court of appeal, providing the last instance in legal proceedings that were initiated on the domestic level.[11] Other models of allocation endow domestic courts with the possibility to ask international courts for preliminary rulings.[12] In other instances, however, jurisdictional interactions between national and international courts remain unregulated, with the ensuing question as to which rules *should* govern them.[13]

How *shared adjudicative functions* are allocated between international and national courts and the way in which the two layers interact determine at least in part whether, and to what extent, their combined effect is to strengthen or to weaken the adjudication of international law. In the words of Thomas M Franck and Gregory H Fox, the sharing of adjudicative functions:

[a]t best [. . .] generates a functional synergy comparable to that found in a mature federal system, with national and provincial courts providing mutual reinforcement of essential norms while also protecting space for varied local experimentation and due deference to socio-cultural sensibilities. Such synergy depends significantly on frank, but respectful discourse between the component judiciaries. At worst, national and international tribunals view one another as interlopers, or even as irrelevant. Then the result is a fractured and weakened normativity.[14]

In between the extremes of a quasi-federal functional synergy and a fractured and weakened normativity, models of allocation between international and domestic courts that have been adopted in actual practice differ greatly, and a closer look at the judicial bodies in question is necessary.

---

[10] Human rights bodies provide for means whereby decisions of national courts can be reviewed as to their compatibility with the respective international or regional human rights standards upon exhaustion of local remedies. For pertinent examples, see eg Human Rights Committee, *Pinto v Trinidad and Tobago*, Communication No 232/1987, UN Doc CCPR/C/39/D/232/1987 (1990) [12.4] ['After careful consideration of the material placed before it, the Committee concludes that the judge's instructions to the jury on 14 June 1985 were neither arbitrary nor amounted to a denial of justice. As the judgment of the Court of Appeal states, the trial judge put the respective versions of the prosecution and the defence fully and fairly to the jury. The Committee therefore finds that in respect of the evaluation of evidence by the trial court there has been no violation of article 14 [of the ICCPR].']; European Court of Human Rights, *Lobo Machado v Portugal*, 15764/89 [1996], Judgment of 20 February 1996, Reports of Judgments and Decisions 1996-I, 206–07 [31] [impossibility for applicant to obtain a copy of the Deputy Attorney-General's opinion, in which it was advocated that his appeal should be dismissed, and to reply to it before judgment was given infringed his right to adversarial proceedings in violation of Article 6 (1) of the ECHR].

[11] See eg Article XXV of the Agreement Establishing the Caribbean Court of Justice, of 14 February 2001, entered into force on 23 July 2002.

[12] Courts of EU member States, for example, interact with the ECJ by way of preliminary rulings (Article 234 (ex Article 177) EC Treaty). These rulings are binding on domestic courts (Article 228 (ex Article 171) EC Treaty).

[13] For examples of unregulated interactions, see Y Shany (n 7) 39–77. For the feasibility of regulation and jurisdiction regulating rules, ibid 125–195.

[14] T M Franck and G H Fox, 'Introduction: Transnational Judicial Synergy' in T M Franck and G H Fox (eds) (n 7) 1–11, 4–5.

For purposes of the present study, however, it suffices to limit our analysis to the relationship between, on the one hand, *domestic criminal* courts called upon to enforce the prohibition of core crimes and, on the other hand, *international criminal* courts and tribunals,[15] set up to enforce the same prohibitions. Forms of allocation between international and domestic courts and tribunals in other areas of law will not be discussed, nor will the relationship between internation-al*ized* criminal courts and tribunals and national criminal jurisdictions, since this relationship raises idiosyncratic questions.[16] The subsequent examination is further limited to those instances in which the question of competence allocation had to be answered in actual practice. In other words, models that have remained a mere theoretical possibility,[17] are discarded. Our analysis is therefore restricted to the relationship between national criminal jurisdictions, on the one hand, and the Nuremberg Tribunal, established after the Second World War,[18] and the two

---

[15] On the definition of an *international* criminal court or tribunal, see (n 2) in Chapter II.

[16] One of these idiosyncrasies is that internationalized criminal courts are at times embedded into domestic judicial systems, which makes them less distinguishable from national criminal jurisdictions. For further discussion, see J K Kleffner and A Nollkaemper, 'The Relationship between Internationalized Courts and National Courts' in C Romano, A Nollkaemper and J K Kleffner (eds) (n 2) 359–378.

[17] Attempts to establish international judicial bodies for the enforcement of international criminal law can be traced back at least to the aftermath of, the First World War, when the victorious allies sought unsuccessfully to try the German *Kaiser* before an international tribunal in accordance with Article 227 of the 1919 Treaty of Versailles. Others assert that early beginnings include the trial of Peter von Hagenbach in 1474: see generally T L H McCormack, 'From Sun Tzu to the Sixth Committee: The Evolution of an International Criminal Law Regime' in T L H McCormack and G J Simpson (eds), *The law of war crimes: National and international approaches* (Kluwer Law International, The Hague, London, Boston 1997) 31–63, 37. The 1937 Convention for the Creation of an International Criminal Court, League of Nations, LN Doc C. 547(I).M.384(I).1937.V (1938) also envisaged the establishment of an International Criminal Court to prosecute the crime of terrorism, but the Convention never entered into force. Similarly, Article VI of the 1948 Genocide Convention foresees an 'international penal tribunal' for the trial of persons accused of genocide; see on the controversial drafting history of the provision, W A Schabas *Genocide in International Law—The Crime of Crimes* (CUP, Cambridge 2000) 368–378. Article V of the 1973 Apartheid Convention also anticipates such an international tribunal. However, these provisions were never put into operation until the inception of the permanent International Criminal Court in accordance with the 1998 Rome Statute, which establishes the ICC's jurisdiction over the crime of genocide (Article 6) and apartheid as a crime against humanity (Article 7 (1)(j)). Early doctrinal proposals for the establishment of international criminal courts and tribunals include the one of Gustave Moynier: '*Note sur la création d'une institution judiciaire internationale propre à prévenir et à réprimer les infractions à la Convention de Genève*', *Bulletin international des Sociétés de secours aux militaires blessés*, Comité international, No 11, avril 1872, 122–131. For a discussion of this proposal, see C K Hall, 'The first proposal for a permanent international criminal court' (1998) 332 IRRC 57–74.

[18] International Military Tribunal for the Trial of the German Major War Criminals, established in accordance with its Charter of 8 August 1945, 82 UNTS 280 (Nuremberg Tribunal).

United Nations ad hoc tribunals for the former Yugoslavia (ICTY)[19] and Rwanda (ICTR),[20] on the other hand.[21]

2.1. The Nuremberg Tribunal

The trials of German war criminals were based on a dispersion of effort and responsibility between the Nuremberg Tribunal (IMT) and the military authorities of the occupying countries and ordinary national courts.[22]

The October 1943 Moscow Declaration (Joint Four-Nation Declaration)[23] contained a 'Statement on Atrocities' of President Roosevelt, Prime Minister Churchill and Premier Stalin in which they expressed the following:

---

[19] The International Tribunal for the Prosecution of Persons Responsible for Serious Violations of International Humanitarian Law Committed in the Territory of the Former Yugoslavia since 1991, established in accordance with UNSC Res 827 (adopted on 25 May 1993) (ICTY).

[20] The International Criminal Tribunal for the Prosecution of Persons Responsible for Genocide and Other Serious Violations of International Humanitarian Law Committed in the Territory of Rwanda and Rwandan citizens responsible for genocide and other violations committed in the territory of neighbouring States, between 1 January 1994 and 31 December 1994, established in accordance with UNSC Res 955 (adopted on 8 November 1994) (ICTR).

[21] The Military Tribunal for the Far East (commonly referred to as Tokyo Tribunal or IMTFE) is at times also considered an 'international tribunal': see for instance the title of its Charter, available at <http://www.yale.edu/lawweb/avalon/imtfech.htm>, referring to 'International Military Tribunal for the Far East'. However, it does not fulfill the first of the abovementioned criteria to speak of an *international* criminal tribunal, namely to be established by an international legal instrument: cf n 15. The Tokyo Tribunal was established by special proclamation of the Supreme Commander for the Allied Powers in Japan, General Douglas MacArthur, acting under orders from the United States' Joint Chiefs of Staff. In so doing, General Douglas MacArthur acted in accordance with US Army Regulations, which provided for the possibility to establish international military commissions consisting of representatives of several States: see United States Law and Practice Concerning Trials of War Criminals by Military Commissions and Military Government Courts, in: *Law-Reports of Trials of War Criminals, The United Nations War Crimes Commission* (Volume I, HMSO, London 1947) 111–124, 116, with an overview of the relevant Army Regulations at 113, <http://www.ess.uwe.ac.uk/WCC/usmillaw.htm>. Although the Tokyo Tribunal resorted to international criminal law in deciding the cases before it and produced a legally binding judgment, it will not be treated as an international criminal tribunal within the meaning employed here. As far as its composition is concerned, it would probably best be described as an early 'internationalized' criminal tribunal. Also, the Special Court for Sierra Leone (SCSL) is not an international tribunal in the present meaning. The SCSL came to a different conclusion in *The Prosecutor v Charles Ghankay Taylor* (Appeals Chamber Decision on motion made under protest and without waiving immunity accorded to a head of state requesting the Trial Chamber to quash the indictment and declare null and void the warrant of arrest and order for transfer of detention, 23 July 2003 (immunity motion)) Case No SCSL-03-01-I-059 (31 May 2004) [37–42]. However, the considerations which led the SCSL to that conclusion were based on a simple juxtaposition of domestic and international courts and tribunals. It failed to distinguish international from *internationalized* criminal courts. Since this book defines an international criminal tribunal as one that draws exclusively on international criminal law in deciding cases before it (cf n 15), the SCSL is more adequately classified as an internationalized criminal court, because its jurisdiction *ratione materiae* extends to both international and domestic offences. For the idiosyncratic dimensions of the relationship between such courts and domestic courts, see J K Kleffner and A Nollkaemper (n 16).

[22] On trials by domestic and occupation courts, see *34–35*.

[23] Available at <http://www.yale.edu/lawweb/avalon/wwii/moscow.htm>.

At the time of granting of any armistice to any government which may be set up in Germany, those German officers and men and members of the Nazi party who have been responsible for or have taken a consenting part in [...] atrocities, massacres and executions will be sent back to the countries in which their abominable deeds were done in order that they may be judged and punished according to the laws of these liberated countries and of free governments which will be erected therein...

Thus, Germans who take part in [atrocities], will know they will be brought back to the scene of their crimes and judged on the spot by the peoples whom they have outraged...

The above declaration is without prejudice to the case of German criminals whose offenses have no particular geographical localization and who will be punished by joint decision of the government of the Allies...[24]

The Moscow Declaration thus envisaged the primary competence of the territorial State, since the accused were to be tried in those states where they had allegedly committed crimes.[25] Such territorial jurisdiction was to be complemented by jurisdiction established by joint decision of the government of the Allies with respect to crimes committed by perpetrators whose offences have no particular geographical localization. At the time, however, this was without express reference to any international tribunal, which only entered the stage with the London Agreement of 8 August 1945[26] and the Charter[27] annexed to it. The establishment of the Nuremberg Tribunal was perceived as the collective exercise of national jurisdiction granted to the parties to the Agreement but effectuated on the international level.[28] The London Agreement clarified in turn that the establishment of the IMT did not prejudice 'the jurisdiction or the powers of any national or occupation court established or to be established in any allied territory or in Germany for the trial of war criminals'.[29] This provision suggests that the various courts and tribunals were to exercise jurisdiction *concurrently* with the IMT. However, a closer look at the principles, which further delineated the respective competences of the IMT and national or occupation courts, is warranted to understand whether and to what extent such a concurrent approach was indeed adopted.

---

[24] Available at <http://www.yale.edu/lawweb/avalon/imt/jackson/jack01.htm>.

[25] A R Carnegie, 'Jurisdiction over Violations of the Laws and Customs of War' (1963) 39 BYIL 402–424, 413.

[26] Agreement by the Government of the United States of America, the Provisional Government of the French Republic, the Government of the United Kingdom of Great Britain and Northern Ireland and the Government of the Union of Soviet Socialist Republics for the Prosecution and Punishment of the Major War Criminals of the European Axis, available at <http://www.yale.edu/lawweb/avalon/imt/proc/imtchart.htm>.

[27] Charter of the International Military Tribunal, available at <http://www.yale.edu/lawweb/avalon/imt/proc/imtconst.htm>.

[28] As the Nuremberg Tribunal put it in its judgment: 'The Signatory Powers created this Tribunal, defined the law it was to administer, and made regulations for the proper conduct of the Trial. In doing so, *they have done together what any one of them might have done singly*; for it is not to be doubted that any nation has the right thus to set up special courts to administer law.' Judgment of the International Military Tribunal for the Trial of German Major War Criminals, Nuremberg, 30 September and 1 October 1946, available at <http://www.yale.edu/lawweb/avalon/imt/proc/judlawch.htm> [emphasis added].

[29] Article 6 of the London Agreement.

A first delineation of the respective competences of the IMT and other courts and tribunals could be found in Article 1 of the London Agreement, which confined the jurisdiction of the IMT to 'war criminals whose offenses have *no particular geographical location'*. Conversely, those offenders whose crimes did have such particular geographical location were beyond the reach of the IMT and exclusively subject to the jurisdiction of national or occupation courts. Furthermore, Article 1 of the Charter of the IMT limited the purpose of the IMT to 'the just and prompt trial and punishment of the *major* war criminals of the European Axis'.[30] In other words, the primary criteria for allocating the respective competences between the IMT and national or occupation courts were *ratione loci* and *personae*: the decisive questions for the jurisdiction of the IMT, which had to be answered, related to the extent and place of the alleged crimes (no particular geographical location) and the qualification of the person as a 'major war criminal of the European Axis'.

A second delineation of the respective competences of the IMT and other courts and tribunals emanates from Control Council Law No 10 of 20 December 1945,[31] which suggests that the IMT was endowed with *primacy* over other courts, in as much as it had the final say over where a particular suspect, who was wanted for trial before both a domestic court and the IMT, would be tried. Control Council Law No 10 acknowledged the right of each occupying power to bring those accused of crimes against peace, war crimes, crimes against humanity and membership in a group or organization declared criminal by the IMT 'to trial before an appropriate tribunal'.[32] The Law also opened the possibility for trials in German courts on the basis of a combination of the active and passive personality principle, in as much as it provided that the appropriate tribunal may be a German Court 'in the case of crimes committed by persons of German citizenship or nationality against other persons of German citizenship or nationality, or stateless persons, ... if authorized by the occupying authorities'.[33] The competent tribunals were to be designated by each Occupation Zone Commander for his respective Zone, but it was clarified that this was without prejudice to 'the Jurisdiction or power of any court or tribunal now or hereafter established in any Zone by the Commander thereof, or of the International Military Tribunal...'.[34] If persons were wanted for trial by the Nuremberg Tribunal, the Committee of Chief Prosecutors, established in accordance with Article 14 of its Charter, had to consent to a trial in another

[30] Available at <http://www.yale.edu/lawweb/avalon/imt/proc/imtconst.htm>. The Charter is annexed to the London Agreement and forms an integral part of that Agreement (compare Article 2 of the London Agreement). Emphasis added.

[31] Control Council Law no 10 of 20 December 1945 [Punishment of Persons Guilty of War Crimes, Crimes Against Peace and Against Humanity], available at <http://www.yale.edu/lawweb/avalon/imt/imt10.htm>.

[32] Ibid. Article III (1)(d), first sentence.

[33] Ibid, Article III (1)(d), second sentence.   [34] Ibid, Article III (2).

forum.[35] This consent was also required if persons were wanted for trial by both the Nuremberg Tribunal and courts in another Zone or outside Germany.[36]

In practice, the application of the aforementioned provisions meant that 24 major figures were indicted before the Nuremberg Tribunal. The verdicts were announced on 30 September and on 1 October 1946. Three of them were acquitted, 12 sentenced to death by hanging and seven sentenced to life imprisonment or to lesser terms.[37] National, military or occupation courts and tribunals adjudicated all other cases.[38]

2.2. The UN ad hoc tribunals for the former Yugoslavia and Rwanda

The Statutes of the two UN ad hoc tribunals for the former Yugoslavia and Rwanda contain identical provisions detailing their relationship to national courts. Both Statutes provide that they 'shall have *concurrent* jurisdiction'[39] while the ad hoc tribunals 'shall have *primacy* over the national courts of all States' with the consequence that '[a]t any stage of the procedure', the tribunals 'may formally request national courts to defer to [the Tribunals'] competence in accordance with the . . . Statute and the Rules of Procedure and Evidence . . .'.[40] The relevant Rules are set forth in Part II of the Rules of Procedure and Evidence of both tribunals.[41] A further manifestation of the primacy of both tribunals can be found in the principle of *ne bis in idem* as laid down in Articles 10 (ICTY) and 9 (ICTR). The provisions stipulate certain exceptions to the prohibition of persons being tried by the ad hoc tribunals if they have already been tried by a national court for acts constituting the three core crimes under the Statutes of genocide, crimes against humanity and war crimes. More in particular, these exceptions allow for a subsequent trial before the ad hoc tribunals if the act for which the accused was tried was characterized as an ordinary crime in the national trial,[42] or if national court proceedings were not impartial or independent, or were designed to shield

---

[35] Ibid, Article III (3).   [36] Ibid, Article III (4) and IV.

[37] The remaining two indictees were Gustav Krupp von Bohlen und Halbach, who was physically unable to appear in court and the charges against him were dropped, and Robert Ley, who committed suicide in the Nuremberg jail on 26 October 1945.

[38] Cf *34–35*.

[39] ICTY Statute Article 9 (1) (n 19); ICTR Statute Article 8 (1) (n 20), emphasis added.

[40] Article 9 (2) ICTY (n 19); Article 8 (2) ICTR (n 20).

[41] Rules 7–13 of the Rules of Procedure and Evidence of the ICTY as amended on 12 July 2007, IT/32/Rev. 40; Rules 8–13 of the Rules of Procedure and Evidence of the ICTR, consolidated text of 15 June 2007. On challenges to the legality of the primacy of the ICTY and the (negative) response of the ICTY, see Appeals Chamber, *Prosecutor v Tadic* (Appeals Decision on the Defence Motion for Interlocutory Appeal on Jurisdiction) IT-94-1-T (2 October 1995) 49–64. For the ICTR, see the similar challenge and reaction of ICTR Trial Chamber 2, *Prosecutor v Kanyabashi* (Decision on the Defence Motion on Jurisdiction) ICTR-96-15 (18 June 1997) 30–32. For a general discussion, including of the early case law of the two ad hoc tribunals on primacy, see B Brown, 'Primacy or Complementarity: Reconciling the Jurisdiction of National Courts and International Criminal Tribunals' (1998) 23 Yale JIL 383–436, 394–416.

[42] Article 10 (2)(a) (ICTY) (n 19); Article 9 (2)(a) (ICTR) (n 20).

the accused from international criminal responsibility, or if the case was not diligently prosecuted.[43]

The concurrent jurisdiction of the UN ad hoc tribunals and national criminal jurisdictions reflect the view, expressed by the UN Secretary-General in his Report Pursuant to Paragraph 2 of Security Council Resolution 808 and which paved the way for the adoption of the ICTY's Statute, that '... it was not the intention of the Security Council to preclude or prevent the exercise of jurisdiction by national courts... Indeed [they] should be encouraged [to do so]'.[44] As we have seen in Chapter II, several States have in fact investigated and prosecuted individuals suspected of having committed core crimes in the former Yugoslavia and Rwanda.[45] While primacy may not have been the only conceivable way to regulate concurrent jurisdiction, through which national criminal jurisdictions can be encouraged to exercise jurisdiction over core crimes, the momentum was such that the situation-specific responses of the Security Council to the crises in the former Yugoslavia and Rwanda allowed for a model with the international enforcement level topping the pyramid.[46] Indeed, an analysis of the subsequent case law of the ad hoc tribunals suggests that they saw primacy as a logical consequence of the nature of the crimes within their jurisdiction. In the words of the ICTY Appeals Chamber in the Tadic Interlocutory Appeal on Jurisdiction:

[...] when an international tribunal such as the present one is created, it must be endowed with primacy over national courts. Otherwise, human nature being what it is, there would be a perennial danger of international crimes being characterised as 'ordinary crimes' [...] or proceedings being 'designed to shield the accused' or cases not being diligently prosecuted [...]. If not effectively countered by the principle of primacy, any one of those stratagems might be used to defeat the very purpose of the creation of an international criminal jurisdiction, to the benefit of the very people whom it has been designed to prosecute. [...]

[The crimes which the International Tribunal has been called upon to try] are really crimes which are universal in nature, well recognised in international law as serious breaches of international humanitarian law, and transcending the interest of any one State. [...]In such circumstances, the sovereign rights of States cannot and should not take precedence over the right of the international community to act appropriately as they affect the whole of mankind and shock the conscience of all nations of the world. There can therefore be no objection to an international tribunal properly constituted trying these crimes on behalf of the international community.[47]

---

[43] Article 10 (2)(b) (ICTY) (n 19); Article 9 (2)(b) (ICTR) (n 20).

[44] Report of the Secretary-General Pursuant to Paragraph 2 of Security Council Resolution 808 (1993), UN Doc S/25704, 3 May 1993 [64].

[45] Cf pages *35–36*.

[46] M El Zeidy, 'The Principle of Complementarity: A New Machinery to Implement International Criminal Law' (2002) 23 Michigan JIL 869–975, 885–887.

[47] ICTY Appeals Chamber, *Prosecutor v Tadic* (Appeals Decision on the Defence Motion for Interlocutory Appeal on Jurisdiction) IT-94-1 App Ch (2 October 1995) [58–59]; see also Separate Opinion of Judge Sidwa on the Defence Motion for Interlocutory Appeal on Jurisdiction [83]. Dusko Tadic was arrested in February 1994 in Germany, where he was then living, on suspicion of

These views, expressed by the ICTY, reflect that its primacy was regarded as both a practical and conceptual necessity: it was considered necessary in order to ensure the punishment of individuals responsible for core crimes and to overcome the obstacles faced by national criminal jurisdictions, as well as to take due account of the international character of core crimes.[48] In practice, however, the allocation of adjudicative functions between both ad hoc tribunals and national criminal jurisdictions has evolved into an instrument for the division of labour, with the international tribunals focusing on those who bear the greatest responsibility,[49] while all other cases are left to national and internationalized[50] criminal courts.

The relationship of the ICTY and ICTR with (national criminal jurisdictions of) the affected States of the former Yugoslavia and Rwanda, respectively, has for a long time been characterized by *relative isolation*,[51] and at times *mutual suspicion* and *antagonism*. However, in addition to the more recent completion strategy for both ad hoc tribunals discussed below,[52] this was subject to some exceptions.

having committed offences at the Omarska camp in the former Yugoslavia in June 1992, including torture and aiding and abetting the commission of genocide, which constitute crimes under German law. Proceedings at the ICTY commenced on 12 October 1994 when the Prosecutor filed an application under Rule 9 of the Rules of Procedure and Evidence. The provision reads: 'Where it appears to the Prosecutor that in any such investigations or criminal proceedings instituted in the courts of any State: (i) the act being investigated or which is the subject of those proceedings is characterized as an ordinary crime; (ii) there is a lack of impartiality or independence, or the investigations or proceedings are designed to shield the accused from international criminal responsibility, or the case is not diligently prosecuted; or (iii) what is in issue is closely related to, or otherwise involves, significant factual or legal questions which may have implications for investigations or prosecutions before the Tribunal, the Prosecutor may propose to the Trial Chamber designated by the President that a formal request be made that such court defer to the competence of the Tribunal.' The formal request to the Federal Republic of Germany was made pursuant to Rule 10, which provides: '(A) If it appears to the Trial Chamber seised of a proposal for deferral that, on any of the grounds specified in Rule 9, deferral is appropriate, the Trial Chamber may issue a formal request to the State concerned that its court defer to the competence of the Tribunal. (B) A request for deferral shall include a request that the results of the investigation and a copy of the court's records and the judgment, if already delivered, be forwarded to the Tribunal. (C) Where deferral to the Tribunal has been requested by a Trial Chamber, any subsequent trial shall be held before another Trial Chamber.'

[48]   Y Shany (n 6) 140.

[49]   Also compare Rule 28 of the Rules of Procedure and Evidence (n 41), which, since April 2004, instructs the Tribunal to determine 'whether the indictment, prima facie, concentrates on one or more of the *most senior leaders* suspected of being most responsible for crimes within the jurisdiction of the Tribunal' (emphasis added). The April 2004 amendment was a result of the Security Council's endorsement of the completion strategy (see below), an element of which was to concentrate on the most senior leaders suspected of being most responsible: see Security Council Resolutions, UNSC Res 1503 (2003) UN Doc S/RES/1503 [Preamble at 7] and UNSC Res 1534 (2004) UN Doc S/RES/1534 [5].

[50]   Internationalized criminal courts have been established in Kosovo in accordance with UNMIK Regulation No 2000/6 and later in Bosnia and Herzegovina; on the latter, see (n 65) and text.

[51]   On the lack of an obligation on States to notify the ICTY or ICTR of their own prosecutions, see eg F Harhoff, 'Consonance or Rivalry? Calibrating the Efforts to Prosecute War Crimes in National and International Tribunals' (1997) 7 Duke JCIL 571–596, 578–579.

[52]   *67–69*.

The first and foremost such exception of a more structural nature existed vis-à-vis core crimes investigations and prosecutions by the judicial authorities in Bosnia and Herzegovina. Here, a specific feature of the relationship of the latter to the ICTY, distinguishing it from the relationship between the two ad hoc tribunals and other national criminal jurisdictions, consists of the so-called 'Rules of the Road' under the Rome Agreement.[53] Under these rules, '[p]ersons, other than those already indicted by the Tribunal, may be arrested and detained for serious violations of international humanitarian law only pursuant to a previously issued order, warrant or indictment that has been reviewed and deemed consistent with international legal standards by the [ICTY]. Procedures will be developed for expeditious decision by the Tribunal and will be effective immediately upon such action.'[54] These procedures have given rise to a system of review and approval of each proposed Bosnian Herzegovinan prosecution by the 'Rules of the Road Unit' within the ICTY's Office of the Prosecutor.[55]

A second exception consists of the few occasions on which charges before the ad hoc tribunals have been withdrawn in accordance with Rule 51 of the Rules of Procedure and Evidence of both tribunals with a view to allowing domestic trials.[56] However, Rule 51 has proved problematic as a legal basis for the deferral of investigations and proceedings by the Tribunal to a national jurisdiction, because, amongst other reasons, the person concerned cannot be released into the custody of any given State once the indictment is withdrawn.[57]

---

[53] The name 'Rules of the Road' stems from the incident, which gave rise to the adoption of the Rome Agreement. On 30 January 1996, General Djukic and Colonel Krsmanovic, of the Republika Srpska Army, were driving near Sarajevo, the capital of Bosnia and Herzegovina. Extensive damage had been done to road signs in Bosnia and Herzegovina during the war, and a damaged sign caused General Djukic and Colonel Krsmanovic to lose their way. They were arrested at a Bosnian Muslim checkpoint and, by virtue only of their military positions, were immediately detained on suspicion of having committed war crimes. They were indicted for war crimes a week later, on 6 February 1996, and it was intended that they be prosecuted in Bosnian Herzegovinan courts. This incident led amongst others to subsequent arbitrary retaliatory arrests and detentions carried out by the formerly opposing forces in the region. In an attempt to devise a mechanism for the prevention of arbitrary arrests and detentions, the signatories of the Dayton Peace Agreement gathered in Rome in February 1996 and adopted the Rome Agreement on 18 February. See generally J Manuell and A Kontic, 'Transitional justice: the prosecution of war crimes in Bosnia and Herzegovina under the "Rules of the Road"' (2000) 5 YIHL 331–343, 333.

[54] Paragraph 5 of the Agreed Measures of the Rome Agreement.

[55] J Manuell and A Kontic (n 53) 335, recounting 'more than 1400 files containing allegations against more than 5000 suspects [which] have been submitted to the Rules of the Road unit for review'.

[56] See for instance *Prosecutor v Nikica Janjic, Dragan Kondic, Goran Lajic, Dragomir Saponja, and Nedjeljko Timarac ('Keraterm Camp')* (Order Granting Leave for Withdrawal of Charges) IT-95-8) (5 May 1998).

[57] Cf ICTR Trial Chamber, *Prosecutor v Ntuyahaga* (Decision on the Prosecutor's Motion to Withdraw the Indictment) ICTR-98–40-T (18 March 1999). The decision concerned an accused who was released after the indictment was withdrawn, although the Belgian authorities had requested he be surrendered to them with a view to prosecuting him for the murder of ten Belgian peacekeepers on 7 April 1994. The Trial Chamber held that 'it does not have jurisdiction to order the release of a person who is no longer under indictment into the custody of any given state', and further held that 'the primacy recognised by the Statute is clear inasmuch as the Tribunal

Notwithstanding the aforementioned limited exceptions, the Statutes and Rules of Procedure and Evidence initially reflected a preoccupation with determining how the ICTY and ICTR could assume jurisdiction over cases. They were silent on whether, and under what conditions, cases over which the ad hoc tribunals have already assumed jurisdiction, could be referred back to national criminal jurisdictions. This model of concurrent jurisdiction of the ICTY and ICTR and domestic courts as a one-way street has been altered in reaction to the *completion strategies* for both tribunals, according to which all investigations were to be completed by the end of 2004, trials at first instance are to be concluded by the end of 2008 and the two tribunals wound up by 2010.[58] As a vital part of the completion strategies, cases in which the indictment has been confirmed by the ICTY or ICTR are transferred to national criminal jurisdictions in accordance with Rule 11 *bis* of the Rules of Procedure and Evidence of both tribunals.[59] Rule 11 *bis* allows such transfers to a State, in whose territory the crime was committed; in which the accused was arrested; or having jurisdiction and being willing and adequately prepared to accept such a case, provided the competent Trial Chamber is satisfied that the accused will receive a fair trial and that the death penalty will not be imposed or carried out.[60] When such a transfer is ordered, the Prosecutors of the ICTY and ICTR must provide to the authorities of the State concerned all of the information relating to the case that the Prosecutor considers appropriate and, in particular, the material supporting the indictment.[61] At the same time, the Prosecutors retain a monitoring role over the

---

may request any national jurisdiction to defer investigations or ongoing proceedings, whereas the reverse, namely the deferral of investigations and proceedings by the Tribunal to any national jurisdiction, is not provided for'.

[58] The completion strategy had first been endorsed by the Security Council: see UNSC Presidential Statement 21 (2002) UN Doc S/PRST/2002/21; UNSC Res 1329 (2000) UN Doc S/RES/1329; and later formally adopted in Security Council Resolutions, UNSC Res 1503 (2003) (n 49) [7] and UNSC Res 1534 (2004) (n 49) [3]. See generally D A Mundis, 'The Judicial Effects of the "Completion Strategies" on the Ad Hoc International Criminal Tribunals' (2005) 99 AJIL 142–157. For the background to the completion strategies, see D Raab, 'Evaluating the ICTY and its Completion Strategy—Efforts to Achieve Accountability for War Crimes and their Tribunals' (2005) 3 JICJ 82–102, 82–88; J-P Fomété, 'Countdown to 2010: A Critical Overview of the Completion Strategy of the International Criminal Tribunal for Rwanda (ICTR)' in E Decaux, A Dieng and M Sow (eds), *From Human Rights to International Criminal Law—Studies in Honour of an African Jurist, the Late Judge Laïty Kama* (Martinus Nijhoff, Leiden/Boston 2007) 345–400.

[59] Rules of Procedure and Evidence (n 41). The possibility to transfer cases to national criminal jurisdictions was first established by the amendments to the Rules of 30 September 2002 (ICTY) and 24 April 2004 (ICTR). Earlier versions of that Rule already provided for the *suspension* of an indictment in case of proceedings before national courts, but not for the transfer of cases: see Rule 11 *bis* as adopted on 12 November 1997 (ICTY) and on 6 July 2002 (ICTR). See generally on the transfer of indictments pursuant to Rule 11 *bis*, S Somers, 'Rule 11 bis of the International Criminal Tribunal for the Former Yugoslavia: Referral of Indictments to National Courts' (2007) 30 Boston College International and Comparative Law Review 175–183; A Marong, C C Jalloh and D Kinnecome, 'Concurrent Jurisdiction and the ICTR: Should the Tribunal Refer Cases to Rwanda?' in E Decaux, A Dieng and M Sow (eds) (n 58) 159–201, 173–200.

[60] Rules of Procedure and Evidence (n 41), Rule 11 *bis* A and C.

[61] Rules of Procedure and Evidence (n 41), Rule 11 *bis* D (iii).

national proceedings[62] and may request the Trial Chamber to revoke an order for transfer at any time before the accused is found guilty or acquitted by a court in the State concerned, requesting the deferral back to the competence of the ad hoc tribunals in accordance with their primacy over national courts.[63]

At the time of writing, since its actual operationalization by the ICTY in 2005, 13 accused persons have been transferred to national criminal jurisdictions pursuant to Rule 11 *bis*.[64] A majority of these cases have been referred to Bosnia and Herzegovina, to be tried by the War Crimes Chamber of the Court of Bosnia and Herzegovina, an internationalized criminal court with specific competence to address war crimes cases.[65] The process of referring cases from the ICTR to national criminal jurisdictions pursuant to Rule 11 *bis* has proved more cumbersome. Following the announcement by the ICTR Prosecutor in December 2005 of the intention to transfer five persons for trial in national criminal jurisdictions,[66] the attempt to refer the first case of *Michel Bagaragaza* to Norway failed, because the latter lacked jurisdiction within the meaning of Rule 11 *bis* A (iii).[67] The Trial Chamber subsequently granted the request of the Prosecutor to refer the case to The Netherlands.[68] That referral met a similar fate, albeit that this time it was not the ICTR that found a lack of jurisdiction of Dutch courts, it was the Dutch courts themselves in another case involving Rwandan Suspect.[69] At the time of writing, the only other requests of the Prosecutor under Rule 11 *bis* granted by an ICTR Trial Chamber have been in the cases of *Munyeshyaka* and *Bucyibaruta*, this time to France.[70] In addition, files involving several individuals have been transferred for trial in national

---

[62] Rules of Procedure and Evidence (n 41), Rule 11 *bis* D (iv).

[63] Rules of Procedure and Evidence (n 41), Rule 11 *bis* F.

[64] Information available at <http://www.un.org/icty/glance-e/index.htm>, visited 13 February 2008.

[65] The Security Council had previously noted that referral of cases to the War Crimes Chamber of the Court of Bosnia and Herzegovina was an essential prerequisite to achieving the objectives of the completion strategy. See S/RES/1503 (2003) (n 49) preambular para 11. The War Crimes Chamber was inaugurated on 9 March 2005.

[66] Letter dated 5 December 2005 from the President of the International Criminal Tribunal for the Prosecution of Persons Responsible for Genocide and Other Serious Violations of International Humanitarian Law Committed in the Territory of Rwanda and Rwandan Citizens Responsible for Genocide and Other Such Violations Committed in the Territory of Neighbouring States between 1 January and 31 December 1994, Security Council, UN Doc S/2005/782 (14 December 2005) [4]. At the time, the Prosecutor considered that approximately forty suspects could be tried in national jurisdictions, ibid [7]. For further information on transfer of persons to national jurisdictions, see ibid [14–15, 34, 40–43].

[67] ICTR, *Prosecutor v Michel Bagaragaza* (Decision on the Prosecution Motion for Referral to the Kingdom of Norway) ICTR-2005-86-R11bis, Trial Chamber, (19 May 2006) [16], confirmed by the Decision of the Appeals Chamber, (Decision on Rule 11 *bis* Appeal) ICTR-05-86-AR11bis (30 August 2006).

[68] *Prosecutor v Michel Bagaragaza* (Decision on Prosecutor's Request for Referral of the Indictment to the Kingdom of the Netherlands) ICTR-2005-86-11bis, Trial Chamber (13 April 2007).

[69] Court of Appeal The Hague (*Gerechtshof 's-Gravenhage*), Judgment of 17 December 2007, LJN: BC0287, 2200612007.

[70] *Prosecutor v Wenceslas Munyeshyaka* (Decision on the Prosecutor's Request for the Referral of Wenceslas Munyeshyaka's Indictment to France) ICTR-2005-87-I, Trail Chamber (20 November

jurisdictions, in particular Rwanda.[71] Rather than being based on Rule 11 *bis*, which is confined to cases in which the indictment has been confirmed, such decisions to transfer files are left to the discretion of the Prosecutor.[72]

In sum, the primacy of the two ad hoc tribunals for the former Yugoslavia and for Rwanda has evolved from a system that primarily reflected a distrust towards national criminal jurisdictions of the former Yugoslavia and Rwanda and the aim of assuring the trial of defendants before the international tribunals into a system that recognizes the need and potential benefits of trials in national criminal jurisdictions. Simultaneously, the current legal regime—and most pertinently Rule 11 *bis*—equally recognizes some of the obstacles faced by national criminal jurisdictions, especially those of States of the former Yugoslavia and of Rwanda, including the risk of domestic proceedings that do not satisfy basic standards of independence and impartiality. The evolution of such a system does not only echo changes on the ground, but also seems, to a fair degree, to be induced by practical necessity in the form of the completion strategies and the tight schedule that they entail for the winding up of the two ad hoc tribunals. The completion strategies in turn are, to a large extent, the result of the unwillingness of the international community to continue to bear the very high costs for the operation of the ad hoc tribunals.[73] While the development of a system of a more conscious and strategized interaction between the ad hoc tribunals and national criminal jurisdictions is to a large extent attributable to these economic considerations, it replaces a system largely characterized by the relative antagonism between, and isolation of, these two levels of adjudicating core crimes.

3. The Emergence of Complementarity

Although the Second World War, and the establishment of the Nuremberg Tribunal,[74] created considerable momentum for the creation of a permanent international criminal jurisdiction within the United Nations, work on a draft statute by the ILC was postponed in 1954,[75] chiefly because States considered an international criminal court to infringe their sovereignty and to interfere in their domestic affairs.[76] This situation prevailed until Trinidad and Tobago reintroduced the idea to the General Assembly in 1989, this time in the context of the UN

2007). *Prosecutor v Laurent Bucyibaruta* (Decision on the Prosecutor's Request for the Referral of Laurent Bucyibaruta's Indictment to France) ICTR-05-85-I, Trial Chamber (20 November 2007).

[71] 'Completion strategy of the International Criminal Tribunal for Rwanda' (n 66) [40]; 'Report on the completion strategy of the International Criminal Tribunal for Rwanda', 20 November 2007, UN Doc S/2007/676 [32].

[72] A Marong, C C Jalloh and D Kinnecome (n 59) 169, 170–172.

[73] For the ICTY, see D Raab (n 58) 95–96.   [74] See *2.1. The Nuremberg Tribunal.*

[75] UNGA Res 898 (IX) (14 December 1954) 512th Plenary Meeting.

[76] Compare the debate of States representatives in the General Assembly's Sixth Committee: UNGA Sixth Committee (1954) 9 GAOR Supp 12, UN Doc A/2645 (1954) 157–162; B Graefrath, 'Universal Jurisdiction and an International Criminal Court' (1990) 1 EJIL 72–75.

Narcotics Convention, and the General Assembly requested that the ILC consider the question of establishing an international criminal court.[77] After an initial report in 1990, the General Assembly requested that the ILC prepare a formal draft statute for an international criminal court 'as a matter of priority' in 1992.[78] Subsequently, a Working Group of the ILC produced the first comprehensive report on a draft statute for an international criminal court in 1993,[79] followed by a new report and draft statute in 1994.[80] The project then moved from the ILC to the Ad Hoc Committee, established by the General Assembly to consider major substantive issues arising from that 1994 Draft Statute, which met twice in 1995 and detailed its deliberations in a Report.[81] The Ad Hoc Committee was subsequently followed up by the Preparatory Committee on the Establishment of an International Criminal Court (PrepCom), established by the General Assembly to prepare a widely acceptable consolidated draft text for submission to a diplomatic conference. The PrepCom, which met from 1996 to 1998, held its final session in March and April of 1998 and completed the drafting of the text.[82] Shortly before the sessions of the PrepCom drew to a close, at its 52nd Session, the General Assembly decided to convene the United Nations Diplomatic Conference of Plenipotentiaries on the Establishment of an International Criminal Court, in

[77] UNGA Res 44/39 (4 December1989) [1] UN GAOR 44th Session Supp No 49, 311.
[78] UNGA Res 47/33 (25 November 1992) [6]; for the ILC's discussion at its 1992 Session, see R Rosenstock, 'The Forty-Fourth Session of the International Law Commission' (1993) AJIL 138–140, 139–140.
[79] ILC, 'Report of the International Law Commission on the Work of its 45th Session' (1993) UN GAOR 48th Session Supp No 10, 255, UN Doc A/48/10 (hereafter 1993 Report) reproduced in 33 ILM 253–296 (1994); see also J Crawford, 'The ILC's Draft Statute for an International Criminal Tribunal' (1994) AJIL 140–152.
[80] ILC, 'Report of the International Law Commission on the Work of its 46th Session' (1994) UN GAOR 49th Session Supp No 10 UN Doc A/49/10 (hereafter 1994 Report) 29–194. See generally J Crawford, 'The Work of the International Law Commission' in A Cassese, P Gaeta and J Jones (eds), *The Rome Statute of the International Criminal Court: A Commentary* (OUP, Oxford 2002) 23–34.
[81] 'Report of the Ad Hoc Committee on the Establishment of an International Criminal Court' (1995) UN Doc A/50/22.
[82] The PrepCom produced the following documents: 'Report of the Preparatory Committee on the Establishment of an International Criminal Court, Vol. I' Proceedings of the Preparatory Committee during March-April and August 1996 (1996) UN GAOR 51st Session Supp No 22 UN Doc A/51/22; 'Report of the Preparatory Committee on the Establishment of an International Criminal Court, Vol. II' Compilation of Proposals (1996) UN GAOR 51st Session Supp No 22 UN Doc A/51/22; 'Decisions taken by the Preparatory Committee at its Session held in New York 11 to 21 February 1997' (1997) UN Doc A/AC.249/1997/L.5; 'Decisions taken by the Preparatory Committee at its Session held in New York 4 to 15 August 1997' (1997) UN Doc A/AC.249/1997/L.8/Rev.1; 'Decisions taken by the Preparatory Committee at its Session held in New York 1 to 12 December 1997' (1997) UN Doc A/AC.249/1997/L.9/Rev.1; 'Report of the Inter-Sessional Meeting From 19 to 30 January 1998 held in Zutphen, The Netherlands' (1998) UN Doc A/AC.249/1998/L.13; 'Report of the Preparatory Committee on the Establishment of an International Criminal Court' (1998) UN Doc A/CONF.183/2: Part I, Draft Statute for the International Criminal Court, and Part II, Draft Final Act of the United Nations Diplomatic Conference of Plenipotentiaries on the Establishment of an International Criminal Court (1998) A/CONF.183/2/Add.1; Part III, Draft rules of procedure for the United Nations Diplomatic Conference of Plenipotentiaries on the Establishment of an International Criminal Court (1998) A/CONF.183/2/Add.2.

Rome, Italy, from 15 June to 17 July 1998, 'with a view to finalizing and adopting a convention on the establishment of an international criminal court'.[83] The United Nations Diplomatic Conference resulted in the adoption of the Rome Statute of the International Criminal Court on 17 July 1998.[84]

The relationship between the ICC and national criminal jurisdictions was a recurring theme in the drafting process. In the following sections, we will trace the evolution of that relationship from the 1993 and 1994 Draft Statutes (3.1. and 3.2.) to the drafting process in the Ad Hoc Committee (3.3.) and in the PrepCom (3.4.), as well as at the Rome Conference (3.5.).

3.1. The 1993 Draft Statute

The 1993 Draft Statute and report touched upon the question of the relationship between national criminal jurisdictions and the envisaged international criminal tribunal in two respects.

First, the commentary to Draft Article 1[85] explained that the purpose of the establishment of the Tribunal was 'to provide a venue for the fair trial of persons accused of crimes of an international character, *in circumstances where other trial procedures may not be available or may be otherwise less preferable*'.[86]

Second, Draft Article 45 dealing with the principle of *ne bis in idem* provided in paragraph 2 that '[a] person who has been tried by another court for acts constituting crimes referred to in articles 22 or 26,[87] may be subsequently tried under this Statute only if: (a) the act in question was characterized as an ordinary crime; or (b) the proceedings in the other court were not impartial or independent or were designed to shield the accused from international criminal responsibility or the case was not diligently prosecuted'. Draft Article 45 thus directly drew upon the principle of *ne bis in idem* as embodied in the Statutes of the two ad hoc tribunals for the former Yugoslavia and Rwanda.[88] As to subparagraph 2 (b), the Commentary stated that it 'reflected the view that the Tribunal should be able to prosecute a person for acts constituting crimes referred to in [the] Statute

---

[83] UNGA Res 52/160 (28 January 1998) [3].

[84] Text of the Rome Statute circulated as document UN Doc A/CONF 183/9 (17 July 1998) and corrected by *procès-verbaux* of 10 November 1998, 12 July 1999, 30 November 1999, 8 May 2000, 17 January 2001 and 16 January 2002. The Statute entered into force on 1 July 2002.

[85] The provision reads: 'There is established an International Criminal Tribunal (hereinafter the Tribunal), whose jurisdiction and functioning shall be governed by the provisions of the present Statute.'

[86] 1993 Report (n 79) 249, Commentary [3]. (Emphasis added).

[87] Draft Article 22 (1993) enumerates genocide, grave breaches of the Geneva Conventions and Additional Protocol I, unlawful seizure of aircraft, unlawful acts against the safety of civil aviation, apartheid and related crimes, crimes against internationally protected persons, hostage-taking, unlawful acts against the safety of maritime navigation and of fixed platforms located on the continental shelf. Article 26 establishes jurisdiction of the Tribunal over other international crimes not covered by Article 22 especially accepted by a State.

[88] Articles 10 (2) (ICTY) (n 19); Article 9 (2) (ICTR) (n 20); see also (nn 42–43).

if the previous criminal proceedings against the same person for the same acts was really a "sham" proceeding, possibly even designed to shield the person from being tried by the Court. In this connection, one member suggested that the need for this provision was demonstrated by some of the war crimes trials in national courts after the First and Second World War. However, other members expressed strong reservations about allowing the Court to review the trial proceedings of national courts as an unacceptable encroachment on State sovereignty'.[89]

No further provision addressing other aspects of the relationship between national criminal jurisdictions and the envisaged international criminal tribunal, such as the issue of concurrent jurisdiction, was included, '[s]ince the jurisdiction of national courts would not be affected unless the Court had actually exercised jurisdiction with respect to the merits...'.[90] The 1993 Report was subsequently commented upon by States and various international and non-governmental organizations and was discussed at the Sixth Committee of the General Assembly during its 48th Session on the report of the ILC.

During the subsequent consideration of the 1993 Report within the ILC, it became apparent that views differed substantially as to the Court's relationship with national courts. Some members of the ILC envisaged the court as supplementing rather than superseding national jurisdiction, while others envisaged it as an option for prosecution in case the State concerned was unwilling or unable to do so. A third group of members suggested providing the court with limited inherent jurisdiction for a core of the most serious crimes, thus presumably envisaging exclusive jurisdiction of the international criminal court for these crimes. Some members also touched upon various other aspects of the role of national criminal jurisdictions in the suppression of international crimes, including the existing treaty obligations to try or extradite offenders of serious crimes; the absence of an implied waiver of national court jurisdiction by virtue of the establishment of the court; the residual nature of the court's jurisdiction as an additional element to the existing regime based on the options of trial, extradition or referral to the court; as well as the possibility of advisory jurisdiction to assist national courts in the interpretation of the relevant treaties. Further suggestions included that the court should have the possibility not to exercise its jurisdiction if the case was not of sufficient gravity or could be adequately dealt with by a national court.[91] Some of the suggestions made during the consideration of the 1993 Report within the ILC found their way into the 1994 Draft Statute.

3.2. The 1994 Draft Statute

The 1994 Draft Statute contains the first express reference to the concept of *complementarity*. More specifically, the Draft Statute's Preamble provided that the

---

[89] 1993 Report (n 79) 308, Commentary [5].
[90] Ibid, Commentary [3].   [91] 1994 Report (n 80) 32 [50].

'court is intended to be complementary to national criminal justice systems in cases where such trial procedures may not be available or may be ineffective'.[92] In the Commentary to this provision, it was stated that the ICC, '[i]n particular is intended to operate in cases where there is no prospect of those persons [accused of crimes of significant international concern] being duly tried in national courts. The emphasis is thus on the Court as a body which will complement existing national jurisdictions and existing procedures for international judicial cooperation in criminal matters and which is not intended to exclude the existing jurisdiction of national courts, or to affect the right of States to seek extradition and other forms of international judicial assistance under existing arrangements.'[93] It was further emphasized that 'the purposes set out in the Preamble were intended to assist in the interpretation and application of the Statute, *and in particular in the exercise of the power conferred by article 35*',[94] while some members of the ILC also suggested that the principles enshrined in the Preamble—and complementarity to national criminal jurisdictions as one of them—should be included in the operative provisions of the Statute, given their importance.[95]

The aforementioned Draft Article 35, being entitled 'issues of admissibility', formed the cornerstone of the complementary nature of the international criminal court in the 1994 Draft Statute. As such, the provision already preluded the manifestation of complementarity in the 1998 Rome Statute as 'issues of admissibility', reflecting the outcome of the discussions on the conceptual distinction between admissibility and jurisdiction.[96]

Article 35 of the 1994 Draft Statute read:

The Court may, on application by the accused or at the request of an interested State at any time prior to the commencement of the trial, or of its own motion, decide, having regard to the purposes of this Statute set out in the preamble, that a case before it is inadmissible on the ground that the crime in question:

(a) has been duly investigated by a State with jurisdiction over it, and the decision of that State not to proceed to a prosecution is apparently well-founded;

(b) is under investigation by a State which has or may have jurisdiction over it, and there is no reason for the Court to take any further action for the time being with respect to the crime; or

(c) is not of such gravity to justify further action by the Court.

---

[92] Ibid, Draft Statute Preamble para 3.
[93] Ibid 44 [1].   [94] Ibid 44 [3], emphasis added.   [95] Ibid [4].
[96] In the words of the ILC in its 1994 Report, admissibility 'goes to the exercise, as distinct from the existence, of jurisdiction', ibid 105 [1]. That approach in the 1994 Draft Statute was questioned by some members of the ILC, who suggested that Article 35 was superfluous as the relevant factors could be taken into account at the level of jurisdiction, especially Draft Articles 20 [Crimes within the jurisdiction of the Court] and 21 [Preconditions to the exercise of jurisdiction]. Others, however, opposed that view and referred to the circumstances of particular cases, which could vary widely and could anyway be substantially clarified after the Court assumed jurisdiction so that a power such as that contained in Article 35 was necessary to fulfil the purpose indicated in the Preamble. Ibid 106 [3].

The ILC's commentary to the provision explained that Draft Article 35 'responds to suggestions made by a number of States, in order to ensure that the Court only deals with cases in the circumstances [...] where it is really desirable to do so'.[97] The ILC summed up the grounds for inadmissibility in Draft Article 35 as being 'that the crime in question has been or is being duly investigated by any appropriate national authorities or is not of sufficient gravity to justify further action by the Court'.[98] As to the question of what constitutes an 'appropriate national authority', the issue of cases in which more than one State have or may have jurisdiction over a given case was also considered and it was understood that the Court may take into account the position of each such State in determining (in)admissibility.[99]

Alongside Draft Article 35, Draft Article 42 on *ne bis in idem* spelled out further aspects of the Court's complementary relationship to national criminal jurisdictions. In reproducing Article 45 of the 1993 Draft Statute[100] with minor modifications, the provision regulated the right of persons not be tried by the Court in cases where that person had already been tried by the International Criminal Court itself (para 1), and in the situation where a person had already been tried by another (in particular domestic) court (para 2). In relation to the latter scenario, Article 42 (2) of the 1994 Draft Statute again provided for two exceptions to the general rule that subsequent trials by the ICC would be barred, namely where the initial trial was for an ordinary crime and in the case of sham proceedings. The ILC nevertheless stressed the exceptional character of allowing a subsequent trial by the ICC in case of sham proceedings, noting that a lack of diligence in the prosecution of a person must be of such a degree as to be calculated to shield the accused from real responsibility. Mere lapses or errors on the part of the earlier prosecution were thus said not to open the way for a subsequent trial.[101]

The 1994 Draft Statute and Report of the ILC also addressed a number of *procedural aspects* for the actual application of complementarity, albeit in a rudimentary form. First, Draft Article 27, on the commencement of prosecution, provided that, if the Prosecutor concludes that a *prima facie* case exists and has filed an indictment, the Presidency of the Court shall examine the indictment and any supporting material, and determine 'whether, *having regard,* inter alia, *to the matters referred to in article 35*, the case should be heard by the Court...'.[102] When the answer is in the affirmative, the Presidency has to confirm the indictment and establish a trial chamber. Second, Draft Article 35 in itself provided some guidance as to how issues of admissibility could be raised before the Court, namely 'on application by the accused or at the request of an interested State at any time prior to the commencement of the trial, or of [the Court's] own motion'.[103] Third, Draft Article 36 provided that '[i]n proceedings under article [...] 35, the accused and the complainant State have the right to be heard', while the proceedings

---

[97] Ibid 105 [1]. [98] Ibid 106 [2].
[99] Ibid 106 [2]. [100] See *72.* [101] 1994 Report (n 80) 119 [7].
[102] Paragraph (2)(b), emphasis added. [103] Cf *chapeau* of Draft Article 35, *74.*

under Article 35 were otherwise to be decided 'by the Trial Chamber, unless it considers, having regard to the importance of the issues involved, that the matter should be referred to the Appeals Chamber'.

The next step was a discussion of these proposals in the Ad Hoc Committee on the Establishment of an International Criminal Court.

3.3. The Ad Hoc Committee 1995

After the first session of the Ad Hoc Committee in April 1995 had focused on issues such as the means of establishing the Court, the scope of its jurisdiction and the definition of crimes,[104] complementarity featured prominently in the discussions during the second session in August 1995.[105] The Report of the Ad Hoc Committee[106] addressed what was referred to as 'The principle of complementarity' under three general headings, namely the 'Significance of the principle of complementarity';[107] the 'implications of the principle of complementarity as regards the list of crimes which would fall under the jurisdiction of an international criminal court';[108] and the 'role of national jurisdiction'.[109]

First, the significance of the principle of complementarity was underlined by describing it as an essential element of the establishment of an international criminal court. However, the provisions in the 1994 Draft Statute of the ILC were regarded as insufficient, and further elaboration of the principle was called for so that its implications for the substantive provisions of the Draft Statute could be fully understood.[110] Views differed as to in whose favour the presumption of complementarity should be created. A number of delegations recalled the advantages of national judicial systems and argued for a strong presumption in favour of national jurisdiction,[111] opposed by those who argued in favour of endowing the ICC with primacy over national criminal jurisdictions.[112] A further point of discussion was whether the principle of complementarity should be reflected in the Preamble or in the operative part of the Statute.[113]

Second, under the heading 'Implications of the principle of complementarity as regards the list of crimes which would fall under the jurisdiction of an international criminal court', the Report of the Ad Hoc Committee revealed the direct link between the scope of the ICC's jurisdiction and complementarity. Some delegations argued in favour of a uniform regime of complementarity for all crimes within the jurisdiction of the Court. It was, however, noted that such an approach would necessitate a limitation of the jurisdiction *ratione materiae*

---

[104] For a summary of the issues considered, see A Bos, 'From the International Law Commission to the Rome Conference (1994–1998)' in A Cassese, P Gaeta and J Jones (eds) (n 80) 35–65, 38–43.
[105] Ibid 43–45.
[106] 'Report of the Ad Hoc Committee on the Establishment of on International Criminal Court' (n 81).
[107] Ibid 6–7 [29–37].   [108] Ibid 7 [38].   [109] Ibid 8–10 [39–51].
[110] Ibid 6 [29].   [111] Ibid 6 [31].   [112] Ibid 6–7 [32]   [113] Ibid 7 [35–37].

of the Court to a few 'hardcore' crimes, because otherwise a multiplicity of jurisdictional mechanisms would have to be established, which was regarded as entailing the risk of endless challenges to the jurisdiction of the Court.[114]

Third, when addressing the general aspect of the role of national jurisdictions, the Report of the Ad Hoc Committee specified a number of areas that required further clarification. One such area was the meaning of 'national jurisdiction' in the context of complementarity, thus addressing the question as to which State should be considered relevant in making the assessment as to whether trial procedures were available and effective, and which State may be considered 'interested' and thereby entitled to apply for a decision of inadmissibility in accordance with the *chapeau* of Article 35 of the 1994 Draft Statute. In the view of some delegations, 'national jurisdiction' should not be understood to be limited to territorial jurisdiction, but should extend to the exercise of jurisdiction by States in accordance with established principles and arrangements. Arrangements expressly referred to in that context were agreements relating to extradition and to the status of forces. These principles and arrangements, according to that view, should be taken into consideration in determining which State had a strong interest and should exercise jurisdiction.[115]

Several aspects of the role of national jurisdictions, which required further clarification, were then identified in the Report under the caption, 'Nature of the exceptions to the exercise of national jurisdiction'.[116] Here, the words 'not available' and 'ineffective' used in the Preamble of the 1994 Draft Statute[117] were widely held to be unclear.[118] It was nevertheless observed that the 1994 Commentary to the Preamble 'clearly envisaged a very high threshold for exceptions to national jurisdiction'.[119] Some delegations also stressed that the exercise of national jurisdiction encompassed decisions not to prosecute, and that, accordingly, that Draft Article 35 should be amended so as to bar subsequent proceedings by the ICC unless decisions by domestic authorities not to prosecute (as much as decisions of acquittal or conviction by national courts) were not well-founded. A further suggestion for amending the provision was to use mandatory, rather than discretionary, language in relation to admissibility, so that the Court *must*—rather than *may*—declare cases inadmissible if the conditions under Draft Article 35 (a) to (c) are met.[120]

Draft Article 42 on *ne bis in idem*[121] proved to be another bone of contention. It was seen by some delegations as being incompatible with what they considered to be the intention of the ILC not to establish a hierarchy between the ICC and national courts or to allow the ICC to pass judgment on the operation of national courts. A particular concern expressed by some delegations in that regard was that the foreseen competence under Draft Article 42 would endow the

---

[114] Ibid 7 [38].   [115] Ibid 8 [39]. See also 33 [160].
[116] Ibid 8–9 [41–47].   [117] See *73–74*.
[118] Report of the Ad Hoc Committee (n 81) 8 [41].   [119] Ibid 8 [42].
[120] Ibid 8 [42]. See also 33 [159].   [121] Cf *75*.

ICC with a supervisory role vis-à-vis national courts.[122] It was further suggested to delete the distinction between ordinary crimes and crimes under international law in that provision.[123]

Discussions within the Ad Hoc Committee also addressed the conditions under which the ICC could set aside national jurisdiction. Several delegations were of the view that such a decision should be made on a case-by-case basis, taking into account, among other factors, the probability that national jurisdiction would be exercised in a particular instance. It appears to have been relatively uncontroversial that the ICC should be able to exercise its jurisdiction in the absence of a functioning judicial system and in case national authorities remained inactive vis-à-vis crimes within its jurisdiction. More cautiously, however, the intervention of the Court in situations where an operating national judicial system was being used as a shield was said to require 'very careful consideration'.[124] In addition, some delegations argued in favour of an express regulation of the issue of national amnesties and the development of guidelines on the matter, which could indicate the circumstances in which the ICC might intervene.[125] A last suggestion made in connection with the nature of the exceptions to the exercise of national jurisdictions was that the Draft Statute should provide for the possibility of States to voluntarily relinquish their jurisdiction in favour of the ICC. Such a waiver-construct was, however, opposed by some delegations, which regarded it as incompatible with the general idea underlying complementarity.[126]

Two further issues were addressed while considering the role of national jurisdictions. First, delegations discussed who should be the *competent authority* to decide on the exceptions to the exercise of national jurisdiction. In this context, the view of some delegations that the ICC should be endowed with primacy comparable with the one foreseen in the Statutes of the two UN ad hoc tribunals for the former Yugoslavia and Rwanda,[127] was opposed by those delegations that did not consider the latter model a suitable option. Some delegations, which shared this latter view, also allocated the burden of proof as to the appropriateness of an exception to the exercise of national jurisdiction on the ICC, thus suggesting a model that differs starkly from the primacy of the UN ad hoc tribunals.[128] Second, some delegations expressed their views on the *timing* of deciding whether exceptions to national jurisdiction should be considered, and noted that this should be done before the Prosecutor of the International Criminal Court initiated an investigation. They also noted that where a case was being investigated or was pending before a national court, the ICC should suspend the exercise of its jurisdiction, notwithstanding the possibility to resume consideration of the case

---

[122] Report of the Ad Hoc Committee (n 81) 9 [43]. See also 34 [177].   [123] Ibid 9 [43].
[124] Ibid 9 [43].   [125] Ibid.   [126] Ibid [47].   [127] Cf 64–66.
[128] Report of the Ad Hoc Committee (n 81) 9–10 [48–49]. Note that the primacy of the ad hoc tribunals entails that they are entitled to request a deferral at any stage of the proceedings without bearing any burden of proof as to the adequacy of national criminal proceedings: cf 64–66.

in accordance with the exceptions to the principle of *ne bis in idem* foreseen in Article 42 of the 1994 Draft Statute.[129]

Finally, the Report of the Ad Hoc Committee also touched upon complementarity in connection with a number of other issues, most importantly that of inherent jurisdiction of the ICC—ie jurisdiction over certain crimes, which States would recognize *ipso facto* without additional consent being required;[130] the subject of State consent requirements and conditions for the exercise of jurisdiction;[131] the State complaint mechanism to trigger the jurisdiction of the court as envisaged in Article 25 of the 1994 Draft Statute;[132] and the role of the Security Council in triggering the jurisdiction of the Court under Article 23 (1) of the 1994 Draft Statute.[133] The Report of the Ad Hoc Committee thereby clearly evinced that complementarity was seen by States as a fundamental principle of the Statute, with implications beyond the procedural issue of admissibility.

3.4. The Preparatory Committee and the Consolidated Draft Statute (1996–1998)

After the Ad Hoc Committee had submitted its report to the General Assembly in 1995, the latter established the Preparatory Committee on the Establishment of an International Criminal Court (PrepCom), in which further discussions were combined with the drafting of new texts on various aspects of the Draft Statute. Complementarity reappeared in the course of these deliberations.

During its first session in March/April 1996, the PrepCom addressed the complementary relationship between the ICC and national jurisdictions in general, and the provisions in the 1994 Draft Statute relating to it in particular.[134]

The *general* comments on complementarity emphasized that a proper balance between the ICC and national jurisdictions was crucial in order to make the Draft Statute acceptable to a large number of States. However, how, where, to what extent and with what emphasis complementarity should be reflected in the Statute was subject to considerable disagreement.[135] Some delegations expressed

---

129 Report of the Ad Hoc Committee (n 81) [51].   130 Ibid 20–21, 22, [91–93, 99].

131 Ibid 23–27, [103–111], [107, 109].

132 Ibid 25–27, [112–119], [112, 114, 116]. Article 25 of the 1994 Draft Statute foresaw States' complaints as the trigger mechanism.

133 Ibid 27–29, [120–126], [120].

134 See the 'Report of the Preparatory Committee on the Establishment of an International Criminal Court, Vol. I' Proceedings of the Preparatory Committee during March-April and August 1996 (n 82) 36–41 [153–178]. Other issues discussed included jurisdiction, definitions of crimes, trigger mechanisms, and general principles of international criminal law during the first session in March/April 1996, and matters such as procedural questions, fair trial and rights of the accused, organizational questions, the relationship of the Court to the SC and the establishment of the Court and its relationship to the United Nations during the second session in August 1996. For an overview, see C K Hall, 'The First Two Sessions of the UN Preparatory Committee on the Establishment of an International Criminal Court' (1997) AJIL 177–187; A Bos (n 104) 46–51.

135 Report of the Preparatory Committee (n 82) 36 [153].

the view that complementarity should more explicitly reflect the ILC's intention that the ICC operate in cases where there was no prospect of the accused being duly tried in national courts, rather than being intended to exclude the existing jurisdiction of national courts or to affect the right of States to seek extradition and other forms of judicial assistance under existing arrangements. This view emphasized the exceptional character of the ICC's jurisdiction, which should defer to domestic investigations and prosecutions as long as these were carried out in good faith. In that connection, the suggestion was also made that the Statute should set forth basic conditions relating to investigations, trials and the handling of requests for extradition and legal assistance as a safeguard against sham trials.[136] The exceptional character of the Court's jurisdiction, which these delegations regarded as inherent in the idea of complementarity, was further supported by the argument that the limited resources of the Court necessitated such an approach, and by the argument that, as a rule, the exercise of police power and penal law is a prerogative of States.[137]

Some delegations approached complementarity from a different angle and conceptualized it by reference to the responsibility of States to investigate vigorously and prosecute criminal cases. They aimed at a reiteration of the obligation of States in this respect in the Preamble. Other delegations opposed the latter proposition, however, albeit not because of a principled objection to the idea that such responsibilities existed, but rather because they feared it might put too much emphasis on national jurisdiction in interpreting complementarity. According to those taking the latter position, the establishment of the ICC should itself be regarded as a manifestation of States exercising their obligations to investigate and prosecute perpetrators of serious crimes.[138]

A third group of States had somewhat different concerns, namely that too strict an approach to complementarity would run the risk of undermining the authority and effectiveness of the Court. They therefore suggested that the Statute specify clear exceptions to complementarity and that the Prosecutor should not be compelled to prove in each and every case that circumstances required the Court's intervention. Although this view did not question the primary responsibility of States to prosecute the perpetrators of the crimes listed in the Statute and acknowledged that attempts should be made to minimize the risk of the Court dealing with a matter that could adequately be addressed on the national level, it was emphasized that 'complementarity should not be used to uphold the sanctity of national courts'.[139] In that context, the earlier proposal to include the principle of complementarity into the operative provisions of the Statute[140] was reiterated and received some support.[141]

---

[136] Ibid [154].　　[137] Ibid [155].　　[138] Ibid [156].　　[139] Ibid [157].
[140] Cf (n 113) and text.
[141] 'Report of the Preparatory Committee on the Establishment of an International Criminal Court, Vol. I' Proceedings of the Preparatory Committee during March-April and August 1996 (n 82) [157].

Delegations also made a number of general suggestions on procedural aspects of complementarity and called for the development of clear conditions, timing and procedures for its invocation and several related aspects.[142] A last general aspect was a reiteration of the need to consider the issue of national reconciliation initiatives.[143]

The Report of the PrepCom subsequently described the debate on specific draft provisions on complementarity.

As far as the *third preambular paragraph* of the 1994 Draft Statute is concerned, some earlier proposals were reiterated,[144] but more significantly, suggestions were made to replace the terms 'unavailable' and 'ineffective' in the Preamble. The latter term in particular was considered too subjective, and some delegations were of the view that it should be replaced because it would put the Court in a position of passing judgment on the penal system of a State. This would impinge on the sovereignty of national legal systems and might be embarrassing to that State to the extent that it might impede its eventual cooperation with the Court. That objection was, however, not extended to the term 'unavailable', which was considered more factual.[145]

A second issue that emerged in the course of discussing the third preambular paragraph was the question of who was to decide on whether the ICC should exercise jurisdiction. Here, one alternative based on the consent of States was opposed by two alternatives, which assigned the task of determining jurisdiction to the Court. The latter differed with regard to the criteria to be applied for this determination. While one view wanted to include precise criteria into the Statute, another envisaged more discretion for the Court.[146]

During the deliberations on *Article 35* of the ILC's 1994 Draft Statute on admissibility, several delegations expressed the view that the three grounds on which to declare a case inadmissible[147] were too narrow. It was suggested that subparagraph (a), according to which a case would be inadmissible if the crime in question 'has been duly investigated by a State with jurisdiction over it, and the decision of that State not to proceed to a prosecution is apparently well-founded', should be broadened to include other national decisions to discontinue the proceedings, such as acquittals or pardons. Furthermore, it was observed that other grounds of inadmissibility, especially those embodied in Draft Article 42 on *ne bis in idem,* could be included into Article 35 so as to streamline the Statute's approach to complementarity. In order to do so, it was proposed that such a future provision should be expanded to include cases which are being or have been prosecuted before national courts, provided that proceedings were conducted impartially and with due diligence.[148]

With respect to the second ground of inadmissibility provided for in Article 35 subparagraph (b), according to which a case is inadmissible if the crime 'is under investigation by a State which has or may have jurisdiction over it, and there is no reason for the Court to take any further action for the time being with respect to the crime', it was observed that this provision should take into account the circumstances under which a crime was investigated and the possibilities of ineffective or unavailable procedures or even sham trials. The possibility for parallel investigations conducted by national authorities and the ICC was also discussed, although the general perception was that parallel procedures should be avoided as far as possible. The necessity for further procedural checks and review was also stressed.[149]

During the deliberations on Draft Article 35, the PrepCom also returned to the problem of the subjectivity of the notion of ineffectiveness, which had already been noted when discussing the third preambular paragraph. Concrete proposals for alternative notions, with a view to develop more stringent and objective criteria, included 'absence of good faith' and 'unconscionable delay' in the conduct of the proceeding on the part of the national authorities, but these notions met with the criticism that they were also vague.[150]

The discussion subsequently focused on procedural aspects of the principle of complementarity, such as the question as to who might raise the issue of inadmissibility, namely only the interested State or also the accused. As to the former, a definition was said to be desirable and suggestions were made that the 'interested State' should be the State of which the accused is a national, the State(s) of which the victim(s) is (or are) national(s), the custodial State, the State of *locus delicti* or any other State which could exercise jurisdiction in respect of the crime.[151] Further procedural aspects were addressed in relation to other draft provisions, most importantly Article 27 on the commencement of prosecution.[152] In that connection, an *ex officio* power of the Prosecutor to examine admissibility upon receipt of a complaint was suggested,[153] in addition to a mechanism of mutual information between the Prosecutor and the State to whose investigation the Prosecutor has deferred.[154]

The Preparatory Committee next turned to the principle of *ne bis in idem* as embodied in Article 42, with the discussions focusing on the exceptions to the

---

[148] 'Report of the Preparatory Committee on the Establishment of an International Criminal Court, Vol. I' Proceedings of the Preparatory Committee during March-April and August 1996 (n 82) [164].

[149] Ibid [165].   [150] Ibid [166].   [151] Ibid [167].

[152] Ibid [175–176]. The links between complementarity and cooperation and judicial assistance also provoked some observations, namely on Article 51 on cooperation and judicial assistance and Article 53 on the transfer of an accused to the Court, Ibid [177–178]. Furthermore, in the course of discussing the principle of *ne bis in idem,* the possibility of preliminary hearings on the question of admissibility was suggested, Ibid [174].

[153] Ibid [175].   [154] Ibid [175–176].

principle, which would allow subsequent proceedings before the Court after a person had been tried before a national court. With regard to the first exception under Article 42 (2)(a), which foresaw the possibility of a subsequent trial if the acts in question were characterized by the national court as an ordinary crime, opinions differed starkly. Some wished further clarification of the notion of 'ordinary crimes', whilst others felt that the term was sufficiently clear and should be retained, and a further group argued in favour of deleting the notion altogether.[155]

Opinions also differed as regards the second exception, which would allow a subsequent trial before the ICC if the proceedings in the other court 'were not impartial or independent or were designed to shield the accused from international criminal responsibility or the case was not diligently prosecuted'.[156] Similar to the issues raised in relation to the notion of 'ineffectiveness' in Draft Article 35, many delegations were concerned about the vagueness and subjectivity of the mentioned criteria. Furthermore, the wording was regarded by some delegations so as to grant an excessive right of control over national jurisdiction to the Court. This view stressed that the ICC should not be regarded as an appellate court. Others, however, considered the article to be sufficiently clear and comprehensive.[157]

A further set of proposals and debates addressed the reach of the exceptions to the principle of *ne bis in idem*. A suggestion was made, for example, to expand further the list of exceptions to include the scenario where a person has already been tried in another court but where the sentence imposed by the national court was manifestly inadequate. As a possible solution, it was suggested that cases would be admissible if the proceedings in the other court manifestly intended to shield the accused from international criminal responsibility.[158] The view was also expressed that the reach of the exceptions should extend to clemency measures, such as parole, pardon and amnesty, but no discussion of the suggestions seems to have taken place.

In reaction to the discussions during the first session of the PrepCom in March and April of 1996, several delegations submitted proposals on various aspects of complementarity, which were collected and published in volume II of its 1996 report.[159] With several key aspects of complementarity still unsettled, the PrepCom did not return to the issue of complementarity until its *August 1997 session*.[160]

[155] Ibid [171].   [156] Cf 75.
[157] 'Report of the Preparatory Committee on the Establishment of an International Criminal Court, Vol. I' Proceedings of the Preparatory Committee during March-April and August 1996 (n 82) [172].
[158] Ibid [173].
[159] 'Report of the Preparatory Committee on the Establishment of an International Criminal Court, Vol. II' Compilation of Proposals (n 82).
[160] After the 1996 Report of the PrepCom, deliberations of delegations, including those on complementarity, are somewhat more difficult to be traced, since the official documents (cf ibid) largely consist of a compilation of different drafting proposals. In the following discussion, we will therefore have to rely primarily on accounts of persons who were present at the various meetings.

As before, the relation between the ICC and national jurisdictions and the question of how the jurisdiction of the Court can be triggered proved to be very controversial. Deliberations on complementarity during the consultations, which largely took place in informal drafting groups and were coordinated by the acting head of the Canadian delegation, John T Holmes, focused on Draft Article 35 and did not address issues such as procedural challenges relating to admissibility, *ne bis in idem*, competing extradition requests, cooperation and clemency measures. The Coordinator produced a Draft Article on complementarity after a week of intense negotiations, and the Committee approved a consolidated provision, which represented consensus subject to several qualifications. First, the actual text of Draft Article 35 was preceded by a general disclaimer explaining that the text represents 'a possible way to address the issue of complementarity and is without prejudice to the views of any delegation. The text does not represent agreement on the eventual content or approach to be included in this article.'[161] Second, a number of explanatory footnotes were added. Some of these detailed outstanding matters, such as the procedural aspects of complementarity,[162] the question as to whether or not complementarity related admissibility requirements may be waived by States[163] and exceptions to the principle of *ne bis in idem,* including the issue of pardons and amnesties.[164] Other footnotes specified the views of delegations on the specific wording of parts of the provision,[165] indicated that the provisions or language of the final version of the draft would depend on the outcome of discussions on other parts of the Statute[166] and addressed some other matters.[167] Third, Mexico introduced an alternative approach in which the ICC would be generally unable to review the genuine nature of the proceedings in as much as '[t]he court has no jurisdiction where the case is being investigated or prosecuted, or has been prosecuted, by a State which has jurisdiction over it'.[168]

Apart from these qualifications, a consolidated text on the *criteria for the admissibility of cases before the Court* emerged. Draft Article 35 provided that cases are inadmissible under four alternative conditions, namely when (a) the case is being investigated by a State which has jurisdiction over it, unless the State is unwilling or unable genuinely to carry out the investigation or prosecution; (b) the case has been investigated by a State which has jurisdiction over it and the State has decided not to prosecute the person concerned, unless the decision resulted from the unwillingness or inability of the State genuinely to prosecute; (c) the person concerned has already been tried for conduct which is the subject of the complaint, and a trial by the Court is not permitted under the exceptions to

---

[161] Decisions taken by the Preparatory Committee at its session held 4 to 15 August 1997 (n 82) Annex I, 'Report of the Working Group on Complementarity and Trigger Mechanism', 10.

[162] Ibid (n 16).   [163] Ibid (n 17). For earlier suggestions in that regard, see (n 126) and text.

[164] (n 82) (n 21).   [165] Ibid (n 22).   [166] Ibid (n 18–20).

[167] Ibid fn 23 [insufficient gravity as ground of inadmissibility should be included elsewhere in the Statute or deleted]; fn 24 [term 'proceedings' in Draft Article 35 (3)(a) covers both investigations and prosecutions].

[168] Ibid 12, margin 11.

the principle of *ne bis in idem,* stipulated under paragraph 2 of Draft Article 42; or (d) the case is not sufficiently grave.[169] In this scenario, the determination of admissibility was left to the ICC.[170]

Although a small group of States retained their reservations vis-à-vis the ICC's competence to review national decisions, Draft Article 35 now reflected an emerging consensus to assign the ICC the role to assume jurisdiction where national jurisdictions were 'unwilling' or 'unable' to carry out the investigation or prosecution. Consequently, a definition of the two notions of 'unwillingness' and 'inability' was considered imperative.

With regard to 'inability', factors such as the total or partial collapse of a State's national judicial system were mentioned, and some proposals contained criteria for determining such a collapse. Other criteria were also suggested, but it was ultimately decided that a further definition of total or partial collapse was not warranted, provided that an additional criterion, the State's inability to secure the presence of the accused or to obtain the necessary evidence or testimony, would be used. To meet concerns that such an approach would be too restrictive, a reference to a State being '[...] otherwise unable to carry out its proceedings' was included.[171] Accordingly, Draft Article 35 (4) defined 'inability' as the situation in which, 'due to a total or partial collapse or unavailability of its national judicial system, the State is unable to obtain the accused or the necessary evidence and testimony or otherwise unable to carry out its proceedings'.[172]

To define 'unwillingness' proved a more controversial matter than 'inability', as some delegations had concerns with regard to State sovereignty and constitutional guarantees in domestic systems against double jeopardy.[173] Earlier difficulties re-emerged, namely the perceived subjectivity of the nature of the test to be used by the ICC and its capacity to function as a quasi-appellate court, passing judgments on the decisions and proceedings of national judicial systems.[174] With a view to accommodating these concerns, the word 'genuinely' was inserted into paragraph 2 of Draft Article 35,[175] as it was regarded as reflecting a more objective connotation.[176] Further discussions focused on detailing the criteria for determining 'unwillingness', and three different manifestations of that notion were identified. The first was proceedings or national decisions 'made for the

---

[169] Draft Article 35 (2).
[170] Cf *chapeau* of Draft Article 35; see also C K Hall, 'The Third and Fourth Session of the UN Preparatory Committee on the Establishment of an International Criminal Court' (1998) AJIL 124–133, 130–131.
[171] J T Holmes, 'The Principle of Complementarity' in R S Lee (ed), *The International Criminal Court, The making of the Rome Statute, Issues, Negotiations, Results* (Kluwer Law Publ, The Hague 1999) 41–78, 48–49.
[172] 'Report of the Working Group on Complementarity and Trigger Mechanism' (n 161) 12.
[173] S A Williams, 'Commentary on Article 17' in O Triffterer (ed) *Commentary on the Rome Statute of the International Criminal Court—Observers' Notes, Article by Article* (Nomos, Baden-Baden 1999) 383–394, margin 12; J T Holmes (n 171) 47–48.
[174] Cf (nn 145, 150 and 157), and accompanying texts.   [175] Cf *84–85.*
[176] For alternative suggestions, see J T Holmes (n 171) 49–50.

purpose of shielding the person concerned from criminal responsibility for crimes within the jurisdiction of the Court',[177] which reflected the view of many delegations that the main purpose of the notion of 'unwillingness' was to avoid sham proceedings. The two other forms of 'unwillingness' that emerged were undue delays in the proceedings which in the circumstances are inconsistent with an intent to bring the person concerned to justice,[178] and 'proceedings which were not or are not being conducted independently or impartially and they were or are being conducted in a manner which, in the circumstances, is inconsistent with an intent to bring the person concerned to justice'.[179] The latter form of a lack of independence and impartiality was considered necessary in order to capture procedural problems in a State that do not amount to the shielding variant of unwillingness.[180]

This text of Draft Article 35 was forwarded to the Rome Conference as Article 15 of the Draft Statute,[181] which formed the basis of the discussions in Rome.

While the intrinsic link between Draft Article 35 and the issue of *ne bis in idem* had already become apparent, the Preparatory Committee did not return to this aspect until its session in March/April 1998, when Draft Article 42 (2) on *ne bis in idem* was largely rewritten. Again, the ordinary crimes exception gave rise to controversy and was ultimately deleted.[182] A further difficulty was resolved more constructively. When the delegations turned to the nature of other national proceedings, which would make cases admissible before the ICC in exception to the principle of *ne bis in idem*, two criteria were used that drew upon the compromise already achieved on complementarity in Draft Article 15. Accordingly, the third paragraph of what became Draft Article 18 in the Draft Statute submitted to the Rome Conference[183] stated two exceptions to the bar to subsequent proceedings for a person that has already been tried by another court. The first related to proceedings in the other court that 'were for the purpose of shielding the person concerned from criminal responsibility for crimes within the jurisdiction of the Court', and the second to those that 'otherwise were not conducted independently or impartially and were conducted in a manner which, in the circumstances, was inconsistent with an intent to bring the person concerned to justice'. While it was acknowledged that this wording might have to be reviewed should Draft Article 15 be modified in Rome,[184] some outstanding issues were included in a footnote, including the question of whether a further exception to the principle of *ne bis in idem* should allow for a trial before the ICC in case the prior proceedings failed to take into account the grave nature of the crime, at either the trial or sentencing stage.[185]

---

[177] Draft Article 35 (3)(a).   [178] Draft Article 35 (3)(b).
[179] Draft Article 35 (3)(c).   [180] J T Holmes (n 171) 50–51.
[181] 'Report of the Preparatory Committee on the Establishment of an International Criminal Court'; Draft Statute & Draft Final Act' (n 82) 48–50.
[182] J T Holmes (n 171) 57–58.   [183] See (n 181) 54.   [184] Ibid (n 58).
[185] Ibid n 59.

As corollary to the Mexican alternative to issues of admissibility in Draft Article 15,[186] an alternative Draft Article 18 precluded the Court from exercising jurisdiction 'where the case in question is being investigated or prosecuted, or has been prosecuted, by a State which has jurisdiction over it'.[187]

Finally, the most controversial part of the negotiations on *ne bis in idem* during the March/April 1998 session related to clemency measures. A proposal was introduced to allow the Court to try a person previously convicted if that person was subsequently pardoned, paroled or had their sentence commuted. However, the provision was too contentious and was therefore submitted to the Rome Conference in brackets. This Draft Article 19 provided that, '[w]ithout prejudice to article 18, a person who has been tried by another court for conduct also proscribed under article 5 may be tried by the Court if a manifestly unfounded decision on the suspension of the enforcement of a sentence or on a pardon, a parole or a commutation of the sentence excludes the application of any appropriate form of penalty'.[188] A footnote was added, stating that further consideration on the content and placement of this provision was needed.

With consensus emerging on criteria for admissibility, the PrepCom delved into *procedural aspects of complementarity* in further detail during its *session in December 1997*. The rudimentary Draft Article 36 of the 1994 ILC Draft Statute[189] formed the basis of the discussions on the regulatory framework for challenges to admissibility and jurisdiction. These discussions evolved around five themes.

The first such theme was *who* should be allowed to make challenges to jurisdiction and admissibility. That the accused should be allowed to do so was relatively uncontroversial, as was the possibility for States to make such challenges and the competence of the Prosecutor to seek a ruling on jurisdiction and admissibility.[190] In contrast, the question as to *which* State or States should be allowed to challenge jurisdiction and admissibility proved divisive. Different views were expressed as to whether such a right should be reserved for States Parties and States that are investigating and prosecuting a case or have already done so, and whether the State of nationality of the accused should be allowed to make a challenge.

The second question related to *when* challenges could be made and how often, with a balance being sought between preventing abuse and delays, on the one hand, and the necessary flexibility to be able to take account of changing situations, on the other.[191] Accordingly, the third paragraph of Draft Article 36 provided that admissibility or jurisdiction may be challenged only once by any person or a State and that such challenges must, as a rule, be made 'prior to or at the

---

[186] See (n 168) and text.
[187] 'Report of the Preparatory Committee on the Establishment of an International Criminal Court, Draft Statute & Draft Final Act]' (n 82) 55.
[188] Ibid   [189] *75–76*.
[190] J T Holmes (n 171) 61–62.   [191] Ibid 62.

commencement of the trial'.[192] However, the Court was given the competence to grant leave for challenges more than once, or at a later time in exceptional cases, although these late challenges (as well as challenges made at the commencement of a trial rather than prior to it) were only allowed to be based on *ne bis in idem*. In addition, Draft Article 36 provided an obligation incumbent upon States to make a challenge 'at the earliest opportunity', although a footnote acknowledged that the consequences, if any, of the failure of a State to do so remained unclear.[193]

Third, the question of *who* could submit their observations regarding jurisdiction and admissibility was discussed. Delegations broadly agreed that those who can submit cases to the Court should be allowed to make such observations, although the matter of who could submit cases, the so-called 'trigger mechanisms', had not yet been decided, with the options being that States, the Security Council and the Prosecutor could do so.[194] Again, the controversy on whether non-party States could challenge jurisdiction and admissibility resurfaced, now in connection to their competence to make observations on these matters, while it was readily agreed that victims should have the right to do so. The relevant part of Draft Article 36 therefore stated that '[i]n proceedings with respect to jurisdiction or admissibility, those having submitted the case [...] as well as victims, may submit observations to the Court' but an extension to 'non-State parties which have jurisdiction over the crimes' was inserted in brackets.[195]

A fourth issue was the *forum* of the Court competent to determine challenges to jurisdiction and admissibility. Mirroring the different stages of proceedings at which such challenges could be made,[196] consensus was reached that the Pre-Trial Chamber was to address challenges prior to the confirmation of the indictment, while the Trial Chamber would rule on such challenges after the indictment has been confirmed.[197]

Fifth and finally, delegations addressed the subject of *appeals and reviews* of decisions on challenges of jurisdiction and admissibility. It was agreed that such decisions should be allowed to be appealed to the Appeals Chamber.[198] In addition, three proposals were introduced, but due to lack of time were, deferred to the Rome Conference. The first proposal would grant the Prosecutor the power to request a review of decisions 'at any time [...] on the grounds that conditions required under article 35 to render the case inadmissible no longer exist or that new facts arose'.[199] The two further proposals were submitted by the Italian delegation. One foresaw a competence of the Prosecutor to monitor domestic

---

[192] 'Decisions taken by the Preparatory Committee at its Session held in New York 1 to 12 December 1997' (n 82) 35.

[193] Draft Article 36 (3) *bis* and ibid (n 21).   [194] Cf ibid (n 17); J T Holmes (n 171) 63.

[195] Draft Article 36 (2), last sentence, ibid.   [196] See (nn 192–193) and text.

[197] Draft Article 36 (4); 'Decisions taken by the Preparatory Committee at its Session held in New York 1 to 12 December 1997' (n 82) 35.

[198] Cf Draft Article 36 (4), last sentence (n 82) 36.

[199] See the bracketed Draft Article 36 (5), ibid.

proceedings, and an obligation of the State concerned to keep the Prosecutor informed about them. In a similar vein, the other proposal envisaged that the Prosecutor should possess the competence to defer an investigation before a formal challenge was made on admissibility and, at the same time, allow him, or her, to request information from the State on the domestic proceedings. Both of these Italian proposals were made partly in reaction to a proposal by the US delegation for an article on preliminary rulings regarding admissibility, which was announced at the beginning of December 1997.[200]

The aforementioned discussions on challenges to jurisdiction and admissibility were reflected in the heavily bracketed text of Draft Article 36,[201] which was submitted to the Rome Conference as Draft Article 17.[202]

Apart from the issue of challenges to admissibility and jurisdiction, another procedural aspect of complementarity emanated from the December 1997 US proposal on *preliminary rulings regarding admissibility* mentioned previously. The US proposed a provision on the matter at the March/April 1998 session. That provision foresaw that the Prosecutor should publicly announce whether s/he had made a determination that there would be a sufficient basis to commence an investigation and to notify States Parties. Within a specified period, States would be allowed to request a deferral to their domestic investigation, a request that would oblige the Prosecutor to defer to such an investigation unless the Pre-Trial Chamber had determined in a preliminary ruling that the requirements of admissibility (unwillingness or inability) were fulfilled. The deferral to a State's investigation was foreseen as being open for review by the Prosecutor and that the latter would be granted the power to request that the State concerned report periodically on the progress of its investigation and on any subsequent prosecution. The lateness of the submission of this proposal forestalled any discussion, however, and the proposal was therefore inserted in brackets as Draft Article 16 of the Draft Statute to be discussed in Rome.[203]

3.5. The Negotiations in Rome

As is readily apparent from the foregoing discussion, the drafting process of the PrepCom yielded a number of draft provisions, which provided the basis for the discussions of complementarity during the Rome Conference,[204] coordinated by

---

[200] J T Holmes (n 171) 65.

[201] 'Decisions taken by the Preparatory Committee at its Session held in New York 1 to 12 December 1997' (n 82) 34–36.

[202] 'Report of the Preparatory Committee on the Establishment of an International Criminal Court, Draft Statute & Draft Final Act]' (n 82) 51–53.

[203] Ibid 50–51. See also J T Holmes (n 171) 69.

[204] For a general description of the negotiations in Rome, see P Kirsch and D Robinson, 'Reaching Agreement at the Rome Conference' in A Cassese, P Gaeta and J Jones (eds), (n 80) 67–91.

John T Holmes. Draft Articles 15 to 19[205] on the criteria for admissibility and procedure of complementarity took centre-stage.[206]

As regards Draft Article 15 on *issues of admissibility*, the Coordinator sought to preserve the compromise already reached and to resist a reopening of the negotiations. To that end, informal consultations, in his view, should be resisted for as long as possible so as to avoid the introduction of new proposals, while such consultations should be held on a new article to address clemency measures since not enough time was devoted to that issue in the PrepCom.[207] The coordinator achieved the first aim by beginning a series of bilateral meetings with those delegations opposed to the text and later, as minor changes were contemplated, with a wider range of delegations. The Mexican proposal[208] was favoured by only two delegations, and as discussions ensued, three main problematic issues emerged. The first repeated the concern that paragraph 2 of Article 15 gave the ICC too much discretion in deciding whether a State was 'unwilling' and was too subjective. In order to address this concern, a passage was ultimately inserted into paragraph 2 containing the words, 'having regard to the principles of due process recognized by international law'. The second concern related to the notion of 'undue delay' in Article 15 (2)(b), which was criticized as being too low a threshold for unwillingness. It was resolved by using the terms 'unjustified delay' instead, while 'unjustified' was understood to establish a higher threshold. Third, the notion of 'partial collapse' was viewed as insufficient to determine 'inability'. It proved more difficult to resolve and ultimately the notion of 'substantial collapse' was used.[209]

Finally, the *chapeau* of Draft Article 15 was amended so as to refer to the proviso in paragraph 10 of the Preamble and in Article 1 of the Rome Statute that the ICC 'shall be complementary to national criminal jurisdictions'. Draft Article 15 subsequently became Article 17 of the Rome Statute, under the title 'Issues of admissibility'.

As far as the relationship between the principle of complementarity and the principle of *ne bis in idem* in what was to become Article 20 (3) of the Rome Statute was concerned, no remarkable discussion on the subject took place. The

---

[205] Report of the Preparatory Committee on the Establishment of an International Criminal Court, Draft Statute & Draft Final Act] (n 82) 48–55.

[206] For summary records of the discussions on these provisions in the Committee of the Whole, see United Nations Diplomatic Conference of Plenipotentiaries on the Establishment of an International Criminal Court (Rome 15 June–17 July 1998) UN GAOR Volume II—Summary records of the plenary meetings and of the meetings of the Committee of the Whole, UN Doc A/CONF.183/13(Vol.II) 2002, 213–221, 295–318, 319–323, 327–348. However, complementarity was also discussed in relation to other aspects of the Draft Statute, particularly the questions of trigger mechanisms and acceptance of jurisdiction: see for instance ibid 182 [30], 201 [109], 204 [52], 187 [15], 189 [42–43], 190 [57], 195 [27], 196 [3], 198 [74, 80], 200 [105], 201 [21], 205 [30], 206 [37] (trigger mechanism and acceptance of jurisdiction); 192 [82, 86] (general principles of criminal law).

[207] J T Holmes (n 171) 51–52.   [208] See (n 168).

[209] J T Holmes (n 171) 52–55.

Draft Article, as consolidated during the 1998 Preparatory Committee, remained largely unchanged, subject to three exceptions. The first such modification was necessitated by the ultimate Articles setting forth the crimes within the jurisdiction of the Court, ie Articles 6 to 8. Second, in order to clarify that the Court could try a person that had already been tried by another court if different conduct was the subject of the prosecution in that latter court, an addition to the *chapeau* was made that no person shall be tried by the ICC if s/he has already been tried by another court for ICC crimes 'with respect to the same conduct'. Finally, a reference to 'norms of due process recognized by international law' was added to paragraph 3 (b), which incorporated the second exception to the principle of *ne bis in idem* as a bar to subsequent proceedings before the ICC if proceedings 'in the other court otherwise were not conducted independently or impartially and were conducted in a manner which, in the circumstances, was inconsistent with an intent to bring the person concerned to justice'.[210] This modification thus rendered paragraph 3 (b) consistent with the wording of Draft Article 15 (2) (Article 17 (2) of the Rome Statute).[211]

The bilateral consultations on the proposal regarding clemency measures proved futile. Views differed too substantially[212] to achieve consensus and Draft Article 19 was dropped.[213] Consequently, the final text contained neither any express regulation of this matter in particular nor of the matter of substitutes for criminal prosecutions in general.

The negotiations on Draft Article 17 concerning *challenges to the jurisdiction of the Court or the admissibility of a case* revisited some of those issues that had proved contentious previously,[214] in particular the question as to which State should be allowed to challenge,[215] the question of the Court reviewing its decision at the request of the Prosecutor over new facts, and the two Italian proposals on the power of the Prosecutor to monitor domestic criminal proceedings and the corollary obligation of States to provide information on such proceedings.[216]

Whilst building on the compromise already reached at the PrepCom's December 1997 session, it was ultimately decided that the right to make chal-

---

[210] Cf n 183 and text.   [211] Cf *90*.

[212] Cf for example the diametrically opposed statements by Belgium, one of the co-sponsors of Draft Article 19, on the one hand: and Afghanistan, on the other hand, United Nations Diplomatic Conference of Plenipotentiaries on the Establishment of an International Criminal Court (Rome 15 June–17 July 1998) UN GAOR Volume II (n 206) 215 [28, 33].

[213] J T Holmes (n 171) 59–60.   [214] See *87–89*.

[215] The two following statements during the Rome Conference may illustrate the two opposing camps on the issue. The UK 'strongly supported the reference to "a State" since, if a State that was not a party was carrying out an effective prosecution in its own territory, there was no reason for the Court to intervene and also conduct a prosecution', United Nations Diplomatic Conference of Plenipotentiaries on the Establishment of an International Criminal Court (Rome 15 June–17 July 1998) UN GAOR Volume II (n 206) 215 at 34. Italy, on the other hand, declared to be 'reluctant to allow States not parties, which did not share the burden of obligations under the Statute, to share the privilege of challenging the jurisdiction of the Court' (n 206) 220 at 27.

[216] Ibid J T Holmes (n 171) 66.

lenges to the admissibility should not be limited to the accused or to a person for whom an arrest warrant, or summons to appear, has been issued and to States Parties. However, it was agreed that non-States Parties could only do so under the condition that they have 'jurisdiction over a case, on the ground that [they are] investigating or prosecuting the case or [have] investigated or prosecuted'. That condition was also extended to States Parties other than those from whom acceptance of jurisdiction is required in accordance with Article 12 (2)(a) and (b) of the Rome Statute,[217] and which wish to make a challenge to jurisdiction or admissibility. In addition, States, from whom acceptance of jurisdiction was required, were granted an independent right to challenge.[218] Broad consensus also emerged on the possibility of a review of a decision on admissibility and on the right of the Prosecutor to request information on a State's domestic proceedings after a deferral. The Italian proposal, which would oblige a State Party to inform the Prosecutor of national proceedings, failed to generate support, however, and was consequently dropped.[219]

Apart from these matters, which were revisited, a new question also emerged, namely whether, and under what conditions, the Prosecutor should be granted any investigative power pending a ruling by the Court on a challenge of admissibility.[220] In that regard, two concerns had to be balanced, namely to avoid simultaneous investigations by both the Prosecutor and States, on the one hand, and the potential of challenges to admissibility to cause delays and frustrate investigations by the Prosecutor, and that valuable evidence could be lost pending a decision on the challenge to admissibility, on the other hand. That balance was struck by providing that, as a rule, a challenge made by a State has a suspensive effect, as far as the investigation by the Prosecutor is concerned, until the Court has ruled on the challenge. As an exception to that rule, however, the Prosecutor may seek authority to take certain measures. Furthermore, it was also agreed that the making of a challenge would not affect the validity of those acts that had already been performed by the Prosecutor prior to the making of the challenge.[221]

The resulting scheme for challenges to the jurisdiction of the Court or the admissibility of a case was ultimately included in the Rome Statute as Article 19.

Due to its late introduction at the PrepCom stage by the US delegation, Draft Article 16 on *preliminary rulings regarding admissibility* underwent the most significant development of all the provisions on complementarity. David Scheffer, Head of the US delegation, introduced the proposed provision in the Committee of the Whole, explaining that it responded to the growing support for the concept

---

[217] Article 12 on preconditions to the exercise of jurisdiction provides in paragraph 2 that in the case of Article 13, paragraph (a) or (c) on the trigger mechanisms of State referrals and *proprio motu* investigations of the Prosecutor, the Court may exercise its jurisdiction if one or more of the following States are Parties to this Statute or have accepted the jurisdiction of the Court in accordance with paragraph 3: (a) the State on the territory of which the conduct in question occurred or, if the crime was committed on board a vessel or aircraft, the State of registration of that vessel or aircraft; (b) the State of which the person accused of the crime is a national.

[218] J T Holmes (n 171) 67.   [219] Ibid.   [220] Ibid 66.   [221] Ibid 68.

of referrals of overall situations to the Court by the Security Council, a State Party, or the Prosecutor acting *proprio motu*. In the view of the US, and '[i]n line with the principle of complementarity, it would then seem necessary to provide for a procedure, at the outset of a referral, which would recognize the ability of national judicial systems to investigate and prosecute the crimes concerned'.[222] He also clarified that the United States' proposal concerned an overall matter referred to the Court at an early stage, when no particular suspects had been identified, and a State's right to launch full-scale investigations.[223]

While retaining the key features of its precursor from the March/April 1998 session of the PrepCom,[224] the proposal[225] had been amended in a number of respects with a view to accommodating the concerns expressed by some States.[226] First, the Prosecutor had to notify a referral not only to States Parties but also to non-States Parties that may have jurisdiction, and s/he was granted the power to do so on a confidential basis where necessary to protect persons or to prevent destruction of evidence. Second, the period in which States must inform the Prosecutor that a domestic investigation is underway was now specified as being six months. Third, the Prosecutor would be granted the power to review the deferral to a State's investigation, not only periodically after six months following the date of the deferral, but also at any time when there had been a significant change of circumstances indicating that the State had become unwilling or unable to genuinely carry out the investigation. Fourth, as far as appeals against preliminary ruling of the Pre-Trial Chamber were concerned, the right to appeal was now also granted to the Prosecutor, and not just the State concerned, as the earlier proposal. Such appeals could be heard on an expedited basis and the Appeals Chamber was granted the power to authorize the Prosecutor to proceed with an investigation while the appeal was pending. Fifth and finally, a new paragraph had been added to the proposal, which provided that, pending a preliminary ruling by the Pre-Trial Chamber, or at any time where the Prosecutor had deferred an investigation, the Prosecutor could, in exceptional cases, seek specific authority from the Pre-Trial Chamber to pursue investigative steps where there was a unique opportunity to obtain important evidence or there was a significant risk that such evidence would not be subsequently available.

Notwithstanding the attempt of the US to adjust the proposal in order to make it more widely acceptable, some delegations retained a number of reservations and

---

[222] United Nations Diplomatic Conference of Plenipotentiaries on the Establishment of an International Criminal Court (Rome 15 June–17 July 1998) UN GAOR Volume II (n 206) 214 [25].

[223] Ibid.   [224] Cf 89.

[225] UN Doc A/CONF.183/C.1/L.25, reproduced in United Nations Diplomatic Conference of Plenipotentiaries on the Establishment of an International Criminal Court (Rome 15 June–17 July 1998) UN GAOR Volume III, Reports and other documents (2002) UN Doc A/CONF. 183/13 (Vol. III) 241–242.

[226] J T Holmes (n 171) 69.

suggested deletion[227] or (substantial) redrafting of (parts of) the provision.[228] However, other delegations supported it.[229] John T Holmes recounts that the issues, which emerged as being central in the quest for agreement, included the question of whether preliminary rulings on admissibility should apply to all trigger mechanisms; the question of public announcements and the addressee States of notifications; the parameters for deferral to national investigations and the conditions for the Prosecutor's power, if any, to proceed regardless of national investigations; the question of review of the decision or ruling to defer; the obligation of States to report periodically on deferred cases; and the relationship between preliminary rulings on admissibility and the right of States to challenge admissibility under what was to become Article 19 of the Rome Statute.[230]

The subsequent consultations revealed the need for a proper balance between the basic idea of complementarity, encapsulating the primary responsibility of national criminal jurisdictions to investigate and prosecute core crimes, on the one hand, and the desire to avoid abuse of preliminary rulings on admissibility by *male fide* States with a view to thwarting investigations by the Prosecutor, on the other. The quest for that balance proved cumbersome,[231] but was ultimately realized. Draft Article 16, which ultimately became Article 18 of the Rome Statute, contained seven paragraphs that set forth the regime for preliminary rulings regarding admissibility. That regime only applies to the two trigger mechanisms of state referral and *proprio motu* investigations of the Prosecutor, and not to Security Council referrals. In the former two cases, the Prosecutor must notify 'all States Parties and those States which, taking into account the information available, would normally exercise jurisdiction over the crimes concerned', while s/he is empowered to do so on a confidential basis and, where necessary to protect persons, prevent destruction of evidence or prevent the absconding of persons, to limit the scope of the information provided to States. In response to the notification, States may, within one month, inform the Court that domestic proceedings are underway with respect to acts which may constitute ICC crimes and which relate to the information provided in the notification by the Prosecutor. These States may request that the Prosecutor defer to their investigation a request with which the Prosecutor must comply unless the Pre-Trial Chamber, on the application of the Prosecutor, decides to authorize the

---

[227] See eg United Nations Diplomatic Conference of Plenipotentiaries on the Establishment of an International Criminal Court (Rome 15 June–17 July 1998) UN GAOR Volume II (n 206) 215 [28] and 306 [13] (Belgium), 216 [36] (Australia), [40] (Finland), [43] (Venezuela), 217 [46] (Poland), 219 [16] (Switzerland), [21] (Norway), [34] (Austria), [35] (Andorra), 221, [46] (Costa Rica), 298 [66] (Sierra Leone), 303 [156] (Mali), 304 [178] (Tanzania), [186] (Germany), 309 [70] (Greece), 317 [38] (Croatia).

[228] Ibid 215 [34] (UK), 217 [1] (Iraq), 220 [26] (Italy).

[229] Ibid 214 [27] (Mexico), 215 [29] (Chile), 218 [2] (Japan), 218 [10] (India), 303 [161] (Jordan), 310 [90] (Egypt).

[230] J T Holmes (n 171) 70.   [231] Ibid 70–73.

investigation. However, the Prosecutor's deferral to a State's investigation is open to review by the Prosecutor six months after the date of deferral, or at any time when there has been a significant change of circumstances based on the State's unwillingness or inability genuinely to carry out the investigation. The provision provides for appeals against rulings of the Pre-Trial Chamber on admissibility, including those on an expedited basis. Subsequent to a deferral, the Prosecutor is empowered to request that the State concerned periodically inform him/her of the progress of its investigations and any subsequent prosecutions. State Parties are under a legal obligation to respond to such requests without undue delay. Furthermore, the exceptional power of the Prosecutor to seek authority from the Pre-Trial Chamber to pursue necessary investigative steps pending a ruling by the Pre-Trial Chamber, or at any time when the Prosecutor has deferred an investigation, was retained.[232] Last but not least, the issue of the relationship between preliminary rulings on admissibility and the right of States to challenge admissibility under what had become Article 19 of the Rome Statute was resolved by allowing States, which have challenged a ruling of the Pre-Trial Chamber under Article 18, to make a subsequent challenge to the admissibility of a case under Article 19 only on the grounds of additional significant facts or a significant change of circumstances.

With the core provisions on complementarity agreed upon, delegations in Rome nevertheless acknowledged that further work was required to operationalize the Statute. It was therefore agreed to establish a Preparatory Commission, which was to elaborate a set of subsidiary instruments, including Rules of Procedure and Evidence.[233] Some of the rules would relate to complementarity.[234]

4. Interim Conclusions

The Rome Statute answers the question as to the relationship between the ICC and national criminal jurisdictions markedly different from the instruments establishing the Nuremburg Tribunal, the ICTY and the ICTR. By providing that the ICC shall be complementary to national criminal jurisdiction, the

---

[232] See (n 225).

[233] Final Act of the United Nations Diplomatic Conference of Plenipotentiaries on the Establishment of an International Criminal Court (17 July 1998) UN Doc A/CONF.183/10, Annex 1, Resolution F. Other instruments to be elaborated by the Preparatory Commission included Elements of Crimes; a relationship agreement between the Court and the United Nations; basic principles governing a headquarters agreement to be negotiated between the Court and the host country; financial regulations and rules; an agreement on the privileges and immunities of the Court; and a budget for the first financial year. The Preparatory Commission was also entrusted with the preparation of proposals for a provision on aggression.

[234] Rules of Procedure and Evidence (RoPE) Doc ICC-ASP/1/3 (part II-A). For a general discussion of the work of the Preparatory Commission, see P Kirsch and V Oosterveld, 'The Post-Rome Conference Preparatory Commission' in A Cassese, P Gaeta and J Jones (eds) (n 80) 93–104.

Statute encapsulates the idea that the latter is the first line of defence in the fight against impunity. The Court, on the other hand, is envisaged as filling the gaps left by ineffective or defunct national judicial systems. Although agreement on this generic idea emerged relatively early in the negotiating process, it was the details of the complementary regime of that proved particularly contentious. The controversies surrounding the questions of whether the Court should be competent to review judgments of national courts and whether the procedural aspects of complementarity should endow the Prosecutor with certain monitoring powers over national proceedings are examples that bear witness to the fact that States were much more concerned about safeguarding their sovereign prerogative to punish these perpetrators than they were in the context of ad hoc international criminal tribunals. The latter are created in response to a particular situation, are endowed with jurisdiction that is limited *ratione temporis, loci* and/or *personae,* and are either imposed by the victor on the vanquished (Nuremberg) or by an organ with supranational powers, most notably the UN Security Council (Yugoslavia, Rwanda). In contrast, the Rome Statute establishes a permanent ICC with prospective jurisdiction, which extends to crimes committed on the territory and by nationals of State Parties. Therefore, the relationship between the ICC and national criminal jurisdictions had to be addressed prospectively for future situations that may implicate States whose nationals, including officials, will potentially be subjected to the ICC's jurisdiction. It comes as no surprise that the detailed content of the complementary relationship between the ICC and national criminal jurisdictions consequently evolved as one of the most controversial elements of the negotiations leading up to the adoption of the Rome Statute. Agreement on the relevant provisions was far more difficult to attain than on the provisions governing the relationship between ad hoc international criminal tribunals and national courts. States regarded complementarity as the core feature through which concerns about their sovereignty could be reconciled with the establishment of an international criminal court, whilst at the same time advancing the cause of punishing perpetrators of genocide, crimes against humanity and war crimes. In so doing, complementarity assumed a vital role in making the Statute as widely acceptable to States as possible and would ultimately influence the degree of support of States, which, in turn, ultimately makes or breaks the effectiveness and legitimacy of the Court. Judging from the number of States that have ratified the Rome Statute in a comparatively short period of time,[235] complementarity in general and the detailed rules that make up its legal regime would appear to encapsulate a balance between State sovereignty and ending impunity that States consider acceptable. This is notwithstanding the fact that some States which were instrumental to the development of complementarity—most notably

---

[235] At the time of writing (February 2008), 105 States were parties to the Rome Statute out of a total of 191 of UN member States.

the United States—have so far considered themselves to be unable to ratify the Statute. However; with more than half of the international community of States, including States on whose territory core crimes have been or are being committed, having become parties: one can conclude that the agreement reached in Rome is regarded as an acceptable solution by a majority of States.

IV

Complementarity as a Legal Principle and as Criteria for Admissibility

1. Introduction

After having traced its evolution in Chapter III, this chapter turns to an exploration of the Preamble and Article 1 and Articles 17 and 20 of the Statute. The Preamble and Article 1 establish complementarity as a legal principle and introduce it as a general notion (2). Articles 17 and 20, on the other hand, translate that principle into criteria for the admissibility of cases before the Court, thus setting forth the material elements of complementarity (3). As such, Articles 17 and 20 have to be distinguished from the procedural aspects of applying and invoking complementarity in the course of ICC proceedings, which we will address in chapter V.

2. Complementarity as a Legal Principle: The Preamble and Article 1

The Statute's Preamble and Article 1 affirm that the International Criminal Court 'shall be complementary to national criminal jurisdictions'.[1] The duplicative reference to complementarity in both the Preamble and the operative provisions of the Statute reflects the fundamental importance that States have attached to it.[2] That importance is further illustrated when considering that Article 1 includes 'complementarity' as one of the three core attributes of the ICC, alongside its *permanence* and its power to exercise jurisdiction over *the most serious crimes of international concern*.

However, both references to complementarity do not specify any automatic legal consequences, nor do they identify their subjects, detailed content

---

[1] Rome Statute of the International Criminal Court (adopted 17 July 1998, as corrected by *procès-verbaux* of 10 November 1998, 12 July 1999, 30 November 1999, 8 May 2000, 17 January 2001 and 16 January 2002, entered into force 1 July 2002) A/CONF.183/9 (Rome Statute) Preamble, para 10 and Article 1, second sentence.

[2] For the emergence of an inclusion of a general reference to the complementary nature of the Court into Article 1, see (n 95, 113, 140–141) and text in Ch III.

or conditions of application. Rather, they are of a programmatory nature and incorporate into the Statute the notion of complementarity as a general goal and a constitutional element on the basis of which the Court is envisaged to function. The Statute's Preamble and Article 1 thus establish 'complementarity' as a legal principle rather than as a legal rule.[3]

The absence of automatic legal consequences, subjects, detailed content and conditions of application in the Preamble and Article 1, however, does not preclude us from identifying generically the envisaged relation between national criminal jurisdictions and the ICC. The ordinary meaning of the adjective 'complementary' can generally be described as 'completing something else' or 'making a pair or a whole'. 'Complementarity', in turn, refers to a relation of different parts and denotes the condition of things that complement one another, while a 'complement' is generally understood as something that completes or perfects something else or supplies the other's deficiencies, or as something that, together with other things, forms a unit.[4] In light of the general meaning of the term employed, the ICC is thus envisaged to supply the deficiencies of national criminal jurisdictions, and together they form a unit in the enforcement of the prohibitions of ICC crimes.

A consideration of the references to the complementary nature of the ICC in the Preamble and Article 1 in the light of a number of preambular provisions further informs the understanding of the envisaged mutual roles of national criminal jurisdictions and the ICC. Thus the Preamble also asserts that the effective prosecution of the most serious crimes of concern to the international

---

[3] For the distinction between the two concepts of legal principles and legal rules, see R Dworkin, *Taking Rights Seriously* (Harvard University Press, Harvard 1977) 22–24, who explains at 24 that 'they differ in the character of the direction they give. Rules are applicable in an all-or-nothing fashion. If the facts a rule stipulates are given, then either the rule is valid, in which case the answer it supplies must be accepted, or it is not, in which case it contributes nothing to the decision.' Principles, on the other hand, 'do not set out legal consequences that follow automatically when the conditions provided are met'. (25). Rather, they incorporate into the law general goals and values, regularly specifying neither their subjects and their content in detail nor their conditions of application (22–23).

[4] Cf the Oxford English Dictionary. Besides these general meanings, the notion of complementarity also acquired more specific connotations in a number of areas. As an epistemological concept, complementarity has its origins in atomic physics. As such, it denotes that two descriptions, though incompatible because describing mutually exclusive observations, are both indispensable and together necessary for an exhaustive description because the conditions of observation influence the object under investigation. Such a conceptualization of complementarity is intrinsically linked to the name of Niels Bohr, a Danish physicist, who initially developed the notion as a response to the epistemological difficulties in understanding the nature of light: see N Bohr, *Atomic Physics and Human Knowledge* (Interscience Publishers, New York 1958) 74. The significance of Bohr's assertion was not confined to atomic physics, however, and was subsequently considered by him as a means to clarify epistemological problems in other sciences, including biology, psychology and philosophy, and was taken up by others in these and other fields. For an overview, see E Rasmussen, *Complementarity and Political Science—An Essay on Fundamentals of Political Science Theory and Research Strategy* (Odense University Press, Odense 1987) 4–12. Another area in which the concept of complementarity has been developed is the theory of colour: see J W Goethe, *Zur Farbenlehre*, 1810.

community as a whole 'must be ensured by taking measures at the national level and by enhancing international cooperation'.[5] The provision thus underlines that impunity must be fought on both fronts, national and international, and further encapsulates the idea that these two layers are mutually reinforcing, and neither the national nor the international component of the enforcement regime can achieve the ultimate aim 'to put an end to impunity for the perpetrators of these crimes and thus to contribute to the prevention of such crimes'.[6] Furthermore, the Preamble recalls 'the duty of every State to exercise its criminal jurisdiction over those responsible for international crimes'.[7] It therefore supposes that the suppression of international crimes in domestic courts is not merely a right but also an obligation of States. Indeed, one way of conceptualizing complementarity, suggested by the preambular reference to the duty to exercise jurisdiction over international crimes, is to understand it as the collective response of State Parties to situations in which States are unwilling or unable to live up to this duty.[8]

Read in conjunction with the aforementioned preambular provisions, the assertion that the ICC 'shall be complementary to national criminal jurisdictions' thus generally denotes a system of international criminal law enforcement that allocates to the latter the *primary responsibility* for the suppression of genocide, crimes against humanity and war crimes. The ICC only assumes the role of a 'permanent reserve court',[9] which completes the 'international criminal order',[10] while national criminal jurisdictions are regarded as remaining indispensable for achieving the ultimate goal of ending impunity. If one were to draw an analogy with existing concepts of jurisdiction, complementarity thus assigns to the ICC a task with some resemblance to the one fulfilled by national criminal jurisdictions basing themselves on the principle of *vicarious jurisdiction (stellvertretende Strafrechtspflege)* in the administration of criminal justice.[11]

---

[5] Rome Statute (n 1) Preambular para 4.

[6] Rome Statute (n 1) Paragraph 5 of the Preamble.

[7] Rome Statute (n 1) Paragraph 6 of the Preamble. The link between the duty to exercise jurisdiction and complementarity had been discussed during the drafting process of the relevant provisions: see eg *80*.

[8] For further discussion, see *Chapter VI: Complementarity and the Obligation to Investigate and Prosecute*, in particular *2. The Preamble*.

[9] A Bos, 'The Role of an International Criminal Court in the Light of the Principle of Complementarity' in E Denters and N Schrijver (eds), *Reflections on International Law from the Low Countries* (Kluwer, The Hague 1998) 249–259, 253.

[10] I Tallgren, 'Completing the "International Criminal Order"' (1998) 67 Nordic JIL 107–137.

[11] Cf eg Section 7 (2) Nr 2 of the German Criminal Code, according to which 'German criminal law shall apply to other acts, which were committed abroad if the act is punishable at the place of its commission or the place of its commission is subject to no criminal law enforcement and if the perpetrator: [. . .] 2. was a foreigner at the time of the act, was found to be in Germany and, although the Extradition Act would permit extradition for such an act, is not extradited, because a request for extradition is not made, is rejected, or the extradition is not practicable.' According to Geoff Gilbert, '[t]he idea behind this form of extraterritorial jurisdiction is that the State exercising it is "stepping into the shoes" of a State with a more pressing claim to prosecute': see G Gilbert, *Transnational Fugitive Offenders in International Law: Extradition and Other Mechanims* (Martinus Nijhoff Publishers, The Hague/Boston/London 1998) 486, 102. See also B Swart, 'La place des

3. Criteria for Admissibility: Articles 17 and 20 (3)

The *principle* of complementarity translates into the more specific legal *rules* of Articles 17 and 20 (3), which set forth the criteria for admissibility.[12] These provisions warrant a number of preliminary observations.

First, the *chapeau* of Article 17 (1) and Articles 17 (2) and (3) clarify that determinations of admissibility are to be made by *the Court*.[13] It is an independent assessment, with the Court as sole arbiter.[14] Declarations of a State referring a situation that has occurred or is occurring on its own territory (auto-referral) to the effect that it considers itself unable, as for instance that made by the Central African Republic,[15] are therefore not binding on the Court. While different organs of the Court,[16] namely the Prosecutor, the Pre-Trial Chamber, the Trial Chamber and the Appeals Chamber, have to *apply* the admissibility criteria, depending on the different procedural stages at which the question of admissibility arises,[17] the Court organs, which *decide on the correct application,* is the Court

critères traditionnels de compétence dans la pursuite des crimes internationaux' in A Cassese and M Delmas-Marty (eds), *Juridictions nationales et crimes internationaux* (Presses Universitaries de France, Paris 2002) 578–580. For the comparison of the principle of vicarious jurisdiction to the principle of complementarity, see F Lattanzi, 'The Rome Statute and State Sovereignty. ICC Competence, Jurisdictional Links, Trigger Mechanisms' in F Lattanzi and W Schabas (eds), *Essays on the Rome Statute of the International Criminal Court* (vol I Ripa Fagnano Alto, Editrice il Sirente 1999) 51–66, 52 ['ICC will perform judicial functions which are vicarious to the functions performed by States' jurisdictions.'].

[12] Cf Rome Statute (n 1) Article 17 (1), which opens with the words 'Having regard to paragraph 10 of the Preamble and article 1', before spelling out the admissibility criteria in more detail; see also M A Newton, 'Comparative Complementarity: Domestic Jurisdiction Consistent with the Rome Statute of the International Criminal Court' (2001) 167 Military Law Review 20–73, 52, referring to the admissibility criteria as implementing the complementarity principle. The need for such a translation into rules of admissibility emerged relatively early during the negotiations: see ILC, 'Report of the international Law Commission on the work of its 46th Session' UN GAOR 49th Session Supp No 10, UN Doc A/49/10, 29–194, 44 [3–4].

[13] Cf the *chapeau* of Rome Statute (n 1) Article 17 (1) ('the Court shall determine') and Articles 17 (2) and (3) ('the Court shall consider').

[14] J T Holmes, 'Complementarity: National Courts *versus* the ICC' in A Cassese, P Gaeta and J Jones (eds) *The Rome Statute of the International Criminal Court: A Commentary* (OUP, Oxford 2002) 667–686, 672.

[15] In its original referral, the *Cour de Cassation*, the country's highest judicial body, asserted that the national justice system was unable to carry out the complex proceedings necessary to investigate and prosecute the alleged crimes: see ICC OTP Press Release, ICC-OTP-PR-20070522-220_EN, 'Prosecutor opens investigation in the Central African Republic', 22 May 2007. See also the background note of the same date: <http://www.icc-cpi.int/library/press/pressreleases/ICC-OTP-BN-20070522–220_A_EN.pdf> 2–3.

[16] Rome Statute (n 1) Article 34 provides that the Court shall be composed of the Presidency, an Appeals Division, a Trial Division and a Pre-Trial Division, the Office of the Prosecutor and the Registry.

[17] For further analysis, see *Chapter V: The Procedural Setting of Complementarity*, in particular *2. The Procedural Phases of Admissibility.*

in its narrow sense, ie the adjudicative entities of the Pre-Trial, Trial and Appeals Chambers.[18]

Article 17 (1) then proceeds to regulate four different situations. The first three relate to investigations and prosecutions by a State that has jurisdiction over a case. They can be distinguished on the basis of what measures a State has taken and how far a case has progressed on the national level. More in particular, a distinction is made according to whether 'the case *is being* investigated or prosecuted',[19] 'the case *has been* investigated [. . .] and the State has decided not to prosecute the person concerned',[20] or '[t]he person concerned *has* already *been tried*'.[21] In these three situations, the inadmissibility of such cases is rebuttable under the following conditions. In the first situation, cases are admissible if 'the State is unwilling or unable genuinely to carry out the investigation or prosecution'.[22] In the second situation, a case is admissible when the decision not to prosecute resulted from the unwillingness or inability of the State genuinely to prosecute.[23] And in the third situation where a person has already been tried, the case is admissible on condition that the proceedings in the other court 'were for the purpose of shielding the person concerned from criminal responsibility for crimes within the jurisdiction of the Court; or otherwise were not conducted independently or impartially in accordance with the norms of due process recognized by international law and were conducted in a manner which, in the circumstances, was inconsistent with an intent to bring the person concerned to justice'.[24] The fourth situation, in which inadmissibility follows, is that '[t]he case is not of sufficient gravity to justify further action by the Court'.[25]

Before we turn to an analysis of these four grounds of inadmissibility, a number of elements of Article 17 (1), which have a bearing on it in its entirety, need to be addressed. These are: first, the question of whether Article 17 also applies in circumstances in which a State does not initiate an investigation and remains completely inactive; second, questions relating to the notion of the 'State' to which reference is made in the provision; and, third, which State or States are relevant in determining admissibility.

As to the first question, whether Article 17 also applies in *circumstances in which a State does not initiate an investigation and remains completely inactive*,[26] the first part of Article 17 (1)(a) refers to a case that is 'being investigated'. It thus

---

[18] M H Arsanjani, 'Reflections on the Jurisdiction and Trigger-Mechanism of the International Criminal Court' in H von Hebel, J Lammers and J Schukking (eds), *Reflections on the International Criminal Court—Essays in Honour of Adriaan Bos* (TMC Asser Press, The Hague 1999) 57–76, 68.

[19] Rome Statute (n 1) Article 17 (1)(a). See *3.1. Cases being investigated or prosecuted: Article 17 (1)(a)*.

[20] Rome Statute (n 1) Article 17 (1)(b). See *3.2. Cases having been investigated and the State has decided not to prosecute: Article 17 (1)(b)*.

[21] Rome Statute (n 1) Article 17 (1)(c). See *3.3. Ne bis in idem: Articles 17 (1)(c) and 20 (3)*.

[22] Rome Statute (n 1) Article 17 (1)(a).   [23] Rome Statute (n 1) Article 17 (1)(b).

[24] Rome Statute (n 1) Article 17 (1)(c) in conjunction with Article 20 (3).

[25] Rome Statute (n 1) Article 17 (1)(d). See *3.4. Insufficient gravity: Article 17 (1)(d)*.

[26] Such inaction has so far proved to be the rule: see J L Balint, 'Conflict, Conflict Victimization, And Legal Redress, 1945–1996 (1996) 59 Law and Contemporary Problems 4 231–247.

contemplates that at least initial steps are taken, such as establishing an investigative unit, securing the site of the alleged crime and collecting evidence.[27] In contrast, the second part of the same sentence provides as an exception that the case is admissible if 'the State is unwilling or unable genuinely to carry out the investigation', which could be read so as to cover equally situations in which no action is taken at all. Considered in isolation, the second part of the sentence would thus imply that Article 17 (1)(a) is of broader application than the first part. However, such an isolated reading would disregard the structure of Article 17 (1)(a) as a whole: the first part provides the rule to which the formulation 'unless the State is unwilling or unable genuinely to carry out the investigation or prosecution' is the exception. Using the terms '*the* investigation' rather than '*an* investigation' implies that the investigation is a specific one, namely the one that renders the case 'being investigated'. In other words, it is the investigation that has already begun and is underway. While subparagraph (a) thus begins to apply as soon as the very first investigative steps are taken, it does not address one situation: the situation in which a State fails to take even initial steps to investigate a case.

The ICC is nevertheless competent to deal with such cases of inaction. For, the Statute is based on the *premise that, as a rule, cases are admissible*, with Article 17 providing the exception (inadmissibility), which in turn can be rebutted by the formula of 'unwilling or unable'.[28] The grounds for rebutting inadmissibility, which are specified in subparagraphs (a) to (c), constitute an exhaustive list[29] of those cases to be admissible that are at least being investigated. In the absence of specific regulation by Article 17, or elsewhere in the Statute, cases are admissible. The following arguments support this general presumption of admissibility.

The *chapeau* of Article 17 (1) specifies the conditions under which a case is *inadmissible* rather than admissible. Were the Statute to be based on inadmissibility, Article 17 (1) would have to specify the conditions under which a case is

---

[27] The exact point in time at which one can speak of the initiation of an investigation depends on the regulation in national criminal (procedural) law and may thus differ from State to State. For example, when a national judicial system allows for criminal complaints to be lodged by (alleged) victims, it may be questionable to speak of an initiation if such a complaint has been lodged but no further steps have been taken by the relevant authorities. This may be different if, in contrast, an interview of the alleged victim follows the lodging of a complaint. Decisive will be that the relevant State authorities take some form of action.

[28] MA Summers, 'A Fresh Look at the Jurisdictional Provisions of the Statute of the International Criminal Court: The Case for Scrapping the Treaty' (2001) 20 Wisconsin ILJ 57–88, 69 ('statutory scheme of the ICC presumes admissibility'); J Meissner, *Die Zusammenarbeit mit dem Internationalen Strafgerichtshof nach dem Römischen Statut* (Verlag C H Beck, Munich 2003) 70–71.

[29] S A Williams, '*Commentary on Article 17*' in 8 *Triffterer (ed), Commentary on the Rome Statute of the International Criminal Court—Observers' Notes, Article by Article* (Nomos, Baden-Baden (1999) 393; J T Holmes (n 14) 675; M Benzing, 'The Complementarity Regime for the International Criminal Court: International Criminal Justice between State Sovereignty and the Fight against Impunity' (2003) 7 Max Planck UNYB 591–632. For a different view, see F Razesberger, *The International Criminal Court—The Principle of Complementarity* (Peter Lang, Frankfurt/Main 2006) 42.

admissible.[30] Furthermore, an assumption of inadmissibility would contradict the Statute's object and purpose as they flow from the Preamble. Paragraph 4 of the Preamble affirms that 'the most serious crimes of concern to the international community as a whole must not go unpunished and that their effective prosecution must be ensured by taking measures at the national level and by enhancing international cooperation.' It thus spells out the object of the Statute, namely the 'effective prosecution [...] by taking measures at the national level and by enhancing international cooperation', whereby it underlines that not all crimes committed can in practice be prosecuted before the ICC, but that measures on the national level are necessary to achieve this object.[31] Preambular paragraph 5, on the other hand, clarifies that the object of effective prosecution is to fulfil the ultimate purpose to 'put an end to impunity for the perpetrators of these crimes and thus to contribute to the prevention of such crimes.'

This object of effective prosecution, and the purpose of ending impunity, would clearly be significantly undermined if cases in which States remained completely inactive were inadmissible. Such an understanding would create an immense gap through which perpetrators could escape punishment precisely because States had abstained from doing anything. It would contradict the very premise on which the ICC is based, namely that the *exercise* in good faith of jurisdiction by States divests it from declaring cases admissible. A teleological interpretation of Article 17 thus equally suggests that cases are admissible if Article 17 does not provide otherwise. Such an interpretation is further supported by Article 18 (2), which limits the right to request a deferral and thus invoke complementarity to States that *are investigating* or *have investigated*. In a similar vein, the right to challenge the admissibility of a case under Article 19 (2)(b) is reserved to States which *are investigating or prosecuting* the case or *have investigated or prosecuted*.[32]

In sum, complete inaction on the national level would thus allow the ICC to take up a case without having to enter into an assessment of the admissibility criteria in Article 17 (1)(a) to (c). The provisions on complementarity only apply once a State takes, at the minimum, initial investigative steps.[33]

---

[30] See also C Stahn, 'Complementarity, Amnesties and Alternative Forms of Justice: Some Interpretative Guidelines for the International Criminal Court' (2005) 3 *JICJ* 695–720, 709 ['Article 17 must be interpreted narrowly, since it is drafted in negative fashion. It regulates exceptions to the principle of admissibility ("the Court shall determine that a case is inadmissible where") and exceptions to the exception (unwillingness and inability to investigate or prosecute). This structure implies that a case is generally admissible before the Court, unless the conditions of a ground of inadmissibility are fulfilled.'].

[31] O Triffterer, 'Preamble' in O Triffterer (ed) (n 29) 11–12, margins 13–14.

[32] For further analysis, see *Chapter V: The Procedural Setting of Complementarity, 2.2. Preliminary Rulings Regarding Admissibility: Article 18 and 2.3. Challenges to the Admissibility of a Case: Article 19.*

[33] See also J T Holmes, 'The Principle of Complementarity' in R S Lee (ed), *The International Criminal Court, The making of the Rome Statute, Issues, Negotiations, Results* (Kluwer Law Publ, The Hague 1999) 77 [It is clear that the Statute's provisions on complementarity are intended to refer to criminal investigations. Thus, where no such investigation occurred, the Court would be free to act]; Paper on some policy issues before the Office of the Prosecutor,

With regard to the second question, the references in Article 17 (1)(a) and (b) to *the State* as the object of a determination of unwillingness or inability need to be clarified. These provisions denote that States are considered as monolithic entities, without differentiating between the sub-organs involved in investigating, prosecuting and adjudicating cases of core crimes, such as police, prosecution services, criminal courts, or between different branches of government. Yet, the reality is often more complex, as State organs do not necessarily behave consistently.[34] If, for example, a blanket amnesty is granted by the executive or the legislature, thereby demonstrating its unwillingness, it is conceivable that the judiciary nevertheless remains (partly) *willing* to investigate and prosecute. Rather, judicial organs would be *unable* to proceed with an investigation and prosecution because, as a matter of national law, they have to apply the amnesty.[35] Another example would be where the military prevents investigations or prosecutions

available at <http://www.icc-cpi.int/library/organs/otp/030905_Policy_Paper.pdf> (2003) 4 ['There is no impediment to the admissibility of a case before the Court where no State has initiated any investigation'.]; Informal Expert Paper for the ICC Office of the Prosecutor: The Principle of Complementarity in Practice, available at <http://www.icc-cpi.int/library/organs/otp/complementarity.pdf>, 7, [17–18]; 'Report of the International Criminal Court to the United Nations General Assembly' (1 August 2005) UN Doc A/60/177 [2]; C Cárdenas, *Die Zulässigkeitsprüfung vor dem Internationalen Strafgerichtshof, Zur Auslegung des Art. 17 IstGH-Statut unter besonderer Berücksichtigung von Amnestien und Wahrheitskommissionen* (Berliner Wissenschaftsverlag, Berlin 2005) 57; B Broomhall, *International Justice and the International Criminal Court: Between Sovereignty and the Rule of Law* (OUP, Oxford 2004) 90–91; S Morel, *La Mise en Oeuvre du Principe de la Complémentarité par la Cour Pénale Internationale—Le Cas Particulier des Amnisties* (PhD thesis, University of Lausanne, Lausanne 2005) 93; P Akhavan, 'The Lord's Resistance Army Case: Uganda's Submission of the First State Referral to the International Criminal Court' (2005) 99 AJIL 403–421, 414; F Razesberger (n 29) 29–30; Pre-Trial Chamber I, Decision Concerning Pre-Trial Chamber I's Decision of 10 February 2006 and the Incorporation of Documents into the Record of the Case against Mr Thomas Lubanga Dyilo, 24 February 2006, Unsealed pursuant to Decision ICC-01/04-01/06-37, ICC-01/04-01/06-8-US-Corr [29].

[34] For a discussion of an alternative model, in which State organs bear international obligations and recent jurisprudence of international courts in support of such a model, see W Ferdinandusse, 'Out of the Black-box? The international obligation of state organs' (2003) 29 Brooklyn Journal of International Law 45–127.

[35] This is notwithstanding the possibility that judicial organs may set aside such amnesties due to their incompatibility with international obligations binding upon the State. If the domestic legal system in question allows for such a possibility, and the judicial organs do not make use of it, it could equally amount to unwillingness, provided the requisite elements of Article 17 (2) are met. Lacking such possibility, however, judicial organs would probably have to be considered 'unable' in the meaning of Article 17 (3). The lack of such possibility may also result from an amnesty law that specifically bars courts from second-guessing its validity. For an example, see the Second Peruvian Amnesty Law No 26492 of 28 June 1995, which declared in Article 2 that an amnesty granted is not subject to review by a judicial authority and in Article 3 stipulated that all Judicial Bodies are under the obligation to apply the general amnesty. Moreover, it expanded the scope of the First Amnesty Law No 26479 of 14 June 1995, granting a general amnesty to all military, police or civilian officials who might be the subject of indictments for human rights violations committed between 1980 and 1995, even though they had not been charged. The effect of the second law was to prevent the judges from determining the legality or applicability of the first amnesty law. For an examination of the compatibility of these laws with Peru's human rights obligations under the Inter-American Convention, see the *Barrios Altos Case*, Judgment of 14 May 2001, IACtHR (Ser C) No 75 (2001), [41–44], available at <http://www1.umn.edu/humanrts/iachr/C/75-ing.html>.

from being carried out against its members, thus effectively blocking the bona fide efforts of the judiciary to carry out proceedings.[36] These examples demonstrate that being 'unwilling' or 'unable' are not mutually exclusive and that a *State*—considered as a whole—may be both at the same time, depending on the attitude of its composite organs.[37] Conversely, however, a State cannot hide behind the positive attitude of one organ in order to have cases declared inadmissible. A domestic criminal court, which meets the criterion of 'willingness', for instance, does not shield the State as a whole from failing the admissibility test, if the police force is unwilling or unable because it fails to arrest the suspect for which that court has issued an arrest warrant. Once an accountability gap that amounts to 'unwillingness' or 'inability' exists, it is irrelevant whether such gap emanates from one or more organs, and the State, as a whole is held 'unwilling' or 'unable' or, indeed, both simultaneously. The analysis of what individual State organs do, or do not do, stands central in the assessment of the (un)willingness and (in)ability of a State.

In addition, the term 'State' in Article 17 (1)(a) and (b) raises the question of whether, and to what extent, it encompasses investigations, prosecutions and decisions not to prosecute by *international and internationalized criminal justice mechanisms*.[38] If such mechanisms involve foreign investigators, prosecutors and judges and take place under the auspices of the UN, as for instance in Kosovo and East Timor, can investigations and prosecutions be considered to be conducted 'by a State'? A similar question would arise if two or more States Parties were to agree to set up an *international* criminal court with jurisdiction over ICC crimes, or if the Security Council set up such a tribunal.

One criterion that can be used in finding an answer to these questions is the degree to which international and regional organizations assume control over the establishment and judicial process of that court. Another determinant is whether, and to what extent, the respective courts are integrated into the domestic legal system of a State.[39] At one end of the spectrum, investigations and prosecutions

---

[36] See for an example the case of General (retired) Fernando Millán, former Commander, Fifth Brigade, for Colombia: Amnesty International, Human Rights Watch and Washington Office on Latin America, 'Colombia Human Rights Certification II', January 2001, on file with author, 5 ['When the Attorney General's Office investigated this case, the army high command prevented prosecutors from questioning Millán, then interposed a jurisdictional dispute, claiming that since Millán was on active service and carrying out his official duties, the case should be tried before a military tribunal. Following a decision by the CSJ, the case was transferred to the military justice system in October 1998. A prosecutor assigned to investigate the May 1998 massacre of eleven people in Barrancabermeja fled the country after receiving threats from General Millán, then-Commander of the Fifth Brigade.'].

[37] See also in this vein the Informal Expert Paper for the ICC Office of the Prosecutor: The Principle of Complementarity in Practice (n 33) 14 [45].

[38] Note that vis-à-vis a completed trial in another court, Article 20 (3) employs broader wording in as much as it only refers to a trial 'by another court': see *125*.

[39] L A Dickinson, 'The Promise of Hybrid Courts' (2003) 97 AJIL 295–310, 309; E Higonnet, 'Restructuring Hybrid Courts: Local Empowerment and National Criminal Justice Reform' (1 March, 2005), *Yale Law School Student Scholarship Series*. Paper 6, available at <http://lsr.nellco.org/

through a fully international criminal tribunal imposed on a State against its will, for instance through Chapter VII measures of the Security Council, would thus presumably fall outside the notion of cases 'being investigated or prosecuted *by a State*' or cases having been investigated '*by a State* [which] has decided not to prosecute the person concerned' and would thus also fall outside the framework of Article 17(1)(a) and (b).[40] Such tribunals could also not be considered to take 'national' decisions in the sense of Article 17 (2)(a) or be regarded as part of a State's 'national judicial system' to which Article 17 (3) refers. At the other end of the spectrum, it would seem that the notion of 'a State' could encompass investigations or prosecutions conducted by internationalized organs that are fully integrated in the domestic judicial system[41] and are established by, and operate under, the overall control of the State concerned.[42]

It remains to be seen, however, how exactly the question of what constitutes 'a State', and whether and to what extent international(ized) investigations and prosecutions fall into that notion, will be answered in between these two ends of the spectrum. It would seem that the aforementioned criteria of control and integration, for instance, would not lead to clear-cut results vis-à-vis such internationalized criminal courts as those established in the context of UN transitional administrations, such as in Kosovo and East Timor.[43]

---

cgi/viewcontent.cgi?article=1005&context=yale/student> 70, 66. But see M Benzing, and M Bergsmo, 'Some Tentative Remarks on the Relationship Between Internationalized Criminal Jurisdictions and the International Criminal Court' in C Romano, A Nollkaemper and J K Kleffner (eds), *International Criminal Courts: Sierra Leane, East Timor, Kosovo, and Combodia* (OUP, Oxford 2004) 407–416, 412, who consider some national involvement to be sufficient.

[40] C Cárdenas (n 33) 60.

[41] Cf Art 2 of the Law on the Establishment of Extraordinary Chambers in the Courts of Cambodia for the Prosecution of Crimes Committed During the Period of Democratic Kampuchea; Art 2 of the Draft Agreement of 17 March 2003 between the United Nations and the Royal Government of Cambodia concerning the Prosecution under Cambodian Law of Crimes committed during the Period of Democratic Kampuchea, which provides that the Extraordinary Chambers will be established in the existing court structure of Cambodia. The Extraordinary Chambers are thus regular Cambodian courts, albeit with some special features, in particular in terms of their composition and the applicable law. On the relationship between national and internationalized courts and the degree to which the latter can be considered to form part of the former, see J K Kleffner and A Nollkaemper, 'The Relationship between Internationalized Courts and National Courts' in C Romano, A Noilkaemper and JK Kleffner (eds), *International Criminal Courts: Sierra Leone, East Timor, Kosovo, and Combodia* (OUP, Oxford 2004).

[42] Cf the discussion of what constitutes a 'national court' within the meaning of Rule 11 *bis* of the Rules of Procedure and Evidence of the ICTY (cf n 59 in Chapter III and text), in *Prosecutor v R Stankovic* (Decision on Referral of Case under Rule 11 *bis*) IT-96-23/2-PT (17 May 2005) 26 ['the phrase 'national court' [means] a court of or pertaining to a nation. The State Court of Bosnia and Herzegovina, of which the War Crimes Chamber is a component, is a court which has been established pursuant to the statutory law of Bosnia and Herzegovina. It is thus a court of Bosnia and Herzegovina, a 'national court.' Bosnia and Herzegovina has chosen to include in the composition of the State Court judges who are not nationals of Bosnia and Herzegovina. That is a matter determined by the legislative authorities of Bosnia and Herzegovina. The inclusion of some non-nationals among the judges of the State Court does not make that court any less a 'national court' of Bosnia and Herzegovina.']. See also C Cárdenas (n 33) 60.

[43] This is amply demonstrated in a dispute between the Government of the Democratic Republic of East Timor and the UN in connection to the indictment of, amongst others, former Indonesian

In a similar vein, the term 'State' excludes those investigations, prosecutions and decisions not to prosecute carried out or taken by non-State actors on the sub-statal level, most notably *organized armed groups,* which are parties to non-international armed conflicts. While this might appear self-evident, a closer look at the legal framework applicable to non-international armed conflicts and the realities in (some) such armed conflicts reveals that this may not be as obvious as it seems. International law recognizes that commanders and superiors of organized armed groups also have certain responsibilities 'to suppress' international crimes committed by their subordinates or to submit such matters 'to the competent authorities for investigation and prosecution'.[44] This follows from the doctrine of command responsibility, which is applicable in international and non-international armed conflicts alike.[45] At times, such responsibilities are also reflected, to varying degrees, by the situation on the ground, namely when organized armed groups dispose of suppressive mechanisms and authorities for investigation and prosecution of (international) crimes.[46] However, regardless of the question of whether such authorities can be considered 'competent'—given

Minister of Defence and Security and Commander of the Armed Forces of Indonesia General Wiranto by prosecutors from Dili's Serious Crimes Unit. On 24 February 2003, UN Spokesperson Mr Fred Eckhard stated that 'those indictments were issued by the Office of the Prosecutor General of Timor-Leste, and not by the United Nations, which merely provides advisory assistance...So, we hope that in the future you'll say, "East Timor indicts", and not "the United Nations indicts".' Daily Press Briefing by the Office of the Spokesman for the Secretary-General, 25 February 2003. This stance was later criticized by civil society. For instance, the National Alliance for an International Tribunal for East Timor, in a letter dated 13 March 2003, addressed to the UN High Commissioner for Human Rights, Mr Sergio Viera de Mello, expressed 'gravest concern' over Eckhard's statements. They pointed out that it was incorrect to say that the indictment had been issued by East Timor alone, because it originated from a 'mixed tribunal, and internationalised court' which includes East Timorese and international staff working together, applying a system of national and international law. The National Alliance derived from this fact that 'one can not say that the indictment issued by the Serious Crimes Unit was issued by East Timor alone. This indictment was issued by the Government of East Timor and the United Nations': National Alliance for International Tribunal Letter to UN High Commissioner for Human Rights (13 March 2003), available at <http://www.etan.org/et2003/march/21/13natnl.htm>.

[44] Cf Rome Statute (n 1) Article 28 (a)(ii) and (b)(iii).

[45] Cf Rome Statute (n 1) Article 28, establishing the responsibility of commanders and superiors for 'crimes within the jurisdiction of the Court', which include crimes committed in internal armed conflicts (cf Rome Statute (n 1) Article 8 (2)(c) and (e)) and expressly referring to 'military commander or person effectively acting as a military commander' (Rome Statute (n 1) Article 28 (a)) and other 'superior and subordinate relationships' (Rome Statute (n 1) Article 28 (b)). For an overview and analysis of the jurisprudence of the two ad hoc tribunals, see E van Sliedregt, The Criminal Responsibility of Individuals for Violations of International Humanitarian Law (TMC Asser Press, The Hague 2003) 175–179, demonstrating that their jurisprudence is evidence that '[c]onflict classification is not relevant as a jurisdictional prerequisite in triggering the application of superior responsibility'. Ibid 179.

[46] A pertinent example is the conflict in El Salvador, in which the FMLN operated its own penal system: see L Zegveld, *Accountability of Armed Opposition Groups in International Law* (CUP 2002) 70–74. More recently, it has also been reported that the Taleban in Afghanistan have subjected the population under their control to quasi-judicial processes: see Amnesty International, 'Afghanistan: All who are not friends, are enemies: Taleban abuses against civilians', AI Index: ASA 11/001/2007, 19 April 2007 at 5.1. Another example are the so-called 'People's Courts' established by the Maoist insurgents (CPN-M) during the Nepalese armed conflict: see J Somer,

that they regularly meet serious objections from a standpoint of impartiality and independence[47]—the availability of such measures do not qualify as investigations, prosecutions and decisions not to prosecute by a 'State'.

It nevertheless needs to be borne in mind that nothing would seem to divest the ICC from the possibility to exercise its jurisdiction in cases where organized armed groups or international(ized) criminal courts, whose proceedings cannot be considered to be conducted 'by a State', carry out proceedings. This follows from our earlier finding that in the absence of specific regulation in Article 17, or elsewhere in the Statute, cases are admissible.[48] As far as international(ized) criminal courts are concerned, it can reasonably be expected, however—and the ICC would in fact be well advised—to assume jurisdiction only when such international(ized) criminal courts prove to be unwilling or unable to investigate and prosecute. Given the ICC's limited capacity and resources, it will have to conceive of itself as part of a larger, multi-layered system of international criminal justice, which includes international(ized) criminal courts, in order to achieve its objective of ending impunity.[49]

As to the third question, which State or States are relevant in determining admissibility, the only hint that Article 17 (1) provides is the reference to an investigation or prosecution by '*a State which has jurisdiction over [a case]*' in subparagraphs (a) and (b).[50] Which, then, are the States that have jurisdiction over a case? This question can only be answered after having determined what is meant by 'jurisdiction'.

'*Jurisdiction*' generally denotes the extent of each State's right to regulate conduct or the consequences of events and the actual regulation of a State in that

---

'Jungle justice: passing sentence on the equality of belligerents in non-international armed conflict' (2007) 89 IRRC 655–690, 681–682.

[47] Accordingly, international bodies have focused on rules of fair trial, which restrain prosecutions and punishments by non-State actors, rather than calling on the latter to prosecute persons suspected of serious violations of international humanitarian law: ibid 68. See also the reaction of Leandro Despouy, the UN Special Rapporteur on the independence of judges and lawyers, to quasi-judicial proceedings carried out by the Taleban: UNCHR Press Release: 'UN Special Rapporteur On Independence Of Judiciary Condemns Public Execution Following Illegal Trial In Afghanistan, 8 June 2006, <http://www.unhchr.ch/huricane/huricane.nsf/view01/5D75CF314F0C8AA7C1257187002F10CD?opendocument>.

[48] Cf *104–105*.

[49] M Benzing and M Bergsmo (n 39) 408–409; Informal Expert Paper for the ICC Office of the Prosecutor: The Principle of Complementarity in Practice (n 33), 5 [9]; C Cárdenas (n 33) 60.

[50] Other provisions of the Statute, which use identical terms, do not elucidate the concept of 'jurisdiction' either. Paragraph 6 of the Preamble only refers generally to 'criminal jurisdiction'. Rome Statute (n 1) Article 18 (1) is similarly vague when it states that the Prosecutor has to notify 'all States Parties and those States which, taking into account the information available, would normally exercise jurisdiction over the crimes concerned'. Likewise, Rome Statute (n 1) Article 19 (2) grants the right to challenge the admissibility of a case to 'a State which has jurisdiction over a case'. For further discussion of the relevant provisions in Article 18 and 19, see *Chapter V: The Procedural Setting of Complementarity, 2.2. Preliminary Rulings Regarding Admissibility: Article 18 and 2.3. Challenges to the Admissibility of a Case: Article 19.*

regard.[51] Traditionally, one distinguishes various *forms* of jurisdiction, according to the *trias politica*, namely legislative, judicial or executive jurisdiction. As far as criminal jurisdiction is concerned, one can additionally distinguish the jurisdiction of different *organs* involved in different phases of criminal proceedings, such as the phase of apprehending a suspect and the investigative, prosecutorial and adjudicative phase. Furthermore, jurisdiction has both an international and a national law *connotation*, the former referring to the permissible limits of a State's jurisdiction and the latter to the extent to which, and manner in which, the State in fact asserts its jurisdiction.[52] With these various facets of jurisdiction in mind, the references in Article 17 (1) to 'a State which has jurisdiction over a case' could thus mean various things, ranging from 'a State which has the right under international law to legislate with regard to conduct as is at stake in the case under consideration', to 'a State which has in fact asserted the right to execute the decisions of its courts with regard to the case under consideration'.

It is clear from the reach of Article 17 (1) what *forms* of jurisdiction the provision envisages, namely the jurisdiction to investigate, prosecute and adjudicate, because the provision is concerned only with investigations, prosecutions and trials.

More difficult to determine is, however, whether the provision contemplates jurisdiction in its *national or* its *international connotation*, or indeed both. The question therefore arises as to whether the jurisdiction to investigate and prosecute is the jurisdiction that a State has in fact asserted, or whether it refers to the jurisdiction that a State is permitted—or obliged—to establish under international law.[53] The first alternative would involve in the process of determining admissibility only those States that could, as a matter of their national law, exercise jurisdiction. Thus, when a person that is alleged to having committed a core crime within the jurisdiction of the ICC is present in the territory of a State, but preliminary investigative steps reveal that the investigative or prosecutorial authorities cannot proceed because they lack jurisdiction—for instance, because the case could only proceed on the basis of universal jurisdiction, while such jurisdictional basis is lacking under national law[54]—such a State would not qualify as 'a State which has jurisdiction' for the purpose of determining admissibility. The second alternative would require a determination of admissibility with regard to all States that possess jurisdiction to investigate and prosecute under

[51] R Jennings and A Watts, *Oppenheim's International Law* (9th edn, vol 1 Longman, London 1996) 456.

[52] Ibid 456–457.

[53] On the question of whether and to what extent international law permits or obliges States to establish jurisdiction, see *Chapter II: National Suppression of Core Crimes, 2.1. Applicable Law. Governing the National Suppression of Core Crimes.*

[54] This could be the case, for instance, if a State finds on its territory a person alleged to have committed grave breaches of the Geneva Conventions, while no further link such as territoriality or (active or passive) nationality to that State exists, and the national law of the latter does not allow it to exercise jurisdiction in these cases.

international law. In the present example, the State would thus be 'a State which has jurisdiction'[55] within the meaning of Article 17 (1), and the Court would have to determine that such a State is either 'unwilling' or 'unable' in order to declare the case admissible.[56]

In order to determine whether Article 17 (1) refers to jurisdiction in its national or international connotation, an important starting point is to consider the assumption on which complementarity is based, namely that States have the possibility to exercise jurisdiction and have taken at least initial investigative steps. It is this instance of concurrence of jurisdiction between the ICC and national criminal jurisdictions that underlies the regulation of admissibility in Article 17. Only the exercise of jurisdiction, taken in good faith, divests the ICC from jurisdiction. Decisive for the ambit of permissible action of national investigative or prosecutorial authorities is that jurisdiction be available under national law.[57] Without such jurisdiction, these authorities cannot proceed and no concurrence of jurisdiction can arise. Assessing the willingness or ability in these situations would thus be a futile exercise. Rather than reinforcing the role of States in the enforcement of the prohibition of the core crimes, it would seek a role for them where they do not have one. Such an understanding finds further support in Articles 18 and 19, which include in the procedure for admissibility only those States that *exercise* jurisdiction.[58] The foregoing discussion suggests that when referring to 'jurisdiction', Article 17 (1) of the Statute refers to the jurisdiction that a State has actually established, and thus a to jurisdiction in its national connotation.

However, this is not the end of the matter. Interpreting 'jurisdiction' exclusively in this manner would disregard an important function of the ICC and its complementarity regime: by deferring to 'a State which has jurisdiction over a case', the ICC endows that State with the presumptive pedigree of being willing

---

[55] Recall that the relevant provisions of the Geneva Conventions *oblige* States to establish and exercise jurisdiction on the basis of the principle of *aut dedere aut judicare*, see *10–11*.

[56] For arguments that could lead one to conclude that legislative gaps, including the lack of jurisdiction under national law, constitutes 'inability', see *3.6. Inability: Article 17 (3)*.

[57] It should be noted, however, that the means of implementing jurisdiction varies considerably, with some States only generally referring to international law for that purpose, while others adopt more specific provisions for individual crimes. The point here is that national authorities need a rule of national law—be it constitutional, statutory or based on common law—which stipulates the available bases for assuming jurisdiction.

[58] More specifically, these provisions refer to 'States which, taking into account the information available, would normally exercise jurisdiction' (Rome Statute (n 1) Article 18 (1)), 'a State [...] that [...] is investigating or has investigated its nationals or others within its jurisdiction' (Rome Statute (n 1) Article 18 (2)) and '[a] State which has jurisdiction over a case, on the ground that it is investigating or prosecuting the case or has investigated or prosecuted' (Rome Statute (n 1) Article 19(2)(b)). On the latter, see also J T Holmes (n 33) 67 [addition that a State must have jurisdiction in the case reflects intention of drafters of the Statute to prevent a State from challenging admissibility when in fact investigation or prosecution was sure to fail because the State lacked jurisdiction as far as its own courts are concerned].

and able whereby it would enhance the legitimacy of the national proceedings.[59] The legitimacy of national proceedings would be seriously undermined, however, if the ICC deferred to States that, while willing and able, have established jurisdiction in violation of international law.[60] Conversely, the legitimacy of national proceedings will be preserved only if the ICC defers cases to States, which have the legal right, under international law, to exercise jurisdiction. In order to do so, the term 'jurisdiction' thus needs to be understood to refer to jurisdiction in its international connotation. Although exactly what forms of jurisdiction conform to international law cannot be derived from the Statute, the application of the phrase 'a State which has jurisdiction over a case' would thereby also bear the potential to incidentally and gradually clarify the boundaries of permissibility under international law.

It follows from the foregoing discussion that the phrase 'a State which has jurisdiction over a case' refers to States which have established domestic jurisdiction in conformity with international law.

With these preliminary observations in mind, we now turn to an analysis of the four different grounds of inadmissibility.

---

[59] See further *Chapter VII: Complementarity as a Catalyst for Compliance, 2. The Legitimacy of Complementarity.*

[60] Maybe the most pertinent example in that regard would be the case in which States establish universal jurisdiction in ways that go beyond what is permissible under international law. It should be noted in that regard that the exact meaning of 'universal jurisdiction' remains a matter of dispute. Considerable differences exist in national and international judicial decisions, national implementing legislation and academic writings. While the term can be defined loosely as 'criminal jurisdiction based solely on the nature of the crime, without regard to where the crime was committed, the nationality of the alleged or convicted perpetrator, the nationality of the victim, or any other connection to the state exercising such jurisdiction' (cf Principle 1 (1) of the Princeton Project on Universal Jurisdiction, The Princeton Principles on Universal Jurisdiction (2001), available at <http://www.law.depaul.edu/centers_institutes/ihrli/downloads/Princeton%20 principles.pdf>), it is particularly controversial whether and to what extent it encompasses universal jurisdiction *in absentia*. Treaty-based universal jurisdiction regularly takes the form of principles.pdf> *aut dedere aut judicare* and thus would seem to require the presence of the suspect or accused. For comprehensive treatment of the subject of universal jurisdiction, see M Henzelin, *Le Principe de l'Universalité en Droit Pénal International, Droit et Obligation pour les États de poursuivre et juger selon le principe de l'universalité* (Helbin & Lichtenhahn, Munich, Geneva, Brussels 2000); L Reydams, *Universal jurisdiction: international and municipal legal perspectives* (OUP, Oxford 2003). See also R O'Keefe, 'Universal Jurisdiction: Clarifying the Basic Concept' (2004) 2 JICJ 735–760. For a synthesis of a number of national approaches, see D Vandermeersch, 'La compétence universelle' in A Cassese and M Delmas-Marty (n 11) 589–611; see also Amnesty International, 'Universal Jurisdiction—The Duty to Enact and Implement Legislation', AI Index IOR 53/002-018/2001, September 2001. Although the ICJ judgment in *Case Concerning the Arrest Warrant of 11 April 2000* (*Democratic Republic of the Congo v Belgium*) [2002] ICJ Rep 3 did not address the issue, a number of declarations, dissenting and separate opinions demonstrate the disagreement of what constitutes universal jurisdiction: see notably Separate Opinion of President Guillaume; Declaration de M Ranjeva; Joint Separate Opinion of Judges Higgins, Kooijmans and Buergenthal [19–65]; Opinion Individuelle de M Rezek, Dissenting Opinion of Judge van den Wyngaert [44–67]. On universal jurisdiction *in absentia,* see M El Zeidy, 'Universal Jurisdiction in Absentia: Is it a Legal Valid Option for Suppressing International Crimes?' (2003) 37 The International Lawyer 835–861; R Rabinovitch, 'Universal Jurisdiction in Absentia' (2005) 28 Fordham International Law Journal 500–530.

3.1. Cases being investigated or prosecuted: Article 17 (1)(a)

Once initial investigative steps have been taken, Article 17 (1)(a) applies. It provides that a case is inadmissible where it 'is being investigated or prosecuted by a State which has jurisdiction over it, unless the State is unwilling or unable genuinely to carry out the investigation or prosecution'. The wording of this provision warrants some clarification.

Article 17 (1)(a) states that, in order for cases to be admissible despite the fact that they are investigated or prosecuted by a State, the State concerned needs to be 'unwilling or unable *genuinely* to carry out the investigation or prosecution'. A preliminary question that arises is whether the term 'genuinely' modifies the verb 'to carry out' or the words 'is unwilling or unable'.[61] In the first hypothesis, the term would increase the threshold of inadmissibility, in as much as it would not only have to be proven that the investigation or prosecution is being or has been carried out, but also that it is being or has been carried out 'genuinely'. In the second hypothesis, the term would increase the threshold of admissibility, because it would not suffice to prove that a State is 'unwilling' or 'unable', but also that the State is 'genuinely' so unwilling or unable. A number of authors have adopted the latter understanding[62] or have understood the term 'genuinely' to only qualify inability.[63] However, while this might be said to find some support in the drafting history of Article 17,[64] two arguments militate against this interpretation. The first argument follows from an interpretation of the term taken in

---

[61] cf L N Sadat and S R Carden, 'The New International Criminal Court: An Uneasy Revolution' (2000) 88 Georgetown LJ 418 ['Does "genuinely" refer to situations where the State's motives are not "genuine" (ie are duplicitous or disingenuous) or situations where the State is 'really' unable or unwilling to prosecute?'].

[62] J T Holmes (n 14) 674 ['[T]he term "genuinely" is attached in Rome Statute (n 1) Article 17 *to both the concepts of unwillingness and inability*. Thus, if doubts are raised about the willingness or ability of a State to investigate or prosecute a case, the entity [fn: Normally, this would be the Prosecutor contesting the State's claim of a *genuine investigation or prosecution*,...] making the allegation must establish to the Court's satisfaction that *the investigation or prosecution was not genuine*.']. See also M El Zeidy, 'The Principle of Complementarity: A New Machinery to Implement International Criminal Law' (2002) 23 Michigan JIL 900 [asserting that the term 'genuinely' refers 'to situations where the State *is really unable or unwilling* to proceed']. M A Newton (n 12) 54 [term 'genuinely' refers to a state being ' "genuinely unwilling" or "genuinely unable" ']. W Schabas, *An Introduction to the International Criminal Court* (2nd edn CUP, Cambridge 2004) 87 ['genuine unwillingness']. F Meyer, 'Complementing Complementarity' (2006) 6 International Criminal Law Review 549–583, 566 ['[...] term 'genuinely' as an attachment to both concepts, inability and unwillingness, to ensure the most objective reading. That suggests 'genuinely' refers to situations where the State *is really unable or unwilling to proceed*.'] All emphases added.

[63] R B Philips, 'The International Criminal Court Statute: Jurisdiction and Admissibility' (1999) 10 Criminal Law Forum, Special Issue on the ICC, 61–85, 77 ['If a State will not *or genuinely cannot* conduct a good faith investigation or prosecution, then the ICC may exercise jurisdiction over the case.'] Emphasis added.

[64] Cf pages 85–86.

its context,[65] which, amongst others, requires identical terms used in different places in a treaty to be presumed to bear the same meaning in each.[66] The term 'genuinely' in Article 17 (1)(b), however, which reads in the relevant parts '[...] unless the decision resulted from the unwillingness or inability of the State *genuinely to prosecute*',[67] clearly relates to the way in which a prosecution is carried out.[68] The second argument is a comparison with the French language version of Article 17(1)(a).[69] It provides that cases are inadmissible '*à moins que cet État n'ait pas la volonté ou soit dans l'incapacité de mener véritablement à bien l'enquête ou les poursuites*', which leaves no doubt that the words '*véritablement à bien*' relate to the words '*mener... l'enquête ou les poursuites*'.[70] These arguments support the view that the term 'genuinely' relates to the phrase 'to carry out the investigation or prosecution'. Such an interpretation overrides a possible conflicting interpretation by reference to its drafting history, which is only a supplementary means of interpretation.[71]

However, the very meaning of the term 'genuinely' also needs to be determined. It replaced alternative proposals that were considered during the drafting process of the provision, and was seen by some delegations as being more objective.[72] While one may doubt whether this assertion withstands scrutiny,[73] the adjective 'genuine' denotes that something is 'properly so called' and 'not a sham',[74] and is also at times described by a myriad of other words ranging from 'actual', 'authentic' and 'bona fide' to 'honest', 'legitimate', 'original', 'pure', 'real', 'sound' and 'true'.[75] John T Holmes recalls that during the negotiations that took place prior to the Rome Conference, he referred to the Oxford Dictionary and notes that 'one aspect of the definition [of the term genuinely] was telling: "Having the supposed character, not sham or feigned."'[76] Sharon Williams, on the other

---

[65] Cf Article 31 (1) of the Vienna Convention on the Law of Treaties (entered into force 27 January 1980*)* 1155 UNTS 331, 8 ILM 679. Note that, according to the *chapeau* of Article 32, the context includes 'the text, including [the] preamble and annexes' of the treaty.

[66] R Jennings and A Watts (n 51) 1273, referring to the case of *Ministry of Defence v Ergialli*, Italy, Court of Venice, judgment of 5 February 1958, 26 ILR (1958-II), 732–734.

[67] Emphasis added.

[68] See also Informal Expert Paper for the ICC Office of the Prosecutor: The Principle of Complementarity in Practice (n 33) 8 [21].

[69] Cf Article 33 (1) and (3) of the Vienna Convention on the Law of Treaties (n 65) which provides that, when a treaty has been authenticated in two or more languages, the text is equally authoritative in each language and that the terms of the treaty are presumed to have the same meaning in each authentic text. On the authentic language versions of the Rome Statute, see Article 128 of the Rome Statute (n 1).

[70] In this vein, see also S Morel (n 33) 100.

[71] Cf Article 32 of the Vienna Convention on the Law of Treaties (n 65).

[72] Cf (n 174–175) and text in Ch III.

[73] As J T Holmes observes, 'this term was, for many delegations, less clear than other terms considered' but that 'it was agreed to in order to achieve broad consensus' (n 33) 50.

[74] The Concise Oxford Dictionary (9th edn, OUP, Oxford 2001).

[75] The New Collins Dictionary and Thesaurus (Collins, London, Glasgow 1987).

[76] J T Holmes (n 33) 50, at n 14 and text.

hand, translates the term 'genuinely' as meaning 'in good faith'.[77] Although this latter understanding would probably move the term closest to a concept that is familiar to international law, it disregards the fact that the insertion of the term 'good faith' was expressly considered during the negotiations, but rejected after some delegations had expressed the view that it was too vague.[78] In contrast, understanding the term 'genuinely' as 'having the supposed character, not sham or feigned' would be more susceptible to an application by reference to objective criteria and thus more in line with the apparent intention of the parties. The 'supposed character' of an investigation and/or prosecution is to establish the guilt or innocence of an accused in accordance with internationally recognized standards for the administration of justice in order to ensure that ICC crimes do not go unpunished.[79] The applicable standards which have to be met in order for proceedings not to be considered a sham or feigned can in turn be derived from 'principles of due process recognized by international law', to which reference is made in the *chapeau* of Article 17 (2).[80] One may very well question, therefore, whether the term 'genuinely' adds anything of substance to the way in which investigations or prosecutions have to be carried out in order for a case to be declared inadmissible, as it merely repeats what the *chapeau* of Article 17 (2) stipulates.

3.2. Cases having been investigated and the State has decided not to prosecute: Article 17 (1)(b)

The second situation that is regulated by Article 17 (1) is when '[t]he case has been investigated by a State which has jurisdiction over it and the State has decided not to prosecute the person concerned, unless the decision resulted from the unwillingness or inability of the State genuinely to prosecute'.[81] Several terms of the provision are identical to those employed in Article 17 (1)(a), and for the purpose of their interpretation, reference can be made to the relevant parts of the previous sections.[82]

What is clear from the wording of Article 17 (1)(b) is that two cumulative requirements have to be fulfilled: first, the case must have been investigated; and

---

[77] See n 29, 392 [22] ('...unless the State is unwilling or unable genuinely, in other words in good faith, to carry such proceedings out...').

[78] 'Report of the Preparatory Committee on the Establishment of an International Criminal Court, Vol I' (Proceedings of the Preparatory Committee during March-April and August 1996 (1996) UN GAOR 51st Session Supp No UN Doc A/51/22 39 [166]. John T Holmes also notes that the term was not acceptable because it was thought to be narrower than genuine (n 14) 674.

[79] In this vein, see R Jensen, 'Complementarity, "Genuinely" and Article 17: Assessing the Boundaries of an Effective ICC' in J K Kleffner and G Kor (eds), *Complementary Views on Complementarity—Proceedings of the International Roundtable on the Complementary Nature of the International Criminal Court, Amsterdam, 25/26 June 2004* (TMC Asser Press, The Hague 2006) 147–170, 160.

[80] For further discussion, see *3.5.1. 'Principles of due process recognized by international law'*.

[81] 17 (1)(b).

[82] These terms are 'State' (*106–110*), 'jurisdiction' (*110–113*) and 'genuinely' (*114–116*).

second, a decision not to prosecute must have been taken. The broad reference to 'the State' also clearly encompasses *all* State organs that can investigate ICC crimes and all such organs in a position to take a decision not to prosecute. The provision is equally clear as to the fact that the investigating State and the State that takes the decision not to prosecute are *one and the same*. This follows from the sequence of 'a State' and 'the State'. For example, in a situation in which State A has investigated a case and extradites a suspect to State B, and the latter subsequently decides not to prosecute that person, the test of Article 17 (1)(b) applies twice. The requested State A has investigated the case and decided not to prosecute (such a decision manifesting itself in the decision to extradite). State B has also investigated the case (at least to the extent so as to make out a *prima facie* case for purposes of the extradition request) and decided not to prosecute (for instance because subsequent investigations revealed insufficient evidence to prosecute).

It furthermore plainly follows from the phrase 'the case has been investigated'—as opposed to 'being investigated' in Article 17 (1)(a)—that the investigation must have been *completed*. Pending further investigative steps, the case at hand is 'being investigated' and thus falls outside the ambit of Article 17 (1)(b). However, does 'the decision not to prosecute' after a completed investigation also have to be *final*? A reasonable starting point appears to be that it must be so.[83] As long as the decision not to prosecute is not final, for instance because an appeal against or judicial review of such a decision is pending, an important opportunity to remedy possible deficiencies of such a decision at the national level would be missed. A determination of admissibility by the ICC based on a decision not to prosecute which is not final would run the risk of being taken prematurely. However, as an exception to this rule that a decision should be final before the ICC determines admissibility, and by analogy with the general rule on the exhaustion of local remedies,[84] the ICC should not be expected to postpone a determination of admissibility until all domestic remedies against a decision not to prosecute are exhausted, if such remedies are not available or are manifestly ineffective.

The notion of 'decisions not to prosecute' also raises the question as to their required *form*. Undoubtedly, there may be instances in which such a decision is clearly manifested, for example when the legislative authorities of a State adopt an amnesty law that not only bars the initiation of investigations, but also extends to cases that have already been investigated,[85] or where the prosecutorial authorities of the investigating State exercise their prosecutorial discretion.[86] However, does

---

[83] In this vein, C Cárdenas (n 33) 74.   [84] See (n 161).

[85] It should be noted in this context that amnesties are frequently adopted without distinguishing whether a case has been investigated or not and apply generally to all crimes that (actually or potentially) were or are subject to criminal proceedings. For an example of such a general amnesty, see the Peruvian Amnesty Law No 26479 (1995) (n 35).

[86] See page 50. For further discussion, see *Chapter VI: Complementarity and the Obligation to Investigate and Prosecute, 3. Prosecutorial Discretion*.

the notion of a 'decision not to prosecute' also extend to 'informal' decisions, and does Article 17 (1)(b) also cover situations, for example, in which a State has investigated the case but the competent authorities subsequently simply fail to take any action? In contrast to a scenario of *complete* inaction,[87] the investigation would have triggered the applicability of Article 17, and the Court would thus have to determine admissibility in accordance with that provision.

Whether such informal decisions not to prosecute would nevertheless fall within the ambit of Article 17 (1)(b) may depend on how clearly the intent not to prosecute is manifested and how definite such a decision can reasonably be expected to be.[88] If a person in a very powerful position makes an official pronouncement at the end of an investigation, indicating that no prosecution will be conducted, and such a pronouncement will in all likelihood be followed by the prosecutorial authorities of a State, notwithstanding the lack of the formal power of that person to issue legally binding decisions to that effect, nothing would seem to preclude such a situation from being subsumed under Article 17 (1)(b). If, on the other hand, it were less clear whether the investigation has indeed been completed and a decision not to prosecute been taken, or it cannot clearly be established whether an informal decision not to prosecute will be implemented, it appears more reasonable to apply Article 17 (1)(a) and thus consider that the investigation is still underway, thus rendering the case as 'being investigated'.

3.3. *Ne bis in idem*: Articles 17 (1)(c) and 20 (3)

The third ground for declaring a case inadmissible is regulated by Article 17 (1)(c), which applies to the situation in which '[t]he person concerned has already been tried for conduct which is the subject of the complaint'. The provision incorporates a reference to Article 20 (3) which regulates the conditions under which a retrial by the ICC is permissible when a person has already been tried 'by another court for conduct also proscribed under article 6, 7 or 8'.[89] This 'upward' *ne bis in idem* principle[90] has to be distinguished from three other situations, in which questions of *ne bis in idem* may arise. First, Article 20 (1) provides that the ICC is barred from trying a person with respect to conduct which has formed the basis of crimes for which the person has been acquitted or convicted by the Court. Second, a prior trial by the ICC also bars a subsequent trial 'by another court'— the 'downward' *ne bis in idem* principle.[91] Third, the question may arise as to

---

[87] Cf *103–104*.

[88] But see C Cárdenas (n 33) 73, who requires a formal decision ['förmliche Entscheidung'].

[89] The other two situations of *ne bis in idem* are regulated in Rome Statute (n 1) Article 20 (1) (trial before the ICC with respect to conduct which formed the basis of crimes for which the person has been convicted or acquitted by the ICC) and 20 (2) (trial before another court for which that person has already been convicted or acquitted by the ICC).

[90] C van den Wyngaert and T Ongena, '*Ne bis in idem* principle, including the issue of amnesty' in A Cassese, P Gaeta and J Jones (eds), (n 14) 705–729, 724–726.

[91] Rome Statute (n 1) Article 20 (2). C van den Wyngaert and T Ongena, ibid 723–724.

whether, and to what extent, a trial by one domestic court bars the courts of another State from subsequently trying the same person for conduct which has formed the basis of crimes for which the person has been acquitted or convicted in the first domestic trial. However, the Rome Statute, being solely concerned with questions of *ne bis in idem* which arise in relation to prior or subsequent proceedings before the ICC, does not address this issue of a 'horizontal' *ne bis in idem* principle.[92]

The 'upward' *ne bis in idem* principle in Article 20 (3) specifies two situations which constitute the exception to the rule that such a subsequent trial before the ICC is impermissible. More specifically, the ICC may try such a person again if the proceedings in the other court '[w]ere for the purpose of shielding the person concerned from criminal responsibility for crimes within the jurisdiction of the Court'[93] or '[o]therwise were not conducted independently or impartially in accordance with the norms of due process recognized by international law and were conducted in a manner which, in the circumstances, was inconsistent with an intent to bring the person concerned to justice'.[94] These two exceptions closely resemble the two forms of unwillingness defined in Article 17 (2)(a) and (c) discussed below.[95]

A preliminary issue that requires clarification is that the prior trial has to be '*for conduct also proscribed under article 6, 7 and 8*' and bars, as a rule, the ICC from trying the person concerned '*with respect to the same conduct*'. The reference to 'conduct' as opposed to 'crimes' seems to indicate that the classification of such conduct as *ordinary crime under domestic law*, eg grievous bodily harm or assault instead of torture as a crime against humanity, is not sufficient to make

---

[92] As a rule, States do not apply the principle of *ne bis in idem* in their mutual horizontal relationship, thus allowing the prosecution of a person again at a later stage for the same offence for which he or she has been convicted or acquitted by the courts of another State. This practice has also been held to be compatible with international human rights requirements, such as Art 14 (7) of the International Covenant on Civil and Political Rights (adopted 16 December 1966, entered into force 23 March 1976) 999 UNTS 171 (ICCPR); see eg Human Rights Committee, *AP v Italy*, Communication 204/1986 (1987) UN Doc CCPR/C/OP/1, 67. This rule may be subject to certain exceptions on the regional level, however. See eg on the regional level: Articles 53–55 of the European Convention on the international validity of criminal judgments (signed in The Hague on 28 May 1970) ETS No 70; Arts 35–37 of the European Convention on the transfer of proceedings in criminal matters, (entered into force 15 May 1972) ETS No 73; European Court of Justice, judgment of 11 February 2003 in Joined Cases C-187/01 and C-385/01 (case governed by the Schengen Convention; held that a person may not be prosecuted in one Member State for the same facts which, in another Member State, have been finally disposed of without recourse to a court). For a general discussion, see C van den Wyngaert and G Stessens, 'The International *Non Bis In Idem* Principle: Resolving Some of the Unanswered Questions' (1999) 48 ICLQ 779, 781–82; O Lagodny, 'Viele Strafgewalten und nur ein transnationales ne-bis-in-idem?' in A Donatsch, M Forster and C Schwarzenegger(eds), *Strafrecht, Strafprozessrecht und Menschenrechte, Festschrift für Stefan Trechsel zum 65* (Geburtstag, Schulthess 2002) 253–267.
[93] Rome Statute (n 1) Article 20 (3)(a).   [94] Rome Statute (n 1) Article 20 (3)(b).
[95] On these related forms of unwillingness and an interpretation of the terms employed and which equally applies in the present context, see *3.5.2. Shielding* and *3.5.4. Lack of Independence and Impartiality*.

Article 20 (3) applicable and thus does not allow for a new trial before the ICC.[96] This conclusion finds support in drawing a comparison with corresponding provisions of the ad hoc tribunals for the former Yugoslavia and Rwanda[97] and the 1996 Draft Code of Offences Against the Peace and Security of Mankind.[98] In contrast to these instruments, the exceptions to the 'upward' *ne bis in idem* principle in the Rome Statute do not include the possibility for the ICC to try a person who has been tried by a national court for acts constituting ICC crimes solely on the ground that the act, for which that person had been tried, was characterized as an ordinary crime. In fact, that possibility had been included in earlier drafts, but was omitted during the March/April 1998 Session of the Preparatory Committee on the Establishment of an International Criminal Court.[99]

The assertion that Article 20 (3) does not allow for subsequent trials before the ICC because of the fact alone that the conduct in question has been characterized as an ordinary crime in the proceedings in another court has been challenged on the basis of the following arguments. First, it has been asserted that, 'in order to become conduct proscribed under articles 6, 7 and 8, such conduct or act should meet the specific requirements listed in those articles'.[100] Second, it is argued that a classification of a crime within the jurisdiction of the ICC as an ordinary crime in a national trial triggers Article 20 (3), if one reads Article 20 (3)(a) in conjunction with Article 22 (1). This follows as the latter provision stipulates that a person 'shall not be criminally responsible under this Statute unless the conduct in question constitutes, at the time it takes place, a crime within the jurisdiction of the Court'. The ICC would not be empowered to exercise its jurisdiction over a domestic crime, because Articles 6, 7 and 8 only cover the international crimes of genocide, crimes against humanity and war crimes.[101]

---

[96] I Tallgren, 'Commentary on Article 20' in O Triffterer (ed) (n 29) 431 at 24 ['The categorization used in the national trial, i.e. whether it relied on definitions of international crimes or crimes under international law, eg murder of several persons, is basically not relevant']; M Benzing (n 29) 614–617; C Cárdenas (n 29) 78–82; F Razesberger (n 29) 153–155.

[97] Article 10 (2)(a) (ICTY); Article 9(2)(a) (ICTR).

[98] Draft Code of Crimes against the Peace and Security of Mankind, ILC, 'Report of the international Law Commission on the work of its 48th session' (6 May–26 July 1996) UN Doc A/51/10 Supplement No 10, Draft Article 12 (2)(a)(i).

[99] J T Holmes (n 33) 57–58.

[100] M El Zeidy (n 62) 933–934. He asserts that the reason why the drafters did not make use of the alternative formulation 'for a crime referred to in article 5' lies elsewhere: '[...] one could argue that the difference of formulation between paragraphs 2 and 3 [of Article 20, the former using the terms 'for a crime referred to in article 5' JK] in this respect suggests that the drafters could not have made reference to the term 'for a crime referred to in article 5' in paragraph 3, since the crime of aggression in article 5 (1)(d) is not defined yet. Furthermore, the drafters intended for paragraph 3 to have the same meaning and purpose as paragraph 2, namely, the crimes set out in Article 5. However, they wanted to widen the interpretation of paragraph 3 to cover specific acts listed under articles 6, 7 and 8 by using the term 'conduct'. It was not therefore possible to identify the acts of aggression because they were not defined yet. There is another reason the drafters did not make reference to the phrase 'a crime referred to in article 5' in paragraph 3. The drafters intended to make reference to the list of acts set out in articles 6, 7 and 8, in order to limit the subjectivity of the Prosecutor's assessment of whether the crime in question, which was subject to a previous trial by a national court, lies within the Court's jurisdiction.'

[101] Ibid 934–935.

However, neither of these arguments appears convincing. The first argument disregards the distinction between fact and law: 'conduct' means 'behaviour'[102] and thus involves a de facto as opposed to a *de jure* appraisal.[103] Accordingly, the 'conduct' of the crime against humanity of murder,[104] for example, is the killing/causing death of one or more persons.[105] It is this conduct which Article 20 (3) requires to be proscribed under both the ICC Statute and the law applicable 'in the other court', in order to bar a subsequent retrial before the ICC, not the legal qualification thereof.[106]

The second argument would equally appear to be open to objection. For one, the ICC does not exercise jurisdiction over a domestic offence by asserting jurisdiction over a crime that has been qualified as an ordinary offence in the domestic proceedings whilst, from an international law perspective, amounting to a crime of genocide, crime against humanity or war crime. The reference to 'crimes within the jurisdiction of the Court' in subparagraph (a) appears to be only logical. For, it is these crimes which provide the basis for the criminal responsibility of perpetrators *as assessed by the ICC* and which consequently provide the yardstick for the ICC to decide whether or not a person has been shielded from such criminal responsibility. Such shielding may occur in trial proceedings in which the conduct is qualified as a domestic as well as an international offence. Finally, one might add that Article 20 (3), interpreted in a way that does not allow a retrial on the sole ground that the conduct in question was qualified as a domestic crime as opposed to a crime referred to in Articles 6 to 8 of the Statute, also conforms to an effective interpretation of the provision. Should one really understand it so as to allow the ICC to spend its resources on retrying persons who have been duly tried and convicted, only because the trial was for an ordinary offence, while many more cases are likely to warrant its action?

While it is submitted that the answer is, in principle, in the negative, the foregoing is not meant to suggest that trials for domestic offences are an optimal response to international crimes. Their prosecution as international crimes can respond to a number of problems, which the ordinary crimes-approach entails.[107]

---

[102] Cf The Concise Oxford English Dictionary (n 74) and The New Collins Dictionary and Thesaurus (n 75).

[103] Cf Elements of Crimes, adopted on 9 September 2002, Doc ICC-ASP/1/3 (Part II-B), General Introduction to the Elements of Crimes, at 7, which, in explaining the structure of the elements of crimes, distinguishes between conduct, consequences and circumstances associated with each crime.

[104] Rome Statute (n 1) Article 7(1)(a).

[105] Cf Elements of Crimes(n 103), Element 1 of Article 7 (1)(a).

[106] Cf also W Schabas (n 62) 88, also noting that the Statute is narrower with respect to the opposite situation in which the ICC has conducted a prior trial, as regulated in Article 20 (2). As the provision specifies that '[n]o person shall be tried by another court *for a crime referred to in article 5* for which that person has already been convicted or acquitted by the Court' [emphasis added], it only excludes a subsequent national trial for genocide, crimes against humanity and war crimes, but allows for such a trial for ordinary domestic offences. On the concurrence of international and domestic offences, see also *30*.

[107] Cf J K Kleffner, 'The Impact of Complementarity on National Implementation of Substantive International Criminal Law' (2003) 1 JICJ 95–100.

An important consideration on the conceptual level is that the prosecution of core crimes *qua* core crimes adequately reflects their very nature. Their international criminalization is based on the premise that such crimes do not only affect the society immediately concerned and individual victims, as ordinary crimes do. Rather, core crimes are of concern to the international community as a whole and, in the words of the Preamble of the Statute, 'threaten the peace, security and well-being of the world'.[108] It is their idiosyncratic constitutive elements—such as the genocidal intent or the contextual elements of a widespread or systematic attack against a civilian population or the existence of an armed conflict—and the specific legal values that they seek to protect which elevate these crimes to the level of *international* crimes and distinguishes them from domestic crimes.[109] International law regulates the suppression of these offences by a body of distinct rules, which reflect their specific gravity and international nature. It does so, for instance, by allowing for, or obliging, the exercise of universal jurisdiction, providing for the non-applicability of statutory limitations, for the doctrine of command responsibility, and rejecting the defence of superior orders.[110] Not recognizing the distinctive features of international crimes and not incorporating them into domestic law may consequently have serious implications for the overall system of international criminal law in which they are embedded. On a more practical level, relying on ordinary crimes entails an increased risk that a narrower range of conduct can be prosecuted domestically than is prescribed on the international plane. This can be the result of a lack of domestic offences, into which international crimes can be 'translated'. It is not immediately obvious, for instance, what could be the 'corresponding' domestic crime for the war crime of making improper use of a flag of truce, of the flag or of the military insignia and uniform of the enemy or of the United Nations, as well as of the distinctive

---

[108] Cf Rome Statute (n 1), Preamble at [3]. See also *26–28*.

[109] See also in this vein ICTR, *Prosecutor v Michel Bagaragaza*, ('Decision on the Prosecution Motion for Referral to the Kingdom of Norway') ICTR-2005-86-R11bis, Trial Chamber, (19 May 2006) [16]: '[. . .] the crimes alleged—genocide, conspiracy to commit genocide and complicity in genocide—are significantly different in term of their elements and their gravity from the crime of homicide, the basis upon which the Kingdom of Norway states that charges may be laid against the Accused under its domestic law. The Chamber notes that the crime of genocide is distinct in that it requires the 'intent to destroy, in whole or in part, a national, ethnical, racial or religious group, as such'. This specific intent is not required for the crime of homicide under Norwegian criminal law. Therefore, in the Chamber's view, the *ratione materiae* jurisdiction, or subject matter jurisdiction, for the acts alleged in the confirmed Indictment does not exist under Norwegian law. Consequently, Michel Bagaragaza's alleged criminal acts cannot be given their full legal qualification under Norwegian criminal law, and the request for the referral to the Kingdom of Norway falls to be dismissed.' The decision was confirmed by the Appeals Chamber in the same case, *Prosecutor v Michel Bagaragaza*, 'Decision on Rule11bis Appeal', 30 August 2006, where the Appeals Chamber added as a further reason that 'the protected legal values are different. The penalization of genocide protects specifically defined groups, whereas the penalization of homicide protects individual lives.' [17].

[110] See also for failure to implement general principles and to establish extraterritorial jurisdiction, especially universal jurisdiction, and the consequences *40–43, 52–53*.

emblems of the Geneva Conventions.[111] Similarly, relying on ordinary crimes may result in the unavailability of general principles of international criminal law and of jurisdictional bases, in particular universal jurisdiction.[112] Such inadequacies of domestic law, which cause national authorities to be able to prosecute less than what the Statute criminalizes, in turn entail the risk that cases are being declared admissible because the national criminal jurisdiction is unable within the meaning of Article 17 (3) of the Statute.[113] Furthermore, when ICC crimes are prosecuted on the basis of ordinary domestic crimes, the process of conversion may result in low sentences. For instance, the determination of the sentence for the grave breach of Additional Protocol I of making cultural property the object of attack and causing extensive destruction thereto[114] may have to be determined by the sentence available for a domestic crime such as damage to property, which in turn entails a sentence that might be said not to reflect adequately the severe nature of a grave breach of Additional Protocol I.[115] There are thus many good reasons for States to implement ICC crimes into their domestic legislation *qua* international crimes.[116] However, the fact remains that the qualification of an international crime as an ordinary domestic offence by another court alone does not automatically trigger Article 20 (3).

[111] Cf Rome Statute (n 1), Article 8 (2)(b)(vii). For an illustrative example of how forced the conversion of an international crime into a domestic offence can be when national authorities rely on domestic offences because international offences have not been implemented, see *Al Dujail Lawsuit* (Case), Iraqi High Criminal Corut (Trial Chamber I), Case No 1/9 First/2005 (2006), Final Decision and Judgment, Part I, 9 p 6, available at <http://www.law.case.edu/saddamtrial/documents/dujail_opinion_pt1.pdf>. The Trial Chamber converted the crime of deportation or forcible transfer of population as a crime against humanity charged against Saddam Hussein into the domestic offence of 'slave labor' and the compelling of a person 'to engage in activities or circumstances other than those … which the law sanctions' under paragraph 325 of Iraq's Penal Code: see Penal Code, No 111, (1969), available at <http://www.law.case.edu/saddamtrial/documents/Iraqi_Penal_Code_1969.pdf>.

[112] As regards the latter, see *Polyukhovich v The Commonwealth of Australia and Another* (1991) High Court of Australia, 172 Commonwealth Law Reports 501 FC 91/026 (14 August 1991), in which it was held that universal jurisdiction was unavailable, because Australian law legislated in terms of serious domestic crimes what internationally are considered war crimes. See also K L Doherty and T L H McCormack, '"Complementarity" as a Catalyst for Comprehensive Domestic Penal Legislation' (1999) 5 UC Davis Journal of International Law and Policy 147–180, 175.

[113] For further analysis, see (nn 293–297) and text.

[114] Cf Article 85 (4)(d) of 1977 Protocol Additional to the Geneva Conventions of 12 August 1949, and relating to the Protection of Victims of International Armed Conflicts (AP I) (adopted 8 June 1977, entered into force 7 December 1978) 1125 UNTS 3–608.

[115] In order to comply with the obligation to provide for effective penal sanctions, States Parties to the Geneva Conventions are obliged to enact legislation which takes into account the severe nature of grave breaches of the Geneva Conventions: see J Pictet (ed), *Commentary to the First Geneva Convention for the Amelioration of the Condition of the Wounded and the Sick in Armed Forces in the Field* (International Committee of the Red Cross, Geneva 1952), commentary on Article 49 I, 364. The same applies to grave breaches of Additional Protocol I. See also F Razesberger (n 29) 51. On the question of whether and under what conditions low sentences may be said to amount to shielding in the sense of Article 17 (2)(a) and thereby may render a case admissible, see further below (nn 187–189) and text.

[116] Indeed, complementarity has a significant effect as a catalyst for States to do so: see *Chapter VII: Complementarity as a Catalyst for Compliance, 333–337.*

Another question that arises, is what is meant by the terms '*has already been tried*' and '*proceedings in the other court*'. More precisely, it is unclear whether the application of Articles 17 (1)(c) and 20 (3) can be based solely on proceedings that were conducted in one single court or whether it would require all internal remedies to be exhausted, including appeal and review. Domestic legal systems adopt differing approaches as to the question of when a person has been tried, with common law jurisdictions regarding a trial as having been terminated once the accused is convicted or acquitted and civil law jurisdictions only doing so once the last appeal decision has been pronounced.[117] With no generally accepted meaning being attached to the terms 'has already been tried', one can also not derive a clear answer from the wording of Article 20 (3). The reference in the English language version of the Statute to '*the* other *court*' would seem to support the position that a trial in one single court would suffice. In contrast, the French version of the Statute refers more broadly to '*juridiction*'[118] rather than '*cour*', which would be the term more precisely corresponding with the English term. Since a comparison of these authentic texts thus discloses a difference in meaning, the meaning that best reconciles the texts, having regard to the object and purpose of the treaty, must be adopted.[119]

It would appear that this objective would best be achieved by approaching the matter with some flexibility. Similar to the above considerations on the question of whether a decision not to prosecute within the meaning of Article 17 (1)(b) has to be final,[120] a State's judicial system should be given the opportunity to remedy deficiencies of proceedings, if, and to the extent that, such means are available and effective. It is conceivable, for instance, that a lower court, with greater proximity to the crime and to the perpetrator, would be more susceptible to bias that amounts to shielding or other inconsistencies with an intent to bring the person concerned to justice, while higher courts may retain their independence and impartiality and reverse the outcome of flawed proceedings. Allowing them to do so would be in line with the recognized need for measures on the national level in order to achieve effective prosecution[121] and with the more general consideration of judicial economy not to overburden the ICC with cases for which other fora are adequately equipped.

The same result is warranted by the possibility that flaws, which satisfy the requirements of the exception to the *ne bis in idem* principle allowing for a subsequent retrial before the ICC, may only occur during proceedings in a national court of higher instance, while the proceedings in the court of first instance were conducted in a way that would make the case inadmissible. To base its decision

---

[117] C Safferling, *Towards an International Criminal Procedure* (OUP, Oxford 2001) 418, 322.

[118] Rome Statute (n 1) Article 20 (3) of the French version reads in relevant parts: 'Quiconque a été jugé par une autre juridiction pour un comportement tombant aussi sous le coup des article 6,7 ou 8 ne peut être judé par la Cour que si la procédure devant l'autre juridiction...'

[119] Cf Article 33 (4) of the Vienna Convention on the Law of Treaties (n 65). For the object and purpose of the Rome Statute, see *104–105*.

[120] Cf (nn 83–84) and accompanying text.   [121] Cf (n 31) and text.

on whether, or not, to apply the principle of *ne bis in idem* or the exception to it on the proceedings in the first instance alone in these cases could, therefore, put the ICC in the position in which it prematurely declares a case inadmissible based on proceedings, which may later be overruled in a way that would make the case admissible. An approach that allows for the exhaustion of local remedies would also be in line with the corresponding admissibility requirement before international courts and tribunals.[122]

However, if domestic remedies are unavailable or ineffective, the ICC should not be expected to delay a determination on admissibility. To do so, for instance when a higher court clearly shows bias prior to the proceedings, or when there is an administrative practice and official encouragement or tolerance of bias,[123] would undermine the object of effective prosecution.

Last but not least, it needs to be emphasized that neither Article 17 (1)(c) nor Article 20 (3) requires the trial to take place in a *national* court. Article 20 (3) merely refers to 'another court'. In contrast to Article 17 (1)(a) and (b), which both raise the question as to whether, and to what extent, they apply in respect to investigations and prosecutions in internationalized or international tribunals,[124] the exception to the *ne bis in idem* principle would thus appear to pertain to 'other courts' regardless of their nature.[125]

3.4. Insufficient gravity: Article 17 (1)(d)

A final ground for declaring a case inadmissible is when it is considered to be 'not of sufficient gravity to justify further action by the Court' as provided for in Article 17 (1)(d). As a matter of *admissibility,* the insufficient gravity test must be distinguished from the *jurisdictional* limitation of the ICC to 'the most serious crimes' of concern to the international community as a whole, which are enumerated in Article 5 and further defined in Articles 6 to 8.[126] The Statute clearly distinguishes between the two concepts of jurisdiction and admissibility, as reflected in the different provisions that address them.[127] The former delimits the material, temporal, geographical and personal realm of the Court's operations, while admissibility is concerned with the subsequent question as to whether matters, over which the Court has jurisdiction, can be considered by it.[128] Article 17 (1)(d), in turn, requires that the crimes within the jurisdiction *ratione materiae* of the ICC also be sufficiently grave in order to justify further action by the Court. In

---

[122] See further below, *132–133*.
[123] See *mutatis mutandis, Cyprus v Turkey* (App no 25781/94) ECHR (6 May 2001) [99].
[124] Cf *107–108*.
[125] In line with Rome Statute (n 1) Article 20 (1) and (2), this is subject to the exception to the *ne bis in idem* principle if the prior trial took place in the ICC itself.
[126] Cf Rome Statute (n 1) Preamble, paragraph 9, Articles 1 and 5.
[127] Cf Rome Statute (n 1) Articles 5–8, 11–16 on jurisdiction, and 17–20 on admissibility.
[128] Cf W Schabas (n 62) 68. For certain aspects of the relationship between the two concepts, see L N Sadat and S R Carden (n 61) 419–421.

other words, the Court can declare cases inadmissible in which the conduct in question amounts to genocide, crimes against humanity or war crimes, but lacks the requisite gravity. The determination of the relative gravity thus takes place in relation to other such crimes rather than crimes that fall outside the Court's jurisdiction.[129] The early practice of the Court suggests that crimes are sufficiently grave only when the conduct in question is systematic or undertaken on a large scale; the person concerned falls within the category of most senior leaders of the situation under investigation, considering his or her position in the State entity, organization or armed group to which s/he belongs; and the person concerned falls within the category of those being most responsible.[130]

Because cases of insufficient gravity are inadmissible without being subject to any exception, such as unwillingness or inability, *all* such cases are left exclusively to national criminal jurisdictions and other mechanisms. They fall outside the framework of complementarity and are beyond the reach of the ICC. This ground of inadmissibility is therefore beyond the present analysis.

3.5. Unwillingness: Article 17 (2)

Article 17 (2) of the Statute defines 'unwillingness'. It provides that:

'[i]n order to determine unwillingness in a particular case, the Court shall consider, having regard to the principles of due process recognized by international law, whether one or more of the following exist, as applicable:

(a) The proceedings were or are being undertaken or the national decision was made for the purpose of shielding the person concerned from criminal responsibility for crimes within the jurisdiction of the Court referred to in article 5;

(b) There has been an unjustified delay in the proceedings which in the circumstances is inconsistent with an intent to bring the person concerned to justice;

(c) The proceedings were not or are not being conducted independently or impartially, and they were or are being conducted in a manner which, in the circumstances, is inconsistent with an intent to bring the person concerned to justice.'

---

[129] See for instance Office of the Prosecutor, Update on Communications Received by the Prosecutor, 10 February 2006, Annex 'Iraq Response', 8–9, available at <http://www.icc-cpi.int/library/organs/otp/OTP_letter_to_senders_re_Iraq_9_February_2006.pdf>. See also L N Sadat and S R Carden (n 61) 419.

[130] Pre-Trial Chamber I, Decision Concerning Pre-Trial Chamber I's Decision of 10 February 2006 and the Incorporation of Documents into the Record of the Case against Mr Thomas Lubanga Dyilo (n 33) [42–63]. See also Paper on some policy issues before the Office of the Prosecutor (n 33); Office of the Prosecutor, Update on Communications Received by the Prosecutor, ibid. But see the slightly different factors listed in the OTP Policy Paper on the Interests of Justice, September 2007, <http://www.icc-cpi.int/library/organs/otp/ICC-OTP-InterestsOfJustice.pdf> at 5 ['scale of the crimes, the nature of the crimes, the manner of their commission and their impact']. On the category of 'those bearing the greatest degree of responsibility', the OTP Policy Paper at 7 enumerates as relevant factors 'the alleged status or hierarchical level of the accused or implication in particularly serious or notorious crimes. That is, the significance of the role of the accused in the overall commission of crimes and the degree of the accused's involvement (actual commission, ordering, indirect participation).'

The reference to due process and the two forms of unwillingness spelled out in subparagraphs (a) and (c) can also be found in very similar terms in Article 20 (3)(a) and (b). The following analysis therefore also applies to the latter provisions to the extent that the terms are identical.[131]

Before analyzing the three different situations that are regulated by subparagraphs (a) to (c), the reference to 'principles of due process recognized by international law' in the *chapeau* of Article 17 (2) warrants further clarification.

3.5.1. *'Principles of due process recognized by international law'*

The *chapeau* of paragraph 2 provides the frame of reference for determining whether the standards for rebutting the presumption of inadmissibility—shielding, unjustified delays or lack of independence and impartiality—are met. This framework consists of 'the principles of due process recognized by international law'. Consequently, the first question that needs to be answered is what these 'principles' actually are. The Statute does not identify them and the drafting history of Article 17 (2) does not elucidate what the drafters of the Statute had in mind when including the notion of 'principles of due process' in the provision.[132]

The similarity between the terms 'principles...recognized by international law' in Article 17 (2) and 'general principles of law recognized by civilised nations' as a source of international law identified in Article 38 (1)(c) of the Statute of the International Court of Justice is striking. At the same time, there are two notable differences: the former provision simply refers to 'principles' as opposed to 'general principles' in the latter provision, and the source of recognition in Article 17 (2) is 'international law' rather than 'civilised nations' (read 'States'[133]). It therefore needs to be clarified whether, and to what extent, the notion of 'general principles of law recognized by civilised nations' corresponds to or differs from the notion of 'the principles of due process recognized by international law'.

Broadly speaking, two alternative conceptualizations of 'general principles of law recognized by civilised nations' have been advanced. The first approach is to derive such principles from *legal principles*, which are transposed to the international legal system after having been *identified in* all or most of the various

---

[131] For the differences in wording, compare the reference to 'principles of due process recognized by international law' in the *chapeau* of Article 17 (2) with the terms 'norms of due process recognized by international law', which, rather than applying to both exceptions to the principle of *ne bis in idem* in Article 20 (3), is only included in one of them, namely subparagraph (b).

[132] The reasons for inclusion of the reference to these principles was to an attempt to further objectify 'unwillingness': see *90*.

[133] It is now generally accepted that the reference to 'civilised nations' should be read as 'all States' or, at least, 'all States member of the UN': see amongst many others: H Mosler, 'General Principles of Law' in R Bernhardt (ed), *Encyclopedia of Public International Law* (vol II Elsevier Science Publ, North Holland 1986) 511–527, 517; W Graf Vitzthum (ed), *Völkerrecht* (De Gruyter, Berlin, New York 1997) 90, margin 144 ['Wegen des Prinzips der souveränen Gleichheit (Art 2 Nr 1 UN-Charta) sind [zu dem Kreis der "Kulturvölker" bzw. "-staaten"] jedenfalls alle UN-Mitglieder zu rechnen.' Footnote omitted].

national systems of law.[134] The second conceptualization is to conceive of 'general principles of law recognized by civilised nations' as referring to *principles of international law*, which are either 'inferred or extracted by way of induction and generalization from conventional and customary rules of international law' or 'peculiar to a particular branch of international law'.[135] In order to determine whether to apply either of these different conceptions of principles of international law in the context of the *chapeau* of Article 17 (2), Article 21 on the applicable law is of assistance.[136] Although the provision is not without ambiguities,[137] it contains a hierarchy of applicable law, with the primary sources being the Statute, Elements of Crimes and Rules of Procedure and Evidence; the secondary sources being 'applicable treaties and the principles and rules of international law';[138] and the tertiary sources being 'general principles of law derived by the Court from national laws of legal systems of the world'.[139] It further contains the general guideline for the Court that '[t]he application and interpretation of law pursuant to [Article 21] must be consistent with internationally recognized human rights, and be without any adverse distinction founded on [any grounds]'.[140] In determining what 'the principles of due process recognized by international law' in the *chapeau* of Article 17 (2) are, Article 21 thus suggests that principles derived from national laws only fill the gaps left by principles of international law as derived from applicable treaties and the principles and rules of international law, the latter being understood to comprise customary international law.[141] Thus understood, such principles have to be extracted primarily from international law regulating due process. This is not to suggest that many such principles are not also recognized in all or most of the various national systems of law and thus are likely to also satisfy the criteria for the first conceptualization of 'general principles of law recognized by civilised nations'.[142] However, should principles established

---

[134] R Jennings and A Watts (n 51) 36–37 ['The intention [of Article 38 (1)(c) of the Statute of the International Court of Justice] is to authorise the Court to apply the general principles of municipal jurisprudence, insofar as they are applicable to relations of states.' Footnote omitted]; see also n 534 36–40 for further references, including to the jurisprudence of the ICJ.

[135] A Cassese, International Law (OUP, Oxford 2001) 152. While Cassese seems to conceive of the two understandings of 'general principles', ie those derived from national legal systems and those of international law proper, as not mutually exclusive (cf 151–152, 155–159), he asserts that the former are subsidiary to the latter ['[...] C]ourts [...] should [...] search first for general principles specific to a certain branch of international law and then general principles of international law. Only at this stage may a court look for general principles of law common to all the major legal systems of the members of the community of nations.' Ibid 158].

[136] See also F Razesberger (n 29) 41.

[137] J Verhoeven, 'Article 21 of the Rome Statute and the ambiguities of applicable law' (2002) 33 NYIL 3–22; A Pellet, 'Applicable Law' in A Cassese, P Gaeta and J Jones (eds) (n 14) 1051–1084.

[138] Para 1 (b).   [139] Para 1 (c).   [140] Para 3.

[141] A Pellet (n 137) 1071 ['there is little doubt that [Article 21(1)(b)] refers, exclusively, to customary international law'].

[142] See for instance N Jayawickrama, *The Judicial Application of Human Rights Law—National, Regional and International Jurisprudence* (CUP, Cambridge 2002) 478–594, with references to decisions of national courts of various States.

according to the first method conflict with those established according to the second, the latter takes precedence.

What, then, are these principles of due process? The concept of 'due process' traditionally evolved as regulating the 'conduct of legal proceedings according to established principles and rules which safeguard the position of the individual charged.'[143] Contemporary international law regulates the matter in a number of principles and rules, most notably those regarding *fair trials*.[144] One pertinent area in that regard comprises those that govern the independence and impartiality of the judiciary. They bear the potential of providing crucial guidance in determining whether 'proceedings were not or are not being conducted independently or impartially' as provided for in Article 17 (2)(c). International legal standards of independent and impartial justice are to be found in conventional undertakings, customary obligations and general principles of law.[145] Their application and interpretation by international and regional human rights bodies, and by UN Special Rapporteurs, first and foremost the Special Rapporteur on the independence of judges and lawyers, provides a useful source for clarifying the notions of 'independence' and 'impartiality' in the context of

---

[143] D M Walker, *The Oxford Companion to Law* (Clarendon Press, Oxford 1980) 381.

[144] Cf Articles 9–11 of the Universal Declaration of Human Rights (1948) UNGA Res 217A (III); Articles 4, 6, 9, 14, 15 of the ICCPR (n 92); Article 7 of the African Charter on Human Peoples' Rights (adopted on 27 June 1981, entered into force 21 October 1986) OAU Doc CAB/LEG/67/3 rev. 5, 21 ILM 58 (AfCHPR); Articles 4, 7–9, 27 of the Inter-American Convention on Human Rights (entered into force 18 July 1978) OAS Treaty Series No 36, 1114 UNTS 123 (IACHR); Articles 5–7, 15 of the European Convention for the Protection of Human Rights and Fundamental Freedoms (entered into force 3 September 1953, as amended by Protocols Nos 3, 5, 8, and 11 which entered into force on 21 September 1970, 20 December 1971, 1 January 1990 and 1 November 1998 respectively) 213 UNTS 222 (ECHR) and Protocols 6 and 7 to the ECHR; Article 3 common to the four 1949 Geneva Conventions for the Amelioration of the Condition of the Wounded and Sick in Armed Forces in the Field (Geneva Convention I), for the Amelioration of the Condition of Wounded, Sick and Shipwrecked Members of Armed Forces at Sea (Geneva Convention II), relative to the Treatment of Prisoners of War (Geneva Convention III) and relative to the Protection of Civilian Persons in Time of War (Geneva Convention IV), (all adopted 12 August 1949, entered into force 21 October 1950) '75 UNTS 31–417, Articles 84–88, 99, 100–107 of Geneva Convention III, Articles 33, 64–77 of Geneva Convention IV, Article 75 of the 1977 API (n 114). Article 6 of the 1977 Protocol Additional to the Geneva Conventions of 12 August 1949, and relating to the Protection of Victims of Non-International Armed Conflicts (AP II) (adopted 8 June 1977, entered into force 7 December 1978) 1125 UNTS 609–699, and the standards in the Statute (Parts 5 and 6) (n 1). Cf also W Schabas (n 62) 86 ['procedural and perhaps even substantive fairness']. See extensively S Trechsel, *Human Rights in Criminal Proceedings* (OUP, Oxford 2005).

[145] For an overview of such standards, see Report of the Special Rapporteur Mr Param Cumaraswamy, 'Independence and impartiality of the judiciary, jurors and assessors and the independence of lawyers', submitted in accordance with Commission on Human Rights resolution 1994/41 (6 February 1995) UN Doc E/CN.4/1995/39, [32–52], and Report of the Special Rapporteur on the independence of judges and lawyers, Dato' Param Cumaraswamy, submitted in accordance with Commission on Human Rights resolution 2002/43 (10 January 2003) UN Doc E/CN.4/2003/65, [46–47], 18–25, and 26–28. See also Informal Expert Paper for the ICC Office of the Prosecutor: The Principle of Complementarity in Practice (n 33) Annex 6, 34.

Article 17 (2)(c).[146] Similarly, the right to be tried without undue delay[147] and the right to a hearing 'within a reasonable time' in the determination of criminal charges,[148] as well as the right to such a hearing in the determination of one's civil rights and obligations,[149] can inspire the determination of whether 'there has been an unjustified delay in the proceedings'.[150]

However, to derive the applicable 'principles of due process recognized by international law' from the aforementioned rules is subject to the important *caveat* that such *rules may at times have to be adapted to the particular situations that are envisaged in Article 17 (2)(a) to (c)*. They cannot simply be mechanically transplanted. For, as a rule subject to only very limited exceptions,[151] Article 17 (2) addresses the situation in which criminal processes are abused *to the benefit* of the suspect or accused. This is diametrically opposed to the general assumption and objective of fair trial guarantees, which are designed to protect individuals against abuses *to their disadvantage*. In fact, in the context of domestic proceedings, the invocation of some of the principles of due process may result in investigations, prosecutions and punishments being barred, either legitimately or by giving such principles a broader meaning than internationally required (or even allowed). The principle of legality (*nullum crimen, nulla poena sine lege*), for example, can be—and has in fact been—used as a bar to criminal punishment of those under investigation for international crimes.[152] This does not render the aforementioned rules irrelevant. It is, however, necessary to transpose them cautiously with a view to adapt them to the notion of 'unwillingness'. Room for such adaptations can be found in the employment of the term 'principles' of due process—as opposed to 'rules', for instance. This choice of words in Article 17 (2) reflects a fair degree of generality and looseness.

Even with these necessary modifications, however, reference to fair trial guarantees may not be sufficient to provide a comprehensive framework for determining the 'principles of due process' which are relevant in the context of determining 'unwillingness'. They can give only limited guidance, if any, when

---

[146] For a more detailed analysis, see *3.5.4. Lack of Independence and Impartiality*.

[147] Cf for instance Article 14 (3)(c) ICCPR (n 92).

[148] Cf Articles 6 (1) ECHR, 8 (1) IACHR, 7 (1)(d) AfCHPR (n 144).

[149] Cf Articles 6 (1) ECHR, 8 (1) IACHR (n 144).

[150] Cf Rome Statute (n 1) Article 17 (2)(b). For further analysis, see *3.5.3. Unjustified Delays*.

[151] See *144–145, 150–152*.

[152] In re Bouterse, the Dutch Supreme Court argued that torture and crimes against humanity had not been criminalized under national law and that a prosecution for such conduct in direct application of customary international law violated the principle of legality as provided for in Article 16 of the Dutch Constitution and Article 1(1) of the Penal Code, notwithstanding the fact that the conduct entailed individual criminal responsibility under international customary law at the time of commission: see Dutch Supreme Court, *In re Bouterse*, 18 September 2001, NJ 2002/559, [6.4]: for an English translation of the judgment, see (2001) 32 NYIL 282–296. See generally on the principle of legality and direct application of core crimes by national courts, W Ferdinandusse, Direct Applications of International Criminal Law in National Courts (TMC Asser Press, The Hague 2006) 221–268.

determining composite elements of 'unwillingness', such as 'shielding'[153] and inconsistencies with 'an intent to bring the person concerned to justice' mentioned in Article 17 (2)(b) and (c). It therefore appears reasonable to look beyond fair trial guarantees and to understand the reference to 'principles of due process recognized by international law' more broadly—and at times less formalistically—to include *principles and standards of international law which are pertinent for duly investigating, prosecuting and punishing crimes in general and international crimes in particular.*[154]

A first set of such principles and standards flows from the concept of a *denial of justice* (*justitia denegata, déni de justice, Rechts- und Justizverweigerung*).[155] In its traditional connotation, which developed from as early as the thirteenth century onwards, this concept denotes any defect in the organization of courts or in the exercise of justice that entails a violation of the international legal duties of States with respect to the judicial protection of aliens.[156] The concept of denial of justice has undergone refinement over the centuries, but it remains of relevance in contemporary international law.[157] It has also developed beyond the protection of aliens to cover situations in which justice is denied to a State's own nationals, a development that can equally prove useful for the present purpose.[158] Of particular relevance for the present purpose of identifying rules that are pertinent for duly investigating, prosecuting and punishing crimes, are the standards for determining a denial of justice in the form of inadequate measures to investigate, apprehend, prosecute and punish persons suspected or guilty of crimes against aliens.[159]

Second, principles and standards of international law pertinent for duly investigating, prosecuting and punishing crimes can be derived from the *obligation*

---

[153] See *3.5.2. Shielding.*

[154] Such an understanding is in line with international courts and tribunals, which have also interpreted the term 'due process' in a broader way than merely referring to conduct of criminal proceedings according to established principles and rules which safeguard the position of the individual charged. See for instance *Mondev Int'l v United States*, Case No ARB (AF) 19813 (11 October 2002) [127], where reference is made to the ICJ judgment in *Elettronica Sicula SpA (ELSI) (United States of America v Italy)* General List No 76 [1989] ICJ Rep 15 [128] ['[...] a Chamber of the Court described as arbitrary conduct that which displays 'a wilful disregard of *due process of law,*... which shocks, or at least surprises a sense of judicial propriety'.[...], emphasis added].

[155] See F Mégret, 'Qu'est ce qu'une juridiction « incapable » ou « manquant de volonté » au sens de l'article 17 du Traité de Rome? Quelques enseignements tirés des théories du déni de justice en droit international', (2004) 17 Revue québécoise de droit international 185–216.

[156] S Verosta, 'Denial of Justice' in R Bernhardt (ed), *EPIL* (vol 1 Elsevier Publ, North Holland 1992) 1007–1010, 1007. For a more detailed account of the historical evolution of denial of justice, see J Paulsson, *Denial of Justice in International Law* (CUP, Cambridge 2005) 10–37.

[157] See for recent decisions for instance *Mondev Int'l v United States* (n 154); ICSID *The Loewen Group, inc and Raymond L Loewen v United States of America* (Award) Case No ARB (AF) 198 3(26 June 2003) [124–137, 142–156]. For detailed discussion of the various manifestations of denial of justice in contemporary international law, J Paulsson, ibid 134–206.

[158] See for instance the position of the Inter-American Commission of Human Rights referred to in *Genie-Lacayo v Nicaragua*, Judgment of 29 January 1997, IACtHR Series C No 30 (1997) [15].

[159] A V Freeman, *The International Responsibility of States for Denial of Justice* (H Vaillant-Carmanne Publ, Liége 1938) 364–388; J Paulsson (n 156) 170–173.

to investigate and prosecute serious violations of human rights, which flows from human rights conventions and to which reference was made earlier.[160] The jurisprudence of human rights bodies elucidates what is required from States in order to meet these human rights obligations. It supplies a further 'principle of due process' in the form of the requirement that States have to use the means at their disposal to carry out a serious investigation of violations committed within their jurisdiction, to identify those responsible and to impose the appropriate punishment.

Third, further guidance on how to duly investigate, prosecute and punish crimes can be found in the law governing the *exhaustion of local remedies* as a requirement for the admissibility of a claim before international courts and tribunals. More specifically, it is today generally accepted that there are certain exceptions to this requirement, to the extent that domestic remedies—including criminal proceedings against human rights violators as one type of such remedies—are ineffective or futile.[161] The jurisprudence on when such remedies must not be pursued for purposes of admissibility of a complaint before international courts and tribunals—and especially before human rights bodies on the ground

---

[160] See *Chapter II: National Suppression of Core Crimes,* at *2.1.4. The Obligation to Prosecute Human Rights Violations.*

[161] See generally C F Amerasinghe, *Local Remedies in International Law* (2nd edn CUP, Cambridge 2004) 200–215; Article 44 (b) of the Articles on Responsibility of States for Internationally Wrongful Acts (2001) UNGA Resolution 56/83 of 12 December 2001, and corrected by document A/56/49 (Vol I)/Corr.4; J Crawford, The International Law Commission's Articles on State Responsibility—Introduction; Text and Commentaries (CUP, Cambridge 2002) 256 at (5). In the context of diplomatic protection, see International Law Commission, Draft Article 15 (a) and (b) on Diplomatic Protection, as adopted on second reading during the 58th Session of the International Law Commission (2006), UN Doc. A/61/10, 76–77 and commentary at 77–80, and Third report on diplomatic protection by Mr John Dugard, Special Rapporteur, International Law Commission, 54th Session Geneva 29 April–7 June and 22 July–16 August 2002 UN Doc A/CN.4/523, 7 March 2002 [18–101]; ICJ, *Case Concerning Ahmadou Sadio Diallo (Republic of Guinea v Democratic Republic of the Congo)* General List No, 103, Judgment of 24 May 2007 [44]. Cf also Article 41 (1)(c) of the ICCPR (n 92); for the jurisprudence of the Human Rights Committee, see *Dermit Barbato v Uruguay* (Communication 84/81) at [9.4], reproduced in S Joseph, J Schultz and M Castan, *The International Covenant on Civil and Political Rights—Cases, Materials, and Commentary* (OUP, Oxford 2000) 80, 80–87 with further references to other case law of the Human Rights Committee. For the European Court for Human Rights, see amongst others, the cases of *Chitayev v Russia* (App no 59334/00), (18 January 2007) [134, 137–141]; *Öcalan v Turkey* (App no 46221/99) [2003] ECHR 125 [69–70]; *Akdivar and others v Turkey* (App no 21893/93) (16 September 1996) [65, 67]; *Cyprus v Turkey* (n 123) [99]; and *Kleyn et al v The Netherlands* (App nos 39343/98, 39651/98, 43147/98 and 46664/99) (6 May 2003) [156], all with further references. For the Inter-American Human Rights System, see also Article 46 (2) (b) of the Inter-American Convention on Human Rights (n 144); Inter-American Court of Human Rights, Judgment of 26 June 1987 in the *Velásquez Rodríguez* case (Preliminary Objections) Series C No 1 [88]; *Godínez Cruz* case, Judgment of 20 January 1989, Series C No 5 [71]; *Fairén Garbi and Solís Corrales* case, Judgment of 15 March 1989, Series C No 6 [93]; and the Court's Advisory Opinion of 10 August 1990, '*Exceptions to the Exhaustion of Domestic Remedies*', Advisory Opinion OC-11/90, 10 August 1990, IACtHR Series A No 11 (1990). For the African system, see Article 50 of the Af CHPR. On relevant jurisprudence of the African Commission on Human and Peoples' Rights, see N J Udombana, 'So far, so fair: The Local Remedies Rule in the Jurisprudence of the African Commission on Human and Peoples' Rights' (2003) 97 AJIL 1–37, 21–34.

that investigations and prosecutions are considered ineffective—thus provides guidance as to what rules govern the appropriate conduct of investigations, prosecutions and trials of crimes.

Fourth, principles and standards that are pertinent for duly investigating, prosecuting and punishing crimes can be drawn from rules regulating *offences against the administration of justice*.[162] While such offences are not, in every situation, the same in relation to the administration of *international* justice as those in relation to *domestic* courts, because the jurisdiction as an international court must take into account its different setting within the basic structure of the international community,[163] Article 70 of the ICC Statute provides a useful starting point for determining additional principles of due process recognized by international law.[164] To the extent that identical or similar[165] offences are committed against or by members of national authorities when core crimes within the jurisdiction of the ICC are investigated, prosecuted or adjudicated on the national level, they result in violations of principles of due process to which the ICC must have regard when determining whether the prerequisites are met for making a finding of unwillingness.

Fifth and finally, rules specifically relevant to the investigation, prosecution and punishment of international crimes can, under certain circumstances, also be distilled from the doctrine of *command responsibility*. The latter has emerged as a form of individual criminal responsibility when commanders knew, or had reason to know, that their subordinates were about to commit international crimes or had done so and the commander failed to take the necessary and reasonable measures to prevent such acts or to initiate disciplinary or penal action against

---

[162] For a brief analysis of the origin of the related notion of the offence of contempt of court, see ICTY Appeals Chamber Judgment of 31 January 2000 on Allegations of Contempt Against Prior Counsel, Milan Vujin [15–16].

[163] Ibid [18].

[164] The provision criminalizes offences such as '[c]orruptly influencing a witness, obstructing or interfering with the attendance or testimony of a witness, retaliating against a witness for giving testimony or destroying, tampering with or interfering with the collection of evidence'; '[i]mpeding, intimidating or corruptly influencing an official of the Court for the purpose of forcing or persuading the official not to perform, or to perform improperly, his or her duties'; [r]etaliating against an official of the Court on account of duties performed by that or another official' and '[s]oliciting or accepting a bribe as an official of the Court in connection with his or her official duties'.

[165] Note for instance the somewhat broader list of offences in Rule 77 of the Rules of Procedure and Evidence of the ICTY as amended on 12 July 2007, IT/32/Rev 40, which also provides for the punishment of '[a]ny person who threatens, intimidates, causes any injury or offers a bribe to, or otherwise interferes with, a witness who is giving, has given, or is about to give evidence in proceedings before a Chamber, or a potential witness, commits a contempt of the Tribunal' (Sub-Rule B); '[a]ny person who threatens, intimidates, offers a bribe to, or otherwise seeks to coerce any other person, with the intention of preventing that other person from complying with an obligation under an order of a Judge or Chamber, commits a contempt of the Tribunal' (Sub-Rule C). It also provides that 'Incitement to commit, and attempts to commit, any of the acts punishable under this Rule are punishable as contempts of the Tribunal with the same penalties' (Sub-Rule D) and reaffirms the Tribunal's 'inherent power [...] to hold in contempt those who knowingly and wilfully interfere with its administration of justice' (Sub-Rule E).

the perpetrators thereof.[166] What such 'necessary and reasonable measures' are depends on the competence of the respective commander and upon his/her degree of effective control, however.[167] The doctrine of command responsibility can therefore only supply principles of due process, which differ from case to case. The doctrine may nevertheless be a subsidiary source for contextual standards which are pertinent for duly investigating, prosecuting and punishing international crimes. For, command responsibility can assist in determining what States, as represented by the commander,[168] have to do in terms of investigating and prosecuting a case under the specific circumstances at hand.

The aforementioned sources of the 'principles of due process recognized by international law' provide the context for a more detailed analysis of the three non-mutually exclusive[169] manifestations of 'unwillingness' stipulated in subparagraphs (a) to (c) of Article 17 (2) to which we now turn.

3.5.2. Shielding

The first form of 'unwillingness' spelled out in Article 17 (2) is where '[t]he proceedings were or are being undertaken or the national decision was made for the purpose of shielding the person concerned from criminal responsibility for

---

[166] Different versions of the doctrine of command responsibility can be found in Articles 87 (3) of Additional Protocol I (n 144), 7 (3) of the Statute of the International Tribunal for the Prosecution of Persons Responsible for Serious Violations of International Humanitarian Law Committed in the Territory of the Former Yugoslavia since 1991 (adopted 25 May 1993) UNSC Res 827 (ICTY), 6 (3) of the Statute of the International Criminal Tribunal for the Prosecution of Persons Responsible for Genocide and Other Serious Violations of International Humanitarian Law Committed in the Territory of Rwanda and Rwandian citizens responsible for genocide and other such violations committed in the territory of neighbouring States, between 1 January 1994 and 31 December 1994, (adopted on 8 November 1994) UNSC Res 955 (ICTR), 6 (3) of the Statute of the Special Court for Sierra Leone, annexed to the Agreement between the United Nations and the Government of Sierra Leone on the Establishment of the Special Court for Sierra Leone, signed on 16 January 2002 (16 January 2002), available at http://www.sc-sl.org/Documents/scsl-statute. html, 28 ICC Statute (n 1). See also n 45.

[167] See eg ICTY Appeals Chamber, *Prosecutor v Delalic et al ('Celebici')* (Appeals Judgment) IT-96-21-A (20 February 2001) 198; ICTY Appeals Chamber, *Prosecutor v T. Blaskic* (Judgment) IT-95-14-A (29 July 2004) 72; ICTY Trial Chamber, *Prosecutor v E Hadzihasanovic and A Kubura* (Judgment) IT-01-47 (15 March 2006) 121–124, 171–178.

[168] If the duty of commanders of national armed forces to punish is violated, State and individual responsibility become two sides of the same coin. The omission of such individual commander is also an omission of an organ of the State concerned, in as much as armed forces are regularly assigned that status under the internal laws of States and thus fulfil the conditions to act on behalf of a State according to international law: cf Article 4 of the Articles on Responsibility of States for Internationally Wrongful Acts (2001) (n 161). A breach of the obligation of military commanders to act, besides establishing individual criminal responsibility, thus also constitutes an international wrongful act attributable to their State: cf Articles 2, 12 of the Articles on State Responsibility (2001). For a more detailed analysis of the relation between individual and state responsibility, see A Nollkaemper, 'Concurrence between individual responsibility and state responsibility in international law' (2003) 52 ICLQ 615–640.

[169] That the different forms of unwillingness are not mutually exclusive is evidenced by the formulation 'one or more' in the *chapeau* of Article 17 (2) Rome Statute (n 1).

crimes within the jurisdiction of the Court […]'.[170] The terms 'proceedings' and 'national decision' in Article 17 (2)(a) refer to those envisaged in Article 17 (1)(a) and (b). In other words, they refer to investigations and prosecutions[171] and decisions not to prosecute made by a State. The term 'proceedings in the other court' in Article 20 (3)(a) on shielding as an exception to the principle of *ne bis in idem*, on the other hand, refers to trial proceedings.[172]

As regards the phrase 'for the purpose of shielding the person concerned from criminal responsibility for crimes within the jurisdiction of the Court', a number of observations are warranted. One such observation relates to the employment of the words '*for the purpose of shielding*'. This formulation implies that the proceedings or the decision in question must be specifically directed at shielding; its rationale, and the intention that the author(s) had when adopting such a cause of (in)action, must have been to shield the person.[173] If one drew an analogy with the concept of intent in criminal law, the 'purpose'-requirement thus would resemble *dolus directus*.[174]

Determining whether the shielding-variant of unwillingness exists involves a determination of the *purpose* of proceedings or decisions, which, in turn, requires an inquiry into the 'state of mind' of a State. In so doing, the obvious difficulty arises as to how the mindset of an abstract entity, such as a State, can be determined. However, such 'state of mind' constructs are not unique to complementarity and are known in other areas of international law. Examples are the concept of States acting in 'good faith'[175] and the requirement that a State 'knows' of the circumstances of an internationally wrongful act to establish that State's responsibility for aiding or assisting in the commission of an internationally wrongful act under Article 16 of the Articles on State Responsibility.[176] The latter is understood to mean that 'a State is not responsible for aid or assistance […] unless

---

[170] Rome Statute (n 1) Article 17 (2)(a).

[171] Cf the explanatory footnote 24 in 'Decisions taken by the Preparatory Committee at its Session held in New York 4 to 15 August 1997' (1997) UN Doc A/AC. 249/1997/L.8/Rev. 1, Annex I, Report of the Working Group on Complementarity and Trigger Mechanism, 11.

[172] See *3.3*. Ne bis in idem: *Articles 17 (1)(c) and 20 (3)*.

[173] Such an understanding is also confirmed by the French version of the provision, which refers to '*la procedure a été ou est engagée ou la decision de l'État a été prise* dans le dessein *de soustraire la personne concernée à sa responsabilité pénale […]*'. Emphasis added.

[174] German criminal law, for instance, distinguishes between different forms of intent. Direct intent (*dolus directus, direkter Vorsatz*) denotes the situation in which the offender acts with the purpose of committing the *actus reus*, while indirect intent (*dolus eventualis, bedingter Vorsatz*) denotes that the offender does not act with that purpose but knows that the *actus reus* is the possible result of his/her actions and willingly accepts that result: see K Lackner, *Strafgesetzbuch mit Erläuterungen* (21st edn C H Beck, Munich 1995) 99–100. Similar distinctions between different forms of intent are made in other legal systems.

[175] See extensively J F O'Connor, *Good faith in international law, Hersch Lauterpacht memorial lectures* (Dartmouth, Aldershot 1991) 148; M Lachs, 'Some thoughts on the role of good faith in international law' in R J Akkerman, P J van Krieken and C O Pannenborg(eds), *Declarations on principles* (A W Stijhoff, Leyden 1977) 47–55.

[176] Cf Article 16 (a) of the Articles on State Responsibility (n 161).

the relevant State organ *intended*, by the aid or assistance given, to facilitate the occurrence of the wrongful conduct [...].'[177]

However, this does not make the actual determination of the requisite 'state of mind' of a State any easier. In the present context, this may ultimately involve an appraisal of the intentions of those individuals who are acting as state organs, such as investigators, prosecutors and judges, as well as an evaluation of the collective will of organs such as legislative bodies. In exceptional cases, the purpose of shielding may be established due to express statements or clearly manifested actions, such as blanket self-amnesties following initial investigatory steps of the relevant national authorities. However, in the absence of such direct proof, the 'devious intent on the part of the State, contrary to its apparent actions'[178] has to be inferred from circumstantial evidence. In these cases, the question arises as to what indicators may constitute such circumstantial evidence. Rule 51 of the Rules of Procedure and Evidence allows the Court to consider '*inter alia*, information that the State referred to in article 17, paragraph 1, may choose to bring to the attention of the Court showing that its courts meet internationally recognized norms and standards for the independent and impartial prosecution of similar conduct, or that the State has confirmed in writing to the Prosecutor that the case is being investigated or prosecuted.'[179] While this information is not determinative and creates at best a rebuttable presumption,[180] it may serve as one such indicator to assess whether proceedings are conducted for the purpose of shielding the person concerned from criminal responsibility. Thus deviations from earlier practices that were compliant with internationally recognized norms and standards for the independent and impartial prosecution of serious crimes would raise the suspicion of proceedings being conducted for the purpose of shielding the person concerned. In addition, the practice of the various organs that apply 'principles of due process'[181] as well as past experiences with national enforcement of international criminal law[182] supply examples of relevant indicators, which, on their own or cumulatively, may reveal that a State conducts proceedings or takes decisions 'for the purpose of shielding'.

Thus, if the court which adjudicates a case 'loses' evidence in its custody,[183] the judge blatantly disregards evidence which no reasonable observer would be able

---

[177] Commentary to Article 16, in: J Crawford (n 161) 149 [5], emphasis added.

[178] L Arbour and M Bergsmo, 'Conspicuous Absence of Jurisdictional Overreach' in H von Hebel, J Lammers and J Schukking (eds) (n 18) 129–140, 131.

[179] The Court may consider such information in considering unwillingness in general. It is not confined to do so only in the context of shielding.

[180] J T Holmes, 'Jurisdiction and Admissibility' in R S Lee (ed), *The International Criminal Court—Elements of Crimes and Rules of Procedure and Evidence* (Transnational Publ, New York 2001) 337.

[181] Cf *129–130*.

[182] See generally *Chapter II: National Suppression of Core Crimes*, at *3.2. Obstacles relating to Enforcement*.

[183] For example, see Report of the Special Rapporteur on the independence of judges and lawyers, Dato' Param Cumaraswamy, submitted in accordance with Commission on Human Rights

to ignore,[184] or a superior knows that a subordinate has committed core crimes and investigates, but does not submit the matter to the competent authorities for further investigation and prosecution in violation of clear regulations and merely tries to have that person replaced or transferred,[185] one can reasonably infer from these circumstances that the proceedings or the decision were for the purpose of shielding the person concerned.[186] Another example would be if the sentence imposed reflects such a purpose because it is manifestly insufficient in light of the gravity of the crime(s) in question and the form of participation of the accused. However, this matter has to be approached with some caution, since there is no universally accepted framework for sentencing ICC crimes. Different sentencing traditions and cultures, also in relation to the core crimes,[187] leave a large margin of appreciation to States in determining what an adequate sentence is.[188] Therefore, the sentencing of ICC crimes in domestic proceedings has to be treated deferentially when determining whether the sentence was imposed for the purpose of shielding a person from criminal responsibility.[189] Nevertheless, when national courts of the same jurisdiction treat comparable cases very differently without any good reason, such differences may be indicative of that purpose.

At the same time, the fact that the proceedings were or are undertaken or decisions had been made for the *purpose* of shielding does not necessarily mean that this shielding is also the *only or ultimate aim*. States may very well pursue different goals and consider the shielding to be necessary in order to attain them. Indeed, such ultimate aims may very well be laudable ones. A permanent stay of proceedings against the leader of an insurrectional movement in exchange for his taking part in a peace process would be a case at hand. Yet, the fact that the shielding is considered a necessary step in the pursuit of a higher goal does not render Article 17 (2)(a) inapplicable. In the same vein, proceedings conducted, or decisions taken for the purpose of shielding, need not necessarily result from breaches of international law by, and/or the bad faith on behalf of, a State.[190] While such

resolution 2001/39, Report on the mission to Guatemala (2001) E/CN.4/2002/72/Add.2 (21 December 2001) [32].

[184] Eg in the Xaman case, referred to in 'Report of the Special Rapporteur on the independence of judges and lawyers, on the mission to Guatemala' (2000) UN Doc E/CN.4/2000/61/Add.1, it was indicated that the patrol in question in this case had fired 288 bullets at unarmed civilians. The judge, however, suggested that the patrol did not intend to kill the civilians: see Report [50].

[185] See eg ICTY Prosecutor v Krstic (Judgment) IT-98-33-T (2 August 2001) 480–482.

[186] For further indicia, see also Informal Expert Paper for the ICC Office of the Prosecutor: The Principle of Complementarity in Practice (n 33) 14 [47] and Annex 4, 28–31.

[187] See generally U Sieber, *The punishment of serious crimes: a comparative analysis of sentencing law and practice* (2 Volumes, Ed Iuscrim, Freiburg, Breisgau 2004).

[188] Cf Article 80, which clarifies that the penalties under the Rome Statute do not affect 'the application by States of penalties prescribed by their national law, nor the law of States which do not provide for penalties prescribed [in the Statute].'

[189] H Olásolo, 'Complementarity Analysis of National Sentencing' in R Haveman and O Olusanya (eds), *Sentencing and Sanctioning in Supranational Criminal Law* (Intersentia, Antwerp 2006) 37–66, 41, 61.

[190] But see C Cárdenas (n 33) 115, who asserts that determining whether a person is shielded necessitates to assess the bona fides of the State.

situations can reasonably be expected to represent the majority of cases, they do not represent the full picture. For instance, a decision not to prosecute a person may be taken for the purpose of shielding that person on the ground that s/he enjoys immunity under international law.[191] Since such immunities do not bar the ICC from exercising its jurisdiction over such a person,[192] the latter could declare such cases admissible in accordance with Article 17 (2)(a). Another example where a decision is taken for the purpose of shielding the person(s) concerned and which does not necessarily result from bad faith is where such a decision is taken on humanitarian grounds, for instance when the alleged perpetrator is unfit to stand trial because of his age, ill-health or mental state.[193] However, such instances of 'bona fide unwillingness' are irrelevant for applying Article 17 (2)(a). A State can be held to be 'unwilling', as long as the *purpose* is to shield the person concerned from criminal responsibility.[194]

A further question is whether it is sufficient for Articles 17 (2)(a) or 20 (3)(a) to be triggered if it can be established that a *particular stage of the proceedings* was conducted for the purpose of shielding the accused, or whether this would have to be established for *all stages*. Different State organs from different branches of government are involved in those proceedings or decisions, which are assessed as to whether they were undertaken or made for the purpose of shielding. These organs enjoy a certain degree of mutual independence and/or exercise mutual control to varying degrees. Different organs may thus conduct proceedings or take decisions for different purposes, with one doing so for the purpose of shielding, while this does not necessarily hold true for other authorities.[195] The latter authorities may then be in a position to reverse the course of action and prevent the purpose of shielding of the initial proceedings or decision from materializing.[196] Finally, the entire political situation may change and remove those who

[191] On the current state of the law, see: pages 51–52. Alternatively, one can construe compliance with such immunities as a form of (legal) inability: see further *3.6. Inability: Article 17 (3), 158.* See also *Chapter VI: Complementarity and the Obligation to Investigate and Prosecute 6.3. Immunities Under International Law.*

[192] Cf Rome Statute (n 1) Article 27 (2). See generally D Akande, 'International Law Immunities and the International Criminal Court' (2004) 98 AJIL 407–433.

[193] Admittedly it is nevertheless highly unlikely that a case in which the alleged perpetrator is unfit to stand trial would be taken up by the ICC, as Article 53 (2)(c) makes explicit reference to the 'age or infirmity of the alleged perpetrator' as one of the factors for determining whether an ICC prosecution is in the interests of justice. See in this vein also, OTP Policy Paper on the Interests of Justice (n 130) 7.

[194] See also *264–265.*

[195] See for instance the *Genie-Lacayo v Nicaragua* Case (n 158), in which the Inter-American Court of Human Rights details the willingness of the Nicaraguan Assistant Attorney-General to investigate the case on various occasions, but finds that 'Nicaraguan military authorities obstructed, or failed to cooperate adequately in, the investigations conducted by the Attorney-General's Office and with the Seventh Judge of the Criminal District of Managua in which the preliminary proceedings took place [...]' [61, 68].

[196] An example is an initial investigation by the military, which amounted to a sham and the civilian justice system has the possibility of assuming jurisdiction and carry out the investigation. See for instance the Guatemalan case of the murder of Edgar Alfredo Ordóñez Porta, 'Report of the Special Rapporteur on the independence of judges and lawyers, Dato' Param Cumaraswamy,

are responsible for shielding to make way for a new regime which is dedicated to bringing perpetrators to justice.[197] In these cases, the ICC will be confronted with the question as to whether or not Articles 17 (2)(a) or 20 (3)(a) are applicable. The answer to this question would appear to depend upon whether the purpose of shielding of one particular stage of a proceeding, or of one particular decision not to prosecute, can effectively be prevented from materializing through subsequent proceedings or through a subsequent decision. In making that determination, the Court would have to consider whether, and to what extent, remedies against proceedings undertaken and decisions made for the purpose of shielding are available and effective, in analogy to what has been discussed above.[198]

3.5.3. Unjustified Delays

'[A]n unjustified delay in the proceedings which in the circumstances is inconsistent with an intent to bring the person concerned to justice'[199] is the second manifestation of unwillingness. In order for cases to be admissible under Article 17 (2)(b), they must meet a threefold test: there must not only be (1) a *delay* in the proceedings, but such a delay also has to be (2) *unjustified,* and such unjustified delay needs to be (3) *inconsistent with an intent to bring the person concerned to justice.* The provision also establishes a contextual framework for assessing whether or not such inconsistency exists by requiring that such an assessment take place in light of the *circumstances.* In contrast to the distinction between 'proceedings' and 'national decision' made in Article 17 (2)(a),[200] the use of the broad term 'proceedings' in Article 17 (2)(b) would seem to indicate that no unjustified delays may occur, regardless of whether the 'proceedings' are of an investigative, prosecutorial, trial, appellate, or any other nature, and that all stages of the proceedings have to be conducted expeditiously.

When, then, are delays unjustified, and when are such delays inconsistent with an intent to bring the person concerned to justice in the circumstances? The first question entails a determination of possible justifications for delays. In that context, the jurisprudence of human rights bodies on the right to be tried 'without undue delay'[201] and to a hearing 'within a reasonable time' in the determination of criminal charges,[202] as well as the right to such a hearing in the determination of one's civil rights and obligations,[203] are helpful. Notwithstanding the differences

submitted in accordance with Commission on Human Rights resolution 2001/39, Addendum, Report on the mission to Guatemala (2001) UN Doc E/CN.4/2002/72/Add.2 [34]. Another example is when a decision not to prosecute is not final, for example because the prosecutor has the possibility to challenge it: cf the Colombian *La Hormiga massacre* case (2000) 3 YIHL 459.

[197] On this scenario and its implications for the procedural setting of complementarity, see also *Chapter V: The Procedural Setting of Complementarity, 2.4. Complementarity at the Post-Admissibility Stage: Referral of Cases Back to National Criminal Jurisdictions?*

[198] See *124–125.*   [199] Rome Statute (n 1) Article 17 (2)(b).

[200] Cf *134–135.*   [201] Cf Articles 14 (3)(c) ICCPR (n 92).

[202] Cf Articles 6 (1) ECHR, 8 (1) IACHR, 7 (1)(d) AfCHPR (n 144).

[203] Cf Articles 6 (1) ECHR, 8 (1) IACHR (n 144).

in wording to Article 17 (2)(b),[204] and the fact that the human rights provisions cannot simply be mechanically transplanted,[205] there is considerable overlap between the notions of an 'unjustified delay' and the human rights norms on 'undue delay' and hearings 'within a reasonable time'. For, when interpreting these human rights norms, supervisory organs assess whether there have been justifications for a delay in deciding that a delay was 'undue' or that a hearing was not held 'within a reasonable time'.[206]

Justifications for a delay depend on the specific circumstances of the case in question and cannot be determined in the abstract.[207] Nevertheless, several clusters of justifying factors can be identified. All human rights bodies agree that one of the relevant factors is the (legal and factual) complexity of the case.[208] The European and Inter-American Courts of Human Rights add that other such factors are the judicial activity of the interested party[209] and the behaviour of the judicial authorities.[210] However, no particular factor is conclusive. Rather, these factors must be examined separately and then their cumulative effect must

[204] Recall that the drafters of the Statute replaced the term 'undue', which appeared in earlier drafts of the provision which later became Article 17 (2)(b), with 'unjustified' during the Rome Conference, because the notion of 'undue delay' was seen as being too low a threshold for unwillingness, *90*.

[205] See *130*.

[206] Cf amongst many others the following cases: Human Rights Committee, *Thomas v Jamaica*, Communication No 614/95 (1999) UN Doc CCPR/C/65/D/614/1995 (25 May 1999) [9.5] ['The Committee [...] notes with regard to the period of 23 months between the trial and appeal that the State party has conceded that such a delay is undesirable, but that it has not offered any further explanation. In the absence of any circumstances *justifying the delay*, the Committee finds that with regard to this period there has been a violation of article 14, paragraph 3 (c), in conjunction with paragraph 5, of the Covenant.' Emphasis added]. European Court of Human Rights, *König v Germany* (App no 6232/73) [1978] ECHR 3 (28 June 1978) [105] ['In an overall assessment of the various factors, the Court concludes that the delays occasioned by the difficulties in the investigation and by the applicant's behaviour do not of themselves *justify* the length of the proceedings. [...] the Court concludes that the "reasonable time" stipulated by Article 6 para. 1 [...] was exceeded.' Emphasis added]. Inter-American Court of Human Rights, *Genie-Lacayo v Nicaragua* Case (n 158) [78] ['[...] the matter under consideration is somewhat complex, since the investigations were very extensive and the evidence copious [...]. All of this could *justify* the fact that the trial, which also involved many incidents and instances, lasted longer than others with different characteristics.' Emphasis added].

[207] See amongst others HRC *Morael v France*, Communication No 207/1986 (1988), UN Doc Supp No 40 (A/44/40) (28 July 1989), at 210 [9.4]; ECHR *König v Germany*, ibid [99].

[208] Ibid; *Genie-Lacayo v Nicaragua* case (n 158) [77]; S Trechsel (n 144) 144–145. As examples for the complexity of a case, Harris, O'Boyle and Warbrick cite the volume of evidence, the number of defendants or charges, the need to obtain expert evidence or evidence from abroad, and the complexity of the legal issues involved: D J Harris, M O'Boyle and C Warbrick, *Law of the European Convention on Human Rights* (Butterworths Publ, London, Dublin, Edinburgh 1995) 224.

[209] See eg ECHR, *König v Germany* (n 206); IACtHR, *Genie-Lacayo v Nicaragua* case (n 158); S Trechsel (n 144) 142-144. D J Harris, M O'Boyle and C Warbrick point out that these judicial activities include, *inter alia,* an applicant's making use of his or her procedural rights and thereby lengthening proceedings, and his or her refusal to appoint a defence lawyer: ibid 224, with further examples 224-225.

[210] See eg ECHR, *König v Germany* (n 206); IACtHR, *Genie-Lacayo v Nicaragua* case (n 158). For examples of factors which are taken into consideration, see S Trechsel (n 144) 146–148; D J Harris, M O'Boyle and C Warbrick ibid 225.

be assessed.[211] On the other side of the equation, the human rights bodies also seem to agree that a number of factors can *not*, as a rule, serve as justifications for delays. This is especially the case as far as economic and administrative restraints are concerned, although there are limited exceptions with regard to a temporary and unforeseeable backlog of cases.[212] The aforementioned factors which may serve as justifications, and those which may not, have also been applied in the context of proceedings in which persons have stood accused of core crimes,[213] thus giving further weight to the argument that they can also be applied in the context of Article 17 (2)(b).

However, the specific contextual elements of core crimes—a pattern of genocidal conduct for genocide,[214] a widespread or systematic attack against the civilian population for crimes against humanity,[215] the existence of an armed conflict for war crimes[216]—add a further dimension to the determination of whether or not a delay is 'unjustified' within the meaning of Article 17 (2)(b). These contexts may make it necessary to identify the *core* of the notions of 'undue delay' or 'reasonable time' if such proceedings take place *during periods in which ICC crimes are still being committed*. For, a State may have proclaimed that it derogates from its human rights obligations in the light of the context of core crimes, which it regards as amounting to a 'public emergency which threatens the life of the nation'.[217] Such derogations are permissible, but only to the extent that they are 'strictly required by the exigencies of the situation', consistent 'with [States'] other

---

[211] For the European Court, see D J Harris, M O'Boyle and C Warbrick ibid 223. Similarly, the IACtHR applies a *'global analysis of the proceeding'*: see for instance *Genie-Lacayo v Nicaragua* case (n 158) [81].

[212] HRC, *Lubuto v Zambia*, Communication No 390/1990 (1995) UN Doc CCPR/C/55/D/390/1990/Rev. 1, at 5.1.–5.3. and 7.3.; as to the limited exceptions, see the jurisprudence of the European Court for Human Rights, which interprets the European Convention as imposing a duty on the contracting parties to organize their legal systems so as to allow the courts to comply with the requirements of Article 6 (1) regardless of costs, but a State is not held liable for delays that result from a backlog of cases that was not reasonably foreseeable provided the State takes reasonably prompt remedial action; for an overview of relevant case law, see D J Harris, M O'Boyle and C Warbrick (n 208) 227–228.

[213] See eg European Commission of Human Rights, 9433/81 (1982); European Court of Human Rights, *Mutimura v France* (App no 46621/99) (8 June 2004) [69–75]. See also the case law of the European Commission referred to in E Mose and C Aptel, 'Trial Without Undue Delay Before the International Criminal Tribunals' in L C Vohrah *et al* (eds), *Man's Inhumanity to Man—Essays on International Law in Honour of Antonio Cassese* (Kluwer, The Hague 2003) 539–566, 543, nn 10, 11.

[214] Cf Elements of Crimes (n 103), Introduction to the Elements of Crime of Article 6 and the fourth Element for each of the prohibited acts.

[215] Cf *chapeau* of Rome Statute (n 1) Article 7.

[216] Cf Elements of Crimes (n 103), Introduction to the Elements of Crimes of Article 8 and the *chapeau* of Article 8 (a) [cross-referring to the Geneva Conventions, common Article 2 of which provides that the Conventions 'shall apply to all cases of declared war or of any other armed conflict which may arise between two or more of the High Contracting Parties'], as well as the *chapeaux* of Article 8 (2)(b) ['international armed conflict'], (c) ['armed conflict not of an international character'] and (e) ['armed conflicts not of an international character'].

[217] Cf Article 4 ICCPR (n 144). Similar provisions are contained in Articles 15 ECHR (n 144) and 27 IACHR (n 92).

obligations under international law' and do 'not involve discrimination solely on the ground of race, colour, sex, language, religion or social origin.'[218] This legal setting for derogating from human rights obligations warrants two comments.

First, as far as situations of armed conflict are concerned, international humanitarian law provides for a number of 'other obligations under international law'[219] on the right to be tried without undue delay. Article 103 (1) of the Third Geneva Convention, for instance, provides that investigations relating to prisoners of war 'shall be conducted *as rapidly as circumstances permit* and so that his trial shall take place *as soon as possible*'.[220] Similarly, Article 71 of the Fourth Geneva Convention provides that '[a]ccused persons who are prosecuted by the

---

[218] Cf Article 4 (1) ICCPR (n 92); limitations to the possibility of derogating from their human rights obligations, which are to a large extent identical to the ones provided for under Article 4 (1) ICCPR are spelled out in Article 15 (1) ECHR (n 144) and 27 (1) IACHR (n 144). On derogations from the right to a fair trial under Article 14 of the ICCPR, see also the Human Rights Committee's General Comment 13, *Article 14*, (Twenty-first session, 1984) UN Doc HRI/GEN/1/Rev.6 at 135 (2003); on states of emergency more generally, see Human Rights Committee, General Comment 29, *States of Emergency (article 4)* UN Doc CCPR/C/21/Rev.1/Add.11 (2001); see also D Weissbrodt, *The Right to a Fair Trial under the Universal Declaration of Human Rights and the International Covenant on Civil and Political Rights* (Martinus Nijhoff Publ, The Hague 2001) 139–141 with further references to relevant case law of the HRC.

[219] Human Rights Committee, General Comment 29 ibid [3] ['During armed conflict [...] rules of international humanitarian law become applicable and help, in addition to the provisions in article 4 and article 5, paragraph 1, of the Covenant, to prevent the abuse of a State's emergency powers.']. Also compare ibid [9] ['[...] article 4, paragraph 1, requires that no measure derogating from the provisions of the Covenant may be inconsistent with the State party's other obligations under international law, particularly the rules of international humanitarian law'] and [11] ['States parties may in no circumstances invoke article 4 of the Covenant as justification for acting in violation of humanitarian law or peremptory norms of international law, for instance by taking hostages, by imposing collective punishments, through arbitrary deprivations of liberty or by deviating from *fundamental principles of fair trial*, including the presumption of innocence'.] Emphasis added. In relation to crimes against humanity, the Human Rights Committee stated: 'In assessing the scope of legitimate derogation from the Covenant, one criterion can be found in the definition of certain human rights violations as crimes against humanity. If action conducted under the authority of a State constitutes a basis for individual criminal responsibility for a crime against humanity by the persons involved in that action, article 4 of the Covenant cannot be used as justification that a state of emergency exempted the State in question from its responsibility in relation to the same conduct.' [12].

[220] Emphases added. The ICRC Commentary explains: 'In order [...] to prevent certain instances of abuse such as occurred during the Second World War, the [...] provision enjoins the authorities concerned to conduct investigations "as rapidly as circumstances permit". The fact that prisoners of war are involved may well make certain procedures more difficult; it was nevertheless desirable to permit some flexibility, in order not to give any semblance of justification for hasty investigation. The text adds: "and so that his trial shall take place as soon as possible". At first sight, this recommendation may seem superfluous since the purpose of the investigations is to prepare the trial. The words clearly demonstrate the intention of the authors of the Convention to keep the period of investigation as short as possible and to protect the prisoner of war during that time from any vexatious or other measures not directly intended to expedite the opening of the trial. In this connection, one should bear in mind the rule that the police authorities are not competent to conduct the investigations and there must be absolute separation between the police and the judicial authorities.' Jean S Pictet (ed), *The Geneva Conventions of 12 August 1949: commentary, Part III, Geneva Convention relative to the treatment of prisoners of war* (International Committee of the Red Cross, Geneva 1960) 477–478.

Occupying Power [...] shall be brought to trial *as rapidly as possible*.'[221] The right to be tried without undue delay provided in these provisions is of customary status and equally applicable during non-international armed conflicts.[222] Therefore, in the context of determining whether or not a delay in criminal proceedings has occurred during armed conflicts, international humanitarian law provides for an important, albeit arguably more flexible, set of obligations with which States have to comply, notwithstanding a derogation from their human rights obligations, to ensure a speedy trial.

Second, in the absence of other obligations under international (humanitarian) law,[223] it is impermissible for States to derogate from their obligations to provide a speedy trial beyond that which is 'strictly required by the exigencies of the situation', and in any case may 'not involve discrimination solely on the ground of race, colour, sex, language, religion or social origin'.[224]

These elements at the core of the right to be tried without undue delay, as flowing from international humanitarian law and the strict exigencies of the situation, may thus become the relevant parameters for determining whether a delay was unjustified within the meaning of Article 17 (2)(b) in times of public emergency.

However, as already noted,[225] the wording of Article 17 (2)(b) suggests that an unjustified delay is, in itself, insufficient for cases to be declared admissible. Rather, such an unjustified delay must also be '*in the circumstances [...] inconsistent with an intent to bring the person concerned to justice*'. As in the context of determining whether a person is shielded from criminal responsibility,[226] Article 17 (2)(b) thus implies a determination of the state of mind of a State, in as much as it necessitates an evaluation of its 'intent'. However, there is an important difference as compared with the 'shielding-variant' of unwillingness. In contrast to the latter, the inconsistency-formula in subparagraph (b) denotes a more objective test. In order for cases to be admissible, the Prosecutor has to show that the unjustified delay is *inconsistent* with an intent to bring the person concerned to justice, rather than providing evidence that such intent does indeed exist.[227]

An unjustified delay will often also be inconsistent with an intent to bring the person concerned to justice. When this is the case, the requirement that such a delay must, in addition, be 'in the circumstances [...] inconsistent with an intent

---

[221] Emphasis added. The ICRC Commentary notes that '[t]his provision is of the utmost importance in time of occupation when delays in the preliminary investigation may tend to prolong the period spent under arrest awaiting trial', Jean S Pictet (ed), *The Geneva Conventions of 12 August 1949: commentary, Part IV, Geneva Convention relative to the protection of civilian persons in time of war* (International Committee of the Red Cross, Geneva 1958) 354.

[222] J M Henckaerts and L Doswald-Beck (eds), *Customary International Humanitarian Law* (Volume I: Rules, CUP, Cambridge 2005) Rule 100, 363–364.

[223] This is the case when the core crimes concerned are crimes against humanity or genocide committed outside the context of an armed conflict.

[224] See (n 218).   [225] Cf *139*.   [226] Cf *135–137*.

[227] Also cf S A Williams (n 29) 393–394 ['A State will be determined by the Court to be unwilling where there has been an unjustifiable delay in the proceedings which in the circumstances *is seen to be inconsistent* with an intent to bring the person concerned to justice.'] Emphasis added.

to bring the person concerned to justice' is met. Yet, starting from the assumption that situations may arise in which the second part of the sentence attains a meaning of its own,[228] there may be delays that cannot be justified by reference to the mentioned factors (complexity of the case, judicial activity of the interested party, behaviour of the judicial authorities), but are nevertheless 'consistent with an intent to bring the person concerned to justice' under the given circumstances.

Scenarios in which this is indeed the case are conceivable. For instance, a State may find itself in a period of transition from a suppressive regime, during which ICC crimes were committed, and the State, while investigating these crimes, intends to arrest and prosecute suspects only after a period during which the fragile political situation consolidates. Another example would be the situation in which a State is embroiled in an internal armed conflict and intends to investigate and prosecute core crimes that have been committed during that armed conflict, but decides not to do so because the necessary evidence can only be found in a part of the territory where the security situation is temporarily so volatile that the risk to which investigators are exposed is regarded as being too high.[229] The Court, when deciding whether an unjustified delay was inconsistent with an intent to bring the person concerned to justice, could thus take such circumstances into account and declare cases inadmissible.

A final observation on Article 17 (2)(b) is that it constitutes an *exception* to the general assumption underlying Article 17 (2) as a whole, which focuses on violations of due process principles to the *advantage* rather than the *disadvantage* of the person concerned.[230] Article 17 (2)(b) seems susceptible to an interpretation that does not only cover situations in which delays in the proceedings are intended to protect the accused from criminal responsibility, as in the case of shielding. Rather, the provision would equally seem to extend to those situations in which unjustified delays work to his or her detriment.[231] Thus a strong argument can be made that delays in the proceedings against persons suspected of having committed core crimes that are left in a limbo for years,[232] without any indication that they will be tried, could fall under Article 17 (2)(b) and thus render cases

---

[228] That assumption follows from the rule of treaty interpretation of *ut res magis valeat quam pereat*: see R Jennings and A Watts (n 51) 1280 ['The parties are assumed to intend the provisions of a treaty to have a certain effect, and not to be meaningless. [...] Therefore, an interpretation is not admissible which would make a provision meaningless, or ineffective.'].

[229] Such a situation could arguably nevertheless amount to inability if one were to conclude that it amounted to an 'unavailability of [a State's] national judicial system' due to which 'the State is unable to obtain the accused or the necessary evidence and testimony or otherwise unable to carry out its proceedings': cf Rome Statute (n 1) Article 17 (3). On that aspect of inability, see further *3.6. Inability: Article 17 (3)*.

[230] Cf *130*.

[231] See also C Cárdenas (n 33) 118–119; F Razesberger (n 29) 41; F Gioia, 'State Sovereignty, Jurisdiction, and "Modern" International Law: The Principle of Complementarity in the International Criminal Court' (2006) 19 LJIL 1095–1123, 1111.

[232] A pertinent example is provided by those persons designated by the US as 'enemy combatants', who are being detained on the Naval base at Guantanamo Bay.

admissible, because they are unjustified and inconsistent with an intent to bring the person concerned to justice.

3.5.4. Lack of Independence and Impartiality

The last form of unwillingness, provided in Articles 17 (2)(c) and 20 (3)(b), are proceedings that were not or are not being conducted independently or impartially, and conducted in a manner which, in the circumstances, is inconsistent with an intent to bring the person concerned to justice. Both Article 17 (2)(c) and 20 (3)(b) contain virtually identical wording,[233] and the main difference between them lies in the fact that the former applies to proceedings prior to the conclusion of a trial and the latter to when a person has already been tried by another court.[234]

'Independence' and 'impartiality' are well-known concepts in human rights law,[235] where they evolved, first and foremost, to protect individuals against abusive proceedings to their disadvantage. However, they have equally been applied in the opposite situation, in which outside interference or bias of judicial organs work to the advantage of a person.[236] Drawing upon the interpretation of the

---

[233] The main difference is that Article 20 (3)(b) contains a reference to 'the norms of due process' which, for Article 17 (2)(c), derives from the *chapeau* of Article 17 (2) Rome Statute (n 1).

[234] On the question as to whether a person 'has been tried by another court' within the meaning of Article 20 (3), see *124–125*.

[235] Cf Articles 14 (1) ICCPR (n 92), 6 (1) ECHR (n 144), 8 (1) IACHR (n 144), 7 (1) and 26 AfCHPR (n 144); see generally S Trechsel (n 144) 45–80. Cf also Articles 84 (2) GC III, 75 (4) AP I (n 144), 6 AP II (n 144). It has been pointed out that the latter two provisions also give valuable indications to help explain the terms 'a regularly constituted court, affording all the judicial guarantees which are recognized as indispensable by civilized peoples' employed in Article 3 (1)(d) common to the Four Geneva Conventions 1949 (n 144): see C Pilloud, J Pictet, Y Sandoz and C Swinarski, *Commentary on the additional protocols of 8 June 1977 to the Geneva Conventions of 12 August 1949* (International Committee of the Red Cross, Nijhoff Publ, Dordrecht 1987) 1625, 878 [3084]. While all the mentioned provisions refer to 'tribunals' or 'courts', it is generally recognized that the notions of 'independence' and 'impartiality' apply to all organs of the judiciary, as evidenced in the various instruments, cited (n 144). On this aspect, see also Human Rights Committee, *Kulomin v Hungary*, Communication No 521/1992 (1996) UN Doc CCPR/C/56/D/521/1992, in which the Human Rights Committee applied the notions to the conduct of the public prosecutor and noted at para. 11.3 that 'it is inherent to the proper exercise of judicial power, that it be exercised by an authority which is independent, objective and impartial in relation to the issues dealt with'. The independence and impartiality of domestic courts have also been factored into the determination as to whether a denial of justice has occurred, cf J Paulsson (n 156) 131–206, and whether local remedies are ineffective or futile and thus do not have to be exhausted in order to render a claim admissible before international courts and tribunals: see CF Amerasinghe (n 161) 208 and Third report on diplomatic protection by Mr John Dugard (n 161) [41, 44].

[236] For examples, see the following reactions to the administration of justice in Colombia: 'Report of the Special Rapporteur on the independence of judges and lawyers, Mr. Param Cumaraswamy, on the mission to Colombia (1998) UN Doc E/CN.4/1998/39/Add.2 [140] [lack of independence because system of military justice allows active-duty officers to try their own subordinates]; IACtHR Annual Report on Colombia 2002, [47–50], available at <http://www.cidh.org/annualrep/2002eng/chap.4.htm#COLOMBIA>, in which matters such as the judicial practices regarding the assignment of competences, the violence or threats against those who investigate or report human rights violations, the lack of progress in the investigation of cases where the responsibility of State agents is involved, and the hasty removal of individual prosecutors on the

two concepts within the field of human rights thus provides crucial guidance for interpreting them in the context of Article 17 (2)(c).

The two concepts, although interrelated, are distinct from each other. *'Independence'*, on the one hand, means independence of the judiciary from the executive and the legislature as well as from the parties. In determining whether such independence exists, matters such as the manner of appointment of members of the judiciary and their terms of office, the existence of guarantees against outside pressures and the question as to whether the judicial organ displays a posture of independence have to be taken into consideration.[237] Independence thus has an institutional dimension as well as relating to a 'state of mind' or attitude in the actual exercise of judicial functions.[238] Both dimensions have to be considered in assessing whether the relevant organ may be reasonably perceived as independent.[239] Examples of a lack of independence are when members of the judiciary are exposed to threats[240] or when the jurisdiction of courts has to be exercised in accordance with decisions of the executive.[241]

'Impartiality', on the other hand, 'implies that judges must not harbour preconceptions about the matter put before them, and that they must not act in

---

verge of bringing formal charges against State agents, particularly high-ranking Army officers, led the Commission to express concern and the hope that the alleged support to the National Human Rights Unit by the Office of the General Prosecutor 'will translate into the *independence, impartiality* [*sic*] and effectiveness of the National Human Rights Unit in its task of clarifying human rights violations', emphasis added.

[237] N Jayawickrama (n 142) 515–518 and S Trechsel (n 144) 53–61, both with further references to relevant case law. See also Human Rights Committee, General Comment 13 (n 218) 14 [3]. On the jurisprudence of the Strasbourg organs, see Harris, O'Boyle and Warbrick (n 208) 231–234. See also Informal Expert Paper for the ICC Office of the Prosecutor: The Principle of Complementarity in Practice (n 33) Annex 4, 29.

[238] N Jayawickrama (n 142) 518.

[239] On this 'perception test', see N Jayawickrama (n 142) 518. For the European Court of Human Rights, see for instance *Belilos v. Switzerland*, (App no 10328/83) [1988] ECHR 4 (29 April 1988). In that case, Mrs Belilos complained, *inter alia*, that the Police Board by which he was convicted of a minor criminal offence was subordinate to the police authorities and thus not independent from the executive. The Swiss Government did not challenge that but argued that the applicant nonetheless received a fair trial [63]. The Court held, however, that 'a number of considerations relating to the functions exercised and to internal organisation are relevant too; even appearances may be important [...]. The ordinary citizen will tend to see [the member of the Lausanne Police Board] as a member of the police force subordinate to his superiors and loyal to his colleagues. A situation of this kind may undermine the confidence, which must be inspired by the courts in a democratic society. In short, the applicant could legitimately have doubts as to the independence and organisational impartiality of the Police Board, which accordingly did not satisfy the requirements of Article 6 § 1 [...] in this respect.' [67].

[240] Concluding observations of the Human Rights Committee: Argentina (1995) UN Doc CCPR/C/79/Add.46; UN Doc A/50/40 [144–165], [155] ['The Committee is concerned about threats to members of the judiciary, which through intimidation seek to compromise the independence of the judiciary as set forth in article 14 of the Covenant.']

[241] European Court of Human Rights, *'The Greek case'* [1969] 12 Yearbook of the European Convention on Human Rights 148.

ways that promote the interests of one of the parties.'[242] In the words of the first Rapporteur on the independence and impartiality of the judiciary, jurors and assessors, and the independence of lawyers, Mr Singhvi, it 'implies freedom from bias, prejudice and partisanship; it means not favouring one more than another; it connotes objectivity and an absence of affection or ill-will. To be impartial as a judge is to hold the scales even and to adjudicate without fear or favour in order to do right [. . .]'.[243] Assessing the impartiality of proceedings thus involves two questions, namely whether a judicial organ objectively offers sufficient guarantees to exclude any legitimate doubt as to its impartiality, combined with the subjective test of whether it can be shown on the facts that a member of the court has in fact acted with personal bias.[244] Clear-cut examples of a lack of impartiality are politically motivated statements made by judges involved in the proceedings at hand[245] and a system of military justice which allows active-duty officers to try their own subordinates.[246] There may, however, also be more subtle ways that may be indicative of bias, for instance when judges allow for broader defences in specific (categories of) cases than in others.[247]

Given the contextual elements of the crimes that fall within the jurisdiction of the ICC,[248] a remark on the independence and impartiality of *military and special courts* seems warranted, since the establishment of such courts with jurisdiction over core crimes is not uncommon.[249]

[242] Human Rights Committee, *Karttunen v Finland*, Communication No. 387/1989 (1992) UN Doc CCPR/C/46/D/387/1989, 7.2.

[243] 'Final report on the independence and impartiality of the judiciary, jurors and assessors, and the independence of lawyers by Mr. Singhvi, submitted to the Sub-Commission on Prevention of Discrimination and Protection of Minorities' (1985) UN Doc E/CN.4/Sub.2/1985/18 and Add.1–6 [79].

[244] S Trechsel (n 144) 61–80, with further references to relevant case law; N Jayawickrama (n 142) 521. As to European Court of Human Rights jurisprudence, see Harris, O'Boyle and Warbrick (n 208) 235–238.

[245] Cf for instance Human Rights Committee, *González del Río v Peru*, Communication No 263/87 (1990) UN Doc CCPR/C/46/D/263/1987 [3.3] and [5.2].

[246] This has been criticized by the Special Rapporteur on the independence of judges and lawyers in his 1998 Report on the mission to Colombia (n 236) [140].

[247] This can take the form, for instance, of adopting the conditional liability approach to the defence of superior orders for nationals and the absolute liability approach with regards to enemy nationals. For this practice, see P Gaeta, 'The Defence of Superior Orders: The Statute of the Ineternational Criminal Court versus Customary International Law' (1999) 10 EJIL 179–180, note 22.

[248] Cf (nn 214–216) and text.

[249] For an overview of several States, see J K Kleffner, 'General Report, The Compatibility of National Legal Systems with the Statute of the Permanent International Criminal Court (ICC), Part II—Procedural Law' (2003) International Society for Military Law and the Law of War, Recueil XVI, vol II 515–516. See also, in the context of the conflict in the Sudan region of Darfur, the special courts set up by the Sudanese government, referred to in Third Report of the Prosecutor of the International Criminal Court to the UN Security Council Pursuant to UNSCR 1593 (2005), 14 June 2006, available at: <http://www.icc-cpi.int/library/cases/OTP_ReportUNSC_3-Darfur_English.pdf>, 3–6 and Annex I; Fourth Report of the Prosecutor of the International Criminal Court to the Security Council pursuant to UNSC 1593 (2005), 14 December 2006, availableat<http://www.icc-cpi.int/library/organs/otp/OTP_ReportUNSC4-Darfur_English.pdf>,

In that regard, the Human Rights Committee, in its General Comment 13 on Article 14 of the ICCPR, which provides for several fair trial guarantees, including independence and impartiality, held that these guarantees 'apply to all courts and tribunals within the scope of that article whether ordinary or specialized.'[250] A similar approach has been taken by the European Court of Human Rights.[251] While neither the Human Rights Committee nor the European Court of Human Rights has declared the establishment of such courts and tribunals impermissible per se, the Committee identified the problem that '[q]uite often the reason for the establishment of such courts is to enable exceptional procedures to be applied which do not comply with normal standards of justice' and that 'such military and special courts do not afford the strict guarantees of the proper administration of justice in accordance with the requirements of article 14' in some countries.[252] It further held that '[i]f States parties decide in circumstances of a public emergency as contemplated by article 4 to derogate from normal procedures required under article 14, they should ensure that such derogations do not exceed those strictly required by the exigencies of the actual situation, and respect the other conditions in paragraph 1 of article 14.'[253]

Thus, if a State decided to establish military or special courts for the purpose of trying core crimes, the applicable criteria for the ICC to determine whether proceedings 'were not or are not conducted independently or impartially' remain the same as for ordinary courts.

Similarly, in times of *armed conflict,* which may be considered by States to require derogations from certain human rights obligations, international humanitarian law supplies important complementary rules that oblige States to conduct proceedings which conform to (at least basic) standards of independence and impartiality.[254] In addition to being considered customary international humanitarian law,[255] such standards derive from Article 84 GC III,

6; and in Situation in Darfur, The Sudan, Prosecutor's Application under Article 58 (7), Public Redacted Version, ICC-02/05, 27 February 2007 [256].

[250] Human Rights Committee, General Comment 13 (n 218) [4].

[251] See instead of many others *Cooper v the United Kingdom* (App no. 48843/99), Judgment of the Grand Chamber, 16 December 2003 [108–110] [determining whether the UK court-martial system meets the requirements of independence and impartiality required under Article 6 (1)].

[252] Human Rights Committee, General Comment 13 (n 218) [4].

[253] Ibid. On derogation, see also *141–143*.

[254] Cf Human Rights Committee, General Comment 219 (n 218), excerpts cited (n 219) as well as the following excerpt from said Comment at para 16: 'As certain elements of the right to a fair trial are explicitly guaranteed under international humanitarian law during armed conflict, the Committee finds no justification for derogation from these guarantees during other emergency situations. The Committee is of the opinion that the principles of legality and the rule of law require that fundamental requirements of fair trial must be respected during a state of emergency. Only a court of law may try and convict a person for a criminal offence. The presumption of innocence must be respected. In order to protect non-derogable rights, the right to take proceedings before a court to enable the court to decide without delay on the lawfulness of detention, must not be diminished by a State party's decision to derogate from the Covenant.'

[255] J M Henckaerts and L Doswald-Beck (eds) (n 222) Rule 100, 354–357.

which requires 'the essential guarantees of independence and impartiality as generally recognized'; from Article 75 (4) of the First Additional Protocol, which refers to 'an impartial and regularly constituted court respecting the generally recognized principles of regular judicial procedure';[256] from Common Article 3, which requires courts to be 'regularly constituted [...] affording all the judicial guarantees which are recognized as indispensable by civilized peoples'; and from Article 6 (2) of the Second Additional Protocol, which contains language similar to Article 84 GC III.

With the foregoing general remarks on the notions of 'independence' and 'impartiality' in mind, Article 17 (2)(c) raises a number of additional issues. First, the question arises as to how the second part of the provision, *'and they were or are being conducted in a manner which, in the circumstances, is inconsistent with an intent to bring the person concerned to justice'* has to be understood. More in particular, is has been doubted whether this part of the provision establishes an additional threshold that needs to be met in order for Article 17 (2)(c) to apply.[257] Indeed, such an interpretation may find some support in the authoritative French version of the Rome Statute, which uses the word *'mais'* to join the first and second part of the provision, rather than 'and'/'y' in the English and Spanish language versions. The French text could therefore be read to mean that the second part of the provision merely clarifies the first part, and epitomizes the fact that any lack of independence or impartiality in the proceedings inevitably leads to their being conducted inconsistently with an intent to bring the person concerned to justice.[258] *Any* lack of independence or impartiality would thus trigger Articles 17 (2)(c) or 20 (3)(b) and render cases admissible.

However, such an interpretation is open to several objections. First, it would make the second part of the provision redundant. If the drafters intended to let any lack of independence and impartiality suffice for cases to be admissible, then why add the second part?[259] Second, the understanding of the word *'mais'* in the French language version of the Statute suggested is not the only possible interpretation. The significance of this word, which contrasts the first to the second

---

[256] According to the ICRC Commentary on the latter provision, it 'emphasizes the need for administering justice as impartially as possible, even in the extreme circumstances of armed conflict, when the value of human life is sometimes small', (n 235) 878 [3084].

[257] C Cárdenas (n 33) 123–124.

[258] The French text of Article 17 (2)(c) reads: 'La procédure n'a pas été ou n'est pas menée de manière indépendante ou impartiale *mais* d'une manière qui, dans les circonstances, est incompatible avec l'intention de traduire en justice la personne concernée.' Emphasis added. According to C Cárdenas, Ibid: '['Bei einem gerichtlichen Verfahren sind Mängel an Unparteilichkeit oder Unabhängigkeit an sich unvereinbar mit der Absicht, den Beschuldigten 'vor Gericht zu stellen', weil Unabhängigkeit und Unparteilichkeit Voraussetzung eines ordnungsgemässen Gerichtsverfahrens sind. Wenn es zu einer Gerichtsverhandlung gekommen ist, dient die zweite Hälfte der Vorschrift nur zur Verdeutlichung der Folge von Mangel an Unparteilichkeit oder Unabhängigkeit. Das 'und', welches in der deutschen, englischen und spanischen Fassung der Norm zwischen dem ersten Teil [...] und dem zweiten Teil [...] zu finden ist, wäre dann als ein 'sondern', wie in der französischen verbindlichen Fassung zu verstehen.']

[259] Cf (n 228) and accompanying text.

part of the provision, can also be understood to *supply further specificity* on how the lack of independence and impartiality needs to manifest itself. Third, the meaning which best reconciles the different language versions, while having regard to the object and purpose of the treaty,[260] is to understand the provision as cumulatively requiring not only a lack of independence and impartiality in conducting proceedings but, in addition, that such proceedings are conducted in a manner which, in the circumstances, is inconsistent with an intent to bring the person concerned to justice. Admittedly, meeting the latter threshold may often be a logical consequence of the lack of independence or impartiality. For instance, a statement of a judge indicating his or her bias in favour of an accused would not only clearly evidence a lack of impartiality, but also be inconsistent with an intent to bring the person concerned to justice. However, there may be instances in which a lack of independence or impartiality is not inconsistent with that intent. This may be the case, for example, when a lack of independence and impartiality is confined to the absence of more general, abstract guarantees, such as an inadequate scheme for financial security of members of the judiciary,[261] the manner in which they are appointed or their terms of office. However, in these cases, it does not automatically follow that proceedings, which these members of the judiciary conduct, are inconsistent per se with an intent to bring the person concerned to justice. They may be flawed on an abstract level, but effective prosecution on the national level may still be possible in such cases, therefore rendering an intervention by the ICC unwarranted. In order to take into account this possibility, Article 17 (2)(c) should be interpreted so as to require that a lack of independence and impartiality must be qualified, in as much as it must also be inconsistent with an intent to bring the person concerned to justice in the circumstances.[262] It is therefore submitted that Articles 17 (2)(c) and 20 (3)(b) need to be understood so as to require that these two criteria are met cumulatively before a case can be declared admissible.

A second issue that needs to be clarified, is whether, and to what extent, Articles 17 (2)(c) and 20 (3)(b) provide room for cases being declared admissible in which a lack of independence and impartiality has resulted in the person concerned being unduly tried and/or convicted.[263] The language employed, and the general context of Article 17 (2), suggests that Articles 17 (2)(c) and 20 (3)(b) are primarily concerned with situations in which flaws in the proceedings work to the advantage of the person concerned.[264] The other side of the equation, ie biased

[260] Cf (n 119).
[261] Cf Basic Principle 11 of the United Nations Basic Principles on the Independence of the Judiciary, adopted by the Seventh United Nations Congress on the Prevention of Crime and the Treatment of Offenders held at Milan from 26 August to 6 September 1985 and endorsed by General Assembly resolutions 40/32 of 29 November 1985 and 40/146 of 13 December 1985.
[262] For an interpretation of the terms *'which, in the circumstances, is inconsistent with an intent to bring the person concerned to justice'*, reference is made to the identical terms in Article 17 (2)(b), *143–144.*
[263] *53–54.*   [264] Cf also *130–131,* but see the exception of 'unjustified delays', *144–145.*

proceedings *to the disadvantage of the person concerned,* however, does not seem to have much occupied the minds of the drafters of the Statute.[265]

Does the notion of unwillingness in general, and its subcategory of a lack of independence and impartiality in particular, nevertheless extend to situations in which individuals are framed for crimes that they did not commit? Does unwillingness cover situations in which they are otherwise tried in violation of fundamental norms of due process in their traditional sense of 'principles and rules which safeguard the position of the individual charged'?[266] In response to that question, some have asserted that the ICC 'is not a human rights court'[267] and that the Court was neither designed nor would be well advised to concern itself with such situations.[268]

Even if one rejected these broad assertions, biased proceedings to the detriment of a person can arguably be brought under Article 17 (2)(c) only in very limited circumstances, or by an interpretation which may at best be considered liberal and at worst be said to stretch the provision beyond its limits. The limited circumstances consist of proceedings against a person other than the real perpetrator, where it could be argued that proceedings are not conducted impartially and are inconsistent with an intent to bring the person concerned (ie the *real* perpetrator) to justice.[269] In other cases, when the person concerned is the real perpetrator but does not receive a fair trial, one would have to give the terms 'to bring the person concerned to justice' an exceptionally broad reading and understand 'justice' in the material rather than the formal sense as implying fairness.[270] This, however, would clearly go beyond the ordinary meaning of the phrase 'to bring someone

---

[265] R B Philips (n 63) 80. For a recount of the drafting history of what eventually became Article 17 (2)(b) and (c) with specific attention to the fact that the drafters of the Statute favoured the intervention of the ICC only when the irregularity of the domestic proceedings worked to the advantage of the person concerned, see E Carnero Rojo, 'The Role of Fair Trial Considerations in the Complementarity Regime of the International Criminal Court: From "No Peace without Justice" to "No Peace with Victor's Justice"?' (2005) 18 LJIL 829–869, 840–854. As an exception during the drafting, where the matter came up, the coordinator of the working group on complementarity and trigger mechanism during the Preparatory Committee's session held 4 to 15 August 1997, John T Holmes recounts as one of the scenarios that was considered as amounting to a lack of independence and impartiality within the meaning of what eventually became Article 17 (2)(c) the deliberate violation of a defendant's rights to taint evidence or testimony: see J T Holmes (n 33) 51.

[266] Cf (n 143).

[267] R E Fife, 'The International Criminal Court—Whence it Came, Where it Goes' (2000) 69 NJIL 63–85, 66–67; M Benzing (n 29) 598; Informal Expert Paper for the ICC Office of the Prosecutor: The Principle of Complementarity in Practice (n 33) 8 [23].

[268] C van den Wyngaert and T Ongena (n 90) 725, who appear to deny that the ICC can intervene in situations where the accused was the victim of partisan justice, because '[t]his would give the task of the Court a totally different dimension and make it a body for the protection of individuals and their basic rights against States'. See also E Carnero Rojo (n 265) 854.

[269] See for instance the Guatemalan case of the murder of Edgar Alfredo Ordóñez Porta, who disappeared on 3 May 1999 and was found dead on 6 May 1999. The military then fabricated a case against two innocent persons who were later acquitted by the court: see (n 196) [34].

[270] In this vein, C Cárdenas (n 33) 123; F Gioia, 'Comments on Chapter 3 of Jann Kleffner' in J K Kleffner and G Kor (eds) (n 79) 105–112, 112. See also (n 196) [34].

to justice', which means to 'arrest and try someone in court for a crime'.[271] The phrase in Article 17 (2)(c) is not 'to do justice to someone', which would imply a concern for the fairness of the proceedings. Finally, it is even more difficult to bring instances under Article 17 (2)(c), in which no crime has been committed at all and a person is framed, for instance, with the aim to eliminate a political opponent. As the Prosecutor has to determine that there is a reasonable basis to proceed,[272] such a basis will be lacking in the absence of any crime. The only incidental factor which provides an argument against proceeding with the case on the national level would be the very fact that the Prosecutor has determined that the information available to him provides no reasonable basis to believe that a crime within the jurisdiction of the Court has been committed.[273] In sum, Article 17 (2)(c)—as well as the provisions on 'unwillingness' as a whole—depicts a considerable blind spot vis-à-vis unfair proceedings that detrimentally affects the rights of suspects, accused or defendants in domestic proceedings.[274]

3.6. Inability: Article 17 (3)

The second ground for rebutting inadmissibility in case criminal proceedings vis-à-vis core crimes are conducted is when States are 'unable'. 'Inability' is defined in Article 17 (3) as a situation in which, 'due to a total or substantial collapse or unavailability of its national judicial system, the State is unable to obtain the accused or the necessary evidence and testimony or otherwise unable to carry out its proceedings.' These terms are of a more objective nature than those employed in connection to 'unwillingness', which was the main reason why

---

[271] The Concise Oxford Dictionary (2001) (n 74).
[272] Cf Rome Statute (n 1) Articles 15 (3) and 53. See also further, *Chapter V: The Procedural Setting of Complementarity, 2.1. Admissibility and the Initiation of an Investigation.*
[273] Cf Rome Statute (n 1) Article 53 (1)(a).
[274] K J Heller, 'The Shadow Side of Complementarity: The Effect of Article 17 of the Rome Statute on National Due Process' (2006) 17 Criminal Law Forum 250–288, 260–263. But see F Gioia (n 231) 1111–1113, who comes to the opposite conclusion by drawing on a number of broader arguments and considerations, including the ICC's role to serve as an international body complementing national jurisdictions in meting out fair punishment for the most serious crimes by abiding by the highest international human rights standards; the objective underlying the reference to 'principles of due process recognized by international law' in Article 17 as circumscribing the Court's discretion; the Prosecutor's mandate according to Article 54 (1) of the Statute to 'extend the investigation to cover all facts and evidence relevant to an assessment of whether there is criminal responsibility under this Statute and, in doing so, investigate incriminating and exonerating circumstances equally' with a view to 'establish[ing] the truth'; Article 21(3) of the Statute, which specifically mandates that the application and interpretation of law by the Court shall 'be consistent with internationally recognized human rights'; and 'the broader architecture of 'modern' international criminal justice, as first implemented by the ad hoc tribunals', including Rule 11 *bis* of the ICTY Rules of Procedure and Evidence. It is submitted, however, that none of these arguments do away with the concern that the actual wording of Article 17 (2) does not lend itself to an application in cases where violation of due process to the detriment of a person, except in the instances previously indicated.

agreement on the notion of 'inability' and its definition in Article 17 (3) could be achieved more easily.[275]

It is clear from the wording that the provision envisages two basic forms of inability—a collapse or unavailability of a State's national judicial system, which causes a State to be 'unable to obtain the accused or the necessary evidence and testimony or otherwise unable to carry out its proceedings'. The structure of Article 17 (3) nevertheless warrants clarification as to *whether the words 'total or substantial' only qualify the word 'collapse' or also the word 'unavailability'*. In the first alternative, the threshold for proving a collapse would differ from the one required to prove unavailability. For the latter, *any* unavailability of a State's judicial system would suffice, as long as such unavailability caused the inability to obtain the accused, the necessary evidence, etc. By contrast, the second alternative would require such unavailability to be, at a minimum, 'substantial'.

The practical relevance of this question may seem somewhat negligible. As long as it can be demonstrated that a State is 'unable to obtain the accused or the necessary evidence and testimony or otherwise unable to carry out the proceedings', it is hardly conceivable that any collapse or unavailability that would cause such inability would not, at least, be 'substantial'. However, should the matter have to be decided, both interpretations are grammatically and syntactically possible.

The intention of the drafters seems to have been not to let *all* situations of such incapability fall into the ICC's reach. This is especially evidenced by the fact that the notion of 'partial collapse' in earlier drafts of the relevant provisions was replaced by the notion of 'substantial collapse'.[276] However, to interpret the provision as establishing the requirement of 'total or substantial' only in relation to 'collapse' is more easily reconcilable with the object of effective prosecution and the purpose of ending impunity.[277] In order to effectively supply the deficiencies of national criminal jurisdictions with a view to ensure accountability of perpetrators of core crimes, *any* unavailability that renders States incapable to obtain the accused or the necessary evidence and testimony or otherwise unable to carry out the proceedings should be within the reach of the ICC. Such an interpretation finds further support in the French and Spanish language versions of the Statute.[278] It is also compatible with the drafting history of Article 17 (3) as a whole and the underlying premise that the notion of inability should not be too restrictive.[279] It follows that *any* unavailability of a State's judicial system suffices

---

[275] Cf *85–86*.   [276] J T Holmes (n 33) 52–55.   [277] See *105*.

[278] French: '[. . .]la Cour considère si l'État est incapable, en raison de l'effondrement *de la totalité ou d'une partie substantielle de son propre appareil judiciaire ou de l'indisponibilité de celui-ci*, de se saisir de l'accusé, de réunir les éléments de preuve et les témoignages nécessaires ou de mener autrement à bien la procédure.' Spanish: '[. . .]la Corte examinará si el Estado, debido al *colapso total o sustancial de su administración nacional de justicia o al hecho de que carece de ella*, no puede hacer comparecer al acusado, no dispone de las pruebas y los testimonios necesarios o no está por otras razones en condiciones de llevar a cabo el juicio.' Emphases added.

[279] This led to the inclusion of the clause 'or otherwise unable to carry out the proceedings': cf (n 171) and accompanying text in Ch III.

provided that such unavailability renders the State unable to obtain the accused or the necessary evidence and testimony, or otherwise unable to carry out the proceedings.

What, then, is meant by the two different *notions of 'collapse' and 'unavailability'* of a State's national judicial system? As a sociological phenomenon, a *collapse* can generally be described as a situation in which *'the police, judiciary and other bodies serving to maintain law and order have either ceased to exist or are no longer able to operate.* In many cases, they are used for purposes other than those for which they were intended.'[280] It is clear from Article 17 (3), however, that the collapse refers to a State's *national judicial system* rather than all State institutions. Admittedly, a collapse of a judicial system often goes hand in hand, as cause and consequence, with the disintegration of other State institutions which do not fulfil any judicial or law-enforcement functions.[281] However, the fact that such other institutions remain operative does not render Article 17 (3) inapplicable. At the same time, the notion of a State's *judicial system* needs to be understood broadly and is not limited to the judiciary *stricto sensu*. This is readily apparent when one considers the envisaged consequence of a collapse (or unavailability), which is that the State concerned is 'unable to obtain the accused or the necessary evidence and testimony or otherwise unable to carry out its proceedings'. This consequence calls for an understanding of the concept of 'a judicial system', which extends to all State authorities which are involved in obtaining the accused or the necessary evidence and testimony, or in carrying out proceedings in any other way, thus including the police, prosecutors, etc.

Article 17 (3) requires a collapse of a State's national judicial system to be *'total or substantial'*. It is clear when a collapse is *total*, namely when the national judicial system has disintegrated in its entirety. Yet, it is difficult to see how initial investigative steps—which, as noted earlier,[282] are required for the complementarity criteria in Article 17 to apply—can be taken when a national judicial system has totally collapsed. The logical consequence of a total collapse is the absence of even initial investigative steps, ie complete inaction (unless such investigative steps have been taken *prior* to the total collapse of a State's judicial system). In the absence of such steps, however, cases are admissible without the need to assess the admissibility criteria in Article 17.[283] The practical relevance of the 'total collapse' type of inability for such an assessment therefore seems questionable at best.

[280] D Thürer, 'The 'failed State' and international law' (1999) 836 IRRC 731–761, 736; first emphasis in the original, second emphasis added, footnote omitted. Thürer refers to 'failed States' rather than 'collapsed States' but notes that he regards the two denominations as interchangeable. See also N L Wallace-Bruce, 'Of Collapsed, Dysfunctional and Disoriented States: Challenges to International Law' (2000) 47 NILR 53–73, 59 ['basic institutions of governance have ceased to function'].
[281] This was the case in Somalia, for instance, where all State institutions, including legislative assemblies, the government *stricto sensu* and the judiciary, as well as the police, had ceased to exist or were unable to operate; N L Wallace-Bruce (n 280) 61 (with further references at n 23).
[282] Cf *103–105*.   [283] Cf *104–105*.

This is different for a *substantial* collapse. A clear example would be the case in which the relevant authorities initiate an investigation against members of an armed opposition group during an internal armed conflict, but the State's national judicial system has collapsed in areas under effective control of that group.[284] It is also conceivable, for instance, that investigative authorities such as the police remain operational and thus able to carry out investigative steps, while the prosecution services or the criminal court system have collapsed.

However, the Statute does not contain any further guidance as to when the threshold of a substantial collapse is met. While a total collapse establishes the high end of the spectrum, a substantial collapse needs to be distinguished from a situation in which a collapse is merely 'partial' at the low end of the spectrum. Such a distinction can be derived from the ordinary meaning of the two terms and is confirmed by the drafting history of Article 17 (3).[285] When shifting resources can compensate such a partial collapse or transfer the trial to other venues, the threshold of a substantial collapse is not met.[286] In a similar vein, it has been asserted that inability 'is not a matter of administrative burden and the Court is not envisioned as an adjunct to a strained national system.'[287] Between these two outer boundaries of the spectrum of a partial and a total collapse, it is, however, difficult to determine in the abstract with a higher degree of precision when the threshold of a *substantial* collapse is met.

Any total or substantial collapse of a State's national judicial system necessarily entails that the second form of inability—*unavailability*—is also met. To the extent that the system has collapsed, it is also unavailable. The two types of inability thus overlap to a certain extent. However, an interpretation of Article 17 (3) must start with the assumption that certain forms of unavailability exist, which cause the State to be unable to obtain the accused or the necessary evidence and testimony, or otherwise be unable to carry out its proceedings while not amounting to a total or partial collapse.[288] An example would be a situation in which a State's national judicial system has not collapsed but is 'unavailable' in as much as it is too weak to carry out proceedings in a safe environment for members of the judiciary, victims, witnesses and/or the perpetrator and thus be 'otherwise unable to carry out its proceedings'.[289] The unwillingness or inability of States other than the one wishing to exercise jurisdiction to provide judicial assistance

---

[284] It should be noted that, as a matter of principle, States remain obliged to investigate and prosecute acts of members of armed opposition groups but that they may be exempted from that obligation to the extent that they have lost effective control. For relevant human rights jurisprudence, see L Zegveld, *Armed Opposition Groups in International Law: The Quest for Accountability* (Thesis, Rotterdam 2000) 79–90.

[285] As to the latter, see J T Holmes (n 33) 55.   [286] J T Holmes (n 14) 677.

[287] R B Philips (n 63) 79. See also J T Holmes (n 14) 677.

[288] See (n 228) and text.

[289] Cf G S McNeal, 'ICC Inability Determinations in Light of the Dujail Case' (2007) 39 Case Western Reserve Journal of International Law 325–350, 342 [inability because security situation and lack of witness protection in Baghdad made it difficult to procure witnesses]. Recall that such a situation need not amount to an 'unjustified delay' (n 229) and text.

or extradite the accused,[290] and the unwillingness of (groups of) persons to participate in the judicial process as witnesses,[291] are other examples. The lack of sufficient qualified personnel to effect a prosecution has also been suggested.[292]

Another manifestation of unavailability results from *gaps in the national legal framework* for the investigation and prosecution of core crimes.[293] However, different types of gaps have to be distinguished. Article 17 (3) does *not* apply when a State has failed to establish its *jurisdiction* over a given crime, as in such a case it would not qualify as 'a State which has jurisdiction over [a case]', thus already precluding entering into the admissibility assessment under Article 17 (1).[294] Furthermore, legislative gaps may constitute a bar to taking even initial investigative steps, which, as noted above, would entail that cases are admissible without having to show unwillingness or inability under Article 17.[295]

However, to the extent that a State has, in principle, jurisdiction over a case and can take at least initial investigative steps, other legislative gaps may render the national system unavailable and, as a consequence, the State may be unable to carry out its proceedings, thus rendering the case admissible in accordance with Article 17 (3).[296] The 1997 Penal Code of the Republic of Paraguay serves to illustrate how *deficiencies* can lead to an 'unavailability' of a State's judicial system: Article 8 of the Penal Code provides, *inter alia,* that Paraguayan penal law shall be applied extraterritorially with regard to 'other acts, that according to an international treaty, the Paraguayan state is obliged to prosecute, even if they were committed in a foreign country'.[297] In principle, the provision would thus

---

[290] Concannon provides examples in respect to the US' unwillingness to cooperate in Haiti's efforts to bring to justice Haitian perpetrators who allegedly were involved in human rights violations during the 1991–94 dictatorship: cf B Concannon, 'Beyond Complementarity: The International Criminal Court and National Prosecutions, a View from Haiti' (2000) 32 Columbia. Human Rights LR 201–250, 219.

[291] This was the case, for instance, in Kosovo after NATO's invasion: see F M M Florenz, 'The Rule of Law in Kosovo: Problems and Prospects' (2000) 11 Criminal Law Forum 130.

[292] J T Holmes (n 14) 678. See also for further examples S Morel (n 33) 133–135.

[293] See generally *Chapter II: National Suppression of Core Crimes, 3.1. Obstacles relating to Implementing Legislation.*

[294] Cf *110–112.*   [295] See *103–105.*

[296] L Condorelli, 'La Cour pénale internationale: un pas géant (pourvu qu'il soit accompli...)' (1999) 103 RGDIP 7–21, 21; K L Doherty and T L H McCormack (n 112) 152; F Lattanzi, 'The International Criminal Court and National Jurisdictions' in M Politi and G Nesi (eds), *The Rome Statute of the International Criminal Court—A Challenge to Impunity* (Ashgate, Dartmouth, Aldershot 2001) 177–223, 181; P Gaeta, 'Official Capacity and Immunities' in A Cassese, P Gaeta and J Jones(eds) (n 14) 975–1002, 998; The Informal Expert Paper for the ICC Office of the Prosecutor on The Principle of Complementarity in Practice (n 33) 15 [50]; Report of the International Commission of Inquiry on Darfur to the United Nations Secretary-General Pursuant to Security Council Resolution 1564 of 18 September 2004, 25 January 2005 [586]. For supporting state practice, see *334–336.* But see C Cárdenas (n 33) 126 [asserting that Article 17 (3) does not apply to situations in which the factors, which constitute 'inability', can be removed by adopting the necessary laws].

[297] Article 8 (1) 7 of the Penal Code of the Republic of Paraguay, Law No 1160/97 Penal Code of the Republic of Paraguay, reproduced in 1 YIHL (1998) 621–623, 622. After Paraguay ratified the Statute on 14 May 2001, becoming the 31st State Party, a presidential decree was passed

allow for the exercise of universal jurisdiction with regard to grave breaches of the Geneva Conventions.[298] And yet, the Penal Code omits a number of these grave breaches.[299] To the extent that such gaps cannot be filled by other means and results in Paraguay's inability to carry out its proceedings, its national judicial system would be unavailable. The same result is warranted in case a State fails to remove statutory limitations for ICC crimes and a prosecution becomes barred on that ground.

Beyond these deficiencies in the implementation of the specific legal framework for the investigation and prosecution of core crimes, it has also been suggested that 'unavailability' covers the lack of implementation in domestic legal orders not only of applicable substantive prescriptions but also of international standards on procedural requirements.[300] These standards, it is argued, include those set forth in the Statute itself 'as referred to in Article 21', entailing that 'unavailability' covers all cases in which national jurisdictions prove to be incapable 'to provide justice in the case'.[301] If, for instance, criminal proceedings in a given judicial system would be carried out in violation of internationally recognized norms of due process,[302] cases would be admissible.

It seems doubtful, however, whether such a reading is consistent with the wording of Article 17 (3), especially in light of the requirement of a causal connection between, on the one hand, the unavailability of a State's judicial system and, on the other hand, a State's inability to obtain the accused or the necessary evidence and testimony, or some other inability to carry out its proceedings.[303] A lack of due process does not entail an inability 'to obtain the accused or the necessary evidence and testimony'. The only possible way would thus be to subsume it under other forms of inability to carry out proceedings, provided one understood the term 'proceedings' to refer to 'fair proceedings'. Such an interpretation would appear to stretch Article 17 (3) beyond its limits, however. The wording of the provision suggests that the unavailability of a State's national judicial system

(No 19.685) on 10 December 2002 that created a committee on implementation of the Rome Statute. Source: <http://www.iccnow.org/countryinfo/theamericas/paraguay.html>.

[298] On the relevant provisions of the Geneva Conventions, see *10–11*.

[299] Paraguay became a party to the Four Geneva Conventions on 23 October 1961 and is therefore under an obligation to enact any legislation necessary to provide effective penal sanctions for persons committing, or ordering to be committed, any of the grave breaches. However, Article 320 of the Parguayan Penal Code (n 297) does not include grave breaches of wilfully depriving a prisoner of war or other protected person of the rights of fair and regular trial and the taking of hostages (Articles 130 of the Third Geneva Convention and 147 of the Fourth Geneva Convention).

[300] F Lattanzi (n 296).   [301] Ibid.

[302] Note that these are understood here in the strict sense as those 'principles and rules which safeguard the position of the individual charged': cf (nn 143–145) and text. The Statute itself includes fair trial standards in Articles 55, 66 and 67. Furthermore, Article 21 of the Statute includes such standards in the form of 'applicable treaties and the principles and rules of international law' (para 1 (b)) and 'internationally recognized human rights' (para 3).

[303] K J Heller (n 274) 264.

must constitute a *bar* to carrying out the proceedings.[304] The lack of due process guarantees does not constitute such a bar, however, but only relates to *the way in which* these proceedings are carried out.

Besides deficiencies in a State's judicial system, which under the aforementioned circumstances fall under Article 17 (3), unavailability may also be caused by other *impediments*. The difference between the latter and deficiencies is that these impediments result from compliance with, rather than inadequate implementation of, international legal norms. This is notably the case when a State, which has jurisdiction over a case and has taken initial investigative steps, is barred from proceeding with an investigation or prosecution because the person concerned enjoys immunity under international law.[305] Another conceivable example would be a resolution of the Security Council under Chapter VII, prohibiting a State or States from prosecuting a given (number of) individual(s).[306]

4. Interim Conclusions

The principle of complementarity, and the criteria for the admissibility of cases into which it translates, bears the potential of responding to many of the obstacles that have hampered—and are likely to continue to hamper—the effective enforcement of the prohibitions of core crimes on the national level. When States remain inactive or are 'unwilling' or 'unable', the ICC is in a position to step in and fill the gap. Conversely, complementarity provides a number of yardsticks for what States have to do in order to retain jurisdiction, namely to conduct investigations, prosecutions and criminal trials that satisfy the criteria of 'willingness' and 'ability'.

However, the foregoing analysis also discloses a number of criticisms. The intention of the drafters of the Statute to achieve a formulation of criteria for admissibility that was as clear and as unsusceptible to subjective interpretation as

---

[304] In the words of John T Holmes, the phrase 'otherwise unable to carry out its proceedings', 'does give the Court some latitude to determine admissibility where unforeseen circumstances *block* national proceedings' as it 'would cover most instances beyond the State's inability to obtain the accused or the necessary evidence or testimony'. [emphasis added]; John T Holmes (n 14) 678.

[305] Cf pages 51–52. As to the requirement for at least initial investigative steps to be taken before issues of admissibility have to be addressed, it needs to be emphasized that international law does not seem to protect (certain) incumbent State officials from certain investigative steps. In the words of the ICJ, when explaining what is meant by 'full immunity from criminal jurisdiction and inviolability', '[...] that immunity and that inviolability protect the individual concerned against *any act of authority of another State which would hinder him or her in the performance of his or her duties*': *Case Concerning the Arrest Warrant of 11 April 2000* (n 60) [54], emphasis added. *A contrario*, as long as investigative steps do not hinder the performance of the duties of the person concerned, such as the questioning of witnesses and the gathering of evidence through non-intrusive means, they can be taken with respect to someone who enjoys immunity under international law.

[306] L Condorelli and S Villalpando, 'Referral and Deferral by the Security Council' in A Cassese, P Gaeta and J Jones (n 14) 627–655, 640. See also pages 165–166.

possible resulted in the detailed and exhaustive *definitions in Article 17 (2) and (3)*. The price for such detail is the *limited flexibility* of the admissibility criteria and the *(potential for) gaps* in these definitions. These problems are amply illustrated by complementarity's neglect of situations in which individuals are subjected to unfair proceedings. With only very limited exceptions, and often only by stretching relevant terms of Article 17, the criteria for admissibility do not provide room for the ICC to assume jurisdiction in cases where there have been violations of norms of due process, disadvantageous to the person concerned. This gap is striking if one considers the extent to which due process guarantees have been incorporated into the Statute for purposes of proceedings before the Court itself[307] and the express inclusion of 'internationally recognized human rights' as part of the ICC's applicable law.[308] In other words, the criteria for admissibility would seem to entail the paradox that violations of norms of due process that protect a suspect or an accused in national proceedings will often be beyond the reach of the ICC with its scrupulous regard for fair trial guarantees. To this extent, the potential of complementarity to supply the deficiencies of national criminal jurisdictions remains incomplete.

Turning to more *specific aspects* of the criteria for admissibility, the *notion of 'unwillingness'* entails a number of problems, both conceptually and in practical terms. *Conceptually*, the *distinction between the three different forms of unwillingness* remains obscure, as they *overlap* to a significant degree. Indeed, the need for the three different forms of unwillingness may be questioned.[309] It would seem that instances of shielding and unjustified delays are only subcategories of proceedings that are neither conducted independently or impartially nor conducted in a manner which, in the circumstances, is consistent with an intent to bring the person concerned to justice.[310] One fails to see in which situation an instance of shielding or of an unjustified delay as defined in Article 17 (2)(a) and (b) can meet the standards of impartiality and independence as they flow from Article 17 (2)(c). Admittedly, Article 17 (2) does not conceive of the different forms of 'unwillingness' as mutually exclusive.[311] However, the need for Article 17 (2)(a) and (b) is doubtful, given that Article 17 (2)(c) contains a broader notion of which the other two forms can easily be conceptualized as derivatives.

The lack of independence and impartiality notion of 'unwillingness' is also less problematic in *practical terms*. This is especially the case in comparison with the unwillingness-variant of undertaking proceedings or making decisions *for the*

[307] Cf Rome Statute (n 1) Articles 55, 63, 66–67.
[308] Cf Rome Statute (n 1) Article 21 (3).
[309] Holmes asserts, for instance, that '[t]he concept of shielding is itself quite broad and an argument could be made that the other criteria, unjustified delay and independence and impartiality, are simply corollaries of the concept. Nevertheless, the drafters of the Statute decided to provide the Court with three separate criteria.' J T Holmes (n 14) 675.
[310] In this vein, see also F Razesberger (n 29) 43.
[311] The *chapeau* Article 17 (2) Rome Statute (n 1) uses the words 'one *or more* of the following' (emphasis added).

purpose of shielding the person concerned in Article 17 (2)(a). In the absence of any express statement to that effect by the relevant State authorities, it will in all likelihood be extremely difficult to establish such 'purpose'. The admissibility criteria in Articles 17 (2)(c) and 20 (3)(b) are at least susceptible to a more objective test in as much as they require a lack of independence and impartiality to be *inconsistent with an intent to bring the person concerned to justice,* rather than requiring the demonstration of the actual lack of such an intent.[312] The notion also bears the additional advantage of incorporating concepts that can be derived, to a large extent, from existing international legal standards. However, it needs to be emphasized that the 'inconsistency-test' bears the potential of only *mitigating* rather than solving the difficulties that an assessment of the subjective motives of a State entails.[313]

Whilst the notion of 'unwillingness' is clearly the more problematic, the notion of *'inability'* can also not evade a number of criticisms. For one, similar to the subcategories of unwillingness, the different forms of inability *overlap*. 'Unavailability' would appear broad enough to cover equally a (total or substantial) collapse of the national judicial system. Second, when a *collapse* is *total*, namely when the national judicial system has disintegrated in its entirety, no initial investigative steps can be taken. Yet, complementarity treats the total collapse-form of the notion of inability in the same manner as any other form of inability, or, for that matter, unwillingness. Also in that regard, Article 17 (1) requires at least initial investigative steps. This logical inconsistency epitomizes that complementarity at times lacks the necessary degree of differentiation, notwithstanding its meticulous provisions.

A *solution of the aforementioned difficulties* would seem possible by considering an *alternative approach* to the definition of the admissibility criteria. It is acknowledged that at this point in time, with the first experience in the application of the existing criteria only emerging, a revision of them may be premature. Given the contentious nature that characterized their drafting process, such a revision also bears the additional risk of leading to a result that puts the admissibility threshold higher than is currently the case. These practical and political considerations

---

[312] Cf (n 228) and text.

[313] See eg J T Holmes (n 33) 75 ['A possible weakness lies in the criteria on which the Court must determine admissibility. [...] [U]navoidably, there were subjective elements included [...]. All three criteria for determining unwillingness require the Court to be satisfied as to the intent of the State in the circumstances. [...] In obvious cases, this will not pose a problem, but a more sophisticated State may be more effective at masking its intentions, thus impinging on the Court's ability to assume jurisdiction.']; see also T van Boven, 'The Principle of Complementarity—The International Criminal Court and National Laws' in J Wouters and H Panken (eds), *De Genocidewet in international perspectief,* Jura Falconis Libri (De Boeck & Larcier Publ, Brussels 2002) 65–74, 67 ['[I]t is questionable whether these notions [of unwillingness and inability] effectively lend themselves as suitable criteria for determining the admissibility of a case. In particular the concept of unwillingness is dubious because, in spite of the circumstances indicated in Article 17 (2) as proof of a State's unwillingness, unwillingness represents a subjective notion about the intent of the State authorities.'].

aside, however, a few cautious and anticipatory suggestions can be made to solve the noted difficulties, overlaps and inconsistencies. These suggestions could be implemented either at the review conference seven years after the entry into force of the Statute or at a review conference '[a]t any time thereafter, at the request of a State Party'.[314]

It is submitted that such an alternative approach should focus on the *effectiveness of national proceedings* as the decisive criterion to determine whether a case is admissible or not.[315] The notion of effectiveness bears a more objective connotation as it can be applied in a result-oriented manner. The effectiveness of proceedings can be determined by reference to the envisaged result that such proceedings are supposed to achieve, which is to determine the guilt or innocence of a person suspected of an ICC crime.

More specifically, admissibility could, and should, be determined on the basis of whether national proceedings ensure the effective investigation and prosecution of perpetrators of international crimes. While the criterion of effectiveness would cover instances of what we now know as 'unwillingness' and 'inability', it would not concentrate on (categories of) *causes* for ineffectiveness, as Article 17 currently does. Rather, the criterion could be defined in reference to the relevant practices that have evolved in international law, such as those of human rights bodies.[316]

Thus defined, a criterion of effectiveness as the cornerstone of complementarity would lend itself to a more objective application, and thereby be in line with the express intention of the drafters of the Statute. Moreover, an approach based on that criterion, with the requirements for such effectiveness clearly identified, would provide more guidance to States on what is required from them when investigating and prosecuting core crimes. Positively spelling out these requirements in order for cases to be inadmissible would contrast with the current approach which uses definitions in Article 17 (2) and (3) that identify inadequacies that render cases admissible. The alternative approach could therefore likely enhance the pull-effect of complementarity as a mechanism that seeks to induce States to investigate and prosecute.[317]

---

[314] Cf Rome Statute (n 1) Article 123 (1) and (2).

[315] Recall the 1994 Draft Article 35 included the notion of 'ineffectiveness', and the terms 'effective' and 'ineffective' also resurfaced during the discussions of a definition of unwillingness: J T Holmes (n 33) 49.

[316] Cf *3.5.1. 'Principles of due process recognized by international law'*.

[317] For further discussion on this pull-effect, see *Chapter VII: Complementarity as a Catalyst for Compliance*.

V

The Procedural Setting of Complementarity

1. Introduction

We will now turn to an analysis of how complementarity is operationalized procedurally. The questions as to when and how the (un)willingness and (in)ability of States has to be determined, who the relevant actors in its application are and how complementarity is applied or invoked by these actors in the course of ICC proceedings are vital in examining the content of complementarity. An examination of this procedural setting also helps to clarify complementarity's consequences for the investigation and prosecution of core crimes by national criminal jurisdictions, because the procedural framework determines how the latter interact with the ICC and, in turn, what impact this interaction may have on national enforcement.

In analyzing the procedural operationalization of complementarity, this chapter begins with an examination of the different phases of ICC proceedings, in which complementarity must or may have to be determined (2). It then turns to a number of related questions of a procedural nature (3).

2. The Procedural Phases of Admissibility

Generally speaking, the Statute distinguishes between three different phases of proceedings, during which admissibility has or may have to be determined. These are the stages of the initiation of an investigation (2.1.), of preliminary rulings on admissibility (2.2.), and of challenges to admissibility (2.3.). In addition, the question arises as to whether and under what conditions a determination on admissibility can be revisited after these stages (2.4.).

Before we address these different phases in detail in the following sections, it needs to be noted at the outset that the procedural setting of complementarity differs in certain respects according to the different trigger mechanisms enumerated in Article 13 of the Statute. In analyzing the procedural setting, we will therefore have to distinguish between referrals of a situation by a State Party,[1] or by the

---

[1] Rome Statute of the International Criminal Court (adopted 17 July 1998, as corrected by *procès-verbaux* of 10 November 1998, 12 July 1999, 30 November 1999, 8 May 2000, 17 January

Security Council[2] and the power of the Prosecutor to initiate an investigation *proprio motu*.[3] In addition, a number of specific questions relating to admissibility arise when States trigger the jurisdiction of the Court by using Article 13 (a) on State referrals to refer situations to the ICC that occur on their own territory (so-called 'auto-referrals'). This way of triggering the jurisdiction of the Court has evolved in the early practice of the Court, but it is not specifically regulated in the Statute. We will address the relationship between admissibility and auto-referrals separately further below (3.2.).

2.1. Admissibility and the Initiation of an Investigation

The first procedural step, which involves a consideration of issues of admissibility, occurs *when the Prosecutor decides whether to initiate an investigation* after having analyzed the information that he/she has gathered *proprio motu*[4] or that was made available to him/her in the course of a referral by a State Party or the Security Council.[5] Both Articles 15 (3) and Article 53 (1) instruct the Prosecutor to determine whether there is a reasonable basis 'to proceed with'[6] or 'to initiate'[7] an investigation. Article 53 (1)(b) in turn provides that, in making that determination, the Prosecutor shall consider whether 'the case is or would be admissible under article 17'.[8] It is clear from the express reference to the factors in Article 53 (1) in Rule 48,[9] which regulates the determination of a reasonable basis to proceed with an investigation under Article 15, paragraph 3, that the

---

2001 and 16 January 2002, entered into force 1 July 2002) A/CONF.183/9 (Rome Statute). Article 13 (a).

[2] Rome Statute (n 1) Article 13 (b).

[3] Rome Statute (n 1) Article 13 (c). The procedural setting for *proprio motu* investigations of the Prosecutor extends to ad hoc declarations of accepting the jurisdiction of the Court by non-State Parties in accordance with Article 12 (3) of the Statute: see C Stahn, M El Zeidy and H Olásolo, 'The International Criminal Court's Ad Hoc Jurisdiction revisited' (2005) 99 AJIL 421–431, 423–426.

[4] Rome Statute (n 1) Article 15 (2) on *proprio motu* investigations provides: 'The Prosecutor shall analyse the seriousness of the information received. For this purpose, he or she may seek additional information from States, organs of the United Nations, intergovernmental or non-governmental organizations, or other reliable sources that he or she deems appropriate, and may receive written or oral testimony at the seat of the Court.'

[5] Cf Rule 104 of the Rules of Procedure and Evidence (12 July 2000) UN Doc PCNICC/2000/ INF/3/Add.1 (RoPE), which allows the Prosecutor to draw upon the same sources of additional information as Article 15 (2).

[6] Rome Statute (n 1) Article 15 (3).   [7] Rome Statute (n 1) Article 53 (1).

[8] Rome Statute (n 1) Article 53 (1)(b). In addition to admissibility, Article 53 (1) also requires the Prosecutor to consider whether the information available provides a reasonable basis to believe that a crime within the jurisdiction of the Court has been or is being committed (cf Article 53 (1)(a)), and whether, taking into account the gravity of the crime and the interests of victims, there are nonetheless substantial reasons to believe that an investigation would not serve the interests of justice (cf Article 53 (1)(c)).

[9] Rule 48 of the RoPE (n 5) provides in full: 'In determining whether there is a reasonable basis to proceed with an investigation under article 15, paragraph 3, the Prosecutor shall consider the factors set out in article 53, paragraph 1 (a) to (c).'

complementarity requirements also have to be assessed in the pre-investigative phase of *proprio motu* investigations by the Prosecutor. These provisions suggest, in short, that admissibility has to be considered by the Prosecutor at the pre-investigative phase *regardless of the trigger mechanism*.[10]

Nevertheless, this latter assertion could be challenged with regard to *Security Council referrals*, in which it takes a distinct position as to the unwillingness and inability of a State, for instance by asserting that proceedings were not or are not being conducted independently or impartially or that a State's judicial system has collapsed. In fact, it has been argued that Security Council referrals can set aside complementarity and endow the Court with primacy over national courts.[11] However, such a claim is open to the objection that both Articles 25 and 103 of the UN Charter, which would provide the legal basis of the overriding force of Security Council resolutions under Chapter VII, address 'Members of the United Nations'.[12] Only States can become members of the United Nations.[13] Hence the wording of the provisions suggests that Chapter VII resolutions are binding only

---

[10] Informal Expert Paper for the ICC Office of the Prosecutor: The Principle of Complementarity in Practice, available at <http://www.ice-cpi.int/library/organs/otp/complementarity.pdf>, 9 [25]; G Turone, 'Powers and Duties of the Prosecutor' in A Cassese, P Gaeta and J Jones (eds) The Rome Statute of the International Criminal Court: A Commentary (OUP, Oxford 2002) 1137–1180, 1146–1147. For further arguments suggesting the same conclusion, see ibid, 1147–1148. For the different trigger mechanisms, see nn 1–3. For the applicability of complementarity to the specific situation in which States refer situations in their own territory, see *3.2. Complementarity and Auto-Referral*.

[11] L Arbour and M Bergsmo, 'Conspicuous Absence of Jurisdictional Overreach' in H von Hebel, J Lammers and J Schukking (eds) *Reflections on the International Criminal Court—Essays in Honour of Adriaan Bos* (TMC Assus Press, The Hague 1999) 139–140 ['It must be expected that the Council will give the Court jurisdictional primacy *vis-à-vis* the relevant national judicial systems when it makes a referral as an enforcement action under Chapter VII. The Security Council's power to conduct international judicial intervention derives from the Charter and is unaffected by the ICC Statute']. See also A Zimmermann, 'The Creation of a Permanent International Criminal Court' (1998) 2 Max Planck UNYB 169–237, 220; International Federation for Human Rights (FIDH)/ Sudan Organisation against Torture (SOAT), 'The Security Council refers the Darfur situation to the International Criminal Court', 4 April 2005, available at <http://www.fidh.org/article.php3?id_article=2336#nh1> ['[A]lthough the ICC is "complementary" to national jurisdictions, the fact that the Security Council brought this matter to the ICC implicitly indicates that the ICC has primacy in prosecuting the suspects: the Sudanese authorities will thus have to abide by the resolution of the UN political body.' Footnote omitted]; G P Fletcher and J D Ohlin, 'The ICC—Two Courts in One?' (2006) 4 JICJ 428–433, 431–433. See further on the controversies surrounding the question of admissibility and Security Council referrals, MA Summers, 'A Fresh Look at the Jurisdictional Provisions of the Statute of the International Criminal Court: The Case for Scrapping the Treaty' (2001) 20 Wisconsin ILJ 57–88, 78–80, 85 and notes 63, 154 with further reference.

[12] Articles 25 and 103 Charter of the United Nations (adopted 26 June 1945, entered into force 24 October 1945) 892 UNTS 119.

[13] Cf Articles 3 and 4 (1) of the 1945 Charter of the United Nations (adopted 26 June 1945, entered into force 24 October 1945) which provide: 'The original Members of the United Nations shall be the *states* which, having participated in the United Nations Conference on International Organization at San Francisco, or having previously signed the Declaration by United Nations of 1 January 1942, sign the present Charter and ratify it in accordance with Article 110.' (Article 3); 'Membership in the United Nations is open to all other peace-loving states which accept the obligations contained in the present Charter and, in the judgment of the Organization, are able and willing to carry out these obligations.' (Article 4 (1)).

on member *States*. If the Security Council, when acting pursuant to Article 13 (b) of the Statute, made a determination on admissibility, such a determination could thus at best have the consequence of divesting States of their right to challenge the admissibility of a case in accordance with Article 19 (2)(b) or (c).[14] In contrast, the Charter neither provides for Chapter VII resolutions to be binding on *international organizations*[15] nor stipulates any power of the Security Council to alter the legal regime governing such an organization. This holds equally true for the ICC, which, besides being an international (judicial) organization, is an autonomous legal entity and not a UN organ.[16]

Consequently, the legal regime governing complementarity and the rules that have to be applied *by the organs of the Court* in that respect, including Article 53, remain unaltered, even if the Security Council makes a determination on admissibility when using its power to refer a situation to the Court.[17]

While issues of admissibility have thus to be addressed by the Prosecutor at this early stage of deciding whether or not to initiate an investigation irrespective of the trigger mechanism, that determination of the Prosecutor is, however, not

[14] G H Oosthuizen, 'Some Preliminary Remarks on the Relationship Between the Envisaged International Criminal Court and the UN Security Council' (1999) 46 NILR 313–342, 328. See eg Informal Expert Paper for the ICC Office of the Prosecutor: The Principle of Complementarity in Practice (n 10) 21–22 [69–70]. On challenges to the admissibility of a case, see *2.3. Challenges to the Admissibility of a Case: Article 19*.

[15] See also in this vein European Court of Justice, Court of First Instance, Case T-184/95 *Dorsch Consult v Council and Commission* [1998] ECR II-667, [74]; Court of First Instance, Case T-306/01 *Yusuf and Al Barakaat International Foundation v Council and Commission* [2005] [242]; and Case T-315/01 *Kadi v Council and Commission* [2005] [192] ['unlike its Member States, the Community as such is not directly bound by the Charter of the United Nations and [. . .] it is not therefore required, as an obligation of general public international law, to accept and carry out the decisions of the Security Council in accordance with Article 25 of that Charter. The reason is that the Community is not a member of the United Nations, or an addressee of the resolutions of the Security Council, or the successor to the rights and obligations of the Member States for the purposes of public international law.'].

[16] D Sarooshi 'Aspects of the Relationship between the International Criminal Court and the United Nations' (2001) 32 NYIL 27–53, 40–41. The autonomy and independence of the ICC from the UN is underlined by Article 2, which requires that '[t]he Court shall be brought into relationship with the United Nations through an agreement to be approved by the Assembly of States Parties to this Statute and thereafter concluded by the President of the Court on its behalf.' See also eg Informal Expert Paper for the ICC Office of the Prosecutor: The Principle of Complementarity in Practice (n 10) 21 [68].

[17] L Condorelli and S Villalpando, 'Referral and Deferral by the Security Council' in A Cassese, P Gaeta and J Jones (eds) (n 10) 637–640 and L Condorelli and S Villalpando, 'Can the Security Council Extend the ICC's Jurisdiction?' in A Cassese, P Gaeta and J Jones (eds) (n 10) 571–583, 577–581, with a reasoning that applies *mutatis mutandis* to altering the complementarity regime. See also P Benvenuti, 'Complementarity of the International Criminal Court to national criminal jurisdictions' in F Lattanzi and W Schabas (eds), *Essays on the Rome Statute of the International Criminal Court* (vol 1 Ripa Fagnano Alto, Editrice il Sirente 1999) 21–50, 41; M H Arsanjani, 'The Rome Statute of the International Criminal Court' (1999) 93 AJIL 22–43, 28; Report of the International Commission of Inquiry on Darfur to the United Nations Secretary-General Pursuant to Security Council Resolution 1564 of 18 September 2004, 25 January 2005 [607]; G H Oosthuizen (n 14) 323–327; J Meissner, Die Zusammenarbeit mit dem Internationale Strefgeriehtshof nuch den Römischer Statut (Verlug CH Beck, Munich 2003) 105–106.

conclusive. Rather, it is subject to *review*, in varying degrees and depending on the trigger mechanism, *by the Pre-Trial Chamber.*

As far as an *initiation of an investigation* by the Prosecutor *proprio motu* is concerned, the Pre-Trial Chamber has to authorize the commencement of an investigation,[18] which it shall do if 'upon examination of the request [of the Prosecutor] and the supporting material, [it] considers that there is a reasonable basis to proceed with an investigation and that the case appears to fall within the jurisdiction of the Court'.[19] Neither the Statute nor the Rules of Procedure and Evidence further clarify the meaning of 'a reasonable basis' for the purpose of the Pre-Trial Chamber authorization. However, it is a logical consequence of the Prosecutor being required to conclude that a case is, or would be, admissible that this issue is equally assessed by the Pre-Trial Chamber in determining whether there is 'a reasonable basis'. The same result is warranted when considering that authorizing the commencement of an investigation by the Pre-Trial Chamber shall be 'without prejudice to subsequent determinations by the Court with regard to the jurisdiction and admissibility of a case'.[20] The reference to admissibility would be superfluous if the Pre-Trial Chamber did not address it in examining the request of the Prosecutor.

A different review procedure applies *when the jurisdiction of the ICC is triggered by a referral of a State Party or the Security Council.* In these instances, no authorization to commence an investigation by the Pre-Trial Chamber is required. Instead, the Prosecutor determines whether there is a reasonable basis to initiate an investigation, and only if he decides *not* to proceed because he concludes that there is no sufficient basis for a prosecution, including for the reason that a case is inadmissible, will the Pre-Trial Chamber be competent to review that decision at the request of the State making a referral or at the request of the Security Council.[21] This review of the *negative* decision of the Prosecutor not to proceed is inapplicable in the case of *proprio motu* investigations.

---

[18] For the procedure for authorization, see Rule 50. According to Rule 50 (4) and (5), the Pre-Trial Chamber may request additional information from the Prosecutor and from victims and 'shall issue its decision, including its reasons, as to whether to authorize the commencement of the investigation in accordance with article 15, paragraph 4, with respect to all or any part of the request by the Prosecutor. The Chamber shall give notice of the decision to victims who have made representations.' The involvement of victims also bears the potential of supplying additional information relating to admissibility, as it may for instance reveal their efforts to obtain justice in the national criminal jurisdiction concerned and any obstacles that they have encountered.

[19] Rome Statute (n 1) Article 15 (4).   [20] Ibid.

[21] Rome Statute (n 1) Article 53 (2) and (3)(a). Note, however, that should the Pre-Trial Chamber come to a different conclusion than the Prosecutor as regards admissibility, the former may only '*request* the Prosecutor to reconsider that decision' (Article 53 (3)(a), emphasis added), which reflects the non-binding nature of the outcome of the review by the Pre-Trial Chamber. See on the non-binding nature of the request, M Bergsmo and P Kruger, 'Article 53' in O Triffterer (ed), *Commentary on the Rome Statute of the International Criminal Court—Observers Notes, Article by Article* (Nomos, Baden-Baden 1999) 712–713, margins 35–36. Nor is the request by a State or the Security Council to the Pre-Trial Chamber to review a decision of the Prosecutor binding on the Pre-Trial Chamber: see G H Oosthuizen (n 14) 325. For the different mechanism for review

Finally, the Prosecutor possesses the power to reconsider whether to initiate an investigation or, subsequently, a prosecution 'at any time [...] based on new facts or information'.[22] He/she thus retains some leeway to take developments subsequent to a decision on whether to initiate an investigation or prosecution into account. If that decision was not to initiate an investigation or prosecution, such developments may also relate to admissibility, for instance where, at the time of the decision by the Prosecutor, the relevant State was investigating ICC crimes but subsequently proved unwilling or unable to carry out domestic investigations. In the reverse situation, where the Prosecutor had decided to initiate an investigation or prosecution, he/she may reconsider for example where that decision was based on the absence of domestic proceedings by a State, and the latter had begun such proceedings after the decision by the Prosecutor had been taken, thus suggesting that cases are, or would be, admissible.

In case the Prosecutor considers that the case is, or would be, admissible in accordance with Article 53 (1)(b) and also otherwise determines that there is a reasonable basis to initiate an investigation, the next procedural phase at which admissibility may arise is a preliminary ruling regarding admissibility under Article 18.

2.2. Preliminary Rulings Regarding Admissibility: Article 18

Article 18 applies '[w]hen a situation has been referred to the Court pursuant to article 13 (a) and the Prosecutor has determined that there would be a reasonable basis to commence an investigation, or the Prosecutor initiates an investigation pursuant to articles 13 (c) and 15'.[23] In other words, it applies *after a determination in accordance with Article 53 (1)*,[24] *before the actual commencement of an investigation* and is *not* applicable to *Security Council referrals*.

The *first step* of the procedure under Article 18 requires the Prosecutor to '*notify* all States Parties and those States which, taking into account the information available, would normally exercise jurisdiction over the crimes concerned.'[25] This notification is the starting point in a dialogue between States and the Prosecutor.[26]

While the provision may seem open to different interpretations as to whether the qualifier, 'would normally exercise jurisdiction over the crimes concerned', applies to both States Parties and other States, it is understood that it only applies

by the Pre-Trial Chamber if the decision of the Prosecutor not to initiate an investigation is solely based on the lack of interests of justice, see Article 53 (3)(b) and Rules 109–110.

[22] Rome Statute (n 1) Article 53 (4).
[23] Rome Statute (n 1) Article 18 (1). For the meaning of the term 'situation', see *3.1.1. Specificity of Proof*.
[24] See M Bergsmo and P Kruger (n 21) 708, margin 18.
[25] Rome Statute (n 1) Article 18 (1).
[26] S N M Young, 'Surrendering the Accused to the International Criminal Court' (2000) 71 BYIL 317–356, 334.

to the latter. Otherwise, the distinction between States Parties and other States would not have been required.[27]

At least two underlying assumptions are reflected in this distinction. First, rather than being of a purely functional nature, confined to States that would 'normally exercise jurisdiction over the crimes concerned', States Parties are seen to form an 'enforcement community'. Notifying all States Parties regardless of whether or not they would 'normally exercise jurisdiction' provides them with the possibility of assisting in the joint effort to bring perpetrators to justice, including means other than through the exercise of jurisdiction. Second, non-States Parties are envisaged to retain their role with respect to investigations and prosecutions of the core crimes and may participate in proceedings regarding admissibility, despite the fact that they do not have any obligation towards the Court in subsequent proceedings. They can thus make use of the *rights* conferred by complementarity, without assuming any consequential obligations.[28]

The reference to States which would '*normally exercise jurisdiction*', however, is somewhat ambivalent. If one were to understand the term 'normally' as a factual description, the group of non-States Parties would be very small, if existent at all, in light of the poor track record of States exercising jurisdiction over core crimes. Indeed, past experience tends to suggest that the *refusal to exercise jurisdiction* describes normality much more adequately.[29] The task to identify those States that would 'normally exercise jurisdiction' by reference to a general pattern of *facts* would therefore likely be futile.

It would also seem that a determination of which States would 'normally exercise jurisdiction' by exclusive reference to the jurisdiction available under international law is of equally little assistance. Nothing in the text of the Statute, or in the negotiating history, suggests that the drafters of the Statute had specific jurisdictional bases—for example, territoriality or active nationality—in mind when referring to such States. Nor can such jurisdictional bases be inferred from Article 12 (2) of the Statute, which makes the exercise of jurisdiction of the ICC conditional on the acceptance of territorial States and States of active nationality. As preconditions to the exercise of jurisdiction *of the ICC*, these bases do not determine the jurisdictional reach of *domestic* criminal proceedings.[30]

It is therefore submitted that a better way to determine those States which would 'normally exercise jurisdiction' is to do so by taking into account the

---

[27] Such an interpretation is also confirmed by the drafting history, see *93–95*.

[28] The *rationale* underlying this involvement of non-States Parties in the procedure under Article 18 is difficult to trace, but it seems safe to assume that the *rationale* can be elucidated by reference to the discussions surrounding the role of non-States Parties in the procedure for challenging admissibility under Article 19. For a discussion of the latter, see *2.3. Challenges to the Admissibility of a Case: Article 19*, especially (nn 110–111) and text.

[29] Cf *Chapter II: National Suppression of Core Crimes, 3.2. Obstacles relating to Enforcement*. See also J L Balint, 'Conflict, Conflict Victimization, And Legal Redress', 1945–1996 (1996) 59 Law and Contemporary Problems 4 231–247.

[30] For further discussion, see (nn 191–202) and accompanying text in Ch VI.

prospect of a State being able to investigate and prosecute core crimes effectively, determined by the jurisdiction that a State has lawfully established under national law,[31] in combination with factors such as its jurisdictional and factual link to the crimes in question, the availability of and access to evidence, and the presence of the suspect.[32] These factors regularly enter the equation when domestic prosecutors decide whether or not to act in relation to a certain crime. Thus understood, 'States which [...] would normally exercise jurisdiction' can be indentified by answering the question as to whether their Prosecutor can reasonably be expected to contemplate conducting proceedings vis-à-vis the ICC crimes concerned. It is to be noted, however, that even non-States Parties that fall outside the category of States, which 'would normally exercise jurisdiction' and therefore do not have to be notified under Article 18 (1), may later challenge the admissibility of a case under Article 19.[33]

The aforementioned aspects of the notification of States by the Prosecutor reflect a positive attitude and a degree of trust in States. They duly reflect the legitimate interests of bona fide States to exercise jurisdiction over the core crimes. However, Article 18 also takes account of the fact that the information supplied by the Prosecutor in the notification may be misused and/or alert persons who could become subjects of an investigation. Accordingly, the Prosecutor may notify States on a confidential basis and may limit the scope of the information provided to States where he/she 'believes it necessary to protect persons, prevent destruction of evidence or prevent the absconding of persons'.[34] Within these potential limitations, Rule 52 of the Rules of Procedure and Evidence nevertheless requires

---

[31] Cf *112–113*. It appears that such an understanding that 'States which, taking into account the information available, would normally exercise jurisdiction over the crimes concerned' also finds support in the early practice of the Office of the Prosecutor. Thus the letters of notification under Article 18 (1) in relation to the situation in the Democratic Republic of the Congo of 22 and 23 June 2004 was reportedly directed to States Parties and all States which *could* [sic] exercise jurisdiction: see Prosecutor's Request for Measures under Article 56, filed on 19 April 2005, at 4 [referred to in Pre-Trial Chamber I, Decision to Hold Consultation under Article 56 of 21 April 2005, 2].

[32] See the Paper on some policy issues before the Office of the Prosecutor, available at <http:// www.ice-cpi.int/library/organs/otp/030905_Policy_Paper.pdf> (2003) 5 ['In a case where multiple States have jurisdiction over the crime in question the Prosecutor should consult with those States best able to exercise jurisdiction (eg primarily the State where the alleged crime was committed, the State of nationality of the suspects, the State which has custody of the accused, and the State which has evidence of the alleged crime) with a view to ensuring that jurisdiction is taken by the State best able to do so.'] See also Informal Expert Paper for the ICC Office of the Prosecutor: The Principle of Complementarity in Practice, available at <http://www.ice-cpi.int/library/organs/ otp/complementarity.pdf> 24 [76] ['The guiding principle in [strengthening the complementarity regime by actively encouraging non-territorial States to exercise jurisdiction] should be to actively encourage those States that provide the most promising prospect for an effective investigation and prosecution. The availability of and access to witnesses, the presence of the alleged perpetrator on a State's territory, and the independence and impartiality of the judiciary are important elements in determining that prospect.']. For further discussion of parameters in identifying the adequate forum for domestic preoceedings vis-à-vis core crimes, see *Chapter VI: Complementarity and the Obligation to Investigate and Prosecute, 5. Addressees of the Obligation to Investigate and Prosecute.*

[33] See *2.3. Challenges to the Admissibility of a Case: Article 19.*

[34] Rome Statute (n 1) Article 18 (1).

that the Prosecutor include in the notification 'information about the acts that may constitute crimes [within the jurisdiction of the Court]' that is relevant for the purposes of a State requesting a deferral in accordance with Article (18)(2).[35] A State may also request 'additional information from the Prosecutor to assist it in the application of article 18, paragraph 2'.[36]

Article 18 (1) and Rule 52 thus clearly reflect the compromise between the necessary and potentially positive role of States, on the one hand, and the risk of abuse of such information by a State acting in bad faith, on the other hand.[37] If one considers different scenarios, then the *problems* inherent in that compromise become obvious.

Consider a situation in which the determination of a reasonable basis under Article 53 (1)(b) has revealed that there is practically no prospect of an investigation and prosecution, for instance due to the blatant unwillingness of a State. Here, the Prosecutor, although allowed to notify States on a confidential basis and to limit the scope of information provided to them, still has to supply information about the acts that may constitute crimes under Article 5, which would provide the blatantly unwilling State with the—merely theoretical—possibility to start an investigation.[38] Even in a situation where one can reasonably assume that that information will in all likelihood be misused to destroy evidence, intimidate witnesses and warn suspects, the Prosecutor does not have the possibility not to notify the State and not to supply any information. Admittedly, the past track record of national suppression of core crimes suggests that States may seek to cover up crimes irrespective of any intervention by foreign or international authorities.[39] In other words, not to require the Prosecutor to notify States where that information will likely be misused to destroy evidence, etc, is no guarantee in preventing such acts from occurring. It would, however, at least prevent the notification from being their trigger.

The dilemma resulting from the compromise between the potentially positive role of States and the risk by a State acting in bad faith of abuse of information supplied by the Prosecutor is especially significant with regard to States that are not parties to the Rome Statute, as they do not have any obligations towards

---

[35] RoPE (n 5) Rule 52 (1).

[36] RoPE (n 5) Rule 52 (2). The same Rule further clarifies that '[s]uch a request does not affect the one-month time limit provided for in article 18, paragraph 2, and shall be responded to by the Prosecutor on an expedited basis'. For the one-month time limit, see below, *172–173*.

[37] Cf J T Holmes, 'Jurisdiction and Admissibility' in R S Lee (ed), *The International Criminal Court—Elements of Crimes and Rules of Procedure and Evidence* (Transnational Publ, New York 2001) 339, noting that 'Rule 52 attempts to balance the legitimate needs of States for information to permit them to determine whether it should request a deferral, with the need to allow the Prosecutor to protect the integrity and speed of the investigations'.

[38] J T Holmes points out that '[t]he addition of the term "acts" [in Rule 52] indicates that the Prosecutor must do more than just inform a State that an investigation is being contemplated. The notice should include specific information, again subject to the article 18 limitations, on the acts to be examined, their location and possible suspects.' Ibid.

[39] See *Chapter II: National Suppression of Core Crimes, 3.2.2. Obstacles during Criminal Proceedings.*

the Court. Consequently, the safeguards against abuse in subsequent phases of the procedure for preliminary rulings regarding admissibility, as limited as they might be, do not apply to them to the same degree as to States Parties, and any subsequent ruling or request by the Court[40] may be disregarded by them.[41]

However, in other scenarios, in which there is a prospect for a State to duly investigate and, if warranted, prosecute, the notification under Article 18 (1) is a logical consequence of the idea of complementarity. If there is a reasonable prospect of States doing so, they should be encouraged to exercise their jurisdiction and be assisted therein by the Prosecutor. The problem in the notification procedure nevertheless remains that, in principle, States with very different intentions and prospects for an effective investigation are treated alike.

The notification under Article 18 (1) provides the basis for the *second step* of the preliminary rulings regarding admissibility, namely the possibility of *deferrals to the investigation of States* regulated in Article 18 (2) and Rules 53 to 55. The primary function of the notification under Article 18 (1) is thus to alert States, to allow them to exercise their jurisdiction and, consequently, to make it superfluous for the ICC to act.[42] Such deferrals may concern States Parties and non-States Parties alike. Accordingly, '[w]ithin one month of receipt of that notification, a State may inform the Court that it is investigating or has investigated its nationals or others within its jurisdiction' with respect to acts contained in the notification to States.[43] A State may so inform the Prosecutor irrespective of whether the notification by the latter has only prompted the State to investigate or whether an investigation had already been started or concluded *prior* to the notification.[44] In any of these situations, the State may request the Prosecutor to 'defer to the State's investigation'[45] a request that must be made in writing and must provide

---

[40] For instance by the Pre-Trial Chamber to authorize the Prosecutor to conduct an investigation despite a request for deferral by a State under Article 18 (2) or a request by the Prosecutor that the State to which an investigation has been deferred to periodically inform him of the progress of the investigation and any subsequent prosecution (cf Rome Statute (n 1) Article 18 (5)), see pages 178–179.

[41] Cf also G Turone (n 10) 1163 ['What is frankly unacceptable about the provision of Article 18, is that the notification has to be forwarded not only to *all* States Parties, but also to those States non-parties which "would normally exercise jurisdiction over the crimes concerned", ie also to those States that—having refused to join the system of the ICC, and being directly involved in the specific situation in which grave breaches of the international humanitarian law are assumed to have occurred—might have no other interest than simply preventing justice from being done'].

[42] See also the Paper on some policy issues before the Office of the Prosecutor (n 32) 5 ['The exercise of the Prosecutor's functions under article 18 of notifying States of future investigations will alert States with jurisdiction to the possibility of taking action themselves.'].

[43] Rome Statute (n 1) Article 18 (2), first sentence. Nsereko rightly points out that, in the light of the strict time limit of one month, the Prosecutor may benefit from ensuring 'that the notification is served personally on the State officials designated to receive it and that such officials issue receipts therefore'. D Nsereko, 'Article 18' in O Triffterer (ed) (n 21) 400, margin 12.

[44] D Nsereko ibid 400, margin 13 ['The spirit and general tenor of the Statute is to give due deference to State jurisdiction. So, a State that has not yet started investigations, but is otherwise able and willing to do so must be given a chance to do so under article 18 para 2.'].

[45] Ibid, second sentence.

information concerning the investigation.[46] The Prosecutor may request add-itional information from the investigating State.[47]

It has been suggested that States, like the Prosecutor, can limit the information to protect the integrity of an investigation, because 'parity exists in the relation-ship [between the Prosecutor and States]'.[48] This assertion undoubtedly holds true with regard to States that are not parties to the Statute and thus not bound by any obligation towards the Court. With regard to States Parties, however, the claim meets with the objection that the rules are silent on the matter, while they are explicit about the Prosecutor's power to limit the information. This sug-gests that any such power for States would also need to be expressly regulated. Furthermore, the power of the Prosecutor is subject to the functional condition that he/she believes such limitation necessary 'to protect persons, prevent destruc-tion of evidence or prevent the absconding of persons'. In order to create parity, these functional limitations would therefore also have to apply to States limiting information. Yet, it is hardly conceivable that the *Prosecutor* misuses information in a way that fulfils these conditions.[49]

As a *rule*, the Prosecutor must *defer* to a State's investigation if the State has so requested. As an *exception* to this rule, the Pre-Trial Chamber, on the *application* of the Prosecutor, has the power to decide *to authorize the investigation*.[50] If the Prosecutor decides to submit such an application for authorization, he/she has to supply the Pre-Trial Chamber with the basis for the application, together with the information concerning the investigation that the State has provided.[51] The Prosecutor is also under an obligation to 'inform that State in writing when he or she makes an application to the Pre-Trial Chamber [. . .] and shall include in the notice a summary of the basis of the application'.[52]

---

[46] RoPE (n 5) Rule 53, first sentence. Until that point, however, ie during the period immedi-ately after sending the notification until the State requests the Prosecutor to defer to its investiga-tion, the Prosecutor may carry out investigative steps. This follows from the wording of Article 18 (1) ['when . . . the Prosecutor initiates an investigation'], which 'clearly shows that he/she is not sup-posed to remain inactive until the term for every State has expired': G Turone (n 10) 1163.

[47] RoPE (n 5) Rule 53, second sentence. It remains unclear, however, what the exact nature of the information to be provided by the State is. In recounting the drafting history of Rule 53, J T Holmes mentions that one of the contentious issues was whether the information must identify the persons concerned. According to J T Holmes, States opposing such an approach pointed out that '[i]t was possible for a State to be conducting an investigation and not know all possible sus-pects until the conclusion of the investigation. The Fact that not all suspects are known by a State at this stage should not automatically give rise to a request of the Prosecutor of an investigation.' Cf J T Holmes (n 37) 340–341.

[48] Ibid 341.

[49] This should not be confused with the possibility for investigating States to provide the infor-mation on a confidential basis in order to protect the integrity of the investigation, either on the national level or by the Prosecutor. Confidentiality does not involve a limitation of the informa-tion, but merely the way in which the later is made available.

[50] Rome Statute (n 1) Article 18 (2), second sentence.   [51] RoPE (n 5) Rule 54 (1).

[52] RoPE (n 5) Rule 54 (2). The term 'summary' denotes that the Prosecutor is allowed to pro-tect information contained in the application relating to the actual investigation: see J T Holmes (n 37) 341.

The Rules of Procedure and Evidence grant the Pre-Trial Chamber a significant degree of leeway in determining the *procedure* to be followed for the purpose of Article 18 (2).[53] The only mandatory parameters for that procedure is that (a) the Pre-Trial Chamber 'shall examine the Prosecutor's application and any observations submitted by a State that requested a deferral in accordance with article 18, paragraph 2, and shall consider the factors in article 17 in deciding whether to authorize an investigation';[54] and (b) that '[t]he decision and the basis for the decision of the Pre-Trial Chamber shall be communicated as soon as possible to the Prosecutor and to the State that requested a deferral of an investigation'.[55] Beyond these constraints, the Pre-Trial Chamber is free to decide on the procedure to be followed and the appropriate measures for the proper conduct of the proceedings.[56] A hearing is not required.[57]

As a limited exception to the rule that the procedural setting for preliminary rulings regarding admissibility is primarily dialogic in character,[58] this procedure following an application by the Prosecutor for an authorization of an investigation despite a request for deferral made by a State may thus involve certain litigious elements.

Several aspects of the deferral procedure warrant clarification. The first such aspect concerns the *States that may request a deferral* to their investigation. Article 18 (2) refers to 'a State [...] that [...] is investigating or has investigated *its nationals or others within its jurisdiction*'. The latter reference to 'others within its jurisdiction' is not entirely clear, especially as regards the concept of 'jurisdiction' employed.[59] A contextual interpretation suggests, however, to read the term 'jurisdiction' together with the term 'is investigating or has investigated' and thus

---

[53] Cf RoPE (n 5) Rule 55.

[54] RoPE (n 5) Rule 55 (2). The obligation of the Pre-Trial Chamber to examine any observations by a State that requested a deferral indicates that, despite the inconclusiveness of Article 18 (2), the rules allow for subsequent observations submitted by such a State directly to the Court. See also J T Holmes (n 37) 342. He notes elsewere, however, that 'the possibility of submitting additional views is not a right and the Chamber is under no obligation to wait for a State to submit additional views': J T Holmes, 'Complementarity: National Courts *versus* the ICC' in A Cassese, P Gaeta and J Jones (eds) (n 9) 682, note 10.

[55] RoPE (n 5) Rule 55 (3).   [56] Cf RoPE (n 5) Rule 55 (1).

[57] Cf ibid, providing that the Pre-Trial Chamber '*may* hold a hearing', emphasis added.

[58] The other exception is an appeal under Rome Statute (n 1) Article 18 (4): see (n 70).

[59] For different notions of 'jurisdictions', see *110–112*. An additional dimension to the term 'others within its jurisdiction' may derive from an interpretation of them in analogy to human rights treaties, which oblige States Parties to respect and to ensure to all individuals within their territory and *subject to* their *jurisdiction* the rights recognized in the respective instruments: cf Article 2 (1) of the International Convenant on Civil and Political Rights (adopted 16 December 1996, entered into force 23 March 1976) 999 UNTS 171 (ICCPR), Article 1 of the Inter-American Convention on Human Rights (entered into force 18 July 1978) OAS Treaty Series No 36, 1144 UNTS 123 (IACHR), Article 1 of the European Convention for the Protection of Human Rights and Fundamental Freedoms (entered into force 3 September 1953, as amended by Protocols Nos 3, 5, 8, and 11 which entered into force on 21 September 1970, 20 December 1971, 1 January 1990, and 1 November 1998 respectively) 213 UNTS 222 (ECHR). For an interpretation of these provisions by human rights bodies, see *25–26*. If one were to apply this interpretation to the terms 'within its jurisdiction' in Article 18 (2), all States could request a deferral which exercise effective control

to refer to investigative jurisdiction. Put differently, States that wish to make a request for deferral must be able to show that they have investigative jurisdiction over the acts in question—under both national and international law[60]—and are exercising that jurisdiction. They do not have to show, however, that the person concerned is *physically* within their jurisdiction. Such an understanding would mean, for instance, that a State may request a deferral where alleged crimes took place in its territory, the State has initiated an investigation, the person has fled to another State and the territorial State has requested the extradition of that person.

The fact that more than one State may possess investigative jurisdiction over acts that relate to the information provided in the notification under Article 18 (1)[61] implies that *several States* may request a deferral. Despite the fact that such a situation has thus far remained the exception to the rule that no State, rather than too many States, express the intention to exercise jurisdiction with respect to international crimes or suspects implicated in such crimes, the phenomenon is not merely theoretical, as demonstrated by the *Pinochet* case.[62] If such a situation arises, the Prosecutor needs to determine eventually *to which State's investigation he or she defers*.[63]

The Statute does not provide any definite guidance in this respect; nor does general international law establish a clear hierarchy of jurisdictional claims beyond the general parameter that jurisdiction is primarily territorial, with the consequence that jurisdictional claims deriving from other bases are generally considered less strong.[64] In the absence of any universally accepted, *a priori* determination of a hierarchical order of jurisdictional claims,[65] the settling of

over persons who are implicated in criminal acts that may constitute crimes under Article 5 of the ICC Statute.

[60] For the underlying rationale of requiring jurisdiction to be available not only under national law but also under international law, cf *112–113*.

[61] Such investigative jurisdiction may be vested in the territorial State, the State of active or passive nationality, or States exercising universal jurisdiction.

[62] Proceedings against Pinochet were initiated in Chile: see (2000) 3 YIHL 447–451. Others were conducted in third States: see on the Pinochet extradition proceedings in English courts, C Warbrick, E M Salgado and N Goodwin, 'The Pinochet Cases in the United Kingdom' (1999) 2 YIHL 91–117. Besides the proceedings in Spanish courts, which gave rise to the aforementioned extradition proceedings, other proceedings against Pinochet had been instituted in Belgium, see (1999) 2 YIHL 335–340, and in Sweden, see (1999) 2 YIHL 414. See generally on conflicting claims of jurisdiction by States within the framework of complementarity, A Klip, 'Complementarity and Concurrent Jurisdiction' in International Criminal Law: *Quo Vadis?* Proceedings of the International Conference held in Siracusa, Italy, 28 November–3 December 2002, on the Occasion of the 30th Anniversary of ISISC (2004) 19 Nouvelles études pénales 173–197, 174–179.

[63] This problem was already apparent from an early stage in the drafting process of complementarity: see eg pages 74–75. For subsequent discussions during the drafting process, see also pages 87 and 91–92.

[64] For further discussion on the context of addressees of an obligation to investigate and prosecute under the Rome Statute, see *Chapter VI: Complementarity and the Obligation to Investigate and Prosecute, 5. Addressees of the Obligation to Investigate and Prosecute.*

[65] Such determinations remain the (geographically limited) exceptions: cf Nordic countries, EUROJUST. See also ICTY Appeals Chamber, *Prosecutor v Jankovic* (Decision on Rule 11 *bis* Referral) IT-96-23-PT (15 November 2005) 34–36.

jurisdictional conflicts remains a matter for *a posteriori* agreement between the States concerned, governed by comity and implemented mainly through the transfer of criminal proceedings on an ad hoc basis.[66]

The deferral procedure nevertheless bears the potential to serve as an informal catalyst for identifying the most suitable forum in case several States request a deferral.[67] Especially Rule 53, requiring the requesting State to provide information concerning its investigation and allowing the Prosecutor to request additional information, may be used as a framework for dialogue between the latter and the different requesting States with a view to settling competing claims of jurisdiction.

At the same time, it is acknowledged that the provisions on the deferral procedure do not provide a satisfactory answer in cases where the attempt to settle jurisdictional conflicts through this informal mechanism fails. Nor is it clear whether the Prosecutor, after having reviewed the deferral to one requesting State and having been authorized by the Pre-Trial Chamber to investigate because of that State's unwillingness or inability,[68] may defer to another State that had requested a deferral rather than conducting the investigation him or herself.[69]

The *third step* in the procedure governing preliminary rulings regarding admissibility concerns the situation in which a deferral to a State's investigation has taken place, either because an application by the Prosecutor for an authorization for an investigation in accordance with Article 18 (2) and Rule 54 is rejected by the Pre-Trial Chamber,[70] or because the Prosecutor does not make

---

[66] On both the absence of hierarchy and the prevalence of *a posteriori* settlement, also as regards international crimes, see M Henzelin, *Le Principe de l'Universalité en Droit Pénal International, Droit et Obligation pour les États de poursuivre et juger selon le principe de l'universalité* (Helbin & Lichtenhahn, Munich, Geneva, Brussels 2000) 227–234; T Vander Beken, 'De moeilijke zoektocht naar het beste forum voor internationale misdrijven—De *ad hoc* tribunalen als ideale oplossing? [*The difficult search for the best forum for international crimes—The* ad hoc *tribunals as ideal solution?*]' in J Wouters and H Panken (eds), *De Genocidewet in international perspectief, Jura Falconis Libri* (De Boeck & Larcier Publ, Brussels 2002) 117–137, 124–126. For the marginal discussion of the power of the ICC to settle conflicts of jurisdiction during the drafting process, see eg 'Report of the Ad Hoc Committee on the Establishment of an International Criminal Court: (1995) UN Doc A/50/22 20, [92].

[67] Cf the Paper on some policy issues before the Office of the Prosecutor (n 32) 5 ['In a case where multiple States have jurisdiction over the crime in question the Prosecutor should consult with those States best able to exercise jurisdiction (eg primarily the State where the alleged crime was committed, the State of nationality of the suspects, the State which has custody of the accused, and the State which has evidence of the alleged crime) with a view to ensuring that jurisdiction is taken by the State best able to do so.']; A Klip (n 62) 175.

[68] Cf Rome Statute (n 1) Article 18 (3) and RoPE (n 5) Rule 56.

[69] See also *227–228* on competing requests.

[70] And, if applicable, the Appeals Chamber has confirmed such a ruling upon appeal by the Prosecutor made in accordance with Article 18 (4), which provides that '[t]he State concerned or the Prosecutor may appeal to the Appeals Chamber against a ruling of the Pre-Trial Chamber, in accordance with article 82. The appeal may be heard on an expedited basis.' In accordance with Article 82 (3), '[a]n appeal shall not of itself have suspensive effect unless the Appeals Chamber so orders, upon request, in accordance with the Rules of Procedure and Evidence'. On the non-suspensive effect of an appeal in the context of Article 18, see D Nsereko (n 43) 403, margin 23.

such an application.[71] In these cases, Article 18 (3) and (5) to (7) provides the Prosecutor with a number of supervisory or monitoring tools, as well as establishing other safeguards to protect the integrity and efficiency of investigations by the Prosecutor and safeguards against abuse of the deferral procedure.

As far as *supervisory or monitoring tools* are concerned, the Prosecutor has the power to *review* the deferral to a State's investigation 'six months after the date of the deferral or at any time when there has been a significant change of circumstances based on the State's unwillingness or inability genuinely to carry out the investigation'.[72] That power thus allows him or her to reconsider the deferral should the State prove to be unwilling or unable in the course of the proceedings to which the Prosecutor has deferred. An important indicator of whether such reconsideration is warranted is the very behaviour of a State in the course of the procedure under Article 18. If, for instance, a State fails to provide information or distorts the information-sharing process under Article 18 (5),[73] provides incomplete or untruthful information, provides information with delay, or prevents the Prosecutor from pursuing the necessary investigative steps if these have been granted in accordance with Article 18 (6),[74] such non-compliance could and should be taken into consideration when making the decision on whether or not there has been 'a significant change of circumstances based on the State's unwillingness or inability genuinely to carry out the investigation', which warrants a review of the Prosecutor's deferral to a State's investigation.

A further monitoring tool available to the Prosecutor is that, according to Article 18 (5), he/she may request the State to whose investigation he/she has deferred to 'periodically *inform* [him/her] of the progress of its investigations and any subsequent prosecutions',[75] and States Parties must respond to these requests 'without undue delay'.[76] Article 18 (5) thereby further underlines the generally dialogic character of the procedure for preliminary rulings regarding admissibility,[77] albeit that such dialogue is not conducted on equal footing in as much as the information gathered by the Prosecutor enables him/her to keep a

---

[71] If, in contrast, the Pre-Trial Chamber authorizes an investigation, and the Appeals Chamber has confirmed the authorization provided the State concerned has appealed against such a ruling in accordance with Article 18 (4), the Prosecutor may investigate in accordance with Articles 54 *et seq*. The same applies when the State does not request a deferral, either because it does not or did not investigate or because it simply refrains from requesting a deferral despite an investigation. Cf D Nsereko ibid 401, margin 14.

[72] Rome Statute (n 1) Article 18 (3).

[73] J T Holmes (n 54) 682 ['[...] the failure of a State to respond adequately [to requests for periodic updates under Article 18 (5)] will likely create a presumption that something untoward is afoot'].

[74] *178–179.*   [75] Rome Statute (n 1) Article 18 (5), first sentence.

[76] Rome Statute (n 1) Article 18 (5), second sentence.

[77] Cf J T Holmes (n 54) 681–682 ['[...] the Statute and the Rules encourage a dialogue between the State and the Prosecutor to ensure that there is no overlap in their respective areas of interest. [...] The notion of dialogue is reinforced by Article 18 (5), which permits the Prosecutor to request States for periodic updates on the progress in investigations.']; and more generally ibid, 683 ['[...] the Statute creates a type of dialogue between States and the Court'].

close eye on the domestic proceedings and to invoke Article 18 (3) if the information supplied (or the lack thereof) indicates that the State concerned is unwilling or unable. With a view to enabling the Prosecutor to analyze the information in the light of the admissibility requirements, it therefore appears reasonable to require that the periodic information supplied by States indicates concrete measures that have been taken, such as steps to gather evidence, to question witnesses and to arrest suspects, as well as giving details about the stage any investigation or prosecution is at, about the length of the different stages, etc.

If, in the view of the Prosecutor, the review reveals that the complementarity threshold has been met, he/she may apply to the Pre-Trial Chamber for an authorization of an investigation in accordance with Article 18 (2).[78] In that case, the information provided by the State in the course of periodically informing the Prosecutor must also be communicated to it in order to provide the Pre-Trial Chamber with a full picture of the State's action.[79]

In addition to the aforementioned tools for the supervision and monitoring of national proceedings, Article 18 contains a number of *safeguards to protect the integrity and efficiency of investigations by the Prosecutor and safeguards against abuse of the deferral procedure.*

First, as previously mentioned,[80] the Prosecutor may notify States on a confidential basis and may limit the scope of the information provided to States.

Second, according to Article 18 (6), 'the Prosecutor may, on an exceptional basis, seek authority from the Pre-Trial Chamber to pursue necessary investigative steps for the purpose of preserving evidence where there is a unique opportunity to obtain important evidence or there is a significant risk that such evidence may not be subsequently available'. A conceivable example of a situation in which the Prosecutor may seek such authority is when it is not (yet) clear whether a delay is unjustified and inconsistent with an intent to bring the person concerned to justice. If a State argued that an unjustified delay is consistent with an intent to bring the person(s) concerned to justice, because investigations and prosecutions will be conducted at a later stage, because they presently pose too great a danger for disrupting a fragile peace,[81] while the Prosecutor cannot conclusively determine whether investigations and prosecutions will indeed be conducted, the Prosecutor may seek authority to pursue necessary investigative steps. The Prosecutor has that opportunity *pending a ruling* by the Pre-Trial Chamber, ie prior to a decision on whether or not to authorize an investigation in accordance with Article 18 (2), and also at any time *when he or she has deferred* an investigation. These provisional

---

[78] RoPE (n 5) Rule 56 (1), which also clarifies that '[t]he application to the Pre-Trial Chamber shall be in writing and shall contain the basis for the application'. Rule 56 (3) provides that the procedure with respect to such an application must also be conducted in accordance with Rules 54 (2) and 55: see nn 54–58 and text.

[79] RoPE (n 5) Rules 56 (2).   [80] *170–171.*

[81] On the room for such delays under Article 17 (2)(b), see *143–144.*

measures under Article 18 (6) shall be considered *ex parte* and *in camera*, and are ruled upon by the Pre-Trial Chamber on an expedited basis.[82]

A third safeguard flows from Article 18 (7), which, with a view to limit the possibility of multiple challenges as regards the admissibility of a case, provides that '[a] State which has challenged a ruling of the Pre-Trial Chamber under [...] article [18] may challenge the admissibility of a case under article 19 on the grounds of additional significant facts or significant change of circumstances'. The provision thus limits the ability of States to bring a subsequent challenge under Article 19 besides making clear that a challenge to a ruling of the Pre-Trial Chamber—namely an appeal in accordance with Article 18 (4) against a ruling authorizing the Prosecutor to investigate despite a State's request for deferral—amounts to a challenge to admissibility.[83] The wording of Article 18 (7) equally clarifies that States are not allowed to request a deferral in accordance with Article 18 (2), again due to 'additional significant facts or significant change of circumstances'. Challenges can only be made in accordance with Article 19. Thus, even if a State argued, for instance, that a changed political climate or the end of hostilities amounts to 'additional significant facts or significant change of circumstances' that renders it willing and able to investigate, and the Court accepts that claim, the State could not request a deferral under Article 18 (2), but could only challenge admissibility in accordance with and within the more limited parameters of Article 19.[84]

Notwithstanding these safeguards, the potential for *delaying* proceedings and/ or for abuse is inherent in Article 18.

One must concede at the outset that delays may be the result of a State's legitimate and bona fide efforts to act in accordance with the fundamental premise of complementarity, that national criminal jurisdictions are those primarily responsible for investigations and prosecutions. The reviews by[85] and periodic information to[86] the Prosecutor may reveal, for instance, that delays result from the complexity of an investigation or difficulties in the gathering of evidence and witness statements. As long as the Prosecutor remains satisfied that a given State undertakes a genuine effort to investigate and prosecute and is able to do so, a case is likely to continue to be investigated at the national level. However, should that situation change at a later stage, for instance because the security situation in the State has deteriorated to an extent that the State is 'unable to obtain the accused or the necessary evidence and testimony'[87] vital time will have been lost.

At least as significantly, the notification in accordance with Article 18 (1)— whether or not on a confidential basis and irrespective of whether the scope of the

---

[82] RoPE (n 5) Rule 57. See further Rome Statute (n 1) Article 56 on the role of the Pre-Trial Chamber in relation to a unique investigative opportunity.

[83] J T Holmes (n 54) 682.

[84] These limitations are that Rome Statute (n 1) Article 19 (4) allows the admissibility of a case to be challenged only once and only in accordance with Article 17 (1)(c): see n 145 and text.

[85] Rome Statute (n 1) Article 18 (3).   [86] Rome Statute (n 1) Article 18 (5).

[87] Cf Rome Statute (n 1) Article 17 (3).

information provided is limited—is likely to alert *male fide* States, which may use the information made available to them to influence or subvert evidence and witnesses and to warn perpetrators.[88] Such States may then use the subsequent procedural steps to further disrupt and delay the proceedings of the Court.[89] They can block further investigation by the Court by requesting a referral and subsequently undermine the Court's efforts to determine whether national proceedings are genuine. Only if the application of the Prosecutor to nevertheless authorize an investigation is successful can the latter proceed.[90] In order to be successful, however, the Prosecutor will have to supply information on which the application to authorize an investigation is based; information that may come to light only *after* the request for deferral has been granted, for instance in the course of the periodic review in accordance with Article 18 (3). Since Article 18 applies at such an early stage that it suffices for a request for deferral that States are starting an investigation,[91] *male fide* States may use several pretexts as to why such an investigation is not progressing when the Prosecutor subsequently reviews the deferral or when subsequently asked to inform the Prosecutor periodically in accordance with Article 18 (5). Besides arguing that an investigation has been conducted but did not reveal a sufficient basis to proceed with the case against a particular person, examples of such pretexts, which *male fide* States can use, are alleged temporary security risks in gathering the necessary evidence or arresting the person(s) concerned; that witnesses are exposed to unacceptably great dangers; or that the person concerned has absconded or the evidence been destroyed.

Given that the Prosecutor will not be able to rely on the cooperative framework of the Statute after the request for a deferral,[92] his/her ability to verify these assertions of and the information supplied by the State is limited. Even if the Prosecutor could rely on independent trial monitors and members of civil society organizations, who may have access to court proceedings, these monitors and members may be unable also to have access to further information, such as case files, evidence and witnesses.

It would also seem that the Prosecutor's ability to seek authority to 'pursue necessary investigative steps'[93] could only mitigate this problem to a rather limited degree. This ability is not only subject to an authorization by the Pre-Trial Chamber but is also 'exceptional'.[94] What is an even more important limitation is that, in the light of the aforementioned problems to have access to information,

---

[88] See also *170–171*.
[89] See for instance J T Holmes, 'The Principle of Complementarity' in Roy S Lee (ed), *The International Criminal Court, The making of the Rome Statute, Issues, Negotiations, Results* (Kluwer Law Publ, The Hague) 76; D Stoelting, 'ICC PreTrial Proceedings: Avoiding Gridlock' (2003) 9 ILSA J Intl & Comp L 413–423, 420–422; D Cassel, 'The Rome Treaty for an International Criminal Court: A Flawed but Essential First Step' (1999) 6 The Brown Journal of World Affairs 41–52, 48; P Benvenuti (n 17) 47; R Dicker and H Duffy, 'National Courts and the ICC' (1999) 6 The Brown Journal of World Affairs 53–63, 59–60.
[90] Rome Statute (n 1) Article 18 (2) and Rules 53–55.   [91] Cf (n 44) and text.
[92] Cf *224–225*.   [93] Rome Statute (n 1) Article 18 (6).   [94] Ibid.

it is not immediately evident how to determine whether 'there is a unique opportunity to obtain important evidence or there is a significant risk that such evidence may not be subsequently available'.[95]

Besides the stage of preliminary rulings regarding admissibility, the procedural framework for complementarity foresees challenges to the admissibility of a case in accordance with Article 19.

2.3. Challenges to the Admissibility of a Case: Article 19

Challenges to the admissibility of a case in accordance with Article 19 and Rules 58 to 62 are the last procedural step specifically designed for the determination of the complementarity threshold.[96] This procedure, which resembles to a certain extent the procedure under Article 18 both in content and underlying *rationale*,[97] foresees the application and invocation of complementarity by a number of actors. First, according to Article 19 (1), the Court[98] has the power to determine 'on its own motion [...] the admissibility of a case in accordance with article 17'.[99] Second, an accused or a person for whom a warrant of arrest or a summons to appear has been issued under Article 58 has the right to challenge admissibility.[100] Third, an identical right is granted to the State that has jurisdiction over a case, on the ground that it is investigating or prosecuting the case or has investigated or prosecuted, and to a State from which acceptance of jurisdiction is required under Article 12.[101] Fourth, the Prosecutor may seek a ruling from the Court regarding a question of admissibility.[102]

Several introductory remarks are warranted with a view to clarifying the provision and its relation to, and differences from, Article 18. First, as the title of the

---

[95] Rome Statute (n 1) Article 18 (6).

[96] Besides regulating challenges to the admissibility of a case, Article 19 also governs challenges to the jurisdiction of the Court. The assertion that Article 19 constitutes the last procedural step specifically designed for the determination of the complementarity threshold is not meant to suggest that complementarity may not also arise at later stages and relate to a number of other provisions of the Statute, although these are not specifically designed to determine admissibility: see *3. Related Questions*.

[97] As to the latter, see *171–172*.

[98] While Article 34 defines 'the Court' as the Presidency, Appeals Division, Trial Division and Pre-Trial Division, the Office of the Prosecutor and the Registry, the term 'Court' has to be understood more narrowly in the present context as only referring to a 'Chamber', which, depending on the circumstances, may be the Pre-Trial Chamber, the Trial Chamber or the Appeals Chamber. This follows amongst other things from Article 19 (6) ['Prior to the confirmation of the charges, challenges to the admissibility of a case or challenges to the jurisdiction of the Court shall be referred to the *Pre-Trial Chamber*. After confirmation of the charges, they shall be referred to the *Trial Chamber*. Decisions with respect to jurisdiction or admissibility may be appealed to the *Appeals Chamber* in accordance with article 82.' Emphasis added].

[99] Rome Statute (n 1) Article 19 (1), second sentence. Note that this facultative power contrasts with the mandatory requirement that the Court 'shall satisfy itself that it has *jurisdiction* in any case brought before it': Article 19 (1), first sentence, emphasis added.

[100] Cf Rome Statute (n 1) Article 19 (2)(a).

[101] Cf Rome Statute (n 1) Article 19 (2)(b) and (c).   [102] Rome Statute (n 1) Article 19 (3).

provision already indicates, it is primarily *litigious* in character. Its core provides a framework for the exchange of claims and counter-claims between States, an accused and the Prosecutor as to admissibility, although this is subject to the qualification that, besides real challenges to the admissibility, both the Court and the Prosecutor have the power to determine or to seek a ruling regarding admissibility. As regards the Court, the emerging practice suggests that this discretionary power is exercised at the stage of issuing an arrest warrant against a particular individual, with the Pre-Trial Chambers making an initial determination on whether the case against a particular individual is admissible as part of the prerequisite to issue such a warrant,[103] if justified by the circumstances of the case, bearing in mind the interest of the person concerned.[104]

Second, the *group of parties who can invoke complementarity* under Article 19 is broader than that under Article 18, as it is not only confined to States but also includes *individuals*, namely 'an accused or a person for whom a warrant of arrest or a summons to appear has been issued under article 58'.[105] While such a right of an individual to invoke the judicial sovereignty of a State is not completely unknown to international criminal proceedings,[106] its express

---

[103] Pre-Trial Chamber II, 'Warrant of Arrest for Joseph Kony issued 8 July 2005 as amended on 27 September 2005', 13 October 2005, ICC-02/04-01/05-53, [38]; 'Warrant of Arrest for Vincent Otti', 13 Ocotbr 2005, ICC-02/04-01/05-54, [38]; 'Warrant of Arrest for Laska Lukwiya', 13 October 2005, ICC-02/04-01/05-55, [26]; 'Warrant of Arrest for Okot Odhiambo', 13 October 2005, ICC-02/04-01/05-56, [28]; 'Warrant of Arrest for Dominic Ongwen', 13 October 2005, ICC-02/04-01/05-57, [26]; Pre-Trial Chamber I, Decision Concerning Pre-Trial Chamber I's Decision of 10 February 2006 and the Incorporation of Documents into the Record of the Case against Mr Thomas Lubanga Dyilo 24 February 2006, Unsealed pursuant to Decision ICC-01/04-01/06-37, ICC-01/04-07/08-8-US-Corr [18].

[104] Pre-Trial Chamber I, Decision on the Prosecution Application under Article 58 (7) of the Statute, 27 April 2007, *Prosecutor v Harun and Kushayb*, ICC-02/05-01/07-1 [18]; Pre-Trial Chamber I, Decision on the evidence and information provided by the Prosecution for the issuance of a warrant of arrest for Germain Katanga, 5 November 2007, *Prosecutor v Germain Katanga*, ICC-01/04-01/07-55, Public Redacted Version of ICC-01/04-01/07-4-US-Exp [17].

[105] Rome Statute (n 1) Article 19 (2)(a).

[106] A (non-statutory) right to invoke the judicial sovereignty before an international criminal tribunal was for the first time recognized in ICTY Appeals Chamber, *Prosecutor v Tadic* (Interlocutory Appeal on Jurisdiction) IT-94-1-A7R2 (2 October 1995) 55 ['[A]n accused, being entitled to a full defence, cannot be deprived of a plea so intimately connected with, and grounded in, international law as a defence based on violation of State sovereignty. To bar an accused from raising such a plea is tantamount to deciding that, in this day and age, an international court could not, in a criminal matter where the liberty of an accused is at stake, examine a plea raising the issue of violation of State sovereignty. Such a startling conclusion would imply a contradiction in terms which this Chamber feels it is its duty to refute and lay to rest.']. This right of an individual to invoke a violation of State sovereignty must be distinguished from the claim made by Tadic in the same case that an accused has a right to be tried by his national courts under his national laws. On this latter point, see ibid, [61–64]. See also M Benzing, 'The Complementarity Regime for the International Criminal Court: International Criminal Justice between State Sovereignty and the Fight against Impunity' (2003) 7 Max Plank UNYB 599 [Article 19 (2)(a) as vesting the accused or suspect with standing to raise an issue that relates to State sovereignty, but not a right to be tried before a domestic court].

incorporation into the Statute of an international criminal court or tribunal is a novelty.[107]

Third, Article 19 grants *several States* the *right to challenge admissibility cumulatively or consecutively*.[108] These States include, first, those that have jurisdiction over a case and are investigating or prosecuting the case or have already done so.[109] All such States may make challenges to the admissibility, whether or not they are parties to the Statute.[110] With this inclusion of non-Party States, the different emphases during the negotiations of those States that sought to preserve the rights of States to investigate and prosecute to the fullest extent possible, on the one hand, and of those that were more concerned about the implications of such an approach for the effective operation of the Court, on the other hand, has been decided in favour of the former.[111]

Besides States which are investigating or prosecuting the case or have already done so, a second group of States are those 'from which acceptance of jurisdiction is required under Article 12',[112] ie the territorial State and State of active nationality. However, in order for these latter States to invoke complementarity successfully, it flows from Article 17 that they equally have to base such a challenge on the fact that they are investigating or have investigated the case in question.[113]

Fourth, when Article 19 refers to the admissibility of '*a case*', it implies that an investigation by the Prosecutor has identified one or more individuals subsequent to the initiation of an investigation of a situation.[114] This is clear not only from Article 19 (2)(a), which grants 'an accused or a person for whom a warrant of arrest or a summons to appear has been issued under article 58' the right to challenge admissibility, but also from the practice of the Pre-Trial Chambers to assess admissibility under Article 19 (1) in the context of deciding on an application by the Prosecutor for an arrest warrant in accordance with Article 58.[115]

Fifth and finally, the fact that Article 19 does not exempt any trigger mechanism from its application indicates that the provisions governing challenges to the

---

[107] G Kor, 'Sovereignty in the dock' in J K Kleffner and G Kor (eds) *Complementary Views on Complementarity—Proceedings of the International Roundtable on the Complementary Nature of the International Criminal Court, Amsterdam, 25/26 June 2004* (TMC Asser Press, The Hague, 2006) 66–67.

[108] J T Holmes (n 54) 684.

[109] Cf Rome Statute (n 1) Article 19 (2)(b). On the notion of 'a State which has jurisdiction over a case', see the discussion *110–113*.

[110] This confirms the participation of non-States parties in the procedure for admissibility: see (n 28) and text. As such, Section 4 of the 1969 Vienna Convention on the Law of Treaties (entered into force 27 January 1980) 1155 UNTS 331, 8 ILM 679, on treaties and third States applies.

[111] The controversy was only resolved in Rome: see *91–92*.

[112] Cf Rome Statute (n 1) Article 19 (2)(c).   [113] Cf *103–105*.

[114] C K Hall, 'Commentary on Article 19' in O Triffterer (ed) (n 21) 407–408, margin 3. For further discussion of what constitutes 'a case' at different stages of admissibility proceedings, see *3.1.1. Specificity of Proof*.

[115] See (n 103).

admissibility of a case are *applicable to all trigger mechanisms*, including Security Council referrals.[116]

The *proceedings under Article 19* are characterized by nearly as much *flexibility* as the deferral procedure under Article 18 (2).[117] Rule 58 grants the Chamber the power to 'decide on the procedure to be followed and [to] take appropriate measures for the proper conduct of the proceedings'.[118]

The mandatory elements under Rule 58 are limited to the requirement that requests or applications[119] made under Article 19 be 'in writing and contain the basis for it',[120] and that the Court 'shall rule on any challenge or question of jurisdiction first and then on any challenge or question of admissibility'.[121] In addition, the Court must transmit 'a request or application received under sub-rule 2' to the Prosecutor and to the accused or person for whom an arrest warrant or a summons to appear has been issued, and who has been surrendered to the Court or has appeared voluntarily.[122] The transmission puts the Prosecutor and accused or person on notice in order to enable them to exercise their right 'to submit written observations to the request or application within a period of time determined by the Chamber'.[123] The sub-rule's reference to 'a request or application received under sub-rule 2' makes clear that the Court is not obliged to transmit to the aforementioned parties information that it is determining the admissibility of a case on its own motion.[124]

Article 19 (3) and Rule 59 also spell out *who may participate* in proceedings with respect to admissibility, namely 'those who have referred the situation under article 13, as well as victims'.[125] These participants may submit observations to the Court after having been informed 'of any question or challenge of [. . .] admissibility which has arisen pursuant to article 19, paragraphs 1, 2 and 3' by

---

[116] J T Holmes (n 54) 683 ['Can these questions [of jurisdiction and admissibility] be raised regardless of the triggering mechanism? The answer is yes. Even where the Security Council has referred a situation and a case emerges, it is still subject to Article 19']. On the question of whether complementarity applies in the case of Security Council referrals, see also *165–166*.

[117] Cf (nn 53–57) and text.

[118] RoPE (n 5) Rule 58 (2). The same Rule also grants the Chamber the facultative powers to hold a hearing and to join the challenge or question concerning its jurisdiction or the admissibility of a case to a confirmation or a trial proceeding as long as this does not cause undue delay. In the latter case, the Chamber 'shall hear and decide on the challenge or question first'.

[119] Holmes points out the difference between requests and applications: '[. . .]If the accused or suspect or a State referred to in article 19, paragraph 2, make a challenge, they must do so by way of application. The Prosecutor must also apply to the Court if he or she seeks a ruling on jurisdiction or admissibility under article 19, paragraph 3, or if he or she seeks authority under article 19, paragraph 8, for investigative steps. However, if the Prosecutor seeks a review of a decision based on article 19, paragraph 10, or if he or she seeks information from a State under article 19, paragraph 11, he or she must do so by way of a request.' J T Holmes (n 37) 345, n 51.

[120] RoPE (n 5) Rule 58 (1).   [121] RoPE (n 5) Rule 58 (4).

[122] RoPE (n 5) Rule 58 (3).   [123] Ibid.

[124] On the meaning of the terms 'request' and 'application', see (n 119).

[125] Rome Statute (n 1) Article 19 (3), second sentence.

the Registrar.[126] Those receiving such information 'may make representation in writing to the competent Chamber within such time limit as it considers appropriate'.[127] As regards victims, these rules affirm the centrality of their interests in the overall structure of the Statute.[128]

The *venue* of proceedings, ie the competent Chamber of the Court, under Article 19 depends on the time at which challenges are made.[129] However, the time for such challenges is limited. According to Article 19 (4), a 'challenge shall take place prior to or at the commencement of the trial. In exceptional circumstances, the Court may grant leave for a challenge to be brought more than once or at a time later than the commencement of the trial'.[130] The rule is thus that challenges can be made up to or at the commencement of the trial. Otherwise, the Court has to expressly authorize them.[131]

Article 19 distinguishes between different venues on the basis of whether challenges are made (1) prior to the confirmation of the charges, in case the Pre-Trial Chamber is competent;[132] (2) after the confirmation of the charges but prior to the constitution or designation of a Trial Chamber, in which case the challenge must 'be addressed to the Presidency, which shall refer it to the Trial Chamber as soon as the latter is constituted or designated';[133] and (3) after the confirmation of the charges and the constitution or designation of a Trial Chamber. In the latter case, the Trial Chamber decides upon challenges.[134] All such decisions may be appealed.[135]

While such an appeal has of itself no suspensive effect,[136] the Prosecutor must suspend the investigation until such time as the Court determines whether or not

---

[126] RoPE (n 5) Rule 59 (1). As far as victims are concerned, Rule 59 (1)(b) further specifies that the Registrar shall inform 'victims who have already communicated with the Court in relation to that case or their legal representatives'.

[127] RoPE (n 5) Rule 59 (3).

[128] See further G Bitti and H Friman, 'Participation of victims in the proceedings' in R S Lee (ed) (n 37) 456–474; D Donat-Cattin, 'The role of victims in ICC proceedings', in F Lattanzi and W Schabas (eds) (n 17) 251–277.

[129] For the venue for requests under Article 19 (10) to review decisions by the Court that a case is inadmissible, see (n 154).

[130] Second and third sentence.

[131] C K Hall suggests that the standard for determining whether 'exceptional circumstances' exist should be that adopted in Article 84 (1)(a) on revision of convictions and sentences, thus requiring that new information has been discovered that: ' (i) Was not available at the time of trial, and such unavailability was not wholly or partially attributable to the party making application; and (ii) Is sufficiently important that had it been proved at trial it would have been likely to have resulted in a different verdict'. He further asserts that 'the closer a case was to trial [before the ICC] the more exceptional the circumstances would have to be to permit a second challenge to admissibility under article 17 para. 1 (a) or (b)': C K Hall (n 114) 412, margin 16.

[132] Rome Statute (n 1) Article 19 (6), first sentence.   [133] RoPE (n 5) Rule 60.

[134] Rome Statute (n 1) Article 19 (6), second sentence.   [135] Ibid, third sentence.

[136] Cf Rome Statute (n 1) Article 82 (3), which provides that '[a]n appeal shall not of itself have suspensive effect unless the Appeals Chamber so orders, upon request, in accordance with the Rules of Procedure and Evidence'. Rule 156 (5), however, grants the party appealing the right to 'request that the appeal have suspensive effect in accordance with article 82, paragraph 3'.

the case is admissible if a State challenges the admissibility of a case under Article 19.[137] A challenge by an individual has no such effect, however.

As with the procedure under Article 18,[138] the procedure for challenges of admissibility contains a number of *safeguards* to protect the integrity and efficiency of investigations by the Prosecutor.

A first safeguard is that the Registrar, when informing those who may participate in proceedings under Article 19[139] about the grounds on which the admissibility of the case has been challenged, must do so 'in a manner consistent with the duty of the Court regarding the confidentiality of information, the protection of any person and the preservation of evidence'.[140] To that end, the information is limited to 'a summary of the grounds'.[141]

Second, the admissibility of a case may be challenged only once by any person who, or State which, is granted the right to challenge admissibility.[142] While the Court may exempt persons or States from this stricture, it is made clear that this is only to occur 'in exceptional circumstances'.[143]

Third, those who are entitled to bring challenges to admissibility cannot claim that a case is being investigated or has been investigated in accordance with Article 17 (1)(a) and (b) if they only bring the challenge at the commencement of a trial, or subsequently with the leave of the Court. In the words of Article 19 (4), such tardy challenges 'may be based only on article 17, paragraph 1 (c)'.[144] This is in contrast to the situation in which challenges to the admissibility of a case are made *prior to* the commencement of the trial. The wording of Article 19 (4) suggests that the limitation to challenges on the basis of Article 17 (1)(c) does not extend to these earlier challenges, which therefore could also be based on Article 17 (1)(a) and (b). Such an understanding is also confirmed by the wording of Article 19 (2)(b), which does not limit the right to challenge admissibility to States, which have already tried a suspect. Rather, that right also extends to States that are still investigating or prosecuting a case.

Fourth, States that are entitled to make challenges to the admissibility of a case must make such a challenge 'at the earliest opportunity',[145] while the same requirement does not apply to a person who may challenge the admissibility of a case. Although the Statute or Rules do not provide expressly for any sanction against States that do not challenge at the earliest moment,[146] the Court is arguably competent to disregard a challenge that is not made 'at the earliest opportunity'.[147] A further incentive for States to challenge admissibility at the earliest opportunity is that they thereby broaden the grounds on which to do

---

[137] Rome Statute (n 1) Article 19 (7). As to the difference in suspensive effects of challenges, on the one hand, and of appeals, on the other, see also C K Hall (n 114) 414, margins 20–21.
[138] *176–179.*   [139] Cf (nn 125–126).   [140] Cf RoPE (n 5) Rule 59 (2).
[141] Ibid. Also cf n 53.   [142] Rome Statute (n 1) 19 (4), first sentence.
[143] Rome Statute (n 1) 19 (4), third sentence.   [144] Ibid.
[145] Rome Statute (n 1) Article 19 (5).   [146] J T Holmes (n 54) 684.
[147] In this vein, see C K Hall (n 114) 413, margin 18.

so: if they make such a challenge prior to the commencement of the trial, they could base the challenge on Article 17 (1)(a) to (c).

Fifth, Article 19 (8) grants the Prosecutor the power to seek authority to pursue necessary investigative steps of the kind referred to in Article 18 (6),[148] a power that is required in light of the suspensive effect of a challenge to admissibility for the applicability of Part 9 of the Statute on international cooperation and judicial assistance.[149] In addition to the steps envisaged in Article 18 (6), Article 19 (8) also permits the Prosecutor '[t]o take a statement or testimony from a witness or complete the collection and examination of evidence which had begun prior to the making of the challenge';[150] and '[i]n cooperation with the relevant States, to prevent the absconding of persons in respect of whom the Prosecutor has already requested a warrant of arrest under article 58'.[151] An application for any such measure is considered *ex parte* and *in camera* and ruled upon on an expedited basis.[152]

A sixth and final safeguard is spelled out in Article 19 (9), which provides that challenging the admissibility of a case 'shall not affect the validity of any act performed by the Prosecutor or any order or warrant issued by the Court prior to the making of the challenge'. The evidence gathered by the Prosecutor in relation to the case against an accused, for instance, is not invalidated by the mere fact that that person has challenged the admissibility of the case against him or her. Similarly, warrants of arrest and surrender issued by the Pre-Trial Chamber in accordance with Article 58 prior to the making of a challenge must be executed.[153]

Similar to Article 18, Article 19 and the applicable Rules also provide for *supervisory or monitoring tools* with regard to national proceedings in situations where the Court has decided that a case is inadmissible or when the Prosecutor defers an investigation. In the former situation, Article 19 (10) provides that 'the Prosecutor may submit a request for a review of the decision when he or she is fully satisfied that new facts have arisen which negate the basis on which the case had previously been found inadmissible under article 17'.[154] The words 'have arisen' need to be understood to refer to 'facts [that] *became known after* the decision rather than

---

[148] Rome Statute (n 1) Article 19 (8)(a). Cf also (nn 81–82) and text.   [149] Cf *225–226*.
[150] Rome Statute (n 1) Article 19 (8)(b).
[151] Rome Statute (n 1) Article 19 (8)(c). See further B Swart, 'Arrest and Surrender' in A Cassese, P Gaeta and J Jones (eds) (n 10) 1639–1703, 1694–1695.
[152] RoPE (n 5) Rule 61 in conjunction with Rule 57: cf (n 82).
[153] B Swart (n 151) 1694. On issues of admissibility arising in the context of surrender proceedings, see *3.3.2. Admissibility and Surrender Proceedings*.
[154] According to RoPE (n 5) Rule 62 (1), such a request must be made 'to the Chamber that made the latest ruling on admissibility. The provisions of rules 58, 59 and 61 shall be applicable.' Rule 62 (2) further specifies that '[t]he State or States whose challenge to admissibility under article 19, paragraph 2, provoked the decision of inadmissibility provided for in article 19, paragraph 10, shall be notified of the request of the Prosecutor and shall be given a time limit within which to make representations'.

that the facts *had to have occurred since* the decision'.[155] Thus, when information becomes available that a State is shielding a person from criminal responsibility, for instance, it is decisive that the Prosecutor *learned about it* after the decision of inadmissibility, regardless of whether the shielding began prior or subsequent to the determination of inadmissibility.

In the situation where the Prosecutor defers an investigation, Article 19 (11) stipulates that 'the Prosecutor may request that the relevant State make available to the Prosecutor information on the proceedings. That information shall, at the request of the State concerned, be confidential. If the Prosecutor thereafter decides to proceed with an investigation, he or she shall notify the State to which deferral of the proceedings has taken place.'[156] While this provision resembles Article 18 (5) to a large degree,[157] it differs in as much as it does not expressly require a State to respond to the Prosecutor's request 'without undue delay'.[158] It has been suggested that, as far as State Parties are concerned, a duty to do so flows from the general duty to cooperate with the Court as provided for in Article 86.[159] However, Part 9, including its opening provision Article 86, does *not* apply as long as investigations are suspended due to a challenge to admissibility.[160] It follows that Article 19 is therefore considerably weaker as far as the supervisory role of the Prosecutor is concerned, in as much as a State would seem to be under no obligation to respond positively to (a) request(s) to make available information on its domestic proceedings.

As in the case of preliminary rulings regarding admissibility, the aforementioned safeguards and supervising tools in Article 19 are no definite guarantees against the procedure's causing *delays* or being *used abusively*.[161]

Again, delays may be the result of a legitimate and *bona fide* effort to exercise jurisdiction as much as they can be the result of a bad faith effort of a given State to thwart proceedings of the Court.[162] Yet, Article 19, in itself as well as

---

[155] C K Hall (n 114) 417 margin 29, emphasis in the original. Hall bases his assertion on a comparison with the French text, which employs the terms '*des faits nouvellement apparus*'.

[156] Rome Statute (n 1) Article 19 (11).   [157] See (n 75) and text.

[158] Cf Rome Statute (n 1) Article 18 (5), second sentence. For the fate of the Italian proposal which would have required a State Party to do so, see pages 88–89 and 92. A second difference is that Article 19 (11) does not expressly specify the information which can be requested, while Article 18 (5), first sentence, in contrast, specifies that the Prosecutor may request 'that the State concerned periodically inform the Prosecutor *of the progress of its investigations and any subsequent prosecutions*' [emphasis added]. However, the only reasonable interpretation of the reference to 'information on the proceedings' in Article 19 (11) is that these proceedings are national proceedings with regard to the case at hand and thus include investigations, any subsequent prosecutions and the outcome thereof.

[159] C K Hall (n 114) 418, margin 31 ['[A] State Party to the Statute [. . .] has a duty to cooperate with the Court under Article 86 and that duty necessarily incorporates a good faith obligation to respond without delay'].

[160] See *225–226*.

[161] The considerations in relation to Rome Statute (n 1) Article 18 (3) and (5) on pages 179–180 apply *mutatis mutandis* to Article 19 (10) and (11).

[162] Ibid.

in combination with Article 18, bears the additional attribute that it may cause delays flowing from *multiple challenges* to the admissibility of a case.

This multiplicity may take two forms. First, a challenge to the admissibility of a case under Article 19 may be made *subsequent to an earlier challenge of a ruling of the Pre-Trial Chamber under Article 18*. States may argue that 'additional significant facts or significant change of circumstances' have arisen and invoke Article 18 (7), allowing them to challenge admissibility and thereby causing further delay.[163] In addition, *male fide* States may hold back facts intentionally to bring about a change of circumstances, or otherwise submit additional facts or a change of circumstances, which reach the level of significance required under Article 18 (7).

It is conceivable, for instance, that a State has requested a deferral in accordance with Article 18 (2) and has subsequently argued that the information available at the time was insufficient to proceed with an investigation. After the review by the Prosecutor (Article 18 (3)), the latter applies to the Pre-Trial Chamber (Rule 56), which authorizes an investigation by the Prosecutor, because it holds the State 'unwilling' or 'unable'. The State maintains that its investigation, while continuing, has not revealed sufficient evidence and, on the basis of that argument, challenges the ruling of the Pre-Trial Chamber before the Appeals Chamber (Article 18 (4)). After the Appeals Chamber has rejected the arguments of the State, it brings a new challenge under Article 19, now arguing that, in the meantime, sufficient evidence has come to light for an investigation of the case at hand.

Second, multiple challenges may result from the *array of those who may make challenges to the admissibility of a case*. Article 19 (2) grants such a right to an accused or a person for whom a warrant of arrest or a summons to appear has been issued; a State which has jurisdiction over a case, on the ground that it is investigating or prosecuting the case or has investigated or prosecuted; the territorial State and the State of active nationality.[164] At least two actors, namely the accused and one State, could thus challenge the admissibility, provided that the investigating State coincides with the territorial State and the State of active nationality. The number of States that may challenge admissibility could multiply if the investigating State differed from the territorial State or from the State of active nationality, or when several States are investigating the case simultaneously.[165]

---

[163] See also D Stoelting (n 89) 420.   [164] See also *182–183*.

[165] Recall that the grounds on which to challenge admissibility are limited to Rome Statute (n 1) Article 17 (1)(c) if such a challenge is made at the commencement of the trial or subsequently with the leave of the Court (n 144 and text). At this late stage, it would not suffice for States to argue that they are investigating or prosecuting the case, but they must assert that they have already tried the person concerned. Multiple challenges by States on this ground would thus assume that a person has been tried more than once in different jurisdictions for the same conduct, which could raise objections from the principle of *ne bis in idem*. Although in principle the prohibition of double jeopardy applies as a fundamental human right, eg under Article 14 (7) ICCPR (n 59), only in relation to judgments emanating from the same jurisdiction (cf eg Human Rights Committee, *AP*

Thus a State which is investigating or prosecuting a case, or has done so on the basis of passive personality or universal jurisdiction, could make such a challenge in accordance with Article 19 (2)(b) as much as the territorial State or State of active nationality, which is conducting or has conducted an investigation or prosecution, could make a challenge, invoking Article 19 (2)(a). If more than one of these challenges to the admissibility of a case proves to be successful, the problem arises of deciding to which State to defer, and the same considerations as in the context of Article 18 apply *mutatis mutandis.*[166]

One could of course understand the provision in Article 19 (4) thus that the admissibility of a case 'may be challenged only once by any person or State referred to in paragraph 2' literally, to mean that *all challenges must be made at the same time.*[167] However, such a reading seems to be contradicted by the wording of the provision, which uses the term 'or' rather than 'and' between 'any person' and 'State'. This choice of words indicates an *alternative* of, on the one hand, admissibility being challenged once by any person and, on the other hand, admissibility being challenged once by a State referred to in paragraph 2.[168] Furthermore, it may at times be hard to reconcile the requirement that all challenges be made at the same time with the requirement that States make them 'at the earliest opportunity'.[169] The 'earliest opportunity' does not necessarily coincide for different States. A situation in which one State is already investigating or has investigated a case while another Article 19 (2)-State, eg the State of active nationality, is still in the process of determining whether or not to initiate an investigation may serve as an example. The 'earliest opportunity' to challenge of the former State will in all likelihood precede the 'earliest opportunity' of the latter.

While the foregoing discussion is not meant to suggest that the Court should not use every opportunity to avoid successive challenges to admissibility, States are in principle allowed to make such challenges. Delays resulting from States making use of that opportunity, whether in good or bad faith, are thus a possibility.

Article 19 constitutes the last procedural phase specifically designed for determining admissibility. As a rule, a declaration of admissibility or inadmissibility

---

v Italy, Communication No 204/1986 (1987) UN Doc CCPR/C/OP/1, 67), some jurisdictions extend its reach to foreign judgments: see eg Section 12 of the Canadian Crimes Against Humanity and War Crimes Act, assented to 29 June 2000; Section 12 (1)(a)(i) of New Zealand's International Crimes and International Criminal Court Act, commenced 1 October 2000; Article 68 (2) Dutch Penal Code; Article 22 of the Code of Criminal Procedure of Mali. See International Society for Military Law and the Law of War, 'Compatibility of National Legal Systems with the Statute of the Permanent International Criminal Court', Recueil XVI (2003) vol I, 210, 313, 323, 378–379.

[166] Cf *175–176*.   [167] In that vein, C K Hall (n 114) 412, margin 15.

[168] The possibility for successive challenges may also be said to find further support in Rome Statute (n 1) Article 19 (6), which refers to 'challenge*s* to the admissibility' in the plural: see D Stoelting (n 89) 422. It is acknowledged, however, that this reference could equally be understood to take account of the possibility that a challenge may be brought more than once 'in exceptional circumstances', as provided for in Article 19 (4), third sentence.

[169] Rome Statute (n 1) Article 19 (5).

in accordance with this provision is the end of the matter.[170] This rule is only subject to the limited exceptions provided for in Article 19 (4)[171] and (10),[172] which provide some leeway for more than one such declaration and for findings on admissibility to be revisited. It is less clear, however, whether the Statute and Rules of Procedure and Evidence provide for the possibility to reconsider cases that have been declared admissible and to refer them back to national criminal jurisdictions.

2.4. Complementarity at the Post-Admissibility Stage: Referral of Cases Back to National Criminal Jurisdictions

The question as to whether, and to what extent, the Statute and Rules of Procedure and Evidence provide room for referring cases that have been declared admissible back to national criminal jurisdictions is of crucial importance. It would bear the advantage of enabling the Court to take into account changed circumstances on the ground which may very well impact on the (un)willingness or (in)ability of a State. The political situation in the State concerned may change, so as to suggest that that State is now inclined to investigate and prosecute ICC crimes domestically, as happened in Uganda subsequent to its auto-referral.[173] In that case, the peace process between the Ugandan government and the Lord's Resistance Army (LRA) led to the Agreement on Accountability and Reconciliation signed on 29 June 2007, and an Annexure to that Agreement signed in early 2008. In these instruments the parties recalled their commitment 'to preventing impunity and promoting redress in accordance with the Constitution and international obligations, and recall[ed], in this connection, the requirements of the Rome Statute of the International Criminal Court (ICC) and in particular the principle of complementarity'.[174] The Annexure to the agreement provides for

---

[170] F Mégret, 'Why would States want to join the ICC? A theoretical exploration based on the legal nature of complementarity' in J K Kleffner and G Kor (eds) (n 107) 1–51, 39–40 ['the ICC regime suggests that a state which is found at one point to be "unwilling or unable" to try certain crimes is, essentially, beyond redemption, that, in other words, engaging its responsibility and ordering it to comply with its obligations would be inadequate or even inappropriate in view of the stakes. Indeed, complementarity does not, for example, even afford the State a second chance. The process whereby a case will be transferred from the national to the international is a one-off, final one, not susceptible to any changes in the relevant states' attitudes.']; B Swart, 'Comments on Chapter 5 by Rod Jensen', ibid 171–175, 174 ['A finding of unwillingness or inability by the ICC, on the other hand, does not seem to entail the possibility for a state to start again with an investigation into the events. The Statute does not provide national criminal jurisdictions of the same state with the possibility to reopen the case or to start a case after a finding of unwillingness or inability, at least not explicitly and unambiguously'].

[171] See (n 130) and text.   [172] See (n 154) and text.

[173] (n 275). See generally on complementarity and auto-referrals, *3.2. Complementarity and Auto-Referral*.

[174] Paragraph 3 of the Preamble to Agreement on Accountability and Reconciliation signed between the Government of the Republic of Uganda and the Lord's Resistance Army/Movement (LRA/M) on 29th June 2007 and Paragraph 5 of the Preamble to the Annexure to the Agreement

the establishment of a special division of the High Court of Uganda to try individuals who are alleged to have committed serious crimes during the conflict[175] and a unit for carrying out investigations and prosecutions in support of trials and other formal proceedings.[176] It further foresees the use of traditional justice mechanisms.[177] These developments clearly demonstrate that the attitude of the Ugandan government has changed from one that had as its aim an intervention by the ICC, to a policy of domestic anti-impunity measures, including criminal proceedings.[178]

In other scenarios, a regime chiefly responsible for the unwillingness of a State may be removed, or the aid and assistance of international donors may bear fruit and result in a reinvigoration of a State's judicial system, which was earlier found to be 'unable', so as to render the State able again.[179] In all of the aforementioned situations, the general presumption encapsulated in complementarity that proceedings in national criminal jurisdictions are given precedence over international proceedings before the ICC suggests that a similar mechanism to the one under Rule 11 *bis* of the Rules of Procedure and Evidence of the ITCY and ICTR[180] is desirable. That desirability further flows from considerations of judicial economy. The ICC should not be forced to spend its limited resources on cases which can be adjudicated effectively on the national level—notwithstanding the fact that the effectiveness of a national criminal jurisdiction may only have evolved after the case had been declared admissible.

No provision of the Statute *expressly* contemplates the possibility of referring cases back to national criminal jurisdictions, however. Nevertheless, some *procedural avenues* would seem to exist which could be used to that effect.

First, nothing in the Statute or the Rules of Procedure and Evidence suggests that the *proprio motu* power of the Court to determine admissibility in accordance

---

on Accountability and Reconciliation signed between the Government of the Republic of Uganda and the Lord's Resistance Army/Movement (LRA/M) on 29th June 2007, signed in Juba on the 19th day of February 2008.

[175] Ibid, Sections 7–9.   [176] Ibid, Sections 10–14.   [177] Ibid, Sections 19–22.

[178] This change in attitude was again confirmed by a public statement by Ugandan President Museveni on 12 March 2008, expressing his preference for local justice initiatives and that '[i]f that's what the community wants, then why would we insist' on a trial in The Hague. He also reportedly stated: 'In that case, we can approach the ICC and say, yes, those people who we have brought to your attention have now come [back] ... Therefore we ask you to withdraw our complaint'. BBC News, 'Museveni rejects Hague LRA trial', 12 March 2008, <http://news.bbc.co.uk/go/pr/fr/-/2/hi/africa/7291274.stm>.

[179] For a practical example of such changed circumstances, see Decision Concerning Pre-Trial Chamber I's Decision (n 103) [35–36], in which the Pre-Trial Chamber noted in relation to the situation in the DRC that, when the President of the DRC sent the letter of referral, it appears that the DRC was unable to undertake the investigation and prosecution of the crimes falling within the jurisdiction of the Court, but 'that since March 2004 the DRC national judicial system has undergone certain changes, particularly in the region of Ituri where a *Tribunal de Grande Instance* has been re-opened in Bunia [...] Therefore, in the Chamber's view, the Prosecution's general statement that the DRC national judicial system continues to be unable in the sense of Article 17 (1)(a) to (c) and (3), of the Statute does not wholly correspond to the reality any longer.'

[180] *68–69.*

with Article 19 (1) could not be utilized to revisit an earlier finding of admissibility. In contrast to Article 19 (4), which is solely concerned with *challenges* to admissibility by those entitled to do so by virtue of Article 19 (2), Article 19 (1) does not stipulate that the Court is allowed to make such *proprio motu* determination only *once*, or that such a determination must be made at a certain point in time.[181] In fact, Rule 58 (2) grants the Court the necessary procedural flexibility in acting on its own motion to that effect.

Second, in a similar vein, Article 19 (3) would seem to allow the Prosecutor to seek a ruling from the Court regarding admissibility more than once and at any stage.[182] If information comes to light which suggests that a case that had earlier been declared admissible would now be inadmissible due to the changed circumstances on the ground, the Prosecutor could seek a further ruling regarding admissibility.

A third and final possible avenue for referring cases back to national criminal jurisdictions flows from the Prosecutor's power under Article 53 (4) to 'reconsider a decision whether to initiate an investigation or prosecution based on new facts or information', which he or she is allowed to do 'at any time'.[183] As we have seen previously, a consideration of admissibility is an integral part of deciding whether or not to initiate an investigation or prosecution.[184] Conversely, the later disappearance of the grounds on which the case was initially found to be admissible would justify a reconsideration of the decision to initiate an investigation or prosecution.

While the Statute thus provides some procedural avenues to refer cases that had earlier been found to be admissible back to national criminal jurisdictions, one cannot fail to notice that these are only crude devices, especially when compared to the mechanism under Rule 11 *bis* procedures within the ICTY and ICTR. The Rome Statute does provide for a legal remedy of an accused against such a decision in accordance with the general provision on appeal against decisions other than those of acquittal, conviction or sentence,[185] thereby resembling Rule 11 *bis* (I) of the ICTY and ICTR Rules of Procedure and Evidence. However, with respect to several other aspects, the regulation of the ad hoc tribunals is far more sophisticated. The ICC Statute does not provide for the modalities for handing over an accused, who is already in the custody of the ICC; for the ICC's sharing information with the national criminal jurisdictions, to which the case is referred

---

[181] Cf Decision Concerning Pre-Trial Chamber I's Decision (n 103) 19–20 [*ex officio* initial determination on admissibility in accordance with Article 19 (1) 'without prejudice to subsequent determinations on jurisdiction or admissibility concerning such case pursuant to Article 19 (1) [sic], (2) and (3) of the Statute'].

[182] Cf also C K Hall (n 114) 411, margin 13.   [183] Cf *168*.

[184] *2.1. Admissibility and the Initiation of an Investigation*.

[185] Cf Article 82 (1)(a), which reads in relevant parts: 'Either party may appeal any of the following decisions in accordance with the Rules of Procedure and Evidence: (a) A decision with respect to jurisdicition or admissibility [...].'

(subject to the limited exception provided for in Article 93 (10)[186]); or for the monitoring of subsequent domestic criminal proceedings by the ICC, beyond what is stipulated in Article 19 (11). Articles 19 (1) and (3) and 53 (4) also do not identify any conditions under which a decision to refer a case back to a national criminal jurisdiction can be revoked. An elaboration of an express procedural mechanism to refer cases back to national criminal jurisdictions therefore appears warranted. This could be done by amendments of the Statute and/or the Rules of Procedure and Evidence, with a view to regulating the aforementioned issues.

3. Related Questions

In addition to the question as to its application during different phases of ICC proceedings, the procedure of complementarity raises a number of related questions. The first set of such questions relates to proving (in)admissibility in the course of ICC proceedings (3.1.). We will then turn to the question as to whether, and to what extent, complementarity applies in the context of auto-referrals, ie referrals that are made by States Parties vis-à-vis crimes that occurred on their own territory (3.2.). The section concludes with a discussion of the links between complementarity and the regime of international cooperation and judicial assistance set forth in Part 9 of the Statute (3.3.).

3.1. Proving Admissibility

The matter of how issues of admissibility have to be proven in ICC proceedings raises three separate issues. First, the *specificity* of proof needs to be clarified, thus warranting a determination *in relation to what* admissibility has to be determined. More in particular, this issue raises the question as to whether and at what procedural stage it is sufficient to prove admissibility in relation to a broader set of circumstances or to a narrow set of circumstances, such as the domestic proceedings against an identified individual (3.1.1.). Second, given that the procedure of complementarity involves a number of parties, which find themselves before the Court arguing or litigating complementarity—most notably the Prosecutor, States requesting a deferral or challenging admissibility, and an accused or person for whom an arrest warrant or summons to appear has been issued, who challenges admissibility—the problem of who bears the *burden* of proving (in)admissibility needs to be addressed (3.1.2.). Third, a determination of the applicable *standard of proof* is necessary (3.1.3.).

---

[186] Rome Statute (n 1) Article 93 (10) provides the Court with the possibility to cooperate with and provide assistance to a State conducting an investigation into or trial in respect of conduct which constitutes a crime within the jurisdiction of the Court. See also (nn 387–388) and text.

3.1.1. *Specificity of Proof*

When considering the question in relation to what admissibility has to be determined, a first glance at the relevant provisions of the Rome Statute suggests that it has to be proven in relation to a 'case'.[187] This term also appears in relation to matters other than admissibility[188] but is further undefined. The reference to a 'case' in the provisions on admissibility has been understood to require that, from the earliest stage of admissibility proceedings, the Prosecutor needs to determine whether sufficient evidence exists to charge at least one individual with the commission of a crime or crimes, and that a State's investigation and/or prosecution corresponds (at least) to that particular individual.[189] Alternatively, it has been argued in relation to the use of the term in Article 53 (1)(b), that '[. . . the Prosecutor] must first identify the potential cases and in each specific case determine in accordance with the criteria in article 53 whether an investigation should be initiated and, subsequently, whether someone should be charged with one or more crimes'.[190] According to these views, admissibility has to be determined with a high degree of specificity. It would not be enough to establish, for instance, that the judiciary as a whole lacks basic guarantees of independence due to the way in which members of the judiciary are appointed, that a given State has a poor record in combating impunity, or that conducted investigations and prosecutions reveal bias in favour of a particular group of suspects, eg from one particular party to an armed conflict. Such general proof on a State's national judicial system would be insufficient, as long as it cannot also be shown that a State's unwillingness or inability manifests itself in the *specific case* under consideration.

However, in opposition to the view that such a high degree of specificity is required whenever admissibility is being determined is the view that the Prosecutor is unlikely always to have identified a particular individual from the outset of the proceedings. Especially when making the determination in the context of whether or not to initiate or proceed with an investigation under Article 53 (1), he/she will often have a more generalized set of facts before him/her, for instance when a State refers a situation to the ICC in accordance with Articles 13 (a) and 14, which covers multiple events that allegedly occurred in a still ongoing armed conflict.[191] In fact, the early practice of the Office of the Prosecutor confirms that

---

[187] Cf Rome Statute (n 1) Articles 15 (4), 17 (1), 18 (7), 19 (1), (2), (4), (6) and (10), 53 (1)(b), 89 (2), 90 (2)(a), (3)–(5), (8).

[188] Except the aforementioned provisions, see amongst others Rome Statute (n 1) Articles 24 (2), 31 (2), 39 (3) and (4), 41 (2), 42 (6) and (7), 55 (2)(c), 57 (3)(d), 64 (3), 65 (3) and (4), 69 (3), 94 (1).

[189] R B Philips, 'The International Criminal Court Statute: Jurisdiction and Admissibility' (1999), 10 Criminal Law Forum, Special Issue of the ICC, 77–78.

[190] H Friman, 'Investigation and Prosecution' in R S Lee (ed) (n 37) 494.

[191] See for instance the letter of Joseph Kabila, referring to the Court 'la situation qui se déroule dans [la République Démocratique du Congo] depuis le 1er juillet 2002, dans laquelle il apparaît que des crimes relevant de la compétence de la Cour Pénale Internationale ont été commis' and requesting the Prosecutor 'd'enquêter sur cette situation, en vue de déterminer si une ou plusieurs personnes devraient être accusées de ces crimes':Letter from Mr Joseph Kabila to the ICC

the object for determining admissibility in accordance with Article 53 (1)(b) can be a broader set of circumstances. Thus, when detailing his reasons for initiating an investigation into the events in Darfur, Sudan, the Prosecutor explained his understanding of Article 53 (1)(b) as requiring him

to consider whether there could be cases that would be admissible within the situation in Darfur [...]. In making this assessment, the Prosecutor takes into account the nature of the alleged crimes, as well as information relating to those who may bear the greatest responsibility for such crimes. For the purpose of analysing the admissibility of cases, the OTP has studied the Sudanese institutions, laws and procedures. [...] The Office has also interviewed more than a dozen individuals and sought information on national proceedings that may have been undertaken in relation to crimes within the jurisdiction of the Court allegedly committed in Darfur, including mechanisms provided to allow individuals to report crimes and have access to justice. The Office has also gathered information regarding multiple ad hoc mechanisms that have been created by the Sudanese authorities in the context of the conflict in Darfur [...]. In light of the information reviewed, the Prosecutor determined, on 1 June 2005, the existence of sufficient information to believe that there are cases that would be admissible in relation to the Darfur situation. [...] *The admissibility assessment is an on-going assessment that relates to the specific cases to be prosecuted by the Court. Once investigations have been carried out, and specific cases selected, the OTP will assess whether or not those cases are being, or have been, the subject of genuine national investigations or prosecutions* [...].[192]

This statement encapsulates the idea that the object of analysis under Article 53 (1)(b) is a broader, more global set of circumstances than a particular case involving one or more identified individuals, and that the required specificity increases with the proximity to an actual prosecution before the ICC. Although the information must be specific enough to allow the Prosecutor to make a determination as to whether a reasonable basis to initiate or to proceed with an investigation exists, the object of analyzing complementarity thus must not be construed too narrowly.[193] In fact, such a lower degree of specificity finds

---

Prosecutor, dated 3 March 2004—Reclassified as public pursuant to Decision ICC-01/04-01/06-46, ICC-01/04-01/06-39-AnxB1, available at <http://www.icc-cpi.int/library/cases/ICC-01-04-01-06-39-AnxB1_French.pdf>.

[192] 'Report of the Prosecutor of the International Criminal Court to the UN Security Council Pursuant to UNSCR 1593' (2005) 29 June 2005, available at <http://www.icc-cpi.int/library/cases/ICC_Darfur_UNSC_Report_29–06-05_EN.pdf>, 3–4. Emphasis added.

[193] See Annex to the 'Paper on some policy issues before the Office of the Prosecutor': Referrals and Communications, available at <http://www.icc-cpi.int/library/organs/otp/policy_annex_final_210404.pdf>, 2–3 ['It would not be reasonable to impose upon the senders of communications the burden of investigating for themselves or conducting an extensive inquiry for the purpose of sending detailed information to the Prosecutor. On the other hand, if the information provided is too broad and unspecific, it might be impossible for the Office to assess its value without launching a full investigation, something the Prosecutor is not allowed to do without authorization from the Pre-Trial Chamber. Likewise, even those States most willing to cooperate may find it impossible to provide substantive information if the questions raised by the Office are too broad and general. Significantly, the reference in Article 42.1 to examination of "substantiated information" indicates the logical assumption of the Statute that the preferred basis for analysis is comparatively detailed

some support in the provisions of, and the Rules of Procedure and Evidence relating to, both Articles 53 (1)(b) and 18, which employ fairly general language. Article 53 (1)(b) requires the Prosecutor to consider whether the case is *or would be* admissible. This wording suggests that the provision extends to situations in which the facts can only be determined with such a degree of generality that the question of whether a case *is* admissible cannot be answered. Furthermore, rulings regarding admissibility under Article 18 are only of a *'preliminary'* nature, and the provision refers in general terms to investigations of a State of 'its *nationals or others within its jurisdiction* with respect to *criminal acts which may constitute crimes'*.[194] This phrase is broad enough to cover multiple individuals and, even more importantly, applies in situations in which the decision as to whether criminal acts do indeed constitute crimes within the jurisdiction of the Court has not necessarily been made. Yet, individual cases can only be selected after such a decision has been made. Article 18 is, however, only applicable *after* determining a reasonable basis under Articles 15 (3) and 53 (1),[195] and it would be illogical to require a higher degree of specificity when applying the latter provisions.

It therefore stands to reason that a gradual increase in the specificity of proving admissibility is required, moving from a comparatively general standard, which addresses broader sets of circumstances, to individual cases. Two alternative constructions of the relevant provisions of the Statute may accommodate an understanding of the required degree of specificity in this way. The first one would be to give the term *'case'* employed in the context of admissibility *different meanings*, depending on the stage of the proceedings concerned. A 'case' in Article 53 (1)(b) would thus not necessarily need to involve one or more identified suspects, while this would be required under Article 19.[196] This construction would be more readily reconcilable with the references to a 'case' in the relevant provisions of the Statute, although it is open to the objection that it would contravene the rule that identical terms in a treaty text should be presumed to carry an identical meaning.[197]

---

and credible information. Accordingly, the Office will analyse the seriousness of all communications received, with the assistance of other information readily available to the Office. The extent of the analysis will be affected by the detail and substantive nature of the available information. The nature of this information will also affect the ability of the Office to make sufficiently focused requests to organisations and States with respect to facts, national investigations and other concrete relevant circumstances, necessary to determine whether there is a reasonable basis to start an investigation']. Cf also Informal Expert Paper for the ICC Office of the Prosecutor: The Principle of Complementarity in Practice (n 10) 9 [26] at (n 10).

[194] Rome Statute (n 1) Article 18 (2). See also Article 18 (1) referring to 'crimes' and 'the absconding of *persons*']; Rule 52 (1) ['information about the acts that may constitute *crimes*'], all emphases added.

[195] Subject to the caveat that it does not apply to Security Council referrals, cf *168*.

[196] Ibid.

[197] R Jennings and A Watts, *Oppenheim's International Law* (9th edn, vol 1 Longman, London 1996) 1273, referring to the case of *Ministry of Defence v Ergialli*, Italy, Court of Venice, judgment of 5 February 1958, 26 ILR (1958-II) 732–734.

The second construction, which it is submitted is the better view, is to *distinguish between 'situations' and 'cases'* as the object of analysis. Accordingly, a determination of admissibility vis-à-vis the former, understood as whole sets of circumstances,[198] suffices for purposes of Articles 53 (1)(b) and 18. In contrast, such a determination vis-à-vis a case, understood narrowly to encompass both the person and the conduct which is the subject of the case before the Court,[199] is required for purposes of Article 19. This distinction draws on the terminology employed in the context of the triggering procedure before the ICC, where the term 'situation' occurs,[200] on the one hand, and the criminal procedure, which is concerned with 'cases', on the other hand.[201] Thus, when determining 'a reasonable basis to proceed' under Article 53 (1), which is part of the triggering procedure, admissibility has to be determined 'in relation to *the whole situation of crisis* [...] *and not only with regard to specific facts that took place within it.*'[202]

---

[198] D Nsereko, in O Triffterer (ed) (n 43) 398, margin 6. See also ICC Pre-Trial Chamber I, Decision on the Applications for Participation in the Proceedings of VPRS 1, VPRS 2, VPRS 3, VPRS 4, VPRS 5 and VPRS 6, public redacted version—17 January 2006 ICC-01/04-101-Corr, [65] ['The Chamber considers that the Statute, the Rules of Procedure and Evidence and the Regulations of the Court draw a distinction between situations and cases in terms of the different kinds of proceedings, initiated by any organ of the Court, that they entail. Situations, which are generally defined in terms of temporal, territorial and in some cases personal parameters, such as the situation in the territory of the Democratic Republic of the Congo since 1 July 2002, entail the proceedings envisaged in the Statute to determine whether a particular situation should give rise to a criminal investigation as well as the investigation as such.' Footnotes omitted].

[199] Pre-Trial Chamber I, Decision Concerning Pre-Trial Chamber I's Decision (n 103) [21], [31], in which the Chamber further clarified that such an interpretation of the term 'case' entails that 'it is *a conditio sine qua non* for a case arising from the investigation of a situation to be inadmissible that national proceedings encompass both the person and the conduct which is the subject of the case before the Court'. See also ICC Pre-Trial Chamber I, Decision on the Applications for Participation in the Proceedings of VPRS 1, VPRS 2, VPRS 3, VPRS 4, VPRS 5 and VPRS 6, ibid ['Cases, which comprise specific incidents during which one or more crimes within the jurisdiction of the Court seem to have been committed by one or more identified suspects, entail proceedings that take place after the issuance of a warrant of arrest or a summons to appear']. See also Situation in Darfur, The Sudan, Prosecutor's Application under Article 58 (7), Public Reducted Version, ICC-02/05, 27 February 2007 [253–267]; Pre-Trial Chamber I, Decision on the Prosecution Application under Article 58 (7) of the Statute, *Prosecutor v Harun and Kushayb* (n 104) [14, 24]; Fifth Report of the Prosecutor of the International Criminal Court to the UN Security Council Pursuant to UNSCR 1593 (2005), 7 June 2007, available at <http://www.icc-cpi.int/library/organs/otp/OTP_ReportUNSC5-Darfur_English.pdf>, 7–9; Pre-Trial Chamber I, Decision on the evidence and information provided by the Prosecution for the issuance of a warrant of arrest for Germain Katanga (n 104) [20]. Cf also C K Hall (n 114).

[200] Cf Rome Statute (n 1) Articles 13 (a) and (b), 14 (1), 15 (5) and (6), 18 (1) and 19 (3). The term 'situation' replaced the term 'matter' 'in light of the change in terminology on questions of jurisdiction': see J T Holmes (n 89) 71 at n 40.

[201] Cf Informal Expert Paper for the ICC Office of the Prosecutor: The Principle of Complementarity in Practice (n 10) 9 [26], n 10. See extensively H Olásolo, 'The Prosecutor of the ICC before the Initiation of Investigations: A Quasi-Judicial or a Political Body' (2003) 3 International Criminal Law Review 87–150; H Olásolo, 'The Triggering Procedure of the International Criminal Court, Procedural Treatment of the Principle of Complementarity, and the Role of Office of the Prosecutor' (2005) 5 International Criminal Law Review 121–146.

[202] H Olásolo, 'The Prosecutor of the ICC before the Initiation of Investigations: A Quasi-Judicial or a Political Body', ibid 99. See also H Olásolo, 'The Triggering Procedure of the

'Situations', in other words, must be 'objectively defined by personal, territorial and temporal parameters'[203] but are not as specific so as to allow the Prosecutor to target 'specific political and military authorities during her preliminary inquiry and subsequent proceedings to open an investigation'.[204] It would thus suffice that 'unwillingness' or 'inability' can be shown in relation to such 'situations' with the consequence that a general lack of independence, widespread impunity and evidence of group bias could satisfy the establishment of 'a reasonable basis' as far as admissibility is concerned. In a similar vein, the preliminary analysis of admissibility under Article 18 has to be applied to 'the ensemble of proceedings initiated in the national criminal jurisdictions of affected States with respect to the crimes allegedly committed in such a situation' and, consequently, 'cannot be as detailed as when the admissibility analysis focuses on a single case',[205] which is required under Article 19. As a possible exception to the rule that admissibility is determined with regard to a *case* under Article 19, it has been argued that the Prosecutor may seek a ruling on admissibility in accordance with Article 19 (3) with regard to an entire situation.[206] However, such a reading appears to ignore both the wording of Rule 59[207] and the context of Article 19 (3).[208] This is not-withstanding that an earlier ruling of admissibility of one case within a particular situation may entail certain presumptions as regards other cases as long

International Criminal Court, Procedural Treatment of the Principle of Complementarity, and the Role of Office of the Prosecutor', ibid 122–123 on underlying reasons for the terminological confusion between 'case' and 'situation', which leads him to conclude that Article 53 refers to a 'situation', and 127–130 for arguments supporting the conclusion that the object of all trigger mechanisms and of the determination as to whether there is a reasonable basis to proceed under Article 53 (1) are 'situations'. See also F Razesberger, *The International Criminal Court—The Principle of Complementarity* (Peter Lang, Frankfurt/Main 2006) 31–33.

[203] H Olásolo, 'The Prosecutor of the ICC before the Initiation of Investigations: A Quasi-Judicial or a Political Body', ibid 99–100. See also 100 at n 44 ['[…] it can be concluded that situations of crisis, and not cases comprised of specific facts, are the subject of the investigations opened in accordance with […] Art 13 (c), 15 and 18'].

[204] H Olásolo, ibid 100. In the view of H Olásolo, a determination of admissibility in relation to situations rather than specific cases is more in line with the explicit intention of the drafters of the Statute to curtail the possibilities for politically motivated investigations of the Prosecutor. See also S Fernandez de Gurmendi, 'The Role of the International Prosecutor' in R S Lee (ed) (n 89) 175–188, 180.

[205] H Olásolo, 'The Triggering Procedure of the International Criminal Court, Procedural Treatment of the Principle of Complementarity, and the Role of Office of the Prosecutor', ibid 129. This is confirmed by the drafting history of Article 18: see (n 223) and text in Ch III.

[206] C K Hall (n 114) 411, margin 13 ['The Prosecutor's ability to "seek a ruling regarding a question of jurisdiction or admissibility" is not limited to a "case", so the Prosecutor could seek a ruling that […] the situation was admissible'].

[207] Note especially that RoPE (n 5) Rule 59 is applicable to '*any question* or challenge of jurisdiction or admissibility which has arisen pursuant to *article 19, paragraphs 1, 2 and 3*' (emphasis added), thus including cases in which the Prosecutor seeks a ruling on admissibility and that sub-rule 1 (b) requires the Registrar to inform 'the victims who have already communicated with the Court *in relation to that case* or their legal representatives' (emphasis added).

[208] As noted earlier, Article 19 applies to the stage where one or more individuals have been identified: see (n 114) and text.

as they confirm a general pattern that also underlay the initial declaration of admissibility.[209]

The aforementioned approach to distinguish between 'situations' and 'cases' as the object of analysis in the context of determining admissibility finds support in the early practice of the Court.[210] However, one cannot fail to note the following *effects*, some of them potentially problematic, of that distinction and the meaning given to the respective terms 'situations' and 'cases'. The first such effect concerns the situation in which a State seeks to request a deferral in accordance with Article 18 (2) on the ground that 'it is investigating or has investigated its national or others within its jurisdiction with respect to criminal acts which may constitute [ICC crimes] and which relate to the information provided in the notification to States'.[211] The broader the 'situation' and the information provided in the notification, the more burdensome it will be for a State to show convincingly that it is carrying out investigations which relate to the information provided in the notification to States, or has done. Conversely, since the preliminary analysis of admissibility under Article 18 has to be applied to *all* proceedings initiated by the requesting State(s) with respect to the crimes allegedly committed, it will not be very demanding for the Prosecutor to establish that a State is inactive, unwilling or unable as long as the requesting State cannot show that it is addressing the situation comprehensively. To consider 'situations' as the object of analysis under Article 18 will therefore have the potential effect that it will be challenging for States to successfully request a deferral. The flip-side of the coin, admittedly, is that it also has the potential effect of serving as an incentive for States wishing to request such a deferral to address the 'situation' as comprehensively as possible, or, at the very least, as an incentive to address all those cases within such a situation that might be of potential interest for the Prosecutor.[212]

The understanding that a 'case', within the meaning of Article 19, must extend to both the person *and the conduct* which is the subject of the case before the Court[213] has similar effects. Given that the Prosecutor is concentrating on those persons who bear the greatest responsibility, there will often be a wide array of conduct which could give rise to charges for crimes under the Statute. National authorities, much as the ICC Prosecutor, will often be faced with the decision as to which crimes to charge. Unless domestic investigations and prosecutions

---

[209] See further (nn 219–222) and text.

[210] See ICC Pre-Trial Chamber I, Decision on the Applications for Participation in the Proceedings (n 198) and Pre-Trial Chamber I, Decision Concerning Pre-Trial Chamber I's Decision (n 199).

[211] See *172–176*.

[212] On prosecutorial policy and sufficient gravity, see *Chapter IV: Complementarity as a Legal Principle and as Criteria for Admissibility, 3.4. Insufficient gravity: Article 17(1)(d)*, and (n 312) and text below. On the limits of of complementarity to serve as an incentive to investigate and prosecute, which emanate from the policy of the ICC Prosecutor to concentrate on those who bear the greatest responsibility, see *323–326*.

[213] See (n 199).

are all-inclusive in as much as they cover *all* conduct of a person who is the subject of a case before the Court, which amounts to crimes within the jurisdiction of the ICC, the Prosecutor will always retain the option to charge crimes relating to conduct other than that which forms the basis of domestic proceedings, and thereby forestall a declaration of inadmissibility under Article 19 (1) or a successful challenge to admissibility under Article 19 (2). The case of *The Prosecutor v Thomas Lubanga Dyilo* is illustrative of the results of that approach. The accused in that case had been arrested and detained by the authorities of the Democratic Republic of the Congo in relation to charges of genocide pursuant to Article 164 of the DRC Military Criminal Code and crimes against humanity pursuant to Articles 166 to 169 of the same code. The charges were later amended to include also the crimes of murder, illegal detention and torture.[214] The case against the accused before the ICC, in contrast, related to the policy/practice of enlisting, conscripting and using to participate actively in hostilities, children under the age of 15.[215] Observing that the warrants of arrest issued by the DRC authorities contained no reference to his alleged responsibility for these latter crimes, the Pre-Trial Chamber concluded that 'the DRC cannot be considered to be acting in relation to the specific case before the Court' and held the case to be admissible.[216] The case demonstrates the potential dilemma faced by those States which are willing and able to investigate and prosecute ICC crimes and make bona fide efforts to bring perpetrators to justice before their domestic courts. Such efforts are no guarantee that jurisdiction over a given case will be retained if a State selects any given number of crimes of a given person, however serious those may be. In relation to all crimes which fall through such a net of domestic prosecutorial discretion, the ICC Prosecutor will face no obstacle to admissibility and can bring such cases before the Court, if he/she so wishes.[217] However, in furtherance of the overall feature of complementarity to serve as a catalyst for domestic proceedings, rather than to discourage them,[218] it is submitted that the Prosecutor would be better advised to grant States a certain margin of appreciation in selecting crimes. If he/she is of the opinion that the crimes charged in domestic proceedings are insufficient, a first step should be to consult with the State concerned to amend domestic charges, instead of frustrating bona fide efforts to conduct domestic criminal proceedings.

The foregoing nevertheless suggests that the required degree of specificity depends on the different procedural steps at which admissibility has to be

---

[214] See Pre-Trial Chamber I, Decision Concerning Pre-Trial Chamber I's Decision (n 103) [33].

[215] Cf Warrant of Arrest, *Prosecutor v Thomas Lubanga Dyilo,* 10 February 2006, Reclassified as public on 17 March 2006 pursuant to decision ICC-01/04-01/06-37, ICC-01/04-01/06-2.

[216] Pre-Trial Chamber I, Decision Concerning Pre-Trial Chamber I's Decision (n 103) [38–40].

[217] See further on the compatibility of the exercise of prosecutorial discretion with the admissibility requirements, *Chapter VI: Complementarity and the Obligation to Investigate and Prosecute, 3. Prosecutorial Discretion.*

[218] See *Chapter VII: Complementarity as a Catalyst for Compliance.*

determined. However, there is an additional set of parameters relevant in that regard, which flows from the *different forms of unwillingness and inability*. Within those degrees of specificity, which apply at different phases of the proceedings, the factual basis of assessing admissibility must nevertheless be sufficiently specific to be able to satisfy the criteria enumerated in Article 17 (2) and (3). However, these criteria lend themselves to different degrees of specificity. A 'shielding of the person concerned', for instance, implies a higher degree of specificity than a 'total or substantial collapse'. When applying the former in the context of Article 19, for instance, the person who is (allegedly) being shielded must be identified. In contrast, a collapse—whether total or substantial—necessarily involves an overall assessment of a State's judicial system.

This is not to suggest, however, that the broader context of a State's past judicial record is irrelevant with regard to proof for 'unwillingness'. Systematic and widespread unwillingness with regard to similar conduct[219]—although not in and of itself determinative[220]—would weigh in favour of admissibility, provided that the steps taken by the State fit into the general pattern of impunity rather than diverting from it. Conversely, it would weigh against admissibility if a past practice of willingness of a judicial system can be shown and if the steps undertaken by the State concerned confirm the pattern. In contrast to proving inability, which can be based on a systemic assessment, the aforementioned factors are indicative when it comes to unwillingness. This approach of drawing on the broader context of a State's past judicial record as evidence for 'unwillingness' also finds support in Rule 51 of the Rules of Procedure and Evidence. For, the provision allows the Court to consider, *inter alia*, 'information [...] showing that [the] courts [of a State which has jurisdiction over a case] meet internationally recognized norms and standards for the independent and impartial prosecution of similar conduct' when assessing unwillingness.[221] Rule 51 was adopted on the express understanding that some general information could be relevant, provided it was linked to particular cases.[222]

---

[219] For an example of showing such past practices, see the 'Report of the UNHCHR to SC on the DR Congo' (16 July 2002) UN Doc S/2002/764, and 'Report of the UNHCHR to SC on the DR Congo' (13 February 2003) UN Doc S/2003/216.

[220] J T Holmes (n 37) 337.

[221] The Rule reads in full: 'In considering the matters referred to in article 17, paragraph 2, and in the context of the circumstances of the case, the Court may consider, *inter alia*, information that the State referred to in article 17, paragraph 1, may choose to bring to the attention of the Court showing that its courts meet internationally recognized norms and standards for the independent and impartial prosecution of similar conduct, or that the State has confirmed in writing to the Prosecutor that the case is being investigated or prosecuted.' Nothing bars organs of the Court, which are faced with an assessment of unwillingness at the pre-investigative stage, to draw upon such information on their own motion even if the State may not (yet) have brought it to the attention of the Court.

[222] Hence the reference to 'the context of the circumstances of the case'. See J T Holmes (n 37) 336.

In sum, the required specificity of proof is generally lower when the Prosecutor makes a determination as to whether a reasonable basis to initiate an investigation exists and at the stage of preliminary rulings on admissibility than under Article 19, which requires admissibility to be assessed in relation to an individual case. However, within these general parameters, different degrees of specificity may be required, depending on whether a claim of admissibility is based on (different forms of) 'unwillingness' or on 'inability'.

3.1.2. Burden of Proof

Who bears the burden of proving (in)admissibility, when States, individuals or the prosecution are raising the matter? An unambiguous answer to this question is not readily discernable from the provisions of the Statute and the matter has given rise to conflicting views. Thus some have asserted that the burden invariably rests on the Prosecutor,[223] others have adopted a more differentiated approach[224] and some suggest that the matter is entirely left to the discretion of the Court.[225] Given that the Court has not had the opportunity to pronounce itself on the issue thus far, we will limit ourselves to some tentative observations in the following.

As a point of departure, the basic rule is that the burden of proof rests on the Party putting forth the claim of (in)admissibility.[226] This general rule of *onus probandi actori incumbit* finds support in the practice of international tribunals and is recognized in virtually every legal system.[227] Accordingly, when the Prosecutor requests an authorization of an investigation in accordance with Article 15 (3), *he/she* will bear the burden of producing the necessary evidence

---

[223] M El Zeidy, 'The Principle of Complementarity: A New Machinery to Implement International Criminal Law' (2002) 23 Michigan JIL 899; B Broomhall, *International Justice and the International Criminal Court: Between Sovereignty and the Rule of Law* (OUP Oxford 2004) 90.

[224] Informal Expert Paper for the ICC Office of the Prosecutor: The Principle of Complementarity in Practice (n 10) 16–18, [53–58]; M Benzing (n 106) 628–629; S N M Young (n 26) 328–329, 334–338; M A Fairlie, 'Establishing Admissibility at the International Criminal Court: Does the Buck Stop with the Prosecutor, Full Stop?' (2005) 29 The International Lawyer 817–842, 822–825, 837–839.

[225] L N Sadat and S R Carden, 'The New International Criminal Court: An Uneasy Revolution' (2000) 88 Georgetown LJ 394.

[226] The Informal Expert Paper for the ICC Office of the Prosecutor: The Principle of Complementarity in Practice (n 10) 16, [54]; M A Fairlie (n 224) 824, 837; J Meissner (n 17) 71. See also the statement of the delegate of the Republic of Korea that '[t]he State Party that raised the question of complementarity should bear the burden of proof': United Nations Diplomatic Conference of Plenipotentiaries on the Establishment of an International Criminal Court (Rome, 15 June–17 July 1998) GAOR Volume II—Summary records of the plenary meetings and of meetings of the Committee of the Whole, UN Doc A/CONF 183/13 (Vol. II) 2002, 69–70, [84].

[227] M Kazazi, Burden of Proof and Related Issues: A study on Evidence Before International Tribunals (Kluwer Law International, London 1996) 406, 53–117, noting at 369 that this 'is the basic rule of the burden of proof'. See also R B Lillich (ed), Fact-Finding Before International Tribunals (Transnational Publ, New York 1990) 34; Third report on diplomatic protection by Mr John Dugard, Special Rapporteur, International Law Commission, 54th Session, Geneva 29 April–7 June and 22 July–16 August 2002, UN Doc A/CN.4/523, 7 March 2002 [102–118].

(burden of production)[228] and persuade the Pre-Trial Chamber (burden of persuasion) that a reasonable basis to proceed with an investigation exists, including that the 'case is or would be admissible under article 17'.[229] If a State requests a deferral in accordance with Article 18 (2), on the other hand, the burden of proving that it is investigating or has investigated its nationals or others within its jurisdiction rests upon that State,[230] while the Prosecutor will again bear the burden of proving admissibility if he/she makes an application for authorizing an investigation in spite of the State's request for deferral[231] or an application following review under Article 18 (3).[232] Furthermore, the Party claiming inadmissibility when making a challenge in accordance with Article 19 (2), ie an accused or person for whom an arrest warrant or a summons to appear has been issued or the State(s) mentioned in subparagraphs (b) and (c) of that provision, bears the burden of proof,[233] while the burden of proving admissibility rests on the Prosecutor when he/she seeks a ruling under Article 19 (3) or when he/she submits a request for a review of a decision of inadmissibility in the light of new facts in accordance with Article 19 (10). In the same vein, the burden of proof in appeals against a ruling in accordance with Article 18 (4), or against decisions under Article 19 (6), rests upon the party making the appeal.

While the general rule of *onus probandi actori incumbit* is the starting point for allocating the burden of proof, this rule may arguably have to be *supplemented* in some respects.

A first such supplementary rule on the burden of proof relates to situations in which the Party, which would not bear that burden according to the *onus probandi actori incumbit* rule, has *exclusive* or *superior access* to the information necessary to make an admissibility determination.[234] Such a rule finds support in the practice of a number of international courts and supervisory bodies, in particular in the field of human rights.[235] It appears particularly relevant in instances where the

---

[228] This burden of production also derives from Article 15 (3), which requires him or her to submit, together with the request for authorization, 'any supporting material collected'.
[229] On the applicability of the criteria in Article 53 (1) to *proprio motu* investigations, see n 9 and text. On the distinction between burden of production and burden of persuasion, which are understood here as distinct elements of the burden of proof, see M Kazazi (n 227) 21–38.
[230] M Benzing (n 106) 628–629. See also RoPE (n 5) Rule 53, which obliges a State making such a request to 'provide information concerning its investigation' while granting the Prosecutor the power to 'request additional information from that State'.
[231] D Nsereko (n 43) 401, margin 16; M A Fairlie (n 224) 824. Cf also RoPE (n 5) Rule 54, which requires the Prosecutor to submit 'the basis for the application' to both the Pre-Trial Chamber and the State.
[232] According to RoPE (n 5) Rule 56 (1), such an application following a review shall equally contain 'the basis for the application'.
[233] C K Hall (n 114) 409, margin 7.
[234] Informal Expert Paper for the ICC Office of the Prosecutor: The Principle of Complementarity in Practice (n 10) 17, [56]; M A Fairlie (n 224) 830.
[235] See eg Human Rights Committee, *Eduardo Bleier v Uruguay*, Communication No R.7/30 (1982) UN Doc Supp No 40 UN Doc A/37/40, 130 (29 March 1982) [13.3] ['With regard to the burden of proof, this cannot rest alone on the author of the communication, especially considering that the author and the State party do not always have equal access to the evidence and that

cooperative regime under Part 9 of the Statute—including the general obligation to cooperate under Article 86 and to comply with requests to provide the forms of cooperation specified in Article 93—does not apply.[236] For, the Prosecutor's ability to gather information on domestic proceedings will then be limited in ways similar to those that gave rise to the development by international (quasi-)judicial bodies of the supplementary evidentiary rule on exclusive or superior access to the relevant information.

An example is the phase after a successful request of a State to defer to its investigation in accordance with Article 18 (2), which postpones the application of Part 9.[237] Accordingly, during this phase the only obligation of State Parties to cooperate derives from Article 18 (5): they have to respond to requests of the Prosecutor for information about the progress of their investigation and any subsequent prosecutions. If the Prosecutor subsequently makes an application for authorizing an investigation following a review in accordance with Article 18 (3) and Rule 56, the starting point will be that he/she bears the burden of proof in accordance with the *onus probandi actori incumbit* rule.[238] However, in such a scenario, the State bears the burden not only of *producing* information, which already derives from Article 18 (5), but arguably also to *persuade* the Pre-Trial Chamber that its domestic investigation and/or prosecution meets the requirements for inadmissibility, to the extent that this can only be established by reference to information to which the State has exclusive or superior access. The general rule that the Prosecutor bears the burden of proof when submitting a

---

frequently the State party alone has access to relevant information. It is implicit in article 4 (2) of the Optional Protocol that the State party has the duty to investigate in good faith all allegations of violation of the Covenant made against it and its authorities, especially when such allegations are corroborated by evidence submitted by the author of the communication, and to furnish to the Committee the information available to it. In cases where the author has submitted to the Committee allegations supported by substantial witness testimony, as in this case, and where further clarification of the case depends on information exclusively in the hands of the State party, the Committee may consider such allegations as substantiated in the absence of satisfactory evidence and explanations to the contrary submitted by the State party.']; European Court of Human Rights, *Salman v Turkey* (App no 21986/93) [2000] ECHR 357 (27 June 2000) [100] ['Where the events in issue lie wholly, or in large part, within the exclusive knowledge of the authorities, as in the case of persons within their control in custody, strong presumptions of fact will arise in respect of injuries and death occurring during such detention. Indeed, the burden of proof may be regarded as resting on the authorities to provide a satisfactory and convincing explanation.']; see also *Ribitsch v Austria* (App no 18896/91) (4 December 1995) [34]; *Chitayev v Russia* (App no 59334/00) (18 January 2007) [149]; *Asan and others v Turkey* (App no 56003/00) (31 July 2007) [69]. See also ICJ, Corfu Channel Case, Judgment of 9 April 1949, ICJ Rep 1949, 18. Here, the ICJ, did not shift the burden of proof when the Party putting forth the claim sought to prove events which lay in the exclusive territorial control exercised by the respondent State within its frontiers, but it nevertheless held that such a situation 'has a bearing upon the methods of proof available to establish the knowledge of that State as to such events. By reason of this exclusive control, the other State, the victim of a breach of international law, is often unable to furnish direct proof of facts giving rise to responsibility. Such a State should be allowed a more liberal recourse to inferences of fact and circumstantial evidence.'

[236] See further *3.3.1. Part 9 and the different procedural stages of complementarity*.
[237] *224–225*.   [238] See (n 231) and text.

request for review of a decision of inadmissibility under Article 19 (10) may possibly have to be similarly qualified. Part 9 would be suspended following a successful challenge to the admissibility of a case,[239] and, furthermore, States are under no obligation to respond positively to requests to make available information on the proceedings under Article 19 (11).[240] Although the Rules of Procedure and Evidence require the Prosecutor's request for review to contain 'the basis for it',[241] the State may bear the burden of proving that the request of the Prosecutor should nevertheless be rejected, provided it has exclusive or superior access to the evidence which is necessary to do so.

Secondly, the *onus probandi actori incumbit* rule may have to be qualified when the conduct of the State concerned justifies to draw *adverse inferences* in relation to the question of admissibility and to thereby facilitate the satisfaction of the burden of proof. This may be the case, for instance, when the Prosecutor, whilst bearing the burden of proof when requesting an authorization of an investigation in accordance with Article 15 (3), can show that a State has sought to prevent information on its domestic proceedings to come to his or her knowledge, or where irregularities in the domestic proceedings suggest that suspicion as to their genuineness is warranted.[242] Similarly, it appears reasonable to allow inferences in favour of admissibility to be drawn when States fail entirely to respond to requests of the Prosecutor to provide information on their proceedings in accordance with Articles 18 (5) or 19 (11), or when they provide information that is incomplete or too unspecific to assess admissibility.[243] On the other hand, it would be equally plausible to draw an opposite inference in favour of *in*admissibility from the fact that a State is forthcoming with comprehensive information or even invites the Office of the Prosecutor to attend the domestic proceedings, etc.

3.1.3. Standard of Proof

A matter closely related to the preceding questions is what the required standard of proving admissibility is. In contrast to the two preceding questions of 'in relation to what has admissibility to be proven?' and 'by whom?', this matter concerns the degree or level of proof demanded for the purpose of ascertaining admissibility.[244] Once the required specificity of proof is established and the party who bears the burden of proof identified, the question of standard of proof arises as an analytically different matter.

---

[239] Cf *225–226*.   [240] Cf (nn 158–160) and text.

[241] RoPE (n 5) Rule 62 (1), second sentence, in conjunction with Rule 58(1).

[242] Informal Expert Paper for the ICC Office of the Prosecutor: The Principle of Complementarity in Practice (n 10) 17–18, [57]. See generally on adverse inferences from non-production of evidence in international tribunals, D V Sandifer, *Evidence Before International Tribunals* (University Press of Virginia, Charlottesville 1975) 519, 147–154.

[243] For such inferences in the context of Article 18, see S N M Young (n 26) 336. See also M Benzing (n 106) 628.

[244] Cf *Black's Law Dictionary* (7th ed, West Group Publ, St Paul 1999) 1413, emphasis added.

In the absence of unequivocal rules in the Statute and the Rules and Procedure and Evidence, jurisprudence by the Court and unequivocal standards in other international courts and tribunals from which comparison could be drawn,[245] it appears impossible to deduce any firm answers to this question. We will therefore limit the ensuing analysis to a number of provisional comments.

One way of addressing the issue would be simply to grant the Court a wide margin of discretion and to leave the required standard of proof largely undetermined. Such an approach would find some support in the practice of other international courts and tribunals, which habitually refrain from articulating precise standards of proof.[246] However, this general approach of other international judicial bodies is certainly not without its criticisms,[247] and would be problematic in the context of ICC admissibility proceedings. The resulting lack of transparency would likely have a detrimental effect on the Court's legitimacy and make it liable to the accusation by the Parties to admissibility proceedings that it acts arbitrarily. Furthermore, the failure to identify the required standard of proof would adversely affect the procedural rights of individuals entitled to invoke complementarity under Article 19 (2)(a).[248]

While a determination of the applicable standard of proving (in)admissibility is therefore generally warranted, the question arises as to *what standard or standards* should be adopted. While we do not suggest that one can readily transplant to admissibility proceedings before the ICC one (or more) of the generally known standards of proof, which have evolved in the context of specific types of proceedings (eg criminal, civil, administrative)—most notably the standards of 'beyond a reasonable doubt', 'by a preponderance of the evidence' or 'a *prima facie* case'[249]—such known standards appear to be a useful point of comparison.

---

[245] M Kazazi and B E Shifman generally assert, for instance, that 'it is generally accepted that the preponderance of the evidence is predominantly applicable in international procedure': M Kazazi and B E Shifman, 'Evidence before International Tribunals—Introduction' (1999) 1 International Law Forum 193–196, 195, [3]. However, besides the standards of 'by a preponderance of the evidence', the standard of 'beyond a reasonable doubt' has also been used in the context of international judicial proceedings: see eg European Court of Human Rights, *Ireland v UK*, 5310/71 [1978] ECHR 1 (18 January 1978) [161]; Iran-US Claims Tribunal, *Oil Field of Texas, Inc v Iran*, Award No 258–43-1 (8 October 1986) 12 Iran-USCTR 308 at 315 ['The burden is on the [Respondent] to establish a defence of alleged bribery in connection with the Lease Agreement. If reasonable doubts remain, such an allegation cannot be deemed to be established']. Furthermore, complementarity being expressed in the form of admissibility, one may be inclined to draw an analogy to the required standard of proof in other *admissibility* proceedings before international courts and tribunals. As far as human rights petitions are concerned, T Zwart infers from the practice of the Human Rights Committee and the European Commission of Human Rights, followed by the European Court of Human Rights, that an applicant is required to establish a *prima facie* case that s/he is the victim of a breach of the Convention for the purposes of admissibility: T Zwart, *The Admissibility of Human Rights Petitions—The Case Law of the European Commission of Human Rights and the Human Rights Committee* (Martinus Nijhoff Publ, Dordrecht/Boston/London 1994) 11 and 31.
[246] M Kazazi (n 227) 325 [standard of proof usually not discussed by international tribunals].
[247] Ibid.   [248] M A Fairlie (n 224) 825.
[249] For an overview over these standards of proof, see M Kazazi (n 227) 323–350.

At the outset, one may be tempted to equate generally the standard of proving (in)admissibility with the one required for establishing the guilt of an individual in the course of criminal proceedings, ie the standard of '*beyond reasonable doubt*'.[250] Such an approach appears to rest on the assumption that this standard should apply throughout the entire proceedings, including those of admissibility, because the ICC is ultimately called upon to determine whether a particular individual is criminally responsible for the crimes of which s/he stands accused. According to such a view, the evidence in favour of admissibility would thus always have to be so strong as to leave only a remote possibility of a case (or, depending on the approach adopted in connection to the specificity of proof, a 'situation'[251]) being inadmissible.[252]

However, such a global approach is open to the objection that the ICC, although undoubtedly an institution which ultimately administers criminal justice, has a broader role than merely determining the innocence or guilt of a particular *individual*. For, before such a determination can be made, an assessment of admissibility entails an incidental finding as to whether and to what extent a given *State* acts and is willing and able to investigate and prosecute ICC crimes. As such, admissibility proceedings resemble more closely proceedings for the determination of State responsibility than individual responsibility.[253] While this is to suggest neither that the standard of proof for State responsibility is clear and uniform,[254] nor that the standard of proof for admissibility before the ICC and the one for State responsibility could simply be equated, the crux for our analysis is that the question of the applicable standard of proof for determining admissibility cannot simply be answered globally by reference to the standard applicable in criminal proceedings.

Rather, the better view, it is submitted, is to address the required standard of proof separately for the different phases of admissibility, thus distinguishing the phase when the Prosecutor decides whether to initiate an investigation (and also when the Pre-Trial Chamber determines whether there is a reasonable basis to proceed with a *proprio motu* investigation in accordance with Article 15 (4)) from

---

[250]   Cf Rome Statute (n 1) Article 66 (3). In this vein, M Benzing (n 106) 629.

[251]   Cf *197*.

[252]   Cf *Miller v Minister of Pensions* [1947] 1 All ER 372, 373–4, *per* Lord Denning ['It need not reach certainty but it must carry a high degree of probability. Proof beyond a reasonable doubt does not mean proof beyond the shadow of a doubt. The law would fail to protect the community if it admitted fanciful possibilities to deflect the course of justice. If the evidence is so strong against a man as to leave only a remote possibility in his favour, which can be dismissed with the sentence, "of course it is possible, but not in the least probable", the case is proved beyond reasonable doubt, but nothing short of that will suffice.']; affirmatively cited in ICTY, *Prosecutor v Zejnil Delalic et al* (*'Celebici'*), IT-96-21-T, T Ch II (16 November 1998) 601.

[253]   See further *248–249*, *318–321*.

[254]   M Kazazi (n 227). For an illustration of the divergent standards of proof, see also (n 245). See also A Nollkaemper, 'Concurrence between individual responsibility and state responsibility in international law' (2003) 52 ICLQ 630, at n 75 for further references.

preliminary rulings regarding admissibility under Article 18 and from challenges to admissibility under Article 19.

Concerning *decisions as to whether to initiate or proceed with an investigation*, an argument in favour of a relatively low standard of proving admissibility under Article 53 (1)(b) draws strength from the fact that the available means of assessing and establishing admissibility are limited at this stage. In the light of the non-applicability of Part 9 at this early stage of the proceedings,[255] the Prosecutor and the Pre-Trial Chamber will have to rely on information available in the public domain or that is voluntarily supplied. Although one cannot derive any specific standard of proof from this fact alone, it nevertheless suggests that such a standard should not be overly demanding for the Prosecutor.[256]

The language employed in Article 53 (1)(b) could be understood to support equally a relatively low standard of proof, in as much as it requires the Prosecutor (and the Pre-Trial Chamber under Article 15 (4)) to consider whether the case is *or would be* admissible. The provision thus appears to render sufficient evidence which is not conclusive, but which is sufficient to establish admissibility in the absence of any evidence to the contrary. Such an understanding of Article 53 (1)(b) would suggest something akin to a *prima facie* test,[257] which finds some support in the early practice of the Office of the Prosecutor. As noted earlier, the Prosecutor expressed his view in the context of the Security Council referral of the situation in Sudan's Darfur Region, that the required standard of proof under Article 53 (1)(b) was 'sufficient information to believe that there are cases that would be admissible in relation to the Darfur situation'.[258]

To require a low standard of proof is further buttressed by drawing an analogy to the standard of proof required under Article 53 (1)(a), which obliges the Prosecutor to consider whether the information available to him or her provides *a reasonable basis to believe* that a crime within the jurisdiction of the Court has been or is being committed. Although the Statute distinguishes between admissibility and jurisdiction,[259] both concepts are concerned with the question as to whether or not the Court can act vis-à-vis a given set of facts. The two concepts therefore bear some resemblance and even overlap in some respects in the Statute.[260] To draw inspiration from the standard under Article 53 (1)(a) when considering the standard of proof under subparagraph (b) of the same provision would thus appear

---

[255] See further *224*.   [256] In this vein, see also F Razesberger (n 202) 54, 69.

[257] Cf also D M Walker, *Oxford Companion to Law* (Clarendon Press, Oxford 1980) 987 ['*Prima facie* evidence exists which is sufficient to establish a fact in the absence of any evidence to the contrary, but is not conclusive'].

[258] Report of the Prosecutor of the International Criminal Court to the UN Security Council (n 192).

[259] On that distinction cf *125–126*.

[260] Cf W Schabas, *An Introduction to the International Criminal Court* (2nd edn CUP, Cambridge 2004) 68–69 [noting the overlap with regard to the jurisdictional limitation on war crimes in Article 8 to those 'in particular when committed as a part of a plan or policy or as part of a large-scale commission of such crimes' and the admissibility threshold of sufficient gravity under Article 17 (1)(d)].

justified. The test under Article 53 (1)(a), in turn, has been identified as amounting to a *prima facie* test.[261] Indeed, a certain similarity between Article 51 (1)(a) and the language employed outside the Statute to define what constitutes *prima facie* evidence[262] is identifiable. Transposed to a consideration of admissibility in the context of Article 53 (1)(b), it would then be required to determine that there is *prima facie* evidence for admissibility, before an affirmative decision on whether to initiate (or proceed with) an investigation can be taken.

The subsequent question is what standard is required when (in)admissibility has to be proven under *Article 18,* a question that requires us to consider the different steps within the procedure for preliminary rulings regarding admissibility.

When a State requests a deferral in accordance with Article 18 (2), it will have to show that it is investigating or has investigated its nationals or others within its jurisdiction with respect to criminal acts which may constitute crimes within the jurisdiction of the Court and which relate to the information provided in the notification to States under Article 18 (1). The question as to *whether* such investigations are indeed underway or have already been concluded is an all or nothing matter: either they are/have or are not/have not. In requesting a deferral and providing information in accordance with Rule 53, the State concerned will thus have to produce evidence capable of convincing the Prosecutor and leaving no doubt that investigations are being or have been conducted.

What, however, is the standard for the Prosecutor to prove that, despite a (request for) deferral, an investigation should be authorized by the Pre-Trial Chamber under Article 18 (2) or (3)? Here, it is submitted, the standard should reflect the balance in these provisions between a certain degree of trust in States requesting a deferral, on the one hand, and the safeguards against abuse by *male fide* requesting States, on the other hand. Striking that balance appears to provide good reasons for requiring a higher standard of proof than at the earlier stage of deciding whether to initiate (or proceed with) an investigation. Indeed, the fact alone that a State requests a deferral and provides information concerning its investigation in accordance with Article 18 (2) and Rule 53 may be regarded as a rebuttal of the evidence for admissibility that was considered sufficient when deciding whether to initiate (or proceed with) an investigation under Article 53 (1)(b). At the same time, the Prosecutor's power to apply for an authorization of the investigation despite a request for deferral by a State or upon review of a deferral also demonstrates that there may be instances in which the Prosecutor will have good reasons for being suspicious of the intentions of the requesting State. In making the case before the Pre-Trial Chamber that this suspicion is supported by the facts, however, he/she will not be able to rely on the

---

[261] G Turone (n 10) 1172–1173. Turone defines the notion of a '*prima facie* case' as an evidentiary situation which at first sight gives the impression of being credible.

[262] For instance, G Turone points out ibid that the ICTY requires for a *prima facie* case 'that there is sufficient evidence to provide *reasonable grounds for believing* that a suspect has committed a crime within the jurisdiction of the Tribunal'. Emphasis added.

cooperative framework under Part 9 of the Statute.[263] It would therefore be too exacting to require the Prosecutor to demonstrate conclusively that the requesting State's investigation(s) do(es) not satisfy the complementarity requirements. Rather, a better view seems to be to require him/her to produce evidence that is weighing in favour of admissibility if compared with the evidence adduced by the requesting State in favour of inadmissibility. The Pre-Trial Chamber would then have to rule in favour of the Party for which the more weighty evidence is available. This, in short, would suggest a standard resembling what is commonly referred to as a 'preponderance of evidence'.[264]

Finally, we have to consider which standard of proving (in)admissibility has to be met by those who bear the burden of doing so under *Article 19*. More in particular, the question is whether the standard further increases under that provision in comparison with the standards under Articles 53 (1)(b) and 18.

The following arguments support such a conclusion. First, given that the specificity of proof under Article 19 requires admissibility to be assessed in relation to a 'case',[265] the Court,[266] those challenging admissibility,[267] and the Prosecutor when s/he seeks a ruling regarding a question of admissibility,[268] all will have specific information available on the domestic proceedings vis-à-vis a particular individual in respect of precise conduct. This would allow for a more concrete assessment of whether domestic proceedings have been, or are being, conducted in relation to that person and conduct, and whether or not they satisfy the complementarity requirements. It will be possible, for instance, to show whether or not a particular individual has been shielded, whether delays in the specific proceedings against that person were justified or not, and whether the judicial organs observed the fundamental requirements of independence and impartiality during these specific proceedings. With that assessment becoming more concrete, however, one may argue that the standard of proof for (in)admissibility should also become more demanding. Second, the litigating parties—namely the Office of the Prosecutor and those entitled to challenge admissibility under Article 19 (2)—have greater access to information about the domestic proceedings. For the States mentioned in Article 19 (2)(b) and (c), this is a logical consequence of their investigating and/or prosecuting the specific person concerned for the concrete conduct at hand. They are therefore in a position to produce all the relevant evidence to make a successful challenge. For the Prosecutor, on the other hand, this follows from the applicability of Part 9 of the Statute during the

[263] See *224–225*.
[264] On the definition of 'preponderance of evidence', see M Kazazi (n 227) 349–350. This standard is also at times referred to as 'balance of probabilites': cf *Black's Law Dictionary* (8th edn, West Publ, London 2004) 1220. For the view that this standard applies in the context of preliminary rulings, see D Nsereko (n 44) 401–402, margins 16, 20; Informal Expert Paper for the ICC Office of the Prosecutor: The Principle of Complementarity in Practice (n 43) 16 [52].
[265] Cf (nn 114–115) and text and pages 197–200.
[266] Cf Rome Statute (n 1) Article 19 (1); for practice of the Pre-Trial Chambers, see (nn 103–104).
[267] Cf Rome Statute (n 1) Article 19 (2).   [268] Cf Rome Statute (n 1) Article 19 (3).

procedure under Article 19[269] by virtue of which he/she can rely on the full range of forms of cooperation envisaged under Article 93.

However, while the foregoing discussion suggests that a higher standard of proving (in)admissibility under Article 19 is a reasonable starting point, it appears imprudent to approach all instances in which admissibility may have to be examined under that provision with a one-size-fits-all standard. For one, the argument that those litigating challenges to the admissibility of a case have improved access to the information does not necessarily hold true. For example, a higher standard of proof may be too demanding when States fail to comply with their obligations to cooperate with the Prosecutor. This may be the case when the State concerned pursues a policy of adjudication by the ICC in the context of an auto-referral.[270] Such a State could also seek to frustrate the efforts to prove inadmissibility of an accused or a person for whom an arrest warrant or a summons to appear has been issued, and fail to cooperate with that person to make his or her case for inadmissibility. The person concerned might then not be in a position to have access to the information necessary to prove to a high standard that his or her case is inadmissible before the ICC. Furthermore, the practice of at least one of the Pre-Trial Chambers when determining on its own motion the admissibility of a case under Article 19 (1) in the context of deciding whether or not to issue an arrest warrant under Article 58[271] suggests a comparably low standard of proof. For, Pre-Trial Chamber II has considered it sufficient that 'without prejudice to subsequent determination, the case [...] appears to be admissible'.[272] In contrast, when the Prosecutor requests a review of a decision that a case is inadmissible under Article 19 (10), the provision explicitly hints at a rather high standard for making such a request in as much as the Prosecutor must be '*fully satisfied* that new facts have arisen which negate the basis on which the case had previously been found inadmissible under article 17'.[273] This wording clearly indicates that the standard is higher than the one applied by the Court in its early practice under Article 19 (1). In fact, an argument could be made that the standard of 'fully satisfied' should also be higher than the standard of proof under Article 19 (2), because the standard for a successful request for review under Article 19 (10) should be more demanding than the one applicable to the earlier finding of inadmissibility which such a request seeks to have reviewed.

We can, therefore, cautiously deduce from the above that the standard of proof under Article 19 (2) and (10) is more demanding than under Articles 53 (1)(b)

---

[269] Cf *225–226*.   [270] On auto-referrals, see *3.2. Complementarity and Auto-Referral*.

[271] On this practice, see (nn 103–104) and text.

[272] Pre-Trial Chamber II, 'Warrant of Arrest for Joseph Kony issued 8 July 2005 as amended on 27 September 2005', 13 October 2005, ICC-02/04-01/05–53, [38]; 'Warrant of Arrest for Vincent Otti', 13 October 2005, ICC-02/04-01/05-54, [38]; 'Warrant of Arrest for Laska Lukwiya', 13 October 2005, ICC-02/04-01/05-55, [26]; 'Warrant of Arrest for Okot Odhiambo', 13 October 2005, ICC-02/04-01/05–56, [28]; 'Warrant of Arrest for Dominic Ongwen', 13 October 2005, ICC-02/04-01/05-57, [26].

[273] Rome Statute (n 1) Article 19 (10), emphasis added.

and 18, but that this does not necessarily hold true for a determination of admissibility under Article 19 (1). Furthermore, the standard of proof under Article 19 should be flexible enough to take account of possible, context-specific situations in which States fail to cooperate. However, further practice of the Court will be required in order to elucidate the relevant standards.

3.2. Complementarity and Auto-Referral

One of the striking features of the early operationalization of the Statute is that State Parties refer situations that occur on their own territory to the ICC. At the time of writing, three situations in relation to which the Prosecutor had opened an investigation emanated from such *auto-referrals*, namely of the Democratic Republic of the Congo (DRC),[274] of Uganda,[275] and of the Central African Republic.[276] If one considers this practice of auto-referrals, one cannot fail to notice its tension with the formal framework of complementarity in general and the procedural setting of complementarity in particular. This formal framework encapsulates the general assumption of the drafters of the Statute that complementarity provides a mechanism for States *to pre-empt* the ICC from acting, centrally by requesting a deferral under Article 18 or challenging admissibility in accordance with Article 19. Complementarity and its regulation in the Statute appears to presuppose that its primary objective is to regulate *competing claims* for the exercise of jurisdiction over ICC crimes, with both claimants—one or more States, on the one hand, and the Prosecutor, on the other hand—being eager to exercise jurisdiction. In these cases, the threat of the Prosecutor opening an investigation into a situation can serve as an important incentive for States to exercise their jurisdiction and to investigate and prosecute those responsible for ICC crimes in accordance with the basic requirements as they flow from the criteria of being 'willing' and 'able'.[277] Auto-referrals, on the other hand, start with the opposite assumption, namely that the State making such a referral *wants* the ICC to carry out proceedings vis-à-vis matters which that State considers to be detrimental to its interests if adjudicated in its own judicial system. Instead of demonstrating that they are willing and able to investigate and prosecute core crimes, they seek to justify their auto-referral by claiming their

---

[274] Letter from Mr Joseph Kabila, dated 3 March 2004—Reclassified as public pursuant to Decision ICC-01/04-01/06-46, ICC-01/04-01/06-39-AnxB1 (n 191).

[275] Letter of referral dated 16 December 2003 from the Attorney-General of the Republic of Uganda, appended as Exhibit A to the Prosecutor's application for Warrants of Arrest under Article 58 dated the 6th day of May 2005, as amended and supplemented by the Prosecutor on the 13th day of May 2005 and on the 18th day of May 2005.

[276] 'Prosecutor receives referral concerning Central African Republic', ICC Press Release, The Hague, 7 January 2005, ICC-OTP-20050107-86-En.

[277] For further discussion of this feature of complementarity, see *Chapter VII: Complementarity as a Catalyst for Compliance, 3. Complementarity as Sanction.*

*in*ability,[278] and are—in the broader sense of the word—unwilling to exercise jurisdiction themselves, but this unwillingness is *compatible* with the intent to bring the person concerned to justice, albeit before the ICC rather than their own courts. This apparent incompatibility between complementarity and auto-referrals demonstrates the need to analyze whether, and to what extent, complementarity in general (3.2.1.), and its procedural framework more in particular (3.2.2.), applies in the context of auto-referrals.

Before turning to these matters, the preliminary remark is warranted that *Articles 13 (a) and 14* on State Party referrals, which are invoked as the basis for auto-referrals,[279] do not stipulate that referrals may only be made by States Parties other than those on whose territory or by whose nationals ICC crimes appear to have been committed. Although the latter situation was undoubtedly at the forefront of the minds of the drafters of the ICC Statute,[280] the provisions merely provide that referrals may be made by *State Parties*. They do not exclude an auto-referral by a State Party, however.

3.2.1. *Applicability of Complementarity*

The most fundamental question is whether complementarity applies at all in the context of auto-referrals, or whether cases of auto-referral would render cases admissible without the need to establish that the referring State is either wholly inactive or unwilling and unable within the meaning of Article 17 (2) or (3). It could be argued that such referrals constitute the voluntary, *a priori* and *ab initio* relinquishment of the right to exercise jurisdiction by the auto-referring State. This understanding appears to underlie the conceptualization of auto-referrals as '*waivers of complementarity*'.[281] However, it appears questionable whether the mere fact that a State makes an auto-referral automatically entails such a waiver. It is generally accepted that waivers or renunciations of claims or rights of States must either be express or unequivocally implied from the conduct of the State alleged to have waived or renounced its right.[282] However, it would

---

[278] Cf Letter from Mr Joseph Kabila (n 191), in which it is claimed that 'les autorités compétentes ne sont malheureusement pas en mesure de mener des enquêtes sure les crimes mentionnés ci-dessus ni d'engager les poursuites nécessaires [...]'.

[279] Cf for instance, ibid.

[280] On the failed attempts to expressly regulate the related question as to whether complementarity could be waived, see (nn 126 and 163) and texts in Ch III. See further M El Zeidy, 'The Ugandan Government Triggers the First Test of the Complementarity Principle: An Assessment of the First State's Party Referral to the ICC' (2005) 5 International Criminal Law Review 83–119, 100.

[281] On this conceptualization, see eg M Benzing (n 106) 629–630; M El Zeidy, ibid 100–110. See also L N Sadat and S R Carden (n 225) 419–420. Also A Y Sheng, 'Analyzing the International Criminal Court Complementarity Principle Through a Federal Courts Lens' (2006) The Berkeley Electronic Press, BePress Legal Series, Paper 1249, <http://law.bepress.com/cgi/viewcontent.cgi?article=5942&context=expresso> 28 [arguing that such 'waivers' are analogous to waivers by States in a federal structure of their right to invoke abstention principles and thereby voluntarily submit to the federal forum].

[282] Cf ICJ, *Certain Phosphate Lands in Nauru (Nauru v Australia)* (Preliminary Objections) General List No 80 [1992] ICJ Rep 240, 247–250, [12–21]; ICJ, *Armed Activities on the Territory*

appear that, in the absence of an express statement to that effect, an unequivocal implied waiver cannot be assumed by the mere fact of an auto-referral alone. This is especially so in light of the fact that the auto-referral—just as any other State referral—concerns a 'situation', rather than specific cases.[283] It was indeed one of the main reasons for the introduction of the term 'situation' to forestall the selective referral of identified persons with a view to avoid politicization of the trigger mechanism of State referrals.[284] A referral, such as the one of the Central African Republic, which sought to refer five named individuals to the Court in April 2006,[285] would therefore fall outside the permissible parameters and the Prosecutor would not be limited to these individuals in his/her investigations.[286] It follows that the auto-referring State cannot be sure that the (group of) persons which it had in mind when making the referral will indeed be the (only) ones who will find themselves before the Court. This was amply illustrated in the context of the Ugandan auto-referral,[287] when the Ugandan President was informed that the Prosecutor would not necessarily limit his investigations to the organized armed group the LRA, which opposes the Ugandan government. He reportedly expressed his readiness 'to be investigated for war crimes', and said that 'if any of our people were involved in any crimes, we will give him up to be tried by the ICC', but then continued to state that 'in any case, if such cases are brought to our attention, we will try them ourselves'.[288]

This statement also illustrates that it may be somewhat over optimistic to assume that '[w]here the Prosecutor receives a referral from the State in which a crime has been committed, the Prosecutor has the advantage of knowing that that State has the political will to provide the Office with all the co-operation within the country that it is required to give under the Statute' and that 'the Prosecutor

of the Congo (Democratic Republic of the Congo v Uganda) General List No 16 [2005] ICJ Rep 1999 [293]; ILC commentary on Article 45 of the Draft Articles on Responsibility of States for Internationally Wrongful Acts, in J Crawford, *The International Law Commission's Articles on State Responsibility—Introduction, Text and Commentaries* (CUP, Cambridge 2002) 267 [5].

[283] For the distinction between 'cases' and 'situations', see pages 198–200.

[284] S Fernandez de Gurmendi (n 204).

[285] 'Hague referral for African pair', BBC News, 14 April 2006, <http://news.bbc.co.uk/go/pr/fr/-/2/hi/africa/4908938.stm>.

[286] Thus, when responding to the letter of referral of Uganda (n 275), in which the latter sought to limit the referred situation to crimes committed by the LRA, the ICC Prosecutor nevertheless concluded that the scope of the referral encompassed all crimes committed in Northern Uganda in the context of the conflict involving the LRA, thus extending to all Parties to the conflict. See Letter by the Chief Prosecutor of 17 June 2004 addressed to the President of the ICC, attached to the Decision of the Presidency Assigning the Situation in Uganda to Pre-Trial Chamber II, 5 July 2004, ICC-02/04-1.

[287] See (n 275).

[288] Remarks by ICC Prosecutor Luis Moreno-Ocampo, 27th meeting of the Committee of Legal Advisors on Public International Law, Strasbourg, 18 March 2004, available at <http://www.coe.int/t/e/legal_affairs/legal_co-operation/Public_international_law/Texts_&_Documents/2004/Speech%20OCAMPO%2027th%20Cahdi%20meeting.asp>.

can be confident that the national authorities will assist the investigation'.[289] It is exactly in scenarios of instrumentalization by the auto-referring State where the cooperation may be limited to those aspects of the investigation and prosecution before the ICC that advances the political goals of the auto-referring State. One can expect the DRC, Uganda and the Central African Republic to do everything in their power to provide the Court with the information necessary to achieve their objectives, but this will not necessarily be the case in relation to information that may be detrimental to them, for instance when investigations target political allies or governmental officials.

Be that as it may, even an *explicit* statement on the part of an auto-referring State that it wishes to waive admissibility would not, and should not, preclude the application of complementarity for the following reasons.

First, excluding the applicability of complementarity by virtue of an explicit waiver is hard to reconcile with the idea encapsulated in *complementarity* to function *as a catalyst for States* to investigate and prosecute ICC crimes.[290] One of the key tasks of complementarity is to improve the performance of States in fulfilling the central role that international law assigns to them in the suppression of ICC crimes. This fundamental objective of complementarity to strengthen domestic proceedings would be seriously undermined if one excluded its application in the context of auto-referrals. Indeed, to take such an approach could perpetuate impunity on the national level in as much as it would present States making an auto-referral with the convenient possibility not to investigate and prosecute ICC crimes, despite the fact that they are neither unwilling nor unable within the meaning of Article 17 (2) and (3).

Second, waivers of admissibility are *incompatible with the obligation to investigate and prosecute ICC crimes,* which, as further explained below, flows from the conjunctive operation of the Preambular phrase that 'it is the duty of every State to exercise its criminal jurisdiction over those responsible for international crimes' and the provisions on complementarity.[291] Notwithstanding assertions to the contrary,[292] it appears doubtful that territorial States can discharge such a duty by making an auto-referral and by arguing that they are ensuring that ICC crimes are investigated and prosecuted, albeit by the ICC rather than their own courts. The sixth paragraph of the Preamble unambiguously refers to the

---

[289] Annex to the 'Paper on Some Policy Issues Before the Office of the Prosecutor': Referrals and Communications (n 193) 5.

[290] M H Arsanjani and W M Reisman, 'The Law-in-action of the International Criminal Court' (2005) 99 AJIL 385–403, 390, 392. For a more detailed analysis of this function of complementarity, see *Chapter VII: Complementarity as a Catalyst for Compliance.*

[291] *Chapter VI: Complementarity and the Obligation to Investigate and Prosecute, 2.4. Preambular Paragraph 6 and Complementarity.*

[292] C Kress, ' "Self-Referrals" and "Waivers of Complementarity", Some Considerations in Law and Policy' (2004) 2 JICJ 944–948, 945–946. In a similar vein, see also M Benzing (n 106) 630; Informal Expert Paper for the ICC Office of the Prosecutor: The Principle of Complementarity in Practice (n 10) 19, note 24; S Morel, *La Mise en Oeuvre du Principe de la complémentarité par la Cour Pénale Internationale—Le cas Particulier des Amnisties* (PhD thesis, University of Lausanne, Lausanne 2005) 141.

exercise of jurisdiction of States ('its jurisdiction'), and the plain terms of the provision contradict its extension to cover the exercise of the ICC's jurisdiction. Even if one rejected this construction and gave the terms a broader meaning, a State making an auto-referral can in no way guarantee that the ICC will indeed exercise its jurisdiction, for instance because it considered the referred situation not to merit its intervention for lack of sufficient gravity (Article 17 (1)(d)) or because an investigation or prosecution of the ICC would not be in the interests of justice (Article 53 (1)(c) and (2)(c)). It is therefore unconvincing to regard this—to some extent discretionary—exercise of jurisdiction by the ICC within the confines that the Statute provides as fulfilment of a State's obligation to investigate and prosecute. To understand the obligation to investigate and prosecute that the Statute imposes on State Parties, as obliging to investigate and prosecute ICC crimes *domestically*, finds further support in a closer analysis of Article 17, which, as indicated, needs to be understood as operating in conjunction with the Preamble when determining the content and reach of the obligation of States Parties to the Statute. The references in that provision to 'a State which has jurisdiction' in subparagraphs (1)(a) and (b) make it quite clear that investigations and prosecutions are envisaged to be conducted on the national level.

Third, to subject auto-referrals to an admissibility assessment diminishes the *risk of politicization* of the Court. States may seek to use auto-referrals (also) as instruments of domestic politics. An illustration is the auto-referral of the DRC by the President, who, it has been suggested, sought to employ the auto-referral as an instrument to sideline political opponents in the run-up to the 2006 elections.[293] Similarly, the Ugandan government initially sought to refer only one party from the conflict, namely the LRA,[294] to the ICC, although the ICC Prosecutor commendably foiled that attempt.[295] By providing a mechanism through which cases are declared inadmissible, which can and are effectively being investigated and prosecuted on the national level, complementarity can contribute to thwarting attempts to selectively externalize the adjudication of cases that are politically or otherwise inconvenient to be investigated and prosecuted domestically.

Fourth, not to apply complementarity in the context of auto-referrals would entail the *risk of overburdening* the Court, notwithstanding some devices, such as prosecutorial policy and the admissibility requirement of sufficient gravity, which may limit the number of cases.[296] The ICC would become the only available forum, in the absence of action of third States and other mechanisms such as internationalized courts for bringing perpetrators to justice. At the same time, the forum, which is envisaged to carry the main burden according to complementarity, ie the active, willing and able national criminal jurisdiction of the

---

[293] W Burke-White, 'Complementarity in Practice: The International Criminal Court as Part of a System of Multi-level Governance in the DemocraticRepublic of Congo' (2005) 18 LJIL 557–590, 563–568.

[294] See letter of referral (n 275). [295] Cf (n 286).

[296] Informal Expert Paper for the ICC Office of the Prosecutor: The Principle of Complementarity in Practice (n 10) 18–19, [60].

auto-referring State, would be unavailable. Not to apply complementarity in the context of an auto-referral would thus divest the Court of a tool to decline the exercise of its jurisdiction, because cases can adequately be addressed on the national level.

The foregoing arguments support the view that auto-referrals are, in principle, subject to the regime of complementarity. It is therefore commendable that the Court appears to have adopted this approach in its early practice. When confronted with the question of admissibility under Article 19 in the case of Mr Thomas Lubanga Dyilo, which emanated from the auto-referral of the DRC, one of the Court's Pre-Trial Chambers assessed the Prosecution's assertion that the DRC's national judicial system was unable in the sense of Article 17 (3) and noted that this 'does not wholly correspond to the reality any longer'.[297] It nevertheless found the case to be admissible, noting that 'no State with jurisdiction over the case . . . is acting, or has acted', because the DRC's criminal proceedings against Mr Lubanga related to conduct different from the policy/practice of enlisting, conscripting and using to participate actively in hostilities, children under the age of 15,[298] which constituted the basis of the ICC Prosecutor's Application for a warrant of arrest; nor had another State become active. The Pre-Trial Chamber continued to state that '[a]ccordingly, in the absence of any acting State, the Chamber need not make any analysis of unwillingness or inability',[299] and thus did not deviate from the ordinary approach according to which the inaction of States entails that the case concerned is admissible.[300] This line of reasoning suggests *a contrario* that the Court would have assessed unwillingness and inability and thus applied complementarity if a State with jurisdiction over the case—including the DRC—had acted vis-à-vis the same person and conduct. Indeed, this scenario may arise should the ICC charges against Mr Lubanga Dyilo be amended to include conduct in relation to which the DRC had initiated criminal proceedings in their domestic courts, most notably the killing of UN peacekeepers on 25 February 2005.[301]

3.2.2. Auto-Referrals and the Procedural Framework of Complementarity

While complementarity is applicable to auto-referrals, some questions as to the operationalization of the procedural framework of admissibility arise. On the

---

[297] Pre-Trial Chamber I, Decision Concerning Pre-Trial Chamber I's Decision of 10 February 2006 and the Incorporation of Documents into the Record of the Case against Mr Thomas Lubanga Dyilo (n 103) [36].

[298] For the requirement that 'a case' relates to the same conduct and the same person, see n 200.

[299] Pre-Trial Chamber I, Decision Concerning Pre-Trial Chamber I's Decision of 10 February 2006 and the Incorporation of Documents into the Record of the Case against Mr Thomas Lubanga Dyilo (n 102) [40].

[300] Cf *104–105*.

[301] On the (conduct subject to) DRC domestic proceedings, see Prosecution's Submission of Further Information and Materials, Reclassified as public on 23 March 2006 pursuant to decision ICC-01/04-01/06-46, ICC-01/04-01/06-32-AnxC, 25 January 2006 [8–10, 22].

one hand, at the stage of deciding whether or not to initiate an investigation in accordance with *Article 53 (1)*, an auto-referral has to be treated no differently than other State referrals. The Prosecutor's role to consider whether 'the case is or would be admissible' is mandatory rather than discretionary.[302] In that regard, it needs to be borne in mind that this assessment by the Prosecutor is independent of the auto-referring State's own perception of whether a case or situation is admissible. An assertion alone that the competent authorities are incapable to investigate and prosecute ICC crimes, for instance,[303] is not determinative.[304]

Auto-referrals may have implications, on the other hand, for several elements of the procedures under *Articles 18 and 19*. Assuming that the Prosecutor has determined that there is a reasonable basis to commence an investigation under Article 53 (1), an auto-referral does not absolve him/her from his/her obligation to 'notify all States Parties and those States which, taking into account the information available, would normally exercise jurisdiction over the crimes concerned' in accordance with the procedure for preliminary rulings regarding admissibility.[305] However, the State making the auto-referral is unlikely, to say the least, to then react to the notification by requesting a deferral in accordance with Article 18 (2). It was after all that State's intention to see the ICC carrying out proceedings vis-à-vis the referred situation rather than itself. In a similar vein, that State may not be inclined to subsequently challenge the admissibility of a case under Article 19 (2)(b) or (c), although that possibility cannot be excluded, for instance when the case concerns an individual who does not belong to the group(s) of persons which the State had in mind when making the auto-referral[306] or when the situation has changed subsequent to the auto-referral.[307] In the absence of requests for deferral or challenges to the admissibility of a case by the auto-referring State, the question arises as to what role third States, an accused or a person for whom an arrest warrant or summons to appear has been issued, the Court and the Prosecutor (should) retain within the framework of Articles 18 and 19.

[302] Recall the opening wording of Rome Statute (n 1) Article 53: 'The Prosecutor *shall...*,' emphasis added. See also M El Zeidy (n 280) 105–106.

[303] Cf Letter from Mr Joseph Kabila (n 191), in which the President of the DRC asserts that 'les autorités compétentes ne sont malheureusement pas en mesure de mener des enquêtes...ni d'engager des poursuites nécessaires'. See also the auto-referral by the Central African Republic's *Cour de Cassation* of 13 April 2006, in which it was reportedly asserted that the persons concerned 'cannot be judged by our [the CAR's] national courts; only the ICC with its reputation and resources can do that': IRIN, 'ICC Reviewing Suit Against Ex-President, Official Says',—26 April 2006, available at <http://allafrica.com/stories/200604260057.html>.

[304] Accordingly, the ICC Prosecutor has applied Article 53 in response to the auto-referral of the DRC: see ICC Press Release, 'Prosecutor receives referral of the situation in the Democratic Republic of Congo', The Hague, 19 April 2004, ICC-OTP-20040419-50-En.

[305] Article 18 (1). For further analysis, see *168–170*.

[306] For example, the statement of the Ugandan President (n 288) and text indicates that, if the ICC Prosecutor were to seek an arrest warrant for a Ugandan governmental official, Uganda might challenge the admissibility of the case.

[307] Again, the Ugandan referral might be a case at hand: cf the developments subsequent to that referral described above (nn 173–177) and text.

As far as the role of *third States* is concerned, we have previously observed that *any* State can inform the Court that it is investigating or has investigated not only its nationals but also 'others within its jurisdiction' and request a deferral under Article 18 (2). Furthermore, States other than those on whose territory or by whose nationals ICC crimes have allegedly been committed can challenge admissibility. At the same time, an auto-referral implies that the referring State wishes the Court to exercise jurisdiction; a wish expressed by the State which can claim the strongest nexus to the crimes by virtue of the territoriality principle. The question therefore arises as to whether States with a weaker nexus or no nexus at all should exercise restraint in requesting a deferral under Article 18 (2) or challenge admissibility under Article 19 (2)(b) or (c) and thereby make it more likely that the wish of the auto-referring State materializes.[308]

On the one hand, there may be good arguments for the exercise of such restraint. The ICC may be in a better position to exercise jurisdiction than the third State, for instance because the auto-referring State has supplied the Court with evidence.[309] On the other hand, there may be circumstances under which proceedings in a third State bear the potential of creating an incentive for the territorial State to investigate and prosecute ICC crimes with a view to foreclosing adjudication in another State.[310] After all, if a third State threatens to forestall an auto-referral by requesting a deferral or challenging the admissibility of a case, the auto-referring State might reconsider its decision not to exercise jurisdiction, because it regards prosecution in the third State as detrimental to its interests. If State A and State B (both State Parties to the Statute) were involved in an international armed conflict and State A sought to auto-refer that armed conflict as a situation to the ICC with a view to have crimes allegedly committed on its territory by members of the armed forces of State B investigated and prosecuted by the ICC, a request for deferral or a challenge to admissibility by State B may cause State A to investigate and prosecute after all. One could therefore argue that States Parties to the Rome Statute should strive to strengthen the overall objective of complementarity to serve as a catalyst for conducting domestic prosecutions by requesting deferrals or challenging admissibility.

If, however, the main objective of an auto-referral is to externalize (a) politically inconvenient case(s) (for instance because the person(s) concerned continue(s)

---

[308] This question has been considered by Germany, where Ignace Murwanashyaka, a senior leader of one of the organized armed groups fighting in the DRC, the Democratic Forces for the Liberation of Rwanda, had been arrested in April 2006. He is believed to have committed numerous international crimes in Congo (as well as Rwanda). After his arrest, it was reported that Germany considered to transferring the case to the ICC: see 'Rwanda: FDLR Leader Could Be Tried At ICC', The New Times (Kigali), 18 April 2006, available at <http://allafrica.com/stories/200604190016.html>.

[309] See eg Informal Expert Paper for the ICC Office of the Prosecutor: The Principle of Complementarity in Practice (n 10) 19, [61]. Cf also and text. See also the auto-referral of the Central African Republic and the statement made by the *Cour de Cassation* (n 303).

[310] Recall that the proceedings against Augusto Pinochet in Spain and the UK appear to have had an impact on renewed efforts to prosecute him in Chile: see on these proceedings (n 62).

to disrupt the domestic political process), a request for deferral or a challenge to admissibility by a third State will unlikely change the attitude of the auto-referring State, because that aim of externalization would be achieved—albeit in a different forum than the one initially envisaged by the State making the auto-referral. The foregoing analysis suggests that the question as to whether third States should exercise restraint in cases of auto-referrals has to be answered contextually rather than in the abstract. However, even if restraint appears a wise cause of (in) action, the guiding principle should be to narrow gaps of impunity rather than to categorically abstain from exercising jurisdiction vis-à-vis all cases emanating from the situation, which was the object of the auto-referral. In other words, there may be room for restraint for the limited number of cases which fall into the reach of the ICC by virtue of the Prosecutor's policy to concentrate on those who bear the greatest responsibility[311] and their gravity under Article 17 (1)(d).[312] Other cases, however, may still have to be prosecuted by third States in order to contribute to ending impunity.

A further question raised by auto-referrals is their possible effect on the procedural right of *an accused or a person for whom an arrest warrant or a summons to appear has been issued* to challenge admissibility, as foreseen in Article 19 (2)(a). Some have suggested that certain elements of this claim of an individual may be 'waived' by the State making an auto-referral. More in particular, it has been argued that to challenge admissibility under Article 17 (1)(a) and (b)—as opposed to a challenge based on the *ne bis in idem* principle embodied in Articles 17 (1)(c) and 20 (3)—does not amount to a *right* of an individual, but merely provides an individual with 'standing to raise an issue that relates to state sovereignty'.[313] This view conceptualizes Article 17 (1)(a) and (b) as protecting the right of States to exercise their jurisdiction over ICC crimes. Drawing on jurisprudence of the ICTY Appeals Chamber in *Prosecutor v Tadic*, the view submits that in such a case, an individual 'cannot claim the rights which have been specifically waived by the State[ ] concerned'.[314] However, even if one assumed that the requirements for such a 'waiver' by a State were met,[315] an auto-referral of a State, which is neither unable nor unwilling in the sense of Article 17, is incompatible with the fundamental assumption underlying complementarity, explained in further detail in Chapter VI, that territorial States are under an *obligation* to

---

[311] Cf Paper on some policy issues before the Office of the Prosecutor (n 32) 7 ['The global character of the ICC, its statutory provisions and logistical constraints support a preliminary recommendation that, as a general rule, *the Office of the Prosecutor should focus its investigative and prosecutorial efforts and resources on those who bear the greatest responsibility, such as the leaders of the State or organisation allegedly responsible for those crimes*'. Emphasis in the original].

[312] Cf *Chapter IV: Complementarity as a Legal Principle and as Criteria for Admissibility, 3.4. Insufficient gravity: Article 17 (1)(d)*.

[313] M Benzing (n 106) 599. See also J Meissner (n 17) 73–75.

[314] ICTY Appeals Chamber, *Prosecutor v Tadic* (Interlocutory Appeal on Jurisdiction) IT-94-I-A7R2 (2 October 1995) 56. Cf J Meissner (n 17) 75. See also S Morel (n 292) 145–146.

[315] Cf (n 282) and text.

investigate and prosecute ICC crimes. What is at issue is thus whether the territorial State complies with that obligation, rather than whether it considers it in its interests not to invoke the right to exercise its jurisdiction. Such an obligation, however, cannot be 'waived'.[316] An accused or a person for whom an arrest warrant or a summons to appear has been issued could, therefore, nevertheless claim that the auto-referring State is neither inactive nor unwilling or unable within the meaning of Article 17 (2) and (3).

An entirely different matter is, of course, whether such a person will in fact invoke admissibility. If, for instance, that person belongs to the group that the referring State sought to eliminate or to sideline (such as the LRA in the case of Uganda or the organized armed groups opposing the government of the DRC), a challenge to admissibility may not be forthcoming, because the person entitled to do so expects his or her chances for a fair trial to be greater if tried by the ICC rather than by domestic courts of the State making the auto-referral. Another reason for an individual not to challenge admissibility under Article 19 (2)(a) may be the fact that the domestic jurisdiction concerned may impose the death penalty for ICC crimes, whereas the ICC cannot impose such a sentence.[317] In short, persons entitled to challenge admissibility may not consider such a challenge to be in their best interest.

In the light of the foregoing analysis, auto-referrals entail the possibility that the sole actors to assess admissibility, after the Prosecutor has determined that there is a reasonable basis to commence an investigation under Article 53 (1), will be the *Court* in exercise of its discretionary power granted under Article 19 (1) or the *Prosecutor* when seeking a ruling in accordance with Article 19 (3).

However, even though complementarity is, in principle, applicable to auto-referrals and (limited) procedural devices are available to apply it, the current system of admissibility does not sit easily with auto-referrals, and one cannot fail to note the *dilemma* which can present itself. If a State remains wholly inactive or abandons proceedings vis-à-vis persons and conduct that it seeks to refer to the Court (and provided that other States also do not act), the Court may find itself in a position as the only available forum for investigating and prosecuting a given case. In such cases, the ICC may be left with no other option than to declare cases admissible, although the auto-referring State could—in theory—conduct domestic criminal proceedings, which meet the requirements of willingness and ability within the meaning of Article 17 (2) and (3). It seems impossible to avoid the ICC effectively being taken hostage in this way within the current system. An express regulation of auto-referrals and their relation to complementarity therefore appears desirable. For the aforementioned reasons,[318] it is submitted that a prudent starting point for such an express regulation is to discourage auto-referrals. At the same time, it should take into account the possibility that

---

[316] M El Zeidy (n 280) 101.   [317] Cf Rome Statute (n 1) Article 77.   [318] *216–217.*

auto-referrals can provide a way to accommodate the genuine wishes of States to have the ICC exercise jurisdiction.[319] If a State delays proceedings against a particular (group of) person(s) because it wishes to allow a fragile peace to consolidate,[320] for instance, an auto-referral to the ICC may be a genuine effort to bring the perpetrator(s) to justice, which merits support from the ICC. Any regulation of auto-referrals should therefore clarify under what conditions auto-referrals are permissible and provide for the necessary flexibility which allows the Court to differentiate between auto-referrals that seek to misuse the ICC and those that are genuinely intended to ensure accountability.

3.3. Complementarity and State Cooperation

A further issue closely related to procedural aspects of complementarity is the cooperation of States with the ICC. The relationship between admissibility and State cooperation raises three questions, which we will examine in the following section. More in particular, we address (1) the general question of whether and to what extent the Statute's regime for international cooperation and judicial assistance in Part 9 applies during the different procedural stages of complementarity; (2) the more specific issue of the role of complementarity in the course of proceedings for the surrender of persons to the Court; and (3) the tension between, on the one hand, the idea of unwilling or unable States, which underlies complementarity, and, on the other hand, the idea of these same States cooperating with the Court.

3.3.1. *Part 9 and the different procedural stages of complementarity*

Part 9 opens with the general obligation incumbent upon State Parties to 'cooperate fully with the Court in its investigation and prosecution of crimes within the jurisdiction of the Court'.[321] This general obligation is then specified further in the following provisions and applicable Rules of Procedure and Evidence.[322] They contain, amongst others, the obligation of States Parties under Article 93 to comply with requests by the Court to provide specific forms of cooperation that are of significant potential relevance to an assessment of issues of admissibility, such as the service of documents, including judicial documents,[323] the provision of records and documents, including those of an official nature,[324] and 'any other

---

[319] Cf Informal Expert Paper for the ICC Office of the Prosecutor: The Principle of Complementarity in Practice (n 10) 19 [61].

[320] Recall that Article 17 (2)(b) provides some leeway for States to do so without being declared 'unwilling': *143–144*.

[321] Rome Statute (n 1) Article 86. See generally A Ciampi, 'The obligation to cooperate' in A Cassese, P Gaeta and J Jones (eds) (n 10) 1607–1638.

[322] Rome Statute (n 1) Article 87–102; RoPE (n 5) Rules 176–197.

[323] Rome Statute (n 1) Article 93 (1)(d).   [324] Rome Statute (n 1) Article 93 (1)(i).

type of assistance which is not prohibited by the law of the requested State'.[325] The applicability of Part 9 to any or all of the procedural steps at which complementarity has to be determined would thus make such forms of cooperation available to the Court while obliging States Parties to comply with requests. Whether this is indeed the case must be assessed in relation to each of the procedural stages of complementarity.

As far as an assessment of admissibility in the course of the *Prosecutor's decision whether to initiate an investigation* is concerned,[326] Part 9 is *not available* to the Prosecutor in order to gather information on which to base his or her decision on admissibility.

Both Article 86 on the general obligation to cooperate and Article 93 enumerating other forms of cooperation are clear in as much as they limit a State's obligations to cooperate with *investigations and prosecutions*, rather than extending them to the pre-investigative stage.[327] Given the clear distinction in the Statute between, on the one hand, an examination of the Prosecutor in order to determine whether a reasonable basis to initiate an investigation exists and, on the other hand, an investigation by the Prosecutor, the former cannot be brought under the term 'investigation or prosecution' in the meaning of Article 86.[328] The Prosecutor would thus have to rely exclusively on the non-compulsory means of gathering information in accordance with Article 15 (2) and Rule 104, ie to *seek* information 'from States, organs of the United Nations, intergovernmental or non-governmental organizations, or other reliable sources'.[329]

The foregoing discussion suggests an affirmative answer to the question of whether Part 9 is available at the stage of *preliminary rulings regarding admissibility* in accordance with Article 18 during the period immediately after sending

---

[325] Rome Statute (n 1) Article 93 (1)(l).

[326] Cf *2.1. Admissibility and the Initiation of an Investigation*.

[327] Cf Rome Statute (n 1) Article 86 ['States Parties shall [...] cooperate fully with the Court in its *investigation and prosecution* of crimes within the jurisdiction of the Court.'] and Article 93 (1) ['States Parties shall [...] comply with requests by the Court to provide the following assistance in relation to *investigations or prosecutions* [...]']; emphases added.

[328] See K Prost and A Schlunck, 'Commentary to Article 93' in O Triffterer (ed) (n 21) 1106, margin 10 ['[...] the specific obligation to comply is limited to the investigation or prosecution context']. In a similar vein, see Informal Expert Paper: Fact-finding and investigative functions of the office of the Prosecutor, including international co-operation, Prepared for the Office of the Prosecutor of the ICC (2003), available at <http://www.icc-cpi.int/library/organs/otp/state_cooperation.pdf>, [22–29] and especially [25], which states that such a view 'corresponds to the desire of States, during the negotiations, to limit the investigative powers of the Prosecutor prior to obtaining judicial authorisation in the case of *proprio motu* investigations. At the same time, the arguments supporting the broad interpretation [according to which Part 9 is applicable, JK] are open to the counter-arguments that Article 86 specifically refers to co-operation in the "investigation and prosecution of crimes", and that Article 15(3) (when read in French ["ouvrir"], Spanish ["abrir"] and Russian ["vozbudit¡"], as well as English) implies that investigations are not opened until Pre-Trial Chamber authorisation has been obtained'].

[329] Rome Statute (n 1) Article 15 (2) and RoPE (n 5) Rule 104. Also cf Rule 47 on testimony under Article 15 (2).

the notification until a State requests the Prosecutor to defer to its investigation.[330] During that period, the Prosecutor may thus request documents, for instance, or 'any other type of assistance'.[331] After a request for deferral by a State, and, if applicable, after such a request is confirmed by the Pre-Trial Chamber, rejecting an application by the Prosecutor for an authorization, however, the application of Part 9 is postponed. This follows from the suspensive effect that a deferral to a State's investigation has on an investigation by the Prosecutor. Such an effect is implied in Article 18 (6), which provides that the Prosecutor '*on an exceptional basis*, seek authority from the Pre-Trial Chamber to pursue necessary *investigative steps* for the purpose of preserving evidence where there is a unique opportunity to obtain important evidence or there is a significant risk that such evidence may not be subsequently available'.[332] In other words, Part 9, being only applicable to investigations and prosecutions of the Prosecutor, is only available to him/her as long as, and to the extent that, such investigative steps are authorized in accordance with Article 18 (6).[333] In all other cases, the Prosecutor can only rely on those cooperative measures that Rule 53 and Article 18 contain.[334] It should be noted, however, that these latter measures, though being more general in as much as they only relate to the providing of *information* by States, might overlap to some extent with measures under Article 93.[335]

As far as *the procedure under Article 19* is concerned, the starting point is that Part 9 is applicable. For, Article 19 only applies after the Prosecutor has already commenced an investigation and carried out at least some investigative steps.[336] Should the Court consider it necessary in the course of determining admissibility on its own motion under Article 19 (1), it can therefore rely on Part 9

---

[330] Cf G Turone (n 46).   [331] Cf (nn 323–325) and text.

[332] Emphasis added. Cf G Sluiter, *International Criminal Adjudication and the Collection of Evidence: Obligations of States* (Intersentia, Antwerp, Oxford, New York 2002) 109; J Meissner (n 17) 93.

[333] See also Informal Expert Paper: Fact-finding and investigative functions of the office of the Prosecutor, including international co-operation (n 328) [46] ['Part 9 co-operation is available for provisional measures in the interim [authorized under Article 18 (6), JK]. While slightly more uncertain, an "investigation" should also be considered commenced for provisional measures explicitly authorised by the Chamber in spite of a deferral (insofar the authorised measures are concerned), and thus Part 9 co-operation would apply'].

[334] Cf *2.2. Preliminary Rulings Regarding Admissibility: Article 18*. See also Informal Expert Paper: Fact-finding and investigative functions of the office of the Prosecutor, including international co-operation, ibid [43] ['Also in case of a deferral, the Prosecutor will have to follow up the national development of the case in question and a State Party may be obliged to submit periodical information on its progress (Article 18(5)). In this case, however, it is hard to claim that the Prosecutor is conducting an "investigation" of a crime and it is very doubtful that the Prosecutor has recourse to any measures of co-operation under Part 9. Hence, the State's own information and information from external sources may be the only material available as a basis for a review of a deferral according to Article 18(3)'].

[335] Thus information concerning a State's investigation (cf Rule 53) or information about the progress of a State's investigation and any subsequent prosecutions (cf Article 18 (5)) would likely contain 'documents, including judicial documents' and 'records and documents, including official records and documents' mentioned in Article 93 (1)(d) and (i).

[336] See (n 114) and text.

of the Statute, for instance. Should States challenge the admissibility under Article 19 (2)(b) or (c), however, the suspensive effect of such a challenge[337] precludes the applicability of Part 9. Only if, and to the extent that, the competent Chamber grants the Prosecutor the authority to take the provisional investigative measures envisaged under Article 19 (8)[338] is Part 9 revived.[339] Furthermore, when a request for assistance has already been made by the Court, Article 95 provides that, when there is an admissibility challenge under consideration by the Court pursuant to article 18 or 19, a requested State may postpone the execution of a request under Part 9 pending a determination by the Court, unless the Court has specifically ordered that the Prosecutor may pursue the collection of such evidence pursuant to Article 18 (6) or 19 (8).[340]

3.3.2. Admissibility and Surrender Proceedings

Another converging point between admissibility and Part 9 of the Statute is when issues of admissibility arise in the course of surrender proceedings. Two such situations are specifically regulated. Under the first circumstance, a 'person sought for surrender brings a challenge before a national court on the basis of the principle of *ne bis in idem* as provided in article 20'.[341] Here, the question arises as to how such challenges are to be entertained. Under the second circumstance, a State Party not only receives a request from the Court to surrender a person, but also receives a request from another State for the extradition of the same person. In this latter situation, admissibility functions as one factor in determining which of the requests prevails.

As far as the situation in which a person sought for surrender brings a '*challenge before a national court on the basis of the principle of* ne bis in idem' is concerned, the right of such a person to do so is a corollary to that right of an accused or a

---

[337] Cf Rome Statute (n 1) Article 19 (7). See also (nn 136–137) and text, and J Meissner (n 17) 95.

[338] See (nn 148–151) and text.

[339] Cf Informal Expert Paper: Fact-finding and investigative functions of the office of the Prosecutor, including international co-operation (n 328) [47] ['Since the "investigation" should only be considered suspended to the extent that provisional measures are not authorised, Part 9 co-operation would be available to the Prosecutor regarding such authorised measures. Moreover, orders and warrants ordered by the Court prior to the challenge continue to be valid (Article 19 (9)) and States Parties continue to be obliged to fulfil requests based on such orders and warrants in accordance with Part 9']. On Article 19 (9), cf (n 153). See also B Swart, 'General Problems' in A Cassese, P Gaeta and J Jones (eds) (n 9) 1589–1605, 1595–1596.

[340] Rome Statute (n 1) Article 95. Note that a challenge to admissibility under Article 18 would take the form of an appeal in accordance with Article 18 (4): cf (n 83) and text. As we have noted previously, such an appeal has in itself no suspensive effect: see (n 136) and text. Article 95 differs from Article 82 (3) in two important respects, however. First, Article 95 is limited to the situation in which a request for assistance has already been made. Second, Article 95 is concerned with the rights and obligations of the *requested State,* rather than the powers of the Court to request assistance, and grants the requested State the power to postpone the execution of such request: see also G Sluiter (n 333) 173–174; J Meissner (n 17) 155.

[341] Rome Statute (n 1) Article 89 (2). Emphasis added.

person for whom an arrest warrant has been issued under Article 58.[342] For, an arrest warrant is the basis on which the Court may request the provisional arrest or the arrest and surrender of the person under Part 9.[343]

However, if a national court could entertain such a challenge and apply the principle of *ne bis in idem*, and especially the exceptions to it contained in subparagraph 3,[344] it would put the national court into the paradoxical position of assessing the unwillingness or inability of its own State, including the judicial system of which itself is a part. Such a competence of national courts would reverse the principle that admissibility is determined independently *by the Court* rather than by States themselves.

In order to avoid such a situation, Article 89 (2) obliges the requested State to 'immediately consult with the Court to determine if there has been a relevant ruling on admissibility. If the case is admissible, the requested State shall proceed with the execution of the request.[345] If an admissibility ruling is pending, the requested State may postpone the execution of the request for surrender of the person until the Court makes a determination on admissibility'.[346] Pending an admissibility ruling, 'the Chamber dealing with the case [...] shall take steps to obtain from the requested State all the relevant information about the *ne bis in idem* challenge brought by the person'.[347] However, such steps are 'without prejudice to the provisions of article 19 and of rules 58 to 62'.[348]

The second situation of *competing requests* is regulated in Article 90.[349] It obliges State Parties to notify the Court and the requesting State of such a competing request.[350] The course of action then taken depends upon a number of parameters, one of which is whether or not the case in respect of which surrender is sought has been declared admissible or such a decision is pending.[351] Other parameters are (1) whether or not the requests relate to the same conduct;[352] (2) whether or not the requesting State is a State Party to the Statute;[353] and

---

[342] See n 105 and text. See also B Swart (n 151) 1693–1695; J Meissner (n 17) 134–137.

[343] Cf Rome Statute (n 1) Article 58 (5).

[344] See *Chapter IV: Complementarity as a Legal Principle and as Criteria for Admissibility, 3.3.* Ne bis in idem: *Articles 17 (1)(c) and 20 (3).*

[345] For the situation in which a case has been declared admissible, but such a decision is under appeal, see C Kress and K Prost, 'Article 89' in O Triffterer (ed) (n 21) 1075–1076, margin 17.

[346] Rome Statute (n 1) Article 89 (2).

[347] RoPE (n 5) Rule 181.

[348] Ibid. On Article 19 and Rules 58 to 62, see *2.3. Challenges to the Admissibility of a Case: Article 19.*

[349] For a detailed analysis, see J Meissner (n 17) 142–154. See also B Swart (n 151) 1695–1698.

[350] Rome Statute (n 1) Article 90 (1).

[351] Cf respectively Rome Statute (n 1) Article 90 (2), (4)–(6) (where there has been a determination on admissibility or the Court makes such a determination pursuant to the requested State's notification), Article 90 (3) [(where such a determination is pending) and Article 90 (8)] [(where, pursuant to a notification, the Court has determined a case inadmissible)].

[352] Rome Statute (n 1) Article 90 (1)–(6) and Article 90 (7) respectively.

[353] Rome Statute (n 1) Article 90 (2)–3) and Article 90 (4)–(6) respectively.

(3) whether or not the requested State is under an international obligation to extradite the person to the requesting State.[354]

When the *requests relate to the same conduct*, the answer to the question as to which of the requests prevails is based on the parameters of, first, whether or not the requesting State is a State Party to the Statute,[355] and, second, whether or not the case in respect of which surrender is sought has been declared admissible or such a decision is pending.[356]

Where the *requesting State is a State Party*, the requested State shall give priority to the request from the Court if the Court has, pursuant to Article 18 or 19, made a *determination that the case* in respect of which surrender is sought *is admissible* and that the determination takes into account the investigation or prosecution conducted by the requesting State in respect of its request for extradition.[357] The same applies if the Court makes such a determination 'pursuant to the requested State's notification' under Article 90 (1).[358] If, in contrast, a *determination of admissibility has not been made but is pending*, the requested State 'may, at its discretion, [...] proceed to deal with the request for extradition from the requesting State but shall not extradite the person until the Court has determined that the case is inadmissible.'[359]

If the *requesting State is not a State Party*, the Statute distinguishes between the situation in which the requested State is under an international obligation to extradite the person to the requesting State and the situation in which no such obligation exists. In the latter case, the requested State is obliged to give priority to the request for surrender from the Court, *if the Court has determined that the case is admissible*.[360] In the *absence of such a determination*, the requested State may, at its discretion, proceed to deal with the request for extradition from the requesting State.[361] If, in contrast, the requested State is under an *existing international obligation to extradite* the person to the requesting State which is not Party to the Statute, and *the Court has determined that the case is admissible*, the requested State has to determine whether to surrender the person to the Court or extradite the person to the requesting State.[362] The Statute contains a non-exhaustive list of factors that the requested State must consider in making its decision, including the respective dates of the requests; the interests of the requesting State including whether the crime was committed in its territory and the nationality of the victims and of the person sought; and the possibility of subsequent surrender between the Court and the requesting State.[363]

---

[354] Rome Statute (n 1) Article 90 (4)–(5), (7)(a) and Article 90 (6), (7)(b) respectively.
[355] Rome Statute (n 1) Article 90 (2)–(3) and Article 90 (4)–(6) respectively.
[356] Rome Statute (n 1) Article 90 (2)–(7) and Article 90 (8) respectively.
[357] Rome Statute (n 1) Article 90 (2)(a).
[358] Rome Statute (n 1) Article 90 (2)(b). As to the notification, see n 351.
[359] Rome Statute (n 1) Article 90 (3), first sentence. According to the second sentence, '[t]he Court's determination shall be made on an expedited basis.'
[360] Rome Statute (n 1) Article 90 (4).   [361] Rome Statute (n 1) Article 90 (5).
[362] Rome Statute (n 1) Article 90 (6).   [363] Ibid, subparagraphs (a) to (c).

When the *requests relate to different conduct*, the decisive criterion is whether or not the requested State is under an existing obligation to extradite the person to the requesting State. If it is not, the requested State must give priority to the request from the Court.[364] If it is, the requested State has to determine whether to surrender the person to the Court or to extradite the person to the requesting State. In making its decision, the requested State must consider the same non-exhaustive list of factors as in the case where the requesting State is not a State Party, 'but shall give special consideration to the relative nature and gravity of the conduct in question'.[365] While it has been suggested that the latter criterion creates a general presumption in support of exercising the discretion in favour of the ICC and to surrender the person rather than to extradite to the requesting State,[366] the better view seems to be that the 'relative nature and gravity of the conduct in question' must be assessed on a case-by-case basis and the conduct in question compared to other ICC crimes. Finally, where pursuant to a notification, the Court has determined a *case* to be *inadmissible*, and subsequently extradition to the requesting State is refused, the requested State shall notify the Court of this decision,[367] namely to the Prosecutor, in order to enable him/her to submit a request for a review of the decision when he/she is fully satisfied that new facts have arisen which negate the basis on which the case had previously been found inadmissible, as provided for in Article 19 (10).[368]

3.3.3. *The tension between complementary and State cooperation*

The foregoing description of the pertinent rules governing the relationship between admissibility and Part 9 would remain incomplete if one failed to note the tension that exists between the complementary nature of the ICC and the latter's reliance on State cooperation as regulated in Part 9. This tension is inherent in the expectation, underlying Part 9, that the very organs that are inactive or have been held by the ICC to be 'unwilling' or 'unable' to investigate and prosecute are expected to be willing and able to cooperate with the Court.

It is admittedly conceivable that a State's judicial system has been found to have substantially collapsed,[369] but certain authorities retain their ability to cooperate with and render assistance to the Court. Similarly, a State's national judicial system may not have collapsed but may be unavailable in the meaning of Article 17 (3),[370] because of its inability to obtain the necessary evidence, for instance, while having a suspect in its custody, and such a State is then willing and able to surrender the person concerned to the ICC. A willingness and ability to cooperate is also not excluded when the unwillingness to investigate and

---

[364] Rome Statute (n 1) Article 90 (7)(a).
[365] Rome Statute (n 1) Article 90 (7)(b); cf (n 363) and text;
[366] In this vein, J Meissner (n 17) 153.   [367] Rome Statute (n 1) Article 90 (8).
[368] RoPE (n 5) Rule 186.   [369] Cf *155*.
[370] On the distinction between a 'total or substantial collapse' and 'unavailability', cf *155–158*.

prosecute takes the form of 'good faith shielding'.[371] However, in the case of a total collapse or *male fide* unwillingness, the possibility of the envisaged willingness and ability to cooperate to materialize seems at best remote.[372]

The Statute seeks to mitigate that problem by granting the ICC some enforcement powers of its own.[373] *Article 99 (4)*, for instance, allows the Prosecutor to take a number of non-compulsory measures, such as the interview of or taking evidence from a person on a voluntary basis and the examination without modification of a public site or other public place, directly on the territory of a State where it is necessary for the successful execution of a request. When the requested State Party is a State on the territory on which the crime is alleged to have been committed, and there has been a determination of admissibility pursuant to Article 18 or 19, the Prosecutor may directly execute such a request following all possible consultations with the requested State Party.[374] In other cases, the Prosecutor may execute such a request following consultations with the requested State Party and subject to any reasonable conditions or concerns raised by that State Party. Where the requested State Party identifies problems with the execution of a request pursuant to this subparagraph, it must, without delay, consult with the Court to resolve the matter.[375]

Furthermore, according to *Article 57 (3)(d)*, the Trial Chamber has the possibility to '[a]uthorize the Prosecutor to take specific investigative steps within the territory of a State Party without having secured the cooperation of that State under Part 9 if, whenever possible having regard to the views of the State concerned,[376] the Pre-Trial Chamber has determined in that case that the State is clearly unable to execute a request for cooperation due to the unavailability of any authority or any component of its judicial system competent to execute the request for cooperation under Part 9'.[377] In contrast to Article 99 (4), which

---

[371] Cf *137–138*. Note that Part 9 contains a specific provision on cooperation with respect to waiver of immunity and consent to surrender (Article 98). This provision provides possible avenues for cooperation when shielding results from respect for international immunities. For further analysis of Article 98, see J Meissner (n 17) 121–134.

[372] It can reasonably be expected that the majority of cases that the Court addresses will be those in which the territorial State is clearly failing to investigate and prosecute, as evidenced in the Paper on some policy issues before the Office of the Prosecutor (n 32) 2 ['As a general rule, the policy of the Office of the Prosecutor will be to undertake investigations only where there is a clear case of failure to act by the State or States concerned'].

[373] Cf Rome Statute (n 1) Articles 57 (3)(d) and 99 (4). See G Sluiter (n 332) 324–327.

[374] Cf Rome Statute (n 1) Article 99 (4)(a).

[375] Rome Statute (n 1) Article 99 (4)(b).

[376] According to RoPE (n 5) Rule 115 (1), the Prosecutor 'may submit a written request to the Pre-Trial Chamber for authorization to take certain measures in the territory of the State Party in question. After a submission of such a request, the Pre-Trial Chamber shall, whenever possible, inform and invite views from the State Party concerned.'

[377] RoPE (n 5) Rule 115 (2) and (3) further specifies: '2. In arriving at its determination as to whether the request is well founded, the Pre-Trial Chamber shall take into account any views expressed by the State Party concerned. The Pre-Trial Chamber may, on its own initiative or at the request of the Prosecutor or the State Party concerned, decide to hold a hearing. 3. An authorization under article 57, paragraph 3 (d), shall be issued in the form of an order and shall state the

concerns scenarios in which the State concerned has the capacity to execute the request, Article 57 (3)(d) is thus applicable when the requested State lacks such capacity.

However, it needs to be emphasized that these powers of the Prosecutor are limited to *investigative steps* and, therefore, do not include matters such as the apprehension of an accused, for instance in cooperation with a peacekeeping force or law enforcement officials of other States. Furthermore, the powers under Article 57 (3)(d) are confined to situations in which a State is 'clearly' unable to execute a request for cooperation due to the unavailability of any authority or any component of its judicial system'. In other words, no such powers are available to the Prosecutor in cases of unwillingness of the State, nor when the inability is not obvious or takes a form other than 'the unavailability of any authority or any component of its judicial system competent to execute the request for cooperation'.[378] These weaknesses as regards to assistance and cooperation may come as no surprise: States were not prepared to yield more executive prerogatives to the Court due to concerns about their sovereignty. However, in light of the complementary nature of the Court, such limitations also bear the potential to weaken considerably the efficacy of the Court.[379]

4. Interim Conclusions

The procedural setting of admissibility renders complementarity a constant feature in the early phases of ICC proceedings. It curtails the discretion of the ICC Prosecutor to conduct investigations, chiefly by requiring the authorization of the Pre-Trial Chamber if the Prosecutor wishes to initiate an investigation *proprio motu* or to conduct an investigation despite a request for deferral by a State that is investigating or has investigated crimes within the jurisdiction of the ICC. This involvement of, and control by, the Pre-Trial and Trial Chambers also serves as a safeguard against the Prosecutor being accused of bias and political manipulation.[380]

While there are certain similarities between the procedures under Articles 18 and 19, the former procedure is principally dialogic in character and only involves limited litigious elements. Article 19, on the other hand, is primarily of a litigious nature, notwithstanding other elements, namely the powers of the Court and the Prosecutor to raise admissibility on their own motion.

---

reasons, based on the criteria set forth in that paragraph. The order may specify procedures to be followed in carrying out such collection of evidence.'

[378] Cf F Guariglia and K Harris, 'Article 57' in O Triffterer (ed) (n 21) 751, margins 17–19. On the various forms of inability, see *Chapter IV: Complementarity as a Legal Principle and as Criteria for Admissibility, 3.6. Inability: Article 17 (3)*.

[379] L N Sadat and S R Carden (n 225) 415.

[380] See also D Nsereko (n 43) 397, margin 3.

Both Articles 18 and 19 provide a framework for interaction between States and the Prosecutor; an interaction that is moderated by and conducted before the Pre-Trial Chamber or Trial Chamber and, in the case of appeal, the Appeals Chamber. The provisions also bestow upon the Prosecutor certain supervisory functions with regard to national proceedings. Encapsulated in these provisions is the general assumption of a fairly antagonistic relationship between States and the ICC, with States being eager to exercise jurisdiction and to forestall the Court from assuming jurisdiction. However, the possibility of a more affable relationship is generally not contemplated. The Statute and the Rules of Procedure and Evidence thus provide only very limited room to differentiate between States with different intentions and prospects for an effective investigation. By and large, the procedural setting is the same for all States, regardless of whether the underlying ground for (potential) admissibility is 'unwillingness' or 'inability',[381] or, indeed, whether the State concerned makes an auto-referral. In principle, the Statute treats alike matters that may in fact be crucially dissimilar. Apart from auto-referrals, the most apparent illustration of this lack of differentiation is to (attempt to) notify, in accordance with Article 18, a State whose national judicial system has totally collapsed, or to imagine any form of meaningful interaction, as envisaged in both Articles 18 and 19, with such a State's judicial system. The detailed and differentiated *criteria for admissibility* are thus not matched with a differentiated *procedural* regime, and one may ask whether this disparity in the Statute should not be reversed.

Apart from its core as embodied in Articles 53, 18 and 19, the procedural setting of complementarity also comprises a number of related issues. As far as the question of how to prove admissibility is concerned, the different procedural phases entail a gradual increase in the required specificity when assessing admissibility, accompanied by a gradual increase in the applicable standard of proof. As a general rule, arguably subject to some exceptions, the burden of proof rests on the Party putting forth the claim of (in)admissibility.

Furthermore, complementarity applies to auto-referrals, although it is unlikely that the procedural framework of complementarity embodied in Articles 18 and 19 is applied to the full extent, and it is indeed possible that auto-referring States render the application of complementarity to such referrals meaningless, leaving the ICC as the only forum for investigations and prosecutions. This situation is not satisfactory and should be remedied by an express regulation in the Statute of auto-referrals and their relation to complementarity.

Finally, the foregoing analysis warrants the following observations in appraising the relationship between admissibility and Part 9 of the Statute. Besides the general dilemma that unwilling and unable States are expected to be willing and able to cooperate and the potential of complementarity to cause delays in cooperating with the Court, these observations are twofold. First, while *States*

[381] For the limited exceptions, see *178–179* and *186–187*.

that are *not Parties* to the Statute may invoke complementarity,[382] these States are under *no obligation to cooperate* with the Court. They may thus benefit from complementarity and, in case the decision of the ICC on the matter is not to their pleasing, 'simply thumb [their] nose[s]'[383] at that decision.[384] While this approach is compatible with the *pacta tertiis* rule,[385] one wonders why raising an admissibility claim was not made conditional on the duty to cooperate, as is the case with non-Party States that specially accept the Court's jurisdiction in accordance with Article 12 (3).[386] The current solution invites abuse of the complementarity regime by non-Party States, while the Court is left empty-handed as far as legal tools to cooperate and/or counter such an abuse are concerned. Second, it is noticeable that the formal framework for *cooperation* under the Statute is primarily *one-sided*, flowing *bottom-up* from States to the Court, rather than top-down from the Court to States.[387] This may come as no surprise *pending a final decision on admissibility*, because cooperation by the Court—let alone an obligation of the Court to cooperate—at this stage would entail the inherent risk of manipulation by States. As long as it is not clear whether States are willing and able, nothing should prevent the Court from making sure that the information gathered by it is not misused for the opposite purpose than the one it is intended to serve. However, one fails to see why the Statute lacks any obligation of the Court to cooperate *after a final decision of inadmissibility*, based on a determination by the Court that the State at hand satisfies the criteria of willingness and ability. In that sense, the Statute adopts 'a curiously non-co-operative form of complementarity'.[388]

---

[382] Cf (nn 110–113) and text.   [383] M Summers (n 11) 77.

[384] This concern was also raised during the negotiations and led some States to argue against the inclusion of non-State Parties into the regime of challenging admissibility: see n 215 in Ch III.

[385] Cf Section 4 of the Vienna Convention on the Law of Treaties (n 110), especially Articles 34–36.

[386] M Summers (n 11) 77–78.

[387] This is only subject to the limited exceptions of (a) the initial notification of States by the Prosecutor, in the course of which the former has to supply information in accordance with Article 18 (1) and Rule 52; and (b) the *facultative* cooperation of the Court to a State conducting proceedings as contemplated in Article 93 (10).

[388] M H Arsanjani, 'Reflections on the Jurisdiction and Trigger-Mechanism of the International Criminal Court' in H von Hebel, J Lammers and J Schukking (eds) (n 11) 71.

VI

Complementarity and the Obligation to Investigate and Prosecute

1. Introduction

In the previous two chapters, we have clarified the formal framework of complementarity in the Rome Statute by interpreting the relevant provisions, which set forth the criteria for admissibility and the procedural aspects of their application. In light of that formal framework, this chapter revisits the question as to whether, and to what extent, the Statute *obliges* rather than merely *entitles* States to exercise their jurisdiction over core crimes.[1] Does the Statute in general, and the provisions on complementarity in particular, add anything to the pre-existing obligations of States to exercise their jurisdiction over core crimes, or does it leave room for States not to initiate proceedings and to abstain from prosecuting these crimes? Only a cursory look at how States and their organs have understood the Statute is illustrative of the fact that an answer to this question is shrouded in controversy. On the one hand, the French *Cour d'appel de Paris*, for instance, has deduced from the Statute a general duty on the part of ratifying states to try defendants for international crimes.[2] The Belgian Tribunal of First Instance Brussels also held that the Rome Statute imposes 'obligations of a jurisdictional character'.[3] South Africa has adopted ICC implementing legislation, which instructs the National Director of Prosecutions, when deciding to prosecute, to

---

[1] For the controversies surrounding the question as to whether States were obliged to investigate and prosecute core crimes prior to and independent of the Rome Statute, see nn 54, 62 and 66 and texts in Ch II, as well as *Chapter II: National Suppression of Core Crimes, 2.1.4. The Obligation to Prosecute Human Rights Violations.*

[2] Cour d'appel de Paris, Judgment of 20 October 2000 (Gadaffi), 105 RGDIP 475–476 ['Moreover, the Preamble to the convention constituting the Statute of the International Criminal Court, [...] says that "it is the duty of every State to exercise its criminal jurisdiction over those responsible for international crimes." [...] That convention recognizes a duty on the part of ratifying states to try defendants for international crimes, [...] including but not limited to crimes against humanity, genocide, apartheid and war crimes [...].']. English translation my own.

[3] Tribunal of First Instance Brussels (*Kamer van Inbeschuldigingstelling*), in re Sharon and Yaron, Judgment of 26 June 2002, reproduced in J Wouters and H Panken (eds) De Genocidewet in international perspectief, Jura Falconis Libri (De Boeck & Larcier Publ, Brussels 2002) 323–339, 332 at 332 ['le Statut de Rome comporte ainsi des obligations à caractère juridictionel'].

'give recognition to the obligation that the Republic, in the first instance and in line with the principle of complementarity [...] has jurisdiction and responsibility to prosecute persons accused of having committed a crime [under the Rome Statute]'.[4] And some States have taken the decision to outlaw the granting of amnesties and other clemency measures in case of ICC crimes in the course of adopting ICC implementing legislation.[5] In contrast to these instances, which are indicative of an obligation to investigate and prosecute ICC crimes, Colombia has asserted that it understood the Statute to be compatible with the granting of amnesties and other clemency measures.[6] Similarly, Trinidad and Tobago has interpreted the Statute so as not to prevent the granting of unfettered prosecutorial discretion to the Attorney-General. For, it has adopted implementing legislation which provides that '[p]roceedings for [ICC crimes] may not be instituted in any Trinidad and Tobago court without the consent of the Attorney General'.[7]

Such practices support the conclusion that States are not obliged to investigate and prosecute ICC crimes. However, the contradictory understandings of States make it all the more pertinent to examine the question as to whether States are obliged to investigate and prosecute ICC crimes. Indeed, such an analysis is a central element in clarifying the content of complementarity and its impact on the suppression of core crimes by national criminal jurisdictions.

Our analysis takes as a starting point the Preamble of the Rome Statute, which provides that 'the most serious crimes of concern to the international community as a whole must not go unpunished and that their prosecution must be ensured by taking measures at the national level and by enhancing international cooperation'[8] and further includes a reference to 'the duty of every State to exercise its criminal jurisdiction over those responsible for international crimes'[9] (2). With a view to elucidating further the content of these preambular provisions, the chapter then returns to Article 17 and determines whether, and to what extent, this provision leaves room for the exercise of discretion by domestic prosecutors (3) and for substitutes of criminal prosecutions, such as amnesties, truth commissions and traditional forms of justice (4). In a subsequent step, we seek to

---

[4] S 5, § 3 of the Implementation of the Rome Statute of the ICC, Act no 27 of 2002.

[5] See eg Panama, Art 115 of the Nuevo Codigo Penal Panameno, adopted 18 May 2007, <http://www.iccnow.org/documents/Panama_nuevo_codigo_penal2.pdf>; Uruguay, Art 8 of the Ley de cooperación con la CPI en materia de lucha contra el genocidio, crímenes de guerra y crímenes de lesa humanidad (No 18.026) of 4 October 2006, <http://www.iccnow.org/documents/Uruguay_ICC_Law_06Oct04.pdf>.

[6] Declaration made on 5 August 2002 upon ratification of the ICC Statute, available at <http://untreaty.un.org/ENGLISH/bible/englishinternetbible/partI/chapterXVIII/treaty10.asp#Declarations>.

[7] Section 13 of the International Criminal Court Act 2006 of 24 February 2006.

[8] Rome Statute of the International Criminal Court (adopted 17 July 1998, as corrected by *procès-verbaux* of 10 November 1998, 12 July 1999, 30 November 1999, 8 May 2000, 17 January 2001 and 16 January 2002, entered into force 1 July 2002) A/CONF. 183/9 (Rome Statute) Paragraph 4 of the Preamble.

[9] Rome Statute (n 8) Paragraph 6 of the Preamble.

determine to whom an obligation to investigate and prosecute is addressed, ie which State or States are bound by an obligation to prosecute ICC crimes (5). Finally, we will attend to the tension between the two opposing poles of, on the one hand, legal requirements to exercise jurisdiction over ICC crimes, and, on the other hand, a number of likely limitations on the capacity of national criminal jurisdictions to comply fully with these requirements. The last section therefore offers some observations on the question of whether, and to what extent, legal avenues for abstaining from complying with the obligation to investigate and prosecute ICC crimes are available to States (6).

2. The Preamble

The Preamble of the Rome Statute refers to 'the duty of every State to exercise its criminal jurisdiction over those responsible for international crimes'.[10] Undoubtedly, the language of this provision denotes that the role of national criminal jurisdictions in the investigation and prosecution of core crimes is obligatory rather than voluntary. Furthermore, the Preamble 'affirm[s] that the most serious crimes of concern to the international community as a whole must not go unpunished and that their prosecution must be ensured by taking measures at the national level and by enhancing international cooperation',[11] thereby suggesting that the punishment of ICC crimes is mandatory. What, however, is the *legal* significance of these provisions?

This section analyzes that question by first addressing the legal force of the Preamble in the abstract (2.1.). It then turns to a determination of the legal force of the two aforementioned preambular provisions (2.2. and 2.3.), before clarifying the relationship between the duty to exercise criminal jurisdiction in Paragraph 6 of the Preamble and the Statute's operative provisions on complementarity (2.4.).

2.1. Legal Force

It is generally accepted that the Preamble has legal force and effect from an *interpretative standpoint*. As an integral part of the treaty text[12], which regularly contains a statement of the motives or objects of the parties in making the treaty, the Preamble of a treaty is a useful guide and aid in interpreting the operative provisions.[13]

---

[10] Rome Statute (n 8) Paragraph 6 of the Preamble.
[11] Rome Statute (n 8) Paragraph 4 of the Preamble.
[12] 1969 Vienna Convention on the Law of Treaties (entered into force 27 January 1980) 1155 UNTS 331, 8 ILM 679, Article 31 (2), *chapeau*.
[13] Cf ICJ, Case Concerning *Rights of Nationals of the United States in Morocco(France v United States)* [1952] ICJ Rep 176, 196; *The Asylum Case (Colombia v Peru)* [1950] ICJ Rep. 266, 282.

In asserting that the prosecution of the most serious crimes of concern to the international community 'must be ensured by taking measures at the national level and by enhancing international cooperation' and that every State has the 'duty [...] to exercise its criminal jurisdiction over those responsible for international crimes', the Preamble clearly reflects a *mandatory role* of national criminal jurisdictions in the investigation and prosecution of international crimes.[14] It is this obligatory exercise of domestic jurisdiction that must be taken to underlie the Statute and inform the interpretation of its relevant operative provisions. Centrally amongst the latter are those that are most directly concerned with domestic criminal proceedings, namely the provisions setting forth the criteria for the admissibility of cases and the procedure for their application.[15]

While the Preamble, including the references to the mandatory role of national criminal jurisdictions in investigating and prosecuting core crimes, is thus of significance for the interpretation of the operative provisions of the Statute, a second question is *whether these preambular provisions possess any legal force, which goes beyond such interpretation.*

A preliminary issue that arises in answering that question is whether a Preamble can, as a matter of principle, contain legal obligations. This question attends to the accuracy of the assertion that the *formal position* of the provisions under consideration in the Preamble, rather than the operative part of the Statute, automatically precludes it from having such legal force.[16] In further support of that contention,

---

[14] Preambular references to duties of States are in fact not unique to the Rome Statute. See for instance the Preamble to the Convention on the Elimination of All Forms of Discrimination against Women (adopted and opened for signature, ratification and accession by General Assembly resolution 34/180 of 18 December 1979, entered into force 3 September 1981) 193 UNTS 135 ['Noting that the States Parties to the International Covenants on Human Rights have *the obligation to ensure the equal rights of men and women to enjoy all economic, social, cultural, civil and political rights*']; 1984 UN Convention against Torture and Other Cruel, Inhuman or Degrading Treatment or Punishment, [adopted 10 December 1984, entered into force 26 June 1987) 1465 UNTS 85 ['Considering the *obligation* of States under the Charter, in particular Article 55, *to promote universal respect for, and observance of, human rights and fundamental freedoms*'] Emphases added.

[15] For analysis, see *Chapter IV: Complementarity as a Legal Principle and as Criteria for Admissibility* and *Chapter V: The Procedural Setting of Complementarity.*

[16] A Seibert-Fohr, 'The Relevance of the Rome Statute of the International Criminal Court for Amnesties and Truth Commissions' (2003) 7 Max Planck UNYB 553–590, 558–559, who asserts that 'the Rome Statute does not include an explicit provision on the obligation to either prosecute or extradite the accused offender'. Despite paragraphs 4 and 6 of the Preamble, in her view, 'there is no provision on prosecuting duties by the States parties in the operative part of the Statute. [...] Though the drafters acknowledged that there were pre-existing responsibilities of the states to prosecute the crimes as defined in art 6 to 8 of the Statute the Statute does not incorporate these obligations.']: Footnotes omitted. On the aforementioned pre-existing obligations, see nn 54, 62 and 66 in Ch II, as well as *Chapter II: National Suppression of Core Crimes, 2.1.4. The Obligation to Prosecute Human Rights Violations.* See also Informal Expert Paper for the ICC Office of the Prosecutor: The Principle of Complementarity in Practice, available at <http://www.ice-cpi.int/library/organs/otp/complementary.pdf>, 19 at fn 24 ['preamble does not as such create legal obligations']; C Tomuschat 'The duty to prosecute international crimes committed by individuals' in H J Cremer and H Steinberger (eds), *Tradition and Weltoffenheit des Rechts: Festschrift für Helmut Steinberger* (Springer, Berlin 2002) 315–349, 338 ['only in preamble']; F Razesberger, *The International Criminal Court—The Principle of Complementarity* (Peter Lang, Frankfurt/Main 2006) 27 ['Preamble creates no direct obligation for States Parties but constructs an inherent

it is submitted that 'it is not the objective of the Rome Statute, which is concerned with international prosecution and not with the international enforcement of state obligations, to deal with prosecuting duties by the States parties'.[17] Accordingly, it is claimed that 'there is no need for a duty of states to prosecute because [the Statute] is based on the idea that if domestic prosecution on which it primarily relies fails the ultimate safeguard is through international prosecution anyway. The ICC is therefore meant to supplement—not to enforce—domestic prosecution.'[18]

While we will return elsewhere to the assertion that the duty to investigate and prosecute is of no concern to the ICC,[19] the view that the formal position of the duty of states to exercise their jurisdiction in the Preamble appears to be at odds with the generally accepted view that the Preamble of a treaty has to be treated as an integral part of the treaty text, which suggests its being on an equal footing with the operative provisions of a treaty.[20] It would indeed be inconsistent with such a premise to reject categorically the possibility that a Preamble can contain legal obligations. Nothing in the law of treaties indicates that provisions have an inferior legal force or no legal force at all, by virtue of the fact alone that they are set forth in the Preamble rather than the *dispositif*.[21] A preambular provision is as *legally binding* as a provision in the operative part.

---

yardstick for the treaty's interpretation, as well as, in case of para. 6, an implicit duty to enact implementing legislation on a national level'] and 30 [drafters laid down goals '*in a non-binding way in the Preamble*'; emphasis added].

[17] A Seibert-Fohr, ibid 560.   [18] Ibid.

[19] Suffice it to say here that the way in which the ICC relates to domestic criminal proceedings by virtue of its complementary nature is a central element in understanding the Statute's objective as not being limited to a regulation of international prosecutions, but also dealing with prosecuting duties by the States Parties. As we have seen in Chapters IV and V, complementarity concerns itself extensively with domestic investigations and prosecutions of core crimes. In so doing, complementarity's role does not exhaust itself in regulating the admissibility of cases before the Court, but also contains a number of other features, including supervisory elements in as much as the Court is called upon to assess whether States fulfil their central role in the enforcement of core crimes prohibitions properly. In fact, such a monitoring role is also acknowledged by A Seibert-Fohr ibid 576. See further *2.4. Preambular Paragraph 6 and Complementarity* and *Chapter VII: Complementarity as a Catalyst for Compliance*.

[20] See (n 12).

[21] See for instance G Scelle, *Précis de droit des gens* (vol II, Sirey Paris 1934) 464; P You, *Le Préambule des Traités Internationaux* (Librairie de L'Université, Fribourg 1941) 67–70; ICJ, *Case Concerning Rights of Nationals of the United States of America in Morocco* (n 13) 184; ICJ, *Case Concerning the Gabcikovo-Nagymaros Project (Hungary v. Slovakia)* [1997] ICJ Sep 7 [151]; G Fitzmaurice, 'The Law and Procedure of the International Court of Justice 1951–1954: Treaty Interpretation and Other Treaty Points' (1957) BYIL 229; S Schepers, 'The legal force of the preamble to the EEC treaty' (1981) 6 European Law Review 356–361, 358, 359; E Suy, 'Le Préambule' in E Yakpo and T Boumedra (eds), *Liber Amicorum Judge Mohammed Bedjaoui* (Kluwer Law International, The Hague 1999) 253–269, 260–261. See also C Rousseau, *Droit International Public, I (Introduction et Sources)* (Paris, 1970) 87, who notes that '[o]n a parfois considéré le préambule des traités comme doué d'une force obligatoire inférieure à celle du dispositif. Mais c'est là une opinion isolée'. An example of such an 'opinion isolée' can be found in N Quoc Dinh, P Daillier and A Pellet, *Droit International Public* (2nd edn 1980) 126, who assert that, while the Preamble constitutes an element in the interpretation of a treaty, it 'ne possède pas de force obligatoire'.

This is not to suggest, however, that the binding character of a provision alone accounts for its ability to effectively dictate what its addressee(s) must do, must not do, or may do. Rather, this *normativity* of a provision is a matter of degree,[22] chiefly determined by two factors, namely the *precision and clarity of its content*, on the one hand, and the *regime for its enforcement*, on the other.[23] The fact that preambular provisions often hold a low degree of normative force or, indeed, lack it completely would thus seem to be attributable to their substance and lack of an enforcement regime. Due to their frequent character as spelling out the motives for the conclusion of the treaty and setting forth the general context for the conclusion of the treaty at hand, while not providing for an enforcement regime, preambular provisions often are not endowed with a high degree of normativity. Such (a lack of) normative force of a provision does not result, however, from its *formal* place in the Preamble. One fails to see, for instance, why the preambular 'duty of every State to exercise its criminal jurisdiction' in the Statute should be considered of a lesser normativity than Article I of the 1948 Genocide Convention, confirming that genocide is a crime under international law, which Contracting Parties to the Convention 'undertake to prevent and to punish'.[24] Nor is it logical to assign a lesser normative value to the statement in the Preamble of the Rome Statute that the ICC 'shall be complementary to national criminal jurisdictions' than to the identical proclamation in Article 1.

The foregoing analysis suggests that, as a matter of principle, preambular provisions can contain legal rules and principles which are legally binding and can possess as much normativity as any other provision in the operative part of the treaty. To what extent this is indeed the case, however, ultimately depends on the individual preambular provision in question.

2.2. Preambular Paragraph 4

When applying the preceding analysis to the two preambular provisions under consideration, the Preamble's affirmation 'that the most serious crimes of concern to the international community as a whole must not go unpunished and that their prosecution must be ensured by taking measures at the national level and by enhancing international cooperation'[25] appears not to raise too many difficulties. This provision undoubtedly sets forth the belief of the drafters that core

[22] See generally P Weil, 'Towards Relative Normativity in International Law?' (1983) 77 AJIL 413–442, 414–415.
[23] See generally Ko Swan Sik, *De verplichting in het volkenrecht, Inaug. Rede uitgresproken bij de aanvaarding van het ambt. van hoogleraar in het internationaal publiek recht aan de Erasmus Universiteit Rotterdam op vrijdag, 22 juni 1990* (TMC Asser Instituut Rotterdam, 's-Gravenhage 1991) 22, 8, 10–14.
[24] On the the operative and non-preambular character of Article I of the 1948 Genocide Convention, see ICJ, *Case Concerning the Application of the Convention on the Prevention and Punishment of the Crime of Genocide (Bosnia and Herzegovina v Serbia and Montenegro)* Judgment of 26 February 2007, General List No 91[162–165].
[25] Rome Statute (n 8) Paragraph 4 of the Preamble.

crimes must be prosecuted and punished and the means which, in their view, are required to implement that belief: measures at the national level and the enhancement of international cooperation. Yet, the language used is of such a general and imprecise nature that it leaves many questions unanswered. What are such 'measures at the national level', which must be taken, and how is international cooperation to be enhanced? It is also not immediately obvious what consequences the Statute foresees in cases where States are non-compliant and abstain from taking measures at the national level and from enhancing international cooperation. By leaving such crucial matters unclarified, the legal significance of the provision would seem to exhaust itself in supplying the general tone for interpreting other provisions of the Statute.

2.3. Preambular Paragraph 6

However, *preambular paragraph 6*, in which the States Parties are 'recalling that it is the duty of every State to exercise its criminal jurisdiction over those responsible for international crimes', deserves a closer analysis.

In using the term '*duty*',[26] the provision is clear on what is expected of States as the response to international crimes: they *must* exercise their criminal jurisdiction. While one may question whether such a duty is of a *moral or political rather than legal* nature,[27] such doubts can easily be removed by referring to the use of the identical term elsewhere in the Statute.[28] These other provisions employ the term 'duty' in its legal sense. The assumption that identical terms in a treaty have an identical meaning[29] suggests that the duty referred to in paragraph 6 of the Preamble is not merely of a moral or political nature. This view is confirmed by the maxim of treaty interpretation that a treaty text must, in principle, be interpreted as consistent with existing law and not in violation of it,[30] and, more particularly in the present context, in harmony with the duties to investigate and

---

[26] Other language versions of the Statute use similarly mandatory terms, such as 'devoir' [French] and 'deber' [Spanish].

[27] Cf The Concise Oxford Dictionary (9th edn OUP, Oxford 2001), which defines a 'duty' *inter alia* as 'a moral or legal obligation'. See also A Klip, 'Complementarity and Concurrent Jurisdiction' in International Criminal Law: *Quo Vadis?* Proceedings of the International Conference held in Siracusa, Italy, 28 November–3 December 2002, on the Occasion of the 30th Anniversary of ISISC (2004) 19 Nouvelles études pénales 173–197, 177 ['Whatever may be said about the reference to 'a duty' in the preamble of the Statute, there is no binding obligation for states to prosecute. If such a duty existed, there would not have been any reason for the establishment of the Court. The Court was created precisely because States do not assume their responsibilities. In the absence of a legally binding duty, we are left with a moral duty only.' Footnotes omitted].

[28] See Rome Statute (n 8) Articles 59 (4) ['duty to surrender'] and 127 (2) ['criminal investigations and proceedings in relation to which the withdrawing State had a duty to cooperate'].

[29] Cf R Jennings and A Watts, *Oppenheim's International Law* (9th edn, vol 1 Longman, London 1996) 1273, referring to the case of Ministry of Defence v Ergialli, Italy, Court of Venice, Judgment of 5 February 1958, 26 ILR (1958-II) 732–734.

[30] Cf ICJ, *Case Concerning Right of Passage over Indian Territory (Portugal v India)* (Preliminary Objections) [1957] ICJ Rep 125, 142.

prosecute, which preceded the Statute and remain applicable independently of it.[31] To understand the term 'duty' as meaning 'legal duty' is equally borne out by the meaning given to the term by the Paris Court of Appeals in the *Gadaffi* case[32] and finds further support in the fact that the drafters of the Statute refused to use a term with less legal connotations, such as 'task', 'role' or ' responsibility'.

While the Preamble thus regards 'the exercise of criminal jurisdiction' as a matter of legal obligation, it is not immediately obvious *whether* preambular paragraph 6 *adds anything to the pre-existing obligations to investigate and prosecute*, which we have already alluded to elsewhere.

An answer in the negative finds support in the wording that the State Parties to the Statute are '*recalling*' the duty of States to exercise their criminal jurisdiction. This would seem to indicate a reference to pre-existing obligations to investigate and prosecute. Thus understood, the Preamble would do nothing more, nor less, than to reaffirm these obligations and to leave them unaltered, notwithstanding the ambiguity surrounding the exact contours of some of them. As far as core crimes subject to the jurisdiction of the ICC are concerned, grave breaches of the Geneva Conventions and a number of other conventional war crimes would therefore remain subject to an obligation to investigate and prosecute on the basis of the principle of *aut dedere aut judicare*,[33] investigating and prosecuting genocide on the basis of territorial jurisdiction would continue to be mandatory,[34] while the question as to whether the exercise of extraterritorial jurisdiction is mandatory or optional would be controversial,[35] and war crimes under customary international law and crimes against humanity as a whole would entail an unequivocal obligation of States to prosecute them only *qua* serious human rights violations if committed in their territory or against individuals subject to their jurisdiction.[36]

---

[31] In the words of the Statute, '[n]othing in [Part II on Jurisdiction, Admissibility and Applicable Law] shall be interpreted as limiting or prejudicing in any way existing or developing rules of international law for purposes other than this Statute'. On prosecuting duties prior to and independent of the Rome Statute, see *Chapter II: National Suppression of Core Crimes, 2.1. Applicable Law Governing the National Suppression of Core Crimes.*

[32] See (n 2).

[33] *10–13*. See also *13–14* on the different treaty regimes governing the suppression of violations of the 1993 Convention on the prohibition of the development, production, stockpiling and use of chemical weapons and on their destruction (adopted 13 January 1993, entered into force 29 April 1997) 32 ILM 800, the 1997 Ottawa Convention on the Prohibition of the Use, Stockpiling, Production and Transfer of Anti-Personnel Mines and on their Destruction (adopted 18 September 1997, entered into force 1 March 1999) 36 ILM 1507–19, and the 1996 Amended Protocol II to the 1980 Certain Conventional Weapons Convention on Prohibitions or Restrictions on the Use of Mines, Booby-Traps and Other Devices (adopted 1996, entered into force 3 December 1998) 35 ILM 1206–17.

[34] *16–17.*   [35] See (n 62) and text in Ch II.

[36] See nn 54 and 64–66 and texts in Ch II, as well as *Chapter II: National Suppression of Core Crimes, 2.1.4. The Obligation to Prosecute Human Rights Violations.* See also 19 on the various treaty regimes governing the suppression of *apartheid* and of acts which, if committed as part of a widespread or systematic attack directed against the civilian population, may amount to crimes against humanity.

A further argument in support of the view that preambular paragraph 6 merely reiterates pre-existing obligations can be derived from the provision's assertion that the exercise of criminal jurisdiction over those responsible for international crimes is the duty of 'every State'. The provision thus differs markedly from other provisions in the Statute, which impose new obligations, because these latter, in conformity with the *pacta tertiis* rule, are only binding on those States that have become parties to the Rome Statute. The Statute, in turn, designates such States consistently as 'State Parties', rather than 'States'. The latter term in preambular paragraph 6 would thus seem to indicate that the drafters are referring to duties which are incumbent on States regardless of whether or not they are Parties to the Statute. Such duties can only be those those exist independent of the Statute, because the latter cannot impose any obligations on non-State Parties.

One may also consider the sweeping reference to '*international crimes*' to support the view that preambular paragraph 6 is merely reaffirming pre-existing obligations to prosecute. The provision is not confined to 'the most serious crimes of concern to the international community as a whole'[37] or 'the most serious crimes of international concern',[38] with which the Statute is otherwise concerned.[39] The category of 'international crimes' is broader than the latter, as it includes not only the core crimes set forth in Articles 5–8 of the Statute, but also other crimes, such as certain terrorist offences or drug trafficking. Such a view would seem to find confirmation in the drafting history of the provision. It originates in a proposal made during the Rome Conference by the Dominican Republic, which emphasized 'that each State *still* has the duty to exercise its penal jurisdiction over individuals responsible for *crimes of international significance*'.[40] Accordingly, it has been pointed out that the purpose of the provision is *not only* to evoke

---

[37] Cf Rome Statute (n 8) Preambular Paragraph 4 and Article 5.

[38] Cf Rome Statute (n 8) Article 1.

[39] Note that the limitation of these two notions to the four broad categories of ICC crimes differs from earlier drafts of the Statute, which included more crimes than aggression, genocide, crimes against humanity and war crimes: see eg the Preamble of the 1994 Draft Statute of the ILC in conjunction with Draft Article 20 (e), 'Report of the International Law Commission on the work of its 46th Session' (1994) UN GAOR 49th Session Supp No 10, UN Doc A/49/10, 70, 78–79. Furthermore, the Rome Statute foresees the eventuality that consensus emerges amongst (some) States Parties to include as 'most serious crimes of concern to the international community as a whole' and 'the most serious crimes of international concern' crimes other than aggression, genocide, crimes against humanity and war crimes: cf Articles 121 (5) and 123 (1).

[40] UN Doc A/CONF.183/C.1/L.25, United Nations Diplomatic Conference of Plenipotentiaries on the Establishment of an International Criminal Court Rome (15 June–17 July 1998) UN GAOR Volume III, Reports and other documents (2002) UN Doc A/CONF 183/13 (Vol Ill) 203, emphasis added. This proposal of the Dominican Republic, introducing for the first time a reference to the duty of States to exercise their penal jurisdiction, then found its way into the rolling text on 10 July 1998 (Official Record vol III, 197) and then into subsequent drafts. On 15 July 1998, the coordinator (Slade) informed the Committee of the Whole that agreement was reached on the Preamble, set out in document UN Doc A/CONF.183/C.1/L.73 United Nations Diplomatic Conference of Plenipotentiaries on the Establishment of an International Criminal Court (15 June–17 July 1998) GA OR Volume II—Summary records of the plenary meetings and of the meetings of the Committee of the Whole (2002) UN Doc A/CONF183/13(Vol II) 351.

the obligation to investigate and prosecute all *core crimes*, but also that there is a class of 'crimes under international law' for which States have an obligation to prosecute even if these crimes do not fall within the jurisdiction of the Court.[41] It would be illogical, however, to conceive of a provision in a treaty that is otherwise solely concerned with a certain category of offences, namely the three core crimes as defined in Articles 6 to 8 of the Statute, to add anything to legal obligations with regard to other offences, which fall outside such a category.

While the aforementioned arguments thus support the view that preambular paragraph 6 exhausts itself in a mere reiteration of pre-existing obligations, the reference in that provision to the duty of States to exercise their criminal jurisdiction over 'international crimes' also creates some doubt as to whether that view is the only reasonable interpretation. By not differentiating between different (categories of) international crimes, the provision reflects the assumption of the drafters of the Statute that a general duty to exercise criminal jurisdiction exists with respect to all international crimes. In other words, the Preamble attaches this duty to the *recognition* of prohibited conduct *as 'international crime'*. The broad category of 'international crimes' undisputedly includes all crimes that fall into the jurisdiction of the ICC. The Statute thereby epitomizes the idea that the general duty to exercise criminal jurisdiction extends to all ICC crimes, which it then 'recalls'. Yet, certain offences, which have been included in the Statute under the rubric of crimes against humanity and war crimes, had not been recognized as international crimes under customary international law or treaty law prior to the adoption and entry into force of the Rome Statute. Rather, they constitute new crimes, 'modernize' crimes or modify some of the constitutive elements of pre-existing crimes so as to change the actual content of the prohibition.[42]

---

[41] M Bergsmo, 'Preamble', margins 16–17 in O Triffterer (ed) *Commentaty on the Rome Statute of the International Criminal Court—Observers' Notes, Article by Article* (Nomos, Baden–Baden 1999) 12–13.

[42] This is notwithstanding the intention of the drafters of the Rome Statute to confine the crimes in Articles 6 to 8 to those which are clearly established under customary law. According to H von Hebel and D Robinson, the Rome Statute was intended 'to be a "procedural, adjectival" instrument, ie an instrument creating a new institution with jurisdiction over existing international crimes. The task facing the delegations at the Rome Conference was to reflect the definition of those crimes under customary international law': H von Hebel and D Robinson, 'Crimes within the jurisdiction of the Court' in R S Lee (ed) *The International Criminal Court, The Making of the Rome Statute, Issues, Negotiations, Results* (Kluwer Law Publ, The Hague 1999) 79–126, 91 at n 40. See also the 1996 PrepCom Report, vol I [51–54] at 78. This view was reiterated by numerous delegations during the Rome Conference: see eg Official Records Volume II (n 40) 67 at 44 (Japan), 149 at 58 (Lesotho), 159 at 55 and 58 (Germany), 184 at 34 (Russian Federation), 166 at 73 (Mexico). However, in the words of James Crawford at the Rome Conference, already 'the revised draft Statute constituted a major effort to consolidate, expand and develop substantive international law, relying only to a very limited extent on *droit acquis*': Official Records Volume II, ibid 71 at 109. Conversely, Articles 7 and 8 also lag behind customary law in other respects: see eg M Boot, *Nullum Crimen Sine Lege and the Subject Matter Jurisdiction of the International Criminal Court—Genocide, Crimes against Humanity, War Crimes* (Intersentia, Antwerp 2002) 603–605; H Fischer, 'The Jurisdiction of the International Criminal Court for War Crimes: Some Observations Concerning Differences between the Statute of the Court and War Crimes Provisions in Other Treaties' in V Epping, H Fischer and W Heintschel von Heinegg (eds), *Brücken*

As regards *crimes against humanity*, the inclusion of the categories of 'forced pregnancy'[43], 'enforced disappearance of persons',[44] the 'crime of apartheid'[45] and the expansion of discriminatory grounds included in the definition of 'persecution' as a crime against humanity under Article 7 (1(h) have been pointed out as being broader than customary international law.[46] Another example is the offence of torture as a crime against humanity,[47] which does not require that the intentional infliction of severe pain or suffering upon a person in the custody or under the control of the accused must be committed for a specific purpose, such as to obtain a statement or a confession, to punish, intimidate or coerce that person. Torture as a crime against humanity under the Rome Statute is therefore wider than customary international law.[48]

In a similar vein, Article 8 on *war crimes* contains a number of offences which differ from pre-existing law. The Statute contains for the first time a war crime of 'intentionally launching an attack in the knowledge that such attack will cause incidental [...] widespread, long-term and severe damage to the natural environment which would be clearly excessive in relation to the concrete and direct overall military advantage anticipated' in international armed conflicts.[49] Likewise,

bauen und begehen: Festschrift für Knut Ipsen zum 65 Geburtstag (Beck, Munich 2000) 77–101, 88–90; R Cryer, *Prosecuting International Crimes—Selectivity and the International Criminal Law Regime* (CUP, Cambridge 2005) 276–277; A Cassese, 'Crimes Against Humanity' in A Cassese, P Gaeta and J Jones (eds) *The Rome Statute of the International Criminal Court: A Commentary* (OUP, Oxford 2002) 353–378, 375–376.

[43] Rome Statute (n 8) Article 7 (1)(g) and 2 (f).

[44] Rome Statute (n 8) Article 7 (1)(i) and 2 (i). See also statement of the UK, Official Records Volume II (n 40) 150 at 91.

[45] Rome Statute (n 8) Article 7 (1)(j) and 2 (h).

[46] A Cassese (n 42) 353–378, 376–377. See also D Robinson, 'Defining "Crimes Against Humanity" at the Rome Conference' (1999) 93 AJIL 43–57, 52–56, who concludes that the definition in Article 7 'sets forth a modernized and clarified definition of crimes against humanity' (57). See further M Bennouna, 'The Statute's Rules on Crimes and Existing or Developing International Law' in A Cassese, P Gaeta and J Jones (eds) (n 42) 1101–1107, 1105–1106. But see R Cryer (n 42) 256–260, who takes the opposite view with regard to some of the crimes against humanity which Cassese has identified as progressive development, relying on the ICTY Trial Chamber Decision on Joint Challenge to Jurisdiction of 12 November 2002 in Hadzihasanovic, Alagic and Kubura, in which it held that 'it is critical to determine whether the underlying conduct at the time of its commission was punishable. The emphasis on conduct rather than on the specific description of the offence in substantive criminal law is of primary relevance.' [62]. Cryer nevertheless concurs with Cassese's assessment of certain persecution-type crimes against humanity: ibid 260.

[47] Rome Statute (n 8) Article 7 (1)(d), incl the applicable Elements of Crimes, adopted on 9 September 2002, Doc ICC-ASP/1/3 (Part II-B), in conjunction with Rome Statute (n 8) Article 7 (2)(e).

[48] G Werle, *Principles of International Criminal Law* (TMC Asser Press, The Hague 2005) 246–247 [719–720] (with further references).

[49] Rome Statute (n 8) Article 8 (2)(b)(iv). M Bothe notes that the criminal sanction of environmental devastation 'constitutes definite progress', M Bothe, 'War Crimes' in A Cassese, P Gaeta and J Jones (eds) (n 42) 379–426, 400. Prior to the Rome Statute, only Article 20 (g) of the 1996 Draft Code of Crimes against the Peace and Security of Mankind, ILC, 'Report of the International Law Commission on the work of its 48th Session' (6th May–26th July 1996) UN Doc A/51/10 Supplement No 10 contained a war crime of environmental devastation, which, however, differs from the provision in Article 8 in as much as it applies to the use of 'methods or means of warfare not justified by military necessity with the intent to cause widespread, long-term

the customary status of the war crimes of 'utilizing the presence of a civilian or other protected person to render certain points, areas or military forces immune from military operations'[50] and of starvation of civilians as a method of warfare,[51] although based on *primary* norms of international humanitarian law which are customary in nature, is at least debatable.[52]

Article 8 also identifies as a war crime to intentionally direct 'attacks against personnel, installations, material, units or vehicles involved in a humanitarian assistance or peacekeeping mission in accordance with the Charter of the United Nations, as long as they are entitled to the protection given to civilians or civilian objects under the international law of armed conflict'.[53] Prior to the Rome Statute, only the Convention on the Safety of United Nations and Associated Personnel, which influenced the inclusion of the mentioned provision into Article 8, contained some criminalizations that were subject to an obligation to prosecute,[54] without, however, identifying such offences as 'war crimes'.[55] Even if one considered such a nomination to be of only secondary significance, a comparison between the war crime under Article 8 and the offences defined in the UN Safety Convention reveal a number of significant differences. In particular, Article 9 (1) of the UN Safety Convention criminalizes '[t]he intentional commission of: (a) A murder, kidnapping or other attack upon the person or liberty of any United Nations or associated personnel; (b) A violent attack upon the *official premises, the private accommodation or the means of transportation* of any United Nations or associated personnel *likely to endanger his or her person or liberty*'.[56] On the contrary, Article 8 (2)(b)(iii) and (e)(iii) extends to intentional attacks against all 'material' and does not require violent attacks against the mentioned objects to be 'likely to endanger his or her person or liberty'. The war crimes under Article 8 (2)(b)(iii) and (e)(iii) thereby go beyond the pre-existing law under the UN Safety Convention.

A last example of differences between Article 8, on the one hand, and pre-existing rules on war crimes, on the other hand, is Article 8 (2)(b)(xvii), which

and severe damage to the natural environment and thereby gravely prejudice the health or survival of the population and such damage occurs'. But see J M Henckaerts and L Doswald-Beck (eds) *Customary International Humanitarian Law* (Volume I: Rules, CUP, Cambridge 2005) Rule 156, 582–583, who seem to base the conclusion that this war crime amounts to customary international law on the fact that 'the inclusion of this war crime was not controversial during the negotiations of the [ICC Statute]'. For arguments against such a construction of customary international law, see *251–253*. This is notwithstanding that the acts prohibited under Article 8 (2)(b)(iv) may very well fall under other customary war crimes, such as the prohibition of attacks against civilian objects: on this point, see J M Henckaerts and L Doswald-Beck, ibid.

[50] Rome Statute (n 8) Article 8 (2)(b)(xxiii).   [51] Rome Statute (n 8) Article 8 (2)(b)(xxv).
[52] Contra customary status: M Bothe (n 49) 402–403 ['new and important development of the present statute'; 'yet another new war crime']; pro: J M Henckaerts and L Doswald-Beck (n 49), Rule 156, 581–582, 584.
[53] Rome Statute (n 8) Article 8 (2)(b)(iii) and (e)(iii).   [54] See *12–13*.
[55] This approach was also followed by the ILC in the 1996 Draft Code (n 49); cf Article 19, which established the offence as an individual crime against the peace and security of mankind 'when committed intentionally and in a systematic manner or on a large scale' rather than a war crime.
[56] Emphasis added.

criminalizes the employment of poison or poisoned weapons, with the criminalization of the use of such weapons under customary international law. In
contrast to the latter, Article 8 (2)(b)(xvii) does not require such weapons to be
'calculated to cause unnecessary suffering'.[57] The wording of Article 8 (2)(b)(xvii)
thus indicates that the weapon in question need not be employed with the specific purpose of causing such suffering. Once the material elements of the prohibition[58] are committed with intent and knowledge, a war crime according to
Article 8 (2)(b)(xvii) is committed. In accordance with Article 30 of the Statute,
in turn, it would suffice for establishing intent that a person is aware that the
consequence of causing death or serious damage to health through the toxic
properties of a given substance will occur in the ordinary course of events.[59]
Consequently, weapons which may not be *calculated* to cause unnecessary suffering, but nevertheless release a substance which is said to cause death or serious
damage to health in the ordinary course of events through its toxic properties,
may fall under the prohibition of Article 8(2)(b)(xvii), while such conduct would
not amount to a war crime under pre-existing law.[60]

A duty to investigate and prosecute these violations of international humanitarian and human rights law, which were not recognized as international crimes
prior to the adoption of the Rome Statute, may very well have flown from a State's
human rights obligations.[61] But if the duty to exercise criminal jurisdiction
attaches to them *qua* international crimes, as suggested by the Preamble, it is difficult to see how such a duty can have existed prior to their being recognized as
such, so that States Parties to the Rome Statute can be 'recalling' it. Their inclusion into the Rome Statute as international crimes for the first time therefore
provokes some hesitation in dismissing that preambular paragraph 6 alters pre-
existing obligations.

[57] Cf Article 3(a) of the Statute of the International Tribunal for the Prosecution of Persons
Responsible for Serious Violations of International Humanitarian Law Committed in the Territory
of the Former Yugoslavia since 1991, established in accordance with UNSC Res 827 (adopted on
25 May 1993) (ICTY). The ICTY Statute was drafted on the assumption that it reflected customary
international law. See also Article 20(c)(i) of the Draft Code (n 49). See on this difference between
Rome Statute (n 8) Article 8 (2)(b)(xvii) and customary international law, H Fischer (n 42) 92–93.
In a similar vein, J M Henckaerts and L Doswald-Beck (n 49), Rule 72, 253 appear to subscribe to
the view that poison must be an 'intended' injury mechanism.

[58] According to the Elements of Crimes (n 47), these material elements are: '(1) The perpetrator
employed a substance or a weapon that releases a substance as a result of its employment. (2) The
substance was such that it causes death or serious damage to health in the ordinary course of events,
through its toxic properties. (3) The conduct took place in the context of and was associated with
an international armed conflict. (4) The perpetrator was aware of factual circumstances that established the existence of an armed conflict.'

[59] Cf Rome Statute (n 8) Article 30(2)(b). See also C Garraway, 'Article 8(2)(b)(xvii)' in R S Lee (ed)
The International Criminal Court: elements of crimes and rules of procedure and evidence (Transnational
Publ, New York 2001) 178 ['It was considered unnecessary to include any additional mental element,
as no deviation was required from the *mens rea* requirement set forth in article 30.'].

[60] H Fischer (n 42) 93.

[61] Cf *Chapter II: National Suppression of Core Crimes, 2.1.4. The Obligation to Prosecute Human
Rights Violations.*

2.4. Preambular Paragraph 6 and Complementarity

The preceding examination reveals some uncertainty in determining the relation of Paragraph 6 of the Preamble to pre-existing obligations to investigate and prosecute ICC crimes. An analysis of that provision in conjunction with the regime of complementarity would, however, seem to tip the balance in favour of the proposition that the Statute alters these pre-existing obligations.

Complementarity is only triggered when States take initial investigative steps vis-à-vis ICC crimes.[62] As a starting point, States wishing to avail themselves of complementarity are thus required to initiate proceedings in order to retain the right to exercise their jurisdiction.[63] Once they have initiated proceedings, the application of the notions of inability and unwillingness genuinely to investigate and prosecute entails an assessment of whether a State's actions satisfy a number of further criteria.[64] The notion of willingness encapsulates the criteria that perpetrators are not shielded, justice is administered without unjustified delay and proceedings are conducted independently and impartially. The notion of ability, on the other hand, sets forth the standard of a functioning national judicial system.[65] 'Willingness' and 'ability' thereby entail important incentives for States to do everything in their power to carry out investigations and prosecutions which meet these criteria. The latter considerably limit the freedom of (in-)action of States vis-à-vis ICC crimes and establish a number of basic benchmarks for States' investigations and prosecutions.[66] However, can one also derive from

---

[62] See pages 104–105.

[63] Note that States may at times not seek to avail themselves of complementarity, notably in cases of auto-referral: see *Chapter V: The Procedural Setting of Complementarity, 3.2. Complementarity and Auto-Referral*. However, the regime of complementarity rests on the assumption that States are in principle inclined to retain jurisdiction: see *213–214* and *Chapter VII: Complementarity as a Catalyst for Compliance, 3. Complementarity as Sanction*.

[64] In the words of Mireille Delmas-Marty, '[c]omplementarity preserves national jurisdiction only on the condition [...] that the state in question is willing and able to adjudicate the crime [...]; the Preamble even speaks of the States Parties "duty" to do so. The concepts of ability and willingness presuppose conditions of validity (legality, effectiveness and legitimacy) that command, via the check of Article 17, an indirect harmonization of national criminal justice systems around common international criteria [...]': M Delmas-Marty, 'Interactions between National and International Criminal Law in the Preliminary Phase of Trial at the ICC' (2006) 4 JICJ 2–11, 4. See also S N M Young, 'Surrendering the Accused to the International Criminal Court' (2000) 71 BYIL 317–356, 323–324.

[65] While inability may be unavoidable, for instance when part of a State's territory is under the control of an armed opposition group, States may very well avoid certain instances of inability, such as the absence of implementing legislation, providing the necessary funds for maintaining a judicial infrastructure, etc. For discussion of different forms of 'inability', see *Chapter IV: Complementarity as a Legal Principle and as Criteria for Admissibility, 3.6. Inability: Article 17 (3)*.

[66] This is notwithstanding the fact that these benchmarks are not exhaustive, because the notions of unwillingness and inability do not cover all inadequacies of national criminal proceedings. Recall that unwillingness does not seem to extend, for instance, to certain violations of fair trial guarantees which work to the disadvantage of a suspect or accused: cf *130* and *144–145*, *150–152* for arguable exceptions. The Rome Statute leaves these obligations of States Parties entirely unaffected and intact (cf Article 10, (n 31)). In fact, the ignorance of the provisions on

this that complementarity is constitutive of a primary legal obligation to investigate and prosecute?

An answer to this question ultimately depends upon the underlying conceptualisation of a '*legal obligation*'. When referring to a 'legal obligation' in the following, this concept is understood generically to denote a legal duty, which, in turn, signifies 'a legal requirement to carry out or refrain from carrying out any act'.[67] The provisions on admissibility themselves, however, do not stipulate that States are required to be willing and, to the extent that it is within their power, able to investigate and prosecute ICC crimes genuinely. Instead, these provisions regulate the consequence for the purpose of ICC proceedings, namely admissibility, in case they are not. The mere fact that the Rome Statute attaches this consequence to not adequately investigating and prosecuting ICC crimes does not mean that States are required to do so. However, paragraph 6 of the Preamble, which, as explained previously, is in principle of equal normative value to other provisions of the Statute,[68] provides unmistakably that States are legally required to exercise their criminal jurisdiction over international crimes, including ICC crimes. Thus understood, the relationship between preambular paragraph 6 and the provisions on complementarity resembles the one between *secondary* and *primary* norms.[69] The obligation in the Preamble provides the principal basis of the system of complementarity,[70] which in turn responds to cases in which national

complementarity in this respect does not seem to be exceptional, if compared with other treaties which are concerned with the obligation to investigate and prosecute international crimes: cf the Convention on the Prevention and Punishment of the Crime of Genocide (adopted 9 December 1948, entered into force 12 January 1951) 78 UNTS 277, albeit that more recent instruments regularly include references to fair trial guarantees, such as Article 7 (3) of the 1984 UN Convention against Torture and Other Cruel, Inhuman or Degrading Treatement or Punishment (n 14), which stipulates that '[a]ny person regarding whom proceedings are brought in connection with any of the offences referred to in Article 4 shall be guaranteed fair treatment at all stages of the proceedings.'

67 *Oxford Reference, A Dictionary of Law* (3rd edn, OUP, Oxford 1994) 137, 271.

68 Cf *2.1. Legal Force*.

69 For that distinction, see J Crawford *The International Law Commission's Article on State Responsibility—Introduction, Text and Commentaries* (CUP, Cambridge 2002) 14–16.

70 Paper on some policy issues before the Office of the Prosecutor, available at <http://icc-cpi. int/library/organs/otp/030905_policy_paper.pdf> (2003) 4 and 5. T van Boven, The Principle of Complementarity—The International Criminal Court and National Laws' in J Wouters and H Panken (eds) (n 3) 65–74, 68 ['It must be inferred from the Rome Statute, both from the Preamble and from the substantive provisions, in particular Article 17 dealing with issues of admissibility, that a State which has jurisdiction on the basis of the territorial or nationality principle is presumed to have an obligation to investigate and prosecute the core crimes covered by the Statute.']. M Politi, 'Le Statut de Rome de la Cour Pénale Internationale: Le Point de Vue d'un Négociateur' (1999) 103 RGDIP 817–850, 843 ['A la lumière des règles sur la "complémentarité" de la Cour, il s'agit en effet d'un principe qui vient souligner l'existence d'une obligation étatique non formelle (mais incluant, au contraire, celle de la mise en place de procédures judiciaries authentiques et efficaces) de poursuivre, sur le plan national, les violations du droit humanitaire.']. A O'Shea, *Amnesty for crime in international law and practice* (Kluwer, The Hague 2002) 257 ['principle of "complementarity"[…] itself appears to rest on the premise that states have an obligation to prosecute those crimes covered by the subject-matter jurisdiction of the court and that are not brought before the court.']; see also G Meintjes and J E Méndez 'Reconciling Amnesties with Universal Jurisdiction'

criminal jurisdictions are not able or willing to fulfil that duty. In so doing, complementarity enhances the normativity of the obligation to investigate and prosecute enshrined in the Preamble by supplying an enforcement mechanism, which induces States to investigate and prosecute ICC crimes.[71]

However, a description of the relationship between preambular paragraph 6 and the provisions on complementarity as the one between primary and secondary norms does not seem to capture all its aspects. For, complementarity also enhances the normativity of the duty to exercise jurisdiction by adding clarity and precision to its actual content by means of the notions of 'unwillingness' and 'inability'.[72] Seen from this angle, the relationship between preambular paragraph 6 and the provisions on complementarity resembles more closely the one between a legal *principle* and legal *rules*.[73]

The Preamble contains the duty to exercise criminal jurisdiction without specifying its subjects beyond the generality that it applies to 'every State'. It is, as Tuiloma Neroni Slade and Roger S Clark so aptly put it, 'delightfully ambiguous',[74] however, as regards the question as to whether such a duty is binding on the territorial State, the State of (active or passive) nationality or, indeed, on all States Parties, it thus obliges them to exercise universal jurisdiction.[75] It also does not determine what exactly the criteria are for States to be considered in compliance with that duty, including whether, and to what extent, States retain room not to exercise their criminal jurisdiction by virtue of prosecutorial discretion or the use of substitutes for criminal proceedings, such as the granting of amnesties or the establishment of a truth commission. As such, preambular paragraph 6 prescribes actions that are distinctly unspecific. By incorporating such a general legal standard, it sets forth a legal principle.

Complementarity, in turn, provides significantly more detail for finding answers to the questions that preambular paragraph 6 leaves open. Although the provisions on complementarity may not conclusively answer each and every

---

(2002) 2 International FORUM du droit international 80–81 [asserting that 'the principle of complementarity [. . . requires] prosecution in future'].

[71] On the relationship between normativity and enforcement, cf *211*. For further discussion of complementarity as a mechanism to induce compliance, see *Chapter VII: Complementarity as a Catalyst for Compliance.*

[72] On the relation between normativity and precision, cf *211*. Cf also Switzerland, *Erläutender Bericht über das Römer Statut des Internationalen Strafgerichtshofs, das Bundesgesetz über die Zusammenarbeit mit dem Internationalen Strafgerichtshof und eine Revision des Strafrechts,* available at <http://www.eda.admin.ch/sub_dipl/g/home/info/trdisc.Par.0001.UpFile.rtf/dt8-Kern-Botschaft.rtf>, at 3.1. ['Indem der Gerichtshof komplementär ausgestattet ist und den Einzelstaaten weiterhin die primäre Verantwortung bei der Verhinderung und der Suppression dieser Verbrechen überlässt, *werden die Staaten stärker als bisher in die Pflicht genommen.*' Emphasis added].

[73] On that distinction, see n 3 in Ch IV.

[74] T N Slade and R S Clark, 'Preamble and final clauses' in R S Lee (ed) (n 42) 421–450, 427. See also C Kress, 'War Crimes Committed in Non-International Armed Conflict and the Emerging System of International Criminal Justice' (2000) 30 Israel Yb HR 103–177, 163.

[75] For further discussion, see *5. Addressees of the Obligation to Investigate and Prosecute.*

one of them,[76] these provisions are applicable in an all-or-nothing fashion: if a 'State which has jurisdiction'[77] investigates and/or prosecutes an ICC crime, such a case is only inadmissible if the State satisfies the criteria of 'willingness' and 'ability'. These criteria are defined meticulously in Articles 17 (2) and (3) and 20 (3), while Articles 53, 18 and 19 and a significant number of Rules of Procedure provide for a detailed procedural framework for applying and invoking them.

In other words, in order to elucidate the content of the legal principle, which encapsulates the obligation of States to exercise their criminal jurisdiction over ICC crimes, reference must be made to the legal rules contained in the provisions on complementarity. The contours of that obligation can be determined with greater specificity by answering the question as to whether and under what conditions non-investigation or non-prosecution entail that a case is admissible.

The foregoing analysis suggests that the duty of States to exercise their criminal jurisdiction in *preambular paragraph 6* operates *in combination with the provisions on complementarity* as far as ICC crimes are concerned.[78] Together they establish a uniform legal requirement—ie an obligation—to investigate and prosecute *all* ICC crimes, because complementarity applies to each of them equally.[79] It is this uniformity which alters the disparate pre-existing obligations to investigate and prosecute.

At the same time, it needs to be emphasized that the uniform obligation imposed jointly by both the Preamble and the rules on complementarity is a *treaty obligation of States Parties to the Rome Statute.* In contrast, some maintain that the obligation to investigate and prosecute ICC crimes, that flows from the Statute has attained the status of customary international law applicable to all

---

[76] This is in particular the case in relation to the question as to how competing claims of jurisdiction by States have to be solved: see *5. Addressees of the Obligation to Investigate and Prosecute.*

[77] Cf Rome Statute (n 8) Article 17 (1)(a) and (b); for discussion, see *110–113*.

[78] J Crawford, P Sands and R Wilde, 'In the Matter of the Statute of the International Criminal Court and in the Matter of Bilateral Agreements Sought by the United States under Article 98(2) of the Statute'—Joint Opinion, 5 June 2003, available at <http://www.humanrightsfirst.org/international_justice/Art98_061403.pdf>, [30] ['In our view it is implicit in the requirements of Article 17(1)(a) and (b) that the ICC Statute imposes upon States Parties a general obligation to investigate allegations relating to the crimes identified in the Statute and, if a case is made out, to ensure that the persons concerned do not escape prosecution. In our view, this general obligation informs the Rome Statute as a whole.']. See also J T Holmes, 'Complementarity: National Courts versus the ICC' in A Cassese, P Gaeta and J Jones (eds) (n 42) 673 '[...] giving recognition to the principle of complementarity, it was decided that Article 17 should obligate the Court to declare the case inadmissible—that is, *to recognise the primary duty of the State to prosecute these types of crimes*' 'principle of complementarity, founded on national sovereignty and the obligations of States to prosecute'], footnote omitted, emphasis added]; Informal Expert Paper for the ICC Office of the Prosecutor: The Principle of Complementarity in Practice (n 16) 19 at fn 24. See also s 5, § 3 of the South African Implementation of the Rome Statute Act (n 4).

[79] The only possible exception may apply to the crime of aggression once defined. At the time of writing, the 'conditions under which the Court shall exercise jurisdiction with respect to this crime' [cf Article 5 (2)] are still under consideration.

States.[80] Admittedly, the plausibility of that assertion depends to some extent on the underlying approach to customary international law.[81] However, it is submitted that this position is to be rejected for the following reasons.

First, inconsistent practice and *opinio juris* of non-Parties in relation to an obligation to investigate and prosecute likely contradicts the existence or formation of a customary obligation, which is co-extensive to the duty of States Parties enshrined in the Statute.[82] Second, the mere adoption of the Statute in Rome by 120 States—less than two-thirds of the international community of States—is in itself not enough to bring about the customary status of this obligation. To assert otherwise would blur the line between the adoption of a treaty text and the entry into force of a treaty. It would make the entry into force of a treaty superfluous as long as an overwhelming majority of States adopted its text. Third, the current number of ratifications is in itself insufficient to consider the provisions of the

[80] See for instance A O'Shea (n 70) 259, who, affirmatively citing Barboza who asserts that '[t]he creation of a permanent international criminal court may be decisive in the definitive consolidation of our subject', explains: 'It may seem surprising that such a recent development as the agreement on the establishment of an international criminal court should constitute the point of emergence of a customary duty of a general nature. However, this is both explicable and fortuitous. It is explicable because, notwithstanding hitherto consistent state practice in the form of treaties and their implementation in relation to disparate crimes, it is the first time that an express, committed, coherent and representative *opinio juris* has emerged for a general duty to prosecute international crimes. It is fortuitous because it brings our understanding of the enforcement of international criminal law firmly within the framework of the most elaborate and comprehensive agreement on the subject to date.' See also A Eser and H Kreicker, *Nationale Strafverfolgung völkerrechtlicher Verbrechen—National Prosecution of International Crimes* (vol 1 Deutschland, edition iuscrim, Freiburg 2003) 440–443. See also with respect to war crimes committed in non-international armed conflicts, C Kress (n 74) [sixth preambular paragraph as affirmation that a customary duty to prosecute crimes under international law has now crystallized] (163). H van der Wilt suggests an alternative basis of such duty binding on all States when he asserts that 'in case of core crimes within the jurisdiction of the ICC, states are not at liberty to decide on the exercise of criminal jurisdiction. States are required, either as a derivative of their state responsibility for international crimes or as a consequence of their membership of the international community, to prosecute the suspects of these crimes and, if found guilty, to punish them': H van der Wilt, 'The International Criminal Court and Domestic Jurisdictions: Competition or Concerted Action' in F Coomans, F Grünfeld, I Westendorp and J Willems (eds), *Rendering Justice to the Vulnerable; Liber Amicorum in Honour of Theo van Boven* (Kluwer Law International, The Hague 2000) 323–338, 334. On an obligation to prosecute emanating from a State's international legal responsibility, see also *249*. Some go as far as suggesting that the duty to investigate and prosecute amounts to an obligation *erga omnes*: see eg F Gioia 'State Sovereignty, Jurisdiction, and "Modern" International Law: The Principle of Complementarity in the International Criminal Court' (2006) 19 LJIC 1095–1123.
[81] See amongst many others J Kammerhofer, 'Uncertainty in the formal Sources of international Law: customary international Law and some of its Problems' (2004) 15 EJIL 523–553; A E Roberts, 'Traditional and modern approaches to customary international law: a reconciliation' (2001) 95 AJIL 757–791; K Wolfke, 'Some persistent controversies regarding customary international law' (1993) 24 NYIL 1–16.
[82] Examples of such practice and/or *opinio juris* can be found in relation to States present in Rome, which have so far abstained from becoming Parties to the Statute. See for instance Official Records Volume II (n 40) 168 [101] (Sudan). See also the decision of the Constitutional Court of Guatemala of 5 February 2005 [BBC News, 5 February 2005, 'Guatemala halts war crimes trial'], overturning earlier jurisprudence on the 1996 amnesty law.

Statute as amounting to customary law in whole or in part,[83] apart from the fact that there is no automaticity between widespread ratification of a treaty and the customary status of its provisions.[84]

The better view, therefore, seems to be to regard the obligation to investigate and prosecute ICC crimes as a treaty obligation flowing from the Statute. It only binds State Parties to it in their mutual relationships as an obligation *erga omnes partes*. As a later treaty, the obligation to investigate and prosecute ICC crimes imposed by the Statute prevails over incompatible earlier treaty rules obliging States to investigate and prosecute these crimes,[85] and the same applies *mutatis mutandis* in relation to such earlier rules under customary international law.[86] State Parties remain, however, bound by such pre-existing obligations in relation to States, which are not Parties to the Rome Statute.[87]

The foregoing discussion leads one to conclude that the significance of paragraph 6 of the Preamble is twofold. First, it reiterates pre-existing duties to exercise criminal jurisdiction over crimes which fall *outside* the jurisdiction of the ICC, either because they relate to crimes other than those spelled out in Articles 6 to 8 of the Statute, or by virtue of the Court's jurisdiction *ratione temporis*[88] or the preconditions to the exercise of jurisdiction in Article 12. The Statute does not affect these obligations.[89]

Second, paragraph 6 of the Preamble, in conjunction with the provisions on complementarity, imposes a uniform obligation to investigate and prosecute ICC crimes on State Parties, with the notions of unwillingness and inability capturing important requirements which States have to satisfy in order to be considered compliant with that obligation.[90] In the following two sections, we will analyze these requirements in relation to two manifestations of non-investigation or non-prosecution: the exercise of prosecutorial discretion and the adoption of substitutes for criminal proceedings, including amnesties and truth commission processes.

[83] On that assertion, see A Eser and H Kreicker (n 80) 440–443. At the time of writing (February 2008), 105 States out of a total of 191 of UN member States were parties to the Rome Statute.

[84] The ICJ requires 'a *very* widespread and representative participation in the convention' for a treaty *rule* to generate customary international law: *North Sea Continental Shelf Cases (Federal Republic of Germany v Denmark; Federal Republic of Germany v The Netherlands)* [1969] ICJ Reports 3, 42 [73], emphasis added. See also on this point, M E Villiger, *Customary International Law and Treaties—A Manual on the Theory and Practice of the Interrelation of Sources* (2nd edn, Kluwer Publ, The Hague 1997) 155–158.

[85] Cf Article 30 (3) and (4)(a) Vienna Convention on the Law of Treaties (n 12).

[86] M E Villiger (n 84) 59, 87.

[87] Cf Article 30 (4)(b) Vienna Convention on the Law of Treaties (n 12); M E Villiger (n 84) 160 at [244].

[88] Cf Rome Statute (n 8) Article 11.   [89] Cf Rome Statute (n 8) Article 10, (n 31).

[90] This should not be understood to mean that all cases which do not qualify for a declaration of admissibility are necessarily flawless, as the inadmissibility requirements contain certain *lacunae*: cf (n 66). Furthermore, cases may be declared inadmissible because they do not meet the gravity-threshold in Article 17 (1)(d) regardless of whether or not the State concerned is willing or able to investigate and prosecute ICC crimes: cf *Chapter IV: Complementarity as a Legal Principle and as Criteria for Admissibility, 3.4. Insufficient gravity: Article 17 (1)(d)*.

While instances of non-investigation or non-prosecution come in a myriad of shapes[91], a focus on these forms of non-investigation and non-prosecution seem justified because they are structural devices, which States employ deliberately in order to avoid investigations or prosecutions of crimes in general and core crimes in particular. They are key mechanisms used to implement certain policies in relation to specific (categories of) cases and crimes. An additional reason to address substitutes for criminal prosecutions is the frequency with which they have been adopted in relation to ICC crimes and the resulting centre stage that they have often taken in the debate about the existence and extent of a legal obligation to investigate and prosecute core crimes.[92]

3. Prosecutorial Discretion

In order to determine the content of the duty of every State Party to exercise its criminal jurisdiction over ICC crimes, a central question that needs to be answered is whether, and to what extent, the Statute's rules on complementarity leave room for the exercise of prosecutorial discretion. Generally speaking, all criminal justice systems, including those which generally follow the principle of mandatory prosecution (*Legalitätsprinzip*), provide the competent authorities with a certain degree of leeway in deciding whether to bring a case to trial; a practice which had led States to call for an express regulation of the matter from an early stage of the drafting of the provisions on complementarity.[93]

It needs to be emphasized at the outset that an analysis of the present question cannot address all aspects of prosecutorial discretion in detail. The diversity of criminal justice systems necessitates a fair degree of generalization. Depending on the criminal justice system at hand, a wide range of possible actors (eg police, military commanders, prosecutors, investigating magistrates) may be involved in deciding whether or not to investigate and/or prosecute a given case. Furthermore, the exercise of prosecutorial discretion can occur at different stages of criminal proceedings. Investigating authorities may be granted the power to

---

[91] For examples, see *Chapter II: National Suppression of Core Crimes, 3. Obstacles to National Suppression.*

[92] For that debate prior to the adoption of the Rome Statute, see amongst many others, D Orentlicher, 'Settling Accounts: The Duty to Prosecute Human Rights Violations of a Prior Regime' (1991) Yale Law Journal, vol 100, 2537–2615, Naomi Roht-Arriaza (ed.), *Impunity and Human Rights in International Law and Practice* (Oxford University Press, New York 1995); L Huyse, 'To Punish or to Pardon: A Devil's Choice' in C C Joyner, M C Bassiouni (eds) *Reining in Impunity for International Crimes and Serious Violations of Fundamental Human Rights: Proceedings of the Siracusa Conference 17–21 September 1998* (1998) 14 Nouvelles Etudes Penales 79–90; J Dugard, 'Is the Truth and Reconciliation process compatible with international law? An unanswered question?' (1997) 13 S. Afr. J. Hum. Rights 258–268; G Meintjes, J E Méndez, 'Reconciling Amnesties with Universal Jurisdiction,' (2000) 2 International Law FORUM du droit international 76–97. On relevant decisions of human rights bodies. See pages 23–24.

[93] Cf page 77.

decline to investigate or to close an ongoing investigation, whereas prosecuting authorities may be able to decide not to prosecute a given person subsequent to a full investigation or to abandon ongoing prosecutions. The diversity between different criminal justice systems also gives rise to varied procedures for the exercise of that discretion and different forms and degrees of checks and balances.[94] Moreover, the complexity of a discussion of prosecutorial discretion increases due to the fact that ICC crimes may be subject to different branches of a State's criminal justice system, for instance civil and military, which in turn may differ as far as investigative and prosecutorial discretion is concerned. Accordingly, when reference is made to the situations in different States in the following, they are only exemplary and used to illustrate different possible scenarios. They are not representative of, or applicable to, every criminal justice system.

With this caveat in mind, one can broadly distinguish between two sets of grounds for the exercise of prosecutorial discretion. Proceedings can be discontinued either due to a lack of evidence or due to policy considerations. The ensuing analysis proceeds on the basis of these generic distinctions.

A first question that arises is whether the Statute leaves room for any discretion—whether under the guise of lack of evidence or due to policy considerations—as to whether or not to *initiate an investigation* after preliminary information has come to the attention of investigative authorities which suggests that one or more ICC crimes may have been committed. As has been noted previously, the Statute implies that cases are admissible, without even entering an assessment of the willingness or ability of a State under Article 17, when the competent authorities fail to initiate an investigation and remain completely inactive in response to such initial information.[95] In order for a State to avail itself of the

[94] See for further information J Verhaegen, 'Legal obstacles to prosecution of breaches of humanitarian law' (1987) 27 IRRC 610–611; R Cryer (n 42) 192–194; D D Ntanda Nsereko, 'Prosecutorial Discretion before National Courts and International Tribunals' (2005) 3 JICJ, 124–144, 126–130. For a concise overview of prosecutorial discretion, see A Hamzah and R M Surachman, *The Prosecutorial Discretion, A Comparative Study, Barcelona Conference on the law of the world* (World Jurist Association, Washington DC 1991) 40, concluding at 6 that '[e]ven in jurisdictions where the public prosecutor's decision in dropping the case needs the consent of the court, most of the time the court will give a positive response to the demand of the public prosecutor'. Also cf 9–10 [exceptions to the mandatory prosecution principle in Germany and the practice in other States which adopt the mandatory prosecution principle (Italy and Austria)]. For a more detailed discussion of the situation in various States, see 'Survey over the Belgian, Dutch, French, German, UK and US prosecution services' (2000) 8 European Journal of Crime, Criminal Law and Criminal Justice 154–295; L Arbour, A Eser, K Ambos and A Sanders (eds), *The Prosecutor of a Permanent International Criminal Court* (edition iuscrim, vol 81, Freiburg 2000) 197–528; answers to question 13 (duty to investigate) in *Compatibility of National Legal Systems with the Statute of the Permanent International Criminal Court*, XVI Recueils of the International Society for Military Law and the Law of War (2003) vol II, 497–498, 557, 561, 565, 569–572, 603, 611, 615, 619, 621–622, 651, 655, 659, 661, 665, 669, 673, 675, 677, 681, 725, 735, 739, 741, 745, 747, 751, 757–759, 781, 785, 787.

[95] Cf pages 104–105. Admissibility is, however, subject to the further conditions of a 'reasonable basis' to proceed in accordance with Rome Statute (n 8) Articles 15 (3) and Article 53 (1)(a) and (c) and Rule 48: see pages 164–165.

grounds for inadmissibility, its investigative authorities would have to ascertain at least whether the available information reveals a reasonable basis for further investigations. A discretionary power of these authorities to decline the initiation of an investigation is thus incompatible with the requirements as they flow from the Statute's regime on admissibility.

A second question is, then, whether the competent authorities are entitled to abandon *an ongoing investigation* for lack of evidence or because of policy considerations, most notably a (perceived) lack of public interest.[96] In other words, does the exercise of these forms of prosecutorial discretion render cases admissible in accordance with Article 17? The most pertinent provision to answer that question is Article 17 (1)(b), in as much as it declares cases inadmissible which have 'been investigated by a State [...] and the State has decided not to prosecute the person concerned, unless the decision resulted from the unwillingness or inability of the State genuinely to prosecute'.[97] It thus most directly relates to the exercise of prosecutorial discretion, while being supplemented by a number of other rules of the Statute which have a more indirect bearing on the question.

It may come as no surprise that, as a matter of principle, Article 17 (1)(b), taken in conjunction with other rules, allows for the exercise of investigative discretion due to *lack of evidence*. Indeed, the ICC Prosecutor is barred from initiating an investigation if there was no 'reasonable basis to believe that a crime within the jurisdiction of the Court has been or is being committed'.[98] Consequently, in the absence of the necessary evidence, matters would not even reach an admissibility assessment. It would also be a waste of resources to require States to investigate matters further, while evidence is insufficient to make a case. Furthermore, such unwarranted investigations could amount to violations of the human rights of the individual concerned, if, for instance, that individual has been arrested: in the absence of the necessary evidence which suggests that the person concerned has committed a crime, the detention of a person is incompatible with the prohibition

---

[96] Generally, this is a possibility in both common law systems and civil law systems: see K Ambos, 'Comparative Summary of National Reports' in L Arbour, A Eser, K Ambos and A Sanders (eds) (n 94) 495–528, 505–509.

[97] Cf Rome Statute (n 8) Article 17 (1)(b). For further analysis of various elements of the provision, *see Chapter IV: Complementarity as a Legal Principle and as Criteria for Admissibility, 3.2. Cases having been investigated and the State has decided not to prosecute: Article 17 (1)(b)*. It has been asserted that, to the extent that the decision to drop cases are subject to a court decision, such exercise would have to be assessed in application of the principle of *ne bis in idem* as regulated in Rome Statute (n 8) Article 17 (1)(c) and Article 20 (3): cf I Tallgren, 'Commentary on Article 20' in O Triffterer (ed) (n 41) 431 at 26. This would seem to disregard that Rome Statute (n 8) Article 20 (3) requires a person to be *tried,* because the trial refers to the phase of the proceedings during which all issues of fact and law are determined. It is therefore submitted that the following also applies to situations in which the exercise of prosecutorial discretion emanates from a court decision rather than a decision of investigative or prosecutorial authorities.

[98] Rome Statute (n 8) Article 53 (1)(a) and Rule 48 of the Rules of Procedure and Evidence (12 July 200) UN Doc PCNICC/2000/INF/3/Add. 1 (RoPE).

of arbitrary arrest and detention.[99] When an investigation reveals insufficient evidence for a prosecution, the competent authorities are thus, in principle, entitled to close the proceedings in accordance with Article 17 (1)(b).

However, complementarity provides for a number of *benchmarks* so as to avoid that flawed investigations can be relied upon as a pretext for the closure of an investigation due to insufficient evidence.[100] These requirements flow from the definitions of 'unwillingness' and 'inability'.[101]

Most fundamentally, in order for a decision not to prosecute due to a lack of evidence to meet these requirements, the State must be able 'to obtain the accused and the necessary evidence and testimony' and otherwise be able 'to carry out the proceedings'. Furthermore, the notion of 'unwillingness' requires an investigation to be in accordance with 'principles of due process recognized by international law',[102] which provide the framework for ascertaining that the decision not to prosecute is not taken for the purpose of shielding the person concerned; that the investigation is carried out without undue delay and conducted independently and impartially so as to be consistent with the intent to bring the person concerned to justice.

As argued in Chapter IV, these 'principles of due process recognized by international law' in the context of complementarity need to be understood broadly to mean *principles and standards of international law which are pertinent for duly investigating, prosecuting and punishing crimes in general and international crimes in particular.* Such principles and standards can be derived from relevant human rights, the concept of a denial of justice, obligations to investigate and prosecute serious violations of human rights, the jurisprudence of the various international and regional human rights bodies on the exhaustion of local remedies requirement, rules regulating offences against the administration of justice and, subsidiarily, the doctrine of command responsibility.[103]

---

[99] Article 9 of the International Covenant on Civil and Political Rights (adopted 16 December 1996, entered into force 23 March 1976) 999 UNTS 171 (ICCPR), Article 5, especially subparagraph (c) of the European Convention for the Protection of Human Rights and Fundamental Freedoms (entered into force 3 September 1953, as amended by Protocols Nos 3, 5, 8, and 11 which entered into force on 21 September 1970, 20 December 1971, 1 January 1990, and 1 November 1998 respectively) 213 UNTS 222 (ECHR), Article 7 of the Inter-American Convention on Human Rights (entered into force 18 July 1978) OAS Treaty Series No 36, 1144 UNTS 123 (IACHR), Article 6 of the African Charter on Human and Peoples' Rights (adopted on 27 June 1981, entered into force 21 October 1986) OAU Doc. CAB/LEG/67/3 rev. 5, 21 ILM 58 (AfCHPR).

[100] Recall that the complementarity framework also requires the factual basis for this assessment to be provided by the State that requests a deferral in accordance with Rule 53 of the Rules of Procedure and Evidence, which requires such States 'to provide information concerning its investigation [. . .]' (n 98).

[101] Cf *248–249.*

[102] Cf *chapeau* of Rome Statute (n 8) Article 17 (2). On these principles, see *Chapter IV: Complementarity as a Legal Principle and as Criteria for Admissibility, 3.5.1. 'Principles of due process recognized by international law'.*

[103] Cf *129–134.*

When applying these principles and standards to the issue under consideration, a decision not to proceed with an investigation due to lack of evidence only withstands the complementarity test when it is carried out diligently by independent and impartial authorities. These authorities must promptly make all reasonable efforts to carry out the investigation and exercise a requisite amount of care with a view to establishing the facts and gathering evidence.[104] States must conduct a thorough and effective investigation capable of leading to the identification and punishment of those responsible rather than an investigation that is a mere formality.[105] Those involved in an investigation (police and judicial authorities, witnesses etc) must be free from undue influence and from obstruction, interference or retaliation, and evidence must be preserved.[106] Furthermore, commanders who learn that ICC crimes have been committed by subordinates under their effective command and control must take all necessary and reasonable measures to investigate so as to enable him or her to suppress such crimes or to submit the matter to the competent authorities for further investigation and prosecution.[107]

[104] A V Freeman *The International Responsibility of States for Denial of Justice* (H Vaillant-Carmanne Publ, Liege 1938) 369–378. See also Human Rights Committee, General Comment No 20, Article 7, adopted during the Committee's 44th session in 1992, Compilation of General Comments and General Recommendations Adopted by Human Rights Treaty Bodies, UN Doc HRI/GEN/1/Rev.6 at 151 (2003)[14].

[105] *Velásquez Rodriguez* Judgment of 29 July 1988, Inter-American Court of Human Rights, (Series C) No 4 (1988)[177]; *Selmouni v France*, 25803/94 [1999] ECHR 66 (28 July 1999) 79; *Kaya v Turkey* 22535/93 [2000] ECHR (28 March 2000) [102–108], detailing the factors that lead the European Court for Human Rights to conclude that it 'is not satisfied that the investigation carried out into the killing of Hasan Kaya and Metin Can was adequate or effective', drawing upon facts such as that the investigation changed hands four times [103]; flaws in the autopsies at the scene of discovery of the bodies and the lack of a forensic examination of the scene or report regarding whether the victims were killed at the scene or how they were deposited at the scene [104]; limited and superficial steps taken by the public prosecutor in response to leads in the investigation [105], and significant delays in the investigation [106]. Human Rights Committee, *Guillermo Ignacio Dermit Barbato et al v Uruguay*, Communication No 84/1981 UN Doc CCPR/C/OP/2 at 112 (1990) [11]. That an investigation must be 'effective' can also be deduced from the generally recognized exceptions to the requirement to exhaust local remedies before cases are admissible before international adjudicate organs: see for relevant jurisprudence (n 161) in Ch IV. See also the Basic Principles and Guidelines on the Right to a Remedy and Reparation for Victims of Gross Violations of International Human Rights Law and Serious Violations of International Humanitarian Law, adopted and proclaimed by UNGA Res 60/147 (16 December 2005), Basic Principle and Guideline II (3)(b) [obligation to '[i]nvestigate violations effectively, promptly, thoroughly and impartially and, where appropriate, take action against those allegedly responsible in accordance with domestic and international law']. While the Basic Principles and Guidelines themselves are not legally binding, they are drawn up on the assumption that they 'do not create new substantive international or domestic legal obligations. They provide for mechanisms, modalities, procedures and methods for the implementation of existing legal obligations under human rights law and international humanitarian law.' Cf Explanatory Comment 1 attached to the Basic Principles and Guidelines, available at <http://www.unhchr.ch/html/menu2/revisedrestitution. doc>. As far as torture is concerned, see also the UN Principles on the Effective Investigation and Documentation of Torture and Other Cruel, Inhuman or Degrading Treatment or Punishment, adopted by UNGA Res 55/89 Annex (4 December 2000).

[106] Cf *133*.

[107] Article 87 (3) of the 1977 Geneva Protocol I Additional to the Geneva Conventions of 12 August 1949, and relating to the Protection of Victims of International Armed Conflicts (AP I)

Only if the exercise of prosecutorial discretion due to a lack of evidence follows an investigation, which satisfies the aforementioned requirements, would it withstand the complementarity test and a case would have to be considered inadmissible. This would certainly not be the case when prosecutorial authorities purposively fail to produce sufficient inculpatory evidence despite the ready availability of that evidence.[108] Nor is it sufficient merely to assert that a person has been interrogated about the allegations and 'there is no case'.[109] In case a State diligently and thoroughly investigates in accordance with the aforementioned requirements, however, the national standard in the legal system in question, which governs the determination whether evidence is sufficient or not, should be treated deferentially, provided it is not manifestly deficient.[110]

However, does the Statute also provide room for States to exercise prosecutorial discretion for *policy reasons* if an investigation reveals that there is sufficient evidence that a crime within the jurisdiction of the Court has been committed and the State concerned is able 'to obtain the accused or the necessary evidence and testimony' and otherwise able 'to carry out its proceedings'[111]? Generally, prosecutorial discretion for policy reasons grants the prosecuting authorities the power to assess whether a prosecution is in the public interest and to abandon proceedings in case such a public interest is lacking.[112] A lack of public interest may emanate from a variety of factors, including the characteristics of the

(adopted 8 June 1977, entered into force 7 December 1978) 1125 UNTS 3–608, Article 7 (3) ICTY (n 57), Article 6 (3) of the Statute of the International Criminal Tribunal for the Prosecution of Persons Responsible for Genocide and Other Serious Violations of International Humanitarian Law Committed in the Territory of Rwanda and Rwandan citizens responsible for genocide and other such violations committed in the territory of neighbouring States, between 1 January 1994 and 31 December 1994, established in accordance with UNSC Res 955 (adopted on 8 November 1994) (ICTR), Article 6 (3) of the Statute of the Special Court for Sierra Leone, annexed to the Agreement between the United Nations and the Government of Sierra Leone on the Establishment of the Special Court for Sierra Leone, signed on 16 January 2002 (16 January 2002), available at http://www.sc-sl.org/Documents/scsl-statute.html, Article 28 of the Rome Statute (n 8). See also pages 133–134.

[108] For a pertinent example prior to the entry into force of the ICC Statute, see D Cohen, 'Intended to Fail—The Trials before the Ad Hoc Human Rights Court in Jakarta' (2003) 74 International Center for Transitional Justice 5.

[109] Cf the statement by the Minister of the Interior of Sudan, Zubeir Bashir Taha, reported in the Sixth Report of the Prosecutor of the International Criminal Court to the UN Security Council Pursuant to UNSCR 1593 (2005), 5 December 2007, available at <http://www.icc-cpi. int/library/organs/otp/OTP-RP-20071205-UNSC-ENG.pdf> [14].

[110] Cf J Gurule, 'United States Opposition to the 1998 Rome Statute Establishing an International Criminal Court: Is the Court's Jurisdiction Truly Complementary to National Criminal Jurisdictions?' (2001) 35 Cornell Intl LJ 1 1–45, 8–9 [arguing for a deferential standard].

[111] Cf Rome Statute (n 8) Article 17 (3).

[112] See generally on the notion of 'public interest' D D Ntanda Nsereko, 'Prosecutorial Discretion before National Courts and International Tribunals' (2005) 3 JICJ 124–144, 130–131. For examples in various States, see the following national reports in L Arbour, A Eser, K Ambos and A Sanders (eds) (n 94): 247 (Canada), 298 (England and Wales), 325 (France), 343 (Germany), 352–353 (Hungary), 364 (Israel), 383 (Japan), 393 (South Korea), 418 (The Netherlands), 427 (Nigeria), 444 (Russia), 452 (Rwanda), 464 (Singapore), 474 (South Africa).

individual accused (eg age, mental state, previous offences),[113] the disinterest of the victim(s)[114] or alternative settlement,[115] competing national interests[116] and the offender's contribution to avert a danger to the existence or security of the State,[117] as well as the relative insignificance of the offence.[118] Theoretically, these policy considerations could also underlie a decision whether or not to prosecute ICC crimes, with the possible exception of the last factor.[119] Thus the competent national authorities could assert, for example, that an individual accused of an ICC crime should not be prosecuted because s/he did not commit any crime previously, or that s/he paid compensation to the (dependents of) the victims of such a crime and the latter have accepted an apology. An equally conceivable contention of these authorities could be not to prosecute because such a prosecution collides with the national interest in maintaining a fragile peace or because the accused has played a vital part in bringing about a settlement of an armed conflict.

And yet, a scenario in which such an exercise of prosecutorial discretion does not result in 'unwillingness' would seem hard to contemplate.[120] A decision not to prosecute for reasons of policy rather than for a lack of evidence would, by definition, be made 'for the purpose of shielding the person concerned from criminal

---

[113] L Arbour, A Eser, K Ambos and A Sanders (eds) (n 94): 298 (England and Wales), 383 (Japan), 393 (South Korea).

[114] L Arbour, A Eser, K Ambos and A Sanders (eds) (n 94): 298 (England and Wales), 325 (France).

[115] L Arbour, A Eser, K Ambos and A Sanders (eds) (n 94): 444 (Russia), 452 (Rwanda).

[116] L Arbour, A Eser, K Ambos and A Sanders (eds) (n 94): 343 (Germany), but note that the rule on prosecutorial discretion for this reason in Section 153 (c)(3) and (4) of the German Code of Criminal Procedure has been modified with the adoption and entry into force of the German *Völkerstrafgesetzbuch* (Code of Crimes against International Law, 26 June 2002), which introduced a new Section 153 (f) into the Code of Criminal Procedure that now governs prosecutorial discretion vis-à-vis ICC crimes.

[117] Ibid.

[118] L Arbour, A Eser, K Ambos and A Sanders (eds) (n 94): 298 (England and Wales), 325 (France), 343 (Germany), 352–353 (Hungary), 383 (Japan), 393 (South Korea).

[119] To argue that acts of genocide, crimes against humanity or war crimes do not merit prosecution because they are too minor would seem to contradict their being recognized as 'most serious crimes of concern to the international community as a whole' (cf Rome Statute (n 8) Preamble, para 4) which 'threaten the peace, security and well-being of the world' (cf Rome Statute (n 8) Preamble, para 3). Technically, the Statute qualifies all ICC crimes as such. This is notwithstanding the fact that there are gradations of gravity between different ICC crimes, exemplified by a comparison of extermination as crime against humanity (Rome Statute (n 8) Article 7 (1)(b)) with the war crime of destroying or seizing the enemy's or adversary's property unless such destruction or seizure be imperatively demanded by the necessities of war or armed conflict (Rome Statute (n 8) Article 8 (2)(b)(xiii) and (e)(xii)), which may take the form, for instance, of a relatively minor seizure, eg a package of cigarettes. One may question whether the latter act is really adequately qualified as one of the most serious crimes of concern to the international community as a whole, which threaten the peace, security and well-being of the world. The Statute nevertheless does not differentiate between different ICC crimes as far as this qualification is concerned. This is notwithstanding the fact that cases which involve allegations of ICC crimes may be declared inadmissible because such cases are not of sufficient gravity to justify further action by the Court. Cf Article 17 (1)(d).

[120] See also *200–202* on the limitations of such prosecutorial discretion emanating from the concept of a 'case'.

responsibility' for ICC crimes.[121] Cumulatively, such a decision sooner or later results in an 'unjustified delay in the proceedings, which in the circumstances is inconsistent with an intent to bring the person concerned to justice'.[122] In this reading, Article 17 (1)(b) only leaves room for decisions not to prosecute, which result from insufficient evidence after an investigation that meets the complementarity requirements. Accordingly, State Parties which develop prosecutorial strategies that involve the setting of priorities and selection of cases run the risk of being branded 'unwilling' vis-à-vis those cases that fall through the net. Notwithstanding other possible avenues to reconcile the exercise of prosecutorial discretion for policy reasons vis-à-vis ICC crimes with the Statute,[123] an interpretation of Article 17 suggests that this form of prosecutorial discretion potentially renders cases admissible. The duty of State Parties to exercise their criminal jurisdiction over ICC crimes, as elucidated by the rules on complementarity, would appear not to leave any room to abandon proceedings with regard to ICC crimes on the basis of policy considerations.[124]

4. Substitutes for Criminal Prosecutions

A second question that needs to be answered in order to further delimit the scope and detailed content of the general duty of every State Party to exercise its criminal jurisdiction over ICC crimes is whether the rules on admissibility provide any room for substitutes for criminal prosecutions. As previously stated, substitutes for criminal prosecutions are a recurring phenomenon in the context of core crimes and may take various forms, ranging from amnesties, pardons and truth commissions to lustration processes, civil proceedings, traditional forms of justice and exclusion from refugee status.[125] An answer as to whether such measures are compatible with the requirements as they flow from complementarity is therefore of particular importance.

The issue of substitutes for criminal prosecutions was too contentious to be expressly regulated in the Statute[126] and remains a matter of controversy. The

---

[121] Rome Statute (n 8) Article 17 (1)(b) in conjunction with (2)(a).

[122] Rome Statute (n 8) Article 17 (1)(b) in conjunction with (2)(b).

[123] For further discussion, see *6. Legal Avenues for Non-Prosecution*.

[124] A possible way to take account of this general incompatibility between the exercise of prosecutorial discretion on policy grounds and the complementarity requirements is the way in which prosecutorial discretion with regard to ICC crimes is regulated under South African law. Cf (n 4).

[125] Cf *Chapter II: National Suppression of Core Crimes, 3.2.1. Substitutes for Criminal Prosecutions*.

[126] For considerations during the drafting process, see pages 83, 87, 90–91. During the Preparatory Commission, South Africa indicated that it intended to submit a draft provision on the matter of amnesties and truth commissions, but this did not materialize: J T Holmes, Complementarity—History of Negotiations, Presentation at the Conference 'The Complementarity Regime of the ICC', 17–19 December 2003, The Hague, The Netherlands, 7 [on file with author].

position taken by the French *Conseil Constitutionnel* and the practice of some States to exclude amnesties and other clemency measures when adopting substantive implementing legislation,[127] on the one hand, and the view expressed by Colombia upon ratification of the Rome Statute, on the other hand, may serve to illustrate this controversy.[128]

Thus, when the French *Conseil Constitutionnel* had to consider the constitutional compatibility of the Rome Statute, it held, *inter alia*, that the provisions on complementarity could result in the ICC's decision to declare cases admissible which are covered by an amnesty law.[129] In contrast, Colombia made a declaration upon ratification of the ICC Statute, expressing its standpoint that '[n] one of the provisions of the Rome Statute concerning the exercise of jurisdiction by the International Criminal Court prevent the Colombian State from granting amnesties, reprieves or judicial pardons for political crimes, provided that they are granted in conformity with the Constitution and with the principles and norms of international law accepted by Colombia. [. . .]'.[130] Colombia seemed to be of the view that these latter norms provided for the possibility to grant amnesties, as evidenced by both the Constitution[131] and an earlier judgment of the Colombian Constitutional Court, which addressed the constitutionality of the two 1977 Additional Protocols to the Geneva Conventions.[132]

---

[127] See (n 5).

[128] See also for an assessment of the position taken by a number of other States, K van der Voort and M Zwanenburg, 'Amnesty and the Implementation of the ICC—Some Country Studies' in R Haveman, O Kavran and J Nicholls (eds), *Supranational Criminal Law: A System Sui Generis* (Intersentia Publ, Antwerp/Oxford/New York 2003) 305–345, 328–340.

[129] Decision of 22 January 1999 (Decision No 98–408 DC, 1999 J.O. 1317, *Traité portant statut de la Cour pénale internationale,* available at <http://www.conseil-constitutionnel.fr/decision/1998/98408/98408dc.htm> ['[. . .] *il résulte du statut que la Cour pénale internationale pourrait être valablement saisie du seul fait de l'application d'une loi d'amnistie [. . .];[. . .] en pareil cas, la France, en dehors de tout manqué de volonté ou d'indisponibilité de l'Etat, pourrait être conduite à arrêter et à remettre à la Cour une personne à raison de faits couverts, selon la loi française, par l'amnistie.*'], English translation in (1999) 2 YIHL 493–505, 503. This view was confirmed by the Chilean Constitutional Court in its decision of 8 April 2002 (Case No 346), unpublished: see the comment on the decision by Rodrigo P and Correa G, 'Chile' (2003) 1 International Journal of Constitutional Law 130–135, 134.

[130] See (n 6). Note, however, that what Colombia called a 'Declaration' may in fact amount to a reservation to the extent that it 'purports to exclude or modify the legal effect of certain provisions of the treaty in their application to [Colombia]': cf Article 2 (1)(d) of the Vienna Convention on the Law of Treaties (n 12). According to Rome Statute (n 8) Article 120 reservations are impermissible.

[131] Cf Article 150, para 17 of the Constitution, available at <http://www.georgetown.edu/pdba/Constitutions/Colombia/col91.html>.

[132] Sentencia No C-574/95, Revisión constitucional del 'Protocolo Adicional a los Convenieos de Ginebra del 12 de agosto de 1949, relativo a la protección de las víctimas de los conflictos armadas sin carácter internacional (Protocolo II)' hecho en Ginebra al 8 junio de 1977, y de la ley 171 del 16 diciembre de 1994, por medio de la cual se apruebra dicho Protocolo [Judgment of 18 May 1995]. For a discussion of the judgment, see F Kalshoven, 'A Colombian view on Protocol II' (1998) 1 YIHL 262–268, 266.

In the absence of any express regulation in the Rome Statute, the question of whether and to what extent the adoption of substitutes for criminal prosecutions renders cases admissible warrants further analysis.

Before doing so, two clarifications are in order. First, the following analysis is confined to situations in which non-criminal responses *replace* criminal proceedings, rather than being applied cumulatively. It will, therefore, not address the complex relationship between criminal prosecutions and alternative responses such as truth commissions, when they operate in conjunction.[133]

Second, substitutes for criminal prosecutions vary widely in form.[134] They may take effect on any, or all, of the procedural stages envisaged in Article 17 (1)(a) to (c), or may bar even initial investigative steps or exonerate persons who have already been duly tried and convicted, whereby they would seem to fall outside the assessment of admissibility in accordance with the complementarity criteria.[135] Last but not least, alternative responses resist a generally valid assessment under one of the specific headings of unwillingness or inability.[136] While all these considerations require us to proceed with a high degree of generalization, the following analysis is based on the broad distinction between, on the one hand, unconditional clemency measures, including amnesties, ie clemency measures which are not dependent on any particular conduct of the beneficiary, such as an admission of guilt, apology to the victim(s), disclosure of facts, etc. (4.1.), and, on the other hand, alternative accountability processes, such as truth commissions, traditional forms of justice, civil and administrative proceedings (4.2.).[137]

---

[133] For discussion of such accumulation of criminal and non-criminal responses to international crimes, see for instance W Schabas 'Internationalized Courts and their Relationship with Alternative Accountability Mechanisms: The Case of Sierra Leone' in C Romano, A Nollkaemper, and J K Kleffner (eds), *Internationalized Criminal Courts: Sierra Leone, East Timor, Kosovo, and Cambodia* (OUP Oxford 2004) 157–180; B S Lyons, 'Getting Untrapped, Struggling for Truth: The Commission for Reception, Truth and Reconciliation (CAVR) in East Timor' in ibid 99–124, 116–121. For an analysis of cumulative truth commissions and criminal processes in the light of the admissibility criteria before the ICC, see C Cárdenas *Die Zulässigkeitsprüfung vor dem Internationalen Strafgerichtshof, Zur Auslegung des Art. 17 IstGH-Statut unter besonderer Berücksichtigung von Amnestien und Wahrheitskommissionen* (Berliner Wissenschaftsverlag, Berlin 2005) 177–180. For an example as to how to regulate such accumulation in practice, see Section 5 of the Annexure to the Agreement on Accountability and Reconciliation signed between the Government of the Republic of Uganda and the Lord's Resistance Army/Movement (LRA/M) on 29th June 2007, signed in Juba on the 19th day of February 2008 ['In the fulfilment of its functions, the body [tasked to inquire into the past] shall give precedence to any investigations or formal proceedings instituted pursuant to the terms of this Agreement. Detailed guidelines and working practices shall be established to regulate the relationship between the body and any other adjudicatory body seized of a case relating to this Agreement.'].

[134] Cf *Chapter II: National Suppression of Core Crimes, 3.2.1. Substitutes for Criminal Prosecutions.*

[135] For an example, see the Peruvian Amnesty Law No 26479 of 14 June 1995, which granted amnesty to all members of the security forces and civilians who had been *accused, investigated, prosecuted or convicted, or who were carrying out prison sentences,* for human rights violations.

[136] Cf *106–107.*

[137] For a more detailed analysis, see for instance C Cárdenas (n 133) 149–186. Amongst further literature addressing the issue of substitutes of criminal prosecutions, see M Scharf, 'The

4.1. Unconditional Clemency Measures, including Amnesties

In principle, the room for the granting of *unconditional amnesties,* ie the decrim-inalization of the acts in question and/or the erasure of the penalty,[138] under *Articles 17 and 20 (3)* seems limited. However, three situations need to be distinguished.

First, *if such an amnesty bars even initial investigative steps,* cases would be admissible without necessitating an assessment in accordance with the admissi-bility regime under Article 17.[139]

Second, unconditional *amnesties, which take effect after the initiation of at least initial investigative steps and prior to the conclusion of a trial,* meet the presump-tion of amounting to 'unwillingness' or 'inability' or both, depending on the State organ under consideration. If the executive or legislature of a State grants such an amnesty for crimes which fall into the jurisdiction of the ICC, the State, represented in this instance by the Parliament, would take a decision not to pros-ecute in the sense of Article 17 (1)(b), and that decision is taken for the purpose of shielding the person concerned from criminal responsibility.[140] Even if the *ultimate aim* of granting an amnesty were something different than shielding the accused, such as to secure the end of hostilities or the transition to a new regime, the *purpose* would remain the shielding of those persons who are envisaged to benefit from the amnesty.[141]

Amnesty Exception to the Jurisdiction of the International Criminal Court' (1999) 32 Cornell ILJ 507–527; N Roht-Arriaza, 'Amnesty and the International Criminal Court' in D Shelton (ed), *International Crimes, Peace, and Human Rights: The Role of the International Criminal Court* (Transnational Publishers, Ardsley, NY 2000) 77–82; J Dugard, 'Possible Conflicts of Jurisdiction with Truth Commissions' in A Cassese, P Gaeta and J Jones (n 42) 693–704; C van den Wyngaert and T Ongena, *'Ne bis in idem* principle, including the issue of amnesty' in A Cassese, P Gaeta and J Jones (eds) (n 42) 726–727; J Gavron, 'Amnesties in the Light of Developments in International Law and the Establishment of the International Criminal Court' (2002) 51 ICLQ 91–117; D Robinson, 'Serving the Interests of Justice: Amnesties, Truth Commissions and the International Criminal Court' (2003) 14 EJIL 481–505.

[138] For that definition, see 'Progress Report on the Question of the Impunity of Perpetrators of Human Rights Violations, prepared by Mr Guissé and Mr Joinet, pursuant to Sub-Commission resolution 1992/23' (19 July 1993) UN Doc E/CN.4/Sub.2/1993/6 [38].

[139] Cf pages 104–105. See also A Seibert-Fohr (n 16) 565.

[140] Rome Statute (n 8) Article 17 (1)(b) in conjunction with Article 17 (2)(a). Cf J Meissner, *Die Zusammenarbeit mit dem Internationalen Strafgerichtshof nach dem Römischen Statut* (Verlag C H Beck, Munich 2003) 84.

[141] Cf *137–138.* See also J Gavron (n 137) 111; C Cárdenas (n 133) 160–161. N Roht-Arriaza fails to make that distinction, when she asserts: 'Amnesties generally by definition shield cer-tain individuals from criminal responsibility, so this provision seems to apply. The affected state could argue an amnesty was not enacted for the *purpose* of shielding, but that shielding is merely a by-product of a decision taken for the purpose of national reconciliation. The Inter-American Commission on Human Rights has found in considering a number of Latin American amnes-ties [...] that the national reconciliation context is not enough to validate the amnesties, but it is unclear how the ICC would rule on this issue.' (n 137) 79, emphasis in the original, footnote omitted.

Sooner or later, an amnesty would also result in an *'unjustified delay* in the proceedings, which in the circumstances is inconsistent with an intent to bring the person concerned to justice'.[142] Admittedly, the provision requires a consideration of whether an unjustified delay is inconsistent with an intent to bring the person concerned to justice *in the circumstances* and thereby allows a certain degree of flexibility.[143] Arguably, it therefore could provide room for a temporary amnesty applicable in a 'cooling-off' period, which enables the parties to an armed conflict to negotiate a peace agreement, while not barring (or indeed expressly providing for) subsequent criminal proceedings at a later stage. When unconditional amnesties foreclose criminal proceedings permanently, however, Article 17 (2)(b) would become applicable sooner or later and cases would be admissible.

Likewise, situations in which courts are competent to review and/or reverse the decision of the executive or legislature to grant such an amnesty, but refuse to do so or defer to these other branches of government,[144] could arguably also fall under Article 17 (2)(c) as 'proceedings [which] were not or are not being conducted independently or impartially, and [...] in a manner which, in the circumstances, is inconsistent with an intent to bring the person concerned to justice'.

In the reverse situation, in which investigative, prosecutorial and judicial organs courts are barred from setting aside such an amnesty and have to follow them as a matter of national law, the national judicial system is unavailable, due to which these organs are 'unable to obtain the accused or the necessary evidence and testimony or otherwise unable to carry out [the] proceedings'.[145] They would therefore result in (legal) inability and fall under Article 17 (3).

Finally, the *ne bis in idem* principle embodied in Article 20 of the Statute equally does not provide a possible avenue to argue inadmissibility. It is unconvincing to understand the notion of being 'tried' to encompass an amnesty granted after a judicial investigation but prior to the conclusion of a trial and thus to trigger Article 20 (3). For, the granting of an amnesty at this stage of criminal proceedings cannot reasonably be equated with a trial.[146] Indeed, it is the very

---

[142] Rome Statute (n 8) Article 17 (2)(b).   [143] Cf pages 143–144.

[144] Such deference could take the form of doctrines and methods of judicial self-restraint, such as the political questions doctrine, the act of state doctrine and judicial deference towards the executive branch. See generally on these doctrines, B Conforti, *International Law and the Role of Domestic Legal Systems* (Martinus Nijhoff Publ, Dordrecht/Boston/London 1993) 13–17; E Benvenisti, 'Judicial Misgivings Regarding the Application of International Law: An Analysis of Attitudes of National Courts' (1993) 4 EJIL 159–183; E Benvenisti, 'Judges and Foreign Affairs: A Comment on the Institut de Droit International's Resolution on "The Activities of National Courts and the International Relations of their State" (1994) 5 EJIL 423–439, 170; H H Koh, 'Why the President (almost) always wins in foreign affairs—lessons of the Iran-Contra Affair' (1988) 97 Yale LJ 1255–1342, 1314–1315.

[145] Cf Rome Statute (n 8) Article 17 (3).

[146] N Ront-Arriaza (n 137) 80. See also C van den Wyngaert and T Ongena (n 137) 726 ['For the purposes of Article 20, national amnesties and pardons obviously do not qualify as "judgments" and would therefore not preclude the ICC from trying the case again.'].

purpose of an amnesty to bar a court from such a trial. Even if one rejected this argument and accepted that an amnesty after a judicial investigation can qualify as a trial, such 'proceedings in the other court' would in any event continue to fall under the exception under Article 20 (3)(a), as they would be for the purpose of shielding the person concerned from criminal responsibility'.[147] Cases would therefore be admissible.

Matters may be different, however, when considering the third situation in which an amnesty may be granted, namely *after* an accused has been *tried and convicted*, or when a pardon is granted, ie an individual is exempted from serving the sentence or from completing it in full by virtue of regalian authority.[148] Article 20 (3) contains a significant *lacuna* in this regard,[149] which has been identified by some as '[p]otentially, the greatest weakness to the complementarity regime':[150] it only addresses flaws *in the conduct of proceedings,* but leaves unaffected measures that take effect *after* an accused has been convicted in proceedings which were *not* for the purpose of shielding the person concerned and were otherwise conducted independently and impartially.[151] Consequently, cases which have been duly conducted and which have led to the conviction of an accused, but in respect of which an amnesty, pardon or parole is subsequently granted, or the sentence is commuted, seem to be beyond the reach of the ICC, unless one were to understand such measures to be an integral part of the 'proceedings in the other court'.[152] The generally non-judicial nature of such clemency measures would, however, militate against such an understanding to bring them into the reach of Article 20 (3).[153]

An argument could be made to the effect that one needs to distinguish between amnesties, pardons and similar measures that *erase* the sentence or the conviction and those that do not.[154] In the former two cases, such measures

---

[147] See also (n 141) and text.

[148] For that definition, cf Progress Report on the Question of the Impunity of Perpetrators of Human Rights Violations (n 138) [38].

[149] Cf W Schabas, *An Introduction to the International Criminal Court* (2nd edn CUP, Cambridge 2004) 88; S Morel, *La Mise en Oeuvre du Principe de la Compleméntarité par la Cour Pénale Internationale—Le Cas Particulier des Amnisties* (PhD thesis, University of Lausanne, Lausanne 2005) 252.

[150] J T Holmes, 'The Principle of Complementarity' in Roy S Lee (ed) (n 42) 76.

[151] C van den Wyngaert and T Ongena (n 137) 727; B Broomhall *International Justice and the International Criminal Court: Between Sovereignty and the Rule of Law* (OUP, Oxford 2004) 100–101; F Razesberger (n 16) 43–45; H Olásolo, 'Complementary Analysis of National Sentencing' in R Haveman and O Olusanya (eds), *Sentencing and Sanctioning in Supranational Criminal Law* (Intersentia, Antwerp 2006) 61–63.

[152] This seems to underlie the argument of the USA in *Case Concerning Avena and Other Mexican Nationals (Mexico v United States of America)* General List No 128 [2004] ICJ Rep 12, 56, [136], where the respondent asserted that '[c]lemency procedures are an integral part of the existing "laws and regulations" of the United States'.

[153] Note that the ICJ pointed at the non-judicial character of clemency procedures: ibid [142].

[154] Cf the Progress Report on the Question of the Impunity of Perpetrators of Human Rights Violations (n 138) [38], which points out that an amnesty typically entails the decriminalization

could then be seen to be comparable in effect to an appeals judgment that quashes an earlier decision of a lower court. And yet, as long as the amnesty, pardon or similar clemency measure only erases the *sentence,* but leaves the criminal *proceedings* as a whole unaffected, the case would remain inadmissible because, in our hypothesis, these were not flawed in a way that would amount to unwillingness or inability. If, on the other hand, a clemency measure had the effect under national law of treating the criminal proceedings as if they had not taken place by expunging the *conviction,*[155] one could argue that these proceedings have to be treated as if they were erased also for purposes of determining the admissibility of a case before the ICC. The granting of such clemency measures could therefore render a case admissible, because the State concerned would have to be regarded as if it had not conducted any proceedings and treated akin to an inactive State.[156]

In sum, Article 20 (3) would seem to provide some room for clemency measures granted *after* a conviction following a trial that satisfies standards of due process, provided such measures leave unaffected the criminal proceedings which led to the conviction. A different conclusion can only be reached by relying on an interpretation that is imaginative to a degree that would broaden the terms of the treaty beyond their ordinary meaning.[157] However, such post-trial measures are the only form of clemency measures that would not render cases admissible.

of the acts in question and the erasure of the penalty. In contrast, a pardon applies to an individual and exempts the beneficiary from serving the sentence or from completing it in full by virtue of regalian authority, which is the prerogative of the Head of State. It thus remits punishment but does not purport to forget or deny an individual's guilt and does not erase the conviction. However, the Report points out that this distinction is somewhat ideal typical and that amnesty and pardon can also apply in combination, for instance if the conviction is erased (amnesty element) through a personal measure independent of the nature of the criminal acts (pardon element).

[155] For an example, see Article 133–9 of the French *Nouveau Code Pénal,* which provides that 'L'amnistie efface les condamnations prononcées. Elle entraîne, sans qu'elle puisse donner lieu à restitution, la remise de toutes les peines. Elle rétablit l'auteur ou le complice de l'infraction dans le bénéfice du sursis qui avait pu lui être accordé lors d'une condamnation antérieure.'

[156] In this vein, A Seibert-Fohr (n 16) 565, who argues that 'taking the underlying idea of the *ne bis in idem* rule there is a reason to argue that a trial which is in fact nullified by a later amnesty does not trigger this rule and therefore cannot render a case inadmissible for the ICC'. [footnotes omitted].

[157] In the words of C van den Wyngaert and T Ongena, 'one could give an unusually broad interpretation of the term "proceedings" in Article 20 [(3)], which would mean that amnesties of this kind would qualify as sham trials'. In the alternative, they suggest that 'it could be argued that there is a customary international law prohibition against amnesty for crimes that come under the jurisdiction of the court, making such amnesties null and void and not binding upon the ICC.' (n 137) 727, footnote omitted. The latter alternative appears open to the objection that it effectively circumvents the admissibility regime of the Statute in as much as it disregards the fact that the list of grounds for admissibility despite domestic proceedings stipulated in Articles 17 and 20 (3) is exhaustive.

4.2. Alternative Accountability Processes

Is the room for *alternative accountability processes,* such as *truth commissions,*[158] *traditional forms of justice,*[159] *lustration processes,*[160] and *civil proceedings,*[161] similarly limited under the rules on complementarity? After all, such substitutes for criminal prosecutions may provide at least some degree of accountability, albeit that such accountability is of a non-criminal nature. In contra-distinction to the aforementioned clemency measures, which regularly seek to *avoid* redressing the wrongs resulting from ICC crimes,[162] States that opt for such substitutes confront these crimes, rather than remaining essentially inactive. Complementarity might, therefore, treat these alternative accountability processes differently from clemency measures.

Yet, it is difficult to reconcile these alternative accountability processes with the requirements of complementarity. Cases which are being or have been addressed in the course of an alternative process, would, as a rule, seem not to bar the Court from declaring cases admissible.

The language employed in relation to issues of admissibility creates a strong presumption that only genuine *criminal* proceedings can render a case inadmissible. A first such indication can be derived from the concept of '*prosecution*' in Article 17 (1) (a) and (b). Article 17 (1)(a) refers to cases that are being 'prosecuted'[163] and the unwillingness or inability to carry out the 'prosecution',[164] while Article 17 (1)(b) employs the identical concept in relation to cases in which a State has decided not to 'prosecute'[165] and such a decision resulted from the unwillingness or inability genuinely to 'prosecute'.[166] Admittedly, one may give the concept of 'prosecution' an exceptionally broad reading to include all proceedings which can result in a sanction, even if that sanction is of a non-penal nature. However, such an understanding would go beyond the ordinary meaning of these terms

---

[158] Note that truth commissions may also involve the granting of conditional amnesties. This was the case, for instance, with regard to the South African Truth Commission. The South African Promotion of National Unity and Reconciliation Act of 1995 (Act 34 of 1995) provides that persons seeking amnesty for gross human rights violations were required to apply to the Committee on Amnesty. The latter could grant amnesty only if it was satisfied that the applicant had committed an act constituting 'a gross violation of human rights', made 'a full disclosure of all relevant facts', and that the act to which the application relates is 'an act associated with a political objective committed in the course of conflicts of the past': Sections 10 (1), 19 (3)(b)(iii) of the Act. Also note that truth commissions have to be distinguished from investigatory commissions, which seek to prepare rather than pre-empt criminal proceedings. See further *46.*

[159] A pertinent example is the setting up of *gacaca* jurisdictions in Rwanda in the wake of the 1994 genocide, see Organic Law No 40/2000 of 26/01/2001 setting up 'Gacaca Jurisdictions' and Organizing Prosecutions for Offences Constituting the Crime of Genocide or Crimes Against Humanity Committed Between October 1, 1990 and December 31, 1994.

[160] Cf page 48.   [161] For an overview, see *47.*

[162] An exception is clemency measures *after* a trial: see *266–268.*

[163] Rome Statute (n 8) Article 17 (1)(a).   [164] Rome Statute (n 8) Article 17 (1)(a).

[165] Rome Statute (n 8) Article 17 (1)(b).   [166] Rome Statute (n 8) Article 17 (1)(b).

of the Statute, which generally denote the pursuit of *criminal proceedings*[167] and would therefore contravene the applicable rules of treaty interpretation. This understanding is also confirmed by different language versions, all of which use terms that are commonly employed in the context of criminal proceedings.[168]

The concept of 'prosecution' in Article 17 thus clearly suggests that the provision envisages criminal proceedings.

The question arises as to whether the same holds true for the concept of an *'investigation'* referred to in Article 17 (a) and (b) or, alternatively, whether it may provide a possible avenue to reconcile alternative accountability mechanisms with the requirements of complementarity. To answer that question essentially depends upon whether such 'investigation' need necessarily be a 'criminal investigation'. The term, read in isolation, is not conclusive and has led some to argue that it could equally cover an investigation in the context of a truth commission process.[169] Cases under consideration in an ongoing truth commission process would then be brought under the heading of cases 'being investigated', and decisions not to prosecute after a completed truth commission process could be cases that 'ha[ve] been investigated' but which the State has decided not to prosecute. That argument could be expanded to equally cover other forms of investigations, for instance those conducted in the course of civil and administrative proceedings. However, placing the term 'investigation' into its context and interpreting it in the light of the object and purpose of the Rome Statute suggests that the provisions on complementarity envisage *criminal* investigations as the only form of investigation that can render cases inadmissible.

As far as the context is concerned, the term in Article 17 (1) (a) and (b) must be interpreted in conjunction with both the formulation of the principle of

---

[167] See also J T Holmes (n 150) 77 ['It is clear that the Statute's provisions on complementarity are intended to refer to criminal investigations...A truth commission and the amnesties it provides may not meet the test of criminal investigation...'].

[168] French: 'poursuite'/'poursuivre'; Spanish: 'enjuiciamento' and 'incoar acción penal'; German (although not an official language of the Statute): 'Strafverfolgung'/'strafrechtlich zu verfolgen'.

[169] M Scharf (n 137) 524–525 ['It is significant that [Article 17 (1)(a) requires an investigation but does not specify a criminal investigation. The concerned state could argue that a truth commission [...] constitutes a genuine investigation.' Footnotes omitted]; J Dugard (n 137) 701–702 ['T]he first part of [Article 17 (1)(b)] might be interpreted imaginatively to cover South African-style amnesty—that is the decision not to prosecute and instead to grant amnesty after an investigation [...].']; N Roht-Arriaza (n 137) 79 ['[A] state that couples an amnesty with a truth commission, such as South Africa, might argue that "investigation" doesn't equal criminal investigation.']; D Robinson (n 137) 499–500 ['[...], the Court could determine that the term "investigation" [in Article 17 (1)(b)] also comprises a diligent, methodical effort to gather the evidence and ascertain the facts relating to the conduct in question, in order to make an objective determination in accordance with pertinent criteria (eg sufficiency of evidence, seriousness of the conduct, role of the perpetrator). These criteria are consistent with typical criminal investigations but might also be satisfied by other forms of investigation, such as those carried out in fulfillment of the 'right to know' (ie, to uncover the truth and determine who was responsible).' Footnote omitted]. B Broomhall (n 151) 101; W Schabas (n 149) 87 [sincere truth commission as a form of investigation that does not suggest 'genuine unwillingness']; S Morel (n 149) 244–246.

complementarity in paragraph 10 of the Preamble and Article 1, as well as the remainder of Article 17.

The principle of complementarity, in turn, clarifies that the ICC 'shall be complementary to national *criminal* jurisdictions'.[170] In other words, the principle as formulated in the Statute suggests that the Court's role in supplying the deficiencies of domestic proceedings under the conditions set forth in Article 17 is limited to domestic criminal proceedings. Conversely, the conditions for inadmissibility in Article 17 can only be met by proceedings conducted by a national criminal jurisdiction.

Furthermore, the references to the concept of 'investigation' in Article 17 (1) have to be read in conjunction with the remainder of that article. Article 17 (2)(a), in turn, defines 'unwillingness' to include 'proceedings [...] undertaken or [...] national decision[s] [...] made for the purpose of shielding the person concerned from *criminal* responsibility for [ICC crimes]'.[171] The term 'proceedings' is the umbrella term for 'investigations' and 'prosecutions' referred to in Article 17 (1)(a), while 'national decision' refers to the decision not to prosecute after an investigation as stipulated in Article 17 (1)(b). It follows that non-criminal accountability processes can only serve as a bar to the admissibility of cases if investigations carried out in the course of such processes were *not* undertaken for the purpose of shielding the person concerned from *criminal* responsibility. Yet, the purpose of non-criminal accountability processes—at least in the present hypothesis that they function as *substitutes* for criminal proceedings—is exactly the opposite. Investigations conducted in the course of such processes are directed at shielding persons from criminal responsibility. Notwithstanding the possibility that the shielding may not be the *ultimate motive*, a State, which replaces criminal proceedings with non-criminal accountability processes, pursues the object of avoiding the imposition of criminal sanctions on those persons who are subjected to these processes.[172] Although the decision to opt for non-criminal accountability processes rather than criminal proceedings may be forced upon the State or may be the only viable alternative to leaving the wrongs committed entirely unaddressed, their *purpose* remains to shield the persons from *criminal* responsibility for ICC crimes.

While non-criminal accountability processes would accordingly render cases admissible in accordance with Articles 17 (1)(a) and (b) in conjunction with Article 17 (2)(a), they would also arguably do so under the two other forms of

---

170   Rome Statute (n 8) Paragraph 10 of the Preamble and Article 1, emphasis added.

171   Rome Statute (n 8) Article 17 (2)(a), emphasis added.

172   Cf *mutatis mutandis* (n 141). Similar to N Roht-Arriaza's argument in relation to amnesties, see ibid, A Seibert-Fohr argues that 'if criminal punishment is waived by a truth commission in the interest of re-establishing peace the purpose is not to shield individual persons but to serve a greater objective at the expense of criminal justice. This suggests that a state in such cases is not unwilling *genuinely* to carry out the prosecution as required by article 17.' [Emphasis in the original] (n 16) 570. Note, however, that the term 'genuinely' in Article 17 does not qualify the 'unwillingness' or 'inability' but rather the verb 'to carry out': see *114–115*.

'unwillingness' in Article 17 (2)(b) and (c) under certain circumstances. Sooner or later, such processes inevitably result in unjustified delays, and the decision of judicial authorities to uphold such processes as substitutes for criminal prosecutions may amount to a lack of independence and/or impartiality.[173]

For, such instances of unjustified delays and lack of independence and impartiality may be said to be 'inconsistent with an intent to bring the person concerned to justice'.[174] Such an interpretation of the terms has been rejected on the basis of the argument that 'to bring someone to justice' does not necessarily mean 'to bring someone to *criminal* justice',[175] a construction which, *prima facie*, does not seem to be incompatible with the terms of the provision. However, the object and purpose of the Statute is the 'effective *prosecution* [of the most serious crimes of concern to the international community as a whole] by taking measures at the national level and by enhancing international cooperation'.[176] Together with paragraph 6 of the Preamble, which recalls the duty of every State to exercise its *criminal* jurisdiction, Article 17 (2)(b) and (c) thus clearly envisages *criminal* as opposed to other forms of domestic justice, a view confirmed by the generally accepted meaning of the phrase 'to bring someone to justice' as denoting 'to put someone on trial' and 'to punish'.[177]

In addition, the employment of the identical terms of 'criminal responsibility' and 'intent to bring the person concerned to justice' in Article 20 (3) would equally support the conclusion that being subjected to a non-criminal

---

[173] The arguments in relation to amnesties (nn 142–144) and text, apply *mutatis mutandis*. Also recall that the notion of 'inability' may also apply in cases in which investigative, prosecutorial and judicial organs courts are legally barred from proceedings with an investigation or prosecution due to an alternative accountability process: cf (n 145) and text.

[174] Rome Statute (n 8) Articles 17 (2)(b) and (c). [175] See eg A Seibert-Fohr (n 16) 569.

[176] Rome Statute (n 8) Preamble, paragraph 4.

[177] Cf *The Concise Oxford Dictionary* (9th edn OUP, Oxford 2001). See also J Dugard (n 137) 702 ['[…] it is difficult to maintain such an interpretation in the face of the second part of the provision [of Article 17 (1)(b)] as the decision "not to prosecute" will result from an "unwillingness" to prosecute, or "to bring the person concerned to justice", because the State has decided to grant amnesty instead of prosecuting!' Footnote omitted]; N Roht-Arriaza, (n 137) 79 ['Unwillingness may be shown where there is an "unjustified delay" or proceedings are "not conducted independently or impartially, and in a manner inconsistent with an intent to bring the person concerned to justice". This clearly suggests that criminal justice is the goal of investigation.']. Also note that the criminal law connotation of the phrase 'to bring someone to justice' is evidenced by the jurisprudence by various human rights bodies on the duty to prosecute (see *23–24*) and the 'right to justice' which emanates from that jurisprudence. In the words of Mr Joinet, this right to *justice* [sic] 'entails obligations for the State: *to investigate violations, to prosecute the perpetrators and, if their guilt is established, to punish them*. Although the decision to prosecute is initially a State responsibility, supplementary procedural rules should allow victims to be admitted as civil plaintiffs in criminal proceedings or, if the public authorities fail to do so, to institute proceedings themselves.' Question of the impunity of perpetrators of human rights violations (civil and political), revised final report prepared by Mr Joinet pursuant to Sub-Commission decision 1996/119 (2 October 1997) UN Doc E/CN.4/Sub.2/1997/20/Rev.1 [27], emphasis added. See also, slightly more cautiously, M Scharf (n 137) 525 ['[…] subsection 2 of [Article 17] suggests that the standard for determining that an investigation is not genuine is whether the proceedings are "inconsistent with an intent to bring the person concerned to justice"—a phrase which might be interpreted as requiring criminal proceedings.' Footnote omitted]. For a contrary argument, see D Robinson (n 137) 500–501.

process would not bar the Court from declaring a case admissible. In addition, Article 20 (3) refers to persons being '*tried*' with respect to conduct amounting to ICC crimes. The ordinary meaning of '*trying*' someone is to subject him or her to criminal proceedings.[178]

Furthermore, the reference to another 'court', by which the person concerned has been tried for conduct amounting to ICC crimes, would exclude from the reach of the *ne bis in idem* principle as a bar to a subsequent trial all those institutions that cannot be qualified as a 'court'. In other words, although civil proceedings or a court-based decision to exclude a person from refugee status may very well qualify as proceedings in a 'court', a truth commission process would meet with the opposite assumption.[179] This room resulting from the word 'court' in Article 20 (3) does not alter the conclusion, however, that the words 'criminal responsibility' and 'intent to bring the person concerned to justice' foreclose court-based non-criminal proceedings to constitute a bar to admissibility.

5. Addressees of the Obligation to Investigate and Prosecute

In addition to the hitherto examined issues, the question as to whom the obligation to investigate and prosecute is addressed arises. It is clear from the foregoing analysis that, to the extent that preambular paragraph 6, together with Article 17, is constitutive rather than declaratory of an obligation to investigate and prosecute, such an obligation can only be binding on State *Parties*.[180] Which State Parties,

---

[178] The New Collins Dictionary and Thesaurus (Collins, London, Glaggow 1987) ['to hear evidence in order to determine the guilt or innocence of an accused'].

[179] M Scharf (n 137) 525 ['[. . .] the provision speaks of trial by "another court", and a truth commission is not a court; second, as with Article 17, Article 20 is not applicable to proceedings "inconsistent with an intent to bring the person concerned to justice" '. Footnote omitted]; J Dugard (n 137) 702 ['This argument [that an amnesty granted after an investigation by a quasi-judicial body such as truth commission qualifies as a prior conviction for the purposes of Article 20] will, however, be difficult to sustain in the light of Article 20 (3)'s requirement that the accused should have been "tried by another court" and in a manner "consistent with an intent to bring the person concerned to justice".']; C van den Wyngaert and T Ongena (n 137) 727 ['[I]t is unlikely that decisions rendered by [truth and reconciliation commissions] will qualify as judgments vis-à-vis the ICC: a "trial" by a truth and reconciliation commission can hardly be seen as a "trial" in the sense of Article 20 of the Rome Statute. The conclusion therefore is that the ICC remains free to try persons who have been amnestied, also if such an amnesty results from a TRC process.']. Whether that assumption can be rebutted essentially depends on the question of what constitutes a 'court' and the individual features of a truth commission process: see A Schlunck, *Amnesty versus Accountability— Third Party Intervention Dealing with Gross Human Rights Violations in Internal and International Conflicts* (Bochumer Schriften zur Friedenssicherung und zum Humanitären Völkerrecht, Band 38, Berlin Verlag 2000) 259 [noting that truth commissions, such as the South African Truth and Reconciliation Commission, may feature a number of court-like parameters, such as rules of procedure, public hearings, questioning of witnesses, the power to subpoena alleged offenders, and the power to take a binding decision, which make them part of a national legal system].

[180] Cf *251–253*. As we have noted, the fact that third States do not incur any obligations under the rules on complementarity does not mean that they may not incur any rights, including to invoke complementarity in the course of the procedures under Articles 18 and 19: see pages 169, 183.

however, are the addressees of the obligation to prosecute? Is such an obligation limited to territorial States,[181] or does it also apply to States of (active and/or passive) nationality,[182] or, indeed, does it extend to States that would have to base the exercise of their criminal jurisdiction on the principle of universality?[183]

These questions cannot be answered easily by reference to paragraph 6 of the Preamble, which only globally refers to the duty 'of every State to exercise its criminal jurisdiction'. However, as argued previously, the contours of that duty can be determined with greater specificity by referring to the provisions on complementarity and answering the question as to whether, and under what conditions, non-investigation or non-prosecution entail that a case is admissible.[184] When adopting such an approach vis-à-vis the matter here under consideration, the relevant wording of the provisions on complementarity suggests that the formulation '*its jurisdiction*' in paragraph 6 of the Preamble is to be understood to refer to the jurisdiction that a given State has established.

Article 17 refers to the 'State which has jurisdiction over [a case]'[185] as the object of determining whether the complementarity requirements of willingness and ability are met. We have earlier clarified that this phrase needs to be understood as referring to States that have established domestic jurisdiction over acts that constitute ICC crimes, which is lawful under international law.[186] According to the procedure under Article 18, State Parties and States which, taking into account the information available, would normally exercise jurisdiction over the

---

[181] In this vein, C Kress (n 74) 163 [customary duty to prosecute crimes under international law of the territorial State has now crystallized]; G Werle, *Völkerstrafrecht* (Mohr Siebeck Publ, Tübingen 2003) 189, [188] [Preamble merely reaffirms duty to prosecute crimes committed on the territory of a State].

[182] In this vein, P Benvenuti, 'Complementarity of the International Criminal Court to national criminal jurisdictions' in F Lattanzi and W Schabas (eds), *Essays on the Rome Statute of the International Criminal Court* (vol 1 Ripa Fagnano Alto, Editrice il Sirente 1999) 22 ['[The duty to exercise jurisdiction] is related to the international responsibility that each State has towards all other States in assuring fundamental values of international concern when it manages its "territorial" or "personal" sovereignty (ie, the duty of States comes from the presence of a territorial link with the crime of a personal link with the wrongdoer).']; T van Boven (n 70) 68. Also compare the 2003 'Interim Report of the Special Rapporteur on the situation of human rights in the Democratic Republic of the Congo' (24 October 2003) UN Doc A/58/534 [55] ['under international customary law, the Democratic Republic of the Congo has an obligation to deliver up to justice the perpetrators of genocide, crimes against humanity and war crimes, at least where those crimes were committed on national territory by Congolese citizens. Since July 2002, when the Rome Statute of the International Criminal Court came into force, this has become a treaty obligation for the Democratic Republic of the Congo.'].

[183] In this vein, L Condorelli, 'La Cour pénale internationale: un pas géant (pourvu qu'il soit accompli...)' (1999) 103 RGDIP 19–20; O Triffterer, 'Legal and Political Implications of Domestic Ratification and Implementation Processes' in C Kress and F Lattanzi (eds), *The Rome Statute and Domestic Legal Orders, vol 1—General Aspects and Constitutional Issues* (Nomos and Ripa di Fagnano Alto: Sirente, Baden Baden 2000) 1–28, 18–19. See also Belgium, Tribunal of First Instance Brussels (*Kamer van Inbeschuldigingstelling*) (n 3); note that the statement that the Rome Statute imposes 'obligations of a jurisdictional character' was made in the specific context of extraterritorial crimes. Also cf A Eser and H Kreicker (n 80) 442–443.

[184] Cf *250–251*.   [185] Cf Rome Statute (n 8) Article 17 (1)(a) and (b).
[186] Cf *112–113*.

crimes concerned[187] are to be notified. All such States may request a deferral provided that they inform the Court that they are investigating or have investigated '[their] nationals or others within [their] jurisdiction with respect to criminal acts which may constitute [ICC crimes]'.[188] Furthermore, challenges to admissibility in accordance with Article 19 may be made by any State 'which has jurisdiction over a case, on the ground that it is investigating or prosecuting the case or has investigated or prosecuted',[189] as well as the territorial State and the State of active nationality.[190] In fact, Article 19 thereby epitomizes that, contrary to what has at times been suggested,[191] the preconditions to the exercise of jurisdiction in Article 12 (2)(a) and (b)—ie the condition that, in case of a State deferral or a *proprio motu* investigation of the Prosecutor, the territorial State or the State of active nationality must be Parties to the Statute—do not limit the jurisdictional grounds for investigating and prosecuting ICC crimes domestically to territoriality and active nationality. The reference to a State 'which has jurisdiction over a case, on the ground that it is investigating or prosecuting the case or has investigated or prosecuted' in Article 19 (2)(b) would be redundant, if only territorial States and States of active nationality could challenge admissibility, because they are expressly mentioned in Article 19 (2)(c). The contrary position that States cannot go beyond territoriality and active nationality thus seems to obscure the distinction between the preconditions to the exercise of jurisdiction *by the Court*, on the one hand, and the jurisdictional bases available to *States,* on the other hand. These preconditions to the exercise of jurisdiction reaffirm the commitment of States Parties to ensure accountability for crimes committed on their territory or by their nationals.[192] Yet, they do not say anything about the question as to whether that accountability has to be effectuated *by* the territorial State or State

---

187   Rome Statute (n 8) Article 18 (1).
188   Cf Rome Statute (n 8) Article 18 (2). For discussion, see *168–170, 175–176.*
189   Rome Statute (n 8) Article 19 (2)(b).
190   Rome Statute (n 8) Article 19 (2)(c) in conjunction with Article 12.
191   Ireland, An Bille Um An gcu' Irt Choiriu' Il Idirna' Isiu' Nta 2003—International Criminal Court Bill 2003—Explanatory and Financial Memorandum, 6 [noting in relation to the envisaged jurisdiction of the Irish court in relation to ICC crimes under Section 12 of the Bill that: '*Subsection (1)* provides for territorial and personal jurisdiction *as required by Article 12 of the Statute*—this means taking jurisdiction for crimes committed on the territory of the State, or by a national of the State outside the State.' Emphasis added]. See also C Tomuschat (n 16) 339, who nevertheless acknowledges that '[i]t may be possible to view universal jurisdiction as implicitly approved by the Rome Statute inasmuch as national tribunals and the Court are supposed to work in close co-operation in accordance with the principle of complementarity': ibid 338.
192   Cf C Stahn, 'Complementarity, Amnesties and Alternative Forms of Justice: Some Interpretative Guidelines for the International Criminal Court' (2005) 3 JICJ 705–706 ['The decision to join the ICC system marks a special commitment to accountability. By ratifying the Statute, a state acknowledges that two types of crimes within the jurisdiction of the Court shall be investigated or prosecuted: crimes committed by its nationals and crimes committed on its territory. The state of the nationality of the accused accepts that crimes committed by its citizens may be subject to investigation or prosecution by the Court, irrespective of where they have been committed. Moreover, victims of crimes situated in the territory of a State Party may be said acquire a right to investigation or prosecution by the accession of the territorial state into the ICC system, which becomes part of an *acquis* of the people [. . .]'].

of active nationality. Nothing would have precluded the drafters of the Statute to endow the ICC with narrower or wider preconditions to the exercise of its jurisdiction, as was in fact suggested in Rome. A far-reaching German proposal on the jurisdiction of the ICC, which was predicated on the assumption that States possessed universal jurisdiction and that the Court should consequently be granted jurisdiction co-extensive to that of States,[193] was rejected in Rome *not* because the concept of universal jurisdiction for core crimes was unanimously rejected. In fact, several delegations expressed support for the concept of universal jurisdiction of national courts over ICC crimes.[194] The contrary statements of the US delegation during the Rome Conference that '[t]he principle of universal jurisdiction was not accepted in the practice of most Governments', and of the Israeli delegation that '[t]he universal nature of a crime did not give a particular body universal jurisdiction'[195] are the only exceptions from which opposition to the concept can be inferred. The sweeping statement of the US is strikingly at odds with the pre-existing jurisdictional regimes vis-à-vis some of the core crimes, most notably a number of treaty-based war crimes which attracted universal jurisdiction in the form of *aut dedere aut judicare*.[196] The fact that the German proposal did not succeed in Rome seems to be attributable first and foremost to the objections of some delegations to the jurisdiction of the ICC over nationals of non-State Parties, which, in the view of these delegations, would have been incompatible with the *pacta tertiis* rule.[197] The idea of an ICC with universal jurisdiction was abandoned to overcome these objections and to reach a compromise,[198] but that compromise did not affect the possibility for States to assert universal jurisdiction over ICC crimes. States can decide to do jointly through an international criminal court or tribunal what each of them may do singly,[199] but the fact that they made the political choice to do less jointly does not mean that they have limited what they may do singly.[200] Indeed, several States Parties have understood the

---

[193] UN Doc A/AC.249/1998/DP.2 (1998).

[194] United Nations Diplomatic Conference of Plenipotentiaries on the Establishment of an International Criminal Court (Rome, 15 July–17 July 1998) GAOR Volume II—Summary records of the plenary meetings and of meetings of the Committee of the Whole, UN Doc A/CONF 183/13 (Vol. II) 2002, 296 at 23 (Trinidad and Tobago), 298 at 60 (Sierra Leone), 299 at 87 (The Netherlands), 302 at 131 (Guinea), at 138 (Malta) and at 143 (Romania), 303 at 153 (Mali), at 175 (Tanzania), 307 at 36 (Burundi), 309 at 79 (Cameroon), 311 at 110 (Djibouti), 315 at 16 (Congo), 330 at 39 (Belgium).

[195] Ibid, 297 at 42 and 310 at 92.   [196] Cf *10–13*.

[197] Cf statements of the US delegation, ibid 297 at 42.

[198] See ibid 300 at 92 (Liechtenstein), 303 at 164 (Republic of Korea) and at 175 (Tanzania), 309 at 79 (Cameroon), 330 at 39 (Belgium).

[199] Cf Judgment of the International Military Tribunal for the Trial of German Major War Criminals, Nuremberg, 30 September and 1 October 1946, available at <http://www.yale.eds/lawweb/avalon/int/proc/judlawch.htm>; D Akande, 'The Jurisdiction of the International Criminal Court over Nationals of Non-Parties: Legal Basis and Limits' (2003) 1 JICJ 618–650, 621–634.

[200] Cf also Rome Statute (n 8) Article 10 (n 31). See also W Schabas (n 149) 67–68 [jurisdiction of the Court narrower than jurisdiction that States are entitled to exercise with respect to the same

system for suppressing ICC crimes established by the Rome Statute as allowing for, or indeed demanding, the establishment of universal jurisdiction in their
ICC implementing legislations in various forms.[201]

One can therefore deduce from the provisions on complementarity that several States are entitled to partake in the procedure on admissibility and invoke
Article 17 or 20 (3) in the course of the proceedings before the ICC. Conversely,
non-investigation or non-prosecution by *all* such States entail that a case is admissible. The central role assigned to States in the suppression of ICC crimes that the
provisions on complementarity encapsulate, is not limited to territorial States,
but extends to States, which may invoke other jurisdictional grounds, including universal jurisdiction.[202] If, for example, a State Party that had established
universal jurisdiction over ICC crimes[203] finds a person suspected of such crimes
on its territory and starts an investigation that coincides with ICC proceedings,
such a State Party could request a deferral and challenge the admissibility of the
resulting case. The same State Party would also be subject to the supervisory
mechanism established by the complementarity regime under the Statute. If its
proceedings did not meet the criteria of willingness and ability, the Court could

crimes]; O Bekou and R Cryer, 'The International Criminal Court and Universal Jurisdiction: A
Close Encounter?' (2007) 56 ICLQ 49–68, 50–51.

[201] The term 'universal jurisdiction' is employed here loosely as jurisdiction without any specific
link to the crime such as territoriality or active or passive nationality. For examples in ICC implementing legislations, see for instance Australia: Section 268.117 (1) of the International Criminal
Court (Consequential Amendments) Act 2002 No 42, 2002, entered into force 28 June 2002;
Belgium: Article 6 (1)(1*bis*) of the Law of 17 April 1878 (Code of Criminal Procedure), as amended
on 7 August 2003; Canada: Section 8 (b) of the Crimes Against Humanity and War Crimes Act,
assented to 29 June 2000; Costa Rica: Article 7 of the Penal Code as amended by Law 8272 of
2 May 2003, published and entered into force on 22 May 2002; Croatia: Article 10 (2) of the Law
on the Application of the Statute of the International Criminal Court, November 2003; Germany:
Section 1 of the Code of Crimes against International Law, 26 June 2002; Malta: Article 5 (1)(d) in
conjunction with Article 54A of the Penal Code as amended by Act XIV 2002.13 of 13 December
2003; The Netherlands: Section 2 (1)(a) of the Wet houdende regels met betrekking tot ernstige
schendingen van het internationaal humanitair recht (Wet internationale misdrijven/International
Crimes Act), 19 June 2003; New Zealand: Section 8 (1)(c) of the International Crimes and
International Criminal Court Act, commenced 1 October 2000; Portugal: Article 5 of the Lei
penal relativa às violações do Direito Internacional Humanitário, annexed to Lei 31/2004 Adapta a
Legislação Penal Portuguesa ao Estatuto do Tribunal Penal Internacional, tipificando as condutas
que constituem crimes de violação do Direito Internacional Humanitário, 22 July 2004; South
Africa: Section 4 (2)(b) and (c) of the Implementation of the Rome Statute of the International
Criminal Court Act, 2002, came into effect on 16 August 2002; Trinidad and Tobago: Section 8
of the International Criminal Court Act 2006 of 24 February 2006; United Kingdom: Sections
51 (2)(b) and 58 (2)(b) of the International Criminal Court Act 2001, entry into force 1 September
2001 and Section 1 (2)(b) of the International Criminal Court (Scotland) Act 2001, passed on 13
September 2001.

[202] Cf Informal Expert Paper for the ICC Office of the Prosecutor: The Principle of
Complementarity in Practice, (n 16) 24. See also the International Court of Justice *Case Concerning
the Arrest Warrant of 11 April 2000*, (Democratic Republic of the Congo v Belgium) Judgment
of 14 February 2002 [2002] ICJ Rep 3, Dissenting Opinion of Judge *ad Hoc* van den Wyngaert
[63–66].

[203] For the implementing practice of States Parties and Signatories of the ICC Statute in relation to universal jurisdiction over ICC crimes, see (n 201).

declare the case admissible (provided that no other State would investigate and prosecute and meet the same criteria).

The foregoing discussion suggests that the Rome Statute, with complementarity as one of its cornerstones, envisages a system of international criminal justice in which all States Parties contribute to the collective endeavour to suppress core crimes, which fall into the jurisdiction of the ICC as defined in the relevant provisions of Part 2 of the Statute.[204] In the words of the Preamble, all State Parties affirm 'that the most serious crimes of concern to the international community as a whole must not go unpunished and that their effective prosecution must be ensured by taking measures at the national level and by enhancing international cooperation'.[205] With a view to achieving the aim to put an end to impunity for the perpetrators of these crimes and thus to contribute to the prevention of such crimes',[206] State Parties and the ICC together constitute an enforcement community, consisting of the two layers of national criminal jurisdictions and the Court, the latter being competent in the case where the former prove unwilling or unable to investigate and prosecute.[207] The aim to ensure criminal accountability for ICC crimes would be seriously undermined, however, if all instances of non-investigation and non-prosecution of territorial States Parties were left to the ICC. Given that the Court will only be able to handle literally a handful of cases,[208] which involve those 'who bear the greatest responsibility',[209] many cases would go unaddressed in case the territorial State proved to be unwilling and/or unable to investigate and prosecute them. A purposive interpretation of the Statute, therefore, supports the view that all States Parties undertake to bring to justice perpetrators of ICC crimes.

The aforesaid considerations go far to understand the duty to exercise jurisdiction in the Preamble, if read in conjunction with the provisions on complementarity, to be *addressed to all States Parties which have established their jurisdiction over ICC crimes.*[210]

---

[204] O Triffterer, 'Kriminalpolitische und dogmatische Überlegungen zum Entwurf gleichlautender "Elements of Crimes" für alle Tatbestände des Völkermordes' in B Schünemann, *Festschrift für Claus Roxin zum 70. Geburtstag am 15. Mai 2001* (2001) 1415–1445, 1416, arguing that complementarity seeks to ensure comprehensive prosecution to achieve the ICC's aim to put an end to impunity.

[205] Rome Statute (n 8) Preamble, Paragraph 4.

[206] Rome Statute (n 8) Preamble, Paragraph 5.

[207] See generally W Burke-White, 'A Community of Courts: Toward a System of International Criminal Law Enforcement' (2002) 24 Mich JIL 1–101, especially 75–76, 91–92. Cf also *168–170.*

[208] This is illustrated by the assumptions of the Office of the Prosecutor, as reflected in the Draft Programme Budget 2005, Doc ICC/ASP/3/2 (26 July 2004), available at <http://www.icc-cpi.int/library/asp/ICC-ASP3-2_budget_English.pdf>. According to these assumptions, there will be three situations under investigation or in the trial phase in 2005, with none of these situations to yield more than two cases: see [161].

[209] Cf (n 130) and text in Ch IV and (nn 311–312) and text in Ch V.

[210] In a similar vein, see Rule 158, second sentence of the ICRC Study on Customary International Humanitarian Law: J M Henckaerts and L Doswald-Beck (n 49), Rule 158, 607 ['[States] must also investigate other war crimes over which they have jurisdiction and, if appropriate, prosecute the

It is nevertheless readily apparent that such an obligation may give rise to jurisdictional conflicts. Yet, the Statute does not provide clear suggestions as to how such conflicts have to be resolved, as it fails to establish a hierarchical order between different States which are under an obligation to investigate and prosecute.[211] Notwithstanding this ambiguity, a number of legal, conceptual, practical and policy considerations provoke the following tentative remarks.

5.1. Territorial States

The obligation to investigate and prosecute is *primarily* directed at the *territorial State*. Territoriality remains the undisputed principal basis for each State's right to regulate conduct or the consequences of events,[212] including (international) crimes.[213] It continues to be 'the point of departure in settling most questions that concern international relations'.[214]

---

suspects.']. Although not confined to an analysis of the Rome Statute, the Summary accompanying Rule 158 refers *inter alia* to the Preamble of the Rome Statute: see ibid 608. See also A Cassese, *International Criminal Law* (OUP, Oxford 2003) 302 ['mandatory for States to exercise jurisdiction on any of the grounds laid down in national law']. On the separate question as to whether and to what extent States Parties are entitled or obliged to establish jurisdiction over ICC crimes, see J K Kleffner, 'The Impact of Complementarity on National Implementation of Substantive International Criminal Law' (2003) 1 JICJ 86–113, 92–94.

[211] Cf also *175–176* and *189–190*. On the potentially negative impact of this ambiguity for compliance with the obligation to investigate and prosecute, see pages 329–330.

[212] See amongst many others, *Case of the SS 'Lotus' (France v Turkey)* PCIJ Rep Series A No 10, 20 (1927); R Jennings and A Watts (n 29) 458, [137]; V Epping and C Gloria, in K Ipsen (ed), *Völkerrecht* (5th edn CH Beck, Munich 2004) 310–311.

[213] A Cassese (n 210) 278 ['The basic principle is that a crime committed in a State's territory is justiciable in that State.']; A Yokaris, 'Les Critères de Compétence des Juridictions Nationales' in H Ascensio, E Decaux and A Pellet (eds), *Droit International Pénal* (Éditions Pedone, Paris 2000) 897–904, 898 at (9); B Swart, La place des critères traditionnels de compétence dans la pursuite des crimes internationaux', in A Cassese, M Delmas Marty, *Juridictions nationales et crimes internationaux* (Presses Universitaires de France, Paris 2002) 567–589, 570, 571–573; H van der Wilt (n 80) 325; Inter-American Commission on Human Rights, Resolution No 1/03 on Trial for International Crimes ['In carrying out this duty, states should consider that even when international crimes are so serious that they affect the entire international community, they primarily have an impact on the state in whose jurisdiction they occur, and especially on the people living in that state. Consequently, the principle of territoriality must prevail in the case of a jurisdictional conflict, provided that there are adequate, effective remedies in that state to prosecute such crimes and guarantee the application of rules of due process for the alleged perpetrators, and that there is an effective will to bring them to justice.'] and at 5 ['the principle of territoriality should prevail over that of nationality in the event that the state where the international crimes occurred wishes to bring them to justice, and that it offers due guarantees of a fair trial to the alleged perpetrators.']. See also Princeton Project on Universal Jurisdiction, The Princeton Principles on Universal Jurisdiction (2001) available at <http://www.law.depaul.edu/centers_institutes/ihrli/downloads/Princeton%20Principles.pdf> 53, Commentary to Principle 8 [judge of the territorial State considered 'natural judge']. The Princeton Principles, while not legally binding, are a restatement of the law on universal jurisdiction by leading scholars, jurists and legal experts from around the world.

[214] *Islands of Palmas Case (Spain v The Netherlands)* (1928) II RIAA 829, 838.

In a similar vein, the territorial State is primarily charged with ensuring compliance with those international legal rules that govern acts occurring on its territory.[215] The acts of organs which are concerned with the application and enforcement of criminal law are, as a rule, territorially limited, to the exclusion of organs of other States. Any extra-territorial competence of such foreign State organs (eg to exercise criminal jurisdiction in relation to crimes committed by or against its nationals or crimes which attract universal jurisdiction, or to investigate crimes committed abroad directly on foreign territory with the agreement of the territorial State) are exceptions to the generally accepted rule of territoriality.[216] Our analysis has to proceed from the same premise and, therefore, takes as a starting point that the obligation to investigate and prosecute is primarily addressed to the State Party on whose territory ICC crimes have been committed (the territorial State).

States Parties' obligation to investigate and prosecute acts of genocide, crimes against humanity and war crimes committed on their territory finds further support in the jurisdictional regime of the Rome Statute: by including as one of the preconditions to the exercise of jurisdiction of the ICC that such crimes must have occurred on the territory of State Parties,[217] the latter reconfirm their commitment to ensuring accountability for crimes committed on their territory and, in case they prove unwilling or unable to effectuate that accountability, for the ICC to take their place.

An additional argument in favour of the view that the territorial State is the primary addressee of the obligation to investigate and prosecute ICC crimes derives from the intended function of criminal prosecutions of these crimes as contributing to the *transition* of the directly affected society towards a peaceful and democratic social order based on the rule of law.[218] Prosecuting ICC crimes in the State where they have occurred and the resulting proximity to the acts in question, the victims and perpetrators, as well as the affected society at large, bear the potential of contributing to the intended process of catharsis more effectively than proceedings abroad. In a similar vein, the deterrent effect of criminal proceedings may be strengthened. Furthermore, on a *practical level*, proceedings in the territorial State generally bear the advantage of easier access to witnesses, crime scenes and evidence, as well as to the alleged perpetrator. Finally, in many cases, such proceedings may also serve to better protect the rights and interests

---

[215] As far as treaty obligations are concerned, Article 29 of the Vienna Convention on the Law of Treaties (n 12) encapsulates this idea in Article 29, providing that '[u]nless a different intention appears from the treaty or is otherwise established, a treaty is binding upon each party in respect of its entire territory'. As 'relevant rules of international law applicable in the relation between the parties', which, together with the context, have to be taken into account when interpreting the obligation to investigate and prosecute ICC crimes (cf Article 31 (3)(c) of the Vienna Convention on the Law of Treaties), obligations to investigate and prosecute human rights violations confirm the primarily territorial character of that obligation: see *25–26*.

[216] Cf *Case of the SS 'Lotus'* (n 212) at 18.   [217] Cf Rome Statute (n 8) Article 12 (2)(a).
[218] Cf pages 30–31.

of an accused, because s/he is familiar with the legal system and speaks the language, and, once arrested, it is easier for his or her family to visit.[219]

While the aforementioned arguments support regarding the territorial State as primary addressee of the obligation to investigate and prosecute ICC crimes, it is the same State that is regularly primarily—though not exclusively—affected by the obstacles to an effective investigation and prosecution of ICC crimes.[220] If any State can reasonably be expected to be prone to be unwilling or unable to effectuate the obligation to investigate and prosecute, it is the State on whose territory such system crimes are or have been committed. At the same time, the ICC's capacity to provide a safety net in these instances and to take the place of the unwilling or unable territorial State is limited.[221] The question therefore arises as to how the obligation to investigate and prosecute of *States Parties, which can base their jurisdiction on grounds other than territorial jurisdiction*, needs to be conceptualized in relation to that obligation of territorial States and in relation to the ICC. In the following section, we will consider a number of parameters that may assist in answering this question.

5.2. States Exercising Extraterritorial Jurisdiction

A first parameter in conceptualizing the relationship between the obligation of territorial State Parties and those exercising extraterritorial jurisdiction is the *nexus* between the ICC crime in question and the State Party concerned. Although a generally accepted, formal hierarchy of jurisdictional claims in criminal matters is absent,[222] the State Party with a weaker nexus to the crime should give way to the exercise of jurisdiction by a State Party with a stronger nexus, provided that the latter is willing and able to investigate and prosecute.[223] This would mean that State Parties, which can base a jurisdictional claim on active or passive nationality, for instance, only exercise that jurisdiction when the territorial State proves unwilling or unable to investigate and prosecute the crime(s) in question. In so doing, the general idea underlying complementarity is transposed to the horizontal relationship between States and informs the allocation of competences between them.[224] Such a construction would serve to ensure accountability while taking due account of the legitimate interests of States with a more direct link to ICC crimes than others. In addition, *horizontal complementarity* also bears the potential of serving a purpose similar to its vertical counterpart embodied in the Rome Statute: it could create an incentive for the territorial State to investigate and prosecute ICC crimes with a view to foreclosing adjudication in another State.[225]

---

[219] On these advantages, see A Cassese (n 210) 278–279.
[220] Cf *Chapter II: National Suppression of Core Crimes, 3.2. Obstacles relating to Enforcement.*
[221] Cf (nn 208–209, and text.)   [222] See pages 175–176.
[223] W Burke-White (n 207) 86–91.
[224] For an example of horizontal complementarity in ICC implementing legislation, see Section 12 (2) of the Canadian Crimes Against Humanity and War Crimes Act, assented to 29 June 2000.
[225] Cf pages *220.*

The same idea of horizontal complementarity can be employed to ascertain the proper role of State Parties exercising *universal jurisdiction*, understood here generically to denote jurisdiction without any specific link to the crime, such as the place of the commission of the crime, the nationality of the offender or the victim, or the interest of the state exercising jurisdiction.[226] Accordingly, such States would provide a forum on the domestic level subsidiary to the jurisdiction of other States with a nexus to the crime, either by virtue of the *locus delicti commissi* or the nationality of the offender or the victim.[227] This idea of subsidiary universal jurisdiction is also borne out by the ICC implementing laws of some States Parties to the Rome Statute[228] and some domestic judgments.[229] In view

---

[226] Cf (n 213). For some general reflections on the relationship between complementarity and universal jurisdiction, see X Philippe, 'The Principles of Universal Jurisdiction and Complementarity: How do the Two Principles Intermesh?' (2006) 88 IRRC 375–398.

[227] J K Kleffner (n 210) 108–109; G De La Pradelle, 'La Compétence Universelle' in H Ascensio, E Decaux and A Pellet (eds) (n 213) 905–918, 905, at 2; S Ratner, 'Belgium's War Crimes Statute: A Postmortem' (2003) 97 AJIL 888–897, 895; International Court of Justice *Case Concerning the Arrest Warrant of 11 April 2000* (n 202) Joint Separate Opinion of Judges Higgins, Kooijmans and Buergenthal [59] [when exercising universal jurisdiction states have to offer to the national State of the prospective accused person the opportunity itself to act upon the charges concerned]; Report of the International Commission of Inquiry on Darfur to the United Nations Secretary-General Pursuant to Security Council Resolution 1564 of 18 September 2004, 25 January 2005 [614]. Cf also Principle 8 (b)–(e) of the Princeton Principles on Universal Jurisdiction (2001) (n 213); Institut de Droit International, Resolution of the Institut de Droit International on 'Universal criminal jurisdiction with regard to the crime of genocide, crimes against humanity and war crimes' adopted at the Session of Krakow—2005 (Seventeenth Session, Rapporteur: M Christian Tomuschat) at 3 (d) ['Any State having custody over an alleged offender, to the extent that it relies solely on universal jurisdiction, should carefully consider and, as appropriate, grant any extradition request addressed to it by a State having a significant link, such as primarily territoriality or nationality, with the crime, the offender, or the victim, provided such State is clearly able and willing to prosecute the alleged offender.']; C Kress, 'Universal Jurisdiction over International Crimes and the Institut de Droit International' (2006) 4 JICJ 579–581. The Rome Statute's provision on competing requests (Article 90) also seems to point in that direction, when it provides that '[t]he interests of the requesting State including, where relevant, whether the crime was committed in its territory and the nationality of the victims and of the person sought' be taken into account when determining whether to surrender the person to the Court or extradite the person to the requesting State if the requesting State is a State not Party to the Statute and the requested State is under an existing international obligation to extradite the person to the requesting State not Party to this Statute: cf Article 90 (6)(b).

[228] See eg Belgium: Article 10, 1°bis (4) and Article 12 bis 4° of the Law of 17 April 1878 (Code of Criminal Procedure), as amended on 7 August 2003; Croatia: Article 10 (2) of the Law on the Application of the Statute of the International Criminal Court, November 2003; Germany: Section 153 f (2) No. 4 of the Code of Criminal Procedure as amended by the Act to Introduce the Code of Crimes against International Law of 26 June 2002. On the practical application of the last-mentioned German provision in the context of a criminal complaint against then US Defense Secretary Donald Rumsfeld and some other high-ranking members of the US military and secret services in relation to crimes committed in the Iraqi Abu Ghraib prison in 2003 and 2004, see F Jessberger, 'Universality, Complementarity, and the Duty to Prosecute Crimes under International Law' in W Kaleck *et al* (eds), *International Prosecution of Human Rights Crimes* (Springer, Berlin 2007) 213–222.

[229] Cf Tribunal Supremo (Supreme Court) of Spain, Judgment on the Peruvian Genocide Case, Judgment No 712/2003 (20 May 2003), 42 ILM (2003), 1200–1206, 1205 [principle of 'necessity of jurisdiction', denoting that 'the necessity of judicial intervention pursuant to the principle of universal jurisdiction remains excluded when territorial jurisdiction is effectively prosecuting

of the fact that a great number of today's ICC crimes are committed *within* State boundaries, and in which the (unwilling and/or unable) territorial State coincides with the State of active and passive nationality, subsidiary universal jurisdiction retains a vital role in ensuring accountability.

However, the notion of subsidiary universal jurisdiction is subject to one important qualification. The coming into existence of the ICC has altered the situation which provided at least part of the conceptual foundation of universal jurisdiction. The latter aims at ensuring the enforcement of meta-national values by prosecuting perpetrators of international crimes in a venue without any nexus to the crime. As such, the exercise of universal jurisdiction is the example *par excellence* for domestic courts acting on behalf of the international community, which lacks any enforcement organs of its own.[230] Yet, since the entry into force of the Rome Statute, States have for the first time established a permanent enforcement organ for (some of) the crimes for which universal jurisdiction had initially been developed. An argument can therefore be made that the ICC, rather than national courts of third States, would be the proper organ to act on behalf of the international community. The Court would probably do so with greater authority than national courts, and may circumvent some of the problems which have so far hampered the exercise of universal jurisdiction.[231] Furthermore, the Court

the crime of universal character in its own country']. This decision conflicts with the Tribunal Supremo's earlier Judgment on the Guatemalan Genocide Case of 25 February 2003, 42 ILM 686–712, 695–696 [application of the subsidiarity principle erroneous, since it was not found in the 1948 Genocide Convention]; see H Ascensio, 'Are Spanish Courts Backing down on Universal Jurisdiction? The Supreme Tribunal's Decision in *Guatemalan Generals*' (2003) 1 JICJ 690–702, 693–697. However, the latter decision was reversed by the Constitutional Tribunal in 2005, reinstating the initial complaint in its entirety and issuing a ringing endorsement of broad universal jurisdiction. It held that neither a nexus to Spain was required, nor that complainants are required to show that the territorial State was unwilling or unable to try the persons concerned, Constitutional Tribunal, Guatemalan Genocide Case, Second Chamber, Judgment of 26 September 2005, No STC/237/2005, summary and discussion by N Roht-Arriaza in (2006) 100 AJIL 207–213.

    230 Cf 26–28.
    231 A H J Swart, 'Universaliteit' [Universality] in T Spronken (ed), *Iets Bijzonders—Liber amicorum aangeboden aan Mischa Wladimiroff ter gelegenheid van zijn 30-jarig jubileum als advocaat* (Sdu Publ, The Hague 2002) 243–262, 254–257; G Bottini, 'Universal Jurisdiction After the Creation of the International Criminal Court' (2004) 36 NYU J Intl L & Pol 503–562, 544–560; G Abi-Saab, 'The Proper Role of Universal Jurisdiction' (2003) 1 JICJ 596–602, 601–602. Cf also Paper on some policy issues before the Office of the Prosecutor (n 70) 5 [Court may have developed superior evidence and expertise relating to a situation, making the Court the more effective forum]. See also *The Special Prosecutor v Col Mengistu Hailemariam and 173 Others* [unreported] Federal High Court, Criminal File No 1/87, Decision of Meskerem 29, 1988 E.C. (9 October 1995 G.C.) ILDC 555 (ET 1995), Comment 2 [principle of complementarity that allows *an international criminal tribunal or a domestic court having universal jurisdiction* to exercise only subsidiary jurisdiction is widely accepted in international law]; Ruling of the National Audience on Jurisdiction of Spanish Justice to Pursue Crimes of Genocide in Chile, Madrid, 5 October 1998, available at <http://www.derechos.org/nizkor/chile/juicio/audi.html>, Section Two [jurisdiction of Spanish courts over crimes of genocide allegedly committed in Chile: 'a State should abstain from exercising jurisdiction over facts giving rise to genocide which have been judged by the courts of the country in which they occur or by an international criminal court.']. For a discussion of this decision and

has the explicit competence to determine whether States are unwilling or unable to exercise their jurisdiction, whereas such a determination by one State vis-à-vis another State is open to the objection that it violates the maxim of *par in parem imperium non habet*.[232]

And yet, this conceptually attractive, and practically sound, approach to rely on the ICC instead of domestic courts exercising universal jurisdiction has its limits. An exclusive reliance on the Court would be likely to result in significant gaps through which perpetrators could escape justice. This may be the case, for instance, if the ICC does not prosecute ICC crimes, either because they do not meet the gravity-threshold[233] or because cases are so numerous that the ICC cannot handle them all,[234] while States with a stronger nexus to the crime are unwilling or unable to do so.[235] Subsidiary universal jurisdiction may still have a role to play in these scenarios.[236] In fact, in such a scenario, the ICC Statute provides for some avenues which, albeit limited, can be used to mitigate against the current

other jurisprudence until December 2000, see M Cottier, 'What relationship between the exercise of Universal and Territorial Jurisdiction' in H Fischer, C Kress and S R Lüder (eds), *International and national prosecution of crimes under international law: current developments* (Spitz, Berlin 2001) 843–857.

[232] This was one of the considerations which led the Spanish Constitutional Tribunal to reject the doctrine of subsidiary universal jurisdiction in its 2005 judgment in the Guatemalan Genocide Case: N Roht-Arriaza (n 229) 208–209. The same argument was used by the Guatemalan Constitutional Court in its decision revoking the arrest of defendants Angel Anibal Guevara and Pedro Arredondo, which had been issued by Spanish courts as a result of the aforementioned judgment of the Spanish Constitutional Tribunal. See Guatemalan Constitutional Court, Judgment of 14 December 2007 (English summary on file with author).

[233] Cf *Chapter IV: Complementarity as a Legal Principle and as Criteria for Admissibility, 3.4. Insufficient gravity: Article 17 (1)(d)*. On that aspect, see O Triffterer (n 183) 17.

[234] An example could be the situation of a collapsed State in which crimes have been committed on a massive scale and perpetrators have fled to neighbouring states in significant numbers. Note that the Prosecutor has a limited discretion to select certain cases for investigation, namely those in which he or she considers it to serve the interests of justice: cf Rome Statute (n 8) Article 53 (1)(c). On that prosecutorial discretion of the ICC prosecutor, see further *290–291*.

[235] Inability could result, for example, from the fact that the State with a stronger nexus cannot obtain the accused because the custodial State, which could exercise universal jurisdiction, refuses to extradite the accused to the State with a stronger nexus because a conviction there may lead to the imposition of the death penalty.

[236] O Triffterer (n 204). See also the Dissenting Opinion of Judge van den Wyngaert in *Case Concerning the Arrest Warrant of 11 April 2000* (n 202) [63–66]. For ICC implementing legislation providing for such a form of subsidiary universal jurisdictional, which takes account of the possibility that proceedings in courts of a State with a stronger nexus *or* before the ICC, may be preferable to the exercise of universal jurisdiction: see Belgium: Article 10, 1°bis (4) and Article 12 bis 4° of the Law of 17 April 1878 (Code of Criminal Procedure), as amended on 7 August 2003; Croatia: Article 10 (2) of the Law on the Application of the Statute of the International Criminal Court, November 2003; Germany: Section 153 f (2) No 4 of the Code of Criminal Procedure as amended by the Act to Introduce the Code of Crimes Against International Law of 26 June 2002, see also Section 28 of the German Law on Cooperation with the International Criminal Court [*Gesetz über die Zusammenarbeit mit dem Internationalen Strafgerichtshof*], providing for the modalities of the transfer of German ICC crimes proceedings to the ICC. In a similar vein, see also F Razesberger (n 16) 38; Institut de Droit International (n 227) at 3 (c) ['Any State having custody over an alleged offender should, before commencing a trial on the basis of universal jurisdiction, ask the State where the crime was committed or the State of nationality of the person concerned whether it is

challenges to the effectiveness of investigations and prosecutions on the basis of universal jurisdiction by allowing the Court to render assistance to a State Party conducting an investigation.[237] The ICC can be expected to develop a high degree of expertise for investigating crimes within its jurisdiction and will have resources at its disposal that are specifically targeted to do so. Its ability to rely on cooperative legislation adopted in accordance with Article 88 of the Statute could thus be used to give teeth to the aim of letting as few perpetrators as possible go unpunished, including using subsidiary universal jurisdiction to that effect.[238]

In sum, States would exercise universal jurisdiction, subject to the conditions that (a) States with a stronger nexus are unable or unwilling to investigate or prosecute (horizontal complementarity/subsidiary universal jurisdiction) and (b) the ICC does not exercise its jurisdiction (reversed vertical complementarity). That would assure that gaps in the enforcement regime are closed without overburdening third States with cases which are adjudicated more effectively in other fora, including the ICC.[239]

Second, considerations of *State responsibility* for ICC crimes may also enter the equation as parameters that may serve to conceptualize the relationship between States Parties *inter se* when fulfilling their obligation to investigate and prosecute these crimes. ICC crimes are breaches of international law which are often attributable to a State, for instance because they were committed by State organs or by persons who are in fact acting on the instructions of, or under the direction or control of, a State.[240] As such, they engage the international responsibility of the State to which such breaches can be attributed.[241]

The international responsibility of that State for the initial crime is closely related to the remedy of prosecuting that crime. For, the investigation of such crimes and the prosecution of alleged perpetrators can be seen as a form of reparation for the internationally wrongful act, which the commission of an ICC crime involves. More in particular, investigation and prosecution is one modality constituting satisfaction for the injury caused by an ICC crime.[242] In other

---

prepared to prosecute that person, unless these States are manifestly unwilling or unable to do so. It shall also take into account the jurisdiction of international criminal courts.'].

[237] Cf especially Rome Statute (n 8) Article 93 (10)(a). See also page 233.

[238] See also the Paper on some policy issues before the Office of the Prosecutor (n 70) 5 [noting that in certain situations, it might be possible and advisable to assist a State genuinely willing to investigate and prosecute by providing it with the information gathered by the Office of the Prosecutor].

[239] J K Kleffner (n 210) 108–109.

[240] Cf Article 2 of the Articles on Responsibility of States for Internationally Wrongful Acts (2001) UNGA Resolution 56/83 of 12 December 2001, and corrected by document A/56/49 (Vol. I)/Corr.4. On rules of attribution, which are particularly relevant in the context of ICC crimes, see Articles 4–5, 8–11.

[241] See generally on the relationship between individual criminal responsibility and State responsibility, A Nollkaemper, 'Concurrence between individual responsibility and state responsibility in international law' (2003) 52 ICLQ 615–640.

[242] Cf Article 37 (2) of the Articles on Responsibility of States for Internationally Wrongful Acts (2001) (n 240). The Commentary to this provision expressly mentions 'penal action against

words, an obligation to investigate and prosecute incumbent upon States can be construed as a manifestation of the obligation to give satisfaction by the State which incurs international responsibility for the commission of an ICC crime.[243] All other things being equal, the exercise of jurisdiction by the willing and able State Party, which is under such an obligation, should take precedence when several States Parties can potentially investigate and prosecute an ICC crime.

A third parameter is the (willingness and ability to secure the) *presence of the defendant and availability of sufficient evidence*.[244] States in which a defendant is present or has already been apprehended and which have gathered sufficient evidence to start proceedings should, in principle, be given priority over those which have to initiate (often lengthy) extradition proceedings or mutual assistance processes. However, this parameter needs to be applied in conformity with the international legal obligations of the requested States. If, under a legal obligation to extradite the person and/or to render mutual assistance (for instance, under a bilateral or multilateral extradition treaty or treaty on mutual assistance in criminal matters), the requested State cannot invoke its willingness and ability to investigate and prosecute as a ground for non-compliance.

The *interests of victims* serve as a fourth parameter. If those who were victimized can easily access and participate in the investigation, prosecution and trial of the perpetrator in a given State, the exercise of jurisdiction by the latter should take precedence over proceedings elsewhere in which victims cannot take part.

Fifth, the *rights of the defendant* may serve as a parameter to conceptualize the relationship between States Parties. A trial in a legal system familiar to the defendant in a language which (s)he understands may simplify compliance with the right to a fair trial.[245] The expected length of the proceedings may also enter the equation. If two States Parties are willing and able to investigate and

---

the individuals whose conduct caused the internationally wrongful act' as a possible form of satisfaction: see J Crawford (n 69) 233 at (5). On the point that the internationally wrongful act need not have caused damage to another State, see ibid 84 at (9), 203 at (6).

[243] Cf M Bothe, 'War crimes in non-international armed conflicts' (1995) 24 Israel Yb HR 241–251, 248; A Nollkaemper (n 241) 636–638; A O'Shea (n 70) 209–213; B Swart, *De berechting van internationale misdrijven* (Gouda Quint, 1996) 17; H van der Wilt (n 80). As to the question as to whom satisfaction is owed, cf Article 33 (1) of the Articles on Responsibility of States for Internationally Wrongful Acts (2001) (n 240), which provides that: 'The obligations of the responsible State set out in [Part Two on the Content of the International Responsibility of a State] may be owed to another State, to several States, or to the international community as a whole, depending in particular on the character and content of the international obligation and on the circumstances of the breach.' Thus the commission of an ICC crime by a State organ of State Party to the ICC Statute A against a national of State Party to the ICC Statute B would give rise to an obligation to give satisfaction in the form of investigation and prosecution owed by A to B, while it is also owed concurrently to the community of States Parties, because the commission of an ICC crime affects them also. On invocation, see also Article 42 of the Articles on Responsibility of States for Internationally Wrongful Acts (2001) ibid.

[244] B Broomhall (n 151) 123–124; Cf also Principle 8 (h) of the Princeton Principles on Universal Jurisdiction (2001) (n 213).

[245] A Cassese (n 210) 278–279.

prosecute an ICC crime, but one of them faces a huge backlog of cases which is likely to result in lengthy pre-trial detention, the other State Party may be a more appropriate forum to effectuate the obligation to investigate and prosecute. Furthermore, certain international legal obligations also limit the possibility of extraditing a suspect to a State which has sufficient evidence, to the extent that complying with an extradition request would result in the requested State violating its human rights obligations.[246]

Finally, besides its implications for the rights of defendants, the consideration of the *available resources* of a State Party may also serve as an independent parameter.[247] It should not be expected of a State whose national legal system is already highly overburdened to also assume extraterritorial jurisdiction over resource-intensive proceedings vis-à-vis ICC crimes, if, all other things being equal, another State has more resources available to assume jurisdiction.

The aforementioned parameters should be understood as practical ways to identify the most suitable forum for prosecution in the light of the concrete circumstances of individual cases. It is not suggested that a hierarchy exists between them. In fact, there may be scenarios in which they may lead to conflicting results. A willing and able territorial State in Africa may request the extradition of a military commander suspected of an ICC crime, who is found in Europe, which could only base the exercise of its jurisdiction on the principle of universality while being legally barred from extraditing the person due to the possibility that the trial in the territorial State may result in the death penalty. At the same time, victims may have fled to a neighbouring African State, which is faced with resource-intensive trials because ICC crimes have been committed in the course of an internal armed conflict occurring on its own territory. This example demonstrates that the suggested parameters will not provide clear-cut answers in all imaginable scenarios. Their cumulative application may nevertheless help to produce reasonable outcomes in many instances and may assist in conceptualizing the relationship between States Parties *inter se,* as well as between States Parties and the ICC, with a view to achieving the overall aim of criminal accountability.

To sum up, if one were to attempt to translate the preceding considerations into an existing legal concept, which captures the obligation of States Parties to exercise extraterritorial jurisdiction, the maxim of *aut dedere aut prosequi* (either extradite or prosecute)[248] would probably come closest. Such States Parties must

---

[246] Cf for instance for States Parties to the European Convention on Human Rights, *Soering v United Kingdom,* (App no 14038/88) [1989] ECHR 14 (7 July 1989) [return of fugitive offender to face death penalty can involve a breach of Article 3 of the ECHR]. Similarly, the extradition of a suspect is barred where there are grounds to believe that the suspects may be subjected to torture or inhuman and degrading treatment under the 1984 UN Convention against Torture (n 14): cf Article 3 of the Convention.

[247] B Broomhall (n 151) 125.

[248] See generally, M C Bassiouni and E M Wise, *Aut dedere aut judicare: the duty to extradite or prosecute in international law* (Nijhoff Publ, Dordrecht 1995) 340.

either (1) extradite a suspect to another State or surrender him or her to the ICC (*dedere*), or (2) prosecute the suspect in their own courts (*prosequi*).

6. Legal Avenues for Non-Prosecution

Despite the obligation to investigate and prosecute ICC crimes outlined in the preceding section, complete investigation and prosecution on the domestic level, primarily to be effectuated by the territorial State, is likely to put the national authorities of the latter in a very difficult, if not practically impossible, position, at least when ICC crimes are committed on a massive scale.[249] Furthermore, given the nature of ICC crimes,[250] non-prosecution is likely to remain a political option on the table in transitional contexts, notwithstanding its *prima facie* incompatibility with the obligation emanating from the Statute.

That the occurrence of non-prosecution can reasonably be expected to persist also after the entry into force of the Rome Statute is already amply apparent from the first situations that the Court has been addressing. At the time of writing, substitutes for criminal prosecution have been contemplated in relation to the situation in the Democratic Republic of Congo,[251] an amnesty had been adopted in relation to crimes committed in Northern Uganda,[252] and the

---

[249] Two examples illustrate this point. First, Rwanda was faced with over 120 000 suspects after the 1994 genocide, and when it enacted its Organic Law on the Organization of Prosecutions for Offenses Constituting the Crime of Genocide or Crimes Against Humanity Committed Since 1 October 1990, Law No 8/96, Rwanda Official Gazette (30 August 1996), approximately 90 000 detainees were still being held in Rwandan prisons awaiting trial: see J Alvarez, 'Crimes of states/ Crimes of hate: lessons from Rwanda' (1999) 24 Yale JIL 365–483, 393. Even if one assumed the Rwandan judicial system to be generally willing and able (an assumption that would seem to be at least doubtful) and that the investigations of everyone of the suspects had revealed *prima facie* evidence, many of the numerous suspects could not be prosecuted without undue delay and thus in accordance with international human rights standards. The resulting backlog had led the Rwandan government to adopt the traditional *gacaca* system, with a view to complement the ordinary criminal justice system and ensure accountability of certain groups of defendants: see n 160). Second, the German judiciary remains faced with Nazi crimes to the present day, almost 60 years after the crimes had been committed, although considerable efforts were made to rebuild the German judicial system and the latter was and is assisted by courts of other States to bring the perpetrators to justice: cf pages 34–35. And yet, there is ample evidence that numerous of the perpetrators of Nazi crimes never faced or will face justice.

[250] See *43–45*.

[251] Cf Article 5 of the *Accord global et inclusif sur la transition en République Démocratique du Congo,* signed in Pretoria on 16 December 2002, <http://www.monuc.org/downloads/accord_de_ Pretoria.pdf>; Article 154 of the Transitional Constitution, adopted 1 April 2003, <http://www. monuc.org/downloads/constitution_transition.pdf>. Both provisions envisage the establishment of a truth and reconciliation commission. Note, however, that the Transitional Constitution has been abrogated by the Constitution of 30 May 2005, <http://www.monuc.org/downloads/consti-tution_RDC.pdf>: cf Article 228.

[252] See the 2000 Ugandan Amnesty Act available at <http://www.c-r.org/our-work/accord/ northern-uganda/documents/2000_Jan_The_Amnesty_Act.doc>. See further page 325. The 2000 Amnesty Act has subsequently been amended.

Security Council, when referring the situation in Sudan's Darfur region to the ICC, expressly encouraged the creation of institutions, such as truth and/or reconciliation commissions.[253]

As much as (complete) investigations and prosecutions may often be unattainable for national authorities of the territorial State, it is similarly unrealistic to expect third States and the ICC to completely fill the resulting void.[254] The system of international criminal justice established by the Rome Statute therefore provides ample room—as a matter of *fact* rather than *law*—*not* to investigate and prosecute ICC crimes domestically. States could do so without the Court's taking their place in bringing perpetrators of ICC crimes to justice.

However, the fact that such cases are beyond the reach of the ICC because of its limited capacity does not mean that States are absolved from the obligation to investigate and prosecute them. The *factual* limitations on the ability of the ICC to act as a vicarious forum for the enforcement of the prohibition of ICC crimes in cases where States are inactive, unwilling or unable to do so must not be misunderstood so as to be co-extensive to the obligation of States Parties to investigate and prosecute these crimes. Whether, and to what extent, *legal* avenues are available to reconcile that obligation with States Parties' abstaining from prosecuting is an entirely different question. In answering this question, we have to differentiate between three types of legal avenues. First, the Rome Statute itself contains rules, which stipulate that the Court can, or must, abstain from carrying out proceedings under certain conditions (6.1.). Second, a number of circumstances may preclude the wrongfulness of not investigating and prosecuting these crimes, which would otherwise not be in conformity with the obligation of States Parties (6.2.). Third, immunities under international law could potentially constitute a legal bar to domestic proceedings vis-à-vis ICC crimes (6.3.).

6.1. The Statute

As far as legal avenues under the Rome Statute are concerned, it is recalled that the notions of unwillingness and inability do not leave any room for the exercise of prosecutorial discretion based on policy grounds and for the substituting of criminal prosecutions with other measures—subject to the important qualification in respect to amnesties, pardons, paroles or the commutation of sentences in cases which have been duly conducted and which have led to the conviction of an accused. Three *other provisions of the Statute*, nevertheless, contain avenues which provide for the possibility of taking into account such prosecutorial discretion and substitutes.

---

[253] Cf UNSC Res 1593 (31 March 2005) UN Doc S/RES/1593 [5]. Note that the Security Council envisages such institutions 'to complement judicial processes'. Whether these institutions, if established, will be a substitute for criminal proceedings therefore remains to be seen.

[254] Cf (n 209) and text.

First, *Article 17 (1)(d)* provides that cases are inadmissible if they are *'not of suffi-cient gravity to justify further action by the Court'*.[255] The provision thereby appears to leave room for States to abstain from prosecuting such crimes without running the risk of cases being declared admissible.[256] Certain individuals, against whom a reasonable suspicion of having committed ICC crimes exists, may, therefore, never find themselves before the Court, because their acts are considered of insuf-ficient gravity. If a national prosecutor decided to exercise his or her prosecutorial discretion with regard to such persons and decided not to pursue such cases, they would remain inadmissible. The same would apply to cases of insufficient grav-ity covered by an amnesty or submitted to an alternative accountability process, such as a truth commission.[257]

Second, *Article 16* empowers the *Security Council* to *defer* an investigation or prosecution for a period of 12 months if it adopts a resolution under Chapter VII of the UN Charter to that effect.[258] Thus, if an investigation or prosecution which comes before the ICC in spite of the adoption of a substitute for criminal prosecution on the national level would, in the view of the Security Council, amount to a threat to the peace, the latter could bar the ICC from proceeding for a period of 12 months. A conceivable example would be where an amnesty was the only way out of (military and political) deadlock to allow for the conclusion of a peace agreement and a non-recognition of that amnesty by the ICC would in all likelihood entail a resumption of hostilities. The Security Council, in making use of its powers under Article 16, does nevertheless not operate in a legal vac-uum, but rather is constrained by a number of requirements:[259] an investigation or prosecution by the ICC in such cases must amount to a situation that fulfils the criteria in Article 39 of the UN Charter;[260] the deferral needs to be necessary to maintain or restore international peace and security;[261] and, in making the deferral, the Security Council must act 'in accordance with the Purposes and

[255] Note that cases of insufficient gravity nevertheless concern the broad categories of ICC crimes (genocide, crimes against humanity and war crimes), but that they fall outside the reach of complementarity: see *Chapter IV: Complementarity as a Legal Principle and as Criteria for Admissibility, 3.4. Insufficient gravity: Article 17 (1)(d)*.

[256] Cf W Schabas (n 149) 87.

[257] C Stahn (n 192) 710 ['The only escape clause for a perpetrator is the de minimis clause in Article 17(1)(d), which allows deference by the Court where "the case is not of sufficient gravity to justify further action by the Court." '].

[258] M Scharf (n 137) 523–524; J Dugard (n 137) 701, noting, however, that this is difficult to accept 'as such a deferral must be made in a resolution under Chapter VII and it is hard, if not impossible, to contemplate a situation in which refusal to recognize a national amnesty could con-stitute a threat to international peace'; N Roht-Arriaza (n 137) 80; D Robinson (n 137) 502–503; A O'Shea (n 70) 328; S Morel (n 149) 238–239.

[259] See generally on these requirements, E de Wet, *The Chapter VII Powers of the United Nations Security Council* (Hart Publishing, Oxford 2004).

[260] Article 39 of the UN Charter requires 'the existence of any threat to the peace, breach of the peace, or act of aggression' and refers to 'measures [...] to maintain or restore international peace and security'. See on this point, L Condorelli and S Villalpando, 'Referral and Deferral by the Security Council' in A Cassese, P Gaeta and J Jones (n 42) 627–655, 630–631.

[261] L Condorelli and S Villalpando, ibid 631–632.

Principles of the United Nations'.[262] A deferral in accordance with Article 16 can only be made or renewed as long as these conditions are fulfilled.[263] The (legal) use of the provision as a *permanent* solution to the problem of the existence of alternative responses, therefore, is doubtful at best.

Third, *Article 53* provides the Prosecutor with a certain degree of *prosecutorial discretion*. More specifically, when deciding whether to initiate an investigation, the Prosecutor may abstain from doing so when '[t]aking into account the gravity of the crime and the interests of victims, there are nonetheless substantial reasons to believe that an investigation would not serve the interests of justice.'[264] Similarly, the Prosecutor may decide that, upon investigation, there is not a sufficient basis for a prosecution because 'a prosecution is not in the interests of justice, taking into account all the circumstances, including the gravity of the crime, the interests of victims and the age or infirmity of the alleged perpetrator, and his or her role in the alleged crime.'[265] The discretion of the ICC Prosecutor is neither unfettered,[266] nor is a decision to abstain from initiating an investigation or from proceeding with a prosecution irreversible.[267] Nevertheless, both provisions create some leeway not to investigate and/or prosecute in disregard

---

[262] Cf Article 24 (2) of the 1945 Charter of the United Nations (adopted 26 June 1945, entered into force 24 October 1945). N Roht-Arriaza (n 137) 80 rightfully notes that the latter requirement may be more problematic, because the purposes and principles of the UN include respect for human rights, concluding that 'if pre-existing law [...] requires prosecution, it is not clear the Security Council can override that law through resolutions aimed at the ICC'. It should nevertheless be noted that there may be circumstances in which the two paradigms of maintaining or restoring international peace and security, on the one hand, and justice for international crimes, on the other hand, may be irreconcilable, eg in a situation where the granting of an amnesty is the *only* way to achieve peace. In these situations the Security Council may be faced with a hard choice and it would seem less than obvious that the choice would have to be for justice rather than peace.

[263] This assertion may be said to disregard political realities, especially the practice of using Article 16 powers for the purpose of shielding members of peacekeeping forces of non-State Parties, notably the US, from ICC jurisdiction; cf SC Resolution 1422. On the latter, see C Stahn, 'The Ambiguities of Security Council Resolution 1422 (2002)' (2003) 14 EJIL 85–104. Note that the Resolution was renewed once by UNSC Res 1487 (12 June 2003) UN Doc S/Res/1487.

[264] Rome Statute (n 8) Article 53 (1)(c). For an elaboration of these factors, see OTP Policy Paper on the Interests of Justice, September 2007, <http://www.icc-cpi.int/library/organs/otp/icc-otp-Interests Of Justice.pdf> 5–6.

[265] Rome Statute (n 8) Article 53 (2)(c). For an elaboration of these factors, see OTP Policy Paper on the Interests of Justice (n 264) 6–7.

[266] Rome Statute (n 8) Article 53 (3)(a) reads: 'At the request of the State making a referral under article 14 or the Security Council under article 13, paragraph (b), the Pre-Trial Chamber may review a decision of the Prosecutor under paragraph 1 or 2 not to proceed and may request the Prosecutor to reconsider that decision.' Subparagraph (b) of the same provision continues: 'In addition, the Pre-Trial Chamber may, on its own initiative, review a decision of the Prosecutor not to proceed if it is based solely on paragraph 1 (c) or 2 (c). In such a case, the decision of the Prosecutor shall be effective only if confirmed by the Pre-Trial Chamber.'

[267] Rome Statute (n 8) Article 53 (4) provides that '[t]he Prosecutor may, at any time, reconsider a decision whether to initiate an investigation or prosecution based on new facts or information'. Thus, if the Prosecutor decides that a given investigation or prosecution is not in the interest of justice because an alternative response can be presumed to fulfil certain minimum criteria of (non-criminal) accountability, but the actual operation of that alternative response turns out to be fundamentally flawed, it would seem that this provision grants the Prosecutor the possibility to

of a given substitute, such as an amnesty or truth commission process, or of the exercise of prosecutorial discretion on policy grounds on the domestic level if the ICC Prosecutor determines such an approach to (better) serve the interests of justice.[268] In developing a policy on the discretion granted under Article 53, the Office of the Prosecutor has emphasized that it will pursue its own judicial mandate independently and does not consider the concept of the interests of justice to 'embrace all issues related to peace and security'.[269] This suggests that the Office does not interpret 'the interests of justice' to be broad enough to determine in a general manner whether, in a given context, 'peace' should prevail over 'justice'. And yet, the exercise of prosecutorial discretion in accordance with Article 53 bears the potential of gradually crystallizing a coherent approach to the room left for alternative responses and for the exercise of prosecutorial discretion on the domestic level.[270]

The aforementioned provisions of the Statute provide legal avenues to accommodate non-prosecution on the domestic level in as much as these provisions remove cases from the reach of the ICC. They, therefore, provide States with some leeway to abstain from prosecuting ICC crimes. However, the fact alone that *the ICC* does not commence or proceed with proceedings vis-à-vis ICC crimes or that it abandons such proceedings by virtue of these provisions does not, in principle, provide *States* with a legal justification or excuse for non-performance of the obligation to prosecute ICC crimes. The application of the mentioned provisions may have the effect of preventing a State Party *to be found* in violation of its obligation to investigate and prosecute by virtue of a declaration of the ICC that that State is inactive, unwilling or unable. They are, however, not determinative of whether the State is in compliance with that obligation.[271]

---

submit relevant evidence to that effect and nevertheless request the opening of an investigation or prosecution.

[268] R J Goldstone and N Fritz, ' "In the Interests of Justice" and Independent Referral: The ICC's Prosecutor's Unprecedented Powers' (2000) 13 LJIL 655–667, 659–666; M Scharf (n 137) 524; N Roht-Arriaza (n 137) 81; J Dugard (n 137) 702; J Gavron (n 137) 110; D Robinson (n 137) 486–488; B Broomhall (n 151) 102; A O'Shea (n 70) 328; M H Arsanjani, 'Reflections on the Jurisdiction and Trigger-Mechanism of the International Criminal Court' in H von Hebel, J Lammers and J Schukking (eds), Reflections on the International Criminal Court—Essays in Honour of Adriaan Bos (T. M. C. Asser Press, The Hague 1999) 57–76, 75–76; T van Boven (n 70) 73–74; Informal Expert Paper for the ICC Office of the Prosecutor: The Principle of Complementarity in Practice (n 16) 22 [71]; S Morel (n 149) 260–269; F Razesberger (n 16) 175–179.

[269] OTP Policy Paper on the Interests of Justice (n 264) 8.

[270] For three propositions for interpreting the reference to 'interests of justice' in Article 53 with regard to alternative responses, see D Robinson (n 137) 488–498. For further interpretative guidelines for the ICC, see also C Stahn (n 192) 699–718; T van Boven (n 70) 74 [suggesting that the terms 'interests of justice' should 'be understood in the light of the last preambular paragraph of the ICC Statute wherein the resolve is expressed to guarantee lasting respect for and the enforcement of international justice'.]. See also OTP Policy Paper on the Interests of Justice (n 264) 7–9.

[271] For the distinction between legal justifications and excuses under the law of State responsibility (grounds precluding wrongfulness) and other arguments, which may have the effect of allowing a State to avoid responsibility, see J Crawford (n 69) 162 at (7). For the similarity between a finding of unwillingness and inability and a finding of State responsibility, see *318–321*.

Under Article 17 (1)(d), cases may be considered to be of insufficient gravity 'to justify further action by the Court', but they nevertheless amount to acts of genocide, crimes against humanity and war crimes—international crimes for which the Statute imposes the duty of States Parties to exercise their criminal jurisdiction. Furthermore, Article 16 limits the power of the Security Council to request *the Court* to defer an investigation or prosecution. Even if the Security Council were to adopt a broader resolution, which equally requested States to defer domestic investigations and prosecutions, such a resolution would have to satisfy the same criteria as the one addressed to the Court[272] and would therefore be equally unlikely to serve as a *permanent* bar to domestic investigations and prosecutions. Finally, it cannot readily be assumed that 'the interests of justice' which govern the ICC Prosecutor in the exercise of his (limited) discretion affects the obligation of State Parties to investigate and prosecute. The practice of the ICC in that regard may eventually provide some guidance for States as to the factual circumstances in which they can adopt substitutes of criminal prosecutions or exercise prosecutorial discretion. An elucidation of the factors to be considered when determining whether an investigation or prosecution is in the interests of justice will indicate to States as to when the gravity of crimes, interests of victims and circumstances of the accused are such that they can abstain from investigating and prosecuting without running the risk of cases being declared admissible before the Court. However, although there may be some overlap, the interpretation of these factors by the Court should not be understood to be identical to the factors to be considered by States when making the decision whether or not to exercise prosecutorial discretion. To say that the crime in question is not sufficiently grave for purposes of the ICC is not the same as saying that only they have reached a threshold of sufficient gravity for the purpose of domestic proceedings. The ICC, with its limited capacity, will necessarily have to be more selective in that regard than national criminal jurisdictions. The same applies to a consideration of the role of the person concerned in the alleged crime. Indeed, in the ultimate equation, a mechanical transposition of the criteria governing the exercise of prosecutorial discretion by the Prosecutor to national criminal jurisdictions would potentially severely curtail the reach of domestic suppression of ICC crimes. For, domestic proceedings—much as ICC proceedings—would become the exclusive province of only that handful of individuals who bear the greatest responsibility for crimes whose scale, nature, manner of commission and impact is such as to justify investigation and prosecution before the ICC. It is therefore submitted that one should not equate the (interpretation of the) criteria for the exercise of prosecutorial discretion of the ICC Prosecutor with those that should govern the decision of domestic authorities whether or not to abstain from investigating and prosecuting ICC crimes. More importantly still, and regardless of the foregoing distinction, it needs to be recalled that one has to distinguish the

---

[272] Cf (nn 260–263) and text.

room for manoeuvre available to domestic authorities created by the exercise of discretion by the ICC Prosecutor, from the question of (non-)compliance with the legal obligation to investigate and prosecute incumbent on States Parties to the Rome Statute.

In sum, neither the fact that crimes do not satisfy the gravity threshold under Article 17 (1)(d), nor a deferral of an ICC investigation of prosecution by the Security Council, nor the exercise of prosecutorial discretion in accordance with Article 53 constitute grounds *in international law* which can *justify* a failure on behalf of national criminal jurisdictions to investigate and prosecute ICC crimes. It is to these legal grounds that we now turn.

6.2. Circumstances Precluding Wrongfulness

As argued previously, the Statute imposes a legal obligation on all State Parties to prosecute ICC crimes, with territorial States being the primary addressees of that obligation. This obligation is owed to the community of State Parties. Non-prosecution, be it in the form of prosecutorial discretion on policy grounds, clemency measures or non-criminal accountability processes, is in breach of that obligation *erga omnes partes*.[273] Such an act (for instance in the form of the adoption of an amnesty law) or omission (for instance by judicial organs abstaining from initiating or completing criminal proceedings) is also attributable to such a State Party. For, it will be that State Party's (legislative, executive or judicial) organs, which act in defiance of the international obligation. In principle, non-prosecution therefore entails the international responsibility of State Parties.[274]

The question nevertheless arises as to whether, and to what extent, State Parties may raise certain circumstances which preclude the wrongfulness of non-prosecution. Since the Rome Statute does not make provision for such circumstances itself, reference must be made to the *lex generalis* on State responsibility.[275] For obligations other than those of a *jus cogens* character,[276] the general law of State

---

[273] It needs to be borne in mind that the occurrence of a breach of the obligation to investigate and prosecute depends on whether or not the intention or knowledge of relevant State organs, or some degree of fault, culpability, negligence or want of due diligence, is required. An answer to this question differs as regards the standards derived from unwillingness, which incorporates subjective elements ('purpose of shielding', 'intent to bring the person concerned to justice'), and inability, which establishes an objective standard requiring States to take all due care to prevent inability. See generally on the point that the question of intent, fault, etc depends on the primary obligation rather than the law of State responsibility, J Crawford (n 69) 81–82 at (3).

[274] Cf Article 2 in conjunction with Article 4 of the Articles on Responsibility of States for Internationally Wrongful Acts (2001) (n 240).

[275] Cf Article 55 of the Articles on Responsibility of States for Internationally Wrongful Acts, ibid.

[276] Cf Article 26 of the Articles on Responsibility of States for Internationally Wrongful Acts, ibid. The obligation to investigate and prosecute ICC crimes is *not* a rule of *jus cogens*, contrary to what is sometimes asserted: see eg International Court of Justice *Case Concerning the Arrest Warrant of 11 April 2000* (n 202) Dissenting Opinion of Judge Al-Khasawneh [7] ['The effective combating of grave crimes has arguably assumed a *jus cogens* character reflecting recognition by

responsibility contains a number of legal justifications and excuses, which, while not annulling or terminating the obligation, preclude the wrongfulness of conduct that would otherwise not be in conformity with the international obligations of the State concerned for as long as the circumstance persists.[277] In its work on the matter, the International Law Commission identified six such circumstances, which found their way into the Articles on Responsibility of States for Internationally Wrongful Acts adopted in 2001.[278] In addition, a number of possible justifications or excuses were not included in the ILC's Articles.[279]

Three circumstances deserve closer analysis as potentially precluding the wrongfulness of the failure to prosecute ICC crimes,[280] in particular when considering the scenario in which the primary addressee of the obligation to investigate and prosecute, ie the territorial State, fails to comply with that obligation.

the international community of the vital community interests and values it seeks to protect and enhance. Therefore when this hierarchically higher norm comes into conflict with the rules on immunity, it should prevail.']. See also in a similar vein, Inter-American Court of Human Rights, *La Cantuta v Peru* Merits, Judgment of 29 November 2006, Reparations and Costs, IACtHR Series C 162 (2006) [157] [prohibition against the forced disappearance of people and the corresponding duty to investigate and punish those responsible has become *jus cogens*]. However, a distinction has to be drawn between the *prohibitions* of ICC crimes, which may very well amount to rules of *jus cogens*, and the *obligation to investigate and prosecute* them. Such a duty is not automatically of the same normative status as the prohibition. In order to attain that status, it would have to undergo the same formative process as other peremptory norms and would thus have to be 'accepted and recognized by the international community of States as a whole as a norm from which no derogation is permitted and which can be modified only by a subsequent norm of general international law having the same character': cf Article 53 of the Vienna Convention on the Law of Treaties (n 12). In the light of the fact that the obligation to investigate and prosecute ICC crimes lacks even customary status and is a treaty obligation of States Parties (cf *251–253*), it cannot have attained that status.

[277] J Crawford (n 69) 160 at (2).

[278] Articles 20–25 of the Articles on Responsibility of States for Internationally Wrongful Acts (n 240). The six grounds are consent (Art 20), self-defence (21), countermeasures (22), *force majeure* (23), distress (24) and necessity (25).

[279] On these and the reasons for their not being included, see J Crawford (n 69) and ILC, 'International Law Commission Report of its 51st Session: Second report on State responsibility' (30 April 1999) UN Doc A/CN.4/498/Add.2 [304–334]. The latter document refers to the following such justifications or excuses: performance in conflict with a peremptory norm (*jus cogens*), '*exceptio inadimplenti non est adimplendum*' and the so-called 'clean hands' doctrine.

[280] While the responsibility of States does not depend on the invocation of that responsibility by another State or States (cf J Crawford (n 69) 254), conceivable scenarios in which such circumstances precluding wrongfulness may be invoked are: a case before the ICJ on diplomatic protection, in which one State Party argues a *déni de justice* to its national due to another State Party's failure to prosecute those responsible for an ICC crime committed against that national; a case between two States Parties which reaches the ICJ by virtue of the dispute settlement procedure envisaged in Article 119 (2) of the Statute; or proceedings in the course of which victims bring a case in a domestic court of the territorial State and request prosecution, arguing that prosecution is mandatory under the Statute. The nature of the obligation to prosecute as an obligation *erga omnes partes* suggests that it is not required that another State point to any specific damage it has suffered by reason of the non-compliance in order to engage the international responsibility of the non-compliant State. For a discussion of whether 'damage' or 'injury' is an integral part of State responsibility, see J Crawford, ibid 84, at (9), noting that 'whether such elements are required depends on the content of the primary obligation, and there is no general rule in this respect'.

These three circumstances are *force majeure* (6.2.1.) necessity (6.2.2.) and performance in conflict with a peremptory norm (*jus cogens*) (6.2.3.).

6.2.1. Force Majeure

Article 23 of the ILC's Articles on Responsibility of States for Internationally Wrongful Acts provides that the wrongfulness of an act of a State not in conformity with an international obligation of that State is precluded if the act is due to *force majeure*. The provision defines *force majeure* as 'the occurrence of an irresistible force or of an unforeseen event, beyond the control of the State, making it materially impossible in the circumstances to perform the obligation'. Accordingly, if an irresistible force or unforeseen event beyond the control of a State Party to the Rome Statute made it materially impossible in the circumstances to investigate and/or prosecute ICC crimes, the wrongfulness of such non-performance of the obligation to do so would be precluded.

In the context in which ICC crimes occur, the occurrence of 'an *irresistible force or an unforeseen event*' which makes it '*materially impossible in the circumstances to perform the obligation*' would certainly seem to be a possibility. Particularly when such crimes occur in the course of an armed conflict, the territorial State concerned may lose control over a portion of its territory as a result of an insurrection or foreign occupation.[281] Similarly, the necessary material infrastructure for conducting investigations and prosecutions, such as police stations, court buildings and prisons, may be destroyed. The necessary personnel may also be unavailable, for instance because police forces are otherwise deployed in order to quell an insurrection or because members of the judiciary have been targeted by the opposing armed forces or groups. In these instances, the State Party concerned could raise *force majeure* as a circumstance precluding the wrongfulness of not investigating and prosecuting ICC crimes. A finding of inability by the ICC in accordance with Article 17 (3) could bear the potential of strengthening such a claim, because the notion of 'inability' incorporates a collapse or unavailability of a national judicial system due to which the State is unable to carry out its proceedings. Such a finding would thus indicate the material impossibility for the State Party to perform the obligation to investigate and prosecute ICC crimes. To the extent that the State Party concerned can show that an irresistible force causes such a collapse or unavailability or unforeseen event beyond its control, a claim of *force majeure* could *prima facie* be successful.

At the same time, there is no automatic correlation between a finding of inability and a successful claim of *force majeure*. Article 23 of the Articles on Responsibility of States for Internationally Wrongful Acts is narrower in application in as much as it requires the occurrence of an '*irresistible* force' or of an

---

[281] Cf also J Crawford (n 69) 170 at (3) [citing loss of control over a portion of the State's territory as a result of an insurrection or devastation of an area by military operations carried out by a third State as examples of material impossibility of performance giving rise to *force majeure*].

'*unforeseen* event' '*beyond the control* of the State'. Excluded from the notion of *force majeure* are thereby constraints which the State was able to avoid or oppose by its own means, events that were foreseen or of an easily foreseeable kind, and forces or events within the control of the State concerned.[282] If the collapse of a national judicial system is, for instance, due to the persecution by a State of a particular ethnic group which was making up the large majority of members of the judiciary and other elites, that State could not subsequently argue *force majeure* as a circumstance precluding the wrongfulness of not investigating or prosecuting those responsible for ICC crimes.

Furthermore, even if a situation were to qualify *prima facie* as *force majeure*, a successful plea of *force majeure* would be precluded by virtue of Article 23 (2)(a), if '[t]he situation of *force majeure* is *due*, either alone or in combination with other factors, *to the conduct of the State invoking it*'.[283] Thus, when the foreign occupation of part of a State's territory is in response to an armed attack by that State and against which the occupying State has acted in self-defence in accordance with the UN Charter, the former State could then not subsequently rely on *force majeure*. If that State were unable to investigate and prosecute ICC crimes due to the foreign occupation in such a situation, it could not argue that the wrongfulness of not investigating or prosecuting ICC crimes is precluded because its conduct had brought about the occupation.

Last but not least, *force majeure* also does not apply if '[t]he *State has assumed the risk* of that situation [of *force majeure*] occurring'.[284] Whether such a risk has been assumed by the State invoking *force majeure* can be deduced *inter alia* from the obligation itself.[285] One could argue that this proviso makes the plea of *force majeure* meaningless as a circumstance precluding the wrongfulness of a failure to investigate and prosecute ICC crimes, because the obligation to investigate and prosecute these crimes already incorporates the risk that the occurrence of these crimes may lead to the inability of the territorial State to comply with that obligation. These ICC crimes incorporate contextual elements, such as the existence of an armed conflict and widespread or systematic attacks against the civilian population, indicating that the existence of circumstances which may give rise to a plea of *force majeure* are anticipated. Furthermore, the Statute may be said to reflect the risk that the occurrence of these crimes may lead to *force majeure*, because State Parties have included Article 17 (3) on 'inability'. They have thereby taken into account that genocide, crimes against humanity and war crimes may cause a partial or complete paralyzation of the judiciary of the State on whose territory they occur.[286] Indeed, the entire system of complementarity rests on the assumption that the ICC serves as a safety net in case States fail to investigate and prosecute ICC crimes, inability being one manifestation of that failure. This

---

[282] J Crawford (n 69) 170 at (2).   [283] Emphasis added.
[284] Article 23 (2)(b) of the Articles on Responsibility of States for Internationally Wrongful Acts (n 240). Emphasis added.
[285] J Crawford (n 69) 173 at (10).   [286] See also *43–45*.

suggests that State Parties, when accepting the obligation to investigate and prosecute ICC crimes, have assumed the risk that the occurrence of ICC crimes may
bring about a situation of *force majeure*. In that hypothesis, *force majeure* could
not serve as a circumstance precluding the wrongfulness of the failure of States
Parties to investigate and prosecute ICC crimes.

One can conclude from the preceding analysis that *force majeure* has, at best,
a very limited aptitude to serve as a circumstance precluding the wrongfulness
of not investigating and prosecuting ICC crimes. If one accepts the argument
that States Parties have assumed the unequivocal risk that the occurrence of core
crimes may lead to a situation of *force majeure,* the latter cannot be invoked. Even
if one rejected that argument, the potential of the plea of *force majeure* as a circumstance precluding the wrongfulness is limited. That potential is confined to
instances in which a State's inability to investigate and prosecute is attributable
to overwhelming factors beyond its control, which are caused by something other
than conduct to which the State itself substantially contributed. Furthermore, as
any circumstance precluding wrongfulness, it only applies as long as the situation
of *force majeure* persists.[287]

6.2.2. Necessity

Another circumstance that needs to be explored as to whether it can serve to
preclude the wrongfulness of not investigating and prosecuting ICC crimes is
necessity, as defined in Article 25 of the ILC's Articles on Responsibility of States
for Internationally Wrongful Acts.[288] This provision, which must be interpreted
narrowly,[289] sets out a number of criteria thatwould have to be satisfied in order
for the international wrongfulness of the failure to prosecute to be precluded.

In particular, the failure to prosecute would have to be 'the *only way for the
State to safeguard an essential interest against a grave and imminent peril*'.[290] The
adoption of an amnesty or another substitute for criminal prosecutions, such as a
truth commission process, for instance, may be the only way by which to secure
the agreement of the opposing sides to end an armed conflict, during which ICC
crimes were committed; or the preparedness of an *ancien régime* of a State, which
was responsible for such crimes, to leave office and to make way for a transition
towards a more peaceful and democratic society. The ending of an armed conflict
or the transition from an oppressive regime may certainly be said to constitute
an 'essential interest' of a State. In a similar vein, if one were to recognize the

---

[287] Cf (n 277).

[288] For the relevance of the necessity argument in the context of a failure to prosecute ICC
crimes, see also G Werle (n 181) 77 at 192.

[289] Cf J Crawford (n 69) 178 at (2); see also International Centre for the Settlement of Investment
Disputes, *CMS Gas Transmission Company v Argentina*, Case No ARB/01/8, 4 ICSID 246 (12
May 2005) [317].

[290] Article 25 (1)(a) of the Articles on Responsibility of States for Internationally Wrongful Acts
(2001) (n 240).

effective functioning of the judicial system to qualify as such an interest,[291] it is conceivable that the exercise of prosecutorial discretion in situations of mass crimes is the only means to safeguard that essential interest against the grave and imminent peril of collapse or deadlock.[292]

Yet, necessity does not only have to satisfy the aforementioned criterion to be the only means by which to safeguard an essential interest of a State, but also must '*not seriously impair an essential interest of the State or States towards which the obligation exists, or of the international community as a whole*'.[293] One essential interest of the State Parties to the Rome Statute, to whom the obligation *erga omnes partes* to investigate and prosecute ICC crimes is owed, is undoubtedly the fight against impunity.[294] In addition, the Preamble seems to suggest that the States Parties to the Rome Statute are inspired by the greater goal of 'peace, security and well-being of the world', as they regard the fight against impunity as part of the endeavour to prevent crimes which threaten these goals.[295]

There may be situations, however, in which the latter are (at least temporarily) undermined rather than furthered by prosecuting ICC crimes. In fact, the choice to be faced may sometimes be the classical one between peace and justice; between, on the one hand, the continuation of the commission of ICC crimes because of the threat of criminal prosecution due to which those responsible for these crimes continue to victimize large sections of a society and, on the other hand, a temporary stay of criminal proceedings, the exercise of prosecutorial discretion or the substitution of prosecution by alternative processes in order to end the perpetration of such atrocities. Opting for the latter may at times provisionally better serve the essential interest of State Parties in achieving the goals of 'peace, security and well-being of the world'.

If both the State concerned and the State Parties to the Rome Statute were to agree[296] in a particular situation that the failure to comply with the obligation to

---

[291] Note, however, that the ICSID rejected the need to avoid a major breakdown, such as a severe economic crisis, as an 'essential interest', (n 289) [319–320].

[292] In exercising prosecutorial discretion, States Parties would nevertheless remain subject to certain constraints, most notably the right to equality before the law, as enshrined in international instruments: see eg Article 7 of the 1948 Universal Declaration of Human Rights (1948) UNGA Res 217A (III), Articles 14 and 26 of the ICCPR (n 99), Article 75 (1) of AP I (n 107). The same guarantee is also incorporated in the ICC Statute: see Article 21(3). The ICTY has interpreted these provisions as prohibiting the exercise of prosecutorial discretion based on impermissible motives such as, *inter alia*, race, colour, religion, opinion, national or ethnic origin, when prosecutors exercise their discretion: see ICTY Appeals Chamber, *Prosecutor v Delalic et al ('Celebici')* (Judgment) IT-96-21-A (20 February 2001) [605–606].

[293] Article 25 (1)(b) of the Articles on Responsibility of States for Internationally Wrongful Acts (2001) (n 240), emphasis added.

[294] Cf Rome Statute (n 8) Preamble, paras 4 and 5. On the former, see also *2.2. Preambular Paragraph 4*.

[295] Rome Statute (n 8) Preamble, paras 3 ['Recognizing that such grave crimes threaten the peace, security and well-being of the world'] and 5.

[296] The States Parties could express their agreement in the form of a resolution adopted by the Assembly of States Parties in accordance with Article 112 (2)(g) of the Statute, which provides

prosecute better serves these essential interests, a plea of necessity may succeed, subject to a number of further conditions discussed below. What, however, if *no* such *agreement* were to be reached? The history of core crimes prosecutions reveals that the territorial State and other (groups of) States or the international community as a whole (as represented by the UN) may at times reach different conclusions as to whether peace or justice should prevail.[297] One would then find oneself in the situation of two competing 'essential interests' or, more precisely, two different views as to how an essential interest is to be safeguarded. States Parties to the Rome Statute could express their view that the essential interests of 'peace, security and well-being of the world' are better served by prosecuting ICC crimes fully, while the territorial State comes to the opposite conclusion. In that case, the cumulative 'and' joining the two conditions for a plea of necessity under Article 25 (1)(a) and (b) of the ILC's Articles on Responsibility of States for Internationally Wrongful Acts suggests that a plea of necessity would fail in such a case. The wrongfulness of the failure to prosecute would not be precluded.

Even if the territorial State Party concerned and other State Parties to the Rome Statute *agreed* that not to prosecute would better serve the aforementioned essential interests, *additional criteria* would nevertheless have to be met for the international wrongfulness of a failure to prosecute to be precluded.[298]

that the Assembly shall '[p]erform any other function consistent with this Statute or the Rules of Procedure and Evidence'.

[297] For a notable example, see the Lomé Peace Agreement between the Government of Sierra Leone and the Revolutionary United Front of Sierra Leone of 7 July 1999, <http://www.sierra-leone.gov.sl/peace_agreement.htm>. The UN special representative for Sierra Leone, when signing the agreement on behalf of the organization, affirmed that 'the United Nations holds the understanding that the amnesty and pardon provision in article IX of the agreement shall not apply to international crimes of genocide, crimes against humanity, war crimes and other serious violations of international humanitarian law': see Report of the Secretary-General to the Security Council, S/1999/836, 2, [7]. See also Avril McDonald, 'Sierra Leone's Uneasy Peace: The Amnesties Granted in the Lomé Peace Agreement and the United Nations' Dilemma' (2000) 1 Humanitäres Völkerrecht 11. In subsequent developments, Sierra Leone abandoned its position and the divergence in views was dissolved. With the adoption of the Statute of the Special Court for Sierra Leone of 16 January 2002, annexed to the Agreement between the United Nations and the Government of Sierra Leone on the Establishment of the Special Court for Sierra Leone, signed on 16 January 2002, '[a]n amnesty granted to any person falling within the jurisdiction of the Special Court [...] shall not be a bar to prosecution' by the Special Court (Article 10). Subsequent decisions of the Special Court have confirmed that view: see chiefly *Prosecutor v Kallon and Kamara* (Appeals Chamber Decision on Challenge to Jurisdiction) Case No SCSL-2004-15AR72(E) and SCSL-2004–16 AR72(E): Lomé Accord Amnesty (14 March 2004).

[298] Such an agreement could be construed as a waiver of the States Parties to invoke the responsibility of the territorial State: cf Article 45 in conjunction with Article 48 (1)(a) and (3) of the Articles on Responsibility of States for Internationally Wrongful Acts (2001) (n 240). This would mean that States Parties would be barred from invoking the responsibility in proceedings such as those mentioned (n 280). However, the consequential loss to *invoke* the responsibility of the States Parties does not affect the responsibility of the territorial State Party as such, because responsibility exists independently of its invocation by another State or States: cf J Crawford (n 69) 254.

First, the obligation to prosecute *must not (explicitly or implicitly) exclude reliance on necessity.*[299] One may argue that the obligation to investigate and prosecute ICC crimes excludes reliance on necessity. Whilst it does not do so expressly, such an exclusion could arguably be inferred from the obligation.[300] For, one could submit that States have intended that the obligation to investigate and prosecute also applies in abnormal situations of peril, such as an armed conflict or other crises.[301]

However, a different conclusion is suggested when considering the object and purpose of the obligation to investigate and prosecute ICC crimes, which stands central in determining whether or not an obligation implicitly excludes reliance on necessity.[302] The object and purpose of the obligation to investigate and prosecute ICC crimes is to ensure that perpetrators of ICC crimes are to be held accountable. That object and purpose does not necessarily mean, however, that this has to occur *while* the abnormal situation of peril endures, regardless of the consequences for a State's essential interests, such as the establishment of peace or the change of an oppressive regime. Indeed, the obligation to investigate and prosecute imposed by the Statute suggests otherwise, when it leaves some room to accommodate a temporary delay of proceedings through the notion of 'unjustified delay in the proceedings which *in the circumstances* is inconsistent with an intent to bring the person concerned to justice'.[303] The better view, therefore, seems to be not to construe the obligation to investigate and prosecute ICC crimes as implicitly excluding the plea of necessity as a circumstance precluding wrongfulness.

Second, the State invoking necessity *must not have contributed to the situation of necessity.*[304] In other words, when the grave and imminent peril to an essential interest of a State has been brought about by the act or omission of that State, it is precluded from invoking necessity as a circumstance precluding the wrongfulness of an act not in conformity with an international obligation. Thus a State which is responsible for the implementation of genocidal practices and provoked the commission of genocide on a massive scale, for instance, cannot later invoke necessity in order to preclude the wrongfulness of its failure to comply with the obligation to investigate and prosecute ICC crimes.

In sum, the narrowly defined conditions required for a successful claim of necessity outlined above renders it a largely hypothetical circumstance precluding the wrongfulness of a failure to investigate and prosecute ICC crimes.

---

[299] Cf Article 25 (2)(a) of the Articles on Responsibility of States for Internationally Wrongful Acts (2001) (n 240).

[300] Cf J Crawford (n 69) 185 at (19) [Certain rules, 'while not explicitly excluding necessity are intended to apply in abnormal situations of peril for the responsible State and plainly engage its essential interests. In such a case the non-availability of the plea of necessity emerges clearly from the object and purpose of the rule.'].

[301] See *mutatis mutandis 296–297.*   [302] Cf J Crawford (n 300).   [303] Cf *143–144.*

[304] Article 25 (2)(b) of the Articles on Responsibility of States for Internationally Wrongful Acts (2001) (n 240).

6.2.3. *Performance in Conflict with a Peremptory Norm (*jus cogens*)*

A last potential circumstance precluding the wrongfulness of an act not in conformity with an international obligation of a State is when the performance of that obligation would produce, or substantially assist in, a breach of a peremptory norm *(jus cogens).*[305] For the purposes of our discussion, this justification would mean that the obligation to investigate and prosecute ICC crimes would give way when compliance with it entails a conflict with a norm of *jus cogens.*

Conceivable scenarios in which such conflicts could arise depend upon the question of what rules of international law amount to *jus cogens,* ie norms accepted and recognized by the international community of States as a whole as a norm from which no derogation is permitted and which can be modified only by a subsequent norm of general international law having the same character.[306] The answer to this question is surrounded by a fair degree of uncertainty, except for a few rules of international law whose *jus cogens* status seems to be generally accepted, such as the prohibition of aggression, genocide and torture.[307] The performance of the obligation to investigate and prosecute is highly unlikely to produce, or substantially assist in, a breach of these norms.

This may be different when one considers certain fundamental human rights which have a bearing on investigations, prosecutions and criminal trials. Compliance with the obligation to investigate and prosecute ICC crimes may very well affect the core content of the right to *habeas corpus*[308] when a State is confronted with a situation in which its judicial system has collapsed, so that persons detained on suspicion of having committed ICC crimes cannot avail themselves of court proceedings in order to have the lawfulness of their detention determined. Such a situation would also make it virtually impossible for the State to comply with the right to be tried without undue delay.[309] Similarly, compliance with the right to be treated with humanity and with respect for the inherent

---

[305] Cf International Law Commission, 51st session (n 279) [306–311], <http://www.law.cam. ac.uk/rcil/ILCSR/498add2e.doc>. Such an occasional conflict with a peremptory norm does not render the entire treaty void, however, because the treaty is not intrinsically unlawful: see ibid at 306 and 311 ['the invalidation of a treaty which does not in terms conflict with any peremptory norm, but whose observance in a given case might happen to do so, seems both unnecessary and disproportionate. In such cases, the treaty obligation is, properly speaking, inoperative and the peremptory norm prevails. But if the treaty can in future have applications not inconsistent with the peremptory norm, why should it be invalidated by such an occasional conflict?'].

[306] Cf Article 53 of the Vienna Convention on the Law of Treaties (n 12).

[307] Cf the position of the International Law Commission, which mentions the prohibitions of aggression, slavery and the slave trade, genocide, racial discrimination, apartheid and torture, in addition to the basic rules of international humanitarian law and the obligation to respect the right of self-determination, while, however, stressing that these examples 'may not be exhaustive': J Crawford (n 69) 246–247 at (4) to (6). For a more extended list, see L Hannikainen, *Peremptory norms (jus cogens) in international law: historical development, criteria, present status* (Finnish Lawyers Publishing Company, Helsinki 1988).

[308] Article 9 (4) ICCPR (n 99).

[309] Article 14 (3)(a) ICCPR, ibid. Cf the Rwandan example referred to in (n 249).

dignity of the human person while being detained[310] is unattainable when prisoners, whether suspects or convicts, can only be detained in overloaded facilities, which do not satisfy even the most basic standards of humane treatment.[311] Or a State may be prevented from securing the right to be tried by a competent, independent and impartial tribunal established by law[312] when members of the judiciary have been targeted in the course of the commission of ICC crimes and, as a consequence, have either fled the country or have been killed, so that the staff required to make up competent, independent and impartial tribunals is unavailable,[313] or consists of unqualified substitutes.

Whether any of the aforementioned rights or others that have a bearing on criminal proceedings possess *jus cogens* status is certainly controversial.[314] None of them is immune from States taking measures derogating from their obligations to the extent strictly required in time of public emergency which threatens the life of the nation.[315] Their derogability contradicts their *jus cogens* status.[316]

---

[310] Article 10 (1) ICCPR (n 99).

[311] As an example, see for the situation in Rwanda in the wake of the 1994 genocide, ICRC, Annual Report 1995, 31 May 1996, Rwanda, available at <http://www.icrc.org/web/eng/siteeng0.nsf/iwpList143/D3B15125343F6B3CC1256B660059C81E>.

[312] Article 14 (1) ICCPR (n 99).

[313] Again, Rwanda may serve as an example: see United States Institute for Peace, 'Rwanda: Accountability for War Crimes and Genocide', Special Report 13, Release Date January 1995, available at <http://www.usip.org/pubs/specialreports/early/rwanda2.html> [In January 1995 only 40 jurists from a total of 300 judges and lawyers staffing the courts of first instance, appellate courts, and Supreme Court and 500 in the provincial courts before the events of April–July 1994 remained in Rwanda].

[314] To illustrate that controversy on the *jus cogens* status of human rights, compare the claim of M McDougal, H Lasswell and L Chen, *Human Rights and World Public Order* (Yale University Press, New Haven 1980) 274 [Universal Declaration of Human Rights has 'the attributes of *jus cogens*'] with the position of several other writers, eg A Cassese, *International Law* (OUP, Oxford 2001) 141 [norms protecting fundamental human rights, in particular prohibition of racial discrimination, torture and the right to self-determination]; G Dahm, J Delbrück and R Wolfrum, *Völkerrecht, Band I/3* (2nd edn De Gruyter, Berlin 2002) 717 at VI.1. [*Achtung elementarer Menschenrechte*]; similarly W Heintschel von Heinegg, in K Ipsen (n 212) 193 at 59; R B Lillich, 'Civil Rights' in T Meron (ed), *Human Rights in International Law—Legal and Policy Issues* (Clarendon Press, Oxford 1984) 115–170, 117–118 ['many human rights'].

[315] Cf Article 4 ICCPR (n 99).

[316] While non-derogability is not identical with the question of whether certain human rights obligations amount to peremptory norms of international law, the two issues are related in as much as the proclamation of certain human rights as being of a non-derogable nature is to be seen partly as recognition of the peremptory nature of some fundamental rights: see Human Rights Committee, General Comment 29, *States of Emergency (article 4)* (2001) UN Doc CCPR/C/21/Rev.1/Add.11 [11]. *A contrario,* the derogability of a human right creates a presumption against its having the status of *jus cogens*. Naturally, this in no way diminishes the acuteness of the dilemma in which a State finds itself when compliance with the obligation to investigate and prosecute under the Statute produces a conflict with human rights norms which are 'ordinary' rules of international law. These conflicts have to be resolved by reference to the principles governing rules of equal rank, including the *lex specialis* and *lex posterior* principles. See on these principles and other aspects of resolving conflicts between rules of international law, the work of the ILC on 'Fragmentation of international law: difficulties arising from the diversification and expansion of international law', Report of the Study Group of the International Law Commission, Finalized by Martti Koskenniemi (13 April 2006) UN Doc A/CN.4/L.682.

However, besides the fact that quite a few of them also apply during armed conflicts by virtue of international humanitarian law,[317] some of them also possess a non-derogable core content.[318] It, therefore, does not appear to be entirely excluded that this core of certain fundamental human rights amounts to rules which are accepted and recognized by the international community of States as a whole as norms from which no derogation is permitted. If this is indeed the case, and the performance of the obligation to investigate and prosecute ICC crimes would produce, or substantially assist in their being breached, the wrongfulness of a failure to prosecute would be precluded.

6.3. Immunities under International Law

Immunities under international law may be a further legal ground for not investigating and prosecuting ICC crimes. Under customary international law, these immunities are granted to high governmental officials, such as heads of States, heads of governments and foreign ministers, with the consequence that States other than their own are barred from exercising their jurisdiction over them. As noted previously,[319] one has to distinguish between international law immunity *ratione personae,* on the one hand, and international law immunity *ratione materiae,* on the other hand. The former attaches to a person by virtue of his/her office or status and, consequently, is available only for the duration of that office or status. Immunity *ratione personae,* therefore, ceases to constitute a bar to domestic legal proceedings after the person concerned has left office and does not enjoy the status of a high governmental official any more. In contrast, immunity *ratione materiae* attaches to acts performed by State officials in their official capacity.

---

[317] Note that Article 4 (1) of the ICCPR (n 99) precludes States from adopting measures that derogate from their 'other obligations under international law'. These obligations include those applicable during armed conflicts under international humanitarian law; for international armed conflicts, see Articles 84, 86–87, 99–108 of the 1949 Geneva Convention relative to the Treatment of Prisoners of War (Geneva Convention III)(adopted 12 August 1949, entered into force 21 October 1950) 75 UNTS 135–285; Articles 71–73, 76, 118 of the Geneva Convention relative to the Protection of Civilian Persons in Time of War (Geneva Convention (IV)(adopted 12 August 1949, entered into force 21 October 1950) 75 UNTS 287–417; Article 75 of AP I (n 107). For non-international armed conflicts, see Article 3 (1) *chapeau* and subpara (d) common to the four 1949 Geneva Conventions for the Amelioration of the Condition of the Wounded and Sick in Armed Forces in the Field (Geneva Convention I), for the Amelioration of the Condition of Wounded, Sick and Shipwrecked Members of Armed Forces at Sea (Geneva Convention II), relative to the Treatment of Prisoners of War (Geneva Convention III) and relative to the Protection of Civilian Persons in Time of War (Geneva Convention (IV), (all adopted 12 August 1949, entered into force 21 October 1950) 75 UNTS 31–417) [humane treatment…civilized peoples]; Articles 4(1) and 6 of the 1977 Protocol Additional to the Geneva Conventions of 12 August 1949, and relating to the Protection of Victims of Non-International Armed Conflicts (AP II) (adopted 8 June 1977, entered into force 7 December 1978) 1125 UNTS 609–699.

[318] Cf Human Rights Committee, General Comment 29 (n 316) [13] (a) and [16] [fundamental requirements of fair trial, only a court of law may try and convict a person for a criminal offence, presumption of innocence, *habeas corpus*].

[319] *51–52.*

Consequently, immunity *ratione materiae* constitutes a legal ground for not initiating domestic proceedings against serving State officials and former officials with respect to acts performed in their official capacity. Customary international law might arguably have evolved to reject functional immunities with respect to core crimes,[320] while personal immunities remain intact. Consequently, domestic proceedings before foreign courts for genocide, crimes against humanity and war crimes are barred with regard to incumbent senior governmental officials.[321]

While the foregoing discussion outlines the legal situation in general (customary) international law, the question arises as to whether the establishment of the ICC in general, and the principle of complementarity in particular, have had an impact in the area of international law immunities vis-à-vis ICC crimes. More precisely, in the light of the obligation to investigate and prosecute,[322] which the Statute imposes on State Parties by virtue of its Preamble and the provisions on complementarity, the issue is whether immunities under international law retain their relevance as a legal bar to domestic legal proceedings in the case of ICC crimes. That question is particularly pertinent in light of the fact that States Parties have adopted ICC implementing legislation which stipulates that no immunities, whether national or international, can constitute a bar to domestic proceedings. An example is the implementing legislation of the Democratic Republic of the Congo.[323] In so doing, the Democratic Republic of the Congo adopted almost verbatim Article 27 (2) of the ICC Statute. That latter provision stipulates that 'immunities or special procedural rules which may attach to the official capacity of a person, whether under national or international law, shall not bar the Court from exercising its jurisdiction over such a person'.[324] Importantly, however, the Congolese implementing legislation converted the provision in the Rome Statute, where it concerns the vertical relation between States and their officials, on the one hand, and the ICC, on the other hand, into a provision that applies in the horizontal relation between States. Admittedly, it is difficult to see how the ICC could declare a case admissible if States were to apply such legislative

---

[320] See page 52.   [321] See ibid.

[322] On the conceptualization of that obligation for States exercising extraterritorial jurisdiction, the relationship between their obligation and the one of the territorial State and between their obligation and the exercise of jurisdiction by the ICC, see *5.2. States Exercising Extraterritorial Jurisdiction*.

[323] Article 21–3 of the Congolese Penal Code, as amended by its 2005 ICC implementing law, *Loi Modifiant et Complétant Certaines Dispositions du Code Pénal, du Code de l'Organisation et de la Compétence Judiciaires, du Code Pénal Militaire et du Code Judiciaire Militaire, en Application du Statut de la Cour International Pénale, September 2005*, which provides: '*Les immunités ou règles de procédures spéciales qui peuvent s'attacher à la qualité officielle d'une personne, en vertu de la loi ou du droit international, n'empêchent pas les juridictions nationales d'exercer leur compétence à l'égard de cette personne en ce qui concerne les infractions non visées par les articles 221 à 224.*' Articles 221–224 implement the prohibitions of genocide, crimes against humanity and war crimes. Law available at <http://www.nottingham.ac.uk/shared/shared_hrlcicju/Democratic_Republic_of_Congo/DRC _Loi_Modifiant_Et_Completant_Certaines_Dispositions_Du_Code_Penal__Du_Code_ Penal_Militaire__2005___French_.pdf>.

[324] Rome Statute (n 8) Article 27 (2).

provisions in concrete cases vis-à-vis high governmental officials of foreign States, provided the State concerned is not otherwise unwilling or unable. Yet, a separate question is whether such an approach finds a sound basis in law and, more generally, is prudent. It is submitted that the answer to both these questions must be in the negative.

The underlying *rationale* for granting immunities *ratione personae* under international law is to ensure the proper functioning of inter-State relations.[325] One may of course question whether the granting of immunities to those who are likely to be most responsible for the planning, organizing, instigating and supervising of ICC crimes, as well as providing political leadership, is unsettling orderly international relations any less than hampering the conduct of a State on the international plane. The assertion in the ICC Statute's Preamble that these crimes 'threaten the peace, security and well-being of the world'[326] is at least indicative of the view of the States Parties to the Rome Statute that these crimes are seriously disruptive of orderly international relations. And yet, in balancing the interests pursued by the granting of immunity with the interest of ensuring accountability through domestic courts, it would seem that States continue to be of the opinion that the former should prevail. This is clearly evidenced in the ICJ's judgment in the *Arrest Warrant* case between the Democratic Republic of the Congo (somewhat curiously the same State that later adopted domestic ICC implementing legislation rejecting international immunities) and Belgium, where the ICJ ascribed the proper functioning of the network of mutual inter-State relations, which immunity was said to guarantee, '*paramount* importance for a well-ordered and harmonious international system'.[327] The ICJ identified 'criminal proceedings before certain international criminal courts' as an exception to the rule that high govermental officials enjoy immunity and referred to Article 27 (2) of the ICC Statute as a pertinent example.[328] However, it did not consider that provision—nor, for that matter, the provisions on complementarity—to alter the rule that *domestic* courts are barred from exercising their jurisdiction. Indeed, this follows from Article 27 (2) of the ICC Statute, which is solely concerned with the effect of immunities on the *ICC's* ability to exercise its jurisdiction, and not the ability of domestic courts. By rejecting immunities only in relation to the ICC's jurisdiction, the provision suggests *a contrario* that the immunities from domestic proceedings in foreign States, which attach to the official capacity of a person under general international law, remain intact.

A possible argument to the effect that States Parties to the ICC Statute have implicitly waived their right to invoke such immunities by recognizing

---

[325] D Akande, 'International Law Immunities and the International Criminal Court' (2004) 98 AJIL 407–433, 410, with further references.

[326] Cf Rome Statute (n 8), Preamble at [3].

[327] International Court of Justice *Case Concerning the Arrest Warrant of 11 April 2000* (n 202) Joint Separate Opinion of Judges Higgins, Kooijmans and Buergenthal [75], emphasis added.

[328] *Case Concerning the Arrest Warrant of 11 April 2000*, ibid [61].

Article 27 (2), which is to be applied by an ICC which is complementary to national criminal jurisdictions, also fails to convince. The mere possibility that cases might have to be declared inadmissible by the ICC if States decided to disregard international law immunities is not enough to meet the threshold that international law requires in order to discern an implied waiver.[329] What is more, in light of the limited number of cases in which international law immunities *ratione personae* are likely to arise (namely only in cases which concern incumbent high governmental officials), there is no need for domestic prosecutions of third States as a matter of practicality. Although it may be unlikely that the State of nationality tries such persons itself or waives the immunity of those persons so as to allow domestic proceedings before courts of another State, the ICC would have the necessary capacity to fully fill the void left by inactive, unwilling or unable national criminal jurisdictions.[330] If third States refuse to initiate proceedings or abandon proceedings against such officials because they are entitled to international law immunities, the Court will be able to rely on Article 17 in order to declare cases admissible. In the former case where a State refuses to take even initial investigative steps, the case would be admissible in any event. In the other scenario where a State abandons ongoing proceedings, the decision not to proceed based on international law immunities could be brought under the heading of either unwillingness, namely what we have previously referred to as 'bona fide unwillingness'[331] or inability.[332]

All of the foregoing analysis suggests that international law immunities *ratione personae* remain a valid legal ground for not acting in conformity with the legal obligation to investigate and prosecute which the Rome Statute imposes on State Parties.

7. Interim Conclusions

The Rome Statute imposes upon all State Parties which have established jurisdiction that conforms to international law a uniform obligation *erga omnes partes* to investigate and prosecute ICC crimes. It thereby alters pre-existing obligations—or the absence thereof—of State Parties in their mutual relations, whilst preserving such obligations in their relations with third States. As long as membership of the ICC does not correspond to other treaties which impose an obligation to investigate and prosecute genocide, crimes against humanity and war

---

[329] See (n 282) and text in Ch V.
[330] This is, of course, without prejudice to the intricate issues of (non-)cooperation of the State of nationality with the ICC. See also *Chapter V: The Procedural Setting of Complementarity, 3.3.3. The tension between complementary and State cooperation.* In the case of incumbent high governmental officials, the risk of a lack of cooperation of the State of nationality is particularly high.
[331] *137–138.*   [332] *158.*

crimes, this means that State Parties are effectively bound by two sets of obligations: an obligation under the ICC Statute and obligations under other treaties, such as the Geneva Conventions.

The detailed content of the obligation imposed by the Statute, as derived from the complementarityrequirements, demands that State Parties conduct effective, genuine, independent and impartial investigations into allegations of ICC crimes without unjustified delays. If such an investigation reveals sufficient evidence, State Parties also have to bring the case to trial and must adjudicate in conformity with the same requirements of effectiveness, genuineness, independence, impartiality and promptness. While this obligation to investigate and prosecute thus generally excludes the exercise of prosecutorial discretion due to policy considerations and substitutions for criminal prosecutions, it does not preclude States Parties from granting certain clemency measures after trial. The enforceability of this obligation finds its limits in the factual constraints of the ICC, legal avenues to reconcile non-prosecution within the Statute, the potential availability of a limited number of temporarily restricted excuses and justifications under the general law of State responsibility, and international law immunities *ratione personae.*

It may be doubted whether the essentially categorical nature of the obligation to investigate and prosecute ICC crimes which the Rome Statute imposes on States Parties is entirely satisfactory. While an obligation to investigate and prosecute may be a well-founded general rule, account should be taken of the fact that there might be exceptions to this rule. Past experiences and the evolving practice in the post-Rome era of international criminal justice suggests that one cannot simply regulate the phenomenon of non-criminal responses to international crimes away. Furthermore, to dismiss categorically non-criminal responses is likely to do injustice to genuine efforts to ensure accountability by means other than criminal prosecution. Undoubtedly, there are good reasons for a fair degree of scepticism towards them, as they have at times proven to be no more than formalized instruments of impunity. And yet, there are exceptions to the rule, for instance when a new, democratically elected government considers an alternative individualized accountability process, such as a truth commission, to be preferable to criminal prosecutions. The South African Truth and Reconciliation Commission is an example at hand.

The failure of the Statute to accommodate genuine alternatives to criminal prosecutions in a structural manner rather than on a case-by-case basis, and even more importantly, its failure to spell out criteria which have to be satisfied in order for them to be considered 'genuine' so as to be distinguished from those which should be considered illegitimate, reflects the controversies surrounding the issue and its political sensitivity. In so doing, it puts States that are genuinely willing and able to ensure accountability, but which are unwilling or unable to conduct criminal prosecutions, in a very difficult position, rather than providing them with clear guidance. Nor does the Statute take due account of the nature of many of the ICC crimes as mass crimes, which may require the exercise of prosecutorial discretion, if only as a matter of pure practicality.

In not setting forth parameters which can lead States in considering whether, and under what conditions, to opt for mechanisms such as truth commissions and traditional forms of justice and to exercise prosecutorial discretion, the Statute seems to reveal a state of denial of the drafters rather than a constructive approach. It is to be hoped that this important *lacuna* of the Statute will be remedied in the future by identifying relevant parameters.[333] That will certainly not be an easy task, but a long and complex process is to be preferred to negating the problem.

---

[333] Possible forms could be an amendment of the Statute in accordance with Articles 121 and 123 or a Protocol to the Statute as suggested by A O'Shea (n 70) 319, 330–336. On relevant criteria, see eg Informal Expert Paper for the ICC Office of the Prosecutor: The Principle of Complementarity in Practice (n 16) 23–24, [73]; C Stahn (n 192) 699–718; S Morel (n 149) 271–293. For a proposal to treat national decisions to impose non-criminal sanctions deferentially, and 'contextual proportionality' as a concept to complement complementarity, see F Meyer, 'Complementing Complementarity' (2006) 6 International Criminal Law Review 549–583.

VII

Complementarity as a Catalyst
for Compliance

1. Introduction

After having analyzed the formal framework for admissibility which complementarity provides (Chapters IV and V), we have argued in Chapter VI that the relevant provisions of the Statute encapsulate an obligation of States Parties to investigate and prosecute ICC crimes over which they have established jurisdiction. In a next step, this chapter analyzes whether, and to what extent, complementarity can serve as a mechanism through which States Parties are induced to and facilitated in complying with that obligation, and more broadly, through which all States, including non-State Parties, are encouraged to act in conformity with the basic premise of complementarity that States retain the primary role in the suppression of ICC crimes.

On a number of occasions, States, the Office of the ICC Prosecutor, academics and other experts have expressed the view that complementarity can be seen as such a catalyst. Thus States have pointed out that the principle of complementarity 'is designed to ensure that national authorities devote serious attention to their obligations to investigate and prosecute [core crimes]'.[1] By virtue of its complementary nature, '[t]he Court can play a twofold role: first, in motivating States to strengthen their judicial mechanisms; and secondly, in assisting States, especially weakened States, during or after a conflict, for instance in delivering justice in accordance with the Rome Statute'.[2]

---

[1] Statement of H E Mr Pfanzelter, Permanent Representative of Austria to the United Nations, at the meeting of the Security Council on Justice and the Rule of Law on 30 September 2003, Security Council 4835th meeting; record of the meeting available at <http://www.un.org/Depts/dhl/resguide/scact2003.htm>.

[2] Statement of H E Mr Wenaweser, Permanent Representative of Liechtenstein to the United Nations, at the same meeting, ibid. Views along comparable lines were expressed by the permanent representatives of Canada ['the ICC will promote national action through the principle of complementarity']; Argentina ['That Court is complementary to national sovereignties. [...] [I]t ensures that local authorities applying accepted principles of justice are universalizing the effective application of the rule of law.']; Austria ['... the International Criminal Court, [...] by means of its subsidiary jurisdiction is designed to ensure that national authorities devote serious attention to their obligations to investigate and prosecute such crimes.'] and Trinidad and Tobago ['[T]he

Similarly, the Office of the Prosecutor expressed its views in support of a conceptualization of complementarity as a catalyst for domestic proceedings by stating that '[a] major part of the external relations and outreach strategy of the Office of the Prosecutor will be to encourage and facilitate States to carry out their primary responsibility of investigating and prosecuting crimes'.[3]

Academics and other experts have likewise pointed to complementarity's potential as a 'powerful incentive to [national courts'] becoming more operational and effective',[4] 'challenging prosecutors and judges to greater zeal in the suppression of serious violation of human rights'.[5] Complementarity, in their view, 'serves as a mechanism to encourage and facilitate the compliance of States with their primary responsibility to investigate and prosecute core crimes'.[6]

International Criminal Court (ICC) can make a significant contribution to international peace and security by requiring that justice be administered at the national level. The ICC operates on the fundamental principle of complementarity: the obligation for the State to prosecute remains, and it is only where national authorities are unwilling or unable to prosecute that the Court may step in.']; Ireland, Explanatory and Financial Memorandum to the International Criminal Court Bill 2003, 2 ['The ICC operates on the principle of complementarity, rather than as a substitute for national criminal justice systems in that it will only take on an investigation where a State is unwilling or genuinely unable to carry out the investigation or prosecution. As such it is an institution to encourage States to prosecute such international crimes rather than seek to diminish States' domestic judicial authority.']; Norway ['The Court is based on the principle that the primary responsibility for prosecution of the most serious international crimes lies with States and it is expected to perform a key function in encouraging States to take this responsibility seriously.']. For an early example of States' view supporting such an understanding of complementarity, see the 'Report of the Ad Hoc Committee on the Establishment of an International Criminal Court' (1995) UN Doc A/50/22 24 [107], where, in the course of the discussion of state consent requirements and conditions for the exercise of jurisdiction, it was noted that this question 'should be examined from the perspective of a basic goal of the planned court: to allow and to encourage States to exercise jurisdiction over the perpetrators of a particular crime' and that such an approach was found by some delegations 'to be consistent with the concept of complementarity'.

³ Paper on some policy issues before the Office of the Prosecutor, available at <http://www.icc-cpi.int/library/organs/otp/030905_Policy_Paper.pdf> (2003) 5 [under the heading 'What does complementarity imply for the Office of the Prosecutor?'].

⁴ A Cassese, *International Criminal Law* (OUP, Oxford 2003) 353. See also A Cassese, 'A Big Step Forward for International Justice' (2003), Crimes of War Magazine, <http://www.crimesofwar.org/icc_magazine/icc-cassese.html> ['powerful incentive to national courts to institute proceedings against alleged criminals'].

⁵ W Schabas, *An Introduction to the International Criminal Court* (2nd edn CUP, Cambridge 2004) 24. See also P Sands, 'International Law Transformed? From Pinochet to Congo…?' (2003) 16 LJIL 37–53, 40 ['incentive for states, encouraging them to develop and then apply their national criminal justice systems as a way of avoiding the exercise of jurisdiction by the ICC'].

⁶ Informal Expert Paper for the ICC Office of the Prosecutor: The Principle of Complementarity in Practice available at <http://www.ice_cpi.int/library/organs/otp/complementarity.pdf> 3. See also J Meyerfeld, 'The Mutual Dependence of External and Internal Justice: The Democratic Achievement of the International Criminal Court' (2001) 12 Finnish YbIL 71–107, 88–89, 92–97; S Chesterman, 'No Justice Without Peace? International Criminal Law and the Decision to Prosecute' in S Chesterman (ed), *Civilians in War* (Lynne Rienner Publishers, Boulder, London 2001) 145–163, 152–153; D Sarooshi, 'The Statute of the International Criminal Court' (1999) 48 ICLQ 387–404, 395; H Duffy and J Huston, 'Implementation of the ICC Statute: International Obligations and Constitutional Considerations' in C Kress and F Lattanzi (eds), *The Rome Statute and Domestic Legal Orders, vol 1—General Aspects and Constitutional Issues* (Nomos and Ripa di Fagnano Alto: Sirente, Baden-Baden 2001) 29–49, 31–32; W Burke-White, 'A Community of Courts: Toward a System of International Criminal Law Enforcement' (2002) 24 Mich JIL 1–101 92; L Arbour,

These statements beg the question as to *how* complementarity can fulfil a catalyst role for States to exercise their jurisdiction over ICC crimes. The following sections address this question by examining different features of complementarity against the background of a variety of explanations which are regularly advanced to understand why, and how, States comply with international law.[7]

More in particular, it will be argued that complementarity can generate a pull-effect towards complying with the obligation to investigate and prosecute, both because it is perceived by States as a principle endowed with a high degree of legitimacy and because it is a vehicle used for bestowing legitimacy on national proceedings (1). Furthermore, some elements of complementarity support it being conceptualized as a coercive mechanism, through which a State that fails to comply with the obligation to investigate and prosecute is reprimanded (2). Complementarity also contains certain features of a managerial model of compliance, in which the ICC engages with State Parties to the Rome Statute and interacts with them in the cooperative venture to ensure accountability of perpetrators (3). Last but not least, complementarity is emerging as the converging point for a process through which its basic premise is gradually internalized into domestic legal systems and political processes of States (4).

It needs to be noted from the outset that these different explanations of why States comply with international law—legitimacy, coercion, management and

---

'Will the ICC have an Impact on Universal Jurisdiction?' (2003) 1 JICJ (2003) 585–588, 585 ['the greatest success of the ICC may consist of encouraging full and fair domestic prosecutions, backed up by the possibility of the international forum taking over if national courts are unwilling or unable to execute the work themselves.']; M H Arsanjani and W M Reisman, The Law-in-action of the International Criminal Court' (2005) AJIL 385–403, 390 ['to develop and expand their national judicial systems to process the crimes enumerated in the Statute' as 'primary objective of the ICC enterprise']; F Razesberger, *The International Criminal Court—The Principle of Complementarity* (Peter Lang, Frankfurt/Main 2006) 28 ['encourage States...to fulfil their implicit obligation under the RS to investigate and to prosecute genuinely']. For an early observation, see the statement of Mr Bernhardt, Observer for the European Court of Human Rights, at the Rome Conference ['The notion of complementarity called to mind the principle of subsidiarity which lay at the heart of the system of the European Convention on Human Rights. The message of the European Court of Human Rights had always been that subsidiarity was a means of ensuring that national courts played their rightful role as far as possible, thus making adjudication at the international level unnecessary. The true function of complementarity in the proposed system of international criminal jurisdiction should be to encourage the competent national courts to carry out their duties, but, if they failed to do so, to ensure that there was no escape for the perpetrators of atrocities.'], United Nations Diplomatic Conference of Plenipotentiaries on the Establishment of an International Criminal Court, (Rome, 15 June–17 July 1998 GAOR Volume II—Summary records of the plenary meetings and of meetings of the Committee of the Whole, UN Doc A/CONF 183/13 (Vol. II) 2002, 79 [102].

   7 For overviews of different compliance theories and the underlying conceptions of international law, see eg A Nollkaemper, 'On the Effectiveness of International Rules' (1992) 27 Acta Politica 49–70, 50–60 [on structural, institutionalist and internal compliance theories]; B Kingsbury, 'The Concept of Compliance as a Function of Competing Conceptions of International Law' (1998) Michigan JIL 345–372; A T Guzman, 'A Compliance-Based Theory of International Law' (2002) 90 California Law Rev 1823–1887, 1830–1840; S R Ratner, 'Overcoming Temptations to Violate Human Dignity in Times of Crisis: On the Possibilities for Meaningful Self-Restraint' (2004) 5 Theoretical Inquiries in Law 81–109, 93–95.

norm internalization—are *not exhaustive*. It goes beyond the purpose of the present study, however, to provide a detailed account of compliance theories in all their facets and nuances. Rather, the present analysis is limited to the main streams of explanations which, while treating international law as relevant in influencing States' behaviour, have had a significant impact on contemporary thinking about compliance with international legal rules and principles.[8]

Moreover, the different theories which are drawn upon in examining complementarity's potential as a catalyst for compliance are *not necessarily mutually exclusive*. Some of them address the phenomenon of (non-)compliance on different levels, overlap in certain respects or build on each other. Nor is it submitted that the factors, which we discuss (legitimacy, sanction, cooperation and consultation, and norm internalization) are equally forceful in inducing compliance, let alone in themselves sufficient to explain complementarity's potential as a mechanism for doing so. Rather, it is their *accumulated* strengths and weaknesses that determine the degree to which complementarity can serve as such a catalyst. The following clear-cut distinction between them thus serves a primarily analytical purpose.

A final caveat is that this chapter's focus is on the *theoretical* basis for such an assessment. It seeks to uncover the *potential* of complementarity to serve as a catalyst for national suppression rather than examining the extent to which and how that potential actually materializes. Although we will draw on some practical examples derived from the early practice under the Rome Statute, a more systematic analysis of complementarity's impact on national enforcement in actual practice will be something for future assessments after more empirical data has become available.[9]

2. The Legitimacy of Complementarity

A first feature of complementarity which supports it being conceptualized as a catalyst for compliance is a twofold link to legitimacy, namely the legitimacy

---

[8] Accordingly, those theories which treat international law as (largely) irrelevant in regulating State behaviour will not be addressed. For such a theory expounded by proponents of the 'classical' American realist tradition in international relations, see amongst others H J Morgenthau, *Politics Among Nations: The Struggle for Power and Peace* (6th edn Alfred A Knopf, New York 1985) 450. See also the reformulation of classical realism in 'neo-' or 'structural realism', eg K Waltz, *Theory of International Politics* (Addison Wesley, Reading 1979) 79–118 [absence of centralized, hierarchical governance structures such as those characterizing domestic authority systems in sovereign States brings about that States must pursue their interests, and above all provide for their own survival, by means of self-help; international law has no transformative impact upon the anarchical structure of the international system]. Another example of such theories includes the one advanced by F A Boyle, 'The Irrelevance of International Law: The Schism Between International Law and International Politics' (1980) 10 California Western ILJ 193–219, 198 ['International law is devoid of any intrinsic significance within the calculus of international political decisionmaking.'].
[9] For a preliminary case study relating to the D R Congo, see W Burke-White, 'Complementarity in Practice: The International Criminal Court as Part of a System of Multi-level Governance in the Democratic Republic of Congo (2005) 18 LJIL 557–590 especially at 568–574.

of complementarity itself and the legitimacy that complementarity can bestow upon national proceedings.

First, *complementarity itself* is endowed with a high degree of legitimacy, a quality which, it is submitted, generates a pull towards compliance.[10] That legitimacy stems from both the *process* through which it has come into being and its *substance*.

With regard to the *process*, the system of the ICC, including complementarity as one of its cornerstones, is based on the *specific consent of States* to the Rome Statute.[11] Non-State Parties do not incur any obligations under the Statute,[12] subject to the limited exception of Security Council referrals to which complementarity equally applies in principle.[13] The assertion that the ICC, and its role in ascertaining whether a given State is 'unwilling' or 'unable', has been created by the wrong process thus carries considerably less weight, if any, than the same challenges made vis-à-vis the UN ad hoc tribunals, which were imposed from the outside and in the absence of the specific consent to their establishment by the former Yugoslavia and Rwanda.[14]

[10] It is acknowledged that the concept of 'legitimacy' has no uniform meaning in international legal scholarship. James Crawford pointedly refers to 'the fuzziness and indeterminacy of 'legitimacy-speak': see J Crawford, 'The Problems of Legitimacy-Speak' (2004) ASIL Proceedings 271–273, 271. However, in the following we will use the concept in accordance with the writings of Thomas Franck. See in particular T Franck, 'Legitimacy in the International Legal System' (1988) 82 AJIL 705–759 [hereafter 'Legitimacy']; T Franck, *The Power of Legitimacy Among Nations* (OUP, New York 1990) 303 [hereafter 'Power of Legitimacy']; T Franck, *Fairness in International Law and Institutions* (Clarendon Press, Oxford 1995) 500. [Hereafter 'Fairness'], especially 25–46; for further references to legitimacy-based explanations of compliance in both national and international law, see T Franck, Legitimacy, 709–710.

[11] On the link between consent and legitimacy, see T Franck, Fairness (n 10) 29 ['state consent is the condition historically deemed necessary, but not necessarily sufficient, for any demonstration of rule legitimacy']; Power of Legitimacy (n 10) 24. See also R Bhattacharyya, 'Establishing a rule-of-law international criminal justice system' (1996) 31 Texas ILJ 58–99, 84–86.

[12] As we have seen in Chapter V, third States only incur rights under the Statute, for instance to invoke complementarity, while nothing in the Statute binds them to comply with the obligations. Unless the Security Council makes use of its referral powers, the Statute is thus fully compatible with the *pacta tertiis* rule: see page 233. The ICC may however exercise jurisdiction over non-Party nationals in accordance with Article 12 of the Statute. On the latter, see amongst others D Akande, 'The Jurisdiction of the International Criminal Court over Nationals of Non-Parties: Legal Basis and Limits (2003), JICJ 618–650.

[13] See *165–166*.

[14] This is not meant to suggest that consent to the UN ad hoc tribunals cannot be construed via the general consent given to the UN Charter and, thereby, to the powers of the UN Security Council under Chapter VII of the UN Charter. Nor is it suggested that the Security Council lacked the authority to establish international criminal tribunals by virtue of Chapter VII. The relevant fact for the present analysis is, however, that the authorization of the Security Council was derived from its general competence to maintain or restore international peace and security. That the establishment of international criminal tribunals under Chapter VII of the UN Charter offers more room for argument as to whether the Security Council was duly authorized and, consequently, the tribunals were established through the right process is amply demonstrated by the arguments advanced by the Defence and rejected in *Prosecutor v Tadić* (Decision on the Defence Motion for Interlocutory Appeal on Jurisdiction) IT-94-1 App Ch (2 October 1995) 9–48. Similar arguments were (and to some extent remain to be) advanced by the (then) Federal Republic of Yugoslavia (now Serbia and

The perception that complementarity has come about in accordance with the right process is not meant to suggest, however, that this aspect of its legitimacy differs from other treaties, including those imposing on State Parties the obligation to investigate and prosecute. Past experience[15] militates against the assumption that complementarity's procedural legitimacy generates a stronger compliance pull than other such treaties or, indeed, treaties in general. Only in comparison with those statutes of international criminal tribunals which have been established without the specific consent of the States concerned does the procedural legitimacy of the ICC Statute have the potential of generating a greater pull towards compliance.

However, in addition to the process through which it has come into being, the legitimacy of complementarity is derived from its *substance*.

First, complementarity *safeguards States' sovereignty*[16] in as much as it reaffirms rather than encroaches upon their primary role in the investigation and prosecution of core crimes.[17] As long as States fulfil the role assigned to them in the

Montenegro). It is telling that this attitude contrasts starkly with the one towards the ICC: the Federal Republic of Yugoslavia ratified the Rome Statute on 6 September 2001 as 38th State. For the rejection of similar arguments against the establishment of the ICTR, ICTR Trial Chamber 2, *Prosecutor v Kanyabashi* (Decision on the Defence Motion on Jurisdiction) ICTR-96–15 (18 June 1997) [9–32]. For the reasons of Rwanda's voting against the establishment of the ICTR, see Statement of the Permanent Representative of Rwanda following the voting, UNSC, *Provisional Verbatim Record, 3453 mtg* UN Doc S/PV.3453 (1994). For the different options of establishing the International Criminal Court, which were suggested in the International Law Commission, see 'Report of the International Law Commission on the work of its 46th Session' (1994) UN GAOR 49th Session Supp No 10, UN Doc A/49/10 [51–52]. For references to subsequent considerations, see O Triffterer 'Preliminary Remarks: The Permanent International Criminal Court—Ideal and Reality' in O Triffterer (ed), *Commentary on the Rome Statute of the International Criminal Court—Observers' Notes, Article by Article* (Nomos, Baden-Baden 1999) 17–50, 33, (n 69).

[15] Cf *Chapter II: National Suppression of Core Crimes, 3. Obstacles to National Suppression.*

[16] The concept of sovereignty has evolved over time, has various facets and is employed in a variety of ways in international legal discourse. However, for purposes of the present analysis sovereignty is understood as a legal status 'within but not above public international law. To rely on sovereignty does not exempt from international law either in the form of general international law or in the form of treaty obligations.' H Steinberger, 'Sovereignty' in R Bernhardt (ed), *Encyclopedia of Public International Law* (vol IV Max Planck Institute for Comparative Public Law and International Law, Amsterdam, Elsevier, 2000) 500–521, 512.

[17] See amongst others F Lattanzi, 'The Rome Statute and State Sovereignty. ICC Competence, Jurisdictional Links, Trigger Mechanisms, in: ICC and State Sovereignty' in F Lattanzi and W Schabas (eds), *Essays on the Rome Statute of the International Criminal Court* (vol I Ripa Fagnano Alto, Editrice il Sirente 1999) 51–66, 53 ['homage to State sovereignty']; T van Boven, 'The Principle of Complementarity—The International Criminal Court and National Laws' in J Wouters and H Panken (eds), *De Genocidewet in internationaal perspectief, Jura Falconis Libri* (De Boeck & Larcier Publ, Brussels 2002) 65–74, 65 ['delicate balance between the fight against impunity and sovereignty']; J Seguin, 'Denouncing the International Criminal Court: An examination of U.S. Objections to the Rome Statute' (2000) 18 Boston University Intl LJ 85–109, 94 ['complementarity maintains state sovereignty by ensuring that the Court will only be a "last resort" which comes into play when national authorities are unable or unwilling to investigate or prosecute a serious crime against humanity']; M El Zeidy, 'The Principle of Complementarity: A New Machinery to Implement International Criminal Law' (2002) 23 Michigan JIL 869–975, 898 ['admissibility criteria . . . establish the critical bulwark that protects the authority and rights of *sovereign* States to

suppression of core crimes, States retain the central sovereign prerogative to exercise their jurisdiction and to organize their judicial processes in a way that they consider appropriate. This makes complementarity one of the central arguments resorted to in order to refute allegations that the ICC is incompatible with State sovereignty.

Second, complementarity benefits from a large degree of *determinacy*. It possesses 'the ability to convey a clear message, to appear transparent in the sense that one can see through the language of a law to its essential meaning.'[18] The essential meaning of the declaration that the ICC is 'complementary to national criminal jurisdictions',[19] while 'it is the duty of every State to exercise its criminal jurisdiction over those responsible for international crimes',[20] leaves no doubt: the primary role of States in the investigation and prosecution of core crimes is preserved and the sole role of the ICC is to supply the deficiencies of national criminal jurisdictions.

This essential meaning is further refined in meticulous rules which together make up complementarity. Detailed definitions of what constitute 'unwillingness' and 'inability' and the various steps for invoking complementarity provide States with rather precise knowledge of what their rights and obligations are.

Naturally, the detail of the rules on complementarity does not remove the need for interpretation and further elucidation by the Court. Here, complementarity does not differ from any international rule, however precisely defined. Furthermore, complementarity lacks determinacy in some respects, for instance regarding the question as to what is expected of States which consider adopting

prosecute these cases in their national courts...']; J T Holmes, 'Complementarity: National Courts *versus* the ICC' in A Cassese, P Gaeta and J Jones (eds) *The Rome Statute of the International Criminal Court: A Commentary* (OUP, Oxford 2002) 667–686, 673 ['principle of complementarity, founded on national sovereignty and the obligations of States to prosecute']. Likewise, some States refer to complementarity when asserting that the ICC is compatible with or a safeguard for State sovereignty: Mongolia, statement at the First Assembly of States Parties, 9 September 2002—['[...] Statute...is based on the principle of respect for sovereignty of States, which is manifested, inter alia, in the principle of complementarity of the Court's jurisdiction.']. See also the excerpts from the meeting of the Security Council on Justice and the Rule of Law on 30 September 2003 of Sierra Leone ['[...The Court] is not a threat to the sovereignty of States. In this delegation's view, the principle of complementarity ensures the sanctity of the sovereignty of States.'] H E Mr Kanu, Permanent Representative of Sierra Leone to the United Nations (n 1). See also the decision of the French *Conseil Constitutionel*, Decision of 22 January 1999 (Decision No 98–408 DC, 1999 J.O. 1317, *Traité portant Statut de la Cour pénale internationale*, available at <http://www.conseil-constitutionnel.fr/decision/1998/98408/98408dc.htm>, English translation in (1999) 2 YIHL 493–505, 502 [stipulations on complementarity are compatible with 'the essential conditions for the exercise of national sovereignty'].

[18] T Franck, Fairness (n 10) 30; Legitimacy (n 10) 713.

[19] Rome Statute of the International Criminal Court (adopted 17 July 1998, as corrected by *procès-verbaux* of 10 November 1998, 12 July 1999, 30 November 1999, 8 May 2000, 17 January 2001 and 16 January 2002, entered into force 1 July 2002) A/CONF.183/9 (Rome Statute). Preamble, para 10 and Article 1, second sentence.

[20] Rome Statute (n 19) Preamble, para 6. On the relationship between complementarity and the duty to exercise jurisdiction, see *Chapter VI: Complementarity and the Obligation to Investigate and Prosecute, 2.4. Preambular Paragraph 6 and Complementarity*.

alternative accountability mechanisms such as truth commissions and which seek to do so in a way that the Prosecutor defers to such a non-criminal response because an ICC investigation or prosecution would not be in the 'interests of justice'.[21] However, a lack of determinacy in the latter respect is the exception which proves the general rule that complementarity has been defined in great detail.

Third, complementarity is bestowed with a high level of *coherence* in as much as it is in keeping with the basic concept underlying the allocation between the national and international realms of regulation and judicial activity.[22] Generally, that concept denotes that action on the international plane is legitimated by grounds which essentially stem from the inadequacy of regulative or adjudicative action on the domestic level.[23]

By subjecting a matter to international regulation, States decide to move it from the national to the international realm. The grounds underlying that decision flow from the perception of States that such regulation is required in order to ensure collective interests, namely the peaceful co-existence of States, their cooperation in matters which cannot adequately be addressed by one State alone, or to ensure and protect meta-national values, such as peace, human dignity and the needs of all mankind.[24] Indeed, it is the question as to whether the grounds provided for international regulation are sound and convincing which today lies at the heart of the debate about State sovereignty.[25] In the absence of such grounds, international regulation is considered unnecessary and the matter at hand left to the national realm of regulation. The clearest articulation of this idea

---

[21] See *Chapter VI: Complementarity and the Obligation to Investigate and Prosecute, 4.2. Alternative Accountability Processes* and *290–291*.

[22] T Franck, Fairness (n 10) 38–41, especially 41 ['The legitimacy of rules is augmented when they incorporate principles of general application. General application requires not only that likes are treated alike, but also that the principles of allocation and exclusion underlying a rule are in general use, so connecting the rule to the skein of the law. This second aspect of coherence, the connectedness of rules as a factor in their legitimacy, reflects the relationship between legitimacy and community. Legitimacy must be manifested by the relationship between any given rule and the rule system of the international community.']; see also J K de Vree, *Order and Disorder in the human universe: the foundations of behavioral and social science* (vol III Prime Press, Bilthoven 1990) 1224. For an instructive perspective on how complementarity is also in keeping with the basic concepts underlying the allocation of American state and federal courts, see A Y Sheng, 'Analyzing the International Criminal Court Complementarity Principle Through a Federal Courts Lens' (2006) The Berkeley Electronic Press, BePress Legal Series, Paper 1249, <http://law.bepress.com/cgi/viewcontent.cgi?article=5942&context=expresso> 6–30.

[23] M Kumm, 'The Legitimacy of International Law: A Constitutionalist Framework of Analysis' (2004) 15 EJIL 907–931, 920–924 [arguing that subsidiarity is one of four principles which together form a constitutional model for thinking about the legitimacy of international law].

[24] These three different areas of regulation correspond to the three moves of international law from a 'relational' law of co-existence to an 'institutional' law of cooperation and the gradual development towards a 'universal' law of the world community. See generally the writings of C Tomuschat, R Neuwirth, A Cassese, J I Charney and D Thürer, referred to in (n111) in ChII and B Conforti, 'Cours général de droit international public' (1988) RdC V, tome 212, 9–210, 25–27.

[25] J H Jackson, 'Sovereignty-Modern: A New Approach to an Outdated Concept' (2003) 97 AJIL 782–802, 790, offering the hypothesis that 'most (but not all) of the time that "sovereignty" is used in current policy debates. It actually refers to questions about the allocation of power; normally "government decision-making power" '. See also M Kumm (n 23) 920–921.

can be found in the notion of 'subsidiarity' within the context of the European Union.[26]

The allocation of concurrent judicial activity between international and national courts, if at all expressly regulated by States,[27] follows the same pattern. There is no need for international adjudicative fora if, and when, national courts can adequately achieve effective adjudication.[28] To the extent that both international and national courts are competent,[29] the latter have, as a rule, the opportunity to remedy wrongs before the matter can be submitted to an international judicial body. This idea is most clearly epitomized by the requirement to exhaust local remedies.[30]

Complementarity, in turn, affirms the same structural elements of the international legal system: only when national criminal jurisdictions are ineffective are cases admissible before the ICC. Indeed, Switzerland has poignantly articulated this view by referring to complementarity as 'an expression of the federalist principle, according to which problems should be solved on the level, on which they can be solved most effectively'.[31]

Whilst the aforementioned analysis demonstrates that complementarity in itself is endowed with a high degree of legitimacy, which generates a compliance-pull, the second link between complementarity and legitimacy is of an entirely different nature, as it concerns complementarity's role as a *vehicle for legitimacy of national proceedings*. Complementarity bestows upon national

---

[26] Cf Article 5 of the Treaty Establishing the European Community (consolidated version following the Treaty of Nice) and Article I-9 (3) of the Draft Treaty Establishing a Constitution for Europe (CIG 86/04) as approved on 18 June 2004.

[27] International law at times does not provide for express allocation rules between national and international courts: see Y Shany, *Regulating Jurisdictional Relations Between National and International Courts* (OUP, Oxford 2007) 39–77. For a useful case study, see Y Shany, 'Contract Claims vs Treaty Claims: Mapping Conflicts Between ICSID Decisions on Multisourced Investment Claims' (2005) 99 AJIL 835–851.

[28] Although the primacy of the two ad hoc tribunals for the former Yugoslavia and Rwanda and the Special Court for Sierra Leone may appear at first sight to contradict this pattern, they rest on the premise that such primacy was necessary because national courts of the States concerned were considered ineffective. For the ICTY and ICTR, see *64–66*. For the Special Court for Sierra Leone, see 'Report of the Secretary General on the Establishment of a Special Court for Sierra Leone' (4 October 2000) UN Doc S/2000/915 [10]. See also [28], clarifying that the lifespan of the Special Court would be depending *inter alia* on 'an indication of the capacity acquired by the local courts', thereby implicitly recognizing their incapacity at the time. See also *The Special Prosecutor v Col Mengistu Hailemariam and 173 Others* [unreported] Federal High Court, Criminal File No 1/87, Decision of Meskerem 29, 1988 E.C. (9 October 1995 G.C.) ILDC 555 (ET 1995), Comment 2.

[29] Recall that there may be areas which fall into the exclusive domain of international courts and tribunals or national courts: cf *58–59*.

[30] Cf *132–133* for further references.

[31] Switzerland, *Botschaft über das Römer Statut des Internationalen Strafgerichtshofs, das Bundesgesetz über die Zusammenarbeit mit dem Internationalen Strafgerichtshof und eine Revision des Strafrechts vom 15 November 2000*, Bundesblatt Nr. 7, 20. February 2001, 391–570, available at <http://www.admin.ch/ch/d/ff/2001/391.pdf>, 417 ['*Der Komplementaritätsgedanke ist Ausdruck des föderalistischen Prinzips, wonach Probleme auf der Stufe geregelt werden sollten, wo sie am besten gelöst werden können. Solange die staatlichen Instanzen zu einer ernsthaften Strafverfolgung im Bereich der Kernverbrechen des Völkerrechts fähig und willens sind, braucht die internationale Instanz nicht einzuschreiten; die Strafhoheit der Vertragsstaaten bleibt unberührt.*'].

proceedings the pedigree of 'willingness' and 'ability' when the Court determines that a case is inadmissible in accordance with Article 17 (1)(a) to (c) of the Statute. Thus, in contrast to the legitimate properties of complementarity analyzed in the preceding paragraphs, the legitimizing function of complementarity stems from its actual application. That legitimizing function bears the potential of inducing and facilitating States to exercise their jurisdiction over core crimes. For, it makes national proceedings less susceptible to the challenge made by actors other than the ICC that they are flawed. If the Court finds that national proceedings did satisfy the criterion of 'willingness', for example, the claim that an acquittal of the person concerned had the purpose of shielding him or her from criminal responsibility would have been authoritatively found to lack a basis.

Moreover, in the case of a declaration of admissibility, the Court would identify the reasons which led itself to that conclusion.[32] In so doing, the Court would pinpoint those areas of a State's national judicial system which were considered unsatisfactory to the degree that they amounted to 'unwillingness' or 'inability'. In response, the State concerned could strive to remedy these deficiencies in order to prevent the Court from coming to the same conclusion in future cases.

Nonetheless, to regard complementarity as a vehicle for the legitimacy of national proceedings is subject to the following important reservation. We have learned in Chapter VI that the notions of 'unwillingness' and 'inability' do not encapsulate all of the conceivable inadequacies of national proceedings. One important such gap results from the neglect of the complementarity requirements for the fair trial of an accused. The criteria for admissibility provide only very limited room for the ICC to assume jurisdiction in cases where there have been violations of norms of due process, which have worked to the disadvantage of the person concerned.[33] To the extent that fair trial notions fall outside the ambit of 'unwillingness' and 'inability', a declaration of inadmissibility must, therefore, not be misunderstood as a finding that the national proceedings were conducted fairly in accordance with due process guarantees.

Although the function of complementarity as a vehicle for legitimacy of national proceedings has thus to be approached with caution, both links between complementarity and legitimacy suggests that it bears the potential of catalysing compliance.

3. Complementarity as Sanction

Second, complementarity bears certain sanctionist features through which it has the potential of inducing States to investigate and prosecute core crimes. These

---

[32] Cf Rome Statute (n 19) Article 74 (5) ['The decision [of the Trial Chamber] shall be in writing and shall contain a full and reasoned statement of the Trial Chamber's findings on the evidence and conclusions.'] and Article 83 (4) ['The judgement [of the Appeals Chamber] shall state the reasons on which it is based.'].

[33] Cf *130, 144–145* and *150–152*.

features chiefly consist of the fact that the failure of a State to investigate and prosecute entails the consequence of a declaration of admissibility.[34] Indeed, thus understood, complementarity can be conceptualized as a procedure for the implementation of the international responsibility, understood *sensu lato*,[35] of State Parties for the breach of the *erga omnes partes* obligation to investigate and prosecute ICC crimes.[36]

As representative of the State Parties to the Statute, which in turn compose the community of States to whom that obligation is owed,[37] the ICC does not only determine whether a State has failed to adequately investigate and prosecute crimes within its jurisdiction. Such a determination alone would not add much to what is already available in the form of an international supervisory mechanism in the field of human rights.[38] Nor is the (possible) imposition of bilateral or multilateral sanctions in response to a failure to investigate and prosecute core crimes unknown outside of the ICC system.[39] Rather, the novelty of complementarity

---

[34] The permanent representatives of Canada put it as follows: 'States will know that, if they do not act, the ICC will act; and they will also know, conversely, that if they do act, the ICC will not act. Certain States that may be unwilling or unable to act will also know that the ICC stands ready to help with extensive checks and balances to prevent abuse.' (n 2).

[35] Strictly speaking, the law on State responsibility is concerned with the responsibility of States for internationally wrongful conduct *as implemented by States*: cf Part 3 (Articles 42–54) of the Articles on Responsibility of States for Internationally Wrongful Acts (2001) UNGA Resolution 56/83 of 12 December 2001, and corrected by document A/56/49 (Vol I)/Corr.4; J Crawford, *The International Law Commission's Articles on State Responsibility—Introduction, Text and Commentaries* (CUP, Cambridge 2002) 254–305. Note, however, that Article 55 of the Articles expressly provides that '[t]hese articles do not apply where and to the extent that the conditions for the existence of an internationally wrongful act or the content or implementation of the international responsibility of a State are governed by special rules of international law.'

[36] On the conceptualization of the relationship between the 'duty to exercise jurisdiction' in paragraph 6 of the Preamble and the provisions on complementarity as the one between primary and secondary norms, see *249–250*. On the *erga omnes partes* character of the obligation to investigate and prosecute, see *251–253*. But see P Benvenuti, 'Complementarity of the International Criminal Court to national criminal jurisdictions' in F Lattanzi and W Schabas (eds), *Essays on the Rome Statute of the International Criminal Court* (vol 1 Ripa Fagnano Alto, Editrice il Sirente 1999) 21–50, 44 [ICC not called upon to determine that the State's behaviour amounts to an internationally wrongful act, and therefore a source of international responsibility]. Yet, P Benvenuti seems to place this assertion on the law on State responsibility in its strict sense as being implemented by States.

[37] Cf G Hafner, K Boon, A Rübesame and J Huston, 'A Response to the American View as Presented by Ruth Wedgwood' (1999) 10 EJIL 108–123, 112–113.

[38] Such human rights bodies monitor compliance of States with obligations flowing from the respective treaties to investigate and prosecute serious human rights violations: see *Chapter II: National Suppression of Core Crimes, 2.1.4. The Obligation to Prosecute Human Rights Violations.*

[39] An example is the threat of sanctions re Sudan/Darfur in UNSC Res 1556 (30 July 2004) UN Doc S/Res/1556 (2004) [6], in which the Security Council '[d]emands that the Government of Sudan fulfil its commitments [...] to bring to justice Janjaweed leaders and their associates who have incited and carried out human rights and international humanitarian law violations and other atrocities, [...] and expresses its intention to consider further actions, including measures as provided for in Article 41 of the [UN Charter] on the Government of Sudan, in the event of non-compliance'. See also US Foreign Operations Appropriations Act for Fiscal Year 2001, Section 563, P.L. 104–208, (2001) 4 YIHL 637 [prohibiting US from giving funds 'to any unit of the security forces of a foreign country if the Secretary of State has credible evidence that such unit has committed gross violations of human rights, unless the Secretary determines that [...] the government of such country is taking effective measures to bring the responsible members of the security forces

lies in the fact that, for the first time in the history of international criminal law, State Parties have agreed *ex ante* that this failure will entail a concrete legal consequence: States forfeiting the claim to exercise jurisdiction, including over their own nationals and officials. The threat of this *sanction*, which such authoritatively determined failure in the form of a declaration of admissibility would involve, bears the potential of coercing State Parties into investigating and prosecuting core crimes.[40] This potential is reinforced by the *reputational costs* in the international arena, which a branding of a State as not satisfying the criteria for cases to be declared inadmissible entails.[41]

This perspective, which places (the threat of) sanctions and reputational costs at the centre of explaining compliance, finds support in the largely *antagonist premise* on which the regime of complementarity is based. States are assumed to be eager, in principle, to retain jurisdiction over cases, while the ICC is being perceived as a threatening institution of shaming and blaming. States are expected to investigate and prosecute because they want to bar the ICC from getting involved. They want to avoid the embarrassment that a declaration of admissibility would entail.[42] States and the Prosecutor would compete for jurisdiction over a given case, with the former 'challenging' admissibility and the two Parties litigating the matter before the Court. In fact, this largely confrontational assumption has led one writer to consider 'complementarity' as somewhat of a misnomer to adequately describe the relationship between the Court and national criminal jurisdictions.[43]

---

unit to justice']. The imposition of such multilateral or bilateral sanctions is nevertheless far from coherent.

[40] On the role of sanctioning violations of international law in order to ensure compliance, cf A T Guzman (n 7) 1845–1846. De Vree (n 22) 1226.

[41] These costs are determined, amongst other things, by the clarity of the obligation and the severity of the violation of that obligation: cf A T Guzman (n 7) 1861–1864.

[42] J Meyerfield (n 6) 88–89 ['To avoid the embarrassment of having their citizens and officials investigated before the Court, ratifying states have an increased incentive to prevent human rights crimes from occurring, and, in case their precautions fail, to prosecute such crimes in national courts. [...] To avoid ICC intervention, member States with fragile protections of human rights [...] will seek to develop bureaucracies more capable of administering justice and upholding the law, reform military and police procedures, institute a program of civic education that emphasizes human rights, and seek to remove the sources of ethnic tensions.'] and 92 ['[T]he Principle of Complementarity is designed to decrease the likelihood that cases are actually heard by the ICC, and to increase the likelihood of their being heard in the courts of those states most directly implicated. States will step up prosecutorial activity to avoid the embarrassment of the ICC's intervention.']. See also S Chesterman (n 6) 152–153 [referring to the threat to establish an international tribunal for East Timor, which induced Indonesia to start domestic proceedings and asserting that these developments 'suggest one way in which the [ICC] might profitably be used: as a tool for pressuring governments to conduct investigations and trials that are "credible"']: A Cassese (n 4) 353 ['[Complementarity's] chief merits lie both in its substantial respect for national courts, and in the indirect but powerful incentive to their becoming more operational and effective, inherent in the power of the ICC to substitute for national judges, whenever they are not in a position to dispense justice or they deliberately fail to do so [...].']; P Sands (n 5); B Broomhall, *International Justice and the International Criminal Court: Between Sovereignty and the Rule of Law* (OUP, Oxford 2004) 86.

[43] W Schabas (n 5) 85 [the two systems function in opposition and to some extent with hostility with respect to each other].

This antagonistic relationship is likely to arise especially as regards cases in which States had earlier made a conscious decision to remain inactive or as regards the majority of cases of '*unwillingness*' in the sense of Article 17 (2).[44] Although the factors which determine complementarity's success or failure as a catalyst for compliance will be context-specific and dynamic, the threat of the ICC to consider matters of admissibility is more likely to lead to a changed attitude on behalf of the State concerned in these cases. More concretely, a change may be the result, for instance, of a State considering the costs of the 'sanction' for non-compliance of forfeiting the right to exercise jurisdiction over a given case, and the reputational costs that a declaration of admissibility would entail, to outweigh the (political or other) costs of conducting investigations and prosecutions.[45]

The catalyst effects which derive from complementarity's sanctionist elements are, however, subject to important *limitations*.

It will be virtually impossible for the coercive components of complementarity to have any impact on *States whose national criminal jurisdictions are 'unable'* within the meaning of Article 17 (3), at least to the extent that such inability results from factors beyond the control of the State concerned.[46] If a State's national judicial system has collapsed, the threat of the ICC declaring a case admissible will not bring about a change in the factual situation on the ground. In fact, it would seem perfectly conceivable, for instance, that such a State would seek the assistance of the ICC in its efforts to rebuild that system and to prosecute perpetrators domestically. Or a State may be willing to bring perpetrators to account but seeks to do so by having a (number of) particularly sensitive case(s) adjudicated by the ICC, and makes an auto-referral with a view to prevent perceptions of bias, which a trial before the given State's domestic courts may provoke, thus paving the way for less sensitive cases to be investigated and prosecuted by national authorities.[47] While the Court may be able to assume a catalyst role in these situations, such scenarios are not encapsulated in complementarity as a coercive mechanism. As such a mechanism, complementarity could only induce compliance vis-à-vis deliberatively inactive and unwilling States.

And yet, even with regard to such States, the catalyst effect of complementarity's coercive facets may further be limited by the *cost–benefit calculation* which underlies the decision of a given State to comply or not.[48] If the (human,

---

[44] On the distinction between complete inaction and 'unwillingness' in the technical sense of Article 17 (2), see *103–104*.

[45] On this cost–benefit analysis, see A T Guzman (n 7) 1844–1851, 1853, 1860–1861, 1866, 1870–1871, also noting at n 149 that '[t]his is not meant to suggest that there is any simple way to aggregate the interests of states to determine when the benefits of a violation outweigh the costs. The point is simply that this will be true in some circumstances, implying that infinite sanctions for violations of the law are inappropriate.'

[46] This will regularly, but not always, be the case, as the examples of certain gaps in the national legal framework governing the investigation and prosecution of ICC crimes (see pages 156–157) illustrate.

[47] On auto-referrals, see generally *Chapter V: The Procedural Setting of Complementarity, 3.2. Complementarity and Auto-Referral*.

[48] Cf A T Guzman (n 45).

economic, political or social) costs for a State to investigate and prosecute core crimes are high, then these costs must be outweighed by the benefits in order for a State to take the decision to comply. In other words, the *higher* the *stakes* at hand, the less likely it will be that the catalyst effect of the coercive elements of complementarity materializes.[49] That this calculation is frequently precarious in matters relating to core crimes is indeed a truism.

If such crimes have been committed by officials of a State in the implementation of a plan developed on the highest level of political authority, for instance, then the perceived costs for that State to comply with the obligation to investigate and prosecute could outweigh the perceived benefits as long as the political regime remains unchanged. Here, the compliance pull of complementarity's coercive aspects will be weak because the stakes at issue are large.[50] The interest of that State's leaders to protect themselves and to stay in power would prevail over the benefits of retaining jurisdiction over the cases at hand[51] and the reputation for compliance. In effect, the very fact that such a political regime had decided to execute a plan of committing core crimes (in spite of probable international protests and condemnations) would be a strong indication that its interests in preserving a reputation for honouring its primary commitment not to commit such crimes is negligible. It would be surprising, to say the least, if that same regime would then be susceptible to any incentive to investigate and prosecute its own (higher) officials as a result of the reputational costs attached to a declaration of admissibility. This limitation of complementarity to serve as a catalyst for compliance, which emanates from the cost–benefit analysis in the context of ICC crimes, appears to be borne out by developments in Sudan. After an initial phase of denial of, and complete inaction, vis-à-vis core crimes by the Sudanese government, the Security Council referral of the situation to the ICC[52] triggered the establishment of various judicial mechanisms by Sudan in an apparent attempt to be able to make use of complementarity. These initiatives to investigate and prosecute crimes committed in Darfur have, however, thus far

[49] See generally on the problem of large stakes, ibid, 1883–1886.

[50] A T Guzman, ibid [arguing that 'many of the most central topics in traditional international law scholarship are the most resistant to influence. Thus, for example, the laws of war, territorial limits (including territorial seas), neutrality, arms agreements, and military alliances are among the areas least likely to be affected by international law. Although agreements with large stakes can be stable, this will rarely be the result of the obligations imposed by international law. Adherence to such agreements is more likely to be the result of a game in which international law plays no more than a small part. The existence of an international legal obligation may be consistent with the outcome, but it is unlikely to alter behavior.'] 1885. Guzman suggests that '[r]ather than concentrating on those topics that are of greatest importance to states, [scholars] might do better to devote more attention to those areas in which international law can yield the greatest benefits'.

[51] While the State would be under an obligation to surrender suspects to the Court after a declaration of admissibility, the cost–benefit analysis would likely result in its refusing to surrender them, similar to what could be witnessed with regard to surrender requests of the ICTY vis-à-vis suspects in the former Yugoslavia.

[52] UNSC Res 1593 (31 March 2005) UN Doc S/RES/1593.

been limited to lower-level perpetrators, and have not reached the highest level of responsibility.[53]

However, the costs of investigating and prosecuting can also outweigh the benefits in scenarios in which the *stakes* are *comparably small*. Consider a State which would have to base itself on universal jurisdiction, because it is faced with the presence of foreign nationals on its territory who are suspected of having committed core crimes abroad against foreign nationals. The costs involved in exercising universal jurisdiction will likely be high: evidence would have to be gathered in a foreign jurisdiction; witnesses may have to be interviewed abroad or must travel to give statements; and the relationship between the State wishing to exercise universal jurisdiction and the territorial State may come under strain. At the same time, the costs of not exercising universal jurisdiction may be lower than in the previous example: the jurisdictional link between the State and the crimes is considerably weaker and universal jurisdiction does not bear the same close relationship to a State's sovereignty as territorial jurisdiction. The threat of the sanction to forfeit the claim to exercise universal jurisdiction may thus generate a weaker pull towards investigating and prosecuting ICC crimes. In fact, to forfeit the claim to exercise universal jurisdiction may not be perceived as a sanction at all. For, the State may very well conceive of the ICC as the more appropriate body to investigate and prosecute core crimes and may thus wish to refrain from exercising jurisdiction.[54] Coupled with the weaker compliance pull of the threat of sanction are the lower reputational costs involved in cases of universal jurisdiction. A violation of that obligation—subsidiary to the exercise of jurisdiction by States with a stronger nexus and by the ICC[55]—is likely to be considered as less severe in terms of the reputational costs involved when compared to a violation of the obligation to investigate and prosecute core crimes committed in their territory.[56]

The potential of the coercive elements of complementarity to fulfil a catalyst function is further limited to the extent to which the (potential) *spheres of action of States and the ICC coincide*. Only if both the Prosecutor *and* the State concerned are eager and capable of investigating a given (number of) case(s) will the threat

[53] 'Report of the Prosecutor of the International Criminal Court to the UN Security Council Pursuant to UNSCR 1593' (2005) 29 June 2005, available at <http://www.icc-cpi.int/library/cases/ICC_Darfur_UNSC_Report_29–06–05_EN.pdf>, 4, noting that the multiple ad hoc mechanisms created by the Sudanese government do not constitute an obstacle to admissibility as 'a result of the absence of criminal proceedings relating to the cases on which the OTP is likely to focus', ie cases involving those who bear the greatest responsibility. See also Statement by Ms Sima Samar, Special Rapporteur on the situation of human rights in the Sudan, 60th Session of the General Assembly Third Committee, Item 71 (c): Human rights situations and reports of special rapporteurs and representatives, New York, 27 October 2005, <http://www.ohchr.org/english/bodies/chr/special/SRSudanstatement.doc>, 5.
[54] Cf *282–284*.   [55] Cf *280–284*.
[56] Cf L Arbour (n 6) 586 ['That assumption [that States Parties will wish to investigate and prosecute] is *certainly likely to hold true* for all crimes over which the ICC has competence but *in which the national court has a direct interest*, such as crimes committed on the territory of that state, or by one of its nationals, or where the victims are nationals of that state, even though they may have suffered elsewhere.' Emphasis added].

of the ICC to declare a case admissible be able to serve to induce compliance by a national criminal jurisdiction. Lacking such a concurrence, however, the pressure on States resulting from the threat of the ICC taking over cannot materialize. Yet, the potential for that concurrence is restricted in two important respects.

First, the potential reach of the ICC is limited through the notion of 'unwillingness' in Article 17 (2), which does not comprehensively capture all possible scenarios in which States may consciously refrain from conducting effective, fair and impartial proceedings. More in particular, the wording of Article 17 (2) does not allow for certain cases to be declared admissible in which violations of due process have occurred to the detriment of the person concerned, except under very limited circumstances.[57] To the extent that Article 17 (2) contains such gaps, the Court will not be able to make use of complementarity in order to threaten States with a declaration of admissibility. If a State conducts proceedings in violation of those norms of due process, which protect the accused from an abuse of legal process, the Court will be unable to coerce that State into compliance to the extent that such a violation falls outside the exceptions to inadmissibility as stipulated in Article 17 (2).

Second, the Court's capacity will be limited to only a small number of cases in each situation, as a matter of practical necessity, prosecutorial policy[58] and the mandatory admissibility requirement of sufficient gravity under Article 17 (1)(d).[59] In turn, the sanctionist components of complementarity can only serve to pressurize States into investigating and prosecuting *these same (categories of)* cases. No threat of declaring cases admissible can materialize with regard to all other cases. This is similar in circumstances in which the mere *possibility* that a given case might be declared admissible induces 'anticipatory' domestic investigations and prosecutions. Complementarity may serve as a catalyst for compliance because the State concerned seeks to pre-empt the Prosecutor from concluding that a preliminary examination reveals a sufficient basis for the initiation of an investigation under Article 53.[60] The criteria for selection used by the Court will provide guidance to States as to what categories of cases will potentially be subject to ICC proceedings. States can thus reasonably expect that the ICC Prosecutor would not pursue cases that fall outside of these categories.[61] With regard to these latter cases, the ICC would not be able to uphold its threat of declaring cases admissible in order to induce States to comply with their duty to exercise jurisdiction.

An ample illustration of how complementarity's potential to serve as a catalyst for compliance is limited in this way is the manner in which Uganda internalized

---

[57]   *130, 144–145, 150–152.*
[58]   See Paper on some policy issues before the Office of the Prosecutor (n 3) 3, 7.
[59]   Cf *Chapter IV: Complementarity as a Legal Principle and as Criteria for Admissibility, 3.4. Insufficient gravity: Article 17 (1)(d).*
[60]   Cf *Chapter V: The Procedural Setting of Complementarity, 2.1. Admissibility and the Initiation of an Investigation.*
[61]   On criteria for selection, see *Ch IV 3.4.* Insufficient gravity: Article 17(1)d.

the ICC Prosecutor's policy not to extend his investigations and prosecutions beyond those persons who bear the greatest responsibility when amending its 2000 Amnesty Act. The latter initially granted amnesty to 'any Ugandan who has at any time since the 26th day of January, 1986 engaged in or is engaging in war or armed rebellion against the government of the Republic of Uganda'.[62] The Act provides that these persons 'shall not be prosecuted or subjected to any form of punishment for the participation in the war or rebellion for any crime committed in the cause of the war or armed rebellion'.[63] The amnesty thus extended to crimes within the jurisdiction of the ICC and would, therefore, have rendered cases admissible under the Rome Statute.[64]

After Uganda made its auto-referral in December 2003,[65] the Ugandan President 'indicated to the Prosecutor his intention to amend [the] amnesty [Act]', according to a Press Release in early 2004.[66] However, the express aim of the amendment was 'to exclude the leadership of the LRA, ensuring that those bearing the greatest responsibility for the crimes against humanity committed in Northern Uganda are brought to justice.'[67] In other words, the prosecutorial policy of limiting the action of the Office of the Prosecutor to a certain category of individuals found reflection in the amendment of the Amnesty Act, thus equally limiting the scope of potential national investigations and prosecutions to these persons.[68] All other persons, however, would still be able to invoke it—as a matter of domestic law—before Ugandan courts whilst also being beyond the reach of the ICC by virtue of the prosecutorial policy and the mandatory admissibility requirement of sufficient gravity under Article 17 (1)(d).

[62] 2000 Ugandan Amnesty Act, available at <www.c-r.org/our-work/accord/northern-uganda/documents/2000_Jan_The_Ammnesty_Act.doc>.

[63] Ibid pt II para 3(2).

[64] Cf *Chapter VI: Complementarity and the Obligation to Investigate and Prosecute, 4.1. Unconditional Clemency Measures, including Amnesties.*

[65] Cf Letter of referral dated 16 December 2003 from the Attorney-General of the Republic of Uganda, appended as Exhibit A to the Prosecutor's application for Warrants of Arrest under Article 58 dated the 6th day of May 2005, as amended and supplemented by the Prosecutor on the 13th day of May 2005 and on the 18th day of May 2005.

[66] ICC Press Release, 'President of Uganda refers situation concerning the Lord's Resistance Army (LRA) to the ICC', The Hague, 29 January 2004, ICC-200400129-44-En. According to news reports, an amendment to this effect was passed by the Ugandan Parliament on 18 April 2006 as the Amnesty Amendment Bill 2003, giving authority to the House to approve names of insurgents and individuals to be excluded from government pardon: see The Monitor (Uganda), 'No Amnesty for Rebel Leaders'—19 April 2006, available at <http://allafrica.com/stories/200604180779.html>.

[67] ICC Press Release, ibid.

[68] Recall that an auto-referral does not pre-empt the operation of complementarity. The fact alone that an auto-referral was made by a State Party, therefore, does not preclude domestic proceedings to the extent that situations or cases are found to be inadmissible by virtue of the fact that the State concerned is willing and able to investigate and prosecute. See *Chapter V: The Procedural Setting of Complementarity, 3.2. Complementarity and Auto-Referral.*

Admittedly, Uganda's amendment to the Amnesty Act in reflection of the Court's limited reach does not emanate from an antagonistic relationship between the ICC and Uganda. Indeed, the making of an auto-referral suggests—at least as far as the LRA is concerned[69]—a cooperative relationship between the two. However, it appears reasonable to assume that a similar effect will *a fortiori* emanate from the limited reach of the ICC if the Court has to rely on complementarity's coercive properties when seeking to pressurize a State into conducting domestic investigations and prosecutions.

In sum, complementarity bears elements of a coercive mechanism to reproach States which fail to investigate and prosecute crimes within the jurisdiction of the ICC. That mechanism bears the potential of inducing compliance with a view to avoiding the sanction of forfeiting jurisdiction over such crimes and the reputational costs that a declaration of admissibility entails. However, the potential of complementarity to induce compliance is limited (1) to States that have consciously decided to be inactive or that are 'unwilling' in the sense of Article 17 (2); (2) to States that have determined that the benefits of investigating and prosecuting outweigh the costs of doing so; and (3) to the extent that the jurisdictional spheres of States and the ICC coincide.

4. Complementarity as Management

A conceptualization of complementarity as a catalyst for compliance finds further support when considering certain features which suggest that it can provide a framework for cooperation and consultation between States and the ICC, with a view to convincing the former to conduct investigations and prosecutions of ICC crimes. In the following, these cooperative and consultative features are referred to as 'management', in line with the 'managerial' theory of compliance as developed by Chayes and Chayes.[70]

The managerial elements of complementarity bear the potential of persuading—rather than coercing—miscreant States to change their conduct and overcome the obstacles to effective national investigations and prosecutions. More specifically, such elements consist of the discursive *interaction* between the ICC and States Parties (and to some degree non-States Parties[71]), and the *supervision*

---

[69] Cf the statement by the Ugandan President referred to on page 215 at (n 288) and text.

[70] A Chayes and A Handler Chayes, *The New Sovereignty—Compliance with International Regulatory Agreements* (Harvard University Press, Cambridge MA 1995) [hereafter 'New Sovereignty']; A Chayes and A Handler Chayes, 'On Compliance' (1993) 47 International Organization 175–205, especially 204–205.

[71] See on non-State Parties in the context of preliminary rulings regarding admissibility, *168–170* and *172–173*, and in the context of challenges to admissibility, *183*.

by the former of the latter.[72] In contrast to the coercive model, these elements establish a more cooperative *modus vivendi* through which the relationship between States and the ICC is moved beyond mere antagonism.

The procedural framework of complementarity provides for *interaction* between the ICC and States. The starting point for such interaction depends upon the trigger mechanism. In the context of *proprio motu* investigations, the current Prosecutor has explained his policy as follows:

In the light of the complementarity regime set out in the Statute and the central role accorded to it in the general policy of the Office, the Prosecutor will generally seek to alert the relevant State of the possibility of taking action itself very early in the process. For this reason, when the Office receives sufficiently detailed and credible information about alleged crimes, the Office will in general consult and seek additional information from the States that would normally exercise jurisdiction, unless there is reason to believe that such consultations may prejudice the future conduct of an analysis or investigation or jeopardize the safety of persons.[73]

Furthermore, for State referrals and investigations *proprio motu*, the notification made under Article 18 (1) sets in motion the back-and-forth between the Prosecutor and States requesting a deferral, which is moderated by and conducted in front of the Pre-Trial Chamber or Trial Chamber and, in case of appeal, the Appeals Chamber.[74] In the case of a Security Council referral, the starting point for this dialogue lies in Article 19.[75] These dialogues converge on the question of whether a State is investigating and prosecuting ICC crimes and whether its criminal proceedings meet the criteria of willingness and ability.

---

[72] These elements of persuasion through interaction and supervision stand central in the managerial theory of compliance: see New Sovereignty (n 70) 26 ['process of "jaw-boning"—the effort to persuade the miscreant to change its ways'; 'fundamental instrument for maintaining compliance with treaties at an acceptable level is an iterative process of discourse among the parties, the treaty organization, and the wider public']; 27 ['dominant atmosphere is one of actors engaged in a cooperative venture, in which performance that seems for some reason unsatisfactory represents a problem to be solved by mutual consultation and analysis, rather than an offense to be punished. States are under the practical necessity to give reasons and justifications for suspect conduct. These are reviewed and critiqued [...]. In the process, the circumstances advanced in mitigation or excuse of non-performance are systematically addressed [...] At all stages, the putative offender is given every opportunity to conform. Persuasion and argument are the principal engines of this process, but if a party persistently fails to respond, the possibility of diffuse manifestations of disapproval or pressures from other actors in the regime is present in the background'; 'justificatory discourse']; 28 ['Inducing compliance through [...] interacting processes of justification, discourse, and persuasion [...]']. The aforementioned elements are not exhaustive, however. On further elements of the managerial theory of compliance, see *328–331*.

[73] See Annex to the 'Paper on some policy issues before the Office of the Prosecutor': Referrals and Communications, available at <http://www.icc-cpi.int/library/organs/otp/policy_annex_final_210404.pdf>, 4.

[74] See *Chapter V: The Procedural Setting of Complementarity, 2.2. Preliminary Rulings Regarding Admissibility: Article 18*.

[75] See *Chapter V: The Procedural Setting of Complementarity, 2.3. Challenges to the Admissibility of a Case: Article 19*.

The interactive features of complementarity are combined with the *supervisory* function of the Court.[76] Although some States expressed their opposition to such a competence of the ICC during the drafting process,[77] it is clearly inherent in the Prosecutor's power to review the deferral to a State's investigation[78] or a decision of inadmissibility;[79] the possibility for him/her to request the State to whose investigation he/she has deferred to inform him/her of the progress of its investigations and any subsequent prosecutions,[80] as well as his/her power to apply to the Pre-Trial Chamber for an authorization of an investigation if, in his/her view, the review reveals that the complementarity threshold has been met.[81]

In combination, interaction and supervision establish complementarity as a mechanism through which the Court can engage States. If 'reasonable grounds'[82] exist which suggest that a State is inactive, unwilling or unable, States are required to give reasons and justifications for such suspect conduct. Throughout the procedures under Articles 18 and 19, the putative non-compliant State is given the opportunity to bring its conduct into compliance with the obligation to investigate and prosecute, and is given the opportunity to convince the Court that it is genuinely investigating and prosecuting the case(s) at hand. However, the efforts of States to do so are reviewed independently by the Court. If a State nevertheless fails to comply, the Court retains the possibility of declaring a case admissible.

While the aforementioned features of complementarity thus suggest that it can induce compliance with the obligation to investigate and prosecute as a managerial framework, the *absence of certain components,* which typify the 'management of compliance' as developed by Chayes and Chayes, potentially weakens complementarity's aptitude to serve as such a framework.

A preliminary missing component is that the Statute is silent as to how to attend to compliance problems through measures of *capacity building*.[83] The interactive and supervisory features of complementarity may serve to identify the sources of a State's non-compliance, but the Statute does not provide for measures of how to address these sources. Admittedly, these sources may at times not require a systemic overhaul of a State's judicial system, for instance if a State has

---

[76] J Meyerfield (n 6) 95–96 ['external check', '*supra*national authority that can monitor government's conduct from the outside and take corrective action when government veers away from the protection of human rights'].

[77] See 'Report of the Ad Hoc Committee on the Establishment of an International Criminal Court' (1995) UN Doc A/50/22, 9, [43]. See also 34, [177].

[78] Rome Statute (n 19) Article 18 (3).   [79] Rome Statute (n 19) Article 19 (10).

[80] Rome Statute (n 19) Article 18 (5) and 19 (11).

[81] Rule 56 (1) of Rules of Procedure and Evidence (12 July 2000) UN Doc PCNICC/2000/INF/3/Add.1 (RoPE).

[82] Cf Rome Statute (n 19) Article 53 (1)(a) to (c) and RoPE, ibid, Rule 48.

[83] On capacity building as an element of the managerial theory of compliance, see New Sovereignty (n 70) 25, 197–201.

been found to be 'unwilling' in one single or a small number of case(s) which proved to be exceptionally politically sensitive, while the national judicial system is otherwise intact. Yet, in other situations, most notably when a State has been found to be 'unable', the Statute does not provide for measures to be taken to improve that State's national judicial system. This is not to suggest that the Court itself should assume an active role in that respect, although this has been advocated by the ICC Prosecutor in the course of developing strategies to facilitate and assist States in investigating and prosecuting ICC crimes, referred to as 'positive complementarity'.[84] If the Court were to be actively engaged in the rebuilding of national criminal jurisdictions, it would run the risk of losing the critical distance to a national criminal jurisdiction that it helped create or shape—a distance that is vital to effectively fulfilling its task of supervising that national criminal jurisdiction. At the very least, the ICC may be perceived to lack the necessary independence and impartiality to do so. Nor does the ICC currently have the budget[85] to play an active role in capacity building. However, the ICC itself is not the only conceivable actor in the endeavour to reinvigorate national judicial systems, as such a role can be—and is in fact being—fulfilled by States and intergovernmental organizations. And yet, the Statute does not link a finding that a State is in need of capacity building with a framework for concerted action, which involves these other actors in the endeavour to satisfy that need.

Second, complementarity lacks clear rules for horizontal *coordination*, which allocates the jurisdictional competences between States.[86] While the Statute imposes an obligation on all State Parties to exercise their jurisdiction, it does not provide clear guidance as to how potential jurisdictional conflicts between

---

[84] An ICC Press Release of May 2003 contained the following statement: 'The principle of complementarity established by the Statute compels the prosecutor's office to collaborate with national jurisdictions in order to help them improve their efficiency. That is the first task of the prosecutor's office: make its best effort to help national jurisdictions fulfil their mission. The prosecutor's office can do this in different ways. In a cooperative way, by giving the state the information received from different public sources or providing the state's personnel with training and technical support.' ICC Press Release, 'OTP—Election of the Prosecutor, Statement by Mr Moreno Ocampo', The Hague, 2 May 2003, ICC-OTP-20030502–10-En, <http://www.icc-cpi.int/press/pressreleases/5. html>. Cf also Paper on some policy issues before the Office of the Prosecutor (n 3) 3–5; Informal Expert Paper for the ICC Office of the Prosecutor: The Principle of Complementarity in Practice (n 6) 3. The ICC Prosecutor has described this positive approach to complementarity as one of the key strategic decisions guiding the work of his Office: see Statement of the Prosecutor Luis Moreno Ocampo to Diplomatic Corps, The Hague, Netherlands, 12 February 2004, <http:// www.icc-cpi.int/library/organs/otp/OTP.SM20040212-EN.pdf>; Office of the Prosecutor, 'Report on Prosecutorial Strategy', 14 September 2006, <http://www.icc-cpi.int/library/organs/ otp/LOM_20040212_En.pdf> 5.

[85] Note that the Draft Programme Budget 2005, Doc ICC/ASP/3/2 (26 July 2004), available at <http://www.icc-cpi.int/library/asp/ICC-ASP3-2_budget_English.pdf>, does not foresee any expenditure for assisting States in rebuilding their national judicial system.

[86] On coordination as an element of the managerial theory of compliance, see A Chayes and A Handler Chayes, New Sovereignty (n 70) 135–142.

several States have to be solved.[87] This ambiguity surrounding the question as to *which* State is responsible for investigating and prosecuting a given case and under what circumstances creates significant room for States to defer to one another, with the risk that none will ultimately investigate and prosecute.[88] In the alternative secnario where two or more States conduct parallel criminal proceedings, the absence of rules on horizontal coordination also entails the risk of wasteful and inefficient parallel proceedings in two or more States, which may produce inconsistent outcomes.[89] The lack of clear rules for horizontal coordination weakens complementarity's propensity to serve as a framework for 'managing' compliance.

The absence of statutory provisions on capacity building and on the horizontal coordination between States does not necessarily exclude the possibility for the Court to assume a role in either of these areas. One may very well argue, for instance, that the Court possesses an implied power to assume a role in the reinvigoration of a given State's national judicial system (subject to the aforementioned caveat that it would be prudent to limit such a role to measures which can be taken without compromising the Court's supervisory role).[90] Such an implied power may be strengthened by a Security Council

---

[87] Cf *278*. Recall that the suggestions as to how competing jurisdictional claims should be settled made in *278–287* are not deduced from the Statute but derive from legal, conceptual, practical and policy considerations outside the Statute.

[88] Cf T Vander Beken, 'De moeilijke zoektocht naar het beste forum voor internationale misdrijven—De *ad hoc* tribunalen als ideale oplossing?' in J Wouters and H Panken (eds) (n17) 117–137, 121, who pointedly describes this phenomenon as the 'black jack-principle' ['*zwarte-pietprincipe*'], through which a *de iure* possibility of prosecution in several States leads to a de facto assertion of jurisdiction of none. In his words, this principle entails that 'collective responsibility in practice ultimately leads to inaction'. ['*[... B]ij internationale misdrijven [...] waarbij vervolging op basis van het universaliteitsbeginsel de iure in een heel aantal landen mogelijk is, maar de facto uitblijft. In politiek gevoelige, en dikwijls de meest ernstige, dossiers speelt het 'zwarte-pietprincipe'vaak een belangrijke rol zodat het bestaan van een collectieve verantwoordelijkheid in de praktijk uiteindelijk tot inertie leidt.*']. See also A Klip, 'Complementarity and Concurrent Jurisdiction' in International Criminal Law: *Quo Vadis?* Proceedings of the International Conference held in Siracusa, Italy, 28 November–3 December 2002, on the Occasion of the 30th Anniversary of ISISC (2004) 19 Nouvelles études pénales 173–197, 176, 178 ['bystander-effect'; 'If many are responsible nobody will feel the individual need to act'; 'one may seriously question whether, in practice, responsibility for *all* leads to responsibility for *no one*.'].

[89] Cf *mutatis mutandis* for these risks as far as the relationship between domestic and international courts and tribunals is concerned, Y Shany, *Regulating Jurisdictional Relations Between National and International Courts* (n 27) 17–20.

[90] It is acknowledged that it may nevertheless be difficult to determine the extent of the powers implied, not the least because the process of determining implied powers (Can they derive only from explicit powers or also from purposes and functions of organizations? Must they be necessary or essential for the organization to perform its functions and, if so, what is actually 'necessary' or 'essential'?) is characterized by a good degree of uncertainty and by inconsistencies: see H Schermers and N Blokker, *International Institutional Law* (4th edn Martinus Nijhoff, Leiden 2003) 177 [233].

referral in accordance with Article 13 (b). The referral of the situation in Darfur to the ICC by the Security Council exemplifies how such a role of the Court could be reinforced in as much as it '*encourages* the Court, as appropriate and in accordance with the Rome Statute, to support international cooperation with domestic efforts to promote the rule of law, protect human rights and combat impunity in Darfur'.[91] Similarly, the Court may assume a more informal catalyst role. This may take the form of generating an impetus for other actors to assist the State concerned in its efforts of judicial reform, for instance, or of using the deferral procedure under Article 18 as a framework for a dialogue between itself and different requesting States with a view to settling competing claims of jurisdiction.[92]

In the words of the Office of the Prosecutor:

The Office will develop formal and informal networks of contacts to encourage States to undertake State action, using means appropriate in the particular circumstances of a given case. For instance, in certain situations, it might be possible and advisable to assist a State genuinely willing to investigate and prosecute by providing it with the information gathered by the Office from different public sources.

The exercise of the Prosecutor's functions under article 18 of notifying States of future investigations will alert States with jurisdiction to the possibility of taking action themselves. In a case where multiple States have jurisdiction over the crime in question the Prosecutor should consult with those States best able to exercise jurisdiction [. . .] with a view to ensuring that jurisdiction is taken by the State best able to do so.[93]

Reliance on implied powers and informal spin-offs of complementarity nevertheless entails the disadvantage of being far less transparent than express provisions. The absence of an agreed upon set of rules on capacity building and the coordination of horizontal jurisdictional competences between States leaves two crucial aspects of an effective 'management' of compliance unaddressed. This lack of transparency is detrimental to compliance, as transparency is in itself an important factor in the promotion of compliance.[94]

---

[91] Paragraph 4 UNSC Res 1593 (n 52).
[92] See *176*. For parameters in identifying the most suitable forum for prosecution, see *280–286*.
[93] Paper on some policy issues before the Office of the Prosecutor (n 3) 5.
[94] New Sovereignty (n 70) 135. Chayes and Chayes identify three important ways in which transparency may operate to promote treaty compliance: coordination, reassurance and deterrence: see ibid and 136–153.

5. Complementarity as Process of Norm Internalization

A fourth and final point in support of conceptualizing complementarity as a catalyst for compliance is to concentrate on its role as a process of norm internalization.[95] Through this process, the underlying premise that States retain the primary role in the suppression of core crimes is internalized into States' domestic legal and political processes, which bears the potential of ultimately resulting in States' compliance with the duty to investigate and prosecute core crimes.[96]

This internalization process is brought about by the interaction between actors involved in matters relating to the ICC, who invoke and interpret, and gradually produce a shared meaning of, complementarity. The procedural framework of complementarity involves States, the ICC and the individual accused, who may invoke complementarity,[97] in addition to victims,[98] intergovernmental and non-governmental organizations.[99] These actors *interact* in a variety of *fora* in which complementarity is interpreted.[100] The most obvious of these fora is the ICC itself. States, the Office of the Prosecutor and an individual accused may invoke complementarity, and the resulting jurisprudence of the Court clarifies

---

[95] This process is also at times referred to as 'transnational legal process', a compliance theory chiefly developed in the writings of H H Koh, 'The 1998 Frankel Lecture: Bringing International Law Home' (1998) 35 Houston LR 623–681. See also H H Koh 'Transnational Public Law Litigation' (1991) 100 Yale LJ 2347–2402 and H H Koh, 'Transnational Legal Process' (1996) 75 Nebraska LR 181. Transnational legal process denotes 'the process whereby an international law rule is interpreted through the interaction of transnational actors in a variety of law-declaring fora, then internalised into a nation's legal system. Through this three-part process of interaction, interpretation, and internalisation, international legal rules become integrated into national law and assume the status of internally binding domestic legal obligations': see 'Bringing International Law Home' 626–627. See also 'Transnational Public Law Litigation' 2371 and 'Transnational Legal Process' 183–84.

[96] Note that Koh distinguishes between 'compliance' (ie awareness of the rule and consciously accepting its influence in order to gain specific rewards or to avoid specific punishments) and 'obedience' (ie adopting rule-induced behaviour because the norm has been internalized and incorporated into the internal value system of the norm-addressee): 'Bringing International Law Home', Ibid 627–633. His notion of 'compliance' is narrower than the one used throughout this chapter. We employ the term more loosely to denote conformity between a State's behaviour and its international legal commitments; see: *309*. See also Ratner (n 7) 85.

[97] Cf Rome Statute (n 19) Article 19 (2).

[98] Eg through their right to 'make representations to the Pre-Trial Chamber', if the Prosecutor concludes that there is a reasonable basis to proceed with an investigation and submits to the Pre-Trial Chamber a request for authorization of an investigation: cf Rome Statute (n 19) Article 15 (3).

[99] For instance, when these organizations submit information to the Prosecutor in support of his/her initiating investigations *proprio motu* and when the Prosecutor requests additional information: cf Rome Statute (n 19) Article 15 (1) and (2).

[100] H H Koh refers to such fora as 'law-declaring fora': cf H H Koh, 'Bringing International Law Home' (n 95) 626–627.

the actual content of complementarity. These and other actors also concern themselves with complementarity in less formal ways and in other contexts. The policy pronouncements of the Office of the Prosecutor on complementarity,[101] declarations of States in intergovernmental fora[102] and of intergovernmental organizations themselves,[103] NGOs[104] or joint fora[105] all add to the substance for an interactive dialogue through which a shared meaning of complementarity evolves.

Even though the jurisprudence of the ICC on complementarity is only evolving, it already appears safe to assert that the central *meaning* of complementarity *shared* by all actors is that States retain the primary responsibility for investigating and prosecuting core crimes and that their capacity to do so should be strengthened. This shared meaning is evidenced not only by statements,[106] but also by its gradual *internalization* into the domestic legal processes of States. In the course of becoming Parties to the Rome Statute, States regularly conduct reviews of their laws which govern the national prosecution of core crimes, with a view to

---

[101] See eg (n 3) and text.   [102] See eg (nn 1–2) and text.

[103] See for instance the Resolution on the ICC taken by the OAU member States during the 31st Ordinary Session of the The African Commission on Human and Peoples' Rights, held in Pretoria, South Africa, from 2nd to 16th May 2002 ['Calls upon the States that have ratified the ICC Statute to rapidly incorporate it into their domestic legislation in order to be able to [. . .] implement the principle of complementarity with their national courts'].

[104] See for instance Amnesty International, 'International Criminal Court: The failure of states to enact effective implementing legislation', available at <http://web.amnesty.org/library/Index/ENGIOR400192004?open&of=ENG-385> ['Under the principle of complementarity [. . .] [t]he implicit bargain [. . .] was that each state party recognized that under international law it had the primary responsibility to bring to justice those responsible for such crimes, with the Court only stepping in when states failed to fulfil their obligations. Indeed, it was implicit in the adoption of the Rome Statute that states parties would do their utmost to carry out their responsibilities to investigate and prosecute cases, otherwise the Court would be so overwhelmed with cases it would not be able to function. States parties have a responsibility to ensure that the Court is able to operate effectively.']; Coalition for the International Criminal Court, 'Implementation of the Rome Statute', available at <http://www.iccnow.org/?mod=romeimplementation> ['[W]hile the Court places itself at the heart of the new international justice system to fight impunity, it also remains a "court of last resort", leaving the primary responsibility to exercise jurisdiction over alleged criminals to national legal systems. This system of complementarity can only work if states undertake the following: ratify or accede to the Rome Statute, fully cooperate with the Court by providing all the necessary judicial assistance in its proceedings, and implement all of the crimes under the Rome Statute into domestic legislation.']

[105] See for instance Déclaration Finale du Séminaire sur la Ratification et la Mise en Oevure du Statut de la Cour Pénale Internationale (Déclaration de Maurice), 27–29 mai 2002. The Seminar was organized by *l'Agence intergouvernementale de la Francophonie* and Parliamentarians for Global Action (PGA) ['Conformément au principe de complémentarité posé par le Statut de la Cour, les Etats qui le ratifient assument la responsabilité première de la poursuite et de la répression des crimes de génocide, des crimes contre l'humanité et des crimes de guerre. Il leur incombe alors d'adapter leur droit interne en conséquence et de prévoir les modalités de coopération avec la Cour pénale internationale.'].

[106] Cf (nn 1–3) and text, (nn 103–105).

assessing their compatibility with the core crimes law contained in the Statute.[107] In various States, these reviews have resulted in the adoption of implementing legislation, while others are in the process of doing so.[108] This fact alone need not necessarily be attributable to the complementary nature of the ICC, as such reviews may be part of the standard procedures for ratification under national law. However, a closer analysis of miscellaneous implementing processes suggests that implementing legislation which enables States to investigate and prosecute core crimes is frequently adopted in direct response to the complementary nature of the ICC.

The Swiss Explanatory Report to the Rome Statute and a Revision of Criminal Law, which analyzes various matters arising in the context of ratifying and implementing the Rome Statute by Switzerland, may serve as an example. An excerpt states:

[...] That the States [...] have to reflect on the matter [of incorporating the crimes in the Statute into their domestic criminal codes and penalize them in the same manner, JK] derives mainly from the principle of complementarity as embodied in Article 17. If States do not want to run the risk to lose their primary competence to the ICC in a particular

---

[107] J Meyerfield (n 6) 88–89 ['Some member states have begun revising their penal codes to include prohibitions on genocide, war crimes, and crimes against humanity as these terms are currently defined; other states are being urged to do so. The Court thus contributes to the "domestication" of international humanitarian law and human rights norms. [...] The Court, having derived its existence from the express authorization of states guided (at least in this instance) by a commitment to human rights, serves in turn to internalize that commitment at the domestic level. It nurtures the values that inspire its creation.'] See also B Broomhall (n 42) 91–92.

[108] The first State to do so known to the author is Congo/Brazzaville, which signed the Statute on 17 July 1998 and subsequently adopted the Law No 8–98 on the definition and the suppression of genocide, war crimes and crimes against humanity on 31 October 1998, available at <http://www.icrc.org/ihl-nat.nsf/WebLAW?OpenView&Start=1&Count=150&Expand=33.6#3 3.6>. For an overview of legislative developments, see the (draft) implementing laws made available at the database of the Coalition for the International Criminal Court (CICC), at <http:// www.iccnow.org/?mod=romeimplementation>; Amnesty International, available at <http://web. amnesty.org/pages/icc-implementation-eng>. For an analysis of ratification and implementation processes in various States, see C Kress and F Lattanzi (n 6); R S Lee, *States' Responses to Issues Arising From the ICC Statute: Constitutional, Sovereignty, Judicial Cooperation and Criminal Law* (Transnational Publ, New York 2005) 313; M Neuner (ed), *National Legislation Incorporating International Crimes—Approaches of Civil and Common Law Countries* (BWV Publ, Berlin 2003) 271; International Society for Military Law and the Law of War, 'Compatibility of National Legal Systems with the Statute of the Permanent International Criminal Court' (2003) Recueil XVI, two volumes; K Ambos and E Malarino, *Persecución Penal Nacional de Crímines Internacionales en América Latina Y España* (Max Planck Institute, Freiburg 2003); see also the volumes published as part of the research project 'Nationale Strafverfolgung völkerrechtlicher Verbrechen—National Prosecution of International Crimes' conducted by the Max Planck Institute for foreign and international criminal law, Freiburg, edited by A Eser and H Kreicker, available at <http://www.iuscrim. mpg.de/forsch/straf/projekte/nationalstrafverfolgung2.html>.

case, they must ensure that the crimes within the jurisdiction of the Court are penalized in their internal legal orders in one way or the other. [...][109]

Similarly, the Uruguayan explanatory memorandum, accompanying the draft ICC implementation law, stated that 'it is not possible to exercise the principle of complementarity if the crimes within the jurisdiction of the Court do not constitute at the same time, punishable conducts within the scope of the jurisdiction of national judges. Accordingly [*del mismo modo*], those crimes should also be established in national law'.[110]

A last example stems from Australia, where the Parliament expressed the purpose of the suggested amendments of the Criminal Code to include the crimes covered by the Rome Statute in the following terms: 'It is the Parliament's intention that the jurisdiction of the International Criminal Court is to be complementary to the jurisdiction of Australia with respect to offences in [the new] Division [268 on genocide, crimes against humanity, war crimes and crimes against the administration of the justice of the International Criminal Court] that are also crimes within the jurisdiction of that Court.'[111] The explanatory memorandum to the 2002 ICC Act further clarified that '[b]y creating crimes in Australian law that mirror the crimes in the Statute, Australia will always be able to prosecute a person accused of a crime under the Statute in Australia rather than surrender that person for trial in the ICC.'[112]

Other statements which indicate a direct relationship between complementarity and states adopting or reviewing national implementing legislation and, where necessary, bringing it into conformity with the Rome Statute, can be found in at

[109] *Botschaft über das Römer Statut des Internationalen Strafgerichtshofs, das Bundesgesetz über die Zusammenarbeit mit dem Internationalen Strafgerichtshof und eine Revision des Strafrechts,* (n 31) 450, translation by author.

[110] 17/01/03—Se Establecen Procedimientos Para La Aplicación En El Ámbito Interno Del Estatuto De Roma De La Corte Penal Internacional, at I, available at <http://www.presidencia.gub.uy/proyectos/2003011701.htm>. ['Del mismo modo, el principio de la complementariedad es de imposible ejercicio si los crímenes de competencia de la Corte no constituyen a la vez conductas punibles en la esfera de competencia de los jueces internos. Para ello, tales crímenes deben estar también consagrados en el derecho nacional.'].

[111] Cf Divisions 268.1 (2) and (3) of the Australian International Criminal Court (Consequential Amendments) Act 2002 No 42, 2002; see also Exposure Draft, International Criminal Court Bill 2001 A Bill for an Act to facilitate compliance by Australia with obligations under the Rome Statute of the International Criminal Court, and for related purposes, The Parliament of the Commonwealth of Australia, House of Representatives/The Senate, 30 August 2001, 2, section 3.

[112] The Parliament of the Commonwealth of Australia, House of Representatives, International Criminal Court (Consequential Amendments) Bill 2002, Explanatory Memorandum, Subdivision A Introductory (Proposed Section 268.1: Purpose of Division).

least the following States: Belgium,[113] Germany,[114] Norway,[115] Senegal,[116] South Africa,[117] Spain,[118] The Netherlands,[119] and Venezuela.[120]

[113] Sénat de Belgique (2 February 2000), Projet de la Loi portant assentiment au statut de la Cour Pénale Internationale fait à Rome le 17 juillet 1998 (exposé des motifs), at [21]: 'Il découle du caractère subsidiaire de la Cour que le Statut invite indirectement les Etats parties à modifier leur droit interne afin de rendre leurs juridictions pénales compétentes pour connaître des faits relevant de la compétence de la Cour elle-même. [...]'.

[114] Germany: 'Gesetzentwurf der Bundesregierung—Entwurf eines Gesetzes zur Einführung des Völkerstrafgesetzbuchs (EGVStGB)', BT-Drucksache 14/8524 (13 March 2002) <http://dip.bundestag.de/btd/14/085/1408524.pdf> 12: 'Das Völkerstrafgesetzbuch hat folgende Ziele: "[...]im Hinblick auf die Komplementarität der Verfolgungszuständigkeit des Internationalen Strafgerichtshofs zweifelsfrei sicherzustellen, dass Deutschland stets in der Lage ist, in die Zuständigkeit des IStGH fallende Verbrechen selbst zu verfolgan [...]"]["[...] to ensure, in the light of the complementary prosecutorial competence of the International Criminal Court, that Germany is always able to prosecute crimes within the jurisdiction of the ICC [...]"].' See also ibid 14.

[115] Comment by Ane Sofie Tømmers (Labour Party) on the Recommendation of the Foreign Affairs Committee on the Law on the Implementation of the Statute of the International Criminal Court of 17 July 1998 (Odelsting Recommendation No 125 (2000–2001)), available at <http://www.legal.coe.int/criminal/icc/docs/Consult_ICC(2001)/ConsultICC(2001)39E.pdf>:   '[...] We must also review our Penal Codes, both the civil and the military ones. We don't have adequate legislation as regards this type of crime. We must look at the substance of the penal provisions. We haven't described this type of crime in our penal codes. We must review our sentencing provisions, where the maximum limits are not in keeping with the Statute of the International Criminal Court. And we must review our provisions on the limitation period. [...]'

[116] Loi 2007 05 du 12 fév 2007 modifiant le Code pénal, Exposé des Motifs ['En incorporant dans le code pénal le crime de génocide, les crimes de guerre, les crimes contre l'humanité [le Sénégal] respected également les exigences de complémentarité.'].

[117] Cf Section 3 (d) of the Implementation of the Rome Statute of the International Criminal Court Act, 2002, which identifies as one of the objects of the Act 'to enable, as far as possible and in accordance with the principle of complementarity [...] the national prosecuting authority of the Republic to prosecute and the High Court of the Republic to adjudicate in cases brought against any person accused of having committed a crime in the Republic and beyond the borders of the Republic in certain circumstances'.

[118] Cf the Spanish Progress report on ratification and implementation of the Rome Statute to the Council of Europe: '[...]Above all, if a State Party wishes successfully to invoke the principle of complementary recognised by the Statute, according to which States have the primary responsibility to prosecute international crimes, then it has to ensure that its law include these crimes and that its courts have jurisdiction to deal over them. [...]', <http://www.legal.coe.int/criminal/icc/docs/Consult_ICC(2001)/ConsultICC(2001)28E.pdf>

[119] Memorie van Toelichting, Regels met betrekking tot ernstige schendingen van het internationaal humanitair recht (Wet internationale misdrijven) (Explanatory Memorandum, International Crimes Act) Kamerstukken II 2001/02, 28 337, nr. 3 (MvT), 2 ['Het Strafhof heeft een bevoegdheid «die complementair is aan de nationale jurisdicties in strafzaken». Dit houdt in dat het Strafhof pas optreedt—dat wil zeggen rechtsmacht kan uitoefenen—indien geen staat bereid of bij machte is het onderzoek of de vervolging daadwerkelijk uit te voeren (zie artikel 17, eerste lid, sub a, Statuut van het Strafhof). Hoewel dit niet uitdrukkelijk in het Statuut is bepaald, is door een meerderheid van staten—waaronder het Koninkrijk—steeds aangenomen dat uit het complementariteitsbeginsel volgt dat de staten die partij zijn bij het Statuut gehouden zijn om de misdrijven die aan de rechtsmacht van het Strafhof zijn onderworpen, in hun nationale strafwetgeving strafbaar te stellen en voorts om extra-territoriale, universele rechtsmacht te vestigen die hun nationale strafgerechten in staat stelt die misdrijven te berechten óók als ze in het buitenland door niet-nationalen zijn gepleegd.']: see also 18.

[120] Propuesta implementación ICC en la legislación penal y militar venezolana, June 2002, 2, fn. 2, on file with author ['El propósito de esta ponencia (Fn: Esta presentación refleja solo la

Most of these pronouncements point towards implementation being motivated by States' seeking to prevent cases from being declared admissible before the ICC. As such, they see implementation as a safeguard against ICC intervention, diminishing 'the risk to lose their primary competence'[121] and being found 'unable' due to the absence or inadequacies of substantive legislation which render a national judicial system unavailable.[122] While States have sometimes offered additional grounds for implementation,[123] the predominance of these motives suggests that complementarity's potential as a catalyst for implementation materializes primarily via its coercive properties and antagonistic assumption.[124]

Evidently, the adoption of such implementing laws will fall short of compliance with the obligation to investigate and prosecute as long as States fail to actually apply and enforce them. In order to attain that goal, the *legislative* internalization may be insufficient, and what is equally indispensable is the internalization of the same premise through *adjudication* and *executive* action as well as its *political and social* internalization.[125] As long as complementarity's meaning acquires

---

opinión del autor) es contribuir con el proceso de implementación (Fn: *Esta implementación se hace indispensable, habida cuenta que la naturaleza de la CPI es complementaria o subsidiaria de la legislación de los países. En otras palabras, si un país no legisla sobre los crímenes y el procedimiento aplicables, la jurisdicción de la CPI es directa e inmediata. En consecuencia, se hace indispensable legislar en la materia.*) del Estatuto de Roma de creación de la Corte Penal Internacional (de ahora en adelante "ER") en la legislación penal y militar venezolana.' Emphasis added].

[121] Cf (n 109) and text. See similarly Australia, Exposure Draft (n 111), ['this Act does not affect the primary right of Australia to exercise its jurisdiction with respect to crimes within the jurisdiction of the ICC'].

[122] On this construction of 'inability', see pages 156–157.

[123] For Germany, see (n 114) 12 [enumerating the following further grounds for implementation: 'das spezifische Unrecht der Verbrechen gegen das Völkerrecht besser zu erfassen, als dies nach allgemeinem Strafrecht derzeit möglich ist; durch Normierungen in einem einheitlichen Regelungswerk die Rechtsklarheit und die Handhabbarkeit in der Praxis zu fördern; [...] durch die Schaffung eines einschlägigen nationalen Regelungswerks das humanitäre Völkerrecht zu fördern und zu seiner Verbreitung beizutragen']; see also statement by H Däubler-Gmelin, quoted in F Jessberger, 'Prosecuting International Crimes in Domestic Courts: A Look Back Ahead' (2001) 12 Finnish YbIL 281–304, 287 (n 28), suggesting a more cooperative mode ['ICC requiring assistance in the form of increased effort on the part of national justice systems']; see also Consultative comments of the Norwegian Director General of Military Prosecutions included in Proposition No 24 (1999–2000) to the Storting (the Norwegian parliament) concerning Ratification of the Rome Statute of the International Criminal Court of 17 July 1998: '[...] the legislation should be examined with a view to establishing penal powers corresponding to those of the Court, even though the power to punish does in fact already exist. In this regard it may be a question of ensuring that the balance of the penalty level is not disturbed because Norway has to apply provisions whose wording covers the case, but which were written with different circumstances in mind. It may also be right in other respects *to stress the seriousness of some categories of crime such as genocide and crimes against humanity by making special penal provisions for them.*' Emphasis added].

[124] Cf 3. *Complementarity as Sanction.*

[125] On the distinction between these three forms of internalization, see H H Koh, 'Why Do Nations Obey International Law?' (1997) 106 Yale LJ 2656–2657 and 'Bringing International Law Home' (n 95) 642–643. For Koh, 'social internalization' occurs when a norm acquires so much public legitimacy that there is widespread general adherence to it; while 'political internalization' occurs when the political elites accept an international norm and advocate its adoption as a matter of government policy.

acceptance by political elites and the general public only *in abstracto*, but not in concrete cases when the actual enforcement of ICC-implementing legislation is at stake, the transnational legal process evolving around complementarity will fail to produce compliance. It is in these areas that one can reasonably expect problems to persist, which are comparable to those already alluded to above.[126] In short, the real test for complementarity as a catalyst for compliance will be whether, and to what extent, it serves as a converging point for norm internalization in the area of actual enforcement.

6. Interim Conclusions

As noted in the Introduction, the different features of complementarity in support of its being conceptualized as a catalyst for compliance are not mutually exclusive. These features address compliance on different levels, with some focusing on external factors which induce compliance—such as coercion and management—while others, most notably the legitimacy-based explanation, take an internal perspective and explicate compliance by reference to the properties of complementarity. Likewise, the different explanations overlap in certain respects. The managerial model and transnational legal process, for instance, encapsulate features of the legitimacy-based explanations and of coercion.[127] Similarly, both embody features of interaction.[128]

As much as the different abstract explanations can thus not be as neatly separated as might appear from the foregoing analysis, is it impossible to pinpoint any single feature of complementarity which is likely to be more effective than others in catalyzing compliance. Rather, all of these features support the view that complementarity can be described as a mechanism which bears the potential of catalyzing States to conduct investigations and prosecutions of core crimes. Whether one or more of them will be predominant will to a large extent be situation-specific and contextual.

Be that as it may, the abstract conceptualization of complementarity as a catalyst for compliance suggests that one of the crucial criteria for assessing the functioning of the ICC, and the principle of complementarity as its cornerstone, is

---

[126] See in particular *321–326*.

[127] New Sovereignty (n 70) 8–9 [overlap between determinacy and transparency]; H H Koh, 'Bringing International Law Home' (n 95) 634 ['complex combination of [...] five factors [...]: *coercion*, self-interest, *rule-legitimacy*, communitarianism, and internalization of rules through socialization, political action, and legal process'. Emphases added]. David Trimble has also pointed out a different link between (legislative) norm internalization and legitimacy [internalization would endow international law with greater legitimacy and, consequently, persuasiveness, because validation of international norms would be achieved through similar processes that produce domestic law]: D Trimble, 'International Law, World Order, and Critical Legal Studies (book review)' (1990) 42 Stanford LR 811–845, 835, 838–845.

[128] *327* and *332–333*.

whether, how and the extent to which it impacts upon national suppression of the core crimes in actual practice. The development of an analytical framework for assessing this impact will be one of the tasks of the Court in the years to come, not least with a view to determining whether, and to what extent, a given strategy for operationalizing complementarity has succeeded or failed.[129] It will, in no small measure, be the answer to the question of whether the Court functions as an institution which induces States to assume their responsibilities in the struggle against impunity that will determine its failure or success. Only if the answer is in the positive will the Court leave a lasting impression in providing justice for the victims of genocide, crimes against humanity and war crimes.

---

[129] For some reflections on such an analytical framework, see J K Kleffner, 'Complementarity as a Catalyst for Compliance' in J K Kleffner and G Kor (eds) *Complementary Views on Complementarity—Proceedings of the International Roundtable on the Complementary Nature of the International Criminal Court, Amsterdam, 25/26 June 2004* (TMC Asser Press, The Hague 2006) 79–104, 99–103.

VIII

Conclusions

1. Introduction

The objective of this book is to clarify the content of complementarity. To that
end, the study has analyzed the formal framework for the admissibility of cases
before the ICC, as well as the wider implications of complementarity for the suppression of ICC crimes in domestic courts. The following concluding observations
aim to synthesize the findings in the previous chapters and revisit the twofold
question posed in the Introduction, namely: what is the potential of complementarity to fill the gap left by ineffective national enforcement of the prohibitions of
ICC crimes (2), and what is the likely impact of complementarity on the suppression of ICC crimes by national criminal jurisdictions (3)? In the final step, I aim
to integrate the findings of the book into the broader systemic question of how to
ensure accountability for ICC crimes (4).

2. The Potential of Complementarity to Fill the Gap

Although, as argued in Chapter VII, complementarity has the aptitude to function as a catalyst for investigating and prosecuting ICC crimes domestically
under certain circumstances, it is more than likely that significant obstacles to an
effective national suppression of ICC crimes will persist. The systemic nature of
these crimes remains unchanged and, as such, so remain the obstacles to national
suppression which result from this systemic nature. This is already apparent from
the situations that are before the ICC at the time of writing, as the obstacles to
national suppression in Uganda, the DRC and Sudan largely correspond to those
which existed in situations prior to the coming into force of the Rome Statute, in
which core crimes were committed. The intention of the drafters of the Statute
was to establish a Court which reconciles the need to ensure that perpetrators
of ICC crimes are brought to justice in responding to these obstacles with the
concerns of States about their sovereign prerogative to enforce domestically the
prohibitions of such crimes. These underlying considerations have yielded an
institution whose intended aim is to supply the deficiencies of national criminal
jurisdictions and to fill the void left by inactive, unwilling or unable States by

virtue of its complementary nature. But does the regulation of complementarity in the Statute provide the ICC with the tools necessary to achieve this aim?

When considering this question in relation to the *criteria for admissibility*, the answer is likely to be affirmative in the majority of conceivable scenarios: if States remain entirely inactive vis-à-vis such crimes, cases would be admissible before the ICC and the latter thus able to step in and ensure that perpetrators are brought to justice. Furthermore, the notions of 'unwillingness' and 'inability' cover most of the obstacles that have hampered effective national suppression of core crimes in the past and are likely to continue to do so in the future. This is notwithstanding that a broader, more flexible notion of 'ineffectiveness' might also have achieved the same aim, while bearing the advantage of avoiding the conceptual and practical problems that the current regulation of the admissibility criteria entail. On balance, however, the existing criteria will often enable the ICC to fill the void left by national criminal jurisdictions, albeit with the qualification that this does not hold true as regards certain scenarios in which the rights of the accused are violated and when convicted persons are granted clemency after a trial, which satisfies the criteria of willingness and ability.

Our assessment of the question as to whether the *procedural setting* of complementarity is well-suited to achieving the aim of supplying the deficiencies of national enforcement suggests a more nuanced answer. The regulation in the Statute and the Rules of Procedure and Evidence epitomize a relationship between national criminal jurisdictions and the ICC which is primarily contemplated to be one of competing claims of jurisdiction and a fair degree of antagonism and mutual suspicion. The procedural framework can reasonably be expected to work better in these situations for which it has been developed than in situations of more cooperative and affable modes of co-existence (eg auto-referrals), the possibility of which was largely neglected during the negotiations. However, this is not to suggest that the procedural setting is flawless even in those situations which were primarily in the drafters' minds. Indeed, much will depend on whether States Parties honour their obligations under the Statute. If so, the interactive elements of complementarity's procedural setting provide room for a frank, but respectful, dialogue between the ICC and States. That dialogue, together with the powers of the Court to supervise national proceedings, helps to determine whether a given national criminal jurisdiction is ineffective and requires States to justify their (in)action before the Court. In conjunction with the framework for cooperation, these devices go a long way to enable the Court to step in and fill the gap left by ineffective national criminal jurisdictions. This is likely to be different, however, when one considers scenarios in which States Parties are unwilling or unable to comply with their obligations under the Statute or when non-State Parties to the Statute are concerned, as the latter incur rights but no obligations under it. Although certain safeguards exist to counter efforts of malevolent States to thwart an intervention by the ICC, the procedural setting contains a number of loopholes for States to abuse the rights granted to them under Articles 18 and 19. In addition, the Court only possesses very limited powers when the real risk that States are unwilling or unable to cooperate with the Court materializes. These weaknesses can lead to a frustration of ICC proceedings and ultimately prevent the Court from supplying the deficiencies of an ineffective national criminal jurisdiction. The absence of the required degree of differentiation between States with different intentions, prospects for effective national enforcement and obligations under the Statute therefore leads one to conclude that the procedural framework may be adequate in some cases, but subject to considerable limitations in others.

This book has also revealed that an appraisal of the potential of complementarity to supply the deficiencies of national enforcement must look beyond the question of whether and how the ICC can step in when national criminal jurisdictions prove to be ineffective, and also assess how the ICC can step *out* or *not step in in the first place* when they are (or when a reasonable prospect exists for them to be) effective. The Court will only be able to use its limited resources efficiently if it is equipped with the necessary mechanisms that allow it to limit its work to situations in which ICC intervention is truly warranted. It is in relation to this question that the Statute and Rules of Procedure and Evidence are to some extent *one-dimensional,* in as much as they principally regulate how cases can reach the Court, seeking to ensure that the ICC can exercise its jurisdiction in spite of efforts of the State concerned to forestall ICC intervention. The formal framework of complementarity is, in certain respects, either ill-equipped or underdeveloped, however, to answer satisfactorily the question as to how the ICC can step out or not step in in the first place. This is amply illustrated by the absence of an express regulation governing the referral of cases, which have earlier been declared admissible, back to national criminal jurisdictions. It is even more conspicuous when considering auto-referrals, through which States can effectively take the ICC hostage and leave the Court as the only remaining forum available for investigating the alleged ICC crimes and, if need be, prosecute them.

More significant still in appraising the potential of complementarity is to acknowledge the *factual and legal constraints*, which make it impossible that all situations and cases in which States prove inactive, unwilling or unable to investigate and prosecute ICC crimes will *in actual practice* be addressed by the Court. The limited resources of the ICC and the mandatory admissibility requirement of sufficient gravity under Article 17 (1)(d) make it more than likely that the ICC will only address a very small fraction of cases, in which national criminal jurisdictions prove to be ineffective. The same results from the operationalization of the Prosecutor's power not to initiate proceedings or to abandon them because they are not 'in the interests of justice', and a prosecutorial policy focusing on those who bear the *greatest* responsibility in situations where there is a *clear* case of failure on the national level to investigate and prosecute. In other words, there is a considerable divide between theory and practice in the potential of complementarity to supply the deficiencies in national suppression.

In sum, our analysis suggests that the regulation of complementarity in the Statute provides the Court with the necessary tools to supply the deficiencies of a national criminal jurisdiction in individual cases. However, complementarity's overall aptitude to ensure that the ICC can effectively fill the void whenever national criminal jurisdictions prove ineffective is subject to considerable limitations, both legal and, perhaps most importantly, factual.

3. The Impact of Complementarity on National Suppression

Turning to the question of the impact of complementarity on national suppression of ICC crimes, it is evident that the Rome Statute establishes a system of international criminal justice in which national criminal jurisdictions retain a central role. However, the implications of complementarity for national suppression are not limited to a mere reiteration of the pre-existing fragmented legal framework governing domestic investigations and prosecutions of different core crimes. Rather, the Statute subjects all ICC crimes, with the current exception of the crime of aggression which remains to be defined,[1] to an *identical* regime of complementarity, under which States run the risk of forfeiting their sovereign prerogative to exercise jurisdiction over them if they do not investigate and prosecute them. Indeed, this book has found that the complementary regime of the ICC Statute postulates an affirmative, *uniform* obligation to investigate and prosecute, which extends *equally* to *all* ICC crimes and is addressed to all States Parties with jurisdiction over such crimes. Although the Statute does not establish an unambiguous hierarchy that can serve to settle jurisdictional conflicts between States, a number of legal, conceptual, practical and policy considerations lead one to conclude that the obligation to investigate and prosecute is primarily addressed to the territorial State, and subsidiarily to States, which would have to exercise extraterritorial jurisdiction.

From a purely normative perspective, the obligation to investigate and prosecute emanating from the Statute is essentially categorical. Only very limited room exists to reconcile instances of non-investigation and non-prosecution with the Statute as a matter of *law*. Nor does general international law provide grounds that would preclude the international wrongfulness not to investigate and prosecute, except under very narrow and, as a rule, temporarily limited circumstances. The Statute thereby affirms the trend in international law in general,

---

[1] The Special Working Group on the Crime of Aggression agreed in 2004 that 'Articles 17, 18 and 19 were applicable in their current wording and the points raised [regarding the applicability of complementarity] merited being revisited once agreement had been reached on the definition of aggression and the conditions for exercise of the Court's jurisdiction'. See Informal inter-sessional meeting of the Special Working Group on the Crime of Aggression, held at the Liechtenstein Institute on Self-Determination, Woodrow Wilson School, at Princeton University, New Jersey, United States, from 21 to 23 June 2004, ICC-ASP/3/SWGCA/INF.1 [20–27].

and international criminal law in particular, that those suspected of genocide, crimes against humanity and war crimes have to undergo criminal proceedings, rather than alternative accountability processes, and may not benefit from clemency measures or the exercise of prosecutorial discretion on policy grounds. That is not to say that States lose any room to manoeuvre as a pure matter of *fact*. In light of the Court's constraints, States can readily assume that many cases are beyond the reach of the ICC and abstain from investigating and prosecuting them without having to fear that the ICC will declare such cases admissible. This does not alter the conclusion, however, that the Statute answers the question of whether States Parties are legally obliged to investigate and prosecute ICC crimes with a resounding 'yes'.

Yet, the impact of complementarity on national suppression of ICC crimes goes beyond the mere imposition of, yet another, obligation to investigate and prosecute. A crucial *difference* between such obligations which international law imposes independent of the Rome Statute, and the obligation that emanates from the Statute, is the *far-reaching legal consequence* foreseen in cases of non-compliance with the latter obligation: a declaration of admissibility and the consequential loss of jurisdiction by the State concerned. The threat of this sanction, in combination with complementarity's high degree of legitimacy, some managerial features of the regime governing admissibility and complementarity's aptitude to serve as a medium for internalizing the premise that States retain the primary role in suppressing ICC crimes into their domestic legal and political processes, suggests that complementarity bears the potential to induce States to carry out criminal proceedings vis-à-vis ICC crimes. As such, the regime for admissibility can be conceptualized as a *catalyst* for compliance, with the underlying obligation of State Parties to investigate and prosecute and, more broadly, as an incentive for all States to conduct criminal proceedings with regard to these crimes.

With the Court only taking the cautious first steps in operationalizing the Statute and in light of the scant empirical data currently available in relation to complementarity, it is too early to determine whether, and to what extent, the potential of complementarity to serve this catalyst function materializes in actual practice. Decisive in that respect will be whether the wide legislative practice in response to complementarity, ie the adoption of implementing laws which allow States to exercise jurisdiction over ICC crimes, will also be followed by the actual enforcement of these laws. However, it is already safe to conclude that complementarity's aptitude to serve as a catalyst for domestic investigations and prosecutions will, in all likelihood, depend to a considerable degree on the factual situation underlying issues of admissibility in a given situation or case. Here, a generic *distinction* can be made *between 'unwilling' or 'unable' States,* although such a distinction serves a primarily analytical purpose because States may be both 'unwilling' and 'unable'.

The Court is likely to be more successful in exerting influence on unwilling but able States to conduct domestic proceedings than it will in helping unable but willing States to overcome the underlying causes for their inability, such as the collapse of its national judicial system. However, even when the Court can draw on complementarity's coercive and managerial properties vis-à-vis unwilling States, the success or failure of complementarity as a catalyst for domestic proceedings will further depend upon what is at stake for the State concerned. Only if the benefits of investigating and prosecuting outweigh the costs of not doing so will there be a reasonable prospect for complementarity to be successful in the endeavour to induce domestic criminal proceedings. Given the nature of ICC crimes, and the Court's focus on those who bear the greatest responsibility, one can reasonably expect that considerable obstacles will persist in States on whose territory ICC crimes have been committed and/or where their nationals (including high-ranking State officials) are implicated in the commission of such crimes. Furthermore, the cost–benefit calculation may lead third States to conclude that an exercise of universal jurisdiction may not be worthwhile, because the costs of doing so would outweigh the costs of abstaining from it. The foregoing discussion suggests that, if considered in isolation, complementarity as regulated in the Statute will be able to function as a catalyst for inducing and facilitating domestic criminal proceedings only in limited circumstances.

However, complementarity and the Court as an institution do not function in isolation. The *broader context* in which they operate can be galvanized in order to mitigate the aforementioned likely limitations of complementarity's potential to function as a catalyst for domestic proceedings. State Parties individually, or collectively (for instance through the Assembly of States Parties), regional and international governmental organizations, and non-governmental organizations all have a role to play in that regard. Vis-à-vis *unwilling but able* States, efforts to increase the costs, both real and reputational, for miscreant States can go a long way to convince States that to conduct criminal proceedings which satisfy internationally recognized standards of due process is more beneficial than it is costly. The economic and political pressure exerted against States of the former Yugoslavia, and the incentive created for them by the prospect of EU membership, are examples that readily come to mind. This pressure and incentive has yielded some positive results in ascertaining the cooperation with, and surrender of suspects to, the ICTY, although the still outstanding arrest and surrender of the two most prominent suspects, Ratko Mladić and Radovan Karadzic, bears witness to the fact that such pressure and incentives equally have their limits. Furthermore, the possibility of having cases referred back to national criminal jurisdictions in accordance with Rule 11 *bis* of the ICTY's Rules of Procedure and Evidence has spurred States of the former Yugoslavia to undertake efforts to satisfy the conditions for such referrals, including establishing jurisdiction, being willing and adequately prepared to conduct proceedings and ensuring a fair trial when doing so. Comparable responses to a State which is unwilling but able to investigate and prosecute ICC crimes may ultimately lead to a State reversing its position in similar ways.

Different responses may be called for in relation to *unable but willing* States. Here, the main challenge for the various actors which constitute the broader 'ICC community' (ICC, States Parties, regional and international intergovernmental organizations, NGOs) will be to effectively fill the void in the Statute as regards capacity building measures and to develop coherent strategies to reinvigorate, or indeed build for the first time, a domestic legal system. It is laudable that the first steps are being taken to meet this challenge,[2] although only the future will show whether such initiatives will also be endowed with the resources necessary for their success. In any event, a role of the ICC in the endeavour to reform and bolster national judicial systems of unable States must not compromise its role as a supervisory organ. Too close an involvement, for instance a direct role of ICC staff in the training of members of the judiciary of the State concerned, entails the risk of negatively impacting on its ability to fulfil that role effectively and credibly. Other relevant actors are, therefore, better placed to fulfil a more active role in capacity building, while the Court's role should be limited to an identification of the problems in situations which merit intervention by the broader ICC community. At the same time, such a 'flagging role' of the ICC should cover situations in which the Court itself possesses jurisdiction but refrains from exercising it. There may very well be situations that fall into the jurisdiction of the ICC and would also be admissible because a State is unable, but nevertheless the Court does not act, for instance because none of the trigger mechanisms foreseen in Article 13 are activated. Yet, any information gathered by the Court, eg received by the Prosecutor in accordance with Article 15 (1) or (2), should nevertheless be made available to other actors, which can subsequently allow this information to be integrated into strategies aimed at improving the national judicial system

---

[2] See eg the *Vancouver Dialogue*, which seeks to bring together the experience, expertise and resources of institutions, governments, civil society and funding organizations involved in international justice. R Adamson and A Vamos-Goldman, 'The Expectation Gap: Summary of the First Meeting of the Vancouver Dialogue' (June 2003), <http://www.gjp.ubc.ca/_media/act/ExpectationGapReport.pdf>. Possible strategies could take the form of internationalizing national courts and linking them to the ICC in order to improve capacity building. See also Stanley Foundation, 'Creating the International Legal Assistance Consortium', <http://www.stanleyfoundation.org/publications/archive/ILAC00p.pdf>. The International Legal Assistance Consortium was formally launched in December 2000, see <http://www.ilac.se/default2.asp?xid=>. See further H Strohmeyer, 'Collapse and Reconstruction of a Judicial System: The United Nations Missions in Kosovo and East Timor' (2001) 95 AJIL 46, 62 [calling for the UN to enhance its own capacity to establish a functioning judiciary as rapidly as possible and suggesting to formulate a 'quick-start package', encompassing 'criminal procedure and criminal codes, as well as a code regulating the activities of the police' for transitional administrations]. See also the Justice Rapid Response Feasibility Study, produced at the request and with support of the governments of Finland, Germany, Liechtenstein, Sweden, Switzerland and United Kingdom, October 2005, 130 pp, on file with author.

concerned. Otherwise, the failure of the ICC to exercise its jurisdiction over situations in which ICC crimes have been committed would run the risk of conveying the erroneous impression that not all such situations deserve a coordinated response with a view to ensuring that the perpetrators are brought to justice.

In summary, complementarity impacts on national suppression in as much as it imposes a uniform obligation to investigate and prosecute ICC crimes and establishes a mechanism which increases the normativity of that obligation. Whether that increased normativity ultimately leads to actual national suppression, however, will depend upon the underlying attitude of the State concerned and on the success or failure of those spin-offs of complementarity, which are developed within the broader ICC community.

4. Complementarity and the Future of Accountability

The entry into force of the Rome Statute marks a critical development in the endeavour to ensure accountability for the core crimes of genocide, crimes against humanity and war crimes. The ICC and national criminal jurisdictions are crucial building blocks, with the principle of complementarity allocating their respective competences in that endeavour. Yet, the term 'complementarity' should not be misunderstood so as to trigger the expectation that the ICC and national criminal jurisdictions together 'complete' a system of accountability. Indeed, one may very well argue that such a 'system', understood in its original meaning of one *unified* whole with each and every component interacting or related to another, is utopian in a world in which sovereign States remain the primary actors and the diversification and expansion of international law is increasingly leading to fragmentation rather than unification.[3] However, to be aware of such realities should encourage rather than dissuade systemic reflections on the relationship between the different fora in which the prohibition of core crimes can be effectuated, and on their integration into a broader setting of *international criminal justice*. Such systemic reflections on international criminal justice, in turn, need to be embedded into a larger scheme of *accountability* for such crimes, which includes modes other than the criminal responsibility of individuals through which the various actors implicated in their occurrence are, or can be, answerable.

The ICC and national criminal jurisdictions are not the only *international criminal justice mechanisms*. Other fora have entered the stage in the form of ad hoc international(ized) criminal courts and tribunals in the past, and it is likely

---

[3] See for instance the work of the ILC on 'Fragmentation of international law: difficulties arising from the diversification and expansion of international law', Report of the Study Group of the International Law Commission, Finalized by Martti Koskenniemi (13 April 2006) UN Doc A/CN.4/L.682.

that such mechanisms will retain their relevance in the future, not least because the ICC's capacity to supply the deficiencies of national criminal jurisdictions will inevitably remain incomplete. As long as the struggle against impunity of those responsible for genocide, crimes against humanity and war crimes continues to rank high on the international agenda, the search for fora to effectuate individual criminal responsibility will continue, and with it the possibility of overlapping jurisdictions. With territorial States, States of active and passive nationality, States exercising universal jurisdiction, ad hoc international(ized) criminal courts and tribunals and the ICC as potential fora, the question of how to regulate their diversifying mutual relationships, on both the vertical and the horizontal level, becomes ever more acute. What should be the relationships between domestic courts of different States, and between different ad hoc international(ized) criminal courts and tribunals? How should the competences of domestic courts relate to ad hoc international(ized) criminal courts and tribunals, and how should the relationship between the ICC and ad hoc international(ized) criminal courts and tribunals be conceptualized? These questions underscore that complementarity, which is confined to the relationship between *national criminal jurisdictions* and the *ICC*, supplies only *one* organizational principle and *not all* of those that would be needed before being able to speak of international criminal justice as a *system*. As such, complementarity incites us to think beyond it, and to confront the challenges ahead, in building such a system.

Finally, as much as complementarity is thus in want of being complemented with a view to organizing the field of international criminal justice, international criminal justice needs to be entrenched into the broader pursuit of *accountability* for genocide, crimes against humanity and war crimes. It is beyond doubt that individual criminal responsibility for these crimes has undergone important developments, to which the establishment of a permanent international criminal court itself bears witness. And yet, these developments, however significant, do not alter the need also to respond to core crimes by other modes of accountability, if the aim of responding effectively to core crimes, and ultimately advancing the cause of preventing them, is to be achieved. On the one hand, such modes of accountability need to respond to the fact that *individuals* commit core crimes. Examples are individual *civil* responsibility, accountability through truth commission and lustration processes, traditional forms of justice and similar such measures. Yet, their mutual relationships, and their relationships with individual criminal responsibility, still require systematization. On the other hand, a system of accountability equally must coherently and comprehensively capture the *collective* context in which core crimes are committed. Rather than as atomized individuals, perpetrators of these crimes regularly act within the broader environment of a State apparatus, or in an organization exercising de facto control, as members of a party to an armed conflict and/or of a particular national, ethnical, racial, religious or other type of group. This renders the need for making more effective the existing modes of collective accountability, most notably State responsibility for ICC crimes, very acute. Perhaps even more importantly, it requires developing new forms of collective accountability of entities other than States, whose implication in the commission of core crimes is a recurring phenomenon. Only once the evolving system under the ICC Statute and its complements for effectuating individual criminal responsibility matures and functions within a comprehensive system of accountability can one expect international law to provide responses to ICC crimes which are effective enough to make a meaningful contribution to their prevention in the future.

Bibliography

1. BOOKS AND MONOGRAPHS

Ahlbrecht, H, '*Geschichte der völkerrechtlichen Strafgerichtsbarkeit im 20. Jahrhundert, unter besonderer Berücksichtigung der völkerrechtlichen Straftatbestände und der Bemühungen um einen Ständigen Internationalen Strafgerichtshof*' (Nomos, Baden-Baden 1999)

Ambos, K, *Der Allgemeine Teil des Völkerstrafrechts: Ansätze einer Dogmatisierung* (Duncker & Humblot, Berlin 2003)

Ambos, K and E Malarino, *Persecución Penal Nacional de Crímines Internacionales en América Latina Y España* (Max Planck Institute, Freiburg 2003)

Amerasinghe, C F, *Local Remedies in International Law* (2nd edn CUP, Cambridge 2004)

Arbour, L, A Eser, K Ambos and A Sanders (eds), *The Prosecutor of a Permanent International Criminal Court* (edition iuscrim, vol 81, Freiburg 2000)

Arendt, H, *Eichmann in Jerusalem—Ein Bericht von der Banalität des Bösen* (7th edn Piper, Munich/Zurich 1964)

Bassiouni, M C, *Crimes Against Humanity in International Criminal Law* (2nd edn Martinus Nijhoff, Dordrecht 1999)

Bassiouni, M C and E M Wise, *Aut dedere aut judicare: the duty to extradite or prosecute in international law* (Nijhoff Publ, Dordrecht 1995)

Bassiouni, M C and P Manikas, *The Law of the International Criminal Tribunal for the Former Yugoslavia* (Transnational Publ, Ardsley New York 1996)

Bilton, M and K Sim, *Four Hours in My Lai* (Penguin Books, London 1992)

Black's Law Dictionary (7th edn, West Group Publ, St Paul 1999)

Black's Law Dictionary (8th edn West Publ, London 2004)

Bohr, N, *Atomic Physics and Human Knowledge* (Interscience Publishers, New York 1958)

Boot, M, *Nullum Crimen Sine Lege and the Subject Matter Jurisdiction of the International Criminal Court—Genocide, Crimes against Humanity, War Crimes* (Intersentia, Antwerp 2002)

Broomhall, B, *International Justice and the International Criminal Court: Between Sovereignty and the Rule of Law* (OUP, Oxford 2004)

Cárdenas, C, *Die Zulässigkeitsprüfung vor dem Internationalen Strafgerichtshof, Zur Auslegung des Art. 17 IstGH-Statut unter besonderer Berücksichtigung von Amnestien und Wahrheitskommissionen* (Berliner Wissenschaftsverlag, Berlin 2005)

Cassese, A, *International Criminal Law* (OUP, Oxford 2003)

Cassese, A, *International Law* (Oxford University Press, Oxford 2001)

Chayes, A and A Handler Chayes, *The New Sovereignty—Compliance with International Regulatory Agreements* (Harvard University Press, Cambridge MA 1995)

Conforti, B, *International Law and the Role of Domestic Legal Systems* (Martinus Nijhoff Publ, Dordrecht/Boston/London 1993)

Crawford, J, *The International Law Commission's Articles on State Responsibility—Introduction, Text and Commentaries* (Cambridge University Press, Cambridge 2002)

Cryer, R, *Prosecuting International Crimes—Selectivity and the International Criminal Law Regime* (CUP, Cambridge 2005)

Dahm, G, J Delbrück and R Wolfrum, *Völkerrecht, Band I/3* (2nd edn De Gruyter, Berlin 2002)

Daniel, J, *Le Problème du Chatiment des Crimes de Guerre d'après les Einseignements de la Deuxième Guerre Mondiale* (Schindler, Cairo 1946)

De Mildt, D W, *Die westdeutschen Strafverfahren wegen nationalsozialistischer Tötungsverbrechen. Eine systematische Verfahrensbeschreibung mit Karten und Registern* (Maarssen, Holland University Press, Munich KG Saur Verlag 1998)

De Vree, J K, *Order and Disorder in the human universe: the foundations of behavioral and social science* (vol III Prime Press, Bilthoven 1990)

De Wet, E, *The Chapter VII Powers of the United Nations Security Council* (Hart Publishing, Oxford 2004)

Drezner, D W (ed), *Locating the proper authorities: the interaction of domestic and international institutions* (University of Michigan Press, Michigan 2003)

Dworkin, A, *Taking Rights Seriously* (Harvard University Press, Harvard 1977)

Erades, L, M Fitzmaurice and C Flinterman (eds), *Interactions between International and Municipal Law—a comparative case law study* (TMC Asser Institute, The Hague 1993)

Eser, A and H Kreicker, *Nationale Strafverfolgung völkerrechtlicher Verbrechen—National Prosecution of International Crimes* (vol 1 Deutschland, edition iuscrim, Freiburg 2003)

Ferdinandusse, W, *Direct Application of International Criminal Law in National Courts* (TMC Asser Press, The Hague 2006)

Franck, T, *The Power of Legitimacy Among Nations* (Oxford University Press, New York 1990)

Franck, T, *Fairness in International Law and Institutions* (Clarendon Press, Oxford 1995)

Freeman, A V, *The International Responsibility of States for Deniel of Justice* (H Valliant-Carmanne Publ, Liége 1938)

Gilbert, G, *Transnational Fugitive Offenders in International Law: Extradition and Other Mechanims* (Martinus Nijhoff Publishers, The Hague/Boston/London 1998)

Goethe, J W, *Zur Farbenlehre*, 1810

Graf Vitzthum W, (ed), *Völkerrecht* (De Gruyter, Berlin, New York 1997)

Haile, D, *Accountability for Crimes of the Past and the Challenges of Criminal Prosecution: The Case of Ethiopia* (Leuven University Press, Leuven 2000)

Hamzah, A and R M Surachman, *The Prosecutorial Discretion, A Comparative Study, Barcelona Conference on the law of the world* (World Jurist Association, Washington DC 1991)

Hankel, G, *Die Leipziger Prozesse—Deutsche Kriegsverbrechen und ihre strafrechtliche Verfolgung nach dem Ersten Weltkrieg* (Hamburger Edition, Hamburg 2003)

Hannikainen, L, *Peremptory norms (jus cogens) in international law: historical development, criteria, present status* (Finnish Lawyers Publishing Company, Helsinki 1988).

Harris, D J, M O'Boyle and C Warbrick, *Law of the European Convention on Human Rights* (Butterworths Publ, London, Dublin, Edinburgh 1995)

Henckaerts, J M and L Doswald-Beck (eds), *Customary International Humanitarian Law* (Cambridge University Press, Cambridge 2005)

Henzelin, M, *Le Principe de l'Universalité en Droit Pénal International, Droit et Obligation pour les États de poursuivre et juger selon le principe de l'universalité* (Helbin & Lichtenhahn, Munich, Geneva, Brussels 2000)

Human Security Centre, *Human Security Report 2005, War and Peace in the 21st Century* (Oxford University Press, Oxford 2005)

ICRC Advisory Service, *Punishing Violations of International Humanitarian Law at the National Level—A Guide for Common Law States* (ICRC, Geneva 2001)

Ipsen, K, *Völkerrecht* (5th edn CH Beck, Munich 2004)

Jäger, H, Makrokriminalität Studien zur Kriminologie kolletiver Gewalt (Suhrkamp, Frankfurt/Main 1989)

Jayawickrama, N, *The Judicial Application of Human Rights Law—National, Regional and International Jurisprudence* (Cambridge University Press, Cambridge 2002)

Jennings, R and A Watts, *Oppenheim's International Law* (9th edn, vol 1 Longman, London 1996)

Joseph, S, J Schultz and M Castan, *The International Covenant on Civil and Political Rights—Cases, Materials, and Commentary* (Oxford University Press, Oxford 2000)

Joyner, C C and M C Bassiouni (eds) *Reining in Impunity for International Crimes and Serious Violations of Fundamental Human Rights: Proceedings of the Siracusa Conference 17–21 September 1998* (1998) 14 Nouvelles Etudes Penales

Karl, W, *Völkerrechtliche Immunität im Bereich der Strafverfolgungen schwerster Menschenrechtsverletzungen* (Nomos, Baden-Baden 2003)

Kazazi, M, *Burden of Proof and Related Issues: A study on Evidence Before International Tribunals* (Kluwer Law International, London 1996)

Ko Swan Sik, *De verplichting in het volkenrecht, Inaug. Rede uitgesproken bij de aanvaarding van het ambt. van hoogleraar in het internationaal publiek recht aan de Erasmus Universiteit Rotterdam op vrijdag, 22 juni 1990* (TMC Asser Instituut Rotterdam, 's-Gravenhage 1991)

Kritz, N, *Transitional justice: How emerging democracies reckon with former regimes* (United States Institute of Peace Press, Washington DC 1995).

Lackner, K, *Strafgesetzbuch mit Erläuterungen* (21st edn C H Beck, Munich 1995)

Lee, R S (ed), *The International Criminal Court: the making of the Rome Statute: issues, negotiations, results* (Kluwer Law International, The Hague 1999)

Lee, R S (ed), *The International Criminal Court: elements of crimes and rules of procedure and evidence* (Transnational Publ, Ardsley, New York 2001)

Lee, R S *States' Responses to Issues Arising From the ICC Statute: Constitutional, Sovereignty, Judicial Cooperation and Criminal Law* (Transnational Publ, New York 2005)

Lillich, R B (ed), *Fact-Finding Before International Tribunals* (Transnational Publ, New York 1990)

Maxwell Fyfe, David (ed), *War Crimes Trials* (William Hodge, London 1948–1952)

McDougal, M, H Lasswell and L Chen, *Human Rights and World Public Order* (Yale University Press, New Haven 1980)

Meissner, J, *Die Zusammenarbeit mit dem Internationalen Strafgerichtshof nach dem Römischen Statut* (Verlag C H Beck, Munich 2003)

Morel, S, *La Mise en Oeuvre du Principe de la Complémentarité par la Cour Pénale Internationale—Le Cas Particulier des Amnisties* (PhD thesis, University of Lausanne, Lausanne 2005)

Morgenthau, H, *Politics Among Nations: The Struggle for Power and Peace* (6th edn Alfred A Knopf, New York 1985)

Mouton, M W, *Oorlogsmisdrijven en het Internationale Recht* (A.A.M. Stols Publ, The Hague 1947)

Neuner, M (ed), *National Legislation Incorporating International Crimes—Approaches of Civil and Common Law Countries* (BWV Publ, Berlin 2003)

O'Connor, J F, *Good faith in international law, Hersch Lauterpacht memorial lectures* (Dartmouth, Aldershot 1991)

O'Shea, A, *Amnesty for crime in international law and practice* (Kluwer, The Hague 2002)

Paulsson, J, *Denial of Justice in International Law* (Cambridge, CUP 2005)

Paust, J, M C Bassiouni, M Scharf *et al* (eds), *International Criminal Law, Cases and Materials* (2nd edn Carolina Academic Press, Durham 2000)

Peyró Llopis, A, *La compétence universelle en matière de crimes contre l'humanité* (Bruylant, Brussels 2003)

Piccigallo, P R, *The Japanese on Trial: Allied War Crimes Operations in the East, 1945– 1951* (Univ of Texas Press, Austin 1980)

Pictet, J (ed), *Commentary to the First Geneva Convention for the Amelioration of the Condition of the Wounded and the Sick in Armed Forces in the Field* (International Committee of the Red Cross, Geneva 1952)

Pictet, J (ed), *The Geneva Conventions of 12 August 1949: commentary, Part III, Geneva Convention relative to the treatment of prisoners of war* (International Committee of the Red Cross, Geneva 1960)

Pictet, J (ed), *The Geneva Conventions of 12 August 1949: commentary, Part IV, Geneva Convention relative to the protection of civilian persons in time of war* (International Committee of the Red Cross, Geneva 1958)

Pilloud, C, J Pictet, Y Sandoz and C Swinarski, *Commentary on the additional protocols of 8 June 1977 to the Geneva Conventions of 12 August 1949* (International Committee of the Red Cross, Nijhoff Publ, Dordrecht 1987)

Quoc Dinh, N, P Daillier and A Pellet, *Droit International Public* (2nd edn 1980)

Randelzhofer, A and C Tomuschat (eds), *State responsibility and the individual: reparation in instances of grave violations of human rights* (Nijhoff, The Hague 1999)

Rasmussen, E, *Complementarity and Political Science—An Essay on Fundamentals of Political Science Theory and Research Strategy* (Odense University Press, Odense 1987)

Ratner, S R and J S Abrams, *Accountability for Human Rights Atrocities in International Law—Beyond the Nuremberg Legacy* (2nd edn OUP, Oxford 2001)

Razesberger, F, *The International Criminal Court—The Principle of Complementarity* (Peter Lang, Frankfurt/Main 2006)

Reydams, L, *Universal jurisdiction: international and municipal legal perspectives* (OUP, Oxford 2003)

Roht-Arriaza, N (ed), *Impunity and Human Rights in International Law and Practice* (Oxford University Press, New York 1995)

Romano, C, A Nollkaemper and J K Kleffner (eds), *Internationalized Criminal Courts: Sierra Leone, East Timor, Kosovo, and Cambodia* (OUP, Oxford 2004)

Rousseau, C, *Droit International Public, I (Introduction et Sources)* (Paris, 1970)

Rückerl, A, *Die Strafverfolgung von NS-Verbrechen 1945–1978* (C F Müller Publ, Heidelberg, Karlsruhe 1979)

Safferling, C, *Towards an International Criminal Procedure* (OUP, Oxford 2001)

Sandifer, D V, *Evidence Before International Tribunals* (University Press of Virginia, Charlottesville 1975)

Scelle, G, *Précis de droit des gens* (vol II Sirey, Paris 1934)

Scelle, G, *Manuel de droit international public* (Domat-Montchrestien, Paris 1948)

Schabas, W, *Genocide in International Law—The Crime of Crimes* (Cambridge University Press, Cambridge 2000)

Schabas, W, *An Introduction to the International Criminal Court* (2nd edn, Cambridge University Press, Cambridge 2004)

Schermers, H and N Blokker, *International Institutional Law* (4th edn Martinus Nijhoff, Leiden 2003)

Schlunck, A, *Amnesty versus Accountability—Third Party Intervention Dealing with Gross Human Rights Violations in Internal and International Conflicts* (Bochumer Schriften zur Friedenssicherung und zum Humanitären Völkerrecht, Band 38, Berlin Verlag 2000)

Shany, Y, *The competing jurisdictions of international courts and tribunals* (Oxford University Press, Oxford 2003)

Shany, Y, *Regulating Jurisdictional Relations between National and International Courts* (Oxford University Press, Oxford 2007)

Sieber, U, *The punishment of serious crimes: a comparative analysis of sentencing law and practice* (2 volumes, Ed Iuscrim, Freiburg, Breisgau 2004)

Sinclair, Sir I, *The Vienna Convention on the Law of Treaties* (2nd edn Manchester University Press, Manchester 1984)

Sluiter, G, *International Criminal Adjudication and the Collection of Evidence: Obligations of States* (Intersentia, Antwerp, Oxford, New York 2002)

Spronken, T (ed), *Iets Bijzonders—Liber amicorum aangeboden aan Mischa Wladimiroff ter gelegenheid van zijn 30-jarig jubileum als advocaat* (Sdu Publ, The Hague 2002)

Swart, B, *De berechting van internationale misdrijven* (Gouda Quint, Arnhem 1996)

Teitel, R, *Transitional Justice* (Oxford University Press, Oxford 2002)

The Concise Oxford Dictionary (9th edn OUP, Oxford 2001)

The New Collins Dictionary and Thesaurus (Collins, London, Glasgow 1987)

Trechsel, S, *Human Rights in Criminal Proceedings* (Oxford University Press, Oxford 2005)

van Alebeek, R, *The Immunities of States and Their Officials in International Criminal Law and International Human Rights Law* (Oxford University Press, Oxford 2008)

van Sliedregt, E, *The Criminal Responsibility of Individuals for Violations of International Humanitarian Law* (TMC Asser Press, The Hague 2003)

Villiger, M E, *Customary International Law and Treaties—A Manual on the Theory and Practice of the Interrelation of Sources* (2nd edn, Kluwer Publ, The Hague 1997)

Walker, D M, *The Oxford Companion to Law* (Clarendon Press, Oxford 1980)

Waltz, K, *Theory of International Politics* (Addison Wesley, Reading 1979)

Weissbrodt, D, *The Right to a Fair Trial, Articles 8, 10 and 11 of the Universal Declaration of Human Rights* (Martinus Nijhoff, The Hague 2001)

Weissbrodt, D, *The Right to a Fair Trial under the Universal Declaration of Human Rights and the International Covenant on Civil and Political Rights* (Martinus Nijhoff Publ, The Hague 2001)

Werle, G, *Völkerstrafrecht* (Mohr Siebeck Publ, Tübingen 2003)

Werle, G, *Principles of International Criminal Law* (TMC Asser Press, The Hague 2005)

Wouters, J and H Panken (eds), *De Genocidewet in internationaal perspectief,* Jura Falconis Libri (De Boeck & Larcier Publ, Brussels 2002)

You, P, *Le Préambule des Traités Internationaux* (Librairie de L'Université, Fribourg 1941)

Zegveld, L, *Armed Opposition Groups in International Law: The Quest for Accountability* (Thesis, Rotterdam 2000)

Zegveld, L, *Accountability of Armed Opposition Groups in International Law* (Cambridge University Press, Cambridge 2002)

Zwart, T, *The Admissibility of Human Rights Petitions—The Case Law of the European Commission of Human Rights and the Human Rights Committee* (Martinus Nijhoff Publ, Dordrecht, Boston, London 1994)

2. ARTICLES IN JOURNALS AND YEARBOOKS

Abi-Saab, G, 'The Proper Role of Universal Jurisdiction' (2003) 1 JICJ 596–602

Akande, D, 'The Jurisdiction of the International Criminal Court over Nationals of Non-Parties: Legal Basis and Limits' (2003) 1 JICJ 618–650

Akande, D, 'International Law Immunities and the International Criminal Court' (2004) 98 AJIL 407–433

Akhavan, P, 'Enforcement of the Genocide Convention: A Challenge to Civilization' (1995) 8 Harvard Human Rights Journal 229–258

Akhavan, P, 'The Lord's Resistance Army Case: Uganda's Submission of the First State Referral to the International Criminal Court' (2005) 99 AJIL 403–421

Alvarez, J, 'Crimes of states/Crimes of hate: lessons from Rwanda' (1999) 24 Yale JIL 365–483

Ambos, K, 'Impunity and International Criminal Law—A case study on Colombia, Peru, Bolivia, Chile and Argentina' (1997) 18 Human Rights Law Journal 1–15

Andries, A, 'Investigations et poursuites des violations du droit des conflits armés: lois et procédures nationals' (1998) 37 *Revue de droit militaire et de droit de la guerre* 179–223

Arbour, L, 'Will the ICC have an Impact on Universal Jurisdiction?' (2003) 1 JICJ (2003) 585–588

Arsanjani, M H, 'The Rome Statute of the International Criminal Court' (1999) 93 AJIL 22–43

Arsanjani, M H and W M Reisman, 'The Law-in-action of the International Criminal Court' (2005) 99 AJIL 385–403

Ascensio, H, 'Are Spanish Courts Backing down on Universal Jurisdiction? The Supreme Tribunal's Decision in *Guatemalan Generals*' (2003) 1 JICJ 690–702

Balint, J L, 'Conflict, Conflict Victimization, And Legal Redress, 1945–1996' (1996) 59 Law and Contemporary Problems 4 231–247

Barboza, J, 'International Criminal Law' (1999) 278 RdC 9–200

Barcroft, B A, 'The Slow Demise of Impunity in Argentina and Chile' ASIL Insight, January 2005

Bassiouni, M C, 'Enslavement as an international crime' (1991) 23 New York University Journal of International Law and Politics 445–517

Bekou, O and R Cryer, 'The International Criminal Court and Universal Jurisdiction: A Close Encounter?' (2007) 56 ICLQ 49–68

Bellinger, J B III and W J Haynes II, 'A US government response to the International Committee of the Red Cross study Customary International Humanitarian Law' (2007) 89 IRRC 443–471

Benvenisti, E, 'Judicial Misgivings Regarding the Application of International Law: An Analysis of Attitudes of National Courts' (1993) 4 EJIL 159–183

Benvenisti, E, 'Judges and Foreign Affairs: A Comment on the Institut de Droit International's Resolution on "The Activities of National Courts and the International Relations of their State"' (1994) 5 EJIL 423–439

Benzing, M, 'The Complementarity Regime for the International Criminal Court: International Criminal Justice between State Sovereignty and the Fight against Impunity' (2003) 7 Max Planck UNYB 591–632

Bhattacharyya, R, 'Establishing a rule-of-law international criminal justice system' (1996) 31 Texas ILJ 58–99

Bothe, M, 'War crimes in non-international armed conflicts' (1995) 24 Israel Yearbook on Human Rights 241–251

Bottini, G, 'Universal Jurisdiction After the Creation of the International Criminal Court' (2004) 36 NYUJ Intl L & Pol 503–562

Boustany, K, 'Brocklebank: A Questionable Decision of the Court Martial Appeal Court of Canada' (1998) 1 YIHL 371–374

Boyle, F A, 'The Irrelevance of International Law: The Schism Between International Law and International Politics' (1980) 10 California Western ILJ 193–219

Brown, B, 'Primacy or Complementarity: Reconciling the Jurisdiction of National Courts and International Criminal Tribunals' (1998) 23 Yale JIL 383–436

Burke-White, W, 'A Community of Courts: Toward a System of International Criminal Law Enforcement' (2002) 24 Mich JIL 1–101

Burke-White, W, 'Complementarity in Practice: The International Criminal Court as Part of a System of Multi-level Governance in the Democratic Republic of Congo' (2005) 18 LJIL 557–590

Carnegie, A R, 'Jurisdiction over Violations of the Laws and Customs of War' (1963) 39 BYIL 402–424

Carnero Rojo, E, 'The Role of Fair Trial Considerations in the Complementarity Regime of the International Criminal Court: From "No Peace without Justice" to "No Peace with Victor's Justice"?' (2005) 18 LJIL 829–869

Cassel, D, 'The Rome Treaty for an International Criminal Court: A Flawed but Essential First Step' (1999) 6 The Brown Journal of World Affairs 41–52

Cassese, A, 'Remarks on Scelles Theory of "Role Splitting" (*dédoublement fonctionnel*) in International Law' (1990) 1 EJIL 1/2, 210–232

Cassese, A, 'On the Current Trends towards Criminal Prosecution and Punishment of Breaches of International Humanitarian Law' (1998) 9 EJIL 2–17

Cassese, A, 'When May Senior State Officials Be Tried for International Crimes? Some Comments on the Congo v. Belgium Case' (2002) 13 EJIL 853–874

Cassese, A, 'A Big Step Forward for International Justice' (2003) Crimes of War Magazine, <http://www.crimesofwar.org/icc_magazine/icc-cassese.html>

Charney, J I, 'Universal International Law' (1993) 87 AJIL 529–551

Charney, J I, 'International criminal law and the role of domestic courts' (2001) 95 AJIL 121–124

Chayes A and A Handler Chayes, 'On Compliance' (1993) 47 International Organization 175–205

Cohen, D, 'Intended to Fail—The Trials before the Ad Hoc Human Rights Court in Jakarta' (2003) 74 International Center for Transitional Justice 5

Concannon, B, 'Beyond Complementarity: The International Criminal Court and National Prosecutions, a View from Haiti' (2000) 32 Columbia Human Rights LR 201–250

Condorelli, L, 'La Cour pénale internationale: un pas géant (pourvu qu'il soit accompli …)' (1999) 103 RGDIP 7–21

Conforti, B, 'Cours général de droit international public' (1988) RdC V, tome 212, 9–210

Conforti, B, 'Notes on the Relationship between International Law and National Law' (2001) 3 International Law FORUM du Droit International 18–24

Correa G R P, 'Chile' (2003) 1 International Journal of Constitutional Law 130–135

Cottier, M, 'Die Anwendbarkeit von völkerrechtlichen Normen im innerstaatlichen Bereich als Ausprägung der Konstitutionalisierung des Völkerrechts' (1999) 9 Schweizerische Zeitschrift für internationales und europäisches Recht 403–440

Crawford, J, 'The ILC's Draft Statute for an International Criminal Tribunal' (1994) AJIL 140–152

Crawford, J, 'The Problems of Legitimacy-Speak' (2004) ASIL Proceedings 271–273

Delmas-Marty, M, 'Interactions between National and International Criminal Law in the Preliminary Phase of Trial at the ICC' (2006) 4 JICJ 2–11

Desch, T, 'The Second Protocol to the 1954 Hague Convention for the Protection of Cultural Property in the Event of Armed Conflict' (1999) 2 YIHL 63–90

Dicker, R and H Duffy, 'National Courts and the ICC' (1999) 6 The Brown Journal of World Affairs 53–63

Dickinson, L, 'The Promise of Hybrid Courts' (2003) 97 AJIL 295–310

Doherty, K L and T L H McCormack, '"Complementarity" as a Catalyst for Comprehensive Domestic Penal Legislation' (1999) 5 UC Davis Journal of International Law and Policy 147–180

Drumbl, M, 'Counseling accused in Rwanda's domestic genocide trials' (1998) 29 Columbia Human Rights LR 545

Dubois, O, 'Rwanda's national criminal courts and the International Tribunal' (1997) 321 IRRC 717–731

Dugard, J, 'Is the Truth and Reconciliation process compatible with international law? An unanswered question' (1997) 13 S Afr J Hum Rights 258–268

Dugard, J, 'South Africa's Truth and Reconciliation Process and International Humanitarian Law' (1999) 2 YIHL 254–263

El Zeidy, M, 'The Principle of Complementarity: A New Machinery to Implement International Criminal Law' (2002) 23 Michigan JIL 869–975

El Zeidy, M, 'Universal Jurisdiction in Absentia: Is it a Legal Valid Option for Suppressing International Crimes?' (2003) 37 The International Lawyer 835–861

El Zeidy, M, 'The Ugandan Government Triggers the First Test of the Complementarity Principle: An Assessment of the First State's Party Referral to the ICC' (2005) 5 International Criminal Law Review 83–119

Fairlie, M, 'Establishing Admissibility at the International Criminal Court: Does the Buck Stop with the Prosecutor, Full Stop?' (2005) 29 The International Lawyer 817–842

Ferdinandusse, W, 'Out of the Black-box? The international obligation of state organs' (2003) 29 Brooklyn Journal of International Law 45–127

Fife, R E, 'The International Criminal Court—Whence it Came, Where it Goes' (2000) 69 NJIL 63–85

Fitzmaurice, G, 'The Law and Procedure of the International Court of Justice 1951–1954: Treaty Interpretation and Other Treaty Points' (1957) BYIL 229

Fletcher, G P and J D Ohlin, 'The ICC—Two Courts in One?' (2006) 4 JICJ 428–433

Fletcher, L E and H M Weinstein, 'Violence and Social Repair: Rethinking the Contribution of Justice to Reconciliation' (2002) 24 Human Rights Quarterly, 573–639

Florenz, F M M, 'The Rule of Law in Kosovo: Problems and Prospects' (2000) 11 Criminal Law Forum 127–142

Flores, J L F, 'Suppression of breaches of the law of war committed by individuals' (1991) 31 IRRC 247–293

Franck, T M, 'Legitimacy in the International Legal System' (1988) 82 AJIL 705–759

Gaeta, P, 'The Defence of Superior Orders: The Statute of the International Criminal Court versus Customary International Law' (1999) 10 EJIL 172–191

Gavron, J, 'Amnesties in the Light of Developments in International Law and the Establishment of the International Criminal Court' (2002) 51 ICLQ 91–117

Gioia, F, 'State Sovereignty, Jurisdiction, and "Modern" International Law: The Principle of Complementarity in the International Criminal Court' (2006) 19 LJIL 1095–1123

Goldstone, R J and N Fritz, ' "In the Interests of Justice" and Independent Referral: The ICC's Prosecutor's Unprecedented Powers' (2000) 13 LJIL 655–667

Graditzky, T, 'Individual criminal responsibility for violations of international humanitarian law committed in non-international armed conflicts' (1998) International Review of the Red Cross 29–56

Graefrath, B, 'Universal Jurisdiction and an International Criminal Court' (1990) 1 EJIL 72–75

Grynfogel, C 'De Touvier a Papon, "la complicité de crime contre l'humanité" ' (1998) 78 Revue de droit pénal et de criminologie 758–779

Gurule, J, 'United States Opposition to the 1998 Rome Statute Establishing an International Criminal Court: Is the Court's Jurisdiction Truly Complementary to National Criminal Jurisdictions?' (2001) 35 Cornell Intl LJ 1–45

Guzman, A T, 'A Compliance-Based Theory of International Law' (2002) 90 California Law Rev 1823–1887

Hafner, G, K Boon, A Rübesame and J Huston, 'A Response to the American View as Presented by Ruth Wedgwood' (1999) 10 EJIL 108–123

Hall, C K, 'The First Two Sessions of the UN Preparatory Committee on the Establishment of an International Criminal Court' (1997) AJIL 177–187

Hall, C K, 'The first proposal for a permanent international criminal court' (1998) 322 IRRC p 101, 57–74

Hall, C K, 'The Third and Fourth session of the UN Preparatory Committee on the establishment of an International Criminal Court' (1998) AJIL 124–133

Harhoff, F, 'Consonance or Rivalry? Calibrating the Efforts to Prosecute War Crimes in National and International Tribunals' (1997) 7 Duke JCIL 571–596

Hayner, P B, 'Fifteen Truth Commissions—1974 to 1994: A Comparative Study' (1994) 16 Human Rights Quarterly 597–655

Heasley, N, R Hurley, K Irwin, A Kaufman, N Moustafa and A Personna, 'Impunity in Guatemala: The State's Failure to Provide Justice in the Massacre Cases' (2001) 16 Am U Intl Rev 1115–1194

Heller, K J, 'The Shadow Side of Complementarity: The Effect of Article 17 of the Rome Statute on National Due Process' (2006) 17 Criminal Law Forum 250–288

Higonnet, E, 'Restructuring Hybrid Courts: Local Empowerment and National Criminal Justice Reform' (1 March 2005), *Yale Law School Student Scholarship Series.* Paper 6, available at <http://lsr.nellco.org/cgi/viewcontent.cgi?article=1005&context=yale/student>

International Society for Military Law and the Law of War, 'Compatibility of National Legal Systems with the Statute of the Permanent International Criminal Court' (2003) Recueil XVI, two volumes, 813

Jackson, J H, 'Sovereignty-Modern: A New Approach to an Outdated Concept' (2003) 97 AJIL 782–802

Jäger, H, 'Makrokriminalität. Studien zur Kriminologie kollektiver Gewalt' (Suhrkamp, Frankfurt/Main 1989) 11

Jessberger, F, 'Prosecuting International Crimes in Domestic Courts: A Look Back Ahead' (2001) 12 Finnish Yearbook of International Law 281–304

Kalshoven, F, 'A Colombian view on Protocol II' (1998) 1 YIHL 262–268

Kammerhofer, J, 'Uncertainty in the formal Sources of international Law: customary international Law and some of its Problems' (2004) 15 EJIL 523–553

Kazazi, M and B E Shifman, 'Evidence before International Tribunals—Introduction' (1999) 1 International Law Forum 193–196

Kingsbury, B, 'The Concept of Compliance as a Function of Competing Conceptions of International Law' (1998) Michigan Journal of International Law 345–372

Kleffner, J K, 'General Report, 'The Compatibility of National Legal Systems with the Statute of the Permanent International Criminal Court (ICC), Part II—Procedural Law' (2003) International Society for Military Law and the Law of War, Recueil XVI, Vol II, 497–523

Kleffner, J K, 'The Impact of Complementarity on National Implementation of Substantive International Criminal Law' (2003) 1 JICJ 86–113

Kleffner, J K, National Enforcement of International Humanitarian Law: A Case Study of War Crimes Prosecutions in Bosnian Domestic Courts in H van Harten and Y Donders (eds), *Gepeperde noten* (U v A Amsterdam 2006) 124–140

Klip, A, 'Complementarity and Concurrent Jurisdiction' in International Criminal Law: *Quo Vadis?* Proceedings of the International Conference held in Siracusa, Italy, 28 November–3 December 2002, on the Occasion of the 30th Anniversary of ISISC (2004) 19 Nouvelles études pénales 173–197

Koh, H H, 'Why the President (almost) always wins in foreign affairs—lessons of the Iran-Contra Affair' (1988) 97 Yale LJ 1255–1342

Koh, H H, 'Transnational Public Law Litigation' (1991) 100 Yale LJ 2347–2402

Koh, H H, 'Transnational Legal Process' (1996) 75 Nebraska LR 181

Koh, H H, 'Why Do Nations Obey International Law?' (1997) 106 Yale LJ 2656–2657

Koh, H H, 'The 1998 Frankel Lecture: Bringing International Law Home' (1998) 35 Houston LR 623–681

Kress, C, 'War Crimes Committed in Non-International Armed Conflict and the Emerging System of International Criminal Justice' (2000) 30 Israel Yb HR 103–177

Kress, C, ' "Self-Referrals" and "Waivers of Complementarity", Some Considerations in Law and Policy' (2004) 2 JICJ 944–948

Kress, C, 'Universal Jurisdiction over International Crimes and the Institut de Droit International' (2006) 4 JICJ 561–585

Kritz, N, 'Coming to Terms with Atrocities: A Review of Accountability Mechanisms for Mass Violations of Human Rights' (1996) 59 Law and Contemporary Problems 4, 127–152

Kumm, M, 'The Legitimacy of International Law: A Constitutionalist Framework of Analysis' (2004) 15 EJIL 907–931

Lampe, E, 'Systemunrecht und Unrechtssysteme' (1994) 106 Zeitschrift für die gesamte Strafrechtswissenschaft 683–745

Landsman, S, 'Alternative Responses To Serious Human Rights Abuses: Of Prosecution and Truth Commissions' (1996) 59 Law and Contemporary Problems 81–92

Mahmoud, M, 'Les leçons de l'affaire Pinochet' (1999) 4 Journal du Droit International, 1021–1041

Manuell, J and A Kontic, 'Transitional justice: the prosecution of war crimes in Bosnia and Herzegovina under the "Rules of the Road" ' (2000) 5 YIHL 331–343

Mayfield, J V, 'The Prosecution of War Crimes and Respect for Human Rights: Ethiopia's Balancing Act' (1995) 9 Emory ILR 553–593

Mazzeschi, R P, 'Reparation claims by individuals for state breaches of humanitarian law and human rights: an overview' (2003) 1 JICJ 339–347

McDonald, A, 'Sierra Leone's Uneasy Peace: The Amnesties Granted in the Lomé Peace Agreement and the United Nations' Dilemma' (2000) 1 Humanitäres Völkerrecht 11

McNeal, G S , 'ICC Inability Determinations in Light of the Dujail Case' (2007) 39 Case Western Reserve Journal of International Law 325–350

Mégret, F, 'Qu'est ce qu'une juridiction « incapable » ou « manquant de volonté » au sens de l'article 17 du Traité de Rome? Quelques enseignements tirés des théories du déni de justice en droit international' (2004) 17 Revue québécoise de droit international 185–216

Meintjes, G and J E Méndez, 'Reconciling Amnesties with Universal Jurisdiction' (2000) 2 International Law FORUM du droit international 76–97

Meron, T, 'Is International Law Moving towards Criminalization?' (1998) 9 EJIL 18–31

Mettraux, G, 'US Courts-Martial and the Armed Conflict in the Philippines (1899–1902): Their Contribution to National Case Law on War Crimes' (2003) JICJ 135–150

Meyer, F 'Complementing Complementarity' (2006) 6 International Criminal Law Review 549–583

Meyerfield, J, 'The Mutual Dependence of External and Internal Justice: The Democratic Achievement of the International Criminal Court' (2001) 12 Finnish YbIL 71–107

Morris, M, 'The trials of concurrent jurisdiction: the case of Rwanda' (1997) 7 Duke JCIL 349–374

Mundis, D A, 'The Judicial Effects of the "Completion Strategies" on the Ad Hoc International Criminal Tribunals' (2005) 99 AJIL 142–157

Neumann, G L, 'Comment, Counter-terrorist Operations and the Rule of Law' (2004) 15 EJIL 1019–1029

Neuwirth, R, 'International Law and the Public/Private Law Distinction' (2000) 55 Austrian Journal of Public and International Law 393–410

Newton, M A, 'Comparative Complementarity: Domestic Jurisdiction Consistent with the Rome Statute of the International Criminal Court' (2001) 167 Military Law Review 20–73

Nollkaemper, A, 'On the Effectiveness of International Rules' (1992) 27 Acta Politica 49–70

Nollkaemper, A, 'Concurrence between individual responsibility and state responsibility in international law' (2003) 52 ICLQ 615–640

Ntanda Nsereko, D D, 'Prosecutorial Discretion before National Courts and International Tribunals' (2005) 3 Journal of International Criminal Justice 124–144

O'Keefe, R, 'Universal Jurisdiction: Clarifying the Basic Concept' (2004) 2 JICJ 735–760

Olásolo, H, 'The Prosecutor of the ICC before the Initiation of Investigations: A Quasi-Judicial or a Political Body?' (2003) 3 International Criminal Law Review 87–150

Olásolo, H, 'The Triggering Procedure of the International Criminal Court, Procedural Treatment of the Principle of Complementarity, and the Role of Office of the Prosecutor' (2005) 5 International Criminal Law Review 121–146

Oosthuizen, G H, 'Some Preliminary Remarks on the Relationship Between the Envisaged International Criminal Court and the UN Security Council' (1999) 46 Netherlands International Law Review 313–342

Orentlicher, D F, 'Settling Accounts: The Duty to Prosecute Human Rights Violations of a Prior Regime' (1991) 100 Yale Law Journal 2537–2615

Osiel, M J, 'Why Prosecute? Critics of Punishment for Mass Atrocities' (2000) 22 Human Rights Quarterly 118–147

Philippe, X, 'The Principles of Universal Jurisdiction and Complementarity: How do the Two Principles Intermesh?' (2006) 88 IRRC 375–398

Philips, R B, 'The International Criminal Court Statute: Jurisdiction and Admissibility' (1999) 10 Criminal Law Forum, Special Issue on the ICC 61–85

Politi, M, 'Le Statut de Rome de la Cour Pénale Internationale: Le Point de Vue d'un Négociateur' (1999) 103 RGDIP 817–850

Raab, D, 'Evaluating the ICTY and its Completion Strategy—Efforts to Achieve Accountability for War Crimes and their Tribunals' (2005) 3 JICJ 82–102

Rabinovitch, R, 'Universal Jurisdiction in Absentia' (2005) 28 Fordham International Law Journal 500–530

Randall, K, 'Universal Jurisdiction under International Law' (1988) 66 Texas Law Review 785–842

Ratner, S, 'Belgium's War Crimes Statute: A Postmortem' (2003) 97 AJIL 888–897

Ratner, S, 'Overcoming Temptations to Violate Human Dignity in Times of Crisis: On the Possibilities for Meaningful Self-Restraint' (2004) 5 Theoretical Inquiries in Law 81–109

Roberts, A E, 'Traditional and modern approaches to customary international law: a reconciliation' (2001) 95 AJIL 757–791

Robinson, D, 'Defining "Crimes Against Humanity" at the Rome Conference' (1999) 93 AJIL 43–57

Robinson, D, 'Serving the Interests of Justice: Amnesties, Truth Commissions and the International Criminal Court' (2003) 14 EJIL 481–505

Roht-Arriaza, N, Constitutional Tribunal, Guatemalan Genocide Case, Second Chamber, Judgment of 26 September 2005, No STC/237/2005 (2006) 100 AJIL 207–213

Romano, C P R, 'The Proliferation of International Judicial Bodies: The Pieces of the Puzzle' (1999) 31 NYU J IntL L & Pol 709–751

Rosenstock, R, 'The Forty-Fourth Session of the International Law Commission' (1993) AJIL 138–140

Sadat, L N and S R Carden, 'The New International Criminal Court: An Uneasy Revolution' (2000) 88 Georgetown LJ 381

Sands, P, 'International Law Transformed? From Pinochet to Congo…?' (2003) 16 LJIL 37–53

Sarooshi, D, 'The Statute of the International Criminal Court' (1999) 48 ICLQ 387–404

Sarooshi, D, 'Aspects of the Relationship between the International Criminal Court and the United Nations' (2001) 32 NYIL 27–53

Satkauskas, R, 'Soviet Genocide Trials in the Baltic States: the Relevance of International Law' (2006) 7 YIHL 388–409

Scelle, G, 'Règles générales du droit de la paix' (1933) 46 Recueil des cours de l'Académie de La Haye IV 327–703

Scelle, G, 'Quelques réflexions sur l'abolition de la compétence de guerre', (1954) RGDIP 7–13

Scharf, M, 'Swapping Amnesty for Peace: Was There a Duty to Prosecute International Crimes in Haiti?' (1996) 31 Texas International Law Journ al 1–41

Scharf, M, 'The Letter of the Law: The Scope of the International Legal Obligation to Prosecute Human Rights Crimes' (1996) 59 Law and Contemporary Problems 41–61

Scharf, M, 'The Amnesty Exception to the Jurisdiction of the International Criminal Court' (1999) 32 Cornell ILJ 507–527

Schepers, S, 'The legal force of the preamble to the EEC treaty' (1981) 6 European Law Review 356–361

Seguin, J, 'Denouncing the International Criminal Court: An examination of U.S. Objections to the Rome Statute' (2000) 18 Boston University Intl LJ 85–109

Seibert-Fohr, A, 'The Relevance of the Rome Statute of the International Criminal Court for Amnesties and Truth Commissions' (2003) 7 Max Planck UNYB 553–590

Shany, Y, 'Contract Claims vs Treaty Claims: Mapping Conflicts Between ICSID Decisions on Multisourced Investment Claims (2005) 99 AJIL 835–851

Sheng, A Y, 'Analyzing the International Criminal Court Complementarity Principle Through a Federal Courts Lens' (2006) The Berkeley Electronic Press, BePress Legal Series, Paper 1249, <http://law.bepress.com/cgi/viewcontent.cgi?article=5942&context=expresso>

Smis, S and K van der Borght, 'Introductory Note to Belgium's Amendment to the Law of June 16, 1993 (As Amended by the Law of February 10, 1999) Concerning the Punishment of Grave Breaches of Humanitarian Law' (2003) 42 ILM 740–748

Somer, J, 'Jungle justice: passing sentence on the equality of belligerents in non-international armed conflict' (2007) 89 International Review of the Red Cross 655–690

Somers, S, 'Rule 11 bis of the International Criminal Tribunal for the Former Yugoslavia: Referral of Indictments to National Courts' (2007) 30 Boston College International and Comparative Law Review 175–183

Stahn, C, 'The Ambiguities of Security Council Resolution 1422 (2002)' (2003) 14 EJIL 85–104

Stahn, C, 'Complementarity, Amnesties and Alternative Forms of Justice: Some Interpretative Guidelines for the International Criminal Court' (2005) 3 JICJ 695–720

Stahn, C, M El Zeidy and H Olásolo, 'The International Criminal Court's Ad Hoc Jurisdiction revisited' (2005) 99 AJIL 421–431

Steven, L A, 'Genocide and the Duty to Extradite or Prosecute: Why the United States is in Breach of Its International Obligations' (1999) 39 Virginia Journal of International Law 425–466

Stoelting, D, 'ICC PreTrial Proceedings: Avoiding Gridlock' (2003) 9 ILSA J Intl & Comp L 413–423

Strohmeyer, H, 'Collapse and Reconstruction of a Judicial System: The United Nations Missions in Kosovo and East Timor' (2001) 95 AJIL 46

Summers, M A, 'A Fresh Look at the Jurisdictional Provisions of the Statute of the International Criminal Court: The Case for Scrapping the Treaty' (2001) 20 Wisconsin ILJ 57–88

Tallgren, I, 'Completing the "International Criminal Order"' (1998) 67 NJIL 107–137

Thürer, D, 'The "failed State" and international law' (1999) 836 IRRC 731–761

Thürer, D, 'Modernes Völkerrecht: Ein System im Wandel und Wachstum—Gerechtigkeitsgedanke als Kraft der Veränderung' (2000) 60 ZaöRV 557–603

Tomuschat, C, 'International Law: Ensuring the Survival of Mankind on the Eve of a New Century' (1999) 281 RdC 9–438

Trimble, D, 'International Law, World Order, and Critical Legal Studies (book review)' (1990) 42 Standford LR 811–845

Udombana, N J, 'So far, so fair: The Local Remedies Rule in the Jurisprudence of the African Commission on Human and Peoples' Rights' (2003) 97 AJIL 1–37

van den Wyngaert, C, and G Stessens, 'The International *Non Bis In Idem* Principle: Resolving Some of the Unanswered Questions' (1999) 48 ICLQ 779

Verhaegen, 'Legal obstacles to prosecution of breaches of humanitarian law' (1987) 27 IRRC 607–620

Verhoeven, J, 'M. Pinochet, la coutume internationale et la compétence universelle, note sous Civ. Bruxelles, 6 novembre 1998' (1999) Journal des Tribunaux 308–315

Verhoeven, J, 'Article 21 of the Rome Statute and the ambiguities of applicable law' (2002) 33 NYIL 3–22

Wallace-Bruce, N L, 'Of Collapsed, Dysfunctional and Disoriented States: Challenges to International Law' (2000) 47 NILR 53–73

Warbrick, C, E M Salgado and N Goodwin, 'The Pinochet Cases in the United Kingdom' (1999) 2 YIHL 91–117

Weil, P, 'Towards Relative Normativity in International Law?' (1983) 77 AJIL 413–442
Wolfke, K, 'Some persistent controversies regarding customary international law' (1993) 24 NYIL 1–16
Young, S N M,'Surrendering the Accused to the International Criminal Court' (2000) 71 BYIL 317–356
Zimmermann, A, 'The Creation of a Permanent International Criminal Court' (1998) 2 Max UNYB 169

3. CONTRIBUTIONS TO COLLECTED WORKS

Ambos, K, 'Comparative Summary of National Reports' in L Arbour, A Eser, K Ambos and A Sanders (eds), *The Prosecutor of a Permanent International Criminal Court* (edition iuscrim, vol 81, Freiburg 2000) 495–528
Ambos, K, 'Superior Responsibility' in A Cassese, P Gaeta and J Jones (eds), *The Rome Statute of the International Criminal Court: A Commentary* (OUP, Oxford 2002) 823–872
Ambos, K and S Wirth, 'Genocide and War Crimes in the Former Yugoslavia Before German Criminal Courts' in H Fischer, C Kress and S R Lüder (eds), *International and national prosecution of crimes under international law: current developments* (Spitz, Berlin 2001) 769–797
Arbour, L and M Bergsmo, 'Conspicuous Absence of Jurisdictional Overreach' in H von Hebel, J Lammers and J Schukking (eds), *Reflections on the International Criminal Court—Essays in Honour of Adriaan Bos* (TMC Asser Press, The Hague 1999) 129–140
Arsanjani, M H, 'Reflections on the Jurisdiction and Trigger-Mechanism of the International Criminal Court' in H von Hebel, J Lammers and J Schukking (eds), *Reflections on the International Criminal Court—Essays in Honour of Adriaan Bos* (TMC Asser Press, The Hague 1999) 57–76
Bassiouni, M C, 'Searching for Peace and Achieving Justice: The Need for Accountability' in C C Joyner and M C Bassiouni (eds), *Reining in Impunity for International Crimes and Serious Violations of Fundamental Human Rights: Proceedings of the Siracusa Conference 17–21 September 1998* (1998) 14 Nouvelles Etudes Penales 45–70
Bassiouni, M C, 'The Sources and Content of International Criminal Law' in C Bassiouni (ed), *International Criminal Law* (vol I (Crimes) 2nd edn Transnational Publ, Ardsley NY 1999) 3–126
Bassiouni, M C, 'L'expérience des premières juridictions pénales internationals' in H Ascensio, E Decaux and A Pellet (eds), *Droit International Pénal* (Éditions Pedone, Paris 2000) 635–659
Bennouna, M, 'The Statute's Rules on Crimes and Existing or Developing International Law' in A Cassese, P Gaeta and J Jones (eds), *The Rome Statute of the International Criminal Court: A Commentary* (2002) 1101–1107
Benvenuti, P, 'Complementarity of the International Criminal Court to national criminal jurisdictions' in F Lattanzi and W Schabas (eds), *Essays on the Rome Statute of the International Criminal Court* (vol 1 Ripa Fagnano Alto, Editrice il Sirente 1999) 21–50

Benzing, M and M Bergsmo, 'Some Tentative Remarks on the Relationship Between Internationalized Criminal Jurisdictions and the International Criminal Court' in C Romano, A Nollkaemper and J K Kleffner (eds), *Internationalized Criminal Courts: Sierra Leone, East Timor, Kosovo, and Cambodia* (OUP Oxford 2004) 407–416

Bergsmo, M and O Triffterer, 'Preamble' in O Triffterer (ed) *Commentary on the Rome Statute of the International Criminal Court—Observers' Notes, Article by Article* (Nomos, Baden-Baden 1999) 1–16

Bergsmo, M and P Kruger, 'Article 53' in O Triffterer (ed), *Commentary on the Rome Statute of the International Criminal Court—Observers' Notes, Article by Article* (Nomos, Baden-Baden 1999)

Bitti, G and H Friman, 'Participation of victims in the proceedings' in R S Lee (ed), *The International Criminal Court—Elements of Crimes and Rules of Procedure and Evidence* (Transnational Publ, New York 2001)

Bos, A, 'The Role of an International Criminal Court in the Light of the Principle of Complementarity' in E Denters and N Schrijver (eds), *Reflections on International Law from the Low Countries* (Kluwer, The Hague 1998) 249–259

Bos, A, 'From the International Law Commission to the Rome Conference (1994–1998)' in A Cassese, P Gaeta and J Jones (eds), *The Rome Statute of the International Criminal Court: A Commentary* (2002) 35–65

Bothe, M, 'Introduction' in M Bothe (ed), *National Implementation of International Humanitarian Law* (Kluwer Academic Publishers, Dordrecht, Boston, London 1990)

Bothe, M, 'War Crimes' in A Cassese, P Gaeta and J Jones (eds), *The Rome Statute of the International Criminal Court: A Commentary* (2002) 379–426

Brody, R and H Duffy, 'Prosecuting Torture Universally, Hissène Habré, Africa's Pinochet?' in H Fischer, C Kress and S R Lüder (eds), *International and national prosecution of crimes under international law: current developments* (Spitz, Berlin 2001) 817–842

Cassese, A, 'Crimes Against Humanity' in A Cassese, P Gaeta and J Jones (eds) *The Rome Statute of the International Criminal Court: A Commentary* (2002) 353–378

Chesterman, S, 'No Justice Without Peace? International Criminal Law and the Decision to Prosecute' in S Chesterman (ed), *Civilians in War* (Lynne Rienner Publishers, Boulder, London 2001) 145–163

Ciampi, A, 'The obligation to cooperate' in A Cassese, P Gaeta and J Jones (eds), *The Rome Statute of the International Criminal Court: A Commentary* (2002) 1607–1638

Condorelli, L and S Villalpando, 'Can the Security Council Extend the ICC's Jurisdiction?' in A Cassese, P Gaeta and J Jones (eds), *The Rome Statute of the International Criminal Court: A Commentary* (2002) 571–583

Condorelli, L and S Villalpando, 'Referral and Deferral by the Security Council' in A Cassese, P Gaeta and J Jones (eds), *The Rome Statute of the International Criminal Court: A Commentary* (2002) 627–655

Cottier, M, 'What relationship between the exercise of Universal and Territorial Jurisdiction' in H Fischer, C Kress and S R Lüder (eds), *International and national prosecution of crimes under international law: current developments* (Spitz, Berlin 2001) 843–857

Crawford, J, 'The Work of the International Law Commission' in A Cassese, P Gaeta and J Jones (eds), *The Rome Statute of the International Criminal Court: A Commentary* (2002) 23–34

De La Pradelle, G, 'La Compétence Universelle' in H Ascensio, E Decaux and A Pellet (eds), *Droit International Pénal* (Éditions Pedone, Paris 2000) 905–918

de Zayas, A M, 'Amnesty Clause' in R Bernhardt (ed), *Encyclopedia of Public International Law* (vol 1 North-Holland, Amsterdam 1992) 148–151

Domb, F, 'Treatment of War Crimes in Peace Settlements—Prosecution or Amnesty' in Y Dinstein, and M Tabory (eds), *War Crimes in International Law* (Martinus Nijhoff Publ, The Hague, Boston, London 1996) 305–320

Dunat-Cattin, D, 'The role of victims in ICC proceedings', in F Lattanzi and W Schabas (eds), *Essays on the Rome Statute of the International Criminal Court* (vol 1 Ripa Fagnano Alto, Editrice il Sirente 1999) 251–277

Drzewicki, K, 'National legislation as a measure for implementation of international humanitarian law' in F Kalshoven and Y Sandoz (eds), *Implementation of International Humanitarian Law* (Martinus Nijhoff Publ, Dordrecht, Boston, London 1989) 109–131

Duffy, H and J Huston, 'Implementation of the ICC Statute: International Obligations and Constitutional Considerations' in C Kress, and F Lattanzi (eds), *The Rome Statute and Domestic Legal Orders, vol 1—General Aspects and Constitutional Issues* (Nomos and Ripa di Fagnano Alto: Sirente, Baden-Baden 2000) 29–49

Dugard, J, 'Possible Conflicts of Jurisdiction with Truth Commissions' in A Cassese, P Gaeta, and J Jones (eds), *The Rome Statute of the International Criminal Court: A Commentary* (OUP, Oxford 2002) 905–918

Epping, V and C Gloria, in K Ipsen, *Völkerrecht* (5th edn CH Beck, Munich 2004) 257–388

Fernandez de Gurmendi, S, 'The Role of the International Prosecutor' in R S Lee (ed), *The International Criminal Court, The making of the Rome Statute issues, negotiations: results* (Kluwer Law Publ, The Hague 1999) 260

Fischer, H, 'The Jurisdiction of the International Criminal Court for War Crimes: Some Observations Concerning Differences between the Statute of the Court and War Crimes Provisions in Other Treaties' in Volker Epping, Horst Fischer and Wolff Heintschel von Heinegg (eds), *Brücken bauen und begehen: Festschrift für Knut Ipsen zum 65 Geburtstag* (Beck, Munich 2000) 77–101

Fomété, J-P, 'Countdown to 2010: A Critical Overview of the Completion Strategy of the International Criminal Tribunal for Rwanda (ICTR)' in E Decaux, A Dieng and M Sow (eds), *From Human Rights to International Criminal Law—Studies in Honour of an African Jurist, the Late Judge Laïty Kama* (Martinus Nijhoff, Leiden/Boston 2007) 345–400

Franck, T M and G H Fox, 'Introduction: Transnational Judicial Synergy' in T M Franck and G H Fox (eds), *International Law Decisions in National Courts* (Transnational Publ, Ardsley NY 1996) 1–11

Friman, H, 'Investigation and Prosecution' in R S Lee (ed), *The International Criminal Court, The making of the Rome Statute, Issues, Negotiations, Results* (Kluwer Law Publ, The Hague 1999) 256

Gaeta, P, 'War Crimes Trials Before Italian Criminal Courts: New Trends' in H Fischer, C Kress and S R Lüder (eds), *International and national prosecution of crimes under international law: current developments* (Spitz, Berlin 2001) 751–768

Gaeta, P, 'Official Capacity and Immunities' in A Cassese, P Gaeta, and J Jones (eds), *The Rome Statute of the International Criminal Court: A Commentary* (OUP, Oxford 2002) 975–989

Garraway, C, 'Article 8(2)(b)(xvii)' in R S Lee (ed) *The International Criminal Court, The making of the Rome Statute: issues, negotiations, results* (Kluwer Law Publ, The Hague 1999) 178

Garwood-Cutler, J L, 'The British War Crimes Trials of Suspected Italian War Criminals, 1945–1947' in J Carey, W V Dunlap and R J Pritchard (eds), *International Humanitarian Law* (vol 1 (Origins) Transnational Publ, Ardsley New York 2003) 89–103

Guariglia, F, and K Harris, 'Article 57' in O Triffterer (ed), *Commentary on the Rome Statute of the International Criminal Court—Observers' Notes, Article by Article* (Nomos, Baden-Baden 1999) 743–752

Hall, C K, 'Commentary on Article 19' in O Triffterer (ed), *Commentary on the Rome Statute of the International Criminal Court—Observers' Notes, Article by Article* (Nomos, Baden-Baden 1999) 405–418

Holmes, J T, 'Jurisdiction and Admissibility' in R S Lee (ed), *The International Criminal Court—Elements of Crimes and Rules of Procedure and Evidence* (Transnational Publ, New York 2001) 321–348

Holmes, J T, 'Complementarity: National Courts *versus* the ICC' in A Cassese, P Gaeta, and J Jones (eds) *The Rome Statute of the International Criminal Court: A Commentary* (OUP, Oxford 2002) 667–686

Holmes, J T, 'The Principle of Complementarity' in R S Lee (ed), *The International Criminal Court, The making of the Rome Statute: issues, negotiations, results* (Kluwer Law Publ, The Hague 1999) 41–78

Huyse, L, 'To Punish or to Pardon: A Devil's Choice' in C C Joyner, and M C Bassiouni (eds) *Reining in Impunity for International Crimes and Serious Violations of Fundamental Human Rights: Proceedings of the Siracusa Conference 17–21 September 1998* (1998) 14 Nouvelles Etudes Penales 79–90

Jäger, H, 'Makroverbrechen als Gegenstand des Völkerstrafrechts' in G Hankel and G Stuby (eds), *Strafgerichte gegen Menschheitsverbrechen: Zum Völkerstrafrecht 50 Jahre nach den Nürnberger Prozessen* (Hamburger Edition, Hamburg 1995) 325–354

Jensen, R, 'Complementarity, "Genuinely" and Article 17: Assessing the Boundaries of an Effective ICC' in J K Kleffner and G Kor (eds), *Complementary Views on Complementarity—Proceedings of the International Roundtable on the Complementary Nature of the International Criminal Court, Amsterdam, 25/26 June 2004* (TMC Asser Press, The Hague 2006) 147–170

Jessberger, F, 'Universality, Complementarity, and the Duty to Prosecute Crimes under International Law' in W Kaleck *et al* (eds), *International Prosecution of Human Rights Crimes* (Springer, Berlin 2007) 213–222

Kidane, W L, 'The Ethiopian "Red Terror" Trials' in M C Bassiouni (ed), Post-Conflict Justice (Transnational Publ, Ardsley New York 2000) 667–694

Kirsch, P and D Robinson, 'Reaching Agreement at the Rome Conference' in A Cassese, P Gaeta, and J Jones (eds), *The Rome Statute of the International Criminal Court: A Commentary* (2002) 67–91

Kirsch, P and V Oosterveld, 'The Post-Rome Conference Preparatory Commission' in A Cassese, P Gaeta and J Jones (eds), *The Rome Statute of the International Criminal Court: A Commentary* (OUP, Oxford 2002) 93–104

Kleffner, J K 'Complementarity as a Catalyst for Compliance' in J K Kleffner and G Kor (eds), *Complementary Views on Complementarity—Proceedings of the International*

Roundtable on the Complementary Nature of the International Criminal Court, Amsterdam, 25/26 June 2004 (TMC Asser Press, The Hague 2006) 79–104

Kleffner, J K, and A Nollkaemper, 'The Relationship between Internationalized Courts and National Courts' in C Romano, A Nollkaemper and J K Kleffner (eds), *Internationalized Criminal Courts: Sierra Leone, East Timor, Kosovo, and Cambodia* (OUP, Oxford 2004) 359–378

Kor, G, 'Sovereignty in the dock' in J K Kleffner and G Kor (eds), *Complementary Views on Complementarity—Proceedings of the International Roundtable on the Complementary Nature of the International Criminal Court, Amsterdam, 25/26 June 2004* (TMC Asser Press, The Hague 2006) 66–67

Kress, C and K Prost, 'Article 89' in O Triffterer (ed) *Commentary on the Rome Statute of the International Criminal Court—Observers' Notes, Article by Article* (Nomos, Baden-Baden 1999) 1075–1076

Lachs, M, 'Some thoughts on the role of good faith in international law' in Robert J Akkerman, Peter J van Krieken and Charles O Pannenborg (eds), *Declarations on principles* (A W Stijhoff, Leyden 1977) 47–55

Lagodny, O, 'Viele Strafgewalten und nur ein transnationales ne-bis-in-idem?' in A Donatsch, M Forster and C Schwarzenegger (eds), *Strafrecht, Strafprozessrecht und Menschenrechte, Festschrift für Stefan Trechsel zum 65* (Geburtstag, Schulthess 2002) 253–267

Lattanzi, F, 'The Rome Statute and State Sovereignty. ICC Competence, Jurisdictional Links, Trigger Mechanisms, in: ICC and State Sovereignty' in F Lattanzi and W Schabas (eds), *Essays on the Rome Statute of the International Criminal Court* (vol I Ripa Fagnano Alto, Editrice il Sirente 1999) 51–66

Lattanzi, F, 'The International Criminal Court and National Jurisdictions' in M Politi and G Nesi (eds), *The Rome Statute of the International Criminal Court—A Challenge to Impunity* (Ashgate, Dartmouth, Aldershot 2001) 177–223

Levie, H S, 'The History and Status of the International Criminal Court' in M Schmitt (ed), *International Law Across the Spectrum of Conflict: Essays in Honour of Professor L.C. Green on the Occasion of His Eightieth Birthday* (Naval War College, Newport 2000) 247–261

Lillich, R B, 'Civil Rights' in T Meron (ed), *Human Rights in International Law—Legal and Policy Issues* (Clarendon Press, Oxford 1984) 115–170

Lukashuk, I I, 'Customary Norms in Contemporary International Law' in J Makarczyk (ed), *Theory of International Law at the Threshold of the 21st Century—Essays in honour of Krzysztof Skubiszewski* (Martin Nijhoff, The Hague 1996) 487–508

Lyons, B S, 'Getting Untrapped, Struggling for Truth: The Commission for Reception, Truth and Reconciliation (CAVR) in East Timor' in C Romano, A Nollkaemper and J K Kleffner (eds), *Internationalized Criminal Courts: Sierra Leone, East Timor, Kosovo, and Cambodia* (OUP, Oxford 2004) 99–124

Marong, A, C C Jalloh, and D Kinnecome, 'Concurrent Jurisdiction and the ICTR: Should the Tribunal Refer Cases to Rwanda?' in E Decaux, A Dieng and M Sow (eds), *From Human Rights to International Criminal Law—Studies in Honour of an African Jurist, the Late Judge Laïty Kama* (Martinus Nijhoff, Leiden/Boston 2007) 159–201

McCormack, T L H, 'From Sun Tzu to the Sixth Committee: The Evolution of an International Criminal Law Regime' in T L H McCormack and G J Simpson (eds), *The law of war crimes: National and international approaches* (Kluwer Law International, The Hague, London, Boston 1997) 31–63

McKay, F, 'Civil reparation in national courts for victims of human rights abuse' in M Lattimer and P Sands (eds), *Justice for crimes against humanity* (Hart Publ, Oxford 2003) 283–302.

Mégret, F, 'Why would States want to join the ICC? A theoretical exploration based on the legal nature of complementarity' in J K Kleffner and G Kor (eds) *Complementary Views on Complementarity—Proceedings of the International Roundtable on the Complementary Nature of the International Criminal Court, Amsterdam, 25/26 June 2004* (TMC Asser Press, The Hague 2006) 1–51

Mose, E and C Aptel, 'Trial Without Undue Delay Before the International Criminal Tribunals' in L C Vohrah *et al* (eds), *Man's Inhumanity to Man—Essays on International Law in Honour of Antonio Cassese* (Kluwer, The Hague 2003) 539–566

Mosler, H, 'General Principles of Law' in R Bernhardt (ed), *Encyclopedia of Public International Law* (vol II Elsevier Science Publ, North Holland 1986) 511–527

Nowak, M, 'The right to reparation of victims of gross human rights violations' in G Ulrich and L Krabbe Boserup (eds), *Human rights in development Yearbook 2001—Reparations: Redressing Past Wrongs* (Kluwer, The Hague 2003) 275–284

Nsereko, D, 'Article 18' in O Triffterer (ed), *Commentary on the Rome Statute of the International Criminal Court—Observers' Notes Article by Article* (Nomos, Baden-Baden 1999)

Olásolo, H, 'Complementarity Analysis of National Sentencing' in R Haveman, and O Olusanya (eds), *Sentencing and Sanctioning in Supranational Criminal Law* (Intersentia, Antwerp 2006) 37–66

Pellet, A, 'Applicable Law', in A Cassese, P Gaeta and J Jones (eds), *The Rome Statute of the International Criminal Court: A Commentary* (2002) 1051–1084

Pritchard, R J, 'International Humanitarian Intervention and Establishment of an International Jurisdiction over Crimes Against Humanity: The National and International Military Trials on Crete in 1898' in J Carey, W V Dunlap and R J Pritchard (eds), *International Humanitarian Law* (vol 1 (Origins) Transnational Publ, Ardsley NY 2003) 1–87

Prost, K, and A Schlunck, 'Commentary to Article 93' in O Triffterer (ed), *Commentary on the Rome Statute of the International Criminal Court—Observers' Notes, Article by Article* (Nomos, Baden-Baden 1999) 1101–1118

Roht-Arriaza, N, 'Punishment, Redress, and Pardon: Theoretical and Psychological Approaches' in N Roht-Arriaza (ed), *Impunity and Human Rights in International Law and Practice* (OUP, Oxford 1995) 13–23

Roht-Arriaza, N, 'Sources in International Treaties of an Obligation to Investicgate, Prosecute, and Provide Radress' in N Roht-Arriaza (ed), *Impunity and Human Rights in International Law and Practice* (OUP, Oxford 1995) 24–38

Roht-Arriaza, N, 'Amnesty and the International Criminal Court' in D Shelton (ed), *International Crimes, Peace, and Human Rights: The Role of the International Criminal Court* (Transnational Publ, Ardsley, New York 2000) 77–82

Röling, B V A, 'The Significance of the Laws of War' in A Cassese (ed), *Current Problems of International Law* (Guiffré, Milan 1975) 137–139

Rosenne, S, 'Antecedents of the Rome Statute of the International Criminal Court Revisited' in M Schmitt (ed), *International Law Across the Spectrum of Conflict: Essays in Honour of Professor L.C. Green on the Occasion of His Eightieth Birthday* (Naval War College, Newport 2000) 387–420

Roth, R and Y Jeanneret, 'Droit Allemand' in A Cassese and M Delmas-Marty (eds), *Juridictions nationales et crimes internationaux* (Presses Universitaires de France, Paris 2002) 7–29

Rückerl, A, 'NS-Prozesse, "Warum erst heute?—Warum noch heute?—Wie lange noch?"' in A Rückerl (ed), *NS-Prozesse, Nach 25 Strafverfolgung: Möglichkeiten, Grenzen, Ergebnisse* (CF Müller Verlag, Karslruhe 1972) 13–34

Rwagasore, S, 'The case of Rwanda, in: ICRC Advisory Service' in C Pellandini (ed), *National Measures to Suppress Violations of International Humanitarian Law (civil law systems), Report on the Meeting of Experts* (ICRC, Geneva 2000) 98–106

Scelle, G, 'Le phénomène juridique du dédoublement fonctionnel', in W Schätzel and HJ Schlochauer (eds), *Rechtsfragen der Internationalen Organisation—Festschrift für H. Wehberg* (Vittorio Klostermann, Frankfurt am Main 1956) 324–342

Schabas, W, 'Internationalized Courts and their Relationship with Alternative Accountability Mechanisms: The Case of Sierra Leone' in C Romano, A Nollkaemper and J K Kleffner (eds), *Internationalized Criminal Courts: Sierra Leone, East Timor, Kosovo, and Cambodia* (OUP Oxford 2004) 157–180

Slade, T N and R S Clark, 'Preamble and final clauses' in R S Lee (ed), *The International Criminal Court, The making of the Rome Statute: issues, negotiations, results* (Kluwer Law Publ, The Hague 1999) 421–450

Slaughter, A-M, 'A Typology of Transjudicial Communication' in Thomas M Franck and Gregory H Fox (eds), *International Law Decisions in National Courts* (Transnational Publ, Ardsley NY 1996) 37–69

Steinberger, H, 'Sovereignty' in R Bernhardt (ed), *Encyclopedia of Public International Law* (vol IV Max Planck Institute for Comparative Public Law and International Law, Amsterdam, Elsevier 2000) 500–521

Suy, E, 'Le Préambule' in E Yakpo and T Boumedra (eds), Liber Amicorum Judge Mohammed Bedjaoui (Kluwer Law International, The Hague 1999) 253–269

Swart, B, 'Arrest and Surrender' in A Cassese, P Gaeta and J Jones (eds), *The Rome Statute of the International Criminal Court: A Commentary* (OUP, Oxford 2002) 1639–1704

Swart, B, 'General Problems' in A Cassese, P Gaeta and J Jones (eds), *The Rome Statute of the International Criminal Court: A Commentary* (OUP, Oxford 2002) 1589–1605

Swart, B, 'La place des critères traditionnels de compétence dans la pursuite des crimes internationaux' in A Cassese and M Delmas Marty (eds), *Juridictions nationales et crimes internationaux* (Presses Universitaires de France, Paris 2002) 567–589

Swart, B, 'Universaliteit' [Universality] in T Spronken (ed), *Iets Bijzonders—Liber amicorum aangeboden aan Mischa Wladimiroff ter gelegenheid van zijn 30-jarig jubileum als advocaat* (Cdu Publ, The Hague 2002) 243–262

Swart, B, 'Comments on Chapter 5 by Rod Jensen' in J K Kleffner and G Kor (eds), *Complementary Views on Complementary—Proceedings of the international Roundtable on the Complementary Nature of the International Criminal Court, Amsterdam, 25/26 June 2004* (TMC Asser Press, The Hague 2006)

Tallgren, I, 'Commentary on Article 20' in O Triffterer (ed) *Commentary on the Rome Statute of the International Criminal Court—Observers' Notes, Article by Article* (Nomos, Baden-Baden 1999) 174–322

Tomuschat, C, 'The duty to prosecute international crimes committed by individuals' in H J Cremer and H Steinberger (eds), *Tradition und Weltoffenheit des Rechts: Festschrift für Helmut Steinberger* (Springer, Berlin 2002) 315–349

Triffterer, O, 'Preliminary Remarks: The Permanent International Criminal Court—Ideal and Reality' in O Triffterer (ed), *Commentary on the Rome Statute of the International Criminal Court—Observers' Notes, Article by Article* (Nomos, Baden-Baden 1999) 17–50

Triffterer, O, 'Legal and Political Implications of Domestic Ratification and Implementation Processes' in C Kress and F Lattanzi, (eds), *The Rome Statute and Domestic Legal Orders, vol. 1—General Aspects and Constitutional Issues* (Nomos and Ripa di Fagnano Alto: Sirente, Baden-Baden 2000) 1–28

Triffterer, O, 'Kriminalpolitische und dogmatische Überlegungen zum Entwurf gleichlautender "Elements of Crimes" für alle Tatbestände des Völkermordes' in B Schünemann, *Festschrift für Claus Roxin zum 70. Geburtstay am 15. Mai 2001* (2001) 1415–1445

Triggs, G, 'National Prosecutions of War Crimes and the Rule of Law' in H Durham and T L H McCormack (eds), *The Changing Face of Conflict and the Efficacy of International Humanitarian Law* (Martinus Nijhoff, The Hague/London/Boston 1999) 175–191

Turone, G, 'Powers and Duties of the Prosecutor' in A Cassese, P Gaeta and J Jones (eds), *The Rome Statute of the International Criminal Court: A Commentary* (2002) 1137–1180

van Boven, T, 'The Principle of Complementarity—The International Criminal Court and National Laws' in J Wouters and H Panken (eds), *De Genocidewet in internationaal perspectief, Jura Falconis Libri* (De Boeck & Larcier Publ, Brussels 2002) 65–74

van den Wyngaert, C, and T Ongena, '*Ne bis in idem* principle, including the issue of amnesty' in A Cassese, P Gaeta and J Jones (eds), *The Rome Statute of the International Criminal Court: A Commentary* (2002) 705–729

van der Voort, K, and M Zwanenburg, 'Amnesty and the Implementation of the ICC—Some Country Studies' in R Haveman, O Kavran and J Nicholls (eds), *Supranational Criminal Law: A System Sui Generis* (Intersentia Publ, Antwerp/Oxford/New York 2003) 305–345

van der Wilt, H, 'The International Criminal Court and Domestic Jurisdictions: Competition or Concerted Action' in F Coomans, F Grünfeld, I Westendorp and J Willems (eds), *Rendering Justice to the Vulnerable; Liber Amicorum in Honour of Theo van Boven* (Kluwer Law International, The Hague 2000) 323–338

Vander Beken, T, 'De moelijke zoektocht naar het beste forum voor internationale misdrijven—De *ad hoc* tribunalen als ideale oplossing ?' in J Wouters and H Panken (eds), *De Genocidewet in internationaal perspectief, Jura Falconis Libri* (De Boeck & Larcier Publ, Brussels 2002) 117–137

Vandermeersch, D, 'La compétence universelle' in A Cassese and M Delmas-Marty (eds), *Juridictions nationales et crimes internationaux* (Presses Universitaires de France, Paris 2002) 589–661

Verosta, S, 'Denial of Justice' in R Bernhardt (ed), *Encyclopedia of Public International Law* (vol 1 Elsevier Publ, North Holland 1992) 1007–1010

von Hebel, H, and D Robinson, 'Crimes within the jurisdiction of the Court' in R S Lee (ed), *The International Criminal Court, The making of the Rome Statute: issues, negotiations, results* (Kluwer Law Publ, The Hague 1999) 79–126

Williams, S A, 'Commentary on Article 17' in O Triffterer (ed), *Commentary on the Rome Statute of the International Criminal Court—Observers' Notes, Article by Article* (Nomos, Baden-Baden 1999) 383–394

Wolfrum, R, 'The Decentralized Prosecution of International Offences Through National Courts' in Y Dinstein and M Tabory (eds), *War Crimes in International Law* (Martinus Nijhoff Publ, The Hague, Boston, London 1996) 233–249

Yokaris, A, 'Les Critères de Compétence des Juridictions Nationales', in H Ascensio, E Decaux and A Pellet (eds), *Droit International Pénal* (Éditions Pedone, Paris 2000) 897–904

Documents

ICC DOCUMENTS

Draft Programme Budget 2005, Doc ICC/ASP/3/2 (26 July 2004), available at <http://www.icc-cpi.int/library/asp/ICC-ASPS-2_budget_English.pdf>

Fifth Report of the Prosecutor of the International Criminal Court to the UN Security Council Pursuant to UNSCR 1593 (2005), 7 June 2007, available at <http://www.icc-cpi.int/library/organs/otp/OTP_ReportUNSC5-Darfur_English.pdf>

Fourth Report of the Prosecutor of the International Criminal Court to the Security Council pursuant to UNSCR 1593 (2005), 14 December 2006, available at <http://www.icc-cpi.int/library/organs/otp/OTP_ReportUNSC4-Darfor_English.pdf>

Informal Expert Paper for the ICC Office of the Prosecutor: The Principle of Complementarity in Practice, available at <http://www.icc-cpi.int/library/organs/otp/complementarity.pdf>

Informal Expert Paper: Fact-finding and investigative functions of the office of the Prosecutor, including international co-operation, Prepared for the Office of the Prosecutor (2003), available at <http://www.icc-cpi.int/library/organs/otp/state_cooperation.pdf>

Informal inter-sessional meeting of the Special Working Group on the Crime of Aggression, held at the Liechtenstein Institute on Self-Determination, Woodrow Wilson School, at Princeton University, New Jersey, United States, from 21 to 23 June 2004 , ICC-ASP/3/SWGCA/INF.1

ICC Press Release, 'OTP—Election of the Prosecutor, Statement by Mr Moreno Ocampo', The Hague, 2 May 2003, ICC-OTP-20030502-10-En, <http://www.icc-cpi.int/press/pressreleases/5.html>

ICC Press Release, President of Uganda refers situation concerning the Lord's Resistance Army (LRA) to the ICC', The Hague, 29 January 2004, ICC-20040129-44-En

ICC Press Release, 'Prosecutor receives referral of the situation in the Democratic Republic of Congo', The Hague, 19 April 2004, ICC-OTP-20040419-50-En

ICC Press Release, 'Prosecutor receives referral concerning Central African Republic', The Hague, 7 January 2005, ICC-OTP-20050107-86-En

ICC Press Release, 'Prosecutor opens investigation in the Central African Republic', 22 May 2007, ICC-OTP-PR-20070522-220_En

Letter by the Chief Prosecutor of 17 June 2004 addressed to the President of the ICC, attached to the Decision of the Presidency Assigning the Situation in Uganda to Pre-Trial Chamber II, 5 July 2004, ICC-02/04-1

Letter from Mr Joseph Kabila to the ICC Prosecutor, dated 03 March 2004—Reclassified as public pursuant to Decision ICC-01/04-01/06-46, ICC-01/04-01/06-39-AnxB1, available at <http://www.icc-cpi.int/library/cases/ICC-01-04-01-06-39-AnxB1_French.pdf>

Paper on some policy issues before the Office of the Prosecutor, available at <http://www.icc-cpi.int/library/organs/otp/030905_Policy_Paper.pdf> (2003)

Paper on some policy issues before the Office of the Prosecutor: Referrals and Communications, available at <http://www.icc-cpi.int/library/organs/otp/policy_annex_final_210404.pdf>

Policy Paper on the Interests of Justice, Office of the Prosecutor, September 2007, <http://www.icc-cpi.int/library/organs/otp/ICC-OTP-InterestsOfJustice.pdf>

Prosecution's Submission of Further Information and Materials, Reclassified as public on 23 March 2006 pursuant to decision ICC-01/04-01/06-46, ICC-01/04-01/06-32-AnxC, 25 January 2006

Sixth Report of the Prosecutor of the International Criminal Court to the UN Security Council Pursuant to UNSCR 1593 (2005), 5 December 2007, available at <http://www.icc-cpi.int/library/organs/otp/OTP-RP-20071205-UNSC-ENG.pdf>

'Remarks by ICC Prosecutor Luis Moreno-Ocampo', 27th meeting of the Committee of Legal Advisors on Public International Law, Strasbourg, 18 March 2004, available at <http://www.coe.int/t/e/legal_affairs/legal_co-operation/Public_international_law/Texts_&_Documents/2004/Speech%20OCAMPO%2027th%20Cahdi%20meeting.asp>

Report of the Preparatory Commission for the International Criminal Court, Addendum Finalized draft text of the Rules of Procedure and Evidence (12 July 2000) UN Doc PCNICC/2000/INF/3/Add.1

Report of the International Criminal Court to the United Nations General Assembly UN Doc A/60/177 (1 August 2005)

Report of the Prosecutor of the International Criminal Court to the UN Security Council Pursuant to UNSCR 1593 (2005) 29 June 2005, available at <http://www.icc-cpi.int/library/cases/ICC_Darfur_UNSC_Report_29-06-05_EN.pdf>

Report on Prosecutorial Strategy, Office of the Prosecutor, 14 September 2006, <http://www.icc-cpi.int/library/organs/otp/OTP_Prosecutorial-Strategy-20060914_English.pdf>

Situation in Darfur, The Sudan, Prosecutor's Application under Article 58 (7), Public Redacted Version, ICC-02/05, 27 February 2007

Statement of the Prosecutor Luis Moreno-Ocampo to Diplomatic Corps, The Hague, Netherlands, 12 February 2004, <http://www.icc-cpi.int/library/organs/otp/OTP.SM20040212-EN.pdf>

Third Report of the Prosecutor of the International Criminal Court to the UN Security Council Pursuant to UNSCR 1593 (2005), 14 June 2006, available at <http://www.icc-cpi.int/library/cases/OTP_ReportUNSC_3-Darfur_English.pdf>

Update on Communications Received by the Prosecutor, Office of the Prosecutor, 10 February 2006, Annex 'Iraq Response', available at <http://www.icc-cpi.int/library/organs/otp/OTP_letter_to_senders_re_Iraq_9_February_2006.pdf>

'Warrant of Arrest for Dominic Ongwen', 13 October 2005, ICC-02/04-01/05-57, [26]

'Warrant of Arrest for Joseph Kony issued 8 July 2005 as amended on 27 September 2005', 13 October 2005, ICC-02/04-01/05-53, [38]

'Warrant of Arrest for Laska Lukwiya', 13 October 2005, ICC-02/04-01/05-55, [26]

'Warrant of Arrest for Okot Odhiambo', 13 October 2005, ICC-02/04-01/05-56, [28]

'Warrant of Arrest for Vincent Otti', 13 October 2005, ICC-02/04-01/05-54, [38]

UNITED NATIONS REPORTS

'Final report on the independence and impartiality of the judiciary, jurors and assessors, and the independence of lawyers by Mr. Singhvi, submitted to the Sub-Commission on Prevention of Discrimination and Protection of Minorities' (1985) UN Doc E/CN.4/Sub.2/1985/18 and Add.1-6

Study concerning the right to restitution, compensation and rehabilitation for victims of gross violations of human rights and fundamental freedoms, Final Report submitted by Mr Theo van Boven, Special Rapporteur (1993) UN Doc E/CN.4/Sub.2/1993/8 (2 July 2 1993)

Report of the United Nations Secretary-General, 'The establishment of the International Criminal Tribunal for the former Yugoslavia (1993) (Report pursuant to paragraph 2 UNSC Res 808)' (3 May 1993) UN Doc S/25704

Progress Report on the Question of the Impunity of Perpetrators of Human Rights Violations, prepared by Mr Guissé and Mr Joinet, pursuant to Sub-Commission resolution 1992/23 (19 July 1993) UN Doc E/CN.4/Sub.2/1993/6

Report of the Special Rapporteur, Mr Param Cumaraswamy, 'Independence and impartiality of the judiciary, jurors and assessors and the independence of lawyers', submitted in accordance with Commission on Human Rights resolution 1994/41, UN Doc E/CN.4/1995/39 (6 February 1995)

Report of the Preparatory Committee on the Establishment of an International Criminal Court, Proceedings of the Preparatory Committee during March-April and August 1996 (1996) UN GAOR 51st Session Supp No 22 UN Doc A/51/22

Report of the Special Rapporteur on the independence of judges and lawyers Mr. Param Cumaraswamy, on the mission to Nigeria (1997) E/CN.4/1997/62/Add.1

Revised final report prepared by Mr Joinet pursuant to Sub-Commission decision 1996/119 (2 October 1997) UN Doc E/CN.4/Sub.2/1997/20/Rev.1

Report of the Inter-Sessional Meeting From 19 to 30 January 1998 held in Zutphen, The Netherlands (1998) UN Doc A/AC.249/1998/L.13

Report of the Special Rapporteur on the independence of judges and lawyers Mr. Param Cumaraswamy, on the mission to Colombia (1998) UN Doc E/CN.4/1998/39/Add.2

Report of the Special Rapporteur on the independence of judges and lawyers, on the mission to Guatemala (2000) UN Doc E/CN.4/2000/61/Add.1

Report of the Secretary-General on the Establishment of a Special Court for Sierra Leone UN Doc S/2000/915(4 October 2000)

Report of the Special Rapporteur on the independence of judges and lawyers Mr Param Cumaraswamy, on the mission to Guatemala (2001) E/CN.4/2002/72/Add.2

Report of the United Nations High Commissioner for Human Rights on the human rights situation in Colombia, UN Doc E/CN.4/2001/15 (8 February 2001)

Report of the Special Rapporteur on the independence of judges and lawyers, Dato' Param Cumaraswamy, submitted in accordance with Commission on Human Rights resolution 2001/39, Report on the mission to Guatemala (2001) E/CN.4/2002/72/Add.2 (21 December 2001)

Report of the UNHCHR to the Security Council on the Democratic Republic of the Congo, UN Doc S/2002/764 (16 July 2002)

Report of the Special Rapporteur on the independence of judges and lawyers, Dato' Param Cumaraswamy submitted in accordance with Commission on Human Rights resolution 2002/43, UN Doc E/CN.4/2003/65 (10 January 2003)

Report of the UNHCHR to the Security Council on the Democratic Republic of the Congo, UN Doc S/2003/216 (13 February 2003)

Interim Report of the Special Rapporteur on the situation of human rights in the Democratic Republic of the Congo, UN Doc A/58/534 (24 October 2003)

ILC MATERIALS

'Report of the International Law Commission on the work of its 45th Session' (1993) UN GAOR 48th Session Supp No 10, 255, UN Doc A/48/10 (1993); reproduced in 33 ILM 253–296

'Report of the International Law Commission on the work of its 46th Session' UN GAOR 49th Session Supp No 10, UN Doc A/49/10

Draft Code of Crimes against the Peace and Security of Mankind, ILC, 'Report of the International Law Commission on the work of its 48th Session' (6 May–26 July 1996) UN Doc A/51/10 Supplement No 10

Yearbook of the International Law Commission, 1996, vol II (2), UN Doc A/CN.4/SER.A/1996/Add.l (Part 2)

'International Law Commission Report of its 51st Session: Second report on State responsibility' (30 April 1999) UN Doc A/CN.4/498/Add.2

Third report on diplomatic protection by Mr. John Dugard, Special Rapporteur, International Law Commission, 54th Session, Geneva 29 April–7 June and 22 July–16 August 2002, UN Doc A/CN.4/523, 7 March 2002

'Report of the International Law Commission on the work of its 58th Session', UN Doc A/61/10

'Fragmentation of international law: difficulties arising from the diversification and expansion of international law', Report of the Study Group of the International Law Commission, finalized by Martti Koskenniemi (13 April 2006) UN Doc A/CN.4/L.682

OTHER DOCUMENTS

Adamson, R and A Vamos-Goldman, 'The Expectation Gap: Summary of the First Meeting of the Vancouver Dialogue' (June 2003), available at <http://www.gjp.ubc.ca/_media/act/ExpectationGapReport.pdf>

Amnesty International, 'International Criminal Court: The failure of states to enact effective implementing legislation', available at <http://web.amnesty.org/library/Index/ENGIOR400192004?open&of=ENG-385>

Amnesty International, 'Universal Jurisdiction—The Duty to Enact and Implement Legislation', AI Index IOR 53/002-018/2001, September 2001

Amnesty International, 'Afghanistan: All who are not friends, are enemies: Taleban abuses against civilians', AI Index: ASA 11/001/2007, 19 April 2007

Crawford, J, P Sands and R Wilde, 'In the Matter of the Statute of the International Criminal Court and in the Matter of Bilateral Agreements Sought by the United States under Article 98(2) of the Statute'—Joint Opinion, 5 June 2003, available at <http://www.humanrightsfirst.org/international_justice/Art98_061403.pdf>

Déclaration Finale du Séminaire sur la Ratification et la Mise en Oevure du Statut de la Cour Pénale Internationale (Déclaration de Maurice), 27–29 May 2002

Gilbert, G, Current Issues in the Application of the Exclusion Clauses, Background Paper for an Expert Round table Discussion on exclusion organised as part of the Global Consultations on International Protection in the context of the 50th anniversary of the 1951 Convention Relating to the Status of Refugees (2001)

Holmes, J T, Complementarity—History of Negotiations, Presentation at the Conference 'The Complementarity Regime of the ICC', 17–19 December 2003, The Hague, The Netherlands

Human Rights First, Rwanda, Prosecuting Genocide in Rwanda: A Human Rights First report on the ICTR and National Trials, available at <http://www.humanrightsfirst. org/pubs/descriptions/rwanda.htm#rwanda> (July 1997)

ICRC, Annual Report 1995, 31 May 1996, Rwanda, available at <http://www.icrc.org/ web/eng/siteeng0.nsf/iwpList143/D3B15125343F6B3CC1256B660059C81E>

International Criminal Tribunal for Rwanda, 'Completion strategy of the International Criminal Tribunal for Rwanda', 30 November 2005, available at <http://65.18.216.88/ ENGLISH/completionstrat/301105.pdf>

Institut de Droit International, Resolution of the Institut de Droit International on 'Immunities from Jurisdiction and Execution of Heads of State and of Government in International Law', adopted at the Session of Vancouver—2001 (Thirteenth Commission, Rapporteur: Mr Joe Verhoeven)

Institut de Droit International, Resolution of the Institut de Droit International on 'Universal criminal jurisdiction with regard to the crime of genocide, crimes against humanity and war crimes' adopted at the Session of Krakow—2005 (Seventeenth Session, Rapporteur: M Christian Tomuschat)

Justice Rapid Response Feasibility Study, produced at the request and with support of the governments of Finland, Germany, Liechtenstein, Sweden, Switzerland and United Kingdom, October 2005, on file with author

Osten, P, 'Der Tokioter Kriegsverbrecherprozeß und seine Rezeption in Japan—Japan und das Völkerstrafrecht' Vortrag gehalten auf den 3. Keio-Tagen, Universität des Saarlands, 2.–5. Dezember 2003, available at <http://www.jura.uni-sb.de projekte/ Bibliothek/texte/Osten.html>

Regional Report: Local Justice, Bosnian-Style' (2001) IWPR's Tribunal Update No 220, 7–12 May 2001

Stanley Foundation, 'Creating the International Legal Assistance Consortium', <http:// www.stanleyfoundation.org/publications/archive/ILAC00.pdf>

Statement by Ms Sima Samar, Special Rapporteur on the situation of human rights in the Sudan, 60th Session of the General Assembly Third Committee, Item 71 (c): Human rights situations and reports of special rapporteurs and representatives, New York, 27 October 2005, <http://www.ohchr.org/english/bodies/chr/special/ SRSudanstatement.doc>

Statement of H E Mr Pfanzelter, Permanent Representative of Austria to the United Nations, at the meeting of the Security Council on Justice and the Rule of Law on 30 September 2003, Security Council 4835th meeting: record of the meeting available at <http://www.un.org/Depts/dhl/resguide/scact2003.htm>

The Princeton Principles on Universal Jurisdiction (2001), available at <http://www.law. uc.edu/morgan/newsdir/unive_jur.pdf>

UNHCHR Press Release: 'UN Special Rapporteur On Independence Of Judiciary Condemns Public Execution Following Illegal Trial In Afghanistan', 8 June 2006, <http://www.unhchr.ch/huricane/huricane.nsf/view01/5D75CF314F0C8AA7C125 7187002F10CD?opendocument>

United Nations Basic Principles on the Independence of the Judiciary, adopted by the Seventh United Nations Congress on the Prevention of Crime and the Treatment of Offenders held at Milan from 26 August to 6 September 1985 and endorsed by General Assembly resolutions 40/32 of 29 November 1985 and 40/146 of 13 December 1985

United States Institute for Peace, 'Rwanda: Accountability for War Crimes and Genocide', Special Report 13, Release Date January 1995, available at <http://www. usip.org/pubs/specialreports/early/rwanda2.html>

Updated Set of principles for the protection and promotion of human rights, Report by Diane Orentlicher updating the Joinet Principles. UN Commission on Human Rights E/CN.4/2005/102/Add.1 Sixty-first session, 8 February 2005

Index